(A.&B.) Pymnt.Sys. ACB—1

American Casebook Series
Hornbook Series and Basic Legal Texts
Black Letter Series and Nutshell Series

of

WEST PUBLISHING COMPANY
P.O. Box 64526
St. Paul, Minnesota 55164–0526

Accounting

FARIS' ACCOUNTING AND LAW IN A NUTSHELL, 377 pages, 1984. Softcover. (Text)

FIFLIS' ACCOUNTING ISSUES FOR LAWYERS, TEACHING MATERIALS, Fourth Edition, 706 pages, 1991. Teacher's Manual available. (Casebook)

SIEGEL AND SIEGEL'S ACCOUNTING AND FINANCIAL DISCLOSURE: A GUIDE TO BASIC CONCEPTS, 259 pages, 1983. Softcover. (Text)

Administrative Law

AMAN AND MAYTON'S HORNBOOK ON ADMINISTRATIVE LAW, Approximately 750 pages, 1993. (Text)

BONFIELD AND ASIMOW'S STATE AND FEDERAL ADMINISTRATIVE LAW, 826 pages, 1989. Teacher's Manual available. (Casebook)

GELLHORN AND LEVIN'S ADMINISTRATIVE LAW AND PROCESS IN A NUTSHELL, Third Edition, 479 pages, 1990. Softcover. (Text)

MASHAW, MERRILL, AND SHANE'S CASES AND MATERIALS ON ADMINISTRATIVE LAW—THE AMERICAN PUBLIC LAW SYSTEM, Third Edition, 1187 pages, 1992. (Casebook)

ROBINSON, GELLHORN AND BRUFF'S THE ADMINISTRATIVE PROCESS, Third Edition, 978 pages, 1986. (Casebook)

Admiralty

HEALY AND SHARPE'S CASES AND MATERIALS ON ADMIRALTY, Second Edition, 876 pages, 1986. (Casebook)

MARAIST'S ADMIRALTY IN A NUTSHELL, Second Edition, 379 pages, 1988. Softcover. (Text)

SCHOENBAUM'S HORNBOOK ON ADMIRALTY AND MARITIME LAW, Student Edition, 692 pages, 1987 with 1992 pocket part. (Text)

Agency—Partnership

DEMOTT'S FIDUCIARY OBLIGATION, AGENCY AND PARTNERSHIP: DUTIES IN ONGOING BUSINESS RELATIONSHIPS, 740 pages, 1991. Teacher's Manual available. (Casebook)

FESSLER'S ALTERNATIVES TO INCORPORATION FOR PERSONS IN QUEST OF PROFIT, Third Edition, 339 pages, 1991. Softcover. (Casebook)

HENN'S CASES AND MATERIALS ON AGENCY, PARTNERSHIP AND OTHER UNINCORPORATED BUSINESS ENTERPRISES, Second Edition, 733 pages, 1985. Teacher's Manual available. (Casebook)

REUSCHLEIN AND GREGORY'S HORNBOOK ON THE LAW OF AGENCY AND PARTNERSHIP, Second Edition, 683 pages, 1990. (Text)

SELECTED CORPORATION AND PARTNERSHIP STATUTES, RULES AND FORMS. Softcover. Revised 1991 Edition, 953 pages.

STEFFEN AND KERR'S CASES ON AGENCY-PARTNERSHIP, Fourth Edition, 859 pages, 1980. (Casebook)

STEFFEN'S AGENCY-PARTNERSHIP IN A NUTSHELL, 364 pages, 1977. Softcover. (Text)

Agricultural Law

MEYER, PEDERSEN, THORSON AND DAVIDSON'S AGRICULTURAL LAW: CASES AND MATERIALS, 931 pages, 1985. Teacher's Manual avail-

List current as of January, 1993

Agricultural Law—Cont'd

able. (Casebook)

Alternative Dispute Resolution

KANOWITZ' CASES AND MATERIALS ON ALTERNATIVE DISPUTE RESOLUTION, 1024 pages, 1986. Teacher's Manual available. (Casebook) 1990 Supplement.

NOLAN-HALEY'S ALTERNATIVE DISPUTE RESOLUTION IN A NUTSHELL, 298 pages, 1992. Softcover. (Text)

RISKIN AND WESTBROOK'S DISPUTE RESOLUTION AND LAWYERS, 468 pages, 1987. Teacher's Manual available. (Casebook)

RISKIN AND WESTBROOK'S DISPUTE RESOLUTION AND LAWYERS, Abridged Edition, 223 pages, 1987. Softcover. Teacher's Manual available. (Casebook)

RISKIN'S DISPUTE RESOLUTION FOR LAWYERS VIDEO TAPES, 1992. (Available for purchase by schools and libraries.)

American Indian Law

CANBY'S AMERICAN INDIAN LAW IN A NUTSHELL, Second Edition, 336 pages, 1988. Softcover. (Text)

GETCHES AND WILKINSON'S CASES AND MATERIALS ON FEDERAL INDIAN LAW, Second Edition, 880 pages, 1986. (Casebook)

Antitrust—see also Regulated Industries, Trade Regulation

BARNES AND STOUT'S ECONOMIC FOUNDATIONS OF REGULATION AND ANTITRUST LAW, 102 pages, 1992. Softcover. Teacher's Manual available. (Casebook)

FOX AND SULLIVAN'S CASES AND MATERIALS ON ANTITRUST, 935 pages, 1989. Teacher's Manual available. (Casebook) 1993 Supplement.

GELLHORN'S ANTITRUST LAW AND ECONOMICS IN A NUTSHELL, Third Edition, 472 pages, 1986. Softcover. (Text)

HOVENKAMP'S BLACK LETTER ON ANTITRUST, Second Edition approximately 325 pages, April 1993 Pub. Softcover. (Review)

HOVENKAMP'S HORNBOOK ON ECONOMICS AND FEDERAL ANTITRUST LAW, Student Edition, 414 pages, 1985. (Text)

POSNER AND EASTERBROOK'S CASES AND ECONOMIC NOTES ON ANTITRUST, Second Edition, 1077 pages, 1981. (Casebook) 1984–85 Supplement.

SULLIVAN'S HORNBOOK OF THE LAW OF ANTITRUST, 886 pages, 1977. (Text)

Appellate Advocacy—see Trial and Appellate Advocacy

Architecture and Engineering Law

SWEET'S LEGAL ASPECTS OF ARCHITECTURE, ENGINEERING AND THE CONSTRUCTION PROCESS, Fourth Edition, 889 pages, 1989. Teacher's Manual available. (Casebook)

Art Law

DUBOFF'S ART LAW IN A NUTSHELL, Second Edition, approximately 325 pages, 1993. Softcover. (Text)

Banking Law

BANKING LAW: SELECTED STATUTES AND REGULATIONS. Softcover. 263 pages, 1991.

LOVETT'S BANKING AND FINANCIAL INSTITUTIONS LAW IN A NUTSHELL, Third Edition, 470 pages, 1992. Softcover. (Text)

SYMONS AND WHITE'S BANKING LAW: TEACHING MATERIALS, Third Edition, 818 pages, 1991. Teacher's Manual available. (Casebook)

Statutory Supplement. *See Banking Law: Selected Statutes*

Bankruptcy—see Creditors' Rights

Business Planning—see also Corporate Finance

PAINTER'S PROBLEMS AND MATERIALS IN BUSINESS PLANNING, Second Edition, 1008 pages, 1984. (Casebook) 1990 Supplement.

Statutory Supplement. *See Selected Corporation and Partnership*

Civil Procedure—see also Federal Jurisdiction and Procedure

AMERICAN BAR ASSOCIATION SECTION OF LITIGATION—READINGS ON ADVERSARIAL JUSTICE: THE AMERICAN APPROACH TO ADJUDICATION, 217 pages, 1988. Softcover. (Coursebook)

CLERMONT'S BLACK LETTER ON CIVIL PROCEDURE, Third Edition, approximately 350 pages, May, 1993 Pub. Softcover. (Review)

COUND, FRIEDENTHAL, MILLER AND SEXTON'S

Civil Procedure—Cont'd

CASES AND MATERIALS ON CIVIL PROCEDURE, Fifth Edition, 1284 pages, 1989. Teacher's Manual available. (Casebook)

COUND, FRIEDENTHAL, MILLER AND SEXTON'S CIVIL PROCEDURE SUPPLEMENT. 476 pages, 1991. Softcover. (Casebook Supplement)

FEDERAL RULES OF CIVIL PROCEDURE—EDUCATIONAL EDITION. Softcover. 761 pages, 1992.

FRIEDENTHAL, KANE AND MILLER'S HORNBOOK ON CIVIL PROCEDURE, Second Edition, approximately 1000 pages, May 1993 Pub. (Text)

KANE AND LEVINE'S CIVIL PROCEDURE IN CALIFORNIA: STATE AND FEDERAL 1992 Edition, 551 pages. Softcover. (Casebook Supplement)

KANE'S CIVIL PROCEDURE IN A NUTSHELL, Third Edition, 303 pages, 1991. Softcover. (Text)

KOFFLER AND REPPY'S HORNBOOK ON COMMON LAW PLEADING, 663 pages, 1969. (Text)

LEVINE, SLOMANSON AND WINGATE'S CALIFORNIA CIVIL PROCEDURE, CASES AND MATERIALS, 546 pages, 1991. Teacher's Manual available. (Casebook)

MARCUS, REDISH AND SHERMAN'S CIVIL PROCEDURE: A MODERN APPROACH, 1027 pages, 1989. Teacher's Manual available. (Casebook) 1991 Supplement.

MARCUS AND SHERMAN'S COMPLEX LITIGATION–CASES AND MATERIALS ON ADVANCED CIVIL PROCEDURE, Second Edition, 1035 pages, 1992. Teacher's Manual available. (Casebook)

PARK AND MCFARLAND'S COMPUTER-AIDED EXERCISES ON CIVIL PROCEDURE, Third Edition, 210 pages, 1991. Softcover. (Coursebook)

SIEGEL'S HORNBOOK ON NEW YORK PRACTICE, Second Edition, Student Edition, 1068 pages, 1991. Softcover. (Text) 1992 Supplemental Pamphlet.

SLOMANSON AND WINGATE'S CALIFORNIA CIVIL PROCEDURE IN A NUTSHELL, 230 pages, 1992. Softcover. (Text)

Commercial Law

BAILEY AND HAGEDORN'S SECURED TRANSACTIONS IN A NUTSHELL, Third Edition, 390 pages, 1988. Softcover. (Text)

EPSTEIN, MARTIN, HENNING AND NICKLES' BASIC UNIFORM COMMERCIAL CODE TEACHING MATERIALS, Third Edition, 704 pages, 1988. Teacher's Manual available. (Casebook)

HENSON'S HORNBOOK ON SECURED TRANSACTIONS UNDER THE U.C.C., Second Edition, 504 pages, 1979, with 1979 pocket part. (Text)

MEYER AND SPEIDEL'S BLACK LETTER ON SALES AND LEASES OF GOODS, Approximately 300 pages, 1993. Softcover. (Review)

NICKLES' BLACK LETTER ON COMMERCIAL PAPER, 450 pages, 1988. Softcover. (Review)

NICKLES, MATHESON AND DOLAN'S MATERIALS FOR UNDERSTANDING CREDIT AND PAYMENT SYSTEMS, 923 pages, 1987. Teacher's Manual available. (Casebook)

NORDSTROM, MURRAY AND CLOVIS' PROBLEMS AND MATERIALS ON SALES, 515 pages, 1982. (Casebook)

NORDSTROM, MURRAY AND CLOVIS' PROBLEMS AND MATERIALS ON SECURED TRANSACTIONS, 594 pages, 1987. (Casebook)

RUBIN AND COOTER'S THE PAYMENT SYSTEM: CASES, MATERIALS AND ISSUES, 885 pages, 1989. Teacher's Manual Available. (Casebook)

SELECTED COMMERCIAL STATUTES. Softcover. 1897 pages, 1992.

SPEIDEL, SUMMERS AND WHITE'S COMMERCIAL LAW: TEACHING MATERIALS, Fourth Edition, 1448 pages, 1987. Teacher's Manual available. (Casebook)

SPEIDEL, SUMMERS AND WHITE'S COMMERCIAL PAPER: TEACHING MATERIALS, Fourth Edition, 578 pages, 1987. Reprint from Speidel et al., Commercial Law, Fourth Edition. Teacher's Manual available. (Casebook)

SPEIDEL, SUMMERS AND WHITE'S SALES: TEACHING MATERIALS, Fourth Edition, 804 pages, 1987. Reprint from Speidel et al., Commercial Law, Fourth Edition. Teacher's Manual available. (Casebook)

SPEIDEL, SUMMERS AND WHITE'S SECURED

Commercial Law—Cont'd

TRANSACTIONS: TEACHING MATERIALS, Fourth Edition, 485 pages, 1987. Reprint from Speidel et al., Commercial Law, Fourth Edition. Teacher's Manual available. (Casebook)

STOCKTON AND MILLER'S SALES AND LEASES OF GOODS IN A NUTSHELL, Third Edition, 441 pages, 1992. Softcover. (Text)

STONE'S UNIFORM COMMERCIAL CODE IN A NUTSHELL, Third Edition, 580 pages, 1989. Softcover. (Text)

WEBER AND SPEIDEL'S COMMERCIAL PAPER IN A NUTSHELL, Third Edition, 404 pages, 1982. Softcover. (Text)

WHITE AND SUMMERS' HORNBOOK ON THE UNIFORM COMMERCIAL CODE, Third Edition, Student Edition, 1386 pages, 1988. (Text)

Community Property

MENNELL AND BOYKOFF'S COMMUNITY PROPERTY IN A NUTSHELL, Second Edition, 432 pages, 1988. Softcover. (Text)

VERRALL AND BIRD'S CASES AND MATERIALS ON CALIFORNIA COMMUNITY PROPERTY, Fifth Edition, 604 pages, 1988. (Casebook)

Comparative Law

BARTON, GIBBS, LI AND MERRYMAN'S LAW IN RADICALLY DIFFERENT CULTURES, 960 pages, 1983. (Casebook)

FOLSOM, MINAN AND OTTO'S LAW AND POLITICS IN THE PEOPLE'S REPUBLIC OF CHINA IN A NUTSHELL, 451 pages, 1992. Softcover. (Text)

GLENDON, GORDON AND OSAKWE'S COMPARATIVE LEGAL TRADITIONS: TEXT, MATERIALS AND CASES ON THE CIVIL LAW, COMMON LAW AND SOCIALIST LAW TRADITIONS, 1091 pages, 1985. (Casebook)

GLENDON, GORDON AND OSAKWE'S COMPARATIVE LEGAL TRADITIONS IN A NUTSHELL. 402 pages, 1982. Softcover. (Text)

Computers and Law

MAGGS, SOMA AND SPROWL'S COMPUTER LAW—CASES, COMMENTS, AND QUESTIONS, 731 pages, 1992. Teacher's Manual available. (Casebook)

MAGGS AND SPROWL'S COMPUTER APPLICATIONS IN THE LAW, 316 pages, 1987. (Coursebook)

MASON'S USING COMPUTERS IN THE LAW: AN INTRODUCTION AND PRACTICAL GUIDE, Second Edition, 288 pages, 1988. Softcover. (Coursebook)

Conflict of Laws

CRAMTON, CURRIE AND KAY'S CASES–COMMENTS–QUESTIONS ON CONFLICT OF LAWS, Fourth Edition, 876 pages, 1987. (Casebook)

HAY'S BLACK LETTER ON CONFLICT OF LAWS, 330 pages, 1989. Softcover. (Review)

SCOLES AND HAY'S HORNBOOK ON CONFLICT OF LAWS, Student Edition, 1160 pages, 1992. (Text)

SIEGEL'S CONFLICTS IN A NUTSHELL, 470 pages, 1982. Softcover. (Text)

Constitutional Law—Civil Rights—see also First Amendment and Foreign Relations and National Security Law

ABERNATHY'S CIVIL RIGHTS AND CONSTITUTIONAL LITIGATION, CASES AND MATERIALS, Second Edition, 753 pages, 1992. (Casebook)

BARNES AND STOUT'S THE ECONOMICS OF CONSTITUTIONAL LAW AND PUBLIC CHOICE, 127 pages, 1992. Softcover. Teacher's Manual available. (Casebook)

BARRON AND DIENES' BLACK LETTER ON CONSTITUTIONAL LAW, Third Edition, 440 pages, 1991. Softcover. (Review)

BARRON AND DIENES' CONSTITUTIONAL LAW IN A NUTSHELL, Second Edition, 483 pages, 1991. Softcover. (Text)

ENGDAHL'S CONSTITUTIONAL FEDERALISM IN A NUTSHELL, Second Edition, 411 pages, 1987. Softcover. (Text)

FARBER AND SHERRY'S HISTORY OF THE AMERICAN CONSTITUTION, 458 pages, 1990. Softcover. Teacher's Manual available. (Text)

FISHER AND DEVINS' POLITICAL DYNAMICS OF CONSTITUTIONAL LAW, 333 pages, 1992. Softcover. (Casebook Supplement)

GARVEY AND ALEINIKOFF'S MODERN CONSTITUTIONAL THEORY: A READER, Second Edition, 559 pages, 1991. Softcover. (Reader)

LOCKHART, KAMISAR, CHOPER AND SHIFFRIN'S CONSTITUTIONAL LAW: CASES–COMMENTS–QUESTIONS, Seventh Edition, 1643 pages,

Constitutional Law—Civil Rights—Cont'd

1991. (Casebook) 1992 Supplement.

LOCKHART, KAMISAR, CHOPER AND SHIFFRIN'S THE AMERICAN CONSTITUTION: CASES AND MATERIALS, Seventh Edition, 1255 pages, 1991. Abridged version of Lockhart, et al., Constitutional Law: Cases–Comments–Questions, Seventh Edition. (Casebook) 1992 Supplement.

LOCKHART, KAMISAR, CHOPER AND SHIFFRIN'S CONSTITUTIONAL RIGHTS AND LIBERTIES: CASES AND MATERIALS, Seventh Edition, 1333 pages, 1991. Reprint from Lockhart, et al., Constitutional Law: Cases–Comments–Questions, Seventh Edition. (Casebook) 1992 Supplement.

MARKS AND COOPER'S STATE CONSTITUTIONAL LAW IN A NUTSHELL, 329 pages, 1988. Softcover. (Text)

NOWAK AND ROTUNDA'S HORNBOOK ON CONSTITUTIONAL LAW, Fourth Edition, 1357 pages, 1991. (Text)

ROTUNDA'S MODERN CONSTITUTIONAL LAW: CASES AND NOTES, Fourth Edition, approximately 1100 pages, April, 1993 Pub. (Casebook)

VIEIRA'S CONSTITUTIONAL CIVIL RIGHTS IN A NUTSHELL, Second Edition, 322 pages, 1990. Softcover. (Text)

WILLIAMS' CONSTITUTIONAL ANALYSIS IN A NUTSHELL, 388 pages, 1979. Softcover. (Text)

Consumer Law—see also Commercial Law

EPSTEIN AND NICKLES' CONSUMER LAW IN A NUTSHELL, Second Edition, 418 pages, 1981. Softcover. (Text)

SELECTED COMMERCIAL STATUTES. Softcover. 1897 pages, 1992.

SPANOGLE, ROHNER, PRIDGEN AND RASOR'S CASES AND MATERIALS ON CONSUMER LAW, Second Edition, 916 pages, 1991. Teacher's Manual available. (Casebook)

Contracts

BARNES AND STOUT'S THE ECONOMICS OF CONTRACT LAW, 127 pages, 1992. Softcover. Teacher's Manual available. (Casebook)

CALAMARI AND PERILLO'S BLACK LETTER ON CONTRACTS, Second Edition, 462 pages, 1990. Softcover. (Review)

CALAMARI AND PERILLO'S HORNBOOK ON CONTRACTS, Third Edition, 1049 pages, 1987. (Text)

CALAMARI, PERILLO AND BENDER'S CASES AND PROBLEMS ON CONTRACTS, Second Edition, 905 pages, 1989. Teacher's Manual Available. (Casebook)

CORBIN'S TEXT ON CONTRACTS, One Volume Student Edition, 1224 pages, 1952. (Text)

FESSLER AND LOISEAUX'S CASES AND MATERIALS ON CONTRACTS—MORALITY, ECONOMICS AND THE MARKET PLACE, 837 pages, 1982. Teacher's Manual available. (Casebook)

FRIEDMAN'S CONTRACT REMEDIES IN A NUTSHELL, 323 pages, 1981. Softcover. (Text)

FULLER AND EISENBERG'S CASES ON BASIC CONTRACT LAW, Fifth Edition, 1037 pages, 1990. (Casebook)

HAMILTON, RAU AND WEINTRAUB'S CASES AND MATERIALS ON CONTRACTS, Second Edition, 916 pages, 1992. Teacher's Manual available. (Casebook)

KEYES' GOVERNMENT CONTRACTS IN A NUTSHELL, Second Edition, 557 pages, 1990. Softcover. (Text)

SCHABER AND ROHWER'S CONTRACTS IN A NUTSHELL, Third Edition, 457 pages, 1990. Softcover. (Text)

SUMMERS AND HILLMAN'S CONTRACT AND RELATED OBLIGATION: THEORY, DOCTRINE AND PRACTICE, Second Edition, 1037 pages, 1992. Teacher's Manual available. (Casebook)

Copyright—see Patent and Copyright Law

Corporate Finance—see also Business Planning

HAMILTON'S CASES AND MATERIALS ON CORPORATION FINANCE, Second Edition, 1221 pages, 1989. (Casebook)

OESTERLE'S THE LAW OF MERGERS, ACQUISITIONS AND REORGANIZATIONS, 1096 pages, 1991. (Casebook) 1992 Supplement.

Corporations

HAMILTON'S BLACK LETTER ON CORPORATIONS, Third Edition, 732 pages, 1992. Softcover. (Review)

HAMILTON'S CASES AND MATERIALS ON CORPORATIONS—INCLUDING PARTNERSHIPS AND

Corporations—Cont'd

LIMITED PARTNERSHIPS, Fourth Edition, 1248 pages, 1990. Teacher's Manual available. (Casebook) 1990 Statutory Supplement.

HAMILTON'S THE LAW OF CORPORATIONS IN A NUTSHELL, Third Edition, 518 pages, 1991. Softcover. (Text)

HENN'S TEACHING MATERIALS ON THE LAW OF CORPORATIONS, Second Edition, 1204 pages, 1986. Teacher's Manual available. (Casebook)

Statutory Supplement. *See Selected Corporation and Partnership*

HENN AND ALEXANDER'S HORNBOOK ON LAWS OF CORPORATIONS, Third Edition, Student Edition, 1371 pages, 1983, with 1986 pocket part. (Text)

SELECTED CORPORATION AND PARTNERSHIP STATUTES, RULES AND FORMS. Revised 1991 Edition, 953 pages. Softcover.

SOLOMON, SCHWARTZ AND BAUMAN'S MATERIALS AND PROBLEMS ON CORPORATIONS: LAW AND POLICY, Second Edition, 1391 pages, 1988. Teacher's Manual available. (Casebook) 1992 Supplement.

Statutory Supplement. *See Selected Corporation and Partnership*

Corrections

KRANTZ' THE LAW OF CORRECTIONS AND PRISONERS' RIGHTS IN A NUTSHELL, Third Edition, 407 pages, 1988. Softcover. (Text)

KRANTZ AND BRANHAM'S CASES AND MATERIALS ON THE LAW OF SENTENCING, CORRECTIONS AND PRISONERS' RIGHTS, Fourth Edition, 619 pages, 1991. Teacher's Manual available. (Casebook)

Creditors' Rights

BANKRUPTCY CODE, RULES AND OFFICIAL FORMS, LAW SCHOOL EDITION. 910 pages, 1992. Softcover.

EPSTEIN'S DEBTOR-CREDITOR LAW IN A NUTSHELL, Fourth Edition, 401 pages, 1991. Softcover. (Text)

EPSTEIN, LANDERS AND NICKLES' CASES AND MATERIALS ON DEBTORS AND CREDITORS, Third Edition, 1059 pages, 1987. Teacher's Manual available. (Casebook)

EPSTEIN, NICKLES AND WHITE'S HORNBOOK ON BANKRUPTCY, Approximately 1000 pages, January, 1992 Pub. (Text)

LOPUCKI'S PLAYER'S MANUAL FOR THE DEBTOR-CREDITOR GAME, 123 pages, 1985. Softcover. (Coursebook)

NICKLES AND EPSTEIN'S BLACK LETTER ON CREDITORS' RIGHTS AND BANKRUPTCY, 576 pages, 1989. (Review)

RIESENFELD'S CASES AND MATERIALS ON CREDITORS' REMEDIES AND DEBTORS' PROTECTION, Fourth Edition, 914 pages, 1987. (Casebook) 1990 Supplement.

WHITE AND NIMMER'S CASES AND MATERIALS ON BANKRUPTCY, Second Edition, 764 pages, 1992. Teacher's Manual available. (Casebook)

Criminal Law and Criminal Procedure—see also Corrections, Juvenile Justice

ABRAMS' FEDERAL CRIMINAL LAW AND ITS ENFORCEMENT, 866 pages, 1986. (Casebook) 1988 Supplement.

BUCY'S WHITE COLLAR CRIME, CASES AND MATERIALS, 688 pages, 1992. Teacher's Manual available. (Casebook)

DIX AND SHARLOT'S CASES AND MATERIALS ON CRIMINAL LAW, Third Edition, 846 pages, 1987. (Casebook)

GRANO'S PROBLEMS IN CRIMINAL PROCEDURE, Second Edition, 176 pages, 1981. Teacher's Manual available. Softcover. (Coursebook)

HEYMANN AND KENETY'S THE MURDER TRIAL OF WILBUR JACKSON: A HOMICIDE IN THE FAMILY, Second Edition, 347 pages, 1985. (Coursebook)

ISRAEL, KAMISAR AND LAFAVE'S CRIMINAL PROCEDURE AND THE CONSTITUTION: LEADING SUPREME COURT CASES AND INTRODUCTORY TEXT. 802 pages, 1992 Edition. Softcover. (Casebook)

ISRAEL AND LAFAVE'S CRIMINAL PROCEDURE—CONSTITUTIONAL LIMITATIONS IN A NUTSHELL, Fourth Edition, 461 pages, 1988. Softcover. (Text)

JOHNSON'S CASES, MATERIALS AND TEXT ON CRIMINAL LAW, Fourth Edition, 759 pages, 1990. Teacher's Manual available. (Casebook)

JOHNSON'S CASES AND MATERIALS ON CRIMI-

Criminal Law and Criminal Procedure—Cont'd

NAL PROCEDURE, 859 pages, 1988. (Casebook) 1992 Supplement.

KAMISAR, LAFAVE AND ISRAEL'S MODERN CRIMINAL PROCEDURE: CASES, COMMENTS AND QUESTIONS, Seventh Edition, 1593 pages, 1990. (Casebook) 1992 Supplement.

KAMISAR, LAFAVE AND ISRAEL'S BASIC CRIMINAL PROCEDURE: CASES, COMMENTS AND QUESTIONS, Seventh Edition, 792 pages, 1990. Softcover reprint from Kamisar, et al., Modern Criminal Procedure: Cases, Comments and Questions, Seventh Edition. (Casebook) 1992 Supplement.

LAFAVE'S MODERN CRIMINAL LAW: CASES, COMMENTS AND QUESTIONS, Second Edition, 903 pages, 1988. (Casebook)

LAFAVE AND ISRAEL'S HORNBOOK ON CRIMINAL PROCEDURE, Second Edition, 1309 pages, 1992 with 1992 pocket part. (Text)

LAFAVE AND SCOTT'S HORNBOOK ON CRIMINAL LAW, Second Edition, 918 pages, 1986. (Text)

LOEWY'S CRIMINAL LAW IN A NUTSHELL, Second Edition, 321 pages, 1987. Softcover. (Text)

LOW'S BLACK LETTER ON CRIMINAL LAW, Revised First Edition, 443 pages, 1990. Softcover. (Review)

SALTZBURG AND CAPRA'S CASES AND COMMENTARY ON AMERICAN CRIMINAL PROCEDURE, Fourth Edition, 1341 pages, 1992. Teacher's Manual available. (Casebook) 1992 Supplement.

SUBIN, MIRSKY AND WEINSTEIN'S THE CRIMINAL PROCESS: PROSECUTION AND DEFENSE FUNCTIONS, Approximately 450 pages, February, 1993 Pub. Softcover. Teacher's Manual available. (Text)

VORENBERG'S CASES ON CRIMINAL LAW AND PROCEDURE, Second Edition, 1088 pages, 1981. Teacher's Manual available. (Casebook) 1990 Supplement.

Domestic Relations

CLARK'S HORNBOOK ON DOMESTIC RELATIONS, Second Edition, Student Edition, 1050 pages, 1988. (Text)

CLARK AND GLOWINSKY'S CASES AND PROBLEMS ON DOMESTIC RELATIONS, Fourth Edition. 1150 pages, 1990. Teacher's Manual available. (Casebook) 1992 Supplement.

KRAUSE'S BLACK LETTER ON FAMILY LAW, 314 pages, 1988. Softcover. (Review)

KRAUSE'S CASES, COMMENTS AND QUESTIONS ON FAMILY LAW, Third Edition, 1433 pages, 1990. (Casebook)

KRAUSE'S FAMILY LAW IN A NUTSHELL, Second Edition, 444 pages, 1986. Softcover. (Text)

KRAUSKOPF'S CASES ON PROPERTY DIVISION AT MARRIAGE DISSOLUTION, 250 pages, 1984. Softcover. (Casebook)

Economics, Law and—see also Antitrust, Regulated Industries

BARNES AND STOUT'S CASES AND MATERIALS ON LAW AND ECONOMICS, 538 pages, 1992. Teacher's Manual available. (Casebook)

GOETZ' CASES AND MATERIALS ON LAW AND ECONOMICS, 547 pages, 1984. (Casebook)

MALLOY'S LAW AND ECONOMICS: A COMPARATIVE APPROACH TO THEORY AND PRACTICE, 166 pages, 1990. Softcover. (Text)

Education Law

ALEXANDER AND ALEXANDER'S PUBLIC SCHOOL LAW, Third Edition, 880 pages, 1992. Teacher's Manual available. (Coursebook)

ALEXANDER AND ALEXANDER'S THE LAW OF SCHOOLS, STUDENTS AND TEACHERS IN A NUTSHELL, 409 pages, 1984. Softcover. (Text)

YUDOF, KIRP AND LEVIN'S EDUCATIONAL POLICY AND THE LAW, Third Edition, 860 pages, 1992. (Casebook)

Employment Discrimination—see also Gender Discrimination

ESTREICHER AND HARPER'S CASES AND MATERIALS ON THE LAW GOVERNING THE EMPLOYMENT RELATIONSHIP, Second Edition, 966 pages, 1992. (Casebook) Statutory Supplement.

JONES, MURPHY AND BELTON'S CASES AND MATERIALS ON DISCRIMINATION IN EMPLOYMENT, (The Labor Law Group). Fifth Edition, 1116 pages, 1987. (Casebook) 1990 Supplement.

PLAYER'S FEDERAL LAW OF EMPLOYMENT DIS-

Employment Discrimination—Cont'd

CRIMINATION IN A NUTSHELL, Third Edition, 338 pages, 1992. Softcover. (Text)

PLAYER'S HORNBOOK ON EMPLOYMENT DISCRIMINATION LAW, Student Edition, 708 pages, 1988. (Text)

PLAYER, SHOBEN AND LIEBERWITZ' CASES AND MATERIALS ON EMPLOYMENT DISCRIMINATION LAW, 827 pages, 1990. Teacher's Manual available. (Casebook) 1992 Supplement.

Energy and Natural Resources Law—see also Oil and Gas

LAITOS' CASES AND MATERIALS ON NATURAL RESOURCES LAW, 938 pages, 1985. Teacher's Manual available. (Casebook)

LAITOS AND TOMAIN'S ENERGY AND NATURAL RESOURCES LAW IN A NUTSHELL, 554 pages, 1992. Softcover. (Text)

SELECTED ENVIRONMENTAL LAW STATUTES—EDUCATIONAL EDITION. Softcover. 1296 pages, 1992.

Environmental Law—see also Energy and Natural Resources Law; Sea, Law of

BONINE AND MCGARITY'S THE LAW OF ENVIRONMENTAL PROTECTION: CASES—LEGISLATION—POLICIES, Second Edition, 1042 pages, 1992. (Casebook)

FINDLEY AND FARBER'S CASES AND MATERIALS ON ENVIRONMENTAL LAW, Third Edition, 763 pages, 1991. Teacher's Manual available. (Casebook)

FINDLEY AND FARBER'S ENVIRONMENTAL LAW IN A NUTSHELL, Third Edition, 355 pages, 1992. Softcover. (Text)

PLATER, ABRAMS AND GOLDFARB'S ENVIRONMENTAL LAW AND POLICY: NATURE, LAW AND SOCIETY, 1039 pages, 1992. Teacher's Manual available. (Casebook)

RODGERS' HORNBOOK ON ENVIRONMENTAL LAW, 956 pages, 1977, with 1984 pocket part. (Text)

SELECTED ENVIRONMENTAL LAW STATUTES—EDUCATIONAL EDITION. Softcover. 1296 pages, 1992.

Equity—see Remedies

Estate Planning—see also Trusts and Estates; Taxation—Estate and Gift

LYNN'S INTRODUCTION TO ESTATE PLANNING IN A NUTSHELL, Fourth Edition, 352 pages, 1992. Softcover. (Text)

Evidence

BERGMAN'S TRANSCRIPT EXERCISES FOR LEARNING EVIDENCE, 273 pages, 1992. Teacher's Manual available. (Coursebook)

BROUN AND BLAKEY'S BLACK LETTER ON EVIDENCE, 269 pages, 1984. Softcover. (Review)

BROUN, MEISENHOLDER, STRONG AND MOSTELLER'S PROBLEMS IN EVIDENCE, Third Edition, 238 pages, 1988. Teacher's Manual available. Softcover. (Coursebook)

CLEARY, STRONG, BROUN AND MOSTELLER'S CASES AND MATERIALS ON EVIDENCE, Fourth Edition, 1060 pages, 1988. (Casebook)

FEDERAL RULES OF EVIDENCE FOR UNITED STATES COURTS AND MAGISTRATES. Softcover. 549 pages, 1992.

FRIEDMAN'S THE ELEMENTS OF EVIDENCE, 315 pages, 1991. Teacher's Manual available. (Coursebook)

GRAHAM'S FEDERAL RULES OF EVIDENCE IN A NUTSHELL, Third Edition, 486 pages, 1992. Softcover. (Text)

LEMPERT AND SALTZBURG'S A MODERN APPROACH TO EVIDENCE: TEXT, PROBLEMS, TRANSCRIPTS AND CASES, Second Edition, 1232 pages, 1983. Teacher's Manual available. (Casebook)

LILLY'S AN INTRODUCTION TO THE LAW OF EVIDENCE, Second Edition, 585 pages, 1987. (Text)

MCCORMICK, SUTTON AND WELLBORN'S CASES AND MATERIALS ON EVIDENCE, Seventh Edition, 932 pages, 1992. Teacher's Manual available. (Casebook)

MCCORMICK'S HORNBOOK ON EVIDENCE, Fourth Edition, Student Edition, 672 pages, 1992. (Text)

ROTHSTEIN'S EVIDENCE IN A NUTSHELL: STATE AND FEDERAL RULES, Second Edition, 514 pages, 1981. Softcover. (Text)

Federal Jurisdiction and Procedure

CURRIE'S CASES AND MATERIALS ON FEDERAL COURTS, Fourth Edition, 783 pages, 1990. (Casebook)

CURRIE'S FEDERAL JURISDICTION IN A NUTSHELL, Third Edition, 242 pages, 1990.

Federal Jurisdiction and Procedure—Cont'd

Softcover. (Text)

FEDERAL RULES OF CIVIL PROCEDURE—EDUCATIONAL EDITION. Softcover. 761 pages, 1992.

REDISH'S BLACK LETTER ON FEDERAL JURISDICTION, Second Edition, 234 pages, 1991. Softcover. (Review)

REDISH'S CASES, COMMENTS AND QUESTIONS ON FEDERAL COURTS, Second Edition, 1122 pages, 1989. (Casebook) 1992 Supplement.

VETRI AND MERRILL'S FEDERAL COURTS PROBLEMS AND MATERIALS, Second Edition, 232 pages, 1984. Softcover. (Coursebook)

WRIGHT'S HORNBOOK ON FEDERAL COURTS, Fourth Edition, Student Edition, 870 pages, 1983. (Text)

First Amendment

GARVEY AND SCHAUER'S THE FIRST AMENDMENT: A READER, 527 pages, 1992. Softcover. (Reader)

SHIFFRIN AND CHOPER'S FIRST AMENDMENT, CASES—COMMENTS—QUESTIONS, 759 pages, 1991. Softcover. (Casebook) 1992 Supplement.

Foreign Relations and National Security Law

FRANCK AND GLENNON'S FOREIGN RELATIONS AND NATIONAL SECURITY LAW, 941 pages, 1987. (Casebook)

Future Interests—see Trusts and Estates

Gender Discrimination—see also Employment Discrimination

KAY'S TEXT, CASES AND MATERIALS ON SEX-BASED DISCRIMINATION, Third Edition, 1001 pages, 1988. (Casebook) 1992 Supplement.

THOMAS' SEX DISCRIMINATION IN A NUTSHELL, Second Edition, 395 pages, 1991. Softcover. (Text)

Health Law—see Medicine, Law and

Human Rights—see International Law

Immigration Law

ALEINIKOFF AND MARTIN'S IMMIGRATION: PROCESS AND POLICY, Second Edition, 1056 pages, 1991. (Casebook)

Statutory Supplement. *See Immigration and Nationality Laws*

IMMIGRATION AND NATIONALITY LAWS OF THE UNITED STATES: SELECTED STATUTES, REGULATIONS AND FORMS. Softcover. 519 pages, 1992.

WEISSBRODT'S IMMIGRATION LAW AND PROCEDURE IN A NUTSHELL, Third Edition, 497 pages, 1992. Softcover. (Text)

Indian Law—see American Indian Law

Insurance Law

DEVINE AND TERRY'S PROBLEMS IN INSURANCE LAW, 240 pages, 1989. Softcover. Teacher's Manual available. (Coursebook)

DOBBYN'S INSURANCE LAW IN A NUTSHELL, Second Edition, 316 pages, 1989. Softcover. (Text)

KEETON'S COMPUTER-AIDED AND WORKBOOK EXERCISES ON INSURANCE LAW, 255 pages, 1990. Softcover. (Coursebook)

KEETON AND WIDISS' INSURANCE LAW, Student Edition, 1359 pages, 1988. (Text)

WIDISS AND KEETON'S COURSE SUPPLEMENT TO KEETON AND WIDISS' INSURANCE LAW, 502 pages, 1988. Softcover. Teacher's Manual available. (Casebook)

WIDISS' INSURANCE: MATERIALS ON FUNDAMENTAL PRINCIPLES, LEGAL DOCTRINES AND REGULATORY ACTS, 1186 pages, 1989. Teacher's Manual available. (Casebook)

YORK AND WHELAN'S CASES, MATERIALS AND PROBLEMS ON GENERAL PRACTICE INSURANCE LAW, Second Edition, 787 pages, 1988. Teacher's Manual available. (Casebook)

International Law—see also Sea, Law of

BERMANN, DAVEY, FOX AND GOEBEL'S CASES AND MATERIALS ON EUROPEAN COMMUNITY LAW, Approximately 1200 pages, 1993. (Casebook) Statutory Supplement. *See European Economic Community: Selected Documents*

BUERGENTHAL'S INTERNATIONAL HUMAN RIGHTS IN A NUTSHELL, 283 pages, 1988. Softcover. (Text)

BUERGENTHAL AND MAIER'S PUBLIC INTERNATIONAL LAW IN A NUTSHELL, Second Edition, 275 pages, 1990. Softcover. (Text)

EUROPEAN ECONOMIC COMMUNITY: SELECTED DOCUMENTS. Approximately 550 pages,

International Law—Cont'd

1993. Softcover

FOLSOM'S EUROPEAN COMMUNITY LAW IN A NUTSHELL, 423 pages, 1992. Softcover. (Text)

FOLSOM, GORDON AND SPANOGLE'S INTERNATIONAL BUSINESS TRANSACTIONS—A PROBLEM-ORIENTED COURSEBOOK, Second Edition, 1237 pages, 1991. Teacher's Manual available. (Casebook) 1991 Documents Supplement.

FOLSOM, GORDON AND SPANOGLE'S INTERNATIONAL BUSINESS TRANSACTIONS IN A NUTSHELL, Fourth Edition, 548 pages, 1992. Softcover. (Text)

HENKIN, PUGH, SCHACHTER AND SMIT'S CASES AND MATERIALS ON INTERNATIONAL LAW, Second Edition, 1517 pages, 1987. (Casebook) Documents Supplement.

INTERNATIONAL LITIGATION AND ARBITRATION: SELECTED TREATIES, STATUTES AND RULES. Approximately 275 pages, 1993. Softcover

INTERNATIONAL ORGANIZATIONS IN THEIR LEGAL SETTING: SELECTED DOCUMENTS. Approximately 500 pages, March, 1993 Pub. Softcover

JACKSON AND DAVEY'S CASES, MATERIALS AND TEXT ON LEGAL PROBLEMS OF INTERNATIONAL ECONOMIC RELATIONS, Second Edition, 1269 pages, 1986. (Casebook) 1989 Documents Supplement.

KIRGIS' INTERNATIONAL ORGANIZATIONS IN THEIR LEGAL SETTING, Second Edition, approximately 1150 pages, March, 1993 Pub. Teacher's Manual available. (Casebook) Statutory Supplement.

LOWENFELD'S INTERNATIONAL LITIGATION AND ARBITRATION, Approximately 875 pages, 1993. (Casebook) Statutory Supplement. *See International Litigation: Selected Documents*

WESTON, FALK AND D'AMATO'S INTERNATIONAL LAW AND WORLD ORDER—A PROBLEM-ORIENTED COURSEBOOK, Second Edition, 1335 pages, 1990. Teacher's Manual available. (Casebook) Documents Supplement.

Interviewing and Counseling

BINDER AND PRICE'S LEGAL INTERVIEWING AND COUNSELING, 232 pages, 1977. Softcover. Teacher's Manual available. (Coursebook)

BINDER, BERGMAN AND PRICE'S LAWYERS AS COUNSELORS: A CLIENT-CENTERED APPROACH, 427 pages, 1991. Softcover. (Coursebook)

SHAFFER AND ELKINS' LEGAL INTERVIEWING AND COUNSELING IN A NUTSHELL, Second Edition, 487 pages, 1987. Softcover. (Text)

Introduction to Law—see Legal Method and Legal System

Introduction to Law Study

HEGLAND'S INTRODUCTION TO THE STUDY AND PRACTICE OF LAW IN A NUTSHELL, 418 pages, 1983. Softcover. (Text)

KINYON'S INTRODUCTION TO LAW STUDY AND LAW EXAMINATIONS IN A NUTSHELL, 389 pages, 1971. Softcover. (Text)

Judicial Process—see Legal Method and Legal System

Jurisprudence

CHRISTIE'S JURISPRUDENCE—TEXT AND READINGS ON THE PHILOSOPHY OF LAW, 1056 pages, 1973. (Casebook)

SINHA'S JURISPRUDENCE (LEGAL PHILOSOPHY) IN A NUTSHELL. Approximately 350 pages, 1993. Softcover. (Text)

Juvenile Justice

FOX'S JUVENILE COURTS IN A NUTSHELL, Third Edition, 291 pages, 1984. Softcover. (Text)

Labor and Employment Law—see also Employment Discrimination, Workers' Compensation

FINKIN, GOLDMAN AND SUMMERS' LEGAL PROTECTION OF INDIVIDUAL EMPLOYEES, (The Labor Law Group). 1164 pages, 1989. (Casebook)

GORMAN'S BASIC TEXT ON LABOR LAW—UNIONIZATION AND COLLECTIVE BARGAINING, 914 pages, 1976. (Text)

LESLIE'S LABOR LAW IN A NUTSHELL, Third Edition, 388 pages, 1992. Softcover. (Text)

NOLAN'S LABOR ARBITRATION LAW AND PRAC-

Labor and Employment Law—Cont'd

TICE IN A NUTSHELL, 358 pages, 1979. Softcover. (Text)

OBERER, HANSLOWE, ANDERSEN AND HEINSZ' CASES AND MATERIALS ON LABOR LAW—COLLECTIVE BARGAINING IN A FREE SOCIETY, Third Edition, 1163 pages, 1986. Teacher's Manual available. (Casebook) Statutory Supplement. 1991 Case Supplement.

RABIN, SILVERSTEIN AND SCHATZKI'S LABOR AND EMPLOYMENT LAW: PROBLEMS, CASES AND MATERIALS IN THE LAW OF WORK, (The Labor Law Group). 1014 pages, 1988. Teacher's Manual available. (Casebook) 1988 Statutory Supplement.

WOLLETT, GRODIN AND WEISBERGER'S COLLECTIVE BARGAINING IN PUBLIC EMPLOYMENT, (The Labor Law Group). Fourth Edition, approximately 600 pages, April, 1993 Pub. (Casebook)

Land Finance—Property Security—see Real Estate Transactions

Land Use

CALLIES AND FREILICH'S CASES AND MATERIALS ON LAND USE, 1233 pages, 1986. (Casebook) 1991 Supplement.

HAGMAN AND JUERGENSMEYER'S HORNBOOK ON URBAN PLANNING AND LAND DEVELOPMENT CONTROL LAW, Second Edition, Student Edition, 680 pages, 1986. (Text)

WRIGHT AND GITELMAN'S CASES AND MATERIALS ON LAND USE, Fourth Edition, 1255 pages, 1991. Teacher's Manual available. (Casebook)

WRIGHT AND WRIGHT'S LAND USE IN A NUTSHELL, Second Edition, 356 pages, 1985. Softcover. (Text)

Legal History—see also Legal Method and Legal System

PRESSER AND ZAINALDIN'S CASES AND MATERIALS ON LAW AND JURISPRUDENCE IN AMERICAN HISTORY, Second Edition, 1092 pages, 1989. Teacher's Manual available. (Casebook)

Legal Method and Legal System—see also Legal Research, Legal Writing

ALDISERT'S READINGS, MATERIALS AND CASES IN THE JUDICIAL PROCESS, 948 pages, 1976. (Casebook)

BERCH, BERCH AND SPRITZER'S INTRODUCTION TO LEGAL METHOD AND PROCESS, Second Edition, 585 pages, 1992. Teacher's Manual available. (Casebook)

BODENHEIMER, OAKLEY AND LOVE'S READINGS AND CASES ON AN INTRODUCTION TO THE ANGLO-AMERICAN LEGAL SYSTEM, Second Edition, 166 pages, 1988. Softcover. (Casebook)

DAVIES AND LAWRY'S INSTITUTIONS AND METHODS OF THE LAW—INTRODUCTORY TEACHING MATERIALS, 547 pages, 1982. Teacher's Manual available. (Casebook)

DVORKIN, HIMMELSTEIN AND LESNICK'S BECOMING A LAWYER: A HUMANISTIC PERSPECTIVE ON LEGAL EDUCATION AND PROFESSIONALISM, 211 pages, 1981. Softcover. (Text)

KEETON'S JUDGING, 842 pages, 1990. Softcover. (Coursebook)

KELSO AND KELSO'S STUDYING LAW: AN INTRODUCTION, 587 pages, 1984. (Coursebook)

KEMPIN'S HISTORICAL INTRODUCTION TO ANGLO-AMERICAN LAW IN A NUTSHELL, Third Edition, 323 pages, 1990. Softcover. (Text)

MEADOR'S AMERICAN COURTS, 113 pages, 1991. Softcover. (Text)

REYNOLDS' JUDICIAL PROCESS IN A NUTSHELL, Second Edition, 308 pages, 1991. Softcover. (Text)

Legal Research

COHEN AND OLSON'S LEGAL RESEARCH IN A NUTSHELL, Fifth Edition, 370 pages, 1992. Softcover. (Text)

COHEN, BERRING AND OLSON'S HOW TO FIND THE LAW, Ninth Edition, 716 pages, 1989. (Text)

COHEN, BERRING AND OLSON'S FINDING THE LAW, 570 pages, 1989. Softcover reprint from Cohen, Berring and Olson's How to Find the Law, Ninth Edition. (Coursebook)

Legal Research Exercises, 4th Ed., for use with Cohen, Berring and Olson, 253 pages, 1992. Teacher's Manual available.

ROMBAUER'S LEGAL PROBLEM SOLVING—ANALYSIS, RESEARCH AND WRITING, Fifth Edition, 524 pages, 1991. Softcover. Teacher's Manual with problems availa-

Legal Research—Cont'd

ble. (Coursebook)

STATSKY'S LEGAL RESEARCH AND WRITING: SOME STARTING POINTS, Fourth Edition, approximately 270 pages, 1993. Softcover. Teacher's Manual available. (Coursebook) Student Workbook.

TEPLY'S LEGAL RESEARCH AND CITATION, Fourth Edition, 436 pages, 1992. Softcover. (Coursebook)

Student Library Exercises, Fourth Edition, 276 pages, 1992. Answer Key available.

Legal Writing and Drafting

CHILD'S DRAFTING LEGAL DOCUMENTS: PRINCIPLES AND PRACTICES, Second Edition, 425 pages, 1992. Softcover. Teacher's Manual available. (Coursebook)

DICKERSON'S MATERIALS ON LEGAL DRAFTING, 425 pages, 1981. Teacher's Manual available. (Coursebook)

FELSENFELD AND SIEGEL'S WRITING CONTRACTS IN PLAIN ENGLISH, 290 pages, 1981. Softcover. (Text)

GOPEN'S WRITING FROM A LEGAL PERSPECTIVE, 225 pages, 1981. (Text)

MARTINEAU'S DRAFTING LEGISLATION AND RULES IN PLAIN ENGLISH, 155 pages, 1991. Softcover. Teacher's Manual available. (Text)

MELLINKOFF'S DICTIONARY OF AMERICAN LEGAL USAGE, 703 pages, 1992. Softcover. (Text)

MELLINKOFF'S LEGAL WRITING—SENSE AND NONSENSE, 242 pages, 1982. Softcover. Teacher's Manual available. (Text)

PRATT'S LEGAL WRITING: A SYSTEMATIC APPROACH, Second Edition, approximately 550 pages, April, 1993 Pub. Teacher's Manual available. (Coursebook)

RAY AND COX'S BEYOND THE BASICS: A TEXT FOR ADVANCED LEGAL WRITING, 427 pages, 1991. Softcover. Teacher's Manual available. (Text)

RAY AND RAMSFIELD'S LEGAL WRITING: GETTING IT RIGHT AND GETTING IT WRITTEN, 250 pages, 1987. Softcover. (Text)

SQUIRES AND ROMBAUER'S LEGAL WRITING IN A NUTSHELL, 294 pages, 1982. Softcover. (Text)

STATSKY AND WERNET'S CASE ANALYSIS AND FUNDAMENTALS OF LEGAL WRITING, Third Edition, 424 pages, 1989. Teacher's Manual available. (Text)

TEPLY'S LEGAL WRITING, ANALYSIS AND ORAL ARGUMENT, 576 pages, 1990. Softcover. Teacher's Manual available. (Coursebook)

WEIHOFEN'S LEGAL WRITING STYLE, Second Edition, 332 pages, 1980. (Text)

Legislation—see also Legal Writing and Drafting

DAVIES' LEGISLATIVE LAW AND PROCESS IN A NUTSHELL, Second Edition, 346 pages, 1986. Softcover. (Text)

ESKRIDGE AND FRICKEY'S CASES AND MATERIALS ON LEGISLATION: STATUTES AND THE CREATION OF PUBLIC POLICY, 937 pages, 1988. Teacher's Manual available. (Casebook) 1992 Supplement.

NUTTING AND DICKERSON'S CASES AND MATERIALS ON LEGISLATION, Fifth Edition, 744 pages, 1978. (Casebook)

STATSKY'S LEGISLATIVE ANALYSIS AND DRAFTING, Second Edition, 217 pages, 1984. Teacher's Manual available. (Text)

Local Government

FRUG'S CASES AND MATERIALS ON LOCAL GOVERNMENT LAW, 1005 pages, 1988. (Casebook) 1991 Supplement.

MCCARTHY'S LOCAL GOVERNMENT LAW IN A NUTSHELL, Third Edition, 435 pages, 1990. Softcover. (Text)

REYNOLDS' HORNBOOK ON LOCAL GOVERNMENT LAW, 860 pages, 1982 with 1990 pocket part. (Text)

VALENTE AND MCCARTHY'S CASES AND MATERIALS ON LOCAL GOVERNMENT LAW, Fourth Edition, 1158 pages, 1992. Teacher's Manual available. (Casebook)

Mass Communication Law

GILLMOR, BARRON, SIMON AND TERRY'S CASES AND COMMENT ON MASS COMMUNICATION LAW, Fifth Edition, 947 pages, 1990. (Casebook)

GINSBURG, BOTEIN AND DIRECTOR'S REGULATION OF THE ELECTRONIC MASS MEDIA: LAW

Mass Communication Law—Cont'd

AND POLICY FOR RADIO, TELEVISION, CABLE AND THE NEW VIDEO TECHNOLOGIES, Second Edition, 657 pages, 1991. (Casebook) Statutory Supplement.

ZUCKMAN, GAYNES, CARTER AND DEE'S MASS COMMUNICATIONS LAW IN A NUTSHELL, Third Edition, 538 pages, 1988. Softcover. (Text)

Medicine, Law and

FISCINA, BOUMIL, SHARPE AND HEAD'S MEDICAL LIABILITY, 487 pages, 1991. Teacher's Manual available. (Casebook)

FURROW, JOHNSON, JOST AND SCHWARTZ' HEALTH LAW: CASES, MATERIALS AND PROBLEMS, Second Edition, 1236 pages, 1991. Teacher's Manual available. (Casebook)

FURROW, JOHNSON, JOST AND SCHWARTZ' BIOETHICS: HEALTH CARE LAW AND ETHICS, Reprint from Furrow et al., Health Law, Second Edition. Softcover. Teacher's Manual available. (Casebook)

FURROW, JOHNSON, JOST AND SCHWARTZ' THE LAW OF HEALTH CARE ORGANIZATION AND FINANCE, Reprint from Furrow et al., Health Law, Second Edition. Softcover. Teacher's Manual available.

FURROW, JOHNSON, JOST AND SCHWARTZ' LIABILITY AND QUALITY ISSUES IN HEALTH CARE, Reprint from Furrow et al., Health Law, Second Edition. Softcover. Teacher's Manual available. (Casebook)

HALL AND ELLMAN'S HEALTH CARE LAW AND ETHICS IN A NUTSHELL, 401 pages, 1990. Softcover (Text)

JARVIS, CLOSEN, HERMANN AND LEONARD'S AIDS LAW IN A NUTSHELL, 349 pages, 1991. Softcover. (Text)

KING'S THE LAW OF MEDICAL MALPRACTICE IN A NUTSHELL, Second Edition, 342 pages, 1986. Softcover. (Text)

SHAPIRO AND SPECE'S CASES, MATERIALS AND PROBLEMS ON BIOETHICS AND LAW, 892 pages, 1981. (Casebook) 1991 Supplement.

Military Law

SHANOR AND TERRELL'S MILITARY LAW IN A NUTSHELL, 378 pages, 1980. Softcover. (Text)

Mining Law—see Energy and Natural Resources Law

Mortgages—see Real Estate Transactions

Natural Resources Law—see Energy and Natural Resources Law, Environmental Law

Negotiation

GIFFORD'S LEGAL NEGOTIATION: THEORY AND APPLICATIONS, 225 pages, 1989. Softcover. (Text)

TEPLY'S LEGAL NEGOTIATION IN A NUTSHELL, 282 pages, 1992. Softcover. (Text)

WILLIAMS' LEGAL NEGOTIATION AND SETTLEMENT, 207 pages, 1983. Softcover. Teacher's Manual available. (Coursebook)

Office Practice—see also Computers and Law, Interviewing and Counseling, Negotiation

HEGLAND'S TRIAL AND PRACTICE SKILLS IN A NUTSHELL, 346 pages, 1978. Softcover (Text)

MUNNEKE'S LAW PRACTICE MANAGEMENT: MATERIALS AND CASES, 634 pages, 1991. Teacher's Manual available. (Casebook)

Oil and Gas—see also Energy and Natural Resources Law

HEMINGWAY'S HORNBOOK ON THE LAW OF OIL AND GAS, Third Edition, Student Edition, 711 pages, 1992. (Text)

KUNTZ, LOWE, ANDERSON AND SMITH'S CASES AND MATERIALS ON OIL AND GAS LAW, Second Edition, approximately 1000 pages, 1993. Teacher's Manual available. (Casebook) Forms Manual. Revised.

LOWE'S OIL AND GAS LAW IN A NUTSHELL, Second Edition, 465 pages, 1988. Softcover. (Text)

Partnership—see Agency—Partnership

Patent and Copyright Law

CHOATE, FRANCIS AND COLLINS' CASES AND MATERIALS ON PATENT LAW, INCLUDING TRADE SECRETS, COPYRIGHTS, TRADEMARKS, Third Edition, 1009 pages, 1987. (Casebook)

HALPERN, SHIPLEY AND ABRAMS' CASES AND MATERIALS ON COPYRIGHT, 663 pages, 1992. (Casebook)

Patent and Copyright Law—Cont'd

MILLER AND DAVIS' INTELLECTUAL PROPERTY—PATENTS, TRADEMARKS AND COPYRIGHT IN A NUTSHELL, Second Edition, 437 pages, 1990. Softcover. (Text)

NIMMER, MARCUS, MYERS AND NIMMER'S CASES AND MATERIALS ON COPYRIGHT AND OTHER ASPECTS OF ENTERTAINMENT LITIGATION—INCLUDING UNFAIR COMPETITION, DEFAMATION, PRIVACY, ILLUSTRATED, Fourth Edition, 1177 pages, 1991. (Casebook) Statutory Supplement. See *Selected Intellectual Property Statutes*

SELECTED INTELLECTUAL PROPERTY AND UNFAIR COMPETITION STATUTES, REGULATIONS AND TREATIES. Softcover.

Products Liability

FISCHER AND POWERS' CASES AND MATERIALS ON PRODUCTS LIABILITY, 685 pages, 1988. Teacher's Manual available. (Casebook)

PHILLIPS' PRODUCTS LIABILITY IN A NUTSHELL, Third Edition, 307 pages, 1988. Softcover. (Text)

Professional Responsibility

ARONSON, DEVINE AND FISCH'S PROBLEMS, CASES AND MATERIALS IN PROFESSIONAL RESPONSIBILITY, 745 pages, 1985. Teacher's Manual available. (Casebook)

ARONSON AND WECKSTEIN'S PROFESSIONAL RESPONSIBILITY IN A NUTSHELL, Second Edition, 514 pages, 1991. Softcover. (Text)

LESNICK'S BEING A LAWYER: INDIVIDUAL CHOICE AND RESPONSIBILITY IN THE PRACTICE OF LAW, 422 pages, 1992. Softcover. Teacher's Manual available. (Coursebook)

MELLINKOFF'S THE CONSCIENCE OF A LAWYER, 304 pages, 1973. (Text)

PIRSIG AND KIRWIN'S CASES AND MATERIALS ON PROFESSIONAL RESPONSIBILITY, Fourth Edition, 603 pages, 1984. Teacher's Manual available. (Casebook)

ROTUNDA'S BLACK LETTER ON PROFESSIONAL RESPONSIBILITY, Third Edition, 492 pages, 1992. Softcover. (Review)

SCHWARTZ, WYDICK AND PERSCHBACHER'S PROBLEMS IN LEGAL ETHICS, Third Edition, approximately 400 pages, 1993. (Coursebook)

SELECTED STATUTES, RULES AND STANDARDS ON THE LEGAL PROFESSION. Softcover. 940 pages, 1992.

SMITH AND MALLEN'S PREVENTING LEGAL MALPRACTICE, 264 pages, 1989. Reprint from Mallen and Smith's Legal Malpractice, Third Edition. (Text)

SUTTON AND DZIENKOWSKI'S CASES AND MATERIALS ON PROFESSIONAL RESPONSIBILITY FOR LAWYERS, 839 pages, 1989. Teacher's Manual available. (Casebook)

WOLFRAM'S HORNBOOK ON MODERN LEGAL ETHICS, Student Edition, 1120 pages, 1986. (Text)

WYDICK AND PERSCHBACHER'S CALIFORNIA LEGAL ETHICS, 439 pages, 1992. Softcover. (Coursebook)

Property—see also Real Estate Transactions, Land Use, Trusts and Estates

BARNES AND STOUT'S THE ECONOMICS OF PROPERTY RIGHTS AND NUISANCE LAW, 87 pages, 1992. Softcover. Teacher's Manual available. (Casebook)

BERNHARDT'S BLACK LETTER ON PROPERTY, Second Edition, 388 pages, 1991. Softcover. (Review)

BERNHARDT'S REAL PROPERTY IN A NUTSHELL, Second Edition, 448 pages, 1981. Softcover. (Text)

BOYER, HOVENKAMP AND KURTZ' THE LAW OF PROPERTY, AN INTRODUCTORY SURVEY, Fourth Edition, 696 pages, 1991. (Text)

BROWDER, CUNNINGHAM, NELSON, STOEBUCK AND WHITMAN'S CASES ON BASIC PROPERTY LAW, Fifth Edition, 1386 pages, 1989. Teacher's Manual available. (Casebook)

BRUCE, ELY AND BOSTICK'S CASES AND MATERIALS ON MODERN PROPERTY LAW, Second Edition, 953 pages, 1989. Teacher's Manual available. (Casebook)

BURKE'S PERSONAL PROPERTY IN A NUTSHELL, Second Edition, approximately 400 pages, May, 1993 Pub. Softcover. (Text)

CUNNINGHAM, STOEBUCK AND WHITMAN'S HORNBOOK ON THE LAW OF PROPERTY, Second Edition, approximately 900 pages, May, 1993 Pub. (Text)

DONAHUE, KAUPER AND MARTIN'S CASES AND MATERIALS ON PROPERTY, AN INTRODUCTION TO THE CONCEPT AND THE INSTITUTION, Third

Property—Cont'd

Edition, approximately 1000 pages, 1993. Teacher's Manual available. (Casebook)

HILL'S LANDLORD AND TENANT LAW IN A NUTSHELL, Second Edition, 311 pages, 1986. Softcover. (Text)

JOHNSON, JOST, SALSICH AND SHAFFER'S PROPERTY LAW, CASES, MATERIALS AND PROBLEMS, 908 pages, 1992. Teacher's Manual available. (Casebook)

KURTZ AND HOVENKAMP'S CASES AND MATERIALS ON AMERICAN PROPERTY LAW, Second Edition, approximately 1350 pages, March, 1993 Pub. Teacher's Manual available. (Casebook)

MOYNIHAN'S INTRODUCTION TO REAL PROPERTY, Second Edition, 239 pages, 1988. (Text)

Psychiatry, Law and

REISNER AND SLOBOGIN'S LAW AND THE MENTAL HEALTH SYSTEM, CIVIL AND CRIMINAL ASPECTS, Second Edition, 1117 pages, 1990. Teacher's Manual available. (Casebook) 1992 Supplement.

Real Estate Transactions

BRUCE'S REAL ESTATE FINANCE IN A NUTSHELL, Third Edition, 287 pages, 1991. Softcover. (Text)

MAXWELL, RIESENFELD, HETLAND AND WARREN'S CASES ON CALIFORNIA SECURITY TRANSACTIONS IN LAND, Fourth Edition, 778 pages, 1992. Teacher's Manual available. (Casebook)

NELSON AND WHITMAN'S BLACK LETTER ON LAND TRANSACTIONS AND FINANCE, Second Edition, 466 pages, 1988. Softcover. (Review)

NELSON AND WHITMAN'S CASES AND MATERIALS ON REAL ESTATE TRANSFER, FINANCE AND DEVELOPMENT, Fourth Edition, 1346 pages, 1992. (Casebook)

NELSON AND WHITMAN'S HORNBOOK ON REAL ESTATE FINANCE LAW, Second Edition, 941 pages, 1985 with 1989 pocket part. (Text)

Regulated Industries—see also Mass Communication Law, Banking Law

GELLHORN AND PIERCE'S REGULATED INDUSTRIES IN A NUTSHELL, Second Edition, 389 pages, 1987. Softcover. (Text)

MORGAN, HARRISON AND VERKUIL'S CASES AND MATERIALS ON ECONOMIC REGULATION OF BUSINESS, Second Edition, 666 pages, 1985. (Casebook)

Remedies

DOBBS' HORNBOOK ON REMEDIES, Second Edition, approximately 1000 pages, April, 1993 Pub. (Text)

DOBBS' PROBLEMS IN REMEDIES. 137 pages, 1974. Teacher's Manual available. Softcover. (Coursebook)

DOBBYN'S INJUNCTIONS IN A NUTSHELL, 264 pages, 1974. Softcover. (Text)

FRIEDMAN'S CONTRACT REMEDIES IN A NUTSHELL, 323 pages, 1981. Softcover. (Text)

LEAVELL, LOVE AND NELSON'S CASES AND MATERIALS ON EQUITABLE REMEDIES, RESTITUTION AND DAMAGES, Fourth Edition, 1111 pages, 1986. Teacher's Manual available. (Casebook)

O'CONNELL'S REMEDIES IN A NUTSHELL, Second Edition, 320 pages, 1985. Softcover. (Text)

SCHOENBROD, MACBETH, LEVINE AND JUNG'S CASES AND MATERIALS ON REMEDIES: PUBLIC AND PRIVATE, 848 pages, 1990. Teacher's Manual available. (Casebook) 1992 Supplement.

YORK, BAUMAN AND RENDLEMAN'S CASES AND MATERIALS ON REMEDIES, Fifth Edition, 1270 pages, 1992. Teacher's Manual available. (Casebook)

Sea, Law of

SOHN AND GUSTAFSON'S THE LAW OF THE SEA IN A NUTSHELL, 264 pages, 1984. Softcover. (Text)

Securities Regulation

HAZEN'S HORNBOOK ON THE LAW OF SECURITIES REGULATION, Second Edition, Student Edition, 1082 pages, 1990. (Text)

RATNER'S SECURITIES REGULATION IN A NUTSHELL, Fourth Edition, 320 pages, 1992. Softcover. (Text)

RATNER AND HAZEN'S SECURITIES REGULATION: CASES AND MATERIALS, Fourth Edition, 1062 pages, 1991. Teacher's Manual available. (Casebook) Problems and Sample Documents Supplement.

Statutory Supplement. *See Securities*

Securities Regulation—Cont'd

Regulation, Selected Statutes

SECURITIES REGULATION, SELECTED STATUTES, RULES, AND FORMS. Softcover. Approximately 1375 pages, 1993.

Sports Law

CHAMPION'S SPORTS LAW IN A NUTSHELL,. Approximately 300 pages, January, 1993 Pub. Softcover. (Text)

SCHUBERT, SMITH AND TRENTADUE'S SPORTS LAW, 395 pages, 1986. (Text)

Tax Practice and Procedure

GARBIS, RUBIN AND MORGAN'S CASES AND MATERIALS ON TAX PROCEDURE AND TAX FRAUD, Third Edition, 921 pages, 1992. Teacher's Manual available. (Casebook)

MORGAN'S TAX PROCEDURE AND TAX FRAUD IN A NUTSHELL, 400 pages, 1990. Softcover. (Text)

Taxation—Corporate

KAHN AND GANN'S CORPORATE TAXATION, Third Edition, 980 pages, 1989. Teacher's Manual available. (Casebook) 1991 Supplement.

SCHWARZ AND LATHROPE'S BLACK LETTER ON CORPORATE AND PARTNERSHIP TAXATION, 537 pages, 1991. Softcover. (Review)

WEIDENBRUCH AND BURKE'S FEDERAL INCOME TAXATION OF CORPORATIONS AND STOCKHOLDERS IN A NUTSHELL, Third Edition, 309 pages, 1989. Softcover. (Text)

Taxation—Estate & Gift—see also Estate Planning, Trusts and Estates

MCNULTY'S FEDERAL ESTATE AND GIFT TAXATION IN A NUTSHELL, Fourth Edition, 496 pages, 1989. Softcover. (Text)

PEAT AND WILLBANKS' FEDERAL ESTATE AND GIFT TAXATION: AN ANALYSIS AND CRITIQUE, 265 pages, 1991. Softcover. (Text)

PENNELL'S CASES AND MATERIALS ON INCOME TAXATION OF TRUSTS, ESTATES, GRANTORS AND BENEFICIARIES, 460 pages, 1987. Teacher's Manual available. (Casebook)

Taxation—Individual

DODGE'S THE LOGIC OF TAX, 343 pages, 1989. Softcover. (Text)

GUNN AND WARD'S CASES, TEXT AND PROBLEMS ON FEDERAL INCOME TAXATION, Third Edition, 817 pages, 1992. Teacher's Manual available. (Casebook)

HUDSON AND LIND'S BLACK LETTER ON FEDERAL INCOME TAXATION, Fourth Edition, 410 pages, 1992. Softcover. (Review)

MCNULTY'S FEDERAL INCOME TAXATION OF INDIVIDUALS IN A NUTSHELL, Fourth Edition, 503 pages, 1988. Softcover. (Text)

POSIN'S FEDERAL INCOME TAXATION, Second Edition, approximately 650 pages, May, 1993 Pub. Softcover. (Text)

ROSE AND CHOMMIE'S HORNBOOK ON FEDERAL INCOME TAXATION, Third Edition, 923 pages, 1988, with 1991 pocket part. (Text)

SELECTED FEDERAL TAXATION STATUTES AND REGULATIONS. Softcover. 1686 pages, 1993.

Taxation—International

DOERNBERG'S INTERNATIONAL TAXATION IN A NUTSHELL, 325 pages, 1989. Softcover. (Text)

KAPLAN'S FEDERAL TAXATION OF INTERNATIONAL TRANSACTIONS: PRINCIPLES, PLANNING AND POLICY, 635 pages, 1988. (Casebook)

Taxation—Partnership

BERGER AND WIEDENBECK'S CASES AND MATERIALS ON PARTNERSHIP TAXATION, 788 pages, 1989. Teacher's Manual available. (Casebook) 1991 Supplement.

BISHOP AND BROOKS' FEDERAL PARTNERSHIP TAXATION: A GUIDE TO THE LEADING CASES, STATUTES, AND REGULATIONS, 545 pages, 1990. Softcover. (Text)

BURKE'S FEDERAL INCOME TAXATION OF PARTNERSHIPS IN A NUTSHELL, 356 pages, 1992. Softcover. (Text)

SCHWARZ AND LATHROPE'S BLACK LETTER ON CORPORATE AND PARTNERSHIP TAXATION, 537 pages, 1991. Softcover. (Review)

Taxation—State & Local

GELFAND AND SALSICH'S STATE AND LOCAL TAXATION AND FINANCE IN A NUTSHELL, 309 pages, 1986. Softcover. (Text)

HELLERSTEIN AND HELLERSTEIN'S CASES AND MATERIALS ON STATE AND LOCAL TAXATION, Fifth Edition, 1071 pages, 1988. (Case-

Taxation—State & Local—Cont'd

book)

Torts—see also Products Liability

BARNES AND STOUT'S THE ECONOMIC ANALYSIS OF TORT LAW, 161 pages, 1992. Softcover. Teacher's Manual available. (Casebook)

CHRISTIE AND MEEKS' CASES AND MATERIALS ON THE LAW OF TORTS, Second Edition, 1264 pages, 1990. (Casebook)

DOBBS' TORTS AND COMPENSATION—PERSONAL ACCOUNTABILITY AND SOCIAL RESPONSIBILITY FOR INJURY, 955 pages, 1985. Teacher's Manual available. (Casebook) 1990 Supplement.

KEETON, KEETON, SARGENTICH AND STEINER'S CASES AND MATERIALS ON TORT AND ACCIDENT LAW, Second Edition, 1318 pages, 1989. (Casebook)

KIONKA'S BLACK LETTER ON TORTS, 339 pages, 1988. Softcover. (Review)

KIONKA'S TORTS IN A NUTSHELL, Second Edition, 449 pages, 1992. Softcover. (Text)

PROSSER AND KEETON'S HORNBOOK ON TORTS, Fifth Edition, Student Edition, 1286 pages, 1984 with 1988 pocket part. (Text)

ROBERTSON, POWERS AND ANDERSON'S CASES AND MATERIALS ON TORTS, 932 pages, 1989. Teacher's Manual available. (Casebook)

Trade Regulation—see also Antitrust, Regulated Industries

MCMANIS' UNFAIR TRADE PRACTICES IN A NUTSHELL, Third Edition, approximately 450 pages, 1993. Softcover. (Text)

SCHECHTER'S BLACK LETTER ON UNFAIR TRADE PRACTICES, 272 pages, 1986. Softcover. (Review)

WESTON, MAGGS AND SCHECHTER'S UNFAIR TRADE PRACTICES AND CONSUMER PROTECTION, CASES AND COMMENTS, Fifth Edition, 957 pages, 1992. Teacher's Manual available. (Casebook)

Trial and Appellate Advocacy—see also Civil Procedure

APPELLATE ADVOCACY, HANDBOOK OF, Second Edition, 182 pages, 1986. Softcover. (Text)

BERGMAN'S TRIAL ADVOCACY IN A NUTSHELL, Second Edition, 354 pages, 1989. Softcover. (Text)

BINDER AND BERGMAN'S FACT INVESTIGATION: FROM HYPOTHESIS TO PROOF, 354 pages, 1984. Teacher's Manual available. (Coursebook)

CARLSON'S ADJUDICATION OF CRIMINAL JUSTICE: PROBLEMS AND REFERENCES, 130 pages, 1986. Softcover. (Casebook)

CARLSON AND IMWINKELRIED'S DYNAMICS OF TRIAL PRACTICE: PROBLEMS AND MATERIALS, 414 pages, 1989. Teacher's Manual available. (Coursebook) 1990 Supplement.

CLARY'S PRIMER ON THE ANALYSIS AND PRESENTATION OF LEGAL ARGUMENT, 106 pages, 1992. Softcover. (Text)

DESSEM'S PRETRIAL LITIGATION IN A NUTSHELL, 382 pages, 1992. Softcover. (Text)

DESSEM'S PRETRIAL LITIGATION: LAW, POLICY AND PRACTICE, 608 pages, 1991. Softcover. Teacher's Manual available. (Coursebook)

DEVINE'S NON-JURY CASE FILES FOR TRIAL ADVOCACY, 258 pages, 1991. (Coursebook)

GOLDBERG'S THE FIRST TRIAL (WHERE DO I SIT? WHAT DO I SAY?) IN A NUTSHELL, 396 pages, 1982. Softcover. (Text)

HAYDOCK, HERR, AND STEMPEL'S FUNDAMENTALS OF PRE-TRIAL LITIGATION, Second Edition, 786 pages, 1992. Softcover. Teacher's Manual available. (Coursebook)

HAYDOCK AND SONSTENG'S TRIAL: THEORIES, TACTICS, TECHNIQUES, 711 pages, 1991. Softcover. (Text)

HEGLAND'S TRIAL AND PRACTICE SKILLS IN A NUTSHELL, 346 pages, 1978. Softcover. (Text)

HORNSTEIN'S APPELLATE ADVOCACY IN A NUTSHELL, 325 pages, 1984. Softcover. (Text)

JEANS' HANDBOOK ON TRIAL ADVOCACY, Student Edition, 473 pages, 1975. Softcover. (Text)

LISNEK AND KAUFMAN'S DEPOSITIONS: PROCEDURE, STRATEGY AND TECHNIQUE, Law School and CLE Edition. 250 pages, 1990. Softcover. (Text)

MARTINEAU'S CASES AND MATERIALS ON APPELLATE PRACTICE AND PROCEDURE, 565 pages, 1987. (Casebook)

Trial and Appellate Advocacy—Cont'd

SONSTENG, HAYDOCK AND BOYD'S THE TRIALBOOK: A TOTAL SYSTEM FOR PREPARATION AND PRESENTATION OF A CASE, 404 pages, 1984. Softcover. (Coursebook)

WHARTON, HAYDOCK AND SONSTENG'S CALIFORNIA CIVIL TRIALBOOK, Law School and CLE Edition. 148 pages, 1990. Softcover. (Text)

Trusts and Estates

ATKINSON'S HORNBOOK ON WILLS, Second Edition, 975 pages, 1953. (Text)

AVERILL'S UNIFORM PROBATE CODE IN A NUTSHELL, Second Edition, 454 pages, 1987. Softcover. (Text)

BOGERT'S HORNBOOK ON TRUSTS, Sixth Edition, Student Edition, 794 pages, 1987. (Text)

CLARK, LUSKY AND MURPHY'S CASES AND MATERIALS ON GRATUITOUS TRANSFERS, Third Edition, 970 pages, 1985. (Casebook)

DODGE'S WILLS, TRUSTS AND ESTATE PLANNING–LAW AND TAXATION, CASES AND MATERIALS, 665 pages, 1988. (Casebook)

MCGOVERN, KURTZ AND REIN'S HORNBOOK ON WILLS, TRUSTS AND ESTATES–INCLUDING TAXATION AND FUTURE INTERESTS, 996 pages, 1988. (Text)

MENNELL'S WILLS AND TRUSTS IN A NUTSHELL, 392 pages, 1979. Softcover. (Text)

SIMES' HORNBOOK ON FUTURE INTERESTS, Second Edition, 355 pages, 1966. (Text)

TURANO AND RADIGAN'S HORNBOOK ON NEW YORK ESTATE ADMINISTRATION, 676 pages, 1986 with 1991 pocket part. (Text)

UNIFORM PROBATE CODE, OFFICIAL TEXT WITH COMMENTS. 863 pages, 1991. Softcover.

WAGGONER'S FUTURE INTERESTS IN A NUTSHELL, 361 pages, 1981. Softcover. (Text)

Water Law—see also Energy and Natural Resources Law, Environmental Law

GETCHES' WATER LAW IN A NUTSHELL, Second Edition, 459 pages, 1990. Softcover. (Text)

SAX, ABRAMS AND THOMPSON'S LEGAL CONTROL OF WATER RESOURCES: CASES AND MATERIALS, Second Edition, 987 pages, 1991. Teacher's Manual available. (Casebook)

TRELEASE AND GOULD'S CASES AND MATERIALS ON WATER LAW, Fourth Edition, 816 pages, 1986. (Casebook)

Wills—see Trusts and Estates

Workers' Compensation

HOOD, HARDY AND LEWIS' WORKERS' COMPENSATION AND EMPLOYEE PROTECTION LAWS IN A NUTSHELL, Second Edition, 361 pages, 1990. Softcover. (Text)

LITTLE, EATON AND SMITH'S CASES AND MATERIALS ON WORKERS' COMPENSATION, 537 pages, 1992. Teacher's Manual available. (Casebook)

WEST'S LAW SCHOOL ADVISORY BOARD

*

CASES, PROBLEMS, AND MATERIALS ON
PAYMENT SYSTEMS

By

Peter A. Alces
Professor of Law
Marshall-Wythe School of Law
The College of William and Mary

Marion W. Benfield, Jr.
University Professor of Law
Wake Forest University School of Law

AMERICAN CASEBOOK SERIES®

WEST PUBLISHING CO.
ST. PAUL, MINN., 1993

610 Opperman Drive
P.O. Box 64526
St. Paul, MN 55164–0526
1–800–328–9352

Library of Congress Cataloging-in-Publication Data

Alces, Peter A.

Cases, problems, and materials on payment systems / by Peter A. Alces and Marion W. Benfield, Jr.

p. cm. — (American casebook series)

Includes index.

ISBN 0–314–01973–1

1. Negotiable instruments—United States—Cases. 2. Payment—United States—Cases. 3. Electronic funds transfers—Law and legislation—United States—Cases. I. Benfield, Marion W. II. Title. III. Series.

KF957.A4A38 1993
346.73'096—dc20
[347.30696] 93–20285
CIP

ISBN 0–314–01973–1

(A.&B.) Pymnt.Sys. ACB

PRINTED ON 10% POST CONSUMER RECYCLED PAPER

Still To Our Parents,
Ramon L. Alces and Shirley M. Alces
Marion W. Benfield and Gazzie Cleo Benfield

*

Preface

This book appears at a time of transition in the payments law. Revised Commercial Code Articles 3, 4, and 4A are displacing the older law, and, particularly in the case of Article 4A, making law where previously there was none. The technology is also changing. The credit card regime, under which no paper is transferred as the charge moves from the merchant to the card issuing bank, will surely sooner or later come to the debit system. Within the next decade or so, check truncation at the bank of first deposit is likely to become common. The book takes account of the changes in payments law by incorporating references to both original and revised Articles 3 and 4, by including substantial coverage of Article 4A, and by providing coverage of related areas such as some of the federal rules applicable to credit cards and electronic funds transfers. Federal Reserve Board Regulations CC and J are treated as well.

The book contains a mix of problems, cases, and expository notes. There are many specific, detailed rules in Articles 3, 4, and 4A: more than is the case in common law subjects, or even in most statutory areas, including Article 2 of the Commercial Code. Problems are used to guide the student through the more basic rules with more economy of time than is possible through the use of cases. At the same time, the problems require the student to become his or her own guide, which helps to develop in the student confidence that he or she, too, can master the material. The book is designed so that the instructor can cover post-revision Articles 3 and 4, pre-revision Articles 3 and 4, or both post- and pre-revision versions of the two articles.

Mastery of payments law involves discovery of the difficulty, uncertainty and malleability of the statutory rules and principles. Many of the problems in the book challenge the student to struggle with the unclear meaning and uncertain application of statutory language. Similarly, many of the cases show lawyers and judges *shaping* the law, within the bounds of a tightly drawn statute, in ways that impart to students a sense of the commercial dynamic. Some of the cases, on the other hand, reveal bad lawyering and alert the student to the difficulty of many of the commercial paper rules. Other cases are included primarily to set the Code rules in the context of actual transactions, so that the student can better appreciate their significance.

The book also endeavors to sensitize the student to the conflict among competing policies that drafters of statutes confront. Developing a sense of the conflicting interests will better prepare the student to judge whether and when courts are likely to pull and tug at the statutory fabric to reach the results that seem most reasonable. The materials posit questions that require the student to evaluate the policy choices made in the Code.

After the introductory chapter, the book begins with holder in due course rules because conceptions of bona fide purchase are at the heart of commercial paper law. The authors recognize, however, that some instructors may wish to first cover liability of parties to instruments. The third chapter covers liability of parties, and an instructor who feels more comfortable doing that chapter first can begin with Chapter 3 and then go back to the holder in due course rules of Chapter 2.

Chapter 4 deals with forgery, alteration and other fraud. Chapter 5 covers bank-customer relations other than issues arising out of forged or altered items. Chapter 6 covers the bank collection process and related issues. Chapters 7 and 8 deal with the so called "New Payment Systems": Chapter 7 with "consumer" transfers governed by the Federal Electronic Funds Transfer Act and credit card law, and Chapter 8 with "wholesale" (wire) transfers and Article 4A of the Code.

The conventions used in the text are designed to make use of thet materials more convenient. The designation OR as a part of a statutory cite (viz OR 3–303) refers to original Article 3; R 3–303 refers to revised Article 3. String citations in cases are frequently omitted without indication of the omission. Similarly, footnotes in cases are omitted without indication. None of the cases in the materials were decided under Revised Article 3 or 4. Each time an opinion cites an Article 3 or 4 section, we have inserted in brackets a cite to the same or comparable revised 3 or 4 section.

Professor Alces acknowledges the thorough and thoughtful research assistance of Serena Carmean, J.D. 1994, The College of William and Mary. Both Professor Alces and Professor Benfield acknowledge their indebtedness to the students in their Spring 1993 Payments System courses who, with industry and good humor, worked through these materials in manuscript and page-proof form.

PETER A. ALCES
Williamsburg, Virginia

MARION W. BENFIELD, JR.
Winston-Salem, North Carolina

April, 1993

Acknowledgements

Beutel, Frederick, The Proposed Uniform [?] Commercial Code Should Not Be Adopted, 61 Yale L.J. 334, 359–63 (1952). Copyright © 1952, The Yale Law Journal Company. Reprinted by permission of The Yale Law Journal Company and Fred B. Rothman & Company from The Yale Law Journal, Vol. 61, pp. 334–363. (p. 24)

Clark, Barkley, The Law of Bank Deposits, Collections and Credit Cards 5–11, 5–12, 5–56, and 5–57 (3d ed. 1990). Copyright © 1990. Reprinted by permission of the publisher, Warren Gorham Lamont. A division of Research Institute of America Inc. (p. 404)

Cooper, Corinne, Uniform Commercial Code Annual Survey—1988, 43 Bus. Lawyer 1327, 1327–34 (1988). Copyright © 1988, American Bar Association. Reprinted by permission of the American Bar Association. (p. 398)

Crenshaw, Albert, Safeway Joins the Charge to Charge It—Supermarket Now Accepts Credit, Debit Payments, The Washington Post, April 13, 1992. Copyright © 1992, The Washington Post. Reprinted with permission. (p. 458)

Farnsworth, E. Allan, Contracts 564–65 (2d ed. 1990). Copyright © 1990, Little, Brown & Co. Reprinted by permission of Little, Brown and Company. (p. 455)

Gilmore, Grant, The Uniform Commercial Code: A Reply to Professor Beutel, 61 Yale L.J. 364, 374–77 (1952). Copyright © 1952, The Yale Law Journal Company. Reprinted by permission of The Yale Law Journal Company and Fred B. Rothman & Company from The Yale Law Journal, Vol. 61, pp. 364–79. (p. 26)

Gilmore, Grant, The Commercial Doctrine of Good Faith Purchase, 63 Yale L.J. 1057 (1954). Copyright © 1954, The Yale Law Journal Company. Reprinted by permission of The Yale Law Journal Company and Fred B. Rothman & Company from The Yale Law Journal, Vol. 63, p. 1057. (p. 102)

Gilmore, Grant, The Good Faith Purchase Idea and the Uniform Commercial Code: Confessions of a Repentant Draftsman, 15 Ga.L.Rev. 605 (1981). Copyright © 1981. Reprinted with permission. (p. 103)

Hillebrand, Gail, Revised Articles 3 and 4 of the Uniform Commercial Code: A Consumer Perspective, 42 Ala.L.Rev. 679, 683–84 (1991). Copyright © 1991 by the University of Alabama. Reprinted by permission. (p. 23)

Leary, Fairfax & Fry, Patricia, A "Systems" Approach to Payment Modes: Moving Towards A New Payments Code, 16 U.C.C.L.J. 283, 286–91 (1984). Copyright © Warren Gorham Lamont. A division of

Research Institute of America Inc. Reprinted by permission of the publisher. (p. 4)

Malcolm, Walter, Article 4—A Battle with Complexity, 1952 Wis.L.Rev. 265, 270–73. Copyright © 1952 Wisconsin Law Review. Reprinted by permission. (p. 18)

Miller, Frederick, Uniform Commercial Code Annual Survey—1984, 39 Bus. Lawyer 1315, 1364–66 (1984). Copyright © 1984 American Bar Association. Reprinted by permission of the American Bar Association. (p. 349)

New York Clearing House, Statement on the Proposed Uniform New Payments Code 10, 11 (1983). Copyright © 1983 by the American Law Institute. Reprinted with the permission of the American Law Institute. (p. 2)

Rapson, Donald, Book Review (Reviewing F. Miller & A. Harrell, The Law of Modern Payment Systems and Notes), 41 Bus. Lawyer 676–77 (1986). Copyright © 1986 American Bar Association. Reprinted by permission of the American Bar Association. (p. 16)

Rubin, Edward, Efficiency, Equity and the Proposed Revision of Articles 3 and 4, 42 Ala.L.Rev. 551, 586–92 (1991). Copyright © 1991 by the University of Alabama. Reprinted by permission. (pp. 28, 274)

Scott, Hal, New Payment Systems Report 88–89 (1977). Copyright © 1977 by the American Law Institute. Reprinted with the permission of the American Law Institute. (p. 21)

Summary of Contents

Table of Contents

Table of Cases

The principal cases are in bold type. Cases cited or discussed in the text are roman type. References are to pages. Cases cited in principal cases and within other quoted materials are not included.

*

Table of Statutes And Regulations

UNITED STATES

UNITED STATES CODE ANNOTATED

15 U.S.C.A.—Commerce and Trade

POPULAR NAME ACTS

ELECTRONIC FUND TRANSFER ACT

EXPEDITED FUNDS AVAILABILITY ACT

TRUTH IN LENDING ACT

UNIFORM COMMERCIAL CODE

UNIFORM COMMERCIAL CODE

ORIGINAL ARTICLE 3

UNIFORM COMMERCIAL CODE ORIGINAL ARTICLE 3

UNIFORM COMMERCIAL CODE ORIGINAL ARTICLE 3

UNIFORM COMMERCIAL CODE
REVISED ARTICLE 3

UNIFORM COMMERCIAL CODE
REVISED ARTICLE 3

UNIFORM COMMERCIAL CODE REVISED ARTICLE 3

UNIFORM COMMERCIAL CODE REVISED ARTICLE 3

UNIFORM COMMERCIAL CODE REVISED ARTICLE 3

UNIFORM COMMERCIAL CODE REVISED ARTICLE 3

UNIFORM COMMERCIAL CODE REVISED ARTICLE 3

UNIFORM COMMERCIAL CODE REVISED ARTICLE 3

UNIFORM COMMERCIAL CODE
REVISED ARTICLE 3

ORIGINAL ARTICLE 4

UNIFORM COMMERCIAL CODE
ORIGINAL ARTICLE 4

UNIFORM COMMERCIAL CODE
ORIGINAL ARTICLE 4

REVISED ARTICLE 4

UNIFORM COMMERCIAL CODE
REVISED ARTICLE 4

UNIFORM COMMERCIAL CODE
REVISED ARTICLE 4

UNIFORM COMMERCIAL CODE REVISED ARTICLE 4

UNIFORM COMMERCIAL CODE REVISED ARTICLE 4

UNIFORM COMMERCIAL CODE
REVISED ARTICLE 4

UNIFORM COMMERCIAL CODE
REVISED ARTICLE 4

UNIFORM COMMERCIAL CODE REVISED ARTICLE 4

UNIFORM CONSUMER CREDIT CODE

UNIFORM FIDUCIARIES ACT

UNIFORM NEGOTIABLE INSTRUMENTS LAW

STATE STATUTES

OFFICIAL CODE OF GEORGIA ANNOTATED

GEORGIA CODE

ILLINOIS SMITH-HURD ANNOTATED

MARYLAND CODE, COMMERCIAL LAW

MICHIGAN COMPILED LAWS ANNOTATED

WISCONSIN ADMINISTRATIVE CODE

CODE OF FEDERAL REGULATIONS

CODE OF FEDERAL REGULATIONS

CASES, PROBLEMS, AND MATERIALS ON

PAYMENT SYSTEMS

*

Chapter 1

THE PAYMENT SYSTEMS *

A. INTRODUCTION

Payment media, the familiar as well as the less familiar devices, facilitate the transfer of value. We do not and could not function in a purely barter economy. Notwithstanding the isolated stories of country doctors accepting chickens for obstetric services, practically all sales of goods or services involve a transfer of money (or a money substitute) as payment. This coursebook focuses on the legal regime governing payment by money substitutes. It also covers credit transactions in which a negotiable promissory note is given. The promissory note is considered along with checks because both are subject to essentially the same legal rules and both are governed by Article 3 of the Uniform Commercial Code (U.C.C.).

The ingenuity of the law merchant and contemporary commercial practices have assured that our law of payment systems is not and will not be static. Bold assertions concerning the demise of paper-based payment systems and the rapid spread of electronic systems are made frequently in the periodicals; and sometimes it is not so difficult to see revolutionary change on the horizon. Only in the last few years have law school courses considered payment systems other than checks, or financing mechanisms besides notes. Electronic or "wire" payment systems of several kinds are increasingly replacing checks as methods of payment. Also, consumers find that in many transactions payment by credit card is more convenient than payment by cash or check. New statutes, both federal and state, deal with many of the problems that arise in the use of payment devices other than the traditional check.

Presently much of the law governing checks and other paperbased payments is found in Articles 3 and 4 of the Commercial Code. Consumer electronic transfers may be partially subject to Article 4 of the Code, but are also subject to the Federal Electronic Funds Transfer Act (E.F.T.A.) and to common law rules. New Article 4A of the Code

* Throughout this text, the designation "OR" refers to an Article in its original form; "R" denotes a revised Article. E.g., OR 3–303 refers to Original Article 3; R 3–303 refers to Revised Article 3.

governs wire transfers other than those governed by the federal E.F.T.A. Credit cards are subject to the Federal Truth in Lending Act, various state statutes, and common law rules. While checks, promissory notes, and wire transfers subject to the U.C.C. are also residually subject to common law rules, the U.C.C. statutory coverage is much more complete than the non-U.C.C. statutory coverage of electronic funds transfers and credit cards. The statutory schemes themselves differ substantially on some issues. One such issue is the effect of a bank customer's negligence on the ability of the bank to debit an unauthorized charge to the customer's account.

Because of the inconsistencies among the bodies of law governing available payment media, the commercial world at one time considered the desirability of providing a single statutory system in which all payment devices would be subject to consistent and coherent treatment. Some practitioners and scholars argued that the "legal framework should not distort user choices among different payment systems, whether they be paper or card based, or electronic." (Memorandum from Professor Hal Scott, Reporter for the Uniform New Payments Code, to National Conference of Commissioners on Uniform State Laws 1 (June 15, 1983)). That is, the consumer's decision to use a credit card rather than a check should be determined by concerns other than the legal rights and liabilities of the parties to the payment transaction. Therefore, according to that line of thought, all payment mechanisms should be subject to essentially the same legal rules. What non-legal considerations bear on the consumer's choice of payment medium?

Even the staunchest traditionalist would admit that a goal of such unitary treatment has some intellectual appeal. The reasons for the legal distinctions that now exist among the available value transfer systems are not intuitively obvious. Each system has the same ultimate goal: to transfer value from A to B. On the other hand, both a Ford and a Lear Jet share the same goal: to get people from point A to point B. But there are differences in the way the two vehicles achieve their objective, and perhaps it is not necessary to impose the same legal rules on both. The New York Clearing House view of the desirability of uniform rules for all payment systems is revealed by the following excerpt.

NEW YORK CLEARING HOUSE, STATEMENT ON THE PROPOSED UNIFORM NEW PAYMENTS CODE

10, 11 (Sept. 29, 1983).

Like payment systems, transportation systems generally have one basic purpose, i.e. to move people or goods from one place to another. The various transportation systems could be said to range from bicycles to planes, with cars, boats and trains in between. While the types of legal issues that must be addressed in fashioning a law to govern each mode of transportation are similar (i.e., who has the right of way; what speed limits, if any, should apply; liability for passengers and parcels), would anyone argue that there is an advantage in calling pilots, captains, engineers and drivers by one functional name ("transport motivators," for instance) or by having one comprehensive code covering all methods of transportation?

Just as transportation systems move people or cargo, each payment system is, at bottom, a method for moving money from one place or person to another. Cash (which is not treated by the NPC [proposed Uniform New Payments Code]), bills and notes including checks, wholesale and retail electronic funds transfers, and credit cards, all serve in primary part to effect this very simple function. While the issues that must be addressed in fashioning a law to govern each of these systems are very similar, each system works differently and the law should reflect those differences. Given the disparate nature of the transportation systems involved, attempts to combine them would necessarily lead to undue complexity.

The drafters of the ill-fated Uniform New Payments Code, a joint project of the American Law Institute and the National Conference of Commissioners on Uniform State Laws, tried to prepare a single comprehensive payments statute. The U.N.P.C. would have integrated the law governing checks with the law governing consumer and commercial electronic transfers. After a relatively short but stormy history, the project was abandoned by the sponsoring organizations. The bank lobby was uncomfortable with the pro-consumer provisions of the U.N.P.C. and consumer groups perceived an over-representation of banking interests.

A committee of the National Conference of Commissioners on Uniform State Laws has revised Article 3 and made conforming amendments to Article 4 of the U.C.C. As of this writing, a substantial number but not yet all of the states have enacted revised Article 3 and the amendments to Article 4. To a significant extent, the revision and amendments respond to problems revealed by over thirty years of practice under original Articles 3 and 4. This book accommodates treatment of both the original and the revised Code. Indeed, many of the new formulations may best be understood in terms of the uncertainties and inadequacies of the prior law.

In these materials, the emphasis is on Articles 3 and 4 of the U.C.C. But because these are dynamic times for the development of payments systems both domestically and internationally, the substance and approach of the laws governing the so-called "new payment systems" is presented in apposition to the U.C.C. rules. There are indications that the paper and electronic payments law will continue to change in the next few years as the law tries to keep pace with technological developments. The approach we use here suggests some of the concerns that are fundamental to understanding the pervasive issues and the recurring questions.

B. PATCHWORK OF PAYMENTS LAW

All payment systems have the same basic goal, the transfer of credit in a financial institution from a debtor or donor to a creditor or donee. Further, as the excerpt from Leary and Fry set out below argues, there may be some basic principles that can be applied to all systems to help in determining the appropriate legal rules.

LEARY & FRY, A "SYSTEMS" APPROACH TO PAYMENT MODES: MOVING TOWARDS A NEW PAYMENTS CODE

16 U.C.C.L.J. 283, 286–91 (1984).

We start with the proposition that the basic purpose of the varying modes mentioned above is to bring about the transfer of deposit institution credit from a debtor or donor to a creditor or donee. This transfer of credit is of immense importance to that larger system we call the economy of the country or of the world. Cash transactions may be the most numerous, but of all monetary value transfers they will amount to approximately one half of one percent. The cash substitute that is the basis for the other 99 percent or more of value transferred is deposit institution credit, whether transferred for the acquisition of goods or real estate, in payment for services, for the acquisition of intangibles as investments or as payment of loans, or to balance for other transfers.

Conceptually, all payment modes are alike in that the ultimate object is the safe transfer of deposit institution credit from the institution used by a debtor or donor to deposit institution credit in the creditor-donee's selected institution. Where both use the same institution, there will be three participants in the transfer, i.e., debtor, creditor, and deposit institution. Where each uses a separate institution, there will be at least four, far more often five or many more, institutions involved. This is because credit cannot, as can cash or gold, be physically transferred. The transfer must be accomplished by entries in mutual accounts. For example, if the creditor and the debtor use the same institution, the transfer is effected by debiting the debtor's account and crediting the creditor's account. If these parties each use a different institution, which have nevertheless mutual institutional accounts, payment is effected by having the debtor's bank debit the debtor's account and credit the account of the creditor's institution. On receipt of notice of this credit, the creditor's institution will internally transfer the credit to the creditor's account and deduct that credit from its usable balance in the other institution. Quite often these institutions either may not have mutual accounts or may find it convenient to use their respective accounts in a third institution, and effect net settlements for a day's business through that institution. There may be even more participants involved and transactions involving other payors and receivers, so that settlements on a "net for the day" basis for all will be more efficient. Thus, all the institutions in a given area or region may send their items to be paid by all other institutions similarly sending items to one place, a clearinghouse, where all sendings and all receipts can be tabulated and netted for settlement purposes. To draw a parallel, a clearinghouse can be called a physical switch and the automated clearinghouse is an electronics switch, but the function is the same. Both notify a clearing bank that then adjusts the net balances among the member banks.

An overview of each payment mode can best be made by examining the essential stages common to all payment modes, thus enabling us to perceive the underlying system. Before a more detailed discussion of each stage, there will be a summation of the stages under the following eight headings:

(1) *Underlying transaction.* A deal between debtor and creditor calling for a payment by the former to the latter;

(2) *Debtor authorization.* An authorization from the debtor to the deposit institution, which may in part precede the initiation of the underlying transaction and in part come after that transaction has been initiated;

(3) *Creditor authorization.* An authorization from the creditor to its deposit institution to accept the payment, which may in part precede the underlying transaction;

(4) *Message transmittal.* The debtor's message to make the payment must be transmitted to the debtor's deposit institution;

(5) *Payor processing time.* Sufficient processing time for the debtor's deposit institution to determine the availability of funds in the account for transfer to others;

(6) *Credit transfer implementation.* The implementation of the necessary credit transfers between deposit institutions;

(7) *Completion signal.* Methods for the deposit institutions to signal completion of the implementation to their respective customers; and

(8) *Retrieval of messages.* Where a question arises about the accuracy or propriety of the payment, a viable retrieval of the message and its implementations, reflecting the successive stopping points of each on its journey.

With the last stage there must be rules for allocating unrecoverable losses. The participants may be stated as three—the debtor, the creditor, and the depositary institution system, or selected sectors thereof. Losses can be allocated to any of these three participants and our present legal framework may not have done this as efficiently and fairly as it could and should have done.

The combined impact of eight principles should govern the allocations of losses. First, each participant should absorb the costs of its own mistakes and misdeeds. Second, losses should be imposed on the participant best able to take cost-effective protective measures. Third, losses should be allocated to the participant best able to spread the impact of the loss by procuring insurance against such loss.

In implementing these principles, where a loss is caused by a person entrusted by a participant with the responsible handling of funds transfer messages or their implementation, a fourth principle, the respondeat superior principle, requires that the entrusting participant should bear the loss. Where this is not the case, but the loss is the result of an intrusion by an independent third party, an interloper, the loss should be allocated in accordance with the second and third principles.

There is a fifth principle: when a participant is made aware of an intrusion or of a strong potential for intrusion in a payment made or in process, there is a duty to warn all other parties in the danger zone. Yet a sixth principle, a principle of repose, must also be considered. The stakes are high, the volume of potential liability mounts daily. Proof of loss caused by delay in instituting claims and giving notices may be most difficult. Therefore, there should be provisions fixing relatively shorter time periods for giving notice of claims than those of the applicable statutes of limitation. But once a claim has been asserted, time should be allowed to work out amicable settlements. Thus, bars to the institution of litigation can be left to the existing statutes of limitation.

A seventh principle of practicality may override the adoption of a loss allocation indicated by an application of the preceding six principles. This principle would continue a rule of longstanding acceptance where the successful legislative adoption of a statute rather clearly would be prevented if the rule were changed. This principle fathered several provisions in the original UCC.

The eighth principle is that the rules of law should, where possible, allocate losses in a way that does not adversely affect creditor acceptability of particular payment modes.

The common elements of payment systems can be illustrated by examining a check transaction. A check is an order drawn on a bank to pay a specified sum. The person writing the check is referred to as the drawer (debtor) and his bank is referred to as the drawee, or payor. The person to whom the check is made out is known as the payee (creditor) and her bank is referred to as the depositary or collecting bank. Between the collecting bank and the drawee bank there may be a number of intermediary banks. In a payment by check, the drawer draws a check payable to the payee and delivers it to him. The payee typically then indorses the check and deposits it in his bank which will collect the check for him. That bank sends the check through the banking system to the drawee bank which will pay the check. Following Diagram 1.1, the physical check moves in a clockwise direction from drawer to payee to collecting bank to drawee (through intermediaries) and back to drawer (subject to truncation, see below). The value moves in a counter-clockwise direction from drawee (through intermediaries) to the collecting bank to the payee.

Diagram 1.1

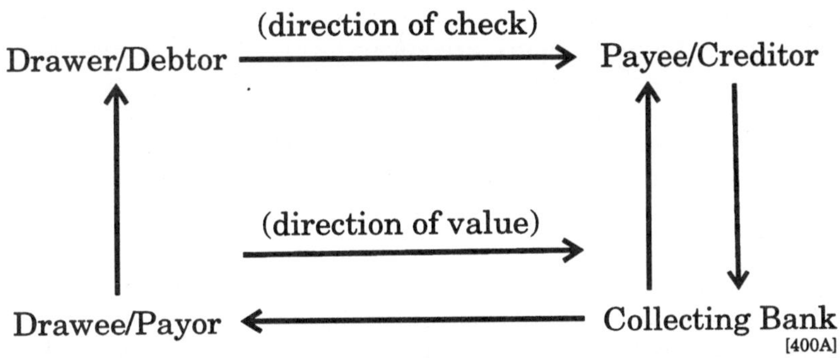

Consider that generic transaction in terms of the Leary and Fry construction: There is, of course, an *underlying contract* giving rise to the transfer of value (the sale of a car, for instance). The debtor *authorizes* his bank, the drawee, to pay the amount on the check by first opening an account with the drawee bank, and then by signing the check ordering payment. Similarly, the creditor (payee) *authorizes* her bank to collect the check by first opening an account with the collecting bank and then by presenting the check for collection. The debtor's *message* to his institution to make payment is accomplished either by forwarding (through intermediaries) the actual check, or by sending an electronic message (point-of-entry truncation) to the drawee. The payor (drawee) *processing* time takes place in the *payor* bank while it determines, inter alia, whether the debtor has sufficient funds to cover the check. The credit *transfer* takes place by debiting the drawer's account with the drawee bank and crediting the account of the collecting bank (or appropriate intermediary). The collecting bank then debits the account of the drawee bank (or appropriate intermediary) and credits the account of the payee. There is no *completion signal* in a check transaction due primarily to the prohibitive cost posed by such a procedure. "No news (of dishonor) is good news." The assumption is that if no word of a problem is received within a set period of time (now governed by Federal Reserve Regulation CC), the check is considered paid. Finally, the drawer *retrieves* the message that the drawee bank honored the order when he receives his statement from the bank, with which, depending on truncation, the canceled check may or may not be enclosed.

The following summary of the several variations on the existing check system provides the basis for contrast and comparison.

1. Check Truncation

Check truncation is already utilized by many banks, savings and loan associations, and credit unions. It is not an independent system, but rather complements the check collection process by expediting payment by check. Somewhere in the check collection process the indispensable information contained in the OR 4–104(1)(g) (R 4–104(a)(9)) "item" is reproduced in electronic form and relayed through the collection channels. There are several different ways in which this can be accomplished. The most common method, drawee bank truncation, allows the drawee/payor to retain the canceled checks drawn on its customer's account and to relay instead only the information necessary to identify the item on the periodic statement sent to the customer. Sometimes called "check-safekeeping," this system does realize cost savings, but falls short of the more radical depositary bank truncation in which the paper is stopped at the financial institution in which it is deposited (first bank with "MICR" encoding capabilities—Magnetic Ink Character Recognition), contemplating that only the pertinent check information (e.g., amount, date, check number) will be forwarded to the drawee. The depositary retains the check, which can, of course, be produced on those rare occasions when a problem arises. More recently, truncation has been accomplished through producing an electronic image of the check that is then encoded and forwarded to the appropriate payor instead of the actual paper. This system avoids the problem inherent in traditional check truncation techniques where there is no physical rendering of the check returned to the consumer, thus making it difficult for the customer to identify specific checks and to recognize forgeries. Digital imaging truncation provides the bank customer with a "hard copy" of the check and may be more palatable to consumers who feel more comfortable with such an assurance.

2. Check Authorization and Guarantee

Check guarantee offers merchants who would like to increase their sales by expanding the forms of payment they will accept for goods and services a more trustworthy means to accept checks. Drafts drawn on a bank pose significant uncertainties: is the check backed by sufficient funds?"; is the drawer "authorized" to access the account? Check guarantee systems provide an electronically sophisticated procedure to shift the risk of accepting payment by check from the merchant to the financial community.

A customer draws a check payable to the merchant or the merchant's order. The customer then inserts a magnetically encoded card ("access device") and personal identification number ("PIN") in an electronic terminal at the merchant's place of business. The transaction data, entered by the merchant, along with the customer information is electronically transmitted to the appropriate financial institution. The decision to guaranty or not to guaranty the instrument is quickly communicated to the merchant terminal.

Check authorization systems differ from check guarantee systems in that the former do not expose the sponsoring organization to liability in the event that there is a problem with the check. Instead, there may merely be a search of the organization's files for negative information concerning the drawer of the check, or at most an inquiry into the drawer's balance with the drawee bank.

Insofar as check guarantee systems involve Article 4 issues, the provisions of the U.C.C. apply. The E.F.T.A. expressly excludes check guarantee systems from its coverage, 15 U.S.C. § 1693a(6)(A). If the guaranteed check accesses a line of credit, the Federal Fair Credit Reporting Act may apply.

3. *Automated Teller Machines*

Automated teller machines (ATMs) have, in many communities, begun to supplant the use of human tellers. In 1990, there were an estimated 80,000 ATMs in service in the United States alone.* The greatest challenge presented by this technology appears to preoccupy those concerned with marketing: as the number of automatic, electronic teller systems proliferates, the number of available acronyms decreases. Now that individual bank systems have formed networks, some state or even nation-wide or world-wide, consumers are deriving substantial benefits. ATMs are customer-activated terminals that effect deposits and withdrawals, respond to balance inquiries, and often make transfers between accounts and initiate payments on continuous accounts (e.g., personal and mortgage loans, utility bills).

The issuing bank provides its customers with a magnetically encoded access device and personal identification number. Depending upon the system, customers then may initiate either on-line (immediate settlement) or off-line (delayed settlement) transactions subject to the E.F.T.A. and perhaps state law. Many ATMs are capable of accessing Visa or MasterCard lines of credit in addition to the more familiar bank-customer services. When customers are permitted to execute inter-bank transactions, there must necessarily be a "switch" or other means of adjusting balances between the banks. Such systems pose legal and procedural problems analogous to those implicated with inter-bank check clearing. The rights and liabilities of the banks will likely be fixed by private agreement, however.

4. *Point of Sale Systems*

Of all the new payment systems, the one that holds the greatest promise to become the next revolutionary step in value transfer is point

* Bank Network News, Sept. 10, 1990, at 1.

of sale. POS systems essentially involve an EFT transaction at the "point of sale," thus eliminating entirely the need for paper to transfer value. Point of sale system transactions are similar to ATM and credit card transactions and provide perhaps the quickest means for a customer to debit her account. Once again, an access device and PIN are all that is needed for a customer to initiate a funds transfer. After the customer inserts the access device, types in the PIN, and has the merchant enter the necessary transaction information, the financial institution that maintains the POS relationship with the merchant either accepts or rejects the transfer. If the transaction is accepted and both the customer's and merchant's accounts are with that financial institution (an "on-us" transaction), the customer's account is debited and the merchant's account will be credited in accordance with the account agreement. If the transaction is "off-us," a "switch" is necessary to effect settlement.

Diagram 1.2

An "Off–Us" POS Transaction

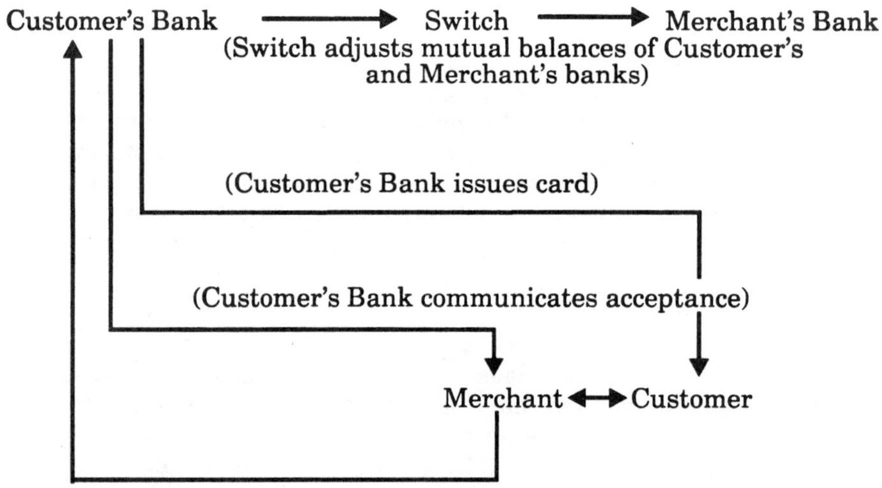

(POS terminal forwards information to Customer's Bank)
[401A]

After initial consumer reluctance to adopt this mode of value transfer, there is now some indication that, if packaged properly, POS will become a more attractive payment medium. In the mid-eighties the Interlink network, a POS system organized by several major California banks, went on-line and now has a volume of some 3 million POS transactions per month.* In 1987, Visa and MasterCard completed plans for a joint debit card program but agreed not to issue the card

* See D. Baker & R. Brandel, The Law of Electronic Fund Transfer Systems, p. 1–24 (1988 & Supp.1992).

following suit by numerous states' attorneys general who alleged that the program would inhibit competition. Each company is now working on a separate card.

5. *Credit/Charge Cards*

Credit/charge cards are perhaps the most familiar form of "new" payment system. Multi-institutional credit cards (e.g. Visa, MasterCard) involve a network of agreements among merchants, their customers, and the financial institutions that issue the cards and process the credits and debits among transactors. When a merchant accepts a particular card to obtain payment for goods or services, a receipt is generated that imprints the customer's and merchant's account numbers. The merchant periodically sends these receipts to its member bank and that bank makes available to the merchant the discounted value of the receipts. The advice of debit is directed through the collection system (often in truncated, electronic form) to the customer's card-issuing bank, which advances funds to the customer's account from a pre-arranged line of credit. When the customer receives the periodic statement, she may pay the entire amount outstanding, or, subject to the account agreement, may amortize the amount over a predetermined term.

Diagram 1.3

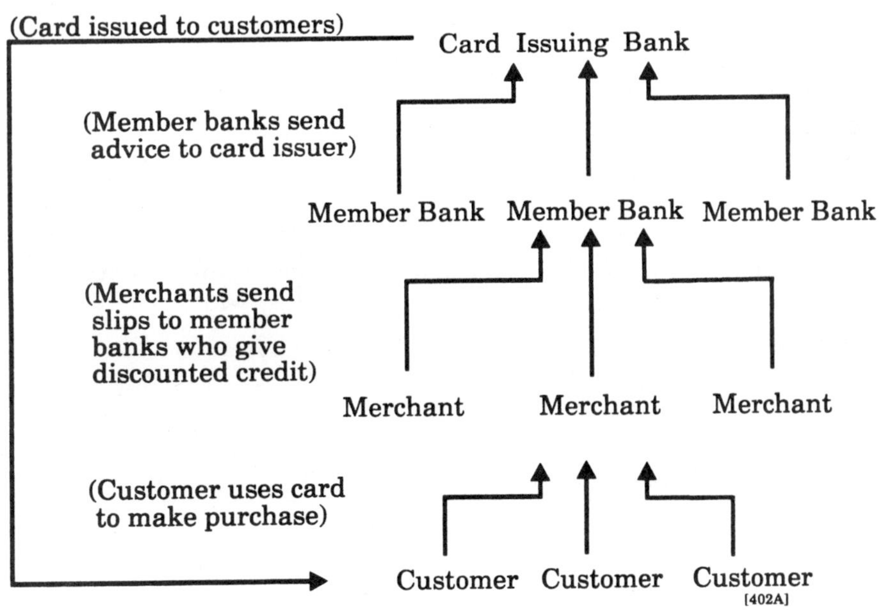

In addition to the private agreements, the Federal Truth in Lending Act, Regulation Z, and the provisions of the Fair Credit Billing Act provide the law governing credit card transactions, all affording the consumer with substantial rights when dealing with the card issuer.

6. *Automated Clearing Houses*

Automated clearing houses (ACH) provide expedited payments and charges of pre-authorized (recurring) credits and debits. Participating financial institutions electronically encode their customers' transfers on magnetic tape and send the tape to the appropriate regional automated clearing house, which charges and credits correspondent Federal Reserve accounts. Alternatively, settlement may be effected by wire transfer. ACH transfers can be useful when a large number of recurring credit entries are made by a customer (e.g., large employer paying salaries), or where a similarly large number of debit entries are handled (e.g. insurance premiums).

Diagram 1.4

ACH Credit Entries

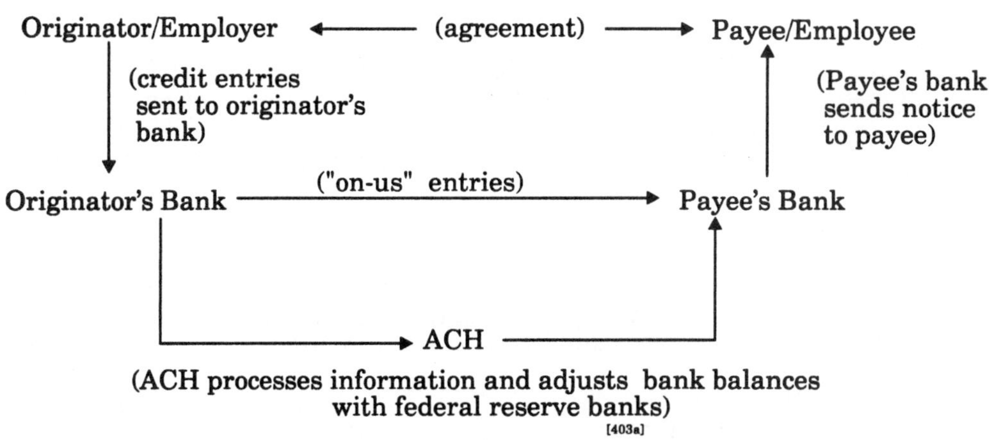

ACH Debit Entries

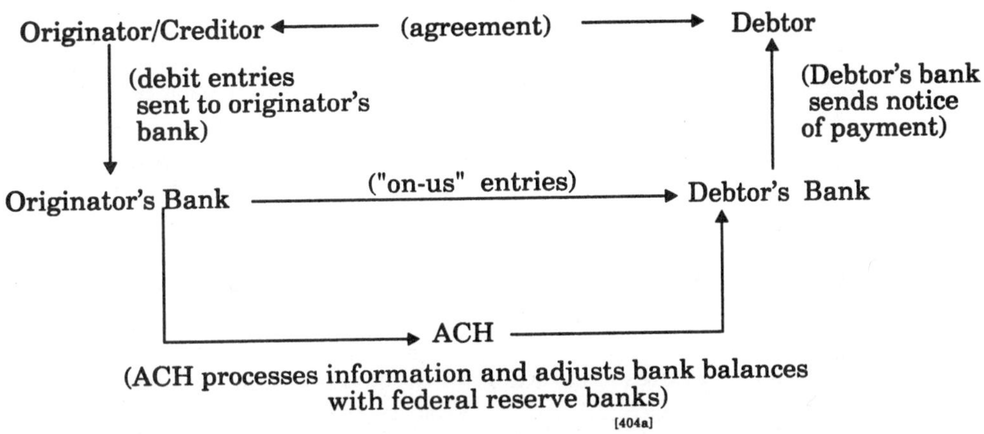

The sources of ACH law are diverse and may lead to inconsistent results. E.F.T.A. and its accompanying Regulation E govern ACH transactions. ACHs also have promulgated their own operating rules that are, necessarily, subject to the E.F.T.A. Private contracts among the transactors, including the Federal Reserve Bank (when it acts as operator of an ACH), complement the federal law, regional ACH operating rules, and, between regional ACH's, National Automated Clearing House Association rules (which, curiously, provide that the U.C.C. is applicable to ACH transfers).

Although it was first thought that ACH would overtake wire transfers in popularity, these conjectures have now largely dissipated. Automated clearing houses have not met their early promise of handling both the high number of transactions involved in the check collection system (without the cumbersome paper) and the high dollar amounts involved in wire transfers. While ACH is a less expensive method of transfer, wire transfers are much faster. Therefore, corporations have continued to rely on the wire transfer system to a large extent.

7. *Wire Transfers*

Wire transfers move the greatest dollar amount of debits and credits, and, arguably, affect the most sophisticated group of transactors. In 1989, the National Conference of Commissioners on Uniform State Laws and the American Law Institute approved an entirely new article, Article 4A ("Funds Transfers"), to govern wire transfers.

A typical wire transfer resembles the check transaction. The following excerpt from the Prefatory Note to Article 4A illustrates the mechanics of a "funds transfer."

> The funds transfer that is covered by Article 4A is not a complex transaction and can be illustrated by the following exam-

ple which is used throughout the Prefatory Note as a basis for discussion. X, a debtor, wants to pay an obligation owed to Y. Instead of delivering to Y a negotiable instrument such as a check or some other writing such as a credit card slip that enables Y to obtain payment from a bank, X transmits an instruction to X's bank to credit a sum of money to the bank account of Y. In most cases X's bank and Y's bank are different banks. X's bank may carry out X's instruction by instructing Y's bank to credit Y's account in the amount that X requested. The instruction that X issues to its bank is a "payment order." X is the "sender" of the payment order and X's bank is the "receiving bank" with respect to X's order. Y is the "beneficiary" of X's order. When X's bank issues an instruction to Y's bank to carry out X's payment order, X's bank "executes" X's order. The instruction of X's bank to Y's bank is also a payment order. With respect to that order, X's bank is the sender, Y's bank is the receiving bank, and Y is the beneficiary. The entire series of transactions by which X pays Y is known as the "funds transfer." With respect to the funds transfer, X is the "originator," X's bank is the "originator's bank," Y is the "beneficiary" and Y's bank is the "beneficiary's bank." In more complex transactions there are one or more additional banks known as "intermediary banks" between X's bank and Y's bank. In the funds transfer the instruction contained in the payment order of X to its bank is carried out by a series of payment orders by each bank in the transmission chain to the next bank in the chain until Y's bank receives a payment order to make the credit to Y's account. In most cases, the payment order of each bank to the next bank in the chain is transmitted electronically, and often the payment order of X to its bank is also transmitted electronically, but the means of transmission does not have any legal significance. A payment order may be transmitted by any means, and in some cases the payment order is transmitted by a slow means such as first class mail. To reflect this fact, the broader term "funds transfer" rather than the narrower term "wire transfer" is used in Article 4A to describe the overall payment transaction.

The characteristics that distinguish the various wire transfer systems pertain to operation and settlement procedures as well as the geographic boundaries recognized by the several systems. Fedwire, operated by the Federal Reserve System, is both a communication and settlement system for instantaneous credit transfers. Member banks request their local Federal Reserve Bank to credit another member bank. The Federal Reserve Bank then debits the message sender's reserve account and credits the payee bank's account. If the payee member is in another reserve district, the receiving Federal Reserve Bank sends the message to the payee's local reserve bank, which debits the sending reserve bank and credits the payee member. Fedwire operates pursuant to Federal Reserve Board Regulation J.

S.W.I.F.T. (Society for Worldwide International Financial Telecommunications) is an international communications system without a settlement component. Member banks communicate credit and debit positions through an international electronic link-up and the parties settle by separate agreement.

C.H.I.P.S. (Clearing House Interbank Payment System) is a communication and settlement system that processes both international and domestic funds transfers. The service is owned by the New York Clearing House and offers same-day settlement by arrangement with the New York Federal Reserve Bank. At the end of each business day net debtors send Fedwires to the New York Federal Reserve Bank to cover their positions and then the New York Fed sends Fedwires through C.H.I.P.S. to net creditors. Operating rules of the New York Clearing House govern the rights and liabilities attending C.H.I.P.S. transactions.

8. *Emerging Technologies*

There is no reason to expect that the technological advances that have brought us the "new payment systems" will not continue to produce improvements on existing payment media. An example is the emergence of the so called "smart cards," which were developed in France and consist of a computer chip embedded in a plastic card that enables merchants to draw on a credit amount retained in the card. Subtracted credit is stored in an electronic "till," which the merchant then brings to the bank to receive credit—thus negating the need for an "on-line" system. Both Visa and MasterCard are currently researching the possibilities of introducing smart card systems in the United States.*

C. EVOLUTION OF THE PAYMENT SYSTEM: LEX LLEWELLYN?

Payment systems and the laws governing them are not static. A study limited to the "black letter" of today's payment systems law would be of only limited use in the years to come because technological, social, and economic factors are sure to alter, not only the physical form taken by future payment systems, but also our perception of the role that payment systems play in society. This process of change has characterized the history of payment systems law. Therefore, an understanding of the legal environment surrounding payment media requires analysis of the forces that have shaped, and continue to shape, the governing rules. A brief examination of the history of U.C.C. Articles 3 and 4 illuminates the role played by changing technology as well as various interest groups in influencing the contemporary law.

* See D. Baker & R. Brandel, The Law Of Electronic Fund Transfer Systems 1–25 to 1–26 (1988).

While the U.C.C. was the product of the work of many attorneys (some of whom were academicians) over the course of many years, it is generally agreed that the Code's primary architect was Karl N. Llewellyn. Professor Llewellyn taught commercial law and jurisprudence at the Yale, Columbia, and University of Chicago law schools. The U.C.C. has been referred to as "Llewellyn's Code," "Code Llewellyn," "Lex Llewellyn," and "Karl's Kode." See William L. Twining, Karl Llewellyn and the Realist Movement 271 (1973). While it is true that the U.C.C. as a whole owes a great deal to Llewellyn's jurisprudential predispositions, it is also true that not all of the articles of the Code follow his realistic style as completely as, say, Article 2 does at several crucial junctures. Indeed, the articles that seem to owe the least to Llewellyn are the Commercial Paper and Bank Deposits and Collections articles. The payments law of the Code betrays perhaps more than any of the other substantive articles the political accommodations necessary to the ultimate promulgation of preemptive commercial legislation.*

In a book review, Donald J. Rapson, a member of the U.C.C. Permanent Editorial Board, remarked upon the dynamics underlying the preparation of the Code's payment provisions.

RAPSON, BOOK REVIEW (REVIEWING F. MILLER & A. HARRELL, THE LAW OF MODERN PAYMENT SYSTEMS AND NOTES)

41 Bus. Lawyer 675, 676–77 (1986).

Surprisingly, Professor William Prosser, the reknowned torts authority, was the reporter for article 3.[4] It is a difficult article, full of

* On the whole, it is difficult to determine with confidence the impact that Llewellyn had on the final version of the Code. He remarked that he had been forced to make some compromises. "I am ashamed of it [the Code] in some ways; there are so many pieces that I could make a little better; there are so many beautiful ideas that I tried to get in that would have been good for the law, but I was voted down." Karl N. Llewellyn, Why a Commercial Code?, 22 Tenn.L.Rev. 779, 784 (1953).

4. Some years ago, I asked Professor Gilmore about the drafting history of arts. 3 and 4. He graciously responded with a fascinating letter which has not previously been made public. About Prosser:

> When I became associated with the Code project (shortly after World War II), the drafting of Article 3 was already well along. Prosser was the Reporter for Article 3 and, I believe, had been from the beginning. He was, of course, an authority on torts (having already published the first edition of his hornbook) but had never, until he agreed to become the Reporter for Article 3, had anything to do with negotiable instruments law. Llewellyn's explanation for his choice of Prosser was that he (Llewellyn) wanted to get a first-rate legal mind (which Prosser obviously was) who, because of his initial ignorance of the field, would be able to take a fresh look at all the problems. Another explanation which occurred to me was that the choice of Prosser made it possible for Llewellyn, who, to start with, knew a great deal more about negotiable instruments law than Prosser did, to control the drafting to a much greater extent than he would have been able to do if the Reporter had been an authority in his own right (say Britton of Illinois or Steffen of Yale). Naturally, Prosser soon acquired the knowledge which he had initially lacked but

antiquarian language drawn almost verbatim from the predecessor negotiable instruments law. Gilmore, who in his last years apparently felt guilty about the U.C.C. enhancement of the position of the good-faith purchaser, including purchasers of negotiable instruments (later "rechristened 'holders in due course' ") minced no words. He described the drafting of article 3 "as the N.I.L. doubled in spades or negotiability *in excelsis,*" calling article 3 "a museum of antiquities—treasure house crammed full of ancient artifacts whose use and function have long since been forgotten."

The drafting of article 4 has a fascinatingly checkered history. The original reporter was Professor Fairfax Leary, Jr., who, for many years, has been a foremost authority on articles 3 and 4. For reasons that have been best explained by Leary, he was replaced. Gilmore stepped into that breach. A few years ago, he recollected that history for me:

> After he [Leary] left I inherited the job and prepared at least one draft (possibly more than one). Article 4 became the bloodiest battleground in the entire history of the Code. While Steffen (and others) attacked it as being "pro-bank," bank counsel (particularly the New York group) attacked it as a Communist plot designed to destroy the American banking system. Eventually, as Fax said in his Temple article, a committee of bank counsel, headed by Walter Malcolm of Boston, was authorized to prepare what became the final (1952) draft—an arrangement I once described as tantamount to appointing a committee of dogs to draw up a protective ordinance for cats (feelings ran high in those days). Malcolm, who was a man of the highest personal integrity, understood that it was his function to do whatever was necessary to placate the New York group (who, nevertheless, refused to be placated.)

This drafting process resulted in two articles that overlap considerably. Article 3 applies to negotiable instruments and a limited form of nonnegotiable instruments. Article 4 treats "items," which include not only negotiable instruments under article 3 but also "any instrument for the payment of money even though it is non-negotiable."

As the above excerpt indicates, Article 3 of the Commercial Code was largely a rewrite of the earlier Uniform Negotiable Instruments Law (N.I.L.), which was promulgated by the then new National Conference of Commissioners on Uniform States Laws in 1896 and by 1924 adopted in all the states. The N.I.L. was itself based upon the English Bills of Exchange Act of 1882. The Bills of Exchange Act was largely a codification of rules developed in the English courts over the 150 years

> my own feeling was that he never felt really at home with the stuff.

Letter from Grant Gilmore to Donald J. Rapson (Oct. 8, 1980); *see also* Mentschikoff, *Reflections of a Drafter,* 43 Ohio St. L.J. 537 (1982).

or so prior to 1882. Therefore, there is some justification for Gilmore's assertion that Article 3 is a "museum of antiquities."

Article 4, however, was not rooted in the past: there was no prior uniform act, though the American Banker's Association had prepared a Bank Collection Code which had been adopted in 19 states. Article 4 was intensively examined and criticized by banking groups and was nearly abandoned as a topic on which a sufficient consensus could not be reached. Though there might still be some disagreement on the issue, the general perception now is that Article 4, more than Article 3, is different in significant ways from the other articles of the U.C.C. Dean Mentschikoff recognized that Article 4 followed more the formalism of the "conveyancing approach," than the open-ended drafting style of some of the other substantive articles. Soia Mentschikoff, Highlights of the Uniform Commercial Code, 27 Mod.L.Rev. 167, 171 n. 9 (1964).

Walter Malcolm is given considerable credit for having brought Article 4 to fruition. In composing the rules of Article 4 to work in combination with Article 3, Malcolm and the other drafters of the Bank Deposits and Collection Law were sensitive to the peculiar interest in certainty and celerity in the banking world.

MALCOLM, ARTICLE 4—A BATTLE WITH COMPLEXITY

1952 Wis.L.Rev. 265, 270–73.

GENERAL APPROACH OF THE CODE

Judging by the end product of Article 4 itself and the Comments to the Article, the general approach adopted in drafting the Article was something as follows. The movement of perhaps 25,000,000 items through bank channels every business day was a volume operation of tremendous proportions. Such operation was primarily mechanical and the rules governing it similarly should be largely mechanical. Rules laid down would probably be of more value if they gave quick, clear-cut answers to the customers and banks interested in the collection of items than if they stated broad general principles from which courts or lawyers could reason their way to a result. An examination of the actual existing rules as they have developed in the last fifty years in Federal Reserve operating letters, in clearing house rules and in state statutes of the kind mentioned above, indicates a marked trend toward such mechanical rules. The Code should follow this trend.

Meritorious though this objective of prescribing clear-cut rules might be, the difficulties attached to it were tremendous. These difficulties might be illustrated by two hypothetical cases.

> *Case 1.* *A* and *B* of Chicago, Illinois, both carry accounts in the X National Bank of Chicago. B owes A $10 and pays this bill by his check for $10 on the X National Bank. A deposits the check for credit to his account in the X National Bank.

Case 2. An orange grower in Morina, California, sells a quantity of oranges to a wholesale grocery concern in Presque Isle, Maine. In payment, the Maine buyer draws its check for $5,000 on the Presque Isle Trust Company payable to the orange grower and mails it to the latter. Upon receipt the orange grower deposits this check in his account with the Morina Trust Company. The Morina Trust Company forwards the check to its correspondent bank in San Diego, the San Diego National Bank, for collection and credit. The San Diego National Bank forwards the check to the Federal Reserve Bank of Los Angeles for collection and credit. The Federal Reserve Bank of Los Angeles forwards the check by air express to the Federal Reserve Bank of Boston for collection and credit. The Federal Reserve Bank of Boston mails the check directly to the Presque Isle Trust Company. The operating letter of the Federal Reserve Bank of Boston under which the item would be forwarded to the Presque Isle Trust Company authorizes payment either by a remittance or by an authorization to charge the account of the Presque Isle Trust Company with the Federal Reserve Bank of Boston, depending upon whether the hypothetical Presque Isle Trust Company is a member of the Federal Reserve System and perhaps other factors.

Case 1 is one of the simple types of bank collection cases, although even this case presents some puzzling problems. Case 2 represents one of the more complicated types of bank collection cases. If one multiplies these two types of bank collection cases many millions of times with an almost infinite variety of combinations of facts and parties, either of the Case 1 or the Case 2 type or somewhere between, and with such types of collection going on all over the entire United States during every business day, a rough mental image of the bank collection problem may arise. Difficulties in framing the rules governing the process arise from the almost infinite number of combinations of parties and facts; from the fact that if one concentrates, for example, on the relationship between the customer and the depositary bank, conclusions drawn from this relationship affect other relationships; from the fact that the status of collecting banks is basically quite different from that of payor banks; and from many other puzzling considerations that continually play tricks on the reasoning process.

Here then was the extremely complex commercial mechanism for which the Code draftsmen undertook to state a uniform set of rules and in doing so to rationalize the process in some degree. From this range of common law, state and Federal statutes, Federal Reserve regulations and operating letters, clearing house rules, agreements and usages there was to be drawn a set of rules suitable for enactment by state legislatures and, perhaps, by Congress. A major task was to decide where to draw the line as between general principles and detailed working rules; or expressed in another way, as between major rules and minor rules.

It might be thought that a major problem was the settlement of issues on class lines, with banks being in one class and their customers in another. To the extent that the writer could observe or assisted in the drafting process, any such "class" problem was of minor significance. In the writer's observation, the major task was consistently that of penetrating the complex maze of the bank collection mechanism; the contest was between the reasoning process and the complexity of the problem. The continuing, difficult, baffling and discouraging task was at all times one of comprehending and understanding the process, isolating the overall and the various subsidiary problems and the stating of accurate rules to solve them.

The history of the development and drafting of Article 4 confirms this conclusion. In instance after instance a rule was stated in a draft which it was hoped would nicely and clearly solve a problem, only to have the draftsman discover himself, or have someone else point out, that the rule simply wouldn't work under some circumstances or in some situations.

In the third paragraph of the foregoing excerpt, Malcolm notes that "[d]ifficulties in framing the rules governing the process arise from the almost infinite number of combinations of parties and facts." Does that distinguish check collection law from sales or secured transactions? From contract or tort? In the final paragraph, Malcolm acknowledges the difficulty of fixing certain and invariable rules. Does he thereby undermine his thesis? How does Article 2 respond to that very problem?

It can be argued that Articles 3 and 4 of the U.C.C. were promulgated at the worst possible time—just before the technological explosion accompanying the computer age. Developments such as magnetic ink character readers and super-efficient computer communication systems have resulted in new and ingenious ways to transfer value. The so called "new payment systems" present questions unanswered by Articles 3 and 4. Further, there has arguably been friction generated between the approaches taken with respect to the new and old payments law because these questions have arisen at a time when an increased emphasis has been placed on the effects of payments systems on the individual consumer. In 1977, Hal Scott, who would later head up the ill-fated Uniform New Payments Code project, drafted a report on the state of new payments law. The following excerpts from the report illustrate both the problem of changing technology and the emerging significance of the consumer viewpoint.

H. SCOTT, NEW PAYMENT SYSTEMS REPORT

Pp. 88–89, 248–52 (1977).

I think, however, it misses the point to stress unduly *conflicts* between Articles 3 and 4 and new statutory treatment or private legal ordering. A more important point is that many of the most important EFT or credit card problems are simply different from those that arise with respect to checks, and are consequently not provided for in Articles 3 and 4. The problem of allocating risk for fraud in the absence of a signature, as in POS and ACH transactions raises new problems. Further, in on-line systems such as POS, there is no possibility of stopping payment; the debit is posted to the customer's account at the time of the transaction. If the Code were strictly applied, see 4–303, any stop payment order made by the customer after completion of the transaction would come too late because final payment would have occurred.

This does not necessarily mean that the consumer should have no right to reverse in such situations. While a strict analogy with Article 4 might suggest that there should be no right to stop payment, because the item had been paid, one might instead conclude that Article 4's provision making the time to stop payment fortuitously turn on the speed of check collection is outdated and that what is needed is a new approach, which starts with the question of whether customers should be able to retain funds pending dispute with merchants in order to correct inequality of bargaining power, or whether reversibility should be conditioned on the ability to effect a chargeback against the merchant account.

* * *

I would recommend that we avoid formulating a comprehensive "reply" to any proposed short-term legislation, either by way of detailed criticism or support, or by way of offering an alternative statute. These proposals are principally addressed to consumer rights issues in NPS [new payment systems], which are likely to be exceedingly controversial and not always subject to rational discourse on the part of either opponents or advocates. As to such matters as reversibility, neither our Committee, nor the ALI possesses special expertise on the question of whether it is or is not desirable, and I believe our direct intervention on the side of one or another position on such an issue will plunge us into the uncomfortable political thicket.

* * *

Having taken this position, however, I should point out a few considerations which may push for a more activist role. First, even in the consumer area, I am not sure that the Congress will be successful in identifying all the NPS issues which do affect consumers. EFT and check guarantee raise a considerable number of consumer issues that cannot be handled by mere application of existing credit card law, with a few refinements. If consumer protection is viewed broadly, we may have a social responsibility to bring these matters to the attention of the Congress and to advocate particular solutions to them.

Second, I think it is wrong to perceive a dichotomy between commercial and consumer issues and worry about the other matters in the future. There is no consumer check law, there is just check law, and it applies to consumers along with everyone else. Most of Articles 3 and 4 are concerned with the rights and liabilities of consumers along with all other users of checks. We would surely view it as odd if it were suggested that we should ignore proposed amendments to Articles 3 and 4 on the allocation of risk for a forged drawer's signature or stop payment.

* * *

Even if it might be desirable to do more, it could not be done in a vacuum with respect to the consumer issues. The retail risk allocation will be a critical element in designing the allocation of risk at the wholesale level. Moreover, drafting such a statute at this time would be premature, both with respect to our ability to anticipate technological change and to grasp proper solutions. A quick fix will not do.

Although the Uniform New Payments Code effort failed to gain acceptance due to political differences between consumer and banking factions, the pressures of changing technology and fear of federal preemption that had precipitated the revision attempt remained. In 1985, new reporters were appointed and efforts to overhaul the Code were revived, culminating in the promulgation in 1990 of a revised Article 3 and a substantially amended Article 4. The same efforts also resulted in a new Article 4A to deal with wire transfers. The official prefatory note to revised Article 3 sheds some light on the forces that shaped the revision.

> The original Articles 3 and 4 and their predecessors were based upon a paper payment system. Literally, there has been an explosion in the volume of paper processed since Articles 3 and 4 were first promulgated. In the early '50s, around 7 billion checks were processed annually. Correctly anticipating an increase in check volume as the result of a retail approach taken by bankers at that time, the American Bankers Association in 1954 placed a team on a research and development project to identify the most efficient method of processing checks mechanically. The eminently successful MICR line technology was the result. Upon its implementation, checks were processed at high rates of speed. In major part as a result of this technology, a seven-fold explosion in check volume has occurred between the '50s and 1988. In 1988, the Federal Reserve Board estimated check volume at 48 billion written annually. In 1987, Congress enacted the Expedited Funds

Availability Act, and the Federal Reserve Board implemented it in 1988 with Regulation CC. Regulation CC covers many aspects of the forward check collection process and all aspects of the return process.

Present Articles 3 and 4, written for a paper-based system, do not adequately address the issues of responsibility and liability as they relate to modern technologies now employed and the procedures required by the current volume of checks and by the "Expedited Funds Availability Act" and Regulation CC. While agreements among parties to particular transactions have provided some relief, such stop-gap measures are no longer adequate.

* * *

The revision of Articles 3 and 4 to update, improve, and maintain their viability is necessary to accommodate these changing practices and modern technologies, the needs of a rapidly expanding national and international economy, the requirement for more rapidly available funds, and the need for more clarity and certainty. Absent such an update, further federal preemption of state law may likely occur.

D. PAYMENT SYSTEMS AND THE CONSUMER MOVEMENT

From the preceding materials we have seen that both the consumer as well as the commercial banking community have a direct interest in the form taken by payment systems law. But how does the law of payment systems affect individual consumers?

HILLEBRAND, REVISED ARTICLES 3 AND 4 OF THE UNIFORM COMMERCIAL CODE: A CONSUMER PERSPECTIVE

42 Ala.L.Rev. 679, 683–84 (1991).

Articles 3 and 4 govern the arcane topics of "negotiable instruments," "commercial paper" (Article 3) and "bank deposits and collections" (Article 4). Consumers are affected by Article 3 because a check is one common type of negotiable instrument. For example, former Article 3 addressed such issues as the effect of postdating a check, the effect of an incomplete check, and the effect of a check with a forged or unauthorized signature. Article 3 also governs a variety of other types of commercial transactions involving negotiable instruments (other than checks) which are not generally used by most consumers. Article 4 governs the manner in which banks process or "collect" checks. It provides specific rules that apply to transactions between banks and it also sets forth some of the rules that create, limit, or affect consumer rights and obligations with respect to checking accounts. According to comments in an earlier draft, the purpose of revised Article 4 is "to continue to be the major source of statutory law for customer-bank relations."

The early history of payments systems law betrays an absence of organized consumer input into the rulemaking process despite organized banking influence. This is perhaps because the rules that provided the foundation of contemporary law were formulated before the advent of the consumer movement. The promulgation of original Articles 3 and 4 was by no means universally praised. There was criticism from academics that the articles, particularly Article 4, were oriented too much toward banking interests at the expense of equity toward consumers. Nowhere was the criticism stronger than in relation to U.C.C. § 4–103.

By its own terms, Article 4 is not the final word on the law governing bank collections. Not only may Federal Reserve regulations and operating letters, clearing house rules, and the like (OR 4–103(2); R 4–103(b)) modify the rights and liabilities of the parties to commercial paper within the collection system, but individual banks and their customers may adjust their legal postures within the limits described in subsection 4–103(1) (R 4–103(a)). The provision explains that the parties may "by agreement" vary the rules of Article 4. Keep in mind the section 1–201(3) definition of "agreement" and consider whether the account agreement distributed to bank customers at the time they open an account would fall within the letter or spirit of the definition. Professor Beutel, not a supporter of the U.C.C. project, was particularly incensed by the operation of Article 4, and no section gave him more trouble than did 4–103.

BEUTEL, THE PROPOSED UNIFORM [?] COMMERCIAL CODE SHOULD NOT BE ADOPTED

61 Yale L.J. 334, 359–63 (1952).

This new Article 4 on Bank Deposits and Collections follows very closely the already discredited American Banker's Association Uniform Bank Collection Code. It even re-enacts the preference articles which have caused that act to be held unconstitutional and which are admittedly contrary to current federal legislation and not, therefore, applicable to National Banks. However, it goes much further than the American Banker's Association in that it provides that all paper deposited with the bank, unless the contracts indicate otherwise, is left for collection and is to be handled entirely at the risk of the customer. The bank, on the other hand, has all the rights of a holder in due course when it is in any danger of suffering loss. All liability of the bank for improper handling of paper so carefully and fairly set up in the earlier drafts is removed. By a trick provision of Section 4–103 and subsection 4, the bank is not bound to follow any of the collection procedures set out in the act. So long as it acts "reasonably," it is only liable for its own lack of good faith and due care; but even due care is limited by other provisions of the "Code," and it is not liable for the acts of any of its agent or associate banks. Damages for the lack of due care and bad faith are carefully held to the minimum, and any action authorized by this Article is specifically made due care for which the bank is not liable.

* * *

The bank may also change by contract any of the rules set out in this act except the duty of due care. Thus the "Code" appears to completely approve the type of surreptitious waivers consistently appearing in fine print on bank forms, in spite of the fact that many courts have refused to enforce "contracts" of this kind. Article 4 and the definitions of contracts found in the "Code" give them blanket approval.

A careful examination of the wording of the act will show that this Article was drafted entirely with the purpose of protecting the banks so that they could carry on their business at the risk of the customer. In most instances they have succeeded, with the aid of their lawyers, in shifting many of the risks of the banking business to their customers, where fairness in bank collections would require that the bank be the insurer of the paper which it is to collect.

* * *

This article is a deliberate sell-out of the American Law Institute and the Commission of Uniform Laws to the bank lobby in return for their support of the rest of the "Code." That this would happen was forecast in the debate before the Institute two years ago when Mr. Schnader in a discussion with the writer said that it would be necessary to make certain concessions to the banking interests in order to get their support for the "Code." And it is significant that Mr. Schnader was very active in pushing the present article through the meeting of the Commissioners and the Institute in September even over the apparent protest of the Editor-in-Chief himself. They not only made concessions to the bankers but delivered everything they asked for. The banks now have a piece of class legislation more favorable to their interests than the American Bankers Association Bank Collections Code which their lobby failed to put over on the legislatures. This one-sided piece of class legislation is now backed by the prestige of the American Law Institute and the Commission on Uniform Laws. Such a sell-out is beneath the dignity of both organizations and is a tremendous blow to their prestige as scientific bodies. It is doubtful if the majority of the members would have approved this article if they had known what they were doing; and, if they do so approve, it raises the question whether the American Law Institute has ceased to be a learned scientific body to become a plush pressure group dominated by reactionary financial interests. The existence of Article 4 alone is enough to condemn in its entirety the adoption of this "Code."

Professor Grant Gilmore, a drafter of Article 9 ("Secured Transactions") and generally a supporter of the Code project, found that he could not disagree completely with Beutel's assessment, particularly with regard to section 4–103.

GILMORE, THE UNIFORM COMMERCIAL CODE: A REPLY TO PROFESSOR BEUTEL

61 Yale L.J. 364, 374–77 (1952).

While I do not agree with many of the details of Beutel's criticism of Article 4, I do not care to urge enactment of the present text of the Article. I shall therefore forego discussion of the provisions of the Article which Beutel draws in question, leaving that task to someone who can undertake it with a better heart.

* * *

The feature of Article 4 as it appears in the final version of the Code which is enough to make the entire Article objectionable is the freedom of contract section, § 4–103. This Section as drafted provides that banks may by general or special agreement contract out of any of the rules laid down in the balance of the Article, provided only that a bank may not disclaim responsibility for the exercise of good faith and ordinary care. The proviso is, however, subject to a double-barrelled exception: 1) banks may agree on what constitutes ordinary care; 2) even in the absence of agreement, any action taken by a bank which is consistent with "a banking usage" is ordinary care. It should be noted further that the "general agreements" by which banks may amend the Article as they see fit, or agree on what ordinary care is, are agreements between banks to which the customer who deposits an item for collection is not a party but by which he will be bound.

This is carrying a good joke too far. The only bright spots are: 1) that a court construing Section 4–103 according to its fair meaning, might be disposed to hold the Article unconstitutional as an improper delegation of legislative power to private interests, 2) that Section 4–103 contains more than one loophole in the drafting on which a court might well seize to limit the scope of "variation by agreement" which the Section was designed to permit.

The principal defense of Section 4–103 runs along these lines: Bank collections is a highly technical field; the operation, because of the enormous number of items handled by banks, must be routinized; as conditions change, new operating procedures become necessary—it would therefore be unwise to freeze any particular procedure by statute; bankers are the only people with a sufficient understanding of the technical processes to establish reasonable rules; it is absurd, fanciful and professorial to imagine that banks would ever take undue advantage of their customers. Parts of this argument are entirely sound. I have not been convinced that it can ever be sound legislative policy to write a blank check to the order of any private interest group in the community.

Let us not overstate the case. I do not believe that it is time to man the barricades. Our way of life will not be in jeopardy even if Article 4 is enacted. Luncheon at the Bankers' Club is not given over to devising ways and means of hoisting the poor customer each day a little higher on his own petard. I do not ascribe to the draftsmen of the final version of Article 4 motives which are in any way improper or malevolent.

A cheap, speedy and efficient collection system is in the private interest of banks as much as it is in the public interest of customers of banks. We may anticipate that in general and in good times banks would use the powers conferred on them under § 4–103 in a good faith effort to improve the collection system. But there are bad times as well as good times; there may even be bad banks as well as good banks. Section 4–103 goes far beyond what is wise or permissible in allowing banks to rewrite the law their way whenever things get tough: say, a general extension of all time limits because of difficulty in finding trained personnel during a war period.

I agree, then, that Article 4 as it now reads should not be enacted, as part of the Code or in any other guise. However, if the present text of Article 4, and particularly of Section 4–103, were revised so as to place appropriate limitations on contracting out of the statute, there would be no insuperable objections to the balance of the Article.

Can you find a "loophole" in section 4–103 that might limit the scope of variation by agreement? Consider Comment 2 to the section.

In the years following the promulgation of Articles 3 and 4, there occurred a change in the way society viewed the relationship between commercial and consumer interests. Writing in the landmark book, *Unsafe at Any Speed,* Ralph Nader foresaw the grass-roots movement he believed was necessary to place sufficient pressure on the commercial establishment to bring about change.

> A great problem of contemporary life is how to control the power of economic interests which ignore the harmful effects of their applied science and technology. The automobile tragedy is one of the most serious of these man-made assaults on the human body. The history of that tragedy reveals many obstacles which must be overcome in the taming of any mechanical or biological hazard which is a by-product of industry or commerce. Our society's

obligation to protect the "body rights" of its citizens with vigorous resolve and ample resources requires the precise, authoritative articulation and front-rank support which is being devoted to civil rights.

Ralph Nader, *Unsafe At Any Speed* xci (1965). The subsequent years saw the rise of the American consumer movement and its concomitant effect on the law of payment systems. Pro-consumer laws such as the Electronic Funds Transfer Act, the Federal Truth in Lending Act, and more recently, the Expedited Funds Availability Act were passed, all of which contain substantial protection for the consumer in payment transactions. The revision of Articles 3 and 4, however, changed little from the consumer standpoint, and in some ways made the consumer even worse off vis-a-vis the banking industry. Professor Edward Rubin offers an explanation in the following excerpt.

RUBIN, EFFICIENCY, EQUITY AND THE PROPOSED REVISION OF ARTICLES 3 AND 4

42 Ala.L.Rev. 551, 586–92 (1991).

The conclusion that a federal statute like the EFTA is more efficient and more equitable than a uniform law promulgated by the American Law Institute seems paradoxical. We all know that Congress is political and the EFTA was, in fact, the product of a highly political process. Essentially, the statute represents a bargain negotiated by the American Bankers Association ("ABA") and the consumer lobby. The ABA had long been the dominant force in any legislative effort involving banks. In the late 1960s, however, the consumer movement suddenly became a powerful force, and the ABA, unprepared for this development, was totally outflanked. As a result, Congress passed a series of heavily consumer-oriented measures, including a statute governing the payment function of credit cards that is probably the most proconsumer legislation ever enacted. The ABA managed to regroup, however, and by the mid–1970s it had regained enough power to counterbalance the consumer lobby. Nevertheless, the ABA was forced to recognize that it had lost enough power so that a careful balancing act was necessary. At the time the EFTA was drafted, the two groups were in relative equipoise and the statute largely reflects the bargain that they struck.

* * * [T]he drafting process for Articles 3 and 4 and their revisions was equally political. Nonetheless, the context was different. The drafting committees were supposed to behave as collections of experts, who put their personal views aside to design good public policy. They had available to them reporters who represented some of the most knowledgeable experts on commercial law. They also had the luxury of time; Congress legislates amidst a whirl of multiple bills, publicity, campaigning, lobbying and all sorts of other pressures, but the U.C.C. drafting process proceeds on its own schedule without time limits or

conflicting demands. If only that drafting process were apolitical, it would do a better job than Congress according to almost all our political theories; even with its politicization, one would hardly expect it to do a worse one. The conclusion [that the U.C.C. Articles 3 and 4 revision process was less successful] reached in the [preceding] section [of this article], therefore, requires an explanation.

One explanation is the inherent advantages that federal legislation possesses. The advantage that springs to mind, of course, is uniformity, but that is not an issue here. The whole point of the U.C.C. is to generate uniform state laws, and for the most part, it has achieved that goal. In any event, the fact that some states saw fit to enact nonuniform provisions is hardly the fault of the drafters. There is, however, a much more important advantage of federal legislation, namely its ability to utilize a regulatory agency. Most modern legislation relies on an agency to draft supplementary rules and to interpret and enforce both the statutory rules and the supplementary ones. This gives the drafters a certain amount of flexibility. They do not need to agonize over every detail, nor do they need to be concerned that every ambiguity will spawn innumerable nonuniform variations, for which the drafters will be excoriated in law review articles and bar association meetings. States have regulatory agencies as well, but reliance on them in a uniform law would destroy its uniformity. The interstices would be filled by different regulations, different interpretations, and different enforcement strategies.

In the case of the EFTA, Congress had access to a particularly effective agency, the Federal Reserve Board. The Federal Reserve Board ranks high among government agencies in terms of its prestige and perceived expertise. While consumer protection is an odd role for a central bank to play, the Federal Reserve Board had been in the business for a decade before the EFTA was enacted and possessed a separate unit that worked exclusively in this field. By relying on the Federal Reserve Board, Congress was able to obtain all the advantages of knowledge and concentrated attention that were the perceived advantages of the U.C.C. drafting process, plus all the detail and flexibility that this regulatory process provides.

But there is a deeper explanation for the superiority of federal legislation, and it lies in the character of representation. At the time the EFTA took shape, both sides of the bank-consumer relationship were well-represented in the political process, the banks by the American Bankers Association, the consumers by various groups such as Consumers Union and the Consumer Federation of America. It may seem odd to ascribe the public policy virtues of a statute to the existence of competing interest groups. Representation is typically regarded as a source of political legitimacy, but not of public policy effectiveness, particularly in an obscure and technical field like the payment system. Moreover, even that legitimacy is generally obtained by proportional, one-person, one-vote representation, not by the additional advantages that certain groups acquire because of the political power of their lobbyists. The conflicting claims of interest groups tend to be portrayed as the very antithesis of intelligent public policy, and the prevalence of these interest groups is perhaps the major source of our prevailing pessimism about our system's capacities for governance.

In fact, representation provided by competing interest groups has major conceptual advantages that often translate into effective public policy. Lobbyists are particularly good at collecting large amounts of information. They need to communicate regularly with their membership in order to obtain financial resources and, in the process, they will naturally be informed of their members' concerns. Listening attentively to these concerns is one of the major services that they provide. More importantly, information is a major tool that lobbyists utilize to influence public policy. Unless its group is extremely powerful, the lobbyist will not want to appear before a decisionmaker and declare, "Do what we want; we have the votes." Rather, he will speak in the public policy terms the decisionmaker must use, and for this he needs information. Of course, all the information that a lobbyist collects and transmits will be favorable to the group it represents. But as long as lobbyists for all relevant interests are on the scene, a full range of information will become available.

Even more important than the availability of the information is the assessment of it. The bankers and bank attorneys who have dominated the U.C.C. drafting process are probably aware of the concerns that consumer representatives would tend to raise. But they evaluate these concerns from their own particular perspective. For example, everyone on the bankers' side was perfectly aware that banks often become involved in disputes with their customers about the propriety of a particular charge that appears on the customer's account statement. Bankers are simply convinced, to the very core of their being, that the customer is generally mistaken or dishonest in these situations. They are equally convinced that if the customer is correct, the bank will realize its error and correct it without any need for sanctions. What consumer lobbyists bring to a drafting session is the equally strong conviction that customers are generally honest, that banks are careless and unresponsive, and that banks will treat their customers fairly only if threatened with substantial liability.

The drafting process for the U.C.C.'s new Article 4A provides a clear example of this difference in perception. One of the crucial issues raised by Article 4A, which deals with wholesale electronic fund transfers, is the mysterious interloper problem; when money disappears from an account by means of an electronic fund transfer, and no one knows who was responsible, who should bear the loss? The banks were persuaded that the customer should bear the loss, since any mysterious transfer would certainly be the result of customer carelessness, and they so provided in the early drafts of Article 4A. At some later date, these drafts came to the attention of the National Corporate Cash Manager's Association, which represents corporate bank customers. The cash managers appeared in force at the next meetings on Article

4A, particularly the meetings of the American Bar Association's advisory group, and brought with them the certainty that the mysterious transfer necessarily resulted from faulty bank design of the security procedures. They did not possess any new information; what they added was a new perception of the information that was already available. There were no votes taken, no explicit exercise of power by either the bankers' or the customers' group. Rather, there was a recognition that each group would need to deal with the other's perception of the world, and that this perception, even though they might not share it, was a possible one that rational people could believe. The final version of Article 4A, not surprisingly, represents a compromise between each side's position.

Representation not only affects the information available and the assessment of that information, but also affects the kinds of solutions that are developed and considered. Drafting a statute is not simply a matter of choosing between existing approaches on the basis of one's political predilections. It also involves the development of new ideas and new statutory devices to deal with perceived problems. The character of this problem solving process will often depend on the perceptions and motivations of the participants. For example, the EFTA's error resolution procedure is new and represents a genuine innovation. It seems unlikely that bank or consumer representatives, acting alone, would have developed this device, even if they had been instructed to favor the opposing side. Most likely, the representatives would have simply shifted liability back and forth, as has been done in all previous statutes in this field. The prescribed dialogue between customer and bank is a product of the interaction between bank and consumer representatives. To trigger this process of innovation, the representation of opposing groups does not need to be equal or in proportion to their underlying strength. It need only be sufficient to present both perspectives forcefully, and strong enough to motivate the drafters to seek new solutions.

To be sure, representation is not a complete solution to the problem of statutory design. For it to work, all the affected groups must be represented, and their representatives must possess roughly equivalent abilities and resources. They must be willing to talk to each other, and imaginative enough to innovate instead of merely compromise. A truly neutral body of experts, committed to good public policy, might still be superior. But neutrality is hard to come by in the real world, and those who claim it most vociferously are often the most deluded or disingenuous. In the absence of neutrality, it is better to rely on representative drafting groups, not only to add political legitimacy, but also to improve the conceptual process of drafting statutes that comport with public policy. The EFTA, for all the political compromises it includes, was drafted by a representative group, while the U.C.C. revisions were not. This is why the EFTA is superior, in terms of both economic efficiency and social equity.

In this chapter we have given you a brief overview of recent developments in payment mechanisms and the legislative responses to those developments. We have also given you a quick look at some of the criticisms that have been made of original Article 4 of the Commercial Code and some similar criticisms of revised Articles 3 and 4. In the following chapters of the book, we turn largely to a careful examination of the commercial paper rules of Articles 3 and 4, the electronic funds transfer rules of the E.F.T.A. and Article 4A, and some coverage of credit card rules. Most commercial paper and EFT problems do not involve the consumerism issues raised by Beutel, Hillebrand, or Rubin. We will, however, encounter them from time to time.

The rules applicable to commercial paper have long historical antecedents going back to the middle ages. Also, codification in the commercial paper area has a rather long history. In England, in 1882 the Bills of Exchange Act was passed making statutory most of the law of commercial paper. The first act promulgated by the newly formed National Conference of Commissioners on Uniform State Laws was the Uniform Negotiable Instruments Law (N.I.L.) (in 1896). That act was ultimately adopted by all the states and remained the governing law until replaced by original Articles 3 and 4 of the Commercial Code. You will see many references to the N.I.L. in the comments to original Article 3 and even some in the comments to revised Article 3.

Before turning to the substantive law of commercial paper, a brief introduction to the basic forms of commercial paper will be helpful to you.

There are two basic instruments: the draft and the promissory note.

The draft is a three party instrument in which the drawer orders a drawee to pay a sum of money to the payee. The check, a draft drawn on a bank and payable on demand, is the most common form of draft. But, as we will see, drafts are often drawn on persons who are not banks and also are often not payable until some specified time, rather than being payable on demand. Drafts payable on demand are essentially always payment mechanisms: that is, the intention of the drawer is that the draft be paid immediately; it is a substitute for cash.

The promissory note is a two party instrument. The signer ("maker") of the note promises to pay the payee a sum of money in the future. The promissory note is always a credit instrument: it evidences a debt that the maker promises to pay in the future.

See R 3–104 concerning promises (a promissory note) and orders (drafts drawn on third parties). See also the subcategories of drafts defined there and compare OR 3–104. Set out below is a copy of a check, a trade draft, and a promissory note.

Personal Check

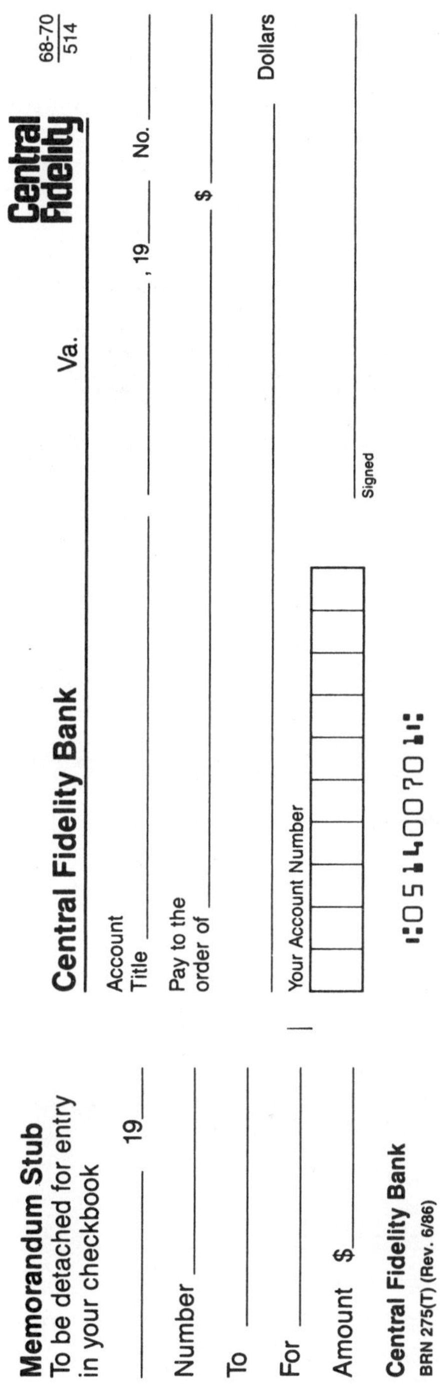

Memorandum Stub
To be detached for entry
in your checkbook
________ 19__
Number ________
To ________
For ________
Amount $ ________
Central Fidelity Bank
BRN 275(T) (Rev. 6/86)

Central Fidelity Bank Va. **Central Fidelity** 68-70/514
Account Title ________, 19__ No. ____
Pay to the order of ________ $ ____
________ Dollars
Your Account Number
Signed ________
⑆051400701⑆

Trade Draft

Bank, at its option, may refuse to honor this draft unless Bill of Sale below is properly filled out. If livestock is encumbered, mortgagee or lienholder must endorse consent of sale and release on reverse.

PAY TO THE ORDER OF BILL OF SALE DRAFT July 26, 1974
HAYDEN RABON AND ROBERT B. BROWN
$6,697.57 $ Six Thousand Six Hundred Ninty-Seven Dollars and 57/100---------------------- DOLLARS
R & R Farms, Inc.
New Ulm State Bank
New Ulm, Texas By B&R Cattle Co (Purchaser Sign Here)

NO.	KIND OR CLASS	Avg. Wt.	BRAND & LOCATION	GR. WEIGHT	% SHRINK.	NET WEIGHT	PRICE	TOTAL $
13	50	162				2,110	40.26	849.57
7	60	215				1,505	33.83	509.18
9	66	497				4,475	34.72	1,554.04
40	22	269				10,765	35.15	3,784.78

KNOW ALL MEN BY THESE PRESENTS: That I, the Seller, signing hereunder and residing in the County of Nueces, State of Texas, in consideration of the payment of the above draft, do bargain and sell, and, by these presents do bargain and sell unto ________ the herein described livestock, and hereby bind myself to warrant and defend the title to said livestock against any person claiming the same or any part of them, and further, warrant that the livestock as described herein is free and clear of any encumbrance or lien whatsoever except those for which consent to said sale and release of said lien is endorsed on this draft as provided for hereon.

________ (Witness) Robert B. Brown by Sally Healy (Seller Signs Here)

FROM: P. O. BOX 1268 ROBSTOWN, TEXAS 78380 88-1590 / 1149

REPORT BY AND DATE July 26, 1974 № 6950

WE ENCLOSE FOR COLLECTION AND RETURN OR CREDIT WHEN PAID

DRAWER	ENDORSER	PAYER	AMOUNT
B & R Cattle Co. Hayden Rabon & Robert B. Brown	State National Bank	R.&R. Farms, Inc.	$6,697.57
KIND OF PAPER draft	DATE DUE sight		

New Ulm State Bank
Box 155
New Ulm, Texas 78950

no authority to pay

SPECIAL INSTRUCTIONS

NO PROTEST

Deliver documents only upon payment. Do not hold after maturity or for convenience of payer.
The proceeds of this collection must not be mingled with your general funds or credited to our account, but you will please remit promptly when collection is made. All funds collected shall remain the property of our depositor, until the proceeds of the remittance are received and finally credited; and the acceptance of any draft for the same, or any portion thereof, is subject to final payment.

Promissory Note

TUSCALOOSA, AL, ________ 19__

FOR VALUE RECEIVED, the undersigned promise(s) to pay to the order of THE FIRST NATIONAL BANK OF TUSKALOOSA

the sum of ________________________________ DOLLARS, negotiable and payable in lawful money of the United States at The First National Bank of Tuskaloosa,

Tuscaloosa, Alabama with interest from date hereof at the rate of ____________

____________________________________ percent______% per annum.

Principal and interest shall be payable as follows:________________________

In the event of default in the payment of this note, or any one or more of any installments, when and as the same fall due, or in the event of death, insolvency of, general assignment by, judgment against, filing of application in any court for receiver for, or issuance of any writ of garnishment or attachment against any party liable hereon, whether maker, endorser, surety or guarantor, or whom the payee, its successors or assigns, shall in good faith and upon reasonable grounds consider the indebtedness insecure, or on the happening of any one or more of said events, the payee, its successors or assigns, shall have the right at its election, and without notice to the undersigned or any endorser hereof, to declare the entire indebtedness evidenced hereby immediately due and payable, and to proceed in any lawful manner for the collection hereof. No delay in making such election shall be construed to waive the right to make the same, and no waiver of any default shall affect any later default.

The parties to this note, whether maker, endorser, surety or guarantor, each for himself, hereby severally waives as to this indebtedness, or any renewal thereof, all rights of exemption under the Constitution and laws of the State of Alabama, or of any other state, as to personal property but shall not waive any consumer protection provision of the Alabama Consumer Credit Act, and they each, jointly and severally, agree to pay all costs of collecting or attempting to collect this note, including, with respect to the original principal amount or original amount financed exceeding $300.00, an Attorney's fee of 15% of the unpaid debt, whether the same be collected or ensured by suit or otherwise. And each maker, endorser, surety and guarantor of this note severally waives demand, presentment, protest, notice of protest, suit and all other requirements necessary to hold them, or any of them, and they severally agree that the time of payment may be extended or a renewal note taken or other indulgence granted without notice or consent to such action, without release of liability as to any such party. The Bank at which this note is payable is hereby authorized to apply, on or after default, to the payment of this debt, any funds or credit held by said Bank on deposit for account of the maker, endorser, surety, guarantor, or any of them, but said Bank shall not be required to make such application unless it shall so elect.

CAUTION: IT IS IMPORTANT THAT YOU THOROUGHLY READ THIS INSTRUMENT BEFORE YOU SIGN IT.

No. ____________ ____________________ (L.S.)
R. No. ____________ ____________________ (L.S.)
Due ____________________ ____________________ (L.S.)

Chapter 2

RIGHTS OF TRANSFEREES, HOLDER IN DUE COURSE*

A. INTRODUCTION

Negotiable Instruments are made to be transferred. At least that is the underlying premise of negotiable instruments law. The law provides, therefore, quick and easy methods of transfer of negotiable instruments and special rules governing the liability of transferors and the rights of transferees. This chapter examines the rules concerning transfer and rights of transferees. In Chapter 3 we deal with the special rules relating to liability of transferors.

Today essentially all contract rights can be assigned. That was not always true: at early common law intangible rights could not be assigned. Therefore, a creditor could not transfer his rights against a debtor to a third party. (As Professor Britton points out, such a rule might have had justification in a time when debtors could be imprisoned for failure to pay their debts. W.E. Britton, Bills & Notes, 2d Ed. 2 (1961)). Also, at early common law, it was conceived that only tangible things, land or goods, could be transferred.

As trade developed in the middle ages, particularly interregional and international trade, the inability to assign rights to payment for goods sold became a serious impediment to its conduct. Merchants, therefore, began to draft instruments which showed on their face that the merchant intended them to be transferred. Such an instrument might be payable to the named payee "or order" or to the named payee or "bearer", or "bearer of this instrument" or simply "bearer". Such instruments might either be promises to pay, like modern promissory notes, or orders to others to pay, like modern checks or drafts. Merchants and their goldsmiths recognized the currency of such instruments. Also, in the middle ages, merchant disputes were commonly

* Throughout this text, the designation "OR" refers to an Article in its original form; "R" denotes a revised Article. E.g., OR 3–303 refers to Original Article 3; R 3–303 refers to Revised Article 3.

resolved by merchant courts sitting at merchants' fairs at various places in England and on the continent. In those merchant courts transferees of such mercantile instruments were allowed to recover on them. So, while in England common law courts still would not recognize the rights of an assignee, the merchant courts were enforcing the rights of transferees of what we would now call negotiable instruments.

By the early 17th century, common law courts also began to recognize the rights of transferees of negotiable instruments. Later the common law courts with some reluctance accepted the idea that any contract claim could be assigned, not just those evidenced by an instrument showing an intention that third parties have a right thereon. However, the separate rules as to negotiable instruments had become firmly fixed in the law and never merged with the later developed law of assignment of general contract claims.

When merchants first developed negotiable instruments that could be freely transferred, use of such instruments as a means of payment greatly facilitated commerce. It would have been inconvenient to transport gold or silver from the place of business of a buyer in, say, Bristol to the place of business of a seller in London. A draft by the Bristol buyer directing a goldsmith in London to deliver gold to the seller was much more convenient. Today paper money meets many of the needs originally met by privately issued commercial paper. But it is still often more convenient to create private "money" by writing a check than it is to pay by governmental legal tender issued in limited denominations which is, in effect, payable to anyone into whose hands it falls. Undoubtedly far more debt is paid by check than is paid by handing over currency.

Just as it is advantageous to commerce to be able to pay debts with negotiable instruments, it is also advantageous to be able to transfer the right to be paid in the future for money loaned or other credit extended. And the merchant rules referred to above also applied to what we today call promissory notes, a writing in which a debtor promises to pay and indicates that he will pay anyone to whom the creditor transfers the paper. That use of commercial paper continues today. When Mr. & Mrs. Smith borrow $100,000 to purchase a new home, they are quite likely to sign a negotiable promissory note evidencing their obligation to repay the loan. Similarly business borrowers often sign promissory notes in which they promise to repay the sums borrowed. While the obligation of Mr. & Mrs. Smith to pay could be assigned even if they did not execute a negotiable note, the use of the note makes transfer easy and the law of negotiable instruments provides transferees with rights that would not be available to ordinary assignees except by special contract arrangement.

B. TAKING FREE OF DEFENSES AND CLAIMS (OF OWNERSHIP)

At first, the fact that certain written instruments were "negotiable" (i.e. transferrable) signified only that the common law prohibition against assignment was overcome. However, in Miller v. Race, a further question was presented. Do certain transferees of negotiable instruments take free of claims of ownership asserted by a prior party?

MILLER v. RACE

97 Eng.Rep. 398 (K.B. 1758).

The cause came on to be tried before Lord Mansfield at the sitting in Trinity term last at Guildhall, London: and upon the trial it appeared that William Finney, being possessed of this bank note on the 11th of December 1756, sent it by the general post, under cover, directed to one Bernard Odenharty, at Chipping Norton in Oxfordshire; that on the same night the mail was robbed, and the bank note in question (amongst other notes) taken and carried away by the robber; that this bank note, on the 12th of the same December, came into the hands and possession of the plaintiff, for a full and valuable consideration, and in the usual course and way of his business, and without any notice or knowledge of this bank note being taken out of the mail.

It was admitted and agreed, that, in the common and known course of trade, bank notes are paid by and received of the holder or possessor of them, as cash; and that in the usual way of negotiating bank notes, they pass from one person to another as cash, by delivery only and without any further inquiry or evidence of title, than what arises from the possession. It appeared that Mr. Finney, having notice of this robbery, on the 13th December, applied to the Bank of England, "to stop the payment of this note": which was ordered accordingly, upon Mr. Finney's entering into proper security "to indemnify the bank."

Some little time after this, the plaintiff applied to the bank for the payment of this note; and for that purpose delivered the note to the defendant, who is a clerk in the bank: but the defendant refused either to pay the note, or to re-deliver it to the plaintiff. Upon which this action was brought against the defendant.

* * *

Sir Richard Lloyd, for the defendant.

The present action is brought, not for the money due upon the note; but for the note itself, the paper, the evidence of the debt. So that the right to the money is not the present question: the note is only an evidence of the money's being due to him as bearer.

The note must either come to the plaintiff by assignment; or must be considered as if the bank gave a fresh, separate, and distinct note to each bearer. Now the plaintiff can have no right by the assignment of a robber. And the bank cannot be considered as giving a new note to each bearer: though each bearer may be considered as having obtained from the bank a new promise.

I do not say whether the bank can, or cannot stop payment; that is another question. But the note is only an instrument of recovery.

Now this note, or these goods (as I may call it), was the property of Mr. Finney who paid in the money: he is the real owner. It is like a medal which might entitle a man to payment of money, or to any other advantage. And it is by Mr. Finney's authority and request that Mr. Race detained it.

* * *

Mr. Williams contra for the plaintiff.

The holder of this bank note, upon a valuable consideration has a right to it, good against the true owner.

1st, the circulation of these notes vests a property in the holder, who comes in the possession of it, upon a valuable consideration.

2dly, this is of vast consequence to trade and commerce; and they would be greatly incommoded if it were otherwise.

3dly, this falls within the reason of a sale in market-overt; and ought to be determined upon the same principle.

First—He put several cases, where the usage, course, and convenience of trade made the law; and sometimes, even against an Act of Parliament.

Secondly—This paper credit has been always, and with great reason, favored and encouraged.

The usage of these notes is, "that they pass by delivery only; and are considered as current cash; and the possession always carries within the property."

A particular mischief is rather to be permitted, than a general inconvenience incurred.

* * *

Lord Mansfield now delivered the resolution of the Court.

* * *

It has been very ingeniously argued by Sir Richard Lloyd for the defendant. But the whole fallacy of the argument turns upon comparing bank notes to what they do not resemble, and what they ought not to be compared to, viz. to goods, or to securities, or documents for debts.

Now they are not goods, not securities, nor documents for debts, nor are so esteemed: but are treated as money, as cash, in the ordinary course and transaction of business, by the general consent of mankind; which gives them the credit and currency of money, to all intents and purposes. They are as much money, as guineas themselves are; or any other current coin, that is used in common payments, as money or cash.

They pass by a will, which bequeaths all the testator's money or cash; and are never considered as securities for money, but as money itself. Upon Ld. Ailesbury's will, [£] 9001. in bank-notes was considered as cash. On payment of them, whenever a receipt is required, the receipts are always given as for money; not as for securities or notes.

So on bankruptcies, they cannot be followed as identical and distinguishable from money: but are always considered as money or cash.

It is a pity that reporters sometimes catch at quaint expressions that may happen to be dropped at the Bar or Bench; and mistake their meaning. It has been quaintly said, "that the reason why money cannot be followed is, because it has no ear-mark": but this is not true. The true reason is, upon account of the currency of it: it can not be recovered after it has passed in currency.

* * *

A bank-note is constantly and universally, both at home and abroad, treated as money, as cash; and paid and received, as cash; and it is necessary, for the purpose of commerce, that their currency should be established and secured.

* * *

Note

1. As you no doubt have already learned, if personal property such as a watch or television set is stolen, the owner from whom it is stolen can recover it or its value from any subsequent person to whom it is transferred, even though the transferee takes in good faith and pays value and even though the particular transferee did not deal with the thief. That is part of the general rule that, unless some exception applies, a transferee cannot get better title than her transferror had. The lawyer for the defendant in *Miller v. Race* argued that the bank note in question should be subject to that rule. Mansfield, however, decided that the bona fide purchaser for value of the bank note took it free of the claim of the person from whom it was stolen and therefore got better title than the thief.

2. Suppose 30 pounds in coin had been stolen from the mails, but the owner of the coins had taken the precaution of making tiny engravings on the coins so that he could identify them. According to Lord Mansfield, could the owner recover them back from a bona fide purchaser for value? What is the reason for the rule adopted by Mansfield?

3. The instrument involved in *Miller v. Race* was a "bank note," an instrument more like today's paper money than like a check or promissory note. More precisely, the "bank note" was a promissory note issued by a bank and payable to bearer. Since Bank of England promises were essentially as "good as gold," its notes passed hand to hand as currency, as Lord Mansfield says. While the instrument in *Miller v. Race* was essentially currency, the commercial advantages of free transferability of non-bank promissory notes and drafts were such that at about the same time as the decision in *Miller v. Race,* such instruments came to be treated in the same way as *bank* notes.

C. REQUIREMENTS FOR HOLDER IN DUE COURSE STATUS

Introductory Note on the Holder in Due Course

In *Miller v. Race* the plaintiff took the instrument for "full and valuable consideration, and in the usual course and way of his business, and without any notice or knowledge of this bank note being taken out of the mail." You will recognize that description as being essentially that of the "good faith purchaser" in current law. In present commercial paper law the "good faith purchaser" is burdened with some very specific requirements and, if he meets those requirements, is called a holder in due course.

As just suggested, the holder in due course doctrine is a part of the larger doctrine of good faith purchase that protects certain innocent purchasers against claims (and sometimes defenses) of prior parties. In the Uniform Commercial Code, Articles 2, 2A, 6, 7, 8, and 9, in addition to Articles 3 and 4, contain provisions protecting bona fide purchasers in certain instances. Those provisions create exceptions to the usual rule that a transferee gets no greater rights than her transferor had. You have probably already learned about U.C.C. §§ 2–403, 2A–304, and 2A–305 which protect certain bona fide purchasers of goods in voidable-title and entrustment-to-merchant cases. Section 9–307 protects certain good faith buyers of goods from merchants against claims of secured parties to whom the merchant had previously given a security interest in the goods. Sections 7–501 and 7–502 protect certain good faith transferees of negotiable documents of title and section 8–302 protects certain good faith transferees of investment securities.

All the other sections of the Code outside of Articles 3 and 4 protecting bona fide purchasers, except sections 2–403(1), 2A–304, and 2A–305 (applying to voidable title cases) and 8–302, require that for the purchaser to be protected she must either buy from a merchant or buy in the ordinary course of business or both. However, a transferee of commercial paper need neither take from a merchant nor take in the ordinary course of business to be a holder in due course. But the transferee of commercial paper, to be a holder in due course, must, in addition to taking in good faith, without notice, and for value, meet several somewhat technical requirements and the paper being transferred must conform with the very technical "formal requisites" for negotiability discussed in the next section of this chapter.

The particular, and fairly complex, features of holder in due course law were developed in the late 18th and early 19th centuries in response to the cash and cash substitute needs of the developing industrial society. The complexities of the rules result from a series of judgments as to the relative desirability of protecting transferees on the one hand, and preserving the claims and defenses of prior parties, on the other. As we work through the holder in due course rules, make your own judgment as to whether the policy choices made continue to be justified in the modern commercial environment. As indicated by

Miller v. Race, the rules protecting holders in due course were (and are) based on the belief that there is an overriding interest in the efficient and free flow of cash substitutes (such as checks) and certain debt instruments (such as promissory notes) that justifies protecting most transferees thereof against most claims and defenses of prior parties.

As noted above there are specific requirements which the transferee of instruments must meet today if she is to gain the rights of a holder in due course. These requirements are:

(1) the instrument must be negotiable,

(2) the transferee must be a holder,

(3) the transferee must give value,

(4) the transferee must acquire the instrument in good faith,

(5) the transferee must acquire the instrument without notice of claims or defenses of prior parties and also without notice of certain other facts that suggest that there may be difficulties in collecting the instrument, and

(6) the instrument must not bear such apparent evidence of forgery or alteration or be otherwise so irregular or incomplete as to call into question its authenticity.

See OR 3–302, OR 3–104(1), R 3–302, R 3–104(a).

1. Form of the Instrument (Formal Requisites)

For several hundred years, first by judicial decision and then by statute, only instruments meeting particular requirements as to form have been treated as negotiable instruments subject to special transfer rules, including the ability of transferees to take free of claims and defenses of prior parties. Those rules are intended to make it easy for persons who execute, transfer, or take instruments to determine whether the instrument is negotiable and therefore subject to the special negotiability rules.

Article 3 of the Code, which states the rules governing negotiable instruments today, provides in section 3–104 the requirements that instruments must meet to be subject to Article 3. Those requirements are elaborated on in revised sections 3–105 through 3–113 and in original sections 3–105 through 3–118. You should take a minute and scan those sections now.

A recent treatise comments as follows on the form requirements for commercial paper:

F. MILLER AND A. HARRELL, THE LAW OF MODERN PAYMENT SYSTEMS AND NOTES*

Pages 2-2 to 2-4 (1992).

The acceptability of a commodity, whether it is gold or a negotiable instrument, is determined in significant measure by the ease of ascertaining whether it is the "real thing." * * * [A] negotiable instrument presumably obtains value from the fact that, even though it is a contract, it is governed by a special body of rules that confer particular benefits not available in an ordinary contract. For example, there is freedom from claims to it and many defenses to its payment, there are procedural advantages, and there may be recourse to one's assignor if the instrument is not paid, to name several. Thus some method must exist for distinguishing the contracts that are negotiable instruments from the contracts that are not. The method chosen by the common law for this purpose was a set of requirements as to the form of the instrument. If the instrument met the requirements, it was governed by special rules. If it did not, it was subject to the general rules that governed ordinary contracts. These form requirements today are continued in Section 3-104 of both Old and Revised Article 3 of the Uniform Commercial Code and are elaborated upon in subsequent sections of that article.

The form requirements themselves originally were established principally to assure that the terms of the instrument would be certain. Certainty was believed necessary to induce the prospective taker of a negotiable instrument to purchase it because, if the terms of the contract were uncertain, it would be difficult to value the contract, and an asset of undeterminable value is not easily saleable. In the years during which the form requirements were being fashioned, the law wished to promote the free transfer of negotiable instruments because negotiable instruments that passed from hand to hand in payment of debts were used to supplement the otherwise inadequate money supply. Uncertainty as to the amount payable, the time of payment, or, worst of all, whether the instrument was absolutely payable without condition, detracted from the goal of creating an easily enforceable right to the payment of money that was divorced from the transaction giving rise to the instrument and which was readily assignable. Ultimately the basic form requirements for negotiable instruments were formulated; legally, to be a negotiable instrument the instrument had to be a written unconditional promise or order to pay a sum certain in money on demand or at a definite time.

* Miller & Harrell, *The Law of Modern Payment Systems and Notes* ¶ 2.01[1] (2d Ed. 1992). © 1992 Anderson Publishing Co., Cincinnati. Used by permission.

a. *Must be Payable to Order or to Bearer*

SUNRIZON HOMES, INC. v. AMERICAN GUARANTY INVESTMENT CORP.

Oklahoma Supreme Court, 1988.
782 P.2d 103, 7 UCC Rep.Serv.2d 796.

KAUGER, J. The * * * issues presented are: (1) Whether an instrument lacking the words "pay to order or to bearer" is a negotiable instrument conferring holder in due course status on a party taking the document by assignment * * *.

We find that: (1) Because an instrument lacking the words "pay to order or to bearer" is nonnegotiable, it does not confer holder in due course status on a party taking the document by assignment; * * *.

FACTS

In October of 1984, the appellant, Apple Homes (Apple–Seller), sold a mobile home to Roland and Rebecca Renault (Buyers). The contract covering the sale was dated December 15, 1984, but the closing on the mobile home did not occur until January 15, 1985. At that time, the buyers executed the installment sales contract and a security agreement in favor of Apple. Thereafter, Apple assigned its contractual rights to American Guaranty Investment Corporation (American Guaranty). American Guaranty took possession of the contract and of the manufacturer's certificate of origin. It issued Apple a check for $39,154.17 dated January 14, 1985 which was not delivered until sometime later. On January 17, 1985, the appellee, Continental Federal Savings and Loan Association (Continental), purchased an assignment of American Guaranty's rights in the installment sales contract for $40,012.42. Continental notified the buyers that their loan payments were to be made to Continental. It filed liens and security agreements to perfect its security interest in the collateral. On approximately February 12, 1985, American Guaranty's check was returned for insufficient funds.

After Apple's efforts to collect on American Guaranty's check were unsuccessful, it filed an action for recission [sic] of the assignment to American Guaranty praying for the restoration of all rights, and for redelivery of all documents. Apple also sought to recover all payments and documents received by Continental under the assignment of the installment sales contract from American Guaranty. Apple asserted that the sales contract was a nonnegotiable instrument, and that Continental had no greater rights than its assignor, American Guaranty. American Guaranty admitted liability and judgment was entered in favor of Apple. Apple and Continental each moved for summary judgment. The trial court granted summary judgment in favor of Continental. The Court of Appeals affirmed the trial court * * *. After the Court of Appeals denied Apple's petition for rehearing, it petitioned for certiorari.

I

AN INSTRUMENT LACKING THE WORDS "PAY TO ORDER OR TO BEARER" IS NONNEGOTIABLE AND DOES NOT CONFER HOLDER IN DUE COURSE STATUS ON A PARTY TAKING THE DOCUMENT BY ASSIGNMENT

The nature of the instrument, i.e., negotiable or nonnegotiable, is essential to determine what rights Continental received under its assignment from American Guaranty. If the contract for sale is a negotiable instrument, Continental may qualify as a holder in due course taking the assignment free of any claim or defense. If the contract for sale is not a negotiable document, Continental stands in the shoes of its assignor, American Guaranty, and the instrument is subject to the defense of failure of consideration—the bad check. Continental asserts that it took the assignment for value, in good faith, without knowledge of any claims or defenses, and that it qualifies as a holder in due course.

Pursuant to 12A O.S. 1981 § 3–302, before one may be a holder in due course, the holder must take an "instrument." Instrument is defined by § 3–102(1)(e) [R 3–104(b)] as a *negotiable* instrument. Section 3–104 [R 3–104] provides that a negotiable instrument must be signed by the maker or drawer,[a] contain an unconditional promise to pay a sum certain in money, and be made payable to order or to bearer.

It is undisputed that the sales contract meets the first two requirements of a negotiable instrument. It is signed by the maker or drawer, and it contains an unconditional promise to pay a sum certain in money. Nevertheless, Apple argues that because the contract does not contain the indispensable words of negotiability, "pay to order or to bearer," Continental is not a holder in due course. The installment sales contract states that the buyer promises "to pay to the Seller" monthly installments for a period of 15 years. Continental argues that this language meets the requirement that the instrument be payable to bearer under 12A O.S. 1981 § 3–111 [R 3–109] which defines an instrument as payable to bearer when it is payable to bearer or the order of bearer, a specified person or bearer, cash or order of cash, or any indication not purporting to designate a specific payee.

The words—order and bearer—place a party on notice that the assignment is negotiable. The general rule in jurisdictions which have considered this question, is that a note payable to a specific person, rather than to order or bearer is nonnegotiable. *The sales contract fails to meet the criteria of § 3–104 [R 3–104] that a negotiable instrument be made payable to order or bearer.* Continental is not a holder in due course of a negotiable instrument, and it is subject to the defense of failure of consideration.

* * *

a. The "signed" requirement is in the definition of "promise" and "order" in Revised Article 3 (R. 3–103(6), (9)). [Ed.]

Certiorari previously granted; opinion of the Court of Appeals vacated; trial court reversed; cause remanded.

Note

Holder in due course compared with ordinary assignee. In *Miller v. Race,* the question was whether a transferee from a thief got good title; in *Sunrison Homes* the question is whether a transferee takes free of the claim of a prior transferor that he was not paid for the instrument as promised. The court holds that since the instrument is not negotiable, the transferee cannot be a holder in due course and is subject to the claim. The court also says that the transferee is subject to defenses of prior parties.

As you may remember from your contracts course, the usual assignment law rule is that a transferee takes subject to (1) all defenses that the obligor has against the assignor which arise out of the transaction assigned and (2) defenses or set-offs against the assignor which arise out of unrelated transactions if the defense or set-off arose before the obligor received notice of the assignment. See 9–318(1) for the Code's statement of that rule in Article 9 security interest cases.

Since the note in this case was not negotiable, the ordinary contract assignment rules would apply. If, for example, the buyers of the mobile home who executed the instrument had a defense against the seller based on a breach of warranty of quality of the home, they would be able to assert that defense against any transferee of the instrument when the transferee demanded that they pay the amount due on the instrument.

If, however, the instrument were negotiable and the transferee were a holder in due course, the buyers of the mobile home would have to pay the full amount due on the instrument to the HDC even though they had a defense against the seller to whom they originally gave the instrument. See OR and R 3–305. We consider those sections in more detail later.

Both original and revised Article 3 require that for the instrument to be negotiable it must be payable "to bearer or to order." How would you modify the instrument in the prior case to make it negotiable? Did the instrument have to say "Pay to order or to bearer" to be negotiable? See R 3–109 and OR 3–110, 3–111.

The court reasons that the words order or bearer put parties on notice that the instrument is negotiable. Presumably, the suggestion is that if the instrument had read "pay to the order of Seller", or pay to "Seller or order" or pay to "Seller or bearer" (for reasons we will see later instruments are almost never made in the latter fashion) the buyers of the mobile home should have known that if the instrument were transferred, they might have to pay the full amount of the instrument to the transferee even though they have a defense against the seller. Similarly, the payee should know that if his transferee further transfers the instrument, the payee might lose the right to reclaim the instrument from a subsequent transferee. Whether signers of negotiable instruments actually understand the consequences of the order or bearer language is doubtful, but the requirement persists.

Essentially all check forms state that the check is payable "to the order of ______." The drawer of the check then fills in the name of a particular payee. Such a check obviously meets the requirement that it be payable to order or to bearer. Suppose that, after this class, you buy a new stereo system and pay for it by a check for $1500.00 on which you strike out the "to the order of" language. It turns out that the stereo is defective and you stop payment on the check. In the meantime, seller indorsed the check over to a supplier for goods delivered. Should the fact that you struck the "to the order of" language on the check prevent supplier from claiming that as holder in due course it can collect the full amount of the check from you in spite of your defense against seller? See R 3–104(c) and comment 2 to R 3–104.

Original 3–805 provides: "This Article applies to any instrument whose terms do not preclude transfer and which is otherwise negotiable within this Article but which is not payable to order or to bearer, except that there can be no holder in due course of such an instrument." Also, original Article 3 has no provision similar to revised 3–104(c). Therefore, under original Article 3, the check with the "pay to the order of" language stricken is subject to Article 3, but there can be no holder in due course of it. Instruments subject to original Article 3 by virtue of 3–805 are further considered in Chapter 3 dealing with liability of parties to instruments.

b. Unconditional Promise or Order

HOLLY HILL ACRES, LTD. v. CHARTER BANK OF GAINESVILLE

Florida Court of Appeal, 1975.
314 So.2d 209.

SCHEB, J. Appellant/defendant appeals from a summary judgment in favor of appellee/plaintiff Bank in a suit wherein the appellee sought to foreclose a note and mortgage given by appellant.

The appellee Bank was the assignee from appellees Rogers and Blythe of a promissory note and purchase money mortgage executed and delivered by the appellant. The note executed April 28, 1972, contains the following stipulation:

> "This note with interest is secured by a mortgage on real estate, of even date herewith, made by the maker hereof in favor of the said payee, and shall be construed and enforced according to the laws of the State of Florida. *The terms of said mortgage are by this reference made a part hereof.*" (Emphasis supplied.)

Rogers and Blythe assigned the promissory note and mortgage in question to the appellee to secure their own note. Appellee sued appellant and joined Rogers and Blythe as defendants alleging a default on their note as well as a default on appellant's note.

Appellant answered incorporating an affirmative defense that fraud on the part of Rogers and Blythe induced the sale which gave rise to the purchase money mortgage. Rogers and Blythe denied the fraud. In opposition to appellee Bank's motion for summary judgment, the appellant submitted an affidavit in support of its allegation of fraud on the part of agents of Rogers and Blythe. The trial court held the appellee Bank was a holder in due course of the note executed by appellant and entered a summary final judgment against the appellant.

The note having incorporated the terms of the purchase money mortgage was not negotiable. The appellee Bank was not a holder in due course, therefore, the appellant was entitled to raise against the appellee any defenses which could be raised between the appellant and Rogers and Blythe. Since appellant asserted an affirmative defense of fraud, it was incumbent on the appellee to establish the non-existence of any genuine issue of any material fact or the legal insufficiency of appellant's affirmative defense. Having failed to do so, appellee was not entitled to a judgment as a matter of law; hence, we reverse.

The note, incorporating by reference the terms of the mortgage, did not contain the unconditional promise to pay required by Fla.Stat. § 673.104(1)(b) [R 3–104(a)]. Rather, the note falls within the scope of Fla.Stat. § 673.105(2)(a) [R 3–106(a)(ii)]. Although negotiability is now governed by the Uniform Commercial Code, this was the Florida view even before the UCC was adopted. E.g., the Supreme Court in Brown v. Marion Mortgage Co., Fla.1932, 145 So. 413, held that certain bonds which were "to be received and held subject to" a certain mortgage were non-negotiable. See also, First Bank of Marianna v. Havana Canning Co., Fla.1940, 195 So. 188; Voges v. Ward, Fla.1929, 123 So. 785; Mason v. Flowers, Fla.1926, 107 So. 334.

Appellee Bank relies upon Scott v. Taylor, Fla.1912, 58 So. 30, as authority for the proposition that its note is negotiable. Scott, however, involved a note which stated: "this note secured by mortgage." Mere reference to a note being secured by mortgage is a common commercial practice and such reference in itself does not impede the negotiability of the note. There is, however, a significant difference in a note stating that it is "secured by a mortgage" from one which provides, "the terms of said mortgage are by this reference made a part hereof." In the former instance the note merely refers to a separate agreement which does not impede its negotiability, while in the latter instance the note is rendered non-negotiable. See Fla.Stat. §§ 673.-105(2)(a) [R 3–106(a)(ii)]; 673.119 [R 3–117, 3–106(a)(6)].[4]

4. Official Comment 5 to Fla.Stat. § 673.119 provides:

"Subsection (2) rejects decisions which have carried the rule that contemporaneous writings must be read together to the length of holding that a clause in a mortgage affecting a note destroyed the negotiability of the note. The negotiability of an instrument is always to be determined by what appears on the face of the

As a general rule the assignee of a mortgage securing a non-negotiable note, even though a bona fide purchaser for value, takes subject to all defenses available as against the mortgagee. 22 Fla.Jur., Mortgages, §§ 555–56. Appellant raised the issue of fraud as between himself and other parties to the note, therefore, it was incumbent on the appellee Bank, as movant for a summary judgment, to prove the non-existence of any genuinely triable issue. Holl v. Talcott, Fla.1965, 191 So.2d 40.

Accordingly, the entry of a summary final judgment is reversed and the cause remanded for further proceedings.

McNulty, C.J., AND Hobson, J., CONCUR.

Note

It is sometimes said that the increased risk of nonpayment and the necessity for determining whether conditions have been satisfied would impair the widespread acceptance of negotiable instruments and that such concern justifies the requirement that the promise be unconditional. However, since the consequences of negotiability are always favorable to the transferee, the fact that transferees might decline to accept certain conditional promises does not really support making such promises nonnegotiable.

A more convincing justification for the requirement that the promise be unconditional is that it protects issuers and transferors by limiting the special rights granted to transferees of negotiable instruments to cases in which the issuer of the instrument has made a simple, unconditional promise to pay. If the promise is conditional so that, on its face, the transferee will be paid only if certain things happen, the transferee will not, in any event, treat the instrument as similar to money and, since that is a function of negotiable instruments, there is no necessity to give the transferee the rights of a holder in due course. However, even that argument does have a weakness. Today transferees do not treat promissory notes as money, if they ever did. Therefore, a justification for the requirement that the promise be unconditional based upon the fact that transferees treat negotiable instruments like money is unrealistic as to promissory notes. Perhaps there is no good justification at all as to promissory notes. Payees and transferees of checks and other drafts usually do treat them as being similar to money, so the rule requiring that the order be unconditional does perhaps have justification as to drafts.

Can you think of other possible justifications for the requirement that a promissory note, to be negotiable, must contain an unconditional promise?

Problem

A promissory note, otherwise negotiable, states that it is payable only from payments the maker receives from the State of Maine on highway

instrument alone, and if it is negotiable in itself a purchaser without notice of a separate writing is in no way affected by it. *If the instrument itself states that it is subject to or governed by any other agreement, it is not negotiable under this Article;* but if it merely refers to a separate agreement or states that it arises out of such an agreement, it is negotiable." (Emphasis supplied.)

contract 9192–15. Is the promise conditional, making the note nonnegotiable? Compare OR 3–105(2)(b) with R 3–106(b)(ii) and see the last paragraph of comment 1 to R 3–106.

c. *Payable on Demand or at a Definite Time*

Problem

A note states that it is payable "five years after Maker receives her J.D. degree." Does the time of payment prevent the note from being negotiable? See R 3–108(b). Compare OR 3–109. If, when the Maker gave the note she was in her final semester of law school and she did in fact graduate on time, would you conclude that, if the issue arose after graduation, the note was payable at a "readily ascertainable time"?

Suppose the note provided that it was payable in 2005, subject to acceleration at the option of the holder at any time after five years from Maker's receipt of her J.D. degree. Is the note negotiable? See *Smith v. Gentilotti,* 371 Mass. 839, 359 N.E.2d 953 (1977).

d. *Fixed Amount of Money*

Original 3–104 requires that the instrument be for a sum certain in money. Revised 3–104(a) requires that the instrument be for a "fixed amount" of money. Presumably the change in language does not change the meaning. Original 3–106 addresses the sum certain requirement in detail. In recent years, a number of courts have held that variable interest rate notes fail the sum certain requirement since 3–106 states that the sum payable is a sum certain even though it is to be paid with *stated* interest. That language suggests that the interest rate has to be clear from the face of the note and that interpretation is supported by the comment to original 3–106 which says that the interest rate computation must be one that can be made from the face of the instrument.

In the 1960s interest rates rose rapidly and later moved precipitously downward. Those quick changes in interest rates led many extenders of credit to offer borrowers variable interest rate loans tied to some market indicator such as the prime rate or the rate on six month United States Treasury notes. Many transferees of such notes wanted the benefits of negotiability and several states amended Article 3 to make certain variable rate notes negotiable. Generally those statutes required that the rate be tied to an easily ascertainable, publicly available index. Revised Article 3 makes variable interest rate notes negotiable without any limitation as to the method used to determine the rate. See R 3–104. Also, revised 3–112, dealing with interest, specifically provides that variable rate notes, without limitation, are negotiable.

Original 3–106 provides that a note is for a sum certain even though it is payable with costs of collection or attorney's fees, or both, on default. Revised 3–104 merely states that the instrument may provide for "other charges described in the promise or order." That language might permit charges which would render the note nonnegotiable under OR 3–106. For example, suppose a note that states an interest rate of 10% also states that the maker will pay any state intangibles tax imposed on the note. The provision for payment of intangibles taxes would no doubt make the note nonnegotiable under original Article 3 but probably would not prevent its being negotiable under revised Article 3.

e. *"Does Not State Any Other Undertaking"*

Problems

1. A note otherwise negotiable made payable to ABC Partnership or order provides that if the maker of the note does not pay the note when due the partnership can terminate the maker's interest in the partnership. Does that provision prevent the note from being negotiable? See *Woodworth v. Richmond Indiana Venture,* 13 U.C.C.Rep.Serv.2d (Callaghan) 1149 (Ohio Com.Pl.1990).

2. A note otherwise negotiable contains the following provision: "For the additional consideration of $10.00 the Borrower hereby agrees to sell to Lender 5% of capital stock of DFW Valet Parking South, Inc." Does that provision render the note nonnegotiable? See *Ford v. Darwin,* 767 S.W.2d 851 (Tex.App.1989).

How would you prepare the documentation in the above two problems if you wished the notes to be negotiable? See R 3–117, OR 3–119.

2. *Holder*

The second requirement for HDC status is that the transferee be a holder. Revised 1–201(20) defines "holder" of a negotiable instrument as "the person in possession if the instrument is payable to bearer, or, in the case of an instrument payable to an identified person, if the identified person is in possession." The drafter of the definition seems to have slipped off the grammatical path in the middle of the sentence. But the intent is that if the instrument is payable to an identified person, only that person can be a holder. Sections 3–201, 3–203, 3–204, 3–205 and 3–206 in both original and revised Article 3 provide rules that control whether particular transferees are holders. Study those sections in relation to the following problems.

Problems

1. Drawer draws a check to the order of Dave Logan. The check is delivered to Dave Logan. Is Dave Logan a holder?

2. Dave Logan signs his name on the back of the check "Dave Logan" and hands over the check to Miles Foy. Is Miles Foy a holder?

3. Without signing his name to the above check, Miles Foy hands over the check to Peter Harms. Is Harms a holder?

4. A check payable to Dave Logan and not yet indorsed by him is stolen by Sam Snitch. Snitch signs Logan's name on the back of the check and takes it to Ace Grocery, where, in front of the cashier, he signs his own name and gives the check to the Grocery. Is Grocery a holder?

The answer to this problem involves one of the central concepts of HDC law. Unfortunately, neither original nor revised Article 3 set out the answer as clearly as they might have—but the answer is clear. The relevant language of revised Article 3 is in 3–201(b). Do you see the controlling language? Hint: Is Sam Snitch a holder?

5. On the facts of problem 4, suppose that Ace Grocery indorses the check and transfers it to Bruce Seafoods. Is Seafoods a holder? Hint: Who is the only possible holder of the check?

6. In Problem 4, if Dave Logan had written his name on the back of the check before it was stolen by Sam Snitch, and Snitch had then indorsed his own name and transferred the check to Ace Grocery, would Grocery be a holder? Would the result be different if Sam Snitch did not sign his own name before the check was transferred to Grocery?

7. Dave Logan indorses the check, Dave Logan, and transfers it to Miles Foy. The check is stolen from Miles Foy by Sam Snitch and transferred by Snitch to Ace Grocery. Is Grocery a holder?

8. Miles Foy, disturbed at your answer to the above question, asks how he can protect himself against loss of the value of the check. Tell him. Hint: The answer is in one of the 3–200 sections cited before this set of problems.

If a transferee is a holder in due course, it takes free of the claim of a prior party that the instrument was stolen from that party. The HDC becomes the owner of the instrument, and the person from whom it was stolen has lost the right to the instrument or its proceeds. But, if the transferee is not a holder in due course, the person from whom the instrument was stolen will be able to recover it or its value from the transferee or possibly from the maker or drawer. (We will consider the question of the rights of the person from whom the instrument was stolen more thoroughly in Chapter 4.)

If the transferee is not a holder, it cannot be a holder in due course. Therefore, even though in the above problems Ace Grocery or Bruce Seafoods act in good faith, give value, and are without notice of any claims or defenses, if they are not holders, they do not get rights superior to those of the person from whom the instrument was stolen.

It would be an intolerable situation if a check or note payable to a particular person could be stolen and then transferred to a bona fide purchaser in such a way as to cut off the ownership rights of the person to whom the instrument is payable. Any check stolen from the mails or from the issuing firm before mailing could be transferred to an HDC, resulting in the loss of the amount of the check by either the drawer or the payee. But the price of protecting the drawer or payee against theft is that transferees run the risk that a prior indorsement may be forged, preventing them from acquiring holder in due course status.

Transferees can protect themselves by knowing the party with whom they deal so that they know that his signature is genuine and that, if any prior signatures are forged they can make a claim against the person with whom they dealt.

If the transferor of the instrument had authority to transfer it, but the transferee is not a holder because the instrument does not have a necessary indorsement, the transferee, of course, is not without rights. As between the transferee and the transferor, the transferee is the owner if transfer of ownership was intended. Unless otherwise agreed, if the transfer is for value, the transferee is entitled to have the indorsement of the transferor so that he may become a holder.

Problem

Arrol Creations was payee of a $150,000 note due on June 1, 1992. On December 1, 1991, it delivered the note to Jim Jones as security for a loan of $150,000. The note, however, was not indorsed because Arrol did not quite trust Jones and expected to pay off the loan before the note came due. On March 1, 1992, Jones learned that the maker of the note had a defense against the note and insisted that Arrol indorse it. Arrol did so. Will Jones be able to collect the note from the maker free of the maker's defense? See OR 3–201(3), R 3–203(c).

Even if the transferee never secures the indorsement of the transferor, he obtains the rights of the transferor (with the exception stated in OR 3–201(1) and R 3–203(b)).

EXCURSUS: PROCEDURAL AND SUBSTANTIVE ADVANTAGES OF NON-HDC HOLDERS OVER ORDINARY ASSIGNEES

Under both original and revised Article 3, a holder, whether or not a holder in due course, has procedural advantages over the assignee of an ordinary contract. Under OR 3–307(2) and R 3–308(b) when signatures are admitted or established, production of the instrument entitles the holder to recover on it unless the defendant establishes a defense. The holder, therefore, does not have to plead and prove that the defendant who signed the instrument became liable as the result of contract, estoppel, or on some other ground that would create an enforceable obligation in favor of an ordinary assignee. Revised 3–308(b) also specifically applies that rule to transferees who are not themselves holders if they have the rights of a prior holder. (See also R 3–301). While OR 3–307(2) does not specifically state that non-holders have such a right, it probably exists because of OR 3–201(1) which gives a transferee the rights of his transferor.

Under revised Article 3, and, in some states, under original Article 3, there is another more substantive advantage for holders who are not holders in due course. The usual contract rule applicable to ordinary assignees is that they take subject not only to defenses that arise out of the contract that has been assigned, *but also to unrelated claims that the obligor could assert against the assignor if the cause of action for the claim arose before the obligor received notice of the assignment.* If, for example, Seller and Buyer entered into two contracts for the sale of widgets, and Seller then assigned his right to be paid under contract A to Bank, if Seller had breached contract B before Buyer learned of the assignment of Seller's rights under contract A to Bank, Buyer could set off as against Bank any damages Buyer suffered as a result of Seller's breach of contract B. That rule is stated in 9–318(a).

However, R 3–305(c) would not permit Buyer to assert breach of contract B as a defense against Bank if Bank is the holder of a negotiable note which Buyer gave Seller for the price of goods sold Buyer under contract A. Original 3–306(b) states that unless the holder has the rights of a holder in due course, she takes subject to "all defenses of any party which would be available on a simple contract." While that language suggests that the ordinary contract rule described above should apply, many courts have held under the original Code that the transferee is subject only to defenses arising out of the contract under which the transferred negotiable instrument was given. See, e.g., *United Overseas Bank v. Veneers, Inc.,* 375 F.Supp. 596 (D.Md. 1973); *Bank of Wyandotte v. Woodrow,* 394 F.Supp. 550 (W.D.Mo.1975). See also the last paragraph of Comment 3 to R 3–305.

3. *Value*

Problems

1. A (maker) signed a negotiable note in which he promised to pay $10,000 to B (payee) on March 1st. On January 15th, B indorsed the note to C who paid B $9,000 for the note. When C asked A to pay the note on March 1st, A claimed that B had not performed the services for which the note was given. Assuming that C is otherwise a holder in due course, is C entitled to recover $10,000 from A, or only $9,000? See *O.P. Ganjo, Inc. v. Tri–Urban Realty,* 108 N.J.Super. 517, 261 A.2d 722 (1969).

2. Suppose in the above problem, C paid B $4,500 of the $9,000 when C received the note and was obligated to pay the balance on February 15th. On February 1, C learned that A had a defense against B, but, nevertheless, paid B the remaining $4,500. To what extent can C be an HDC? $10,000,

$5,500, $5,000, or $4,500. OR & R 3–303. See O.P. Ganjo, Inc., just cited and R 3–302(d), R 3–303.

3. Seller has contracted to sell to Buyer a printing press specially designed for Buyer, and, as payment, Buyer has indorsed to A a note for $10,000 payable to Buyer. After Seller has spent $3,000 building the machine, Seller learns that the maker of the note has a defense against Buyer. To what extent can Seller be a holder in due course of the note? What additional facts, if any, do you need? How would the fact that the materials used so far can be sold for salvage for $500 affect your answer? See *Saka v. Mann Theatres,* 94 Nev. 137, 575 P.2d 1335 (1978).

SALEMY v. DIAB

New Jersey Superior Court, Appellate Division, 1991.
246 N.J.Super. 274, 587 A.2d 305.

BRODY, J.A.D. The trial judge held that plaintiff is a holder in due course of a $75,000 note payable August 10, 1989. Defendants Diab and Golden, makers of the note, had made the note payable to third-party defendant Anderson who assigned it to plaintiff on May 25, 1989, to satisfy Anderson's $70,000 antecedent debt to plaintiff and plaintiff's wife. In return for the note, plaintiff's attorney sent to Anderson's attorney a written release of Anderson's debt with a covering letter containing the following instruction: "Please hold [the release] in escrow pending my client's receipt of the sum of $75,000." Diab and Golden have raised several defenses to the note that are not available if plaintiff is a holder in due course.

Defendants argue that plaintiff is not a holder in due course. The precise issue they raise is whether plaintiff gave value for the note in view of the conditional nature of his release of Anderson's debt. Judge Lawrence Weiss granted plaintiff's motion for partial summary judgment, holding that plaintiff had given value. The judge relied on Altex Aluminum Supply Co. v. Asay, 72 N.J.Super. 582, 585, 178 A.2d 636 (App.Div.1962), a case governed by the Negotiable Instruments Law, where we said:

> "It is settled law that a party taking a negotiable instrument in payment of, or as security for, an antecedent debt, is a holder in due course. Citrin v. Tansey, 107 N.J.L. 368 [153 A. 523] (E. & A.1931). Cf. Colozzi v. Bevko, Inc., 17 N.J. 194, 209 [110 A.2d 545] (1955). This is so even though satisfaction of the antecedent debt is conditioned on actual payment of the note. Citrin v. Tansey, supra; Ahern v. Towle, 310 Mass. 695, 39 N.E.2d 561 (Sup.Jud.Ct. 1942); Brannan, Negotiable Instruments Law (7th ed. 1948), § 25, pp. 515–516."

Defendants contend that a change in the definition of value brought about by adoption of the Uniform Commercial Code, N.J.Super. 12A:1–101 et seq., requires a different result. We disagree and affirm.

Value is defined in N.J.S.A. 12A:3–303 [R 3–303], which provides:

* * *

These definitions are disjunctive. Plaintiff took the note for value as defined in § 3–303(b) [R 3–303(a)(3)], whose wording is essentially identical to our courts' construction of the Negotiable Instruments Law.

Defendants mistakenly direct our attention to the § 3–303(a) [R 3–303(a)(1)] definition, whose wording has the effect of withholding holder-in-due-course status from a holder who has taken a negotiable instrument in return for making an unperformed promise. Uniform Commercial Code Comment 3 to § 3–303 [R 3–303] explains the new meaning given to the § 3–303(a) [R 3–303(a)(1)] definition:

> "Paragraph (a) resolves an apparent conflict between the original Section 54 and the first sentence of the original Section 25 [of the Negotiable Instruments Law], by requiring that the agreed consideration shall actually have been given. An executory promise to give value is not itself value, except as provided in paragraph (c). The underlying reason of policy is that when the purchaser learns of a defense against the instrument or of a defect in title he is not required to enforce the instrument, but is free to rescind the transaction for breach of the transferor's warranty (Section 3–417) [R 3–417]. There is thus not the same necessity for giving him the status of a holder in due course, cutting off claims and defenses, as where he has actually paid value. A common illustration is the bank credit not drawn upon, which can be and is revoked when a claim or defense appears."

Defendants confuse the § 3–303(a) [R 3–303(a)(1)] definition of value with the § 3–303(b) [R 3–303(a)(3)] definition. At first blush there appears to be little difference between a promisor's unexecuted promise of performance, such as a promise to extend credit, and a creditor's release of an antecedent debt. In both cases the holder may sustain no loss if the negotiable instrument is dishonored. But that is not always so. A holder-promisor who has not yet performed before the dishonor has lost nothing, but a holder-creditor who has released a debt before the dishonor has lost an earlier opportunity to collect it. It is difficult, if not impossible, in some cases for a creditor to measure the loss attributable to forbearance. Section 3–303(b) [R 3–303(a)(3)] therefore protects the creditor in all cases by treating the release of an antecedent debt as the giving of value.

Another cause of confusion arises from the conditional nature of the release in this case. Section 3–303(b) [R 3–303(a)(3)] applies when the negotiable instrument is taken "in payment" of an antecedent claim. Defendants contend that because the release given here expressly postpones payment of the antecedent claim until the instrument is paid, plaintiff never treated the debt as paid and therefore did not give value.

The argument is flawed because, unless the parties have otherwise agreed, whenever a holder takes a negotiable instrument in payment of an antecedent debt, the underlying obligation is restored should the instrument be dishonored. N.J.S.A. 12A:3–802(1)(b) [R 3–310(b)]. Thus the condition in the release adds nothing to the rights plaintiff had even if the release had been unconditional. If a holder taking a negotiable instrument in payment of an antecedent debt lost his status as a holder in due course because his release of the debt was conditioned upon payment of the instrument, § 3–303(b) [R 3–303(a)(3)] would be rendered a nullity.

Defendants find support for their argument in opinions from other jurisdictions. See State Bank of Broonton v. Am. Nat. Bank, 266 N.W.2d 496 (Minn.1978); Wilson Supply Co. v. West Artesia Transmission Co., 505 S.W.2d 312 (Tex.Civ.App.1974), aff'd 511 S.W.2d 261 (Tex.1974); Halbert v. Horton, 29 Mich.App. 208, 185 N.W.2d 76 (1970). However, the holdings in those cases have been criticized as "of questionable merit" because they overlook the effect of § 3–802(1)(b) [R 3–310(b)]. Hawkland & Lawrence, Uniform Commercial Code Series, § 3–303:06 (1990).

Affirmed.

LYNNWOOD SAND & GRAVEL, INC. v. BANK OF EVERETT

Washington Court of Appeals, 1981.
29 Wash.App. 686, 630 P.2d 489.

JAMES, JUDGE.

Plaintiff Lynnwood Sand and Gravel, Inc. (Lynnwood) appeals entry of summary judgment in favor of defendant Bank of Everett (Everett) in a suit to recover the amount of a check drawn by Lynnwood and paid by Everett over a stop payment order. We affirm.

On December 23, 1977, Lynnwood issued its check No. 1555 in the amount of $30,000 drawn on Everett and payable to Western Cedar Products (Western). Western deposited the check in its checking account at Peoples National Bank (Peoples) the same day. Also on December 23, Peoples gave provisional credit for the check, reducing an existing overdraft of $32,328.71 in Western's account by the full amount of the check.

Lynnwood contends it issued a stop payment order to Everett on December 27, with respect to check No. 1555. For purposes of the summary judgment motion, it was assumed that a valid stop payment order was given. On December 28, Everett returned the check to Peoples with the notation, "non-collected funds, refer to maker." On January 5, 1978, Peoples resubmitted the check to Everett, and Everett paid the check.

If Peoples was a holder in due course of the check, Everett is subrogated to its rights. RCW 62A.4–407 [R 4–407] provides:

> If a payor bank has paid an item over the stop payment order of the drawer or maker * * *, to prevent unjust enrichment and only to the extent necessary to prevent loss to the bank by reason of its payment of the item, the payor bank shall be subrogated to the rights
>
> (a) of any holder in due course on the item against the drawer or maker; * * *

Because Lynnwood presented no defense valid against a holder in due course, Lynnwood cannot recover against Everett if Peoples was a holder in due course. A holder in due course is defined by RCW 62A.3–302 [R 3–302], which states:

> (1) A holder in due course is a holder who takes the instrument
>
> (a) for value; and
>
> (b) in good faith; and
>
> (c) without notice that it is overdue or has been dishonored or of any defense against or claim to it on the part of any person.

That Peoples acted in good faith and was without notice of dishonor or of claims or defenses regarding the check when provisional credit was given is not disputed. Lynnwood does, however, contend that Peoples did not take the instrument for value. RCW 62A.3–303 [R 3–303] provides:

> A holder takes the instrument for value
>
> (a) to the extent that the agreed consideration has been performed or that he acquires a security interest in or a lien on the instrument otherwise than by legal process; or
>
> (b) when he takes the instrument in payment of or as security for an antecedent claim against any person whether or not the claim is due; * * *

RCW 62A.4–209 [R 4–211] provides:

> For purposes of determining its status as a holder in due course, the bank has given value to the extent that it has a security interest in an item provided that the bank otherwise complies with the requirements of RCW 62A.3–302 [R 3–302] on what constitutes a holder in due course.

RCW 62A.4–208 [R 4–210] provides:

> (1) A bank has a security interest in an item and any accompanying documents or the proceeds of either

(a) in case of an item deposited in an account to the extent to which credit given for the item has been withdrawn or applied;

(b) in case of an item for which it has given credit available for withdrawal as of right, to the extent of the credit given whether or not the credit is drawn upon and whether or not there is a right of charge-back; or

(c) if it makes an advance on or against the item.

Lynnwood contends that Peoples neither allowed a withdrawal nor applied credit given for the item by merely granting a provisional credit to its depositor, and thus did not take for value. Everett responds that value was given because the credit was applied to reduce an existing overdraft in the depositor's account. The issue, then, is whether a bank takes an item for value for purposes of becoming a holder in due course by giving provisional credit for the item which is applied against an existing overdraft in the depositor's account. We conclude that a bank does give value and becomes a holder in due course under these circumstances.

It is well established that the mere granting of provisional credit, without more, does not constitute a taking for value. But it is also well established that a depository bank gives value when it allows its depositor to make withdrawals against uncollected checks for which the bank has given credit.

A bank makes a loan to its customer by allowing an account overdraft. *State v. Larson,* 119 Wash. 259, 205 P. 373 (1922). This creates an "antecedent claim" within the meaning of RCW 62A.3–303(b) [R 3–303(a)(3)]. By applying credit given for a check to reduce an existing overdraft in the depositor's account, a bank gives value for the check, even if the credit is provisional. Peoples became a holder in due course no later than when it granted provisional credit for the check and applied that credit to reduce an existing overdraft in Western's account.

Lynnwood relies primarily upon *Marine Midland Bank v. Graybar Electric Co.,* [41 N.Y.2d 703, 363 N.E.2d 1139, 395 N.Y.S.2d 403 (1977)]. The case is distinguishable. There, the depositor of a check had both a checking account and an independent loan from the bank. The bank applied credit for a subsequently dishonored check against the depositor's loan obligation. The court reasoned that because the depositor's loan and checking account were not interconnected, the bank did not take the check in satisfaction of an antecedent claim but merely took unilateral action to protect its security. Here, Peoples granted provisional credit against an overdraft in Western's checking account for a check deposited in Western's account.

Citing RCW 62A.4–202(1)(b) [R 4–202(a)(2)], Lynnwood finally contends that Peoples, if a holder in due course, lost that status by breaching its duty of ordinary care through failing to reverse the provisional credit upon receipt of the notice of dishonor and by failing to return the item. We do not agree.

Subsequent notice of infirmities in the instrument has no effect upon the rights of a holder in due course, absent a showing of bad faith. *Sullivan v. United Dealers Corp.*, 486 S.W.2d 699 (Ky.Ct.App.1972); 11 Am.Jur.2d Bills & Notes section 428 (1963). There is no contention that Peoples acted in bad faith. Moreover, RCW 62A.4–202(1)(b) [R 4–202(a)(2)] is designed for the protection of the bank's customer. When returning an item, the collecting bank (here Peoples) acts as agent for the owner of the item, RCW 62A.4–201 [R 4–201], who is the depositor (here Western). *Belsheim v. First Nat'l Bank*, 77 Wash. 552, 137 P. 1055 (1914). See generally Comments, RCW 62A.4–201 [R 4–201]. The statute does not provide that failure to use ordinary care deprives the bank of holder in due course status as to a check on which a third party is obligated.

The judgment is affirmed.

DURHAM-DIVELBISS and WILLIAMS, JJ., concur.

Note

Under OR and R 3–303, taking an instrument in return for an executory promise does not constitute value, but taking an instrument in payment of or as security for an antecedent claim against any person, whether or not the claim is due, does constitute taking for value. The policy justifying denying holder in due course status to one who has given only an executory promise is explained in Comment 2 to R 3–303 as follows: "The policy basis for [the rule] is that the holder who gives an executory promise of performance will not suffer an out-of-pocket loss to the extent that the executory promise is unperformed at the time the holder learns of dishonor of the instrument."

A person who takes an instrument as security for an antecedent claim could be said to be within this rationale; he has given up nothing of value and has not detrimentally changed his position unless he discharges the underlying debt, grants an extension, or takes some such action. Yet both OR and R 3–303 protect him as a holder in due course whether or not he gives additional consideration.

Section 25 of the Negotiable Instruments Law also stated that: "An antecedent or pre-existing debt constitutes value; and is deemed such whether the instrument is payable on demand or at a future time." Prior to section 25, state laws conflicted as to whether taking an instrument as security for an antecedent debt constituted value. In *Coddington v. Bay,* 20 Johns. (N.Y.) 637 (1822), the court said that an antecedent debt is not value because it is not consideration. See also *Stalker v. McDonald,* 6 Hill (N.Y.) 93 (1848), where the Court said:

> * * * [w]here he has received [a note] for an antecedent debt, either as a nominal payment or as a security for payment, without giving up any security for such debt which he previously had, or paying any money, or giving any new consideration, he is not a holder of the note for a valuable consideration, so as to give him any equitable right

to detain it from its lawful owner. This principle, of protecting the bona fide holder of negotiable paper who has paid value for it, or who has relinquished some available security or valuable right on the credit thereof, is derived from the doctrines of the courts of equity in other cases where a purchaser has obtained the legal title without notice of the equitable right of a third person to the property. It has been uniformly held by the courts of equity in such cases that the purchaser who has obtained the legal title as a mere security or payment of a pre-existing debt, without parting with anything of value, is not entitled to hold the property as against the prior equitable owner. And, if he has paid part of the consideration or value of the property, he is only entitled to be considered as a bona fide purchaser pro tanto.

The leading case holding that an antecedent debt did constitute value was *Swift v. Tyson,* 41 U.S. (16 Pet.) 1, 10 L.Ed. 865 (1842). The Supreme Court emphasized the commercial necessity for such a holding, and noted that the usual course of trade or business is to receive negotiable instruments in payment of or as security for antecedent indebtedness. The Court said:

> And why upon principle should not a pre-existing debt be deemed such a valuable consideration? It is for the benefit and convenience of the commercial world to give as wide an extent as practicable to the credit and circulation of negotiable paper, that it may pass out not only as security for new purchases and advances, made upon the transfer thereof, but also in payment of and as security for pre-existing debts. The creditor is thereby enabled to realize or to secure his debt, and thus may safely give a prolonged credit, or forbear from taking any legal steps to enforce his rights. The debtor also has the advantage of making his negotiable securities of equivalent value to cash. But establish the opposite conclusion, that negotiable paper cannot be applied in payment of or as security for pre-existing debts, without letting in all the equities between the original and antecedent parties, and the value and circulation of such securities must be essentially diminished, and the debtor, driven to the embarrassment of making a sale thereof, often at a ruinous discount, to some third person, and then by circuity to apply the proceeds to the payment of his debts. What, indeed, upon such a doctrine, would become of that large class of cases, where new notes are given by the same or by other parties, by way of renewal or security to banks in lieu of old securities discounted by them, which have arrived at maturity? Probably more than one-half of all bank transactions in our country, as well as those of other countries, are of this nature. The doctrine would strike a fatal blow at all discounts of negotiable securities for pre-existing debts.

Britton agreed with this rationale: "An antecedent debt must constitute consideration because the conception serves such a useful business purpose that it would be unwise to abandon it." W. Britton, Handbook of the Law of Bills and Notes § 94, at 222 (2d ed. 1961).

Section 25 of the N.I.L. codified the *Swift v. Tyson* rule and Article 3 continues it.

(2) The *Lynnwood* court distinguishes the *Marine Midland* decision, which had held that when a depository bank sets off a deposited item against a separate loan obligation, the bank has not given value because the bank has not parted with anything it could not recover. That is, the depositary bank is no worse off after the deposited item is dishonored than it was before the item was presented. The court in *Marine Midland* reached that conclusion by finding that "the credit given to [customer/debtor's] account was provisional because the bank could and did reverse the credit after notice of the stop payment order, thereby reinstating that portion of the loan against which the credit was set-off." See *Marine Midland Bank v. Graybar Electric Co., Inc.,* 41 N.Y.2d 703, 712, 395 N.Y.S.2d 403, 409, 363 N.E.2d 1139, 1145, 21 UCC Rep.Serv. (Callaghan) 1094, 1102 (1977). Is the distinction between *Lynnwood* and *Marine Midland* convincing? Could the depositary bank in *Marine Midland* have improved its position if it had not reversed the credit to the loan balance when the check was returned to it unpaid by the drawee bank? Cf. *Serve v. First Nat'l Bank of Atlanta,* 143 Ga.App. 239, 237 S.E.2d 719 (1977) (bank could sue customer on OR 3–414 [R 3–415] indorser liability when it credited customer with amount of deposited item against loan balance and did not reverse credit when item was later dishonored).

Note on Consumer Drawers and Holder in Due Course Status of Depositary Banks

A holder in due course takes free of all personal defenses and all claims to a negotiable instrument. The operation of the Code's value rules in the context of bank collections, [OR 4–208 and 4–209 and R 4–210 and 4–211] can operate to bring about results that a consumer drawer may not anticipate. First, a consumer may not be aware of how the HDC rule works. It would not be surprising to find that few consumers understand that they may have liability on a check after they have issued a stop payment order, even if their bank has honored the stop order. Also, a consumer drawer may be surprised to discover that his payee's depositary bank could be the plaintiff in an action to enforce the consumer drawer's liability on the check. Further, the rights of that depositary bank might very well mature as a result of the Code's first-in/first-out rule of OR 4–208(2) and R 4–210(b).

> For example, assume that Customer on January 2 opens an account with a cash deposit of $10,000. On January 5 Customer deposits a check for $10,000 and on January 7 deposits $10,000 in cash. The account now contains $30,000. On January 9 the bank pays a check for $20,000 against the account. Now $10,000 remains in the account. On January 11, the January 5 check is returned unpaid. The bank is treated as having paid the January 9 check against the January 2 cash deposit and the January 5 check deposit. If the bank meets the good faith and without notice tests of U.C.C. § 3–302 [R 3–302], the bank is a holder in due course and is entitled to enforce the January 5 check against the drawer free of any defenses the drawer might have against the payee. The bank can enforce the January 5 check even though, when the check was returned, the bank could have charged the check against the $10,000 balance still in the account.

Marion W. Benfield, Jr., *The New Payments Code and the Abolition of Holder in Due Course Status as to Consumer Checks,* 40 Wash. & Lee L.Rev. 11, 18, n. 26 (1983). See also Albert J. Rosenthal, *Negotiability: Who Needs It?,* 71 Colum.L.Rev. 375, 382–88 (1971). While both of those commentaries acknowledge that the depositary bank in the foregoing hypothetical would likely charge back the amount of the check against its customer/depositor, the bank would have the option and right to seek reimbursement from the consumer drawer though the depositary institution in no real way relied on the payment of the check. Under OR and R 3–303 taking for antecedent debt is value, but the use of the first-in/first-out rule in OR 4–208 and 4–209 and R 4–210 and 4–211, at least arguably, goes beyond the reasons for the antecedent debt rule.

Problem

Seller contracted to sell to Buyer his (controlling) interest in Finance Company. Under the agreement, Buyer was to secure a release of Seller from his guarantee of the debt of Finance Company and the stock representing Seller's interest in the company was to be placed in escrow with Seller's attorney pending the releases. The brief escrow agreement provided simply that the attorney would deliver the stock to Buyer upon receipt of written advice from Seller that Seller had been released from his guarantee liability.

Buyer paid for the purchase with a cashier's check payable to Buyer and indorsed by Buyer over to Seller. The Bank drawer-drawee of the check has discovered that Buyer received the cashier's check by fraud. Seller can recover from Bank free of the fraud defenses if Seller is a holder in due course.

1. Did Seller, by placing the stock in the escrow account, perform the promise?
2. Has Seller made an "irrevocable obligation to a third party" by placing the stock in escrow?

See *Crest Finance Co., Inc. v. First Bank of Westmont,* 37 Ill.2d 243, 226 N.E.2d 369 (1967).

4. Good Faith and Lack of Notice of Claims or Defenses

The Code requires that a holder, to be a holder in due course, must take in good faith and without notice of claims or defenses. OR 3–302(1)(b), (c); R 3–302(a)(2). While the statute treats good faith and lack of notice of claims or defenses as separate requirements, they are so closely related, if not identical, that they are considered together here.

Prior to the promulgation of the Uniform Negotiable Instruments Law in 1896 there had been differing views as to whether good faith was to be determined by a purely subjective or by an objective test. Under the subjective test, often stated as the "pure heart, empty head" test, the question was whether the transferee himself had any suspicion that prior parties had a defense or claim to the instrument, that is, the question was actual bad faith. Under the objective test, the rule was that a "purchaser of a negotiable instrument must exercise reasonable care and caution and if the circumstances were such as ought to have excited the suspicion of a prudent and careful man, and he made no inquiry, he did not act in good faith" [1] The idea underlying both tests is that a transferee is in bad faith if he asserts that he is entitled to take free of a defense or claim if he knew (subjective test) or had reason to know (objective test) that there was a likelihood of an outstanding claim or defense.

The N.I.L., as does the Code, imposed the double requirement that the holder in due course take in good faith *and* without notice of claims or defenses. It did not define good faith, but it did define notice as "* * * actual knowledge of the infirmity or defect, or knowledge of such facts that [the] action in taking the instrument amounts to bad faith." Courts generally concluded under the N.I.L. that the test for good faith was the same as that for notice: that is, a subjective pure heart, empty head test.

The Commercial Code definition of notice in 1–201(25) seems to depart from the N.I.L.'s purely subjective definition of notice. Section 1–201(25) reads:

"A person has 'notice' of a fact when

(a) he has actual knowledge of it; or

(b) he has received a notice or notification of it; or

(c) from all the facts and circumstances known to him at the time in question he has reason to know that it exists."

Subsection (c) of the definition sounds very much like the suspicious circumstances test that some courts had adopted for good faith prior to the enactment of the N.I.L. Consistently with the Code definition of notice, the 1952 draft of the Code provided that "good faith" included honesty in fact and the observance of reasonable commercial standards of fair dealing, a test with objective elements. Bankers, however, objected to including observance of reasonable commercial standards as a part of the good faith test for holder in due course status and, to meet their objections, the Code was amended to define good faith as "honesty in fact." Therefore, the Code had inconsistent tests, a subjective test for good faith but an apparent objective test for notice of claims or defenses. (Two states, New York and Virginia, tried to eliminate the inconsistency by changing the notice test to a subjective one by adding a subjection (7) to 3–304 providing that a holder does not have notice of a claim or defense unless the holder has knowledge of the claim or defense or knowledge of such facts that his action in taking the instrument amounts to bad faith.)

1. 2 New York Law Revision Commission Report, Study of the Uniform Commercial Code 125 (1956).

Revised Article 3 in 3–103(a)(4) defines "good faith" as "honesty in fact and the observance of reasonable commercial standards of fair dealing." It, therefore, returns to the 1952 Code in imposing an objective standard for both notice and good faith.

The following cases were decided under original Article 3. As you read them, consider whether the new definition of good faith would change either the analysis or the result.

FUNDING CONSULTANTS, INC. v. AETNA CASUALTY & SURETY CO.

Connecticut Supreme Court, 1982.
187 Conn. 637, 447 A.2d 1163.

PETERS, J. In this suit on a promissory note, the dispositive issue is whether a maker of a note may introduce expert testimony to challenge the good faith of a person seeking to enforce the note as a holder in due course. The plaintiff, Funding Consultants, Inc., brought an action, initially only against the defendant Aetna Casualty and Surety Co., Inc., but ultimately also against the defendant Benjamin C. Preisner, as co-makers of a promissory note in the amount of $68,000. Aetna Casualty, in the interim, had impleaded Preisner by a third party complaint alleging that Aetna Casualty as surety was entitled to indemnification from Preisner if Aetna Casualty were held liable to Funding Consultants. See General Statutes § 52–102a; Practice Book § 117. After a trial to a jury, judgments were rendered in favor of the plaintiff against both defendants, and in favor of the third party plaintiff against the third party defendant. Only the appeal of Preisner as defendant and third party defendant is being pursued in this court.

The present action is a suit on a promissory note which was given to Paul King, Jr. in connection with the 1974 sale of the Paul King, Jr. Insurance Company to the defendant Preisner. On this note, hereinafter the Preisner note, Preisner and Aetna Casualty were co-makers, although Aetna Casualty's status was that of an accommodation party for Preisner. The Preisner note was a $68,000 non-interest bearing negotiable instrument calling for four equal instalments to be paid annually beginning on November 1, 1975, and ending on November 1, 1978.

King sold the Preisner note to the plaintiff Funding Consultants, Inc. on January 18, 1975, for $5000 cash and a promissory note. This note, hereinafter the Funding note, was a $35,000 noninterest bearing negotiable instrument calling for four equal installments to be paid at bi-monthly intervals beginning on March 20, 1975, and ending on September 20, 1975.

The defendant Preisner, after formal demand, refused to make any payments on the Preisner note because, he alleged, the execution of the note had been induced by fraudulent misrepresentations about the financial condition of the Paul King, Jr. Insurance Company. The plaintiff Funding Consultants thereupon, on December 1, 1975, in reliance upon an acceleration clause contained in the Preisner note, declared the whole amount of that note to be then due and payable. This litigation ensued.

At the trial, the plaintiff sought to recover on the Preisner note as a holder in due course. Only a holder in due course may enforce a negotiable instrument without regard to the maker's assertion of a personal defense such as fraud in the inducement. General Statutes § 42a–3–305(2) [R 3–305(a)(1)]; cf. Land Finance Corporation v. Menzies, 114 Conn. 694, 699, 160 A. 168 (1932) (under pre-Uniform Commercial Code law); see E. Peters, A Negotiable Instruments Primer (2d Ed.1974) § I, pp. 33–34; White & Summers, Uniform Commercial Code (2d Ed.1980) § 14–9. Evidence of the existence of a personal defense does, however, shift to the holder of the instrument the burden of proving his due course status. General Statutes § 42a–3–307(3) [R 3–308(b)]; cf. Hartford National Bank & Trust Co. v. Credenza, 119 Conn. 368, 370, 177 A. 132 (1935) (under pre-Uniform Commercial Code law); see Peters, op. cit., § J, p. 34. That burden requires the holder to prove his taking of the instrument "(a) for value; and (b) in good faith; and (c) without notice that it is overdue or has been dishonored or of any defense against or claim to it on the part of any person." General Statutes § 42a–3–302 [R 3–302 has similar language]; cf. Parsons v. Utica Cement Mfg. Co., 82 Conn. 333, 339, 73 A. 785 (1909) (under pre-Uniform Commercial Code law); see Peters, loc. cit.; White & Summers, op. cit., § 14–6.

In order to establish its due course status, the plaintiff relied on the testimony of its president, Richard R. Splain. When the good faith of the plaintiff's purchase was put into issue, Splain testified that he had little knowledge about or experience in the purchase of negotiable instruments. The defendant sought to counter this testimony by offering, as an expert witness, Michael Schaeffer of the Connecticut Bank & Trust Company to testify that the plaintiff had given inadequate consideration for its purchase of the Preisner note. Such testimony would furnish some evidence, according to the defendant, that Splain had testified untruthfully about the good faith of the plaintiff's purchase. The plaintiff objected to admission of the testimony as irrelevant and prejudicial. After a hearing, the trial court sustained the plaintiff's objection on the ground of prejudice.

The case was submitted to the jury with one special interrogatory. In response to that interrogatory, the jury found the plaintiff to be a holder in due course with respect to the Preisner note. The defendant's appeal has assigned the exclusion of the expert testimony as error.

The disagreement of the parties on this appeal is a narrow one. On the one hand, the defendant concedes that the standard of good faith under the Uniform Commercial Code is, as it was under the prior

Negotiable Instruments Law, a subjective standard. "Good faith," as used in General Statutes § 42a–3–302(1)(b) [R 3–302(a)], is defined in General Statutes § 42a–1–201(19) as "honesty in fact in the conduct or transaction concerned." Both the language of other sections of the Code and the Code's drafting history incontrovertibly demonstrate that this standard is one that imposes no duty of due care on the holder. The test is honesty in fact rather than negligence. On the other hand, the plaintiff does not dispute that application of this test calls for the factfinder to determine the inferences appropriately to be drawn from all of the evidence, including testimony "regarding the relationship between the plaintiff and the [transferor of the negotiable instrument], and the circumstances surrounding the purchase of this paper * * *." Williams & Co. v. Wiltz, 106 Conn. 147, 152, 137 A. 759 (1927). A defendant who wishes to overcome the plaintiff's own testimony in support of its good faith perforce must introduce evidence to contradict the plaintiff's assertions of honesty in fact. See Favors v. Yaffe, 605 S.W.2d 342, 345 (Tex.Civ.App.1980).

The issue that does divide the parties, here as in the trial court, is what evidence is admissible to test the holder's subjective good faith. In order to decide whether a holder of an instrument acted in good faith, the trier of fact must determine the intent or state of mind of the party concerned. Breslin v. New Jersey Investors, Inc., supra; Community Bank v. Ell, supra. As in other determinations concerning intent, the trier is entitled to consider not only the testimony of the interested party but also evidence of surrounding circumstances that inferentially illuminate his honesty in fact in view of his actual knowledge. "Although mere negligence or failure to make the inquiries which a reasonably prudent person would make does not of itself amount to bad faith, if a party fails to make an inquiry for the purpose of remaining ignorant of facts which he believes or fears would disclose a defect in the transaction, he may be found to have acted in bad faith." Community Bank v. Ell, supra, 428; Hollywood National Bank v. International Business Machines Corporation, 38 Cal.App.3d 607, 614–15, 113 Cal. Rptr. 494 (1974). Similarly, if a party pays for an instrument an amount far less than its face value, such evidence is a factor that a trier may reasonably consider in weighing whether a purchase was made in good faith. The sale of an instrument at a substantial discount may in fact have alerted a prospective purchaser to a possible defense to which he may not wilfully close his eyes. We therefore hold that the defendant was entitled to introduce evidence in this case to show that there was such inadequacy of consideration that this factor, among others, should have been weighed by the jury in its determination of the plaintiff's good faith.

Even if evidence of inadequacy of consideration is generally admissible, the question still remains whether the particular evidence offered by this defendant was sufficiently probative so that it should not have been excluded. The plaintiff had bought a $68,000 noninterest bearing note. The expert testimony was offered by the defendant to show what a commercial bank would have paid for the Preisner note and what the effective rate of return on the plaintiff's investment would have been. It is not an answer to this offer of proof that the plaintiff's president had testified about his inexperience with the purchase of negotiable paper and his ignorance of the practices and procedures of commercial banks. The jury might have chosen to disregard some or all of this testimony. The expert's evidence would have provided the jury with some basis for assessing the present value of both the Preisner note and the Funding note. It is not unreasonable to offer a lay jury expert assistance in the proper calculation of values that are not obvious on the face of the instruments to be compared. The proffered evidence was relevant because it would have enabled the jury to make a more accurate assessment of whether the plaintiff took the Preisner note in good faith.

The trial court's decision to exclude the expert testimony impliedly agreed with the defendant that the testimony would have been relevant since the court made its determination on the ground that the testimony was too prejudicial to be admissible. The only basis advanced by the plaintiff for the finding of prejudice is the argument that evidence about mathematical projections by a commercial bank would unfairly bring into play the objective criteria of good faith which the Uniform Commercial Code has repudiated. As we have noted above, there is no inherent inconsistency between a subjective standard of good faith and a reasonable inquiry into the actual known circumstances surrounding a purchase of negotiable paper. The price actually paid, the present value of the instrument actually bought, are elements which may be considered in determining a holder's good faith. Although in most instances admission of expert testimony and questions of relevancy and prejudice rest within the sound discretion of the trial court; Going v. Pagani, 172 Conn. 29, 34–35, 372 A.2d 516 (1976); Katsetos v. Nolan, 170 Conn. 637, 651–52, 368 A.2d 172 (1976); in this case the court's action was clearly erroneous. Because exclusion of the expert testimony kept admissible evidence from the jury, the defendant is entitled to a new trial.

* * *

There is error, the judgment is set aside, and the case is remanded for a new trial in accordance with this opinion.

In this opinion the other judges concurred.

Note

Do you think that under the new definition of good faith the jury can consider what the banker would have done as directly relevant to the issue of plaintiff's observance of reasonable commercial standards of fair dealing?

On page 67, Judge Peters says that the honesty in fact test imposes no duty of care on the holder and that the test is honesty rather than negligence. It would be natural to assume that the revised Article 3 requirement that reasonable commercial standards of fair dealing be observed as a part of good faith is an adoption of a suspicious circumstances test and that a suspicious circumstances test is fairly called a negligence test. However, revised Article 3 distinguishes between the observance of reasonable commercial standards of *fair dealing* and *the exercise of ordinary care.* In 3–103(7) ordinary care is defined as "in the case of a person engaged in business [the] observance of reasonable commercial standards prevailing in the area in which the person is located with respect to the business in which the person is engaged." Comment 4 to 3–103 explains:

> The definition [of good faith] requires not only honesty in fact but also 'observance of reasonable commercial standards of fair dealing.' Although fair dealing is a broad term that must be defined in context, it is clear that it is concerned with fairness of conduct rather than with the care with which an act is performed. Failure to exercise ordinary care in conducting a transaction is an entirely different concept than failure to deal fairly in conducting the transaction. Both fair dealing and ordinary care * * * are to be judged in the light of reasonable commercial standards, but these standards in each case are directed to different aspects of commercial conduct."

How plausible would be an argument by plaintiff in the principal case that it might have been careless but it was not acting in bad faith in buying at a steep discount? As the following excerpted case indicates, Preisner might have also asserted that plaintiff had notice from all the facts and circumstances (i.e. the willingness of King to sell at a steep discount) that Preisner had a defense.

WINTER AND HIRSCH v. PASSARELLI

Illinois Supreme Court, 1970.
122 Ill.App.2d 372, 259 N.E.2d 312.

[Plaintiff purchased a note from the payee, Equitable, immediately after the note had been executed. The note was in the amount of $16,260 and was payable in installments over 60 months. Plaintiff paid $11,000 for the note. The difference between $11,000 and $16,260 was greater than the interest allowable under the Illinois usury statute. In fact, the defendant makers had been loaned only $10,000 by the payee, and the loan transaction did in fact violate the usury statute thereby giving the defendants a defense. Plaintiff, however, claimed that it was a holder in due course and took free of the defense. The court acknowledged that usury statutes do not apply to purchase of notes at a discount, but it concluded that plaintiff was not a holder in due course under the circumstances.

Some excerpts from the opinion follow.]

McCormick, Judge * * *

We feel we are justified in saying that where it appears from the facts and circumstances of the particular transaction under review that a reasonably prudent businessman would have found the purchase suspicious, he should inquire as to the truth. One should become suspicious when, as here, he is himself able to purchase paper at a price which is in itself so far below the amount to be repaid from the borrower that because of that differential the contract would have been usurious had it been the original transaction. The suspicion should be all the more compelling when the paper is bought from a broker or other company that is in the business of selling such paper. Since brokers are in the business of selling loan contracts for a profit, they are likely to have loaned out less than the amount for which they are willing to sell the contract to another. Thus, if one is able to buy a loan contract from a broker for $11,000, it is more than likely that the broker had loaned some figure less than the $11,000, and the broker's profit then becomes the difference between the amount he actually loaned and that for which he sold the contract. It would then appear likely that when this difference is itself usurious, the original transaction was also. * * *

Under the circumstances, if the plaintiff was a purchaser, as it claims to be, it was on notice of a defense, since section 3–304 [R 3–302(a)], chapter 26 of Illinois Rev. Statutes 1965 provides:

> "(1) The purchaser has notice of a claim or defense if
>
> "(a) the instrument is so incomplete, bears such visible evidence of forgery or alteration, or is otherwise so irregular as to call into question its validity, terms or ownership or to create an ambiguity as to the party to pay; * * *."

This code provision is consistent with the earlier definition of "notice" found in section 1–201(25), chapter 26, providing:

> "A person has 'notice' of a fact when
>
> " * * *
>
> "(c) from all the facts and circumstances known to him at the time in question he has reason to know that it exists."

The intendment of these provisions would seem to be an attempt to prevent those dealing in the commercial world from obtaining various rights when, from a reasonable inquiry into the true facts that person would have discovered that a fact existed which prevented him from obtaining the rights which he was seeking. Under the circumstances in the present case, it is fair to say that the plaintiff had "reason to know" there was a good defense against the note in question. Even the earlier cases point out that notice of usury destroyed one's rights in the note.

We have already pointed out that on the basis of the dates when plaintiff issued its check to Equitable and when Equitable issued the note to the defendants, it is apparent that plaintiff was not a purchaser at all, but rather had advanced the very money to Equitable which Equitable, in turn, gave to the defendants. That being the case, plaintiff was a cooriginator of the note, and a defense against that note would be good against the plaintiff. Accepting plaintiff's statement that the dates are in error and that it paid out the money only after it had already seen the note, we would still hold that plaintiff was on notice of the defense for the reasons stated. Under either theory, plaintiff was not a holder in due course of the note, and the trial court was in error when it found otherwise. The trial court's judgment must be reversed.

* * *

The judgment of the Circuit Court is reversed, and the cause is remanded with directions to enter a judgment for defendants and for further proceedings in conformity with this opinion.

Reversed and remanded with directions.

EXCURSUS: COMPLETE AND REGULAR ON ITS FACE

Problem 1

Bruce Naylor is the proprietor of a gasoline station in College Town. Professor Solid (who has an irreproachable reputation) has been a Naylor customer for ten years. On a Saturday morning Professor Solid presents Naylor a check payable to Solid on which, it is clear from its face, the amount has been erased. The sum now written in is $200.00. Naylor cashed the check but, when he presented it for payment, he found that payment had been stopped. Drawer claims that the check was originally issued for $75.00. Naylor's lawyer claims that Naylor is entitled to recover $75.00 since he took in good faith. (See OR and R 3–407). Drawer's lawyer claims that Naylor is not entitled to anything since any fool should have known not to take a check with an erased amount. In a jury trial must Naylor show anything other than good faith? See OR 3–304, OR 3–307(3), R 3–302, R 3–308(b), R 3–407.

Suppose that Naylor testifies that he was so busy that day that he merely asked Professor Solid what the amount of the check was without looking at it. Does that affect the result? Would failing to look be a lack of good faith? Remember the distinction drawn in revised Article 3 between good faith and ordinary care. Would Naylor's failure to look at the check be relevant to whether he was on notice of a claim or defense?

The above problem raises the issue of the extent to which the requirement that the instrument be complete and regular on its face is a test for holder in due course status independent of the good faith and notice requirements. Original 3–304(1)(a) reads:

"The purchaser has notice of a claim or defense if

(a) the instrument is so incomplete, bears such visible evidence of forgery or alteration, or is otherwise so irregular as to call into question its validity, terms or ownership or to create an ambiguity as to the party to pay. * * *"

Completeness and regularity is, therefore, treated as a part of the notice rules.

In R 3–302(a) the requirement that the instrument be complete and regular is independent of the notice and good faith rules: there can be a holder in due course of the instrument only if "the instrument when issued or negotiated to the holder does not bear such apparent evidence of forgery or alteration or is not otherwise so irregular or incomplete as to call into question its authenticity." Further, R 3–302(a)(2)(iv) requires that for a holder to be a holder in due course, he must take the instrument "without notice that the instrument contains an unauthorized signature or has been altered."

Should the character and reputation of the transferor of the instrument be taken into account in deciding whether the authenticity of the instrument (R 3–302(a)(1)) has been called into question?

Does R 3–302(a)(2)(iv) in any event require a holding that Naylor was not a holder in due course? Can Naylor recover the $75.00 for which the check was originally drawn without meeting all the requirements for HDC status. See R 3–407(c).

Problem 2

On January 5, 1992, drawer draws a $10,000 check and misdates it January 5, 1991. She then notices the error, and strikes through 1991 and writes 1992. Later drawer claims that because of the obvious change in date a transferee of the check cannot be a holder in due course and is subject to a defense drawer has against payee. See OR 3–304 comment 2. That comment was not carried over to R 3–302. Does R 3–302(a)(2)(iv) suggest that the transferee cannot be a holder in due course? Construct an argument that even under revised Article 3, the change in date does not prevent a transferee of the check from being a holder in due course.

EXCURSUS: OVERDUE INSTRUMENTS

In 1849 Chief Judge Shaw of Massachusetts said: "Where a negotiable instrument is found in circulation after it is due, it carries suspicion on the face of it. The question immediately arises, why is it in circulation,—why is it not paid? Here is something wrong. Therefore, although it does not give the [indorsee] notice of any specific matter of defense such as setoff, payment, or fraudulent acquisition, yet it puts him on inquiry; he takes only such title as the indorser himself had, and subject to any defense which would be made if the suit were brought by the indorser." *Fisher v. Leland,* 4 Cush (Mass.) 456, 50 Am.Dec. 805, quoted in W. Britton, Bills & Notes, 2d Ed. 302 (1961).

While the more likely explanation for the non-payment of an overdue instrument is that the obligor does not have any money, which is, of course, not a defense, the rule continues that takers with notice that the instrument is overdue are not holders in due course. See OR 3–302(1)(c), R 3–302(a)(2)(iii).

If the instrument is payable on a stated date, presumably a person taking after that date would always be on notice from the face of the instrument that it is overdue. If a transferee takes an installment note after some installments are past due, the question is whether she knows or has notice that some of those installments were not paid. OR 3–304(3), R 3–302(a)(2)(iii), R 3–304(b).

Sometimes negotiable notes are payable on demand, and checks always are. In the case of checks, both original and revised Article 3 state rules which help in determining whether a check is overdue. Original 3–304(3)(c) states a *presumption* that a check is overdue after 30 days from its *issue.* Revised 3–304(a)(2) replaces the presumption of original Article 3 with the rule that a check *is* overdue 90 days after its *date.* Demand notes are issued in such varying circumstances that it is not possible for the statute to state anything other than that the issue is up to the finder of fact under very general guidelines furnished by the statute. See OR 3–304(3)(c), R 3–304(a)(3).

KAW VALLEY STATE BANK & TRUST CO. v. RIDDLE

Kansas Supreme Court, 1976.
219 Kan. 550, 549 P.2d 927.

FROMME, J.

This action was brought by The Kaw Valley State Bank and Trust Company (hereinafter referred to as Kaw Valley) to recover judgment against John H. Riddle d/b/a Riddle Contracting Company (hereafter referred to as Riddle) on two notes and to determine the priority of conflicting security agreements. The two notes were covered by separate security agreements and were given to purchase construction equipment. The Planters State Bank and Trust Company (hereafter referred to as Planters) held a note and security interest on the same and other construction equipment acquired by Riddle. Kaw Valley had acquired the two notes and the security agreements by assignment from Co–Mac, Inc. (hereafter referred to as Co–Mac), a dealer, from whom Riddle purchased the construction equipment.

In a trial to the court Kaw Valley was found not to be a holder in due course of one of the notes. Its claim on said note, totaling $21,904.64, was successfully defended on the grounds of failure of consideration. It was stipulated at the trial that none of the construction equipment for which the note was given had ever been delivered by Co–Mac. Kaw Valley has appealed.

The facts underlying this controversy are lengthy and complex but they must be set forth to adequately understand the issues on appeal. The parties submitted the case to the trial court upon a written stipulation of facts supplemented by testimony and exhibits. The following facts are taken from either the stipulation or the facts found by the trial court.

Prior to the transactions in question Riddle had purchased construction equipment and machinery from the dealer, Co–Mac. A number of these purchases had been on credit and discounted to Kaw Valley by Co–Mac. Including the Riddle transactions, Kaw Valley had purchased over 250 notes and security agreements from Co–Mac during the prior ten year period. All were guaranteed by Co–Mac and by its president personally.

In May, 1971, Riddle negotiated for the purchase of a model 6–c Caterpillar tractor, a dozer and a used 944 Caterpillar wheel tractor with a two yard bucket. Riddle was advised that this machinery could be delivered but it would first be necessary for Co–Mac to have a signed note and security agreement to complete the transaction. An installment note, security agreement and acceptance of delivery of the machinery were mailed to Riddle. These were signed and returned to Co–Mac. Ten days later, the machinery not having been delivered, Riddle called Co–Mac and inquired about purchasing a D–8 Caterpillar and a # 80 Caterpillar scraper in place of the first machinery ordered. Co–Mac agreed to destroy the May 11, 1971 papers and sell this larger machinery to Riddle in place of that previously ordered.

The sale of this substitute machinery was completed and the machinery was delivered after the execution of an additional note and security agreement. However, the May 11, 1971 papers were not destroyed. The note had been discounted and assigned to Kaw Valley prior to the sale of the substitute machinery. Thereafter Co–Mac, who was in financial trouble, made regular payments on the first note to Kaw Valley. The note was thus kept current by Co–Mac and Riddle had no knowledge of the continued existence of that note. The 6–c Caterpillar tractor, dozer and the used 944 Caterpillar wheel tractor were never delivered to Riddle. Riddle received no consideration for the May 11, 1971 note and no lien attached under the security agreement because the machinery never came into possession of Riddle. (See K.S.A. 84–9–204). The debtor never had rights in any of the collateral.

On February 24, 1972, representatives of Riddle, Co–Mac and Kaw Valley met for the purpose of consolidating the indebtedness of Riddle on machinery notes held by Kaw Valley and guaranteed by Co–Mac. Riddle was behind in some of his payments and wanted to consolidate the notes and reduce his monthly payments to $4,500.00. Kaw Valley disclosed eight past due machinery notes, each representing separate purchase transactions by Riddle. Riddle objected to one of these notes dated July 16, 1971, because the machinery purchased under this particular transaction had been previously returned to Co–Mac.

It was agreed by Kaw Valley that Riddle did not owe for this machinery because of the previous settlement between Co–Mac and Riddle. Kaw Valley cancelled the $5,000.00 balance shown to be due from Riddle.

Thereupon a renewal note and security agreement for $44,557.70 dated February 24, 1972, was drawn consolidating and renewing the seven remaining notes. Riddle then asked Kaw Valley if this was all that it owed the bank and he was assured that it was. The renewal note was then executed by Riddle.

It was not until March 12, 1972, that Riddle was advised by Kaw Valley that it held the note and security agreement dated May 11, 1971, which Riddle believed had been destroyed by Co–Mac. This was within a week after a receiver had been appointed to take over Co–Mac's business affairs. Riddle explained the machinery had never been delivered and Co–Mac promised to destroy the papers. No demand for payment of the May 11, 1971 note was made on Riddle until this action was filed.

* * *

The primary point on appeal questions the holding of the trial court that Kaw Valley was not a holder in due course of the note and security agreement dated May 11, 1971.

K.S.A. 84–3–306 [R 3–305] provides that unless a holder of an instrument is a holder in due course he takes the instrument subject to the defenses of want or failure of consideration, nonperformance of any condition precedent, nondelivery or delivery for a special purpose. It was undisputed in this case that Riddle received no consideration after executing the note. The machinery was never delivered and he was assured by Co–Mac that the papers would be destroyed. The parties so stipulated. If Kaw Valley was not a holder in due course the proven defense was a bar to recovery by Kaw Valley.

K.S.A. 84–3–302 [R 3–302] states that a holder in due course is a holder who takes the instrument (1) for value, (2) in good faith and (3) without notice of any defense against it. It was not disputed and the court found that Kaw Valley took the note for value so the first requirement was satisfied. The other requirements were subject to dispute. The trial court concluded:

> Kaw Valley State Bank and Trust Company is not a holder in due course of the note and security agreement, dated May 11, 1971 for the reason that it did not establish in all respects that it took said instruments in good faith and without notice of any defense against or claimed to it on the part of John H. Riddle, and Kaw Valley State Bank and Trust Company therefore took said instruments subject to the defense of failure of consideration.

So we are confronted with the question of what is required for a holder to take an instrument "in good faith" and "without notice of defense." We will consider the two parts of the question in the order mentioned.

"Good faith" is defined in K.S.A. 84–1–201(19) as "honesty in fact in the conduct or transaction concerned." The first draft of the Uniform Commercial Code (UCC) as proposed required not only that the actions of a holder be honest in fact but in addition it required the actions to conform to *reasonable commercial standards.* This would have permitted the courts to inquire as to whether a particular commercial standard was in fact reasonable. (See *Uniform Commercial Code, Proposed Final Draft* [1950], § 1–201, 18, p. 30.) However, when the final draft was approved the test of reasonable commercial standards was excised thus indicating that a more rigid standard must be applied for determining "good faith." (See White and Summers, *Uniform Commercial Code* [1972], § 14–6, pp. 471, 472.)

From the history of the Uniform Commercial Code it would appear that "good faith" requires no actual knowledge of or participation in any material infirmity in the original transaction.

The second part of our question concerns the requirement of the UCC that a holder in due course take the instrument without notice of any defense to the instrument. K.S.A. 84–1–201(25) provides:

* * *

As is apparent from reading the above statute the standard enunciated is not limited to the rigid standard of actual knowledge of the defense. Reason to know appears to be premised on the use of reasonable commercial practices. Since "good faith" and "no notice of defense" are both required of a holder to claim the status of a holder in due course it would appear that the two standards are not in conflict even though the standards of conduct may be different.

There is little or no evidence in the present case to indicate that Kaw Valley acted dishonestly or "not in good faith" when it purchased the note of May 11, 1971. However, as to "notice of a defense" the court found from all the facts and circumstances known to Kaw Valley at the time in question it had reason to know a defense existed. The court found:

> During the period 1960 to May, 1971, plaintiff purchased from Co–Mac over 250 notes and secured transactions and held at any given time between $100,000.00 and $250,000.00 of such obligations. All of which were guaranteed by Co–Mac and personally guaranteed by D.J. Wickern, its president. Conant Wait personally handled most if not all of such transactions for plaintiff. Mr. Wait was aware that Co–Mac was making warranties and representations as to fitness to some purchasers of new and used equipment. Mr. Wait further knew that some transactions were in fact not as they would appear to be in that the money from Kaw Valley would be used by Co–Mac to buy the equipment that was the subject matter of the sale. Further, that delivery to the customer of said purchased equipment was sometimes delayed 60 to 90 days for repairing and/or overhauling of same. The plaintiff obviously on many transactions was relying on Co–Mac to insure payment of the obligations and contacted Co–Mac to collect delinquent payments. Some transactions involved delivery of coupon books to Co–Mac

rather than the debtor so Co–Mac could bill service and parts charges along with the secured debt. Co–Mac collected payments directly from debtors in various transactions and paid plaintiff. Plaintiff did not concern itself with known irregularities in the transactions as it clearly was relying on Co–Mac.

The coupon book on the May 11, 1971 transaction was not sent to defendant Riddle; no payments on same were made by defendant Riddle; the payments were made by Co–Mac until January 25, 1972; prior to early March, 1972, defendant Riddle did not know plaintiff had the May 11, 1971 secured transaction; knowledge of said transaction came to defendant Riddle on March 12, 1972 when Mr. Wait contacted defendant Riddle's manager; that Co–Mac had shortly before been placed in receivership; that no demand for any payment on said transaction was made by plaintiff to defendant Riddle until September 1972.

To further support its holding that Kaw Valley had reason to know that the defense existed the court found that when Kaw Valley, Co–Mac and Riddle met on February 24, 1972, to consolidate all of Riddle's past due notes Kaw Valley recognized Co–Mac's authority to act for it. Co–Mac had accepted return of the machinery on one of the eight transactions and Kaw Valley recognized its authority as their agent to do so and cancelled the $5,000.00 balance remaining due on the note held by the bank.

The cases dealing with the question of "reason to know a defense exists" seem to fall into four categories.

The first includes those cases where it is established the holder had information from the transferor or the obligor which disclosed the existence of a defense. In those cases it is clear if the holder takes an instrument having received prior or contemporaneous notice of a defense he is not a holder in due course. (*Billingsley v. Mackay,* 382 F.2d 290.) Our present case does not fall in that category for there is no evidence that Co–Mac or Riddle informed Kaw Valley that the machinery had not been delivered when the note was negotiated.

The second group of cases are those in which the defense appears in an accompanying document delivered to the holder with the note. For example, when a security agreement is executed concurrently with a note evidencing an indebtedness incurred for machinery to be delivered in the future. In such case the instrument may under certain circumstances disclose a defense to the note, such as nondelivery of the machinery purchased. Our present case does not fall in this category because Riddle had signed a written delivery acceptance which was handed to Kaw Valley along with the note and security agreement.

A third group of cases are those in which information appears in the written instrument indicating the existence of a defense, such as when the note on its face shows that the due date has passed or the note bears visible evidence of alteration and forgery or the note is clearly incomplete. In our present case the instrument assigned bore nothing unusual on its face and appeared complete and proper in all respects.

In the fourth category of cases it has been held that the holder of a negotiable instrument may be prevented from assuming holder in due course status because of knowledge of the business practices of his transferor or when he is so closely aligned with the transferor that the transferor may be considered an agent of the holder and the transferee is charged with the actions and knowledge of the transferor.

Under our former negotiable instruments law containing provisions similar to the UCC this court refused to accord holder in due course status to a machinery company receiving notes from one of its dealers because of its knowledge of the business practices of the dealer and the company's participation and alignment with the dealer who transferred the note. (*International Harvester Co. v. Watkins,* 127 Kan. 50, Syl. ¶ 3, 272 Pac. 139, 61 A.L.R. 687 (1982).)

In *Unico v. Owen,* 50 N.J. 101, 232 A.2d 405 (1967), the New Jersey court refused to accord holder in due course status to a financing partnership which was closely connected with the transferor and had been organized to finance the commercial paper obtained by the transferor and others. The financing partnership had a voice in setting the policies and standards to be followed by the transferor. Under such circumstances the court found that the holder must be considered a participant in the transaction and subject to defenses available against the payee-transferor. In *United States Finance Company v. Jones,* 285 Ala. 105, 229 So.2d 495 (1969), it was held that a finance company purchasing a note from a payee for fifty percent of its face value did not establish holder in due course status and must be held subject to defenses inherent in the original transaction. Other jurisdictions have followed the rationale of *Unico.* See *American Plan Corp. v. Woods,* 16 Ohio App.2d 1, 240 N.E.2d 886 (1968), where the holder supplied forms to the payee, established financing charges and investigated the credit of the maker of the note; *Calvert Credit Corp. v. Williams,* 244 A.2d 494 (D.C.App.1968), where the holder exerted total control over payee's financial affairs; and *Jones v. Approved Bancredit Corp.,* 256 A.2d 739 (Del.1969), where ownership and management of the holder and payee were connected.

In the present case Kaw Valley had worked closely with Co–Mac in over 250 financing transactions over a period of ten years. It knew that some of these transactions were not for valuable consideration at the time the paper was delivered since the bank's money was to be used in purchasing the machinery or equipment represented in the instruments as already in possession of the maker of the note. Kaw Valley had been advised that delivery to Co–Mac's customers was sometimes delayed from 60 to 90 days. Kaw Valley continued to rely on Co–Mac to assure payment of the obligations and contacted it to collect delinquent payments. Some of these transactions, including the one in question, involved the use of coupon books to be used by the debtor in making payment on the notes. In the present case Kaw Valley did not notify Riddle that it was the holder of the note. It delivered Riddle's coupon book to Co–Mac as if it were the obligor or was authorized as its collection agent for this transaction. Throughout the period from May 11, 1971, to February 25, 1972, Kaw Valley received and credited the monthly payments knowing that payments were being made by Co–Mac and not by Riddle. Then when Riddle's loans were consolidated, the May 11, 1971 transaction was not included by Kaw Valley, either by oversight or by intention, as an obligation of Riddle. Co–Mac occupied a close relationship with Kaw Valley and with its knowledge and consent acted as its agent in collecting payments on notes held by Kaw Valley. The working relationship existing between Kaw Valley and Co–Mac was further demonstrated on February 24, 1972, when the $5,000.00 balance due on one of Riddle's notes was cancelled when it was shown that the machinery for which the note was given had previously been returned to Co–Mac with the understanding that no further payments were due.

KSA 84–3–307(3) [R 3–308(b)] provides:

> After it is shown that a defense exists a person claiming the rights of a holder in due course has the burden of establishing that he or some person under whom he claims is in all respects a holder in due course.

In the present case the court found that the appellant, Kaw Valley, had not sustained its burden of proving that it was a holder in due course. Under the evidence in this case the holder failed to advise the maker of the note of its acquisition of the note and security agreement. It placed the payment coupon book in the hands of Co–Mac and received all monthly payments from them. A close working relationship existed between the two companies and Co–Mac was clothed with authority to collect and forward all payments due on the transaction. Agency and authority was further shown to exist by authorizing return of machinery to Co–Mac and terminating balances due on purchase money paper. We cannot say under the facts and circumstances known and participated in by Kaw Valley in this transaction it did not at the time in question have reason to know that the defense existed. This was a question of fact to be determined by the trier of fact which if supported by substantial competent evidence must stand.

* * *

The judgment is affirmed.

Note

On page 76, the court says that Kaw Valley knew that Co–Mac took notes for goods not yet delivered. Does knowledge that the transferror has not yet performed the obligation for which the note is given prevent a transferee from being a holder in due course? See OR 3–304(4)(a). That provision is not continued in revised Article 3. Does the principle of OR 3–304(4)(a) still obtain in revised Article 3?

Suppose a transferee of a negotiable instrument taken by a farm implement seller for the price of a combine knows that the dealer is being sued for breach of contract by another buyer of a combine. Would that knowledge prevent the transferee from being a holder in due course? See *Waterbury Savings Bank v. Jaroszewski,* 4 Conn.Cir. 620, 238 A.2d 446 (1967).

Thousands of sellers of goods and land take installment notes from their purchasers and then transfer the notes to banks or finance companies. The transferees usually are recurring buyers of the notes and commonly do not transfer them further. It is convenient for such transferees to provide the forms to be used because that relieves them of the burden of reading instruments prepared by others. Often, sellers will want to know before they make the sale that their bank or finance company will buy the resulting negotiable instrument. Therefore, they will ask the transferee to approve the credit of the maker of the notes before the sale is made.

Many courts have denied holder in due course status to transferees who regularly buy the negotiable instruments of a dealer. Some courts have tried to fit that result within the Article 3 provisions by concluding that such a transferee had notice of a claim or defense of the maker, as did the court in *Kaw Valley,* or that such a transferee was not in good faith. See *Arcanum Nat'l Bank v. Hessler,* 69 Ohio St.2d 549, 433 N.E.2d 204 (1982). Other courts have denied such transferees holder in due course status without making any reference to the specific holder in due course rules of Article 3. Following is such a case.

JONES v. APPROVED BANCREDIT CORP.

Delaware Supreme Court, 1969.
256 A.2d 739.

[The court, applying what it called the "party to the transaction rule," denied holder in due course status to a transferee that was a related corporation of the transferor. The court did not discuss the good faith or notice requirements of the N.I.L. which was in force in Delaware at the time.]

HERRMANN, JUSTICE * * *

In dealing with the holder in due course status, a basic problem has been recognized by the courts in cases involving the financing of installment sales, especially of consumer goods and household improvements. The problem arises from the increasingly apparent need for a balancing of the interest of the commercial community in the unrestricted negotiability of commercial papers, on the one hand, against the interest of the installment buyers of the community, on the other hand, in the preservation of their normal remedy of withholding payment whenever there has been misrepresentation, failure of consideration, or other valid reason for refusal to pay. This problem and this need have given rise to this concept: the more the holder knows about the underlying transaction which is the source of the paper, the more he controls or participates in it, the less he fits the role of good faith purchaser for value; and the less justification there is for according to him the protected status of holder in due course considered necessary for the free flow of paper in the commercial world.

The rule, balancing the needs of the installment-buying community and the commercial community, has evolved in various ways. Many courts have solved the problem by denying holder in due course status to the finance company where it maintains a close business relationship with the dealer whose paper it buys; where the financer is closely connected with the particular credit transaction under scrutiny; or where the financer prescribes to the dealer the forms of the papers, the buyer signs the purchase agreement and the note concurrently, and the dealer endorses the note and assigns the contract immediately thereafter. In such situations, many courts look upon the transaction as a species of tri-partite transaction; and the tenor of the cases is that the finance company, in such situation, should not be permitted to hide behind "the fictional fence" of the UNIL or the UCC and thereby achieve an unfair advantage over the purchaser. See Unico v. Owen, 50 N.J. 101, 232 A.2d 405 (1967); Buffalo Industrial Bank v. DeMarzio, 162 Misc. 742, 296 N.Y.S. 783 (1937).

The rule of balance thus evolved is exemplified by Mutual Finance Co. v. Martin, Fla., 63 So.2d 649 (1953). There a finance company was held not to be a holder in due course where it appeared that the finance company furnished to the payee electrical appliance dealer the form of conditional sales contract and promissory note with its name imprinted thereon; that before the sales transaction occurred the finance company had investigated the purchaser's credit standing, had approved the proposed terms and agreed to purchase the contract and note in the event the transaction was consummated; that over a period of years immediately prior to the transaction, the finance company had provided much financing for the dealer in other transactions. In holding that, under those circumstances, the finance company was sufficiently a party to the transaction to deprive it of holder in due course status, the Supreme Court of Florida stated:

> "* * * It may be that our holding here will require some changes in business methods and will impose a greater burden on the finance companies. We think the buyer—Mr. & Mrs. General Public—should have some protection somewhere along the line. We believe the finance company is better able to bear the risk of the dealer's insolvency than the buyer and in a far better position to protect his interests against unscrupulous and insolvent dealers. * * *
>
> "If this opinion imposes great burdens on finance companies it is a potent argument in favor of a rule which will afford protection

to the general buying public against unscrupulous dealers in personal property. * * *."

* * *

EQUICO LESSORS, INC. v. RAMADAN

Florida Court of Appeal 1986.
493 So.2d 516.

[Defendant leased a computerized energy management system for his office building from Hastings. Plaintiff is assignee from Hastings. Hastings guaranteed that the equipment would produce specific energy savings. When plaintiff sued for unpaid lease payments, defendant asserted as a defense that the guarantee had been breached. The lease contained the following "waiver of defenses" clause: "It is understood that Lessor contemplates assigning this Agreement, and that said assignee may assign the same * * *. The assignee's rights shall be free from all defenses, set-offs or counterclaims which Lessee may be entitled to assert against Lessor. * * *" The trial court applied the close-connectedness doctrine to deny effect to the waiver of defenses clause. On Appeal Reversed.]

BARFIELD, JUDGE * * *

Equico's assistant vice president testified while it supplied the printed forms used to execute the lease, [sic] there was no prior agreement that the lease would indeed be assigned to Equico. Equico assumed the lease would be assigned and prepared the lease and related documents on that assumption. Ramadan testified he did not know Equico was a potential party to the lease until he signed the lease. However, he had been contacted by Equico during the credit check. * * *

Florida's Uniform Commercial Code contains a provision that validates waiver of defenses clauses in contracts or leases.[2] The purpose of this statutory provision is to treat the assignee like a holder in due course of a negotiable instrument. *See* 19C Fla.Stat.Ann. 240, (1966), Uniform Commercial Code Comment. Such clauses are designed to facilitate financing of transactions by insulating an innocent or unknowing purchaser of the contract, lease or financing note from disputes over the underlying transaction. Such clauses reduce the risk to assignees in taking such assignments and thereby encourage the financ-

2. Section 679.206, Florida Statutes, provides that:

(1) Subject to any statute or decision which establishes a different rule for buyers or lessees of consumer goods, an agreement by a buyer or lessee that he will not assert against an assignee any claim or defense which he may have against the seller or lessor is enforceable by an assignee who takes his assignment for value, in good faith and without notice of a claim or defense, except as to the defense of a type which may be asserted against a holder in due course of a negotiable instrument under the chapter on commercial paper.

ing of transactions by assuring a market for those wishing to assign contracts and leases.

However, because of the great protection such a clause gives an assignee, such as Equico, it is only valid when the assignment is taken for value, in good faith and without knowledge of a defense or claim. *Leasing Service Corp. v. River City Construction, Inc.*, 743 F.2d 871 (11th Cir.1984). The close connection doctrine acts as an evidentiary rule by which the good faith of an assignee is tested. *Are v. Barnett Bank of Miami Beach, NA,* 330 So.2d 250 (Fla. 3rd DCA1976). It is not a rule of law that says if a close connection appears, then the assignee will be denied the benefit of a waiver of defenses clause. In a commercial setting, more than just a close connection must be shown before an assignee will be denied the status of a holder in due course under § 679.206(1), Florida Statutes.

* * *

Courts in other jurisdictions also require a greater showing of close connection between the assignee and the assignor and the underlying commercial transaction before invalidating a particular waiver of defenses clause. In *Leasing Service Corp. v. River City Construction Inc.*, 743 F.2d at 871, the 11th Circuit said the defendant needed to show the assignee's knowledge of the seller's fraudulent acts or its significant participation in the original transaction. The assignee's supplying the forms for the underlying lease was not sufficient as such a practice was common in commercial transactions.

* * *

Here, the evidence of a close connection consisted of Equico's supplying preprinted forms for the lease between Hastings Capital and Ramadan; the lease and personal guaranty contained pre-printed assignment clauses naming Equico as assignee; and Equico conducted a credit check on Ramadan before the lease was executed. Equico had taken assignments of approximately 30 leases from Hastings in the past with a total value of $250,000. However, there was no evidence of a standing agreement that Hastings Capital would assign to Equico all the leases it executed or that Equico agreed to take all assignments from Hastings Capital.

There was no showing in this transaction that Equico had knowledge of the performance guarantee made by Hastings. Equico had no knowledge of the equipment's failure before the assignment or of Ramadan's potential claims. Further, Equico did not solicit Ramadan but only agreed to finance the arrangement after Hastings Capital representatives had arranged the transaction.

The evidence offered by Ramadan was insufficient to justify setting aside the waiver of defenses clause. The trial court therefore erred in entering judgment for Ramadan. The final judgment is REVERSED and the case is REMANDED to the trial court to enter judgment for appellant.

Note

It is common in financing transactions like that in the *Equico* case to use a waiver of defenses clause in the contract, rather than a negotiable note, to gain the benefit of freedom from buyer's defenses against the seller. U.C.C. § 9–206, as you see from the case, applies holder-in-due-course-like rules to determine the rights of assignees who claim rights under a waiver of defenses clause.

5. The Payee as Holder in Due Course (A Little Third Party Beneficiary Law)

As we have just seen, if a seller, A, takes a negotiable note or check payable to itself for the price of the thing sold and then indorses that note or check over to B, B may be a holder in due course. Suppose A, instead of having the buyer make the negotiable instrument payable to A, has it made payable directly to B and has buyer hand it to B. Can B as payee be a holder in due course? Under the N.I.L., some cases held that a payee could not be a holder in due course. But, on the above facts, it seems somewhat peculiar to make B's HDC status turn on whether the negotiable instrument is made payable to A and then indorsed over to B, or made payable directly to B. Original 3–302(2) says simply: "A payee may be a holder in due course." Revised Article 3 does not continue that language but comment 4 to R 3–302 says it was not continued because it is not necessary. The comment goes on: "The payee of an instrument can be a holder in due course, but use of the doctrine by the payee of an instrument is not the usual situation."

Problems

1. A sells 1,000 widgets to B and takes a negotiable note for $10,000 from B for the price. B does not pay and A sues B on the note. B claims that the widgets were defective. A responds that A is a holder in due course and takes free of B's defense. Is A's argument sound? See *Mansion Carpets, Inc. v. Marinoff,* 24 A.D.2d 947, 265 N.Y.S.2d 298 (1965).

2. Suppose that in problem 1, A has B make the note payable to C, a creditor of A. Can C be a holder in due course? Does it make any difference whether the note is given to A who then mails it to C, or is sent by B directly to C?

3. Suppose that Brown approaches Bank requesting a loan of $50,000. Bank says it will make the loan only if Brown can find a good customer of Bank who will co-sign the note. Brown approaches his friend White and induces White to become co-signer by giving White what Brown says is a first mortgage on Brown's home to secure White's possible duty to pay the note. The mortgage is in fact a worthless third mortgage. Brown is insolvent and Bank sues White. White defends that he was defrauded by Brown into signing the note. Can Bank be a holder in due course and take free of White's defense of fraud?

4. A delivered his automobile to X, owner of a used car business, for sale on commission, X to receive 10% of the sales price. X, to induce a sale, told Buyer that the automobile had a new transmission. It did not.

X told Buyer to make out his check for the purchase price to A. Buyer discovers that the transmission is bad and stops payment on the check. Can A recover from Buyer on the check free of Buyer's defense? Would it make any difference if Buyer's check had been payable to X and then X had indorsed it to A? Would the result be different if the arrangement between A and X had been that X could keep any excess above $5000 that he received for the automobile?

6. Transferees From Fiduciaries and Notice of Claims or Defenses

Problem

Mary Jones is treasurer of the Salem Lions Club with power to sign checks issued by, and to indorse checks payable to, the Club. In all of the following transactions, the transferee-holders of the checks in question knew that Jones was the treasurer of the club. In each case, Mary was embezzling club funds. In each case consider whether the transferee's knowledge that Jones is the treasurer prevents the transferee from taking the check free of the claim of the club that Jones was embezzling the funds? See OR 3–304(2), R 3–307.

(a) Jones draws a check for $400 payable to Sears and uses it to pay the price of a new washing machine to be delivered to her home.

(b) Jones draws a check for $4,000 payable to American Express in payment of her American Express bill.

(c) Jones draws a check for $400 payable to herself and takes it to Sears and indorses it over to Sears in payment of a washing machine to be delivered to her home.

(d) Jones draws a check for $1,000 payable to First Bank, which is also the bank on which the check is drawn, and receives $1,000 cash for it at First Bank.

(e) Jones draws a check for $1,000 payable to First Bank and deposits it in her personal account at the bank.

(f) Jones indorses in blank on behalf of the Lions Club a check for $2,000 payable to the club and deposits the check in her personal account at First Bank.

As to problems (e) and (f), the Uniform Fiduciaries Act (UFA), promulgated by the Uniform Law Commissioners in 1922 and adopted in 24 states and the District of Columbia, provides (Section 9) that a bank is not liable to the principal for allowing the fiduciary to deposit fiduciary funds in the fiduciary's personal account unless it had actual knowledge of the wrongdoing or was otherwise acting in bad faith. The bank, therefore, under UFA, has no per se liability if the fiduciary deposits fiduciary funds in her personal account and then misappropriates them. Original Article 3 in 3–304(2) does not speak clearly to the issue. Revised 3–307, however, reverses the rule of the Uniform Fiduciaries Act.

In states which do not have the Uniform Fiduciaries Act, the cases are split as to whether a bank is automatically liable to the principal if the bank allows a fiduciary to deposit funds in the fiduciary's personal account and the fiduciary later misappropriates the funds. Two cases reaching opposite results on nearly identical facts came from New York and Washington, respectively. Both cases involved a father, guardian of funds belonging to a child, who deposited the funds in his personal account and then misappropriated them. The New York case, *Matter of Knox,* 64 N.Y.2d 434, 488 N.Y.S.2d 146, 477 N.E.2d 448 (1985) held that the bank was not liable. The court said that a bank may in general assume that a fiduciary will act properly and need not make an investigation to assure that a misappropriation will not occur. The Washington case, *Smith v. Olympic Bank,* 103 Wash.2d 418, 693 P.2d 92 (1985) held that the bank knew that the father had negotiated the check in a transaction for his own benefit and that, therefore, the bank could not be a holder in due course.

What do you think as to the policy. Should banks be liable on the facts of problems (e) and (f)? See the further discussion, infra, at pages 257–263.

DOUGLASS v. WONES

Illinois Court of Appeals, 1983.
120 Ill.App.3d 36, 76 Ill.Dec. 114, 458 N.E.2d 514.

[Plaintiff sued Wones, Michael Douglas, and three banks, Glenview, First National, and Citizens, to recover losses caused by the fraud of defendant Douglas.]

HOPF, JUDGE * * *

On September 23, 1980, defendant Douglas requested and received from plaintiff Douglass the following three checks drawn on Douglass Development's in-State account: $5,000 to Glenview, $6,600 to First National and $54,000 to Citizens. In exchange, Michael Douglas gave Douglass [an] out-of-State check for $65,600 made payable to Douglass Development, which Douglass deposited.

On each of these two occasions, defendant Douglas represented to plaintiffs that his two checks payable to Douglass Development represented good funds. Plaintiffs issued their checks in reliance upon Douglas' representations. All of the checks drawn by Douglass were paid to the payees named thereon. Defendant Douglas' two checks payable to Douglass Development were returned for insufficient funds.

* * *

Next, we consider whether counts XII through XX of plaintiffs' amended complaint, alleging causes of action in conversion, rescission of negotiation, and unjust enrichment against Citizens, First National and Glenview, were properly dismissed for failing to state causes of action. In all of these counts, plaintiffs alleged "on information and belief" that defendants "knew or had reason to know" of Douglas' fraudulent inducement because plaintiffs neither had a business or other relationship with them nor owed them money. In addition, as against Citizens, the complaint also alleged it had knowledge or notice because the check payable to it was in payment of an indebtedness created by an earlier bad check of Douglas.

Initially, we consider the question whether these payee defendants are entitled to the protection afforded to holders in due course under the Uniform Commercial Code. (Ill.Rev.Stat.1979, ch. 26, par. 3–305.) Under the Code, a "holder in due course" is a holder who takes an instrument for value in good faith, and without notice of any defense against or claim to it on the part of any person. (Ill.Rev.Stat.1979, ch. 26, par. 3–302(1) [R 3–302].) A "holder" is a person who has possession of an instrument payable to his order or to bearer in blank. (Ill.Rev. Stat.1979, ch. 26, par. 1–201(20).) It is clear in the present case that the payee banks were "holders" of the checks in question. In Illinois it has been held that a payee who accepts a check from one who is indebted to him but who is not the drawer, without knowledge of any fraud which the debtor may have practiced to induce the drawer to write the check in favor of the payee is a holder in due course who takes the instrument free from any defenses claimed by the drawer. (Ill.Ann.Stat., ch. 26, par. 3–302(2) [omitted in revised Article 3], Illinois Code Comment, at 140 (Smith–Hurd 1963); Drumm Construction Co. v. Forbes (1922), 305 Ill. 303, 137 N.E. 225.) However, a special situation exists where the payee is a bank who accepts a check from one who is not the drawer and that person requests that the bank credit his personal account with the proceeds. In this situation, the bank is held to a higher standard than is the individual in a private transaction, and notice is deemed to have been given by the terms of the instrument itself. (Milano v. Sheridan Trust & Savings Bank (1926), 242 Ill.App. 362, 368.) Explaining the distinction between individuals and banks under these circumstances, the court in Milano stated:

> "There is a marked difference between the obligations of a banking institution receiving funds and an individual. The latter does not ordinarily receive checks payable to his order from persons not indebted to him; he is not the custodian of funds in which he has no interest; nor is he a depositary for such members of the public as wish to avail themselves of his services. On the other hand, a bank is all of these. The public is invited to use its conveniences as places of deposit; it holds itself out as trustworthy for such purposes; when it is named as the payee in a check by a party not indebted to it, it will be presumed that it accepts the same subject to the directions of the drawer and not to the directions of a stranger to the paper who happens to present it." (242 Ill.App. 362, 369. Accord, People ex rel. Nelson v. Peoples Bank & Trust Co. (1933), 271 Ill.App. 41.)

Thus, under these circumstances the bank is required to hold the proceeds of the instrument subject to the order of the drawer, and not the presenter, and it generally cannot be a holder in due course as against the drawer if it has permitted the presenter to withdraw or otherwise use the proceeds of the check without taking precautions to determine the authority of the person to receive them. People ex rel.

Nelson; Milano; Ill.Ann.Stat., ch. 26, par. 3–302(2) [omitted in revised Article 3], Illinois Code Comment, at 140–41 (Smith–Hurd 1963).

Glenview argues that an inquiry here would have been fruitless since plaintiffs intended Douglas to receive the proceeds and were not aware at the time of negotiation of any defense which they had upon the instrument. While this may be true, the pleadings do not indicate either the point at which plaintiffs became aware of Douglas' fraud or the time when the checks were cashed. Thus, we are unable to conclude with any degree of certainty that an inquiry by the payee banks here would have been fruitless. It is conceivable that had the banks contacted plaintiffs, plaintiffs would have been advised of Douglas' financial position and could have averted this controversy. Further, we do not consider the results of the inquiry as being determinative of whether the duty to inquire exists in the first instance. The duty in our opinion arises from the face of the instrument itself and not from the information which would be obtained from the drawer. We therefore conclude that the payee banks here are not entitled to assert holder in due course status as a defense to plaintiffs' claims. They were merely holders of the instruments and as such took subject to all claims against them. Ill.Rev.Stat.1979, ch. 26, pars. 3–306 [R 3–306], 1–201.

Note

Douglass v. Wones goes beyond R 3–307 since the wrongdoer was not a fiduciary of plaintiff. In a state which has no authority on the issue, is a court more, or less, likely to follow Douglass under revised Article 3 than under original Article 3? Note that R 3–307 applies only if the transferee knows that the transferor is a fiduciary.

7. The FDIC and Federal Holder in Due Course Rules.

SUNBELT SAVINGS, FSB, DALLAS, TEXAS v. MONTROSS

United States Court of Appeals, Fifth Circuit, 1991.
923 F.2d 353.

GEE, CIRCUIT JUDGE. Today we decline to extend the federal holder in due course doctrine to protect the FDIC or its successors from the personal defenses of makers of non-negotiable promissory notes, holding that as a matter of federal common law the doctrine does not apply to non-negotiable instruments. Having announced this rule, we go on to conclude that the defendant did submit sufficient evidence to avoid summary judgment on his prevention of performance claim. We also conclude that a summary judgment ruling on defendant's other affirmative defenses would be premature. Accordingly, we reverse and remand for consistent proceedings.

BACKGROUND

On March 18, 1986, George Montross executed a $1.1 million variable interest promissory note in favor of Sunbelt Savings (Old

Sunbelt). Mr. Montross defaulted on the note. Old Sunbelt foreclosed, purchased the security at foreclosure sale, and, on May 24, 1988, filed suit against Mr. Montross for the deficiency. Shortly after filing suit, Old Sunbelt failed. The FSLIC (now FDIC) assumed control and established Sunbelt Savings, FSB (New Sunbelt). Mr. Montross defended against the deficiency suit on two grounds: (1) Old Sunbelt prevented him from transferring the note to a new debtor as allowed by the deed of trust, thus, excusing his performance; and (2) as an affirmative defense, he satisfied the conditions in the deed of trust, thus, absolving him of personal liability for the note. New Sunbelt, having intervened as plaintiff, moved for summary judgment on the grounds that the federal holder in due course doctrine barred all of Mr. Montross' defenses and that Mr. Montross had failed to produce evidence to establish a genuine dispute over a material fact. Mr. Montross countered that the federal holder in due course doctrine should not apply to the non-negotiable instrument at issue in this case and that he had either presented sufficient evidence to avoid summary judgment or had been denied the opportunity for effective discovery so as to do so. The district court granted New Sunbelt's motion, ruling that the federal holder in due course doctrine applies to non-negotiable instruments, and bars all Mr. Montross' defenses as a matter of law. The district court, however, did not evaluate the summary judgment evidence and dismissed the discovery dispute as moot. Mr. Montross appeals. * * *

THE FEDERAL HOLDER IN DUE COURSE DOCTRINE AND NON-NEGOTIABLE INSTRUMENTS

The district court granted summary judgment in favor of New Sunbelt after concluding that the federal holder in due course doctrine applies to non-negotiable instruments and, thus, bars all of Mr. Montross' defenses. This conclusion presents us with an issue of first impression: whether the federal holder in due course doctrine protects the FDIC and its successors from personal defenses to the enforcement of non-negotiable instruments.

The federal holder in due course doctrine bars makers of promissory notes from asserting personal [1] defenses against the FDIC and its successors in connection with purchase and assumption transactions involving troubled financial institutions. See FSLIC v. Murray, 853 F.2d 1251, 1256 (5th Cir.1988). The FDIC enjoys this protection as a matter of federal common law so that it may achieve the congressional mandate of the "sound, effective, and uninterrupted operation of the [nation's] banking system with resulting safety and liquidity of bank deposits." S.Rep. No. 1269, 81st Cong., 2d Sess., reprinted in 1950 U.S.Code Cong. & Admin.News 3765, 3765–66; see also Campbell Leasing, 901 F.2d at 1244–46. The federal holder in due course doctrine facilitates uninterrupted operation of the banking system by allowing the FDIC to complete purchase and assumption transactions quickly

1. We have differentiated personal and real defenses by reference to state law. See Campbell Leasing, Inc. v. FDIC, 901 F.2d 1244, 1249 (5th Cir.1990); see also Tex.Bus. & Comm.Code § 3.305 [R 3–305].

and based on the face value of a failed bank's negotiable instruments, obviating the need to scrutinize the instruments for personal defenses. The doctrine also prevents makers from using personal defenses to gain priority over the failed bank's creditors' and depositors' rights to the note proceeds.

To date, our holdings have been limited. In Murray, we held that the "FSLIC has at least the rights of a holder in due course when it acquires a negotiable instrument in a purchase and assumption transaction." Murray, 853 F.2d at 1256.

In Campbell Leasing, we extended the ambit of federal holder in due course doctrine by holding that the FDIC and its successors may be federal holders in due course without meeting the technical state-law requirements for holder in due course status. Campbell Leasing, 901 F.2d at 1249. In Campbell the defendant had argued that the federal holder in due course doctrine should not apply to the FDIC when notes are acquired in bulk transfers. Under Texas law bulk transferees do not enjoy holder in due course status. Campbell rejected this requirement, recognizing that the FDIC receives notes by bulk transfer involuntarily and as a matter of course, thus, such a technical state-law requirement cannot be allowed to defeat the policy behind federal holder in due course doctrine. Likewise the "for value," "without notice of prior dishonor," and "without notice of contrary claims" requirements of state-law should also be waived when the FDIC assumes control of negotiable instruments. * * *

After carefully reviewing our decisions and the policy underlying them, we decline to extend federal holder in due course status to the FDIC or its successor in cases in which it acquires non-negotiable instruments through purchase and assumption transactions. Respecting our decisions, Murray's holding was expressly limited to *negotiable instruments* acquired by purchase and assumption. Campbell Leasing did not deal with negotiability at all. It merely excused the FDIC from compliance with the bulk transfer exclusion of Texas holder in due course law. CTS, being off point, carries little weight.

Turning to the policy analysis, we conclude that a judicial extension of the federal holder in due course doctrine to non-negotiable instruments is unwarranted. We recognize the vital role of the FDIC in ensuring the sound, effective, and uninterrupted operation of our banks. We also recognize that the FDIC requires some special protections to enable it to perform this function effectively. For example, the FDIC must be protected from the effect of secret agreements. See D'Oench, Duhme & Co., Inc. v. FDIC, 315 U.S. 447, 62 S.Ct. 676, 86 L.Ed. 956 (1942); 12 U.S.C. § 1823(e) (1988). Likewise, we recognize that, because of the circumstances surrounding purchase and assumption transactions, the FDIC must be accorded holder in due course status when it takes a negotiable instrument in a bulk transfer even if this does not meet the technical requirements of state law. See Campbell Leasing, 901 F.2d at 1249; Murray, 853 F.2d at 1255–56. The

FDIC also reminds us that many banks in our Circuit have large numbers of variable-interest—and thus non-negotiable—notes.

At first blush, these policy justifications seem to apply with equal force to non-negotiable instruments. On closer examination, however, we conclude that applying the doctrine to non-negotiable instruments is fundamentally different from the earlier protections that we have afforded the FDIC. Murray, Campbell Leasing, D'Oench, and section 1823(e) all act to prevent the FDIC from being disadvantaged when it is forced to assume control of a troubled financial institution. Under these decisions, the FDIC is protected from the disadvantages attendant upon its role, but the nature of the assets the FDIC receives from the institutions remains unchanged. Conversely, extending federal holder in due course protection to non-negotiable instruments would bestow a benefit on the FDIC by changing the assets' nature—actually enhancing their value.

We do not view negotiability as a technical requirement. Negotiability is the foundation underlying all of Article Three and of holder in due course status in particular. Under Article Three of the Uniform Commercial Code, negotiable instruments enjoy various protections, including the possibility that they will come into the possession of a holder in due course. When the negotiable note is in the hands of a holder in due course, the maker is left with few defenses, thus, the instrument's value is enhanced. Non-negotiable instruments, however, are contractual obligations, which do not enjoy holder in due course protections. The makers of variable interest rate notes sign only a contractual obligation to repay their debt; they had no expectation that holder in due course doctrine would strip them of their defenses.

Extending holder in due course status to the FDIC and its successors respecting non-negotiable instruments is both unnecessary and undesirable. When the FDIC assumes control of an institution, the assets are what they are—negotiable instruments, contracts, real property, and so on. We agree that the FDIC should not be disadvantaged by the circumstances of its assumption of control, but this policy does not require giving the FDIC the ability to transmute lead into gold. Allowing the FDIC to transform contracts into negotiable instruments would defeat the reasonable commercial expectations of the variable interest note makers. Carried only a little further, this transformation would affect all contracts and even the title to real property. Alchemy is the province of Congress; therefore, we decline to extend Murray and Campbell Leasing to non-negotiable instruments.

* * *

CONCLUSION

We hold that the federal holder in due course doctrine does not protect the FDIC or its successors from personal defenses asserted by the makers of non-negotiable instruments. We also conclude that Mr. Montross presented sufficient evidence to avoid summary judgment on the issue whether Old Sunbelt prevented his performance under the non-negotiable note. Finally, respecting Mr. Montross' affirmative defenses to New Sunbelt's deficiency action, we conclude that a summary judgment ruling is premature. Accordingly, we reverse and remand for consistent proceedings.

The 5th Circuit granted an en banc rehearing. Following is the en banc decision.

RESOLUTION TRUST CORP. v. MONTROSS

United States Court of Appeals, Fifth Circuit, 1991.
944 F.2d 227.

PER CURIAM. The panel held that the federal holder in due course status of Sunbelt Savings, transferee of the notes from the Federal Savings and Loan Insurance Corporation as receiver for the insolvent former Sunbelt Savings, does not protect Sunbelt from personal defenses of the maker of a promissory note which was not negotiable from its inception. The panel opinion at 923 F.2d 353 is reinstated, except that we take no position on the effect of the variable interest rate on the negotiability of the note. The maker of the note gave other reasons for the note being non-negotiable, and the case was presented on the appeal with both parties accepting the non-negotiability of the note. Sunbelt's contention to the contrary before the en banc court comes too late. See Najarro v. First Federal Savings & Loan Ass'n of Nacogdoches, Texas, 918 F.2d 513, 516 (5th Cir.1990); Moore v. United States, 598 F.2d 439, 441 (5th Cir.1979).

The personal defenses to which the maker is entitled must, of course, be based on documents of the savings institution at the time of its insolvency and not upon secret agreements unenforceable under D'Oench, Duhme & Co. v. FDIC, 315 U.S. 447, 62 S.Ct. 676, 86 L.Ed. 956 (1942). See Howell v. Continental Credit Corp., 655 F.2d 743 (7th Cir.1981).

As recited in the conclusion of the panel opinion, the summary judgment in favor of Sunbelt Savings was premature. The case is remanded for further proceedings.

Reversed and remanded.

D. RIGHTS OF TAKER FROM HOLDER IN DUE COURSE—THE SHELTER PRINCIPLE

KOST v. BENDER

Michigan Supreme Court, 1872.
25 Mich. 515.

The declaration in this case is upon a promissory note which was given to the plaintiff by the defendant as part payment on a purchase of land supposed to be valuable for the production of mineral oil. The defense is, that the defendant was defrauded in the sale, and has sustained damages in consequence, which he is entitled to recoup.

The note is negotiable, and was transferred by the plaintiff, before it fell due, to a party who, he claims, was a *bona fide* purchaser, without notice of any infirmity, and who afterward, for a new consideration, sold it back to him. And the plaintiff further claims, that the note having once passed to a *bona fide* holder, in whose hands it was subject to no defense of fraud in inception, or defect in consideration, is forever thereafter discharged of such defense, into whose hands soever it may afterward come.

It is perfectly true as a general rule, that the *bona fide* holder of negotiable paper has a right to sell the same, with all the rights and equities attaching to it in his own hands, to whoever may see fit to buy of him, whether such purchaser was aware of the original infirmity or not. Without this right he would not have the full protection which the law merchant designs to afford him, and negotiable paper would cease to be a safe and reliable medium for the exchanges of commerce. For if one can stop the negotiability of paper against which there is no defense, by giving notice that a defense once existed while it was held by another, it is obvious that an important element in its value is at once taken away.

But I am not aware that this rule has ever been applied to a purchase by the original payee, nor can I perceive that it is essential to the protection of the innocent indorsee, that it should be. It can not be very important to him, that there is one person incapable of succeeding to his equities, and who consequently would not be likely to become a purchaser. If he may sell to all the rest of the community, the market value of his security is not likely to be affected by the circumstance that a single individual can not compete for its purchase, especially when we consider that the nature of negotiable securities is such that their market value is very little influenced by competition. Nor do I perceive that any rule or principle of law would be violated by permitting the maker to set up this defense against the payee, when he becomes indorsee, with the same effect as he might have done before it had been sold at all, or that there is any valid reason against it.

The ground of defense is, the claim for damages which the maker has, by reason of the fraud alleged to have been practiced upon him. It is not pretended that this claim is extinguished by the sale of the note, but only that it is thereby separated from the note and incapable of again becoming annexed to it. After the payee had sold the note, he might have been sued upon this claim, and when he again becomes the holder, he is indisputably liable in some form. The question, then, seems to be, whether the maker shall be compelled to submit to judgment on his note, and then resort to a separate action for damages, or whether all disputes growing out of the one transaction shall be submitted to one jury.

In general, the policy of the law is to avoid circuity of action, wherever it can be done without confusion; and cases of a counterclaim like this, are always held to be proper cases for the application of this rule of policy. And if we do not apply it in this case, it must be because of a purely technical reason, and not because the interests of justice would be prejudiced.

The technical reason is, that by the sale of the note to a *bona fide* holder the claim for damages has been severed from it, and the payee when he again becomes holder, will sue upon it in his character of indorsee, and can not have his demand reduced by a claim which could only be offset because of its being an incident to the debt, and which ceased to be an incident when the first transfer took place. But there are many cases in which the law, to avoid circuity of action, disregards such intermediate transactions, and remits the parties to their original rights and equities, with a view to the most speedy and effectual remedy. When this defense was severed from the note by the first transfer, it was done by means of the plaintiff's own wrong. If the defendant had a legal and just defense to the note, either in whole or in part, arising from the conduct of the plaintiff, it was the duty of the latter to recognize and allow it, and he had no moral right to cut it off, or to attempt so to do, by any transfer. But, having done so, and afterward acquired the note a second time, the law, we think, will not permit him to take advantage of this wrong, but will remit the defendant to his original rights. Such, we think, should be the rule; because it avoids circuity of action, expense to the parties, and inconvenience to the courts, without, at the same time, endangering any substantial rights.

For the Article 3 position on the issues raised in *Kost,* see OR 3–201(1), R 3–203(b).

E. DEFENSES TO WHICH AN HDC IS SUBJECT—"REAL DEFENSES"

The materials up to this point in the chapter have focused attention on the elements of HDC status and the policies that inform the applications and limitations of the doctrine. For the most part we have seen HDCs enforce their rights free of the defenses of parties obligated on negotiable instruments. But, as noted at the outset, there are limits to the courts' willingness to vindicate the general interests of commerce at the expense of individual transactors. The primary limitations are described in the very section which provides the due course status of certain holders. Review OR 3–305 and R 3–305 and R 3–306 before considering the materials that follow.

The previous sections of this chapter considered the ways in which the drafters and the courts have circumscribed the opportunities for assertion of HDC status by their promulgation and construction of the particular requisites to the prosecution of due course rights. This section treats those impediments to the enforceability of a payment obligation that not even the social and financial force of the HDC doctrine can overcome.

SCHAEFFER v. UNITED BANK & TRUST CO. OF MARYLAND

Maryland Court of Special Appeals, 1976.
32 Md.App. 339, 360 A.2d 461 aff'd 280 Md. 10, 370 A.2d 1138 (1977).

MOORE, J.

The ultimate question presented here is whether the Circuit Court for Prince George's County properly granted appellee-payee's motion for a directed verdict in an action upon an installment note where there was evidence that appellant, an accommodation maker, was unable to read and had been told by the accommodated party, who had been his supervisor and friend, that the document he was signing was a "character reference."

I

In early 1973 James and Marie Estepp, husband and wife, sought a debt consolidation loan from the United Bank and Trust Company of Maryland. The bank was unwilling to make them an unsecured loan for the amount they desired without the additional signature of a real property owner in Prince George's County. To that end Mr. Estepp then approached appellant, Marvin O. Schaeffer, whom he supervised at work at the Tantallon Country Club and who owned real property in Clinton. On May 19, 1973, the Estepps signed the face of an "Unsecured Installment Note" in the amount of $5,622.69 and appellant signed the reverse side which was blank. The note contained a standard confession of judgment clause.

After the Estepps had made a few of the required monthly installments of $192.93, the payments ceased and the bank communicated with appellant. Appellant advised the bank of Mr. Estepp's new telephone number and place of employment, in Las Cruces, New Mexico. The bank contacted Estepp there but, his assurances to the contrary notwithstanding, no further payments were ever received.

In due course, appellant was invited to the bank "to make arrangements for him to start paying on the loan." He endeavored, unsuccessfully, to have the Estepps resume the payments and the bank ultimately obtained judgment by confession against him in the amount of $5,313.83. Appellant's motion to vacate the confessed judgment was granted (Couch, J.) and appellant filed a general issue plea. He also alleged that the bank obtained the note "by misrepresentation and without consideration to or from the defendant" and "in violation of the Federal Consumer Protection Act and Article 49 of the Annotated Code of Maryland" [now §§ 12–106 and 12–114(b) of the Commercial Law Article], which provides that lenders must furnish borrowers with certain information concerning the terms of the loan. Appellant also prayed a jury trial.

At the conclusion of its case the bank moved for a directed verdict, which the court denied. At the conclusion of the entire case, the bank renewed its motion and it was granted. The court stated:

> It is unfortunate that he may have a limited education and the Court can sympathize with him, *but I do not think that the United Bank did anything wrong in this case in its dealings and I have not seen any evidence here today that it committed any kind of fraud on this particular defendant.* I have given you all the latitude that I can to try to show some fraud or misrepresentation. You have not been able to do it to my satisfaction.
>
> I do not think that I should submit this case to a jury and that is how I feel about it. I do not think they should be allowed to speculate on this because you have not met the burden that the Court of Appeals has made out to show some kind of fraud or misrepresentation.

(Emphasis added.)

It is manifest that the court overlooked evidence of fraud on the part of the maker, James Estepp, and herein resides reversible error.

II

When the trial court was required—by the bank's motion for a directed verdict—to rule upon the legal sufficiency of the evidence for submission to the jury of appellant's liability on the note, it had to assume the truth of all credible evidence and of all inferences fairly deducible therefrom and consider them in the light most favorable to appellant as the party against whom the motion was made. It is only when such evidence and inferences lead to conclusions from which reasonable minds could not differ, that the issue is one of law for the court and not one of fact for the jury. *Holloway v. Hauver,* 22 Md.App. 303, 322 A.2d 890 (1974); *Lauer v. Scott,* 12 Md.App. 555, 280 A.2d 917 (1971).

During the course of the brief trial below, appellant was called by the bank as its own witness. He identified his signature on the reverse side of the note but also stated that he had only a third grade education and had limited reading ability. "I can't sit down and read a newspaper or nothing." He was asked by the bank's counsel why he did not consider himself responsible for the debt and the following colloquy ensued:

> **Q.** Well, Mr. Schaeffer, will you tell us please why you do not feel apparently that you should pay this debt?
>
> **A.** Because Jim Estepp when he told me to sign that paper it wasn't for paying a debt.
>
> **Q.** Well now, you are saying Jim Estepp. You are not saying United Bank and Trust Company; is that correct?
>
> **A.** No, Jim told me that when he filled the application out to sign and I signed it. He said it was a character witness.
>
> * * *
>
> **Q.** Are you stating nobody explained to you that this was a note?
>
> **A.** No, sir.

Under questioning by his own counsel, appellant testified that he had known Estepp for approximately eight years, that Estepp had been his boss at the Tantallon Country Club and had assisted him in the making of funeral arrangements at the time of appellant's wife's death. "I thought he was a wonderful guy," he said.

The officer in charge of installment loans on the date of the transaction with the Estepps explained the circumstances surrounding appellant's signing of the note:

> **A.** Well, I told Mr. Schaeffer that he would—that he was responsible for the loan if he signed the note and he didn't say anything and then he and Mr. Estepp started talking about something and I felt that the man maybe didn't know, I don't know, that he was signing as an endorser so I thought that they should talk it over and I left. When I came back I asked them if it was straight, if everything was all right, and he signed the note. That's all I know.

In appellant's own case, his stepmother testified that the vision in his right eye had been impaired by a bottle explosion, that he had attended school only until the third grade, had a learning disability and could not read or write. His brother-in-law testified that he had completed the job application for appellant's then employment as a groundskeeper and mechanic because "He can't read and write."

Under the established rule, previously stated, the evidence in the light most favorable to the appellant would establish (1) that he was almost illiterate, (2) that the nature of the transaction was not explained to him by the bank, (3) that he did not understand that he was assuming any financial responsibility when he signed the note and (4) that Mr. Estepp falsely and fraudulently misrepresented the document. This evidence mounts up to fraud in the factum.

Fraud in the factum, unaccompanied by negligence, is one of the most potent defenses in the realm of commercial law. When it is successfully interposed it bars recovery not only by the promisee on a simple contract (Restatement, Contracts § 475), but also by a holder in due course, § 3–305 [R 3–305], Commercial Law Article.

In discussing the elements of fraud in the factum, official comment 7 [comment 1 to R 3–305] to § 3–305 of the Commercial law Article is instructive:

> The test of the defense here stated is that of excusable ignorance of the contents of the writing signed. The party must not only have been in ignorance, but must also have had no reasonable opportunity to obtain knowledge. In determining what is a reasonable opportunity all relevant factors are to be taken into account, including the age and sex of the party, his intelligence, education and business experience; his ability to read or to understand English, the representations made to him and his reason to rely on them or to have confidence in the person making them; the presence or absence of any third person who might read or explain the instrument to him, or any other possibility of obtaining independent information; and the apparent necessity, or lack of it, for acting without delay.

Here appellant was a man of limited intelligence, little education, and virtually no ability to read English. His supervisor at work, who had assisted him in the funeral of his wife, and in whom he "had complete confidence in what he said" at the time the note was signed, misrepresented the very essence of the transaction.

In a strikingly similar case, a New Jersey court observed:

> The evidence supports the trial court's finding that De Paul signed the note in issue in reliance upon the false representation made to him by the maker, Ronald Perkowsky, that he was signing only a "character reference" which Perkowsky needed in connection with the purchase of merchandise from Bushberg Brothers of Union City, the payee of the instrument. Because of his subnormal mentality, his only schooling having been in a "special class" of the public school, De Paul was not able to read, except small words, and then he needed reading glasses for this purpose. When he signed this note, he did not read it; he had no reading glasses with him, and the note was not read to him by Perkowsky or the representative of Bushberg Brothers who witnessed his signature. It seems clear, therefore, that the district court was correct in finding that De Paul's signature was obtained as the result of fraud in the factum, without any negligence on his part.
>
> * * *
>
> The rationale of the defense is the fundamental of contract law that one cannot be bound on an obligation he does not know he is entering into. Restatement, Contracts, § 475, *Amsterdam v. De Paul,* 70 N.J.Super. 196, 175 A.2d 219, 200 (App.Div.1961). See also, *Kearney v. Commerce Investment Co.,* 262 A.2d 804 (D.C.App. 1970).

Here, of course, the bank was not a holder in due course, but the same considerations lead us to the conclusion that appellant was a victim of fraud in the factum.

In Amsterdam the plaintiff holder in due course argued that since the fraud was perpetrated by a maker upon a comaker rather than by the payee, "the defense was not available as against the payee or its transferee, the plaintiff." 175 A.2d at 221. In the instant case the bank correctly argues that "there was no testimony or evidence of fraud perpetrated by the appellee on the appellant." This argument is, however, irrelevant. When the individual charged on a note successfully interposes the defense of fraud in the factum it is immaterial *who* perpetrated the fraud. As the New Jersey court said in Amsterdam:

> [W]e find no validity in such a distinction. A negotiable instrument which is the product of fraud in the factum, unaccompanied by negligence, as distinguished from an instrument which is the product of fraud in the treaty, is void, and not merely voidable. As stated in 17 C.J.S. Contracts § 140, p. 495:
>
> > Where some trick is used to substitute another instrument for the one which it is intended to sign, as where a note is substituted for a receipt, and in like cases, the signature has no legal effect, * * * Hence there is no agreement which can give rights to anyone, except where the signer is estopped by negligence or otherwise to set up the truth as against bona fide third persons * * *.
>
> In *McDonald v. Central R.R. Co.,* 89 N.J.L. 251, 254, 98 A. 391, 392 (E. & A.1916) the court said:
>
> > A misrepresentation of the contents of a document by which one is induced to sign a paper thinking it is other than it really is is the typical case of fraud in the execution; it is a case where the defrauded party may properly say, "I never agreed to that, and hence the document is not my deed." 175 A.2d at 221.

Because there was evidence in this case from which a jury could have found appellant not liable on the note, it was error for the court to grant a directed verdict for the bank. In so holding, we are mindful that counsel for the appellant did not argue here—nor in the court below—the issue of fraud on the part of Mr. Estepp. This is not a situation governed by Maryland Rule 1085, under which the scope of our review is limited to questions which "have been tried and decided by the lower court." The motion by the bank for a directed verdict was made on the ground that Mr. Schaeffer had failed to prove any fraud or misrepresentation on the part of the bank. As we have seen, however, the absence of fraudulent conduct on the part of the payee was not dispositive of the case. It was incumbent on the trial court, in its consideration of the motion for a directed verdict, to consider the sufficiency of *all* the evidence on the issue of Schaeffer's liability on the note in the light of the pleadings. The defense of fraud in the factum was within the ambit of the general issue plea, since that plea properly encompasses any defense other than those which must be specially pleaded under the provisions of a statute or rule. Md.Rule 342; *Herrick v. Swomley,* 56 Md. 439, 456 (1881); 2 Poe, *Pleading and Practice,* §§ 606–608 (6th ed. 1970).

III

Appellant makes several arguments that require consideration, although only minimal, because a new trial must be ordered.

Much is made of the fact that two witnesses, Mr. Buckingham and his predecessor at the bank, Betty R. Coleman, characterized appellant as being an "endorser" of the note. Since the note provided that

> It is agreed by any person, firm or corporation who writes his, her or its name or signature on the face or back of this instrument, that they and each of them shall be regarded as makers as between them and each of them and any holder hereof.

and because § 3–402 [R 3–204(a)] of the Commercial Law Article, Annot Code of Md. (1975) provides that "Unless the instrument clearly indicates that a signature is made in some other capacity it is an endorsement," it is clear that appellant was, if anything, a maker of the note. It seems to us, however, that it is of little moment whether appellant was a maker or an endorser since the contract and warranty liabilities of each class of signatories to a note are not so dissimilar as to predicate appellant's liability here upon the distinction between a maker and an endorser. Commercial Law Art, §§ 3–413, 3–414, 3–417 [R 3–412, 3–414, 3–415, 3–416, 3–417].

Appellant is also off the mark in his stubborn pursuit of the trial court's refusal to permit him to elicit testimony concerning the fact that he had received no consideration from the bank for the note. As a leading text states:

> At the outset one should understand that an accommodation party's failure to receive dollars in his pocket from the creditor is not a defense. Time and again sureties respond to a holder's suit by arguing, "I am a surety and I did not receive consideration for my contract." This is a losing argument. Section 3–415(2) [R 3–419(b)] specifically provides that the surety is liable to a taker (and a fortiori, holders and holders in due course) when the instrument is taken for value before it is due. Regardless whether the surety signs gratuitously or receives compensation, his obligation is supported by the consideration which moves from the creditor to the principal debtor. (Footnotes omitted.)

White and Summers, *Uniform Commercial Code,* § 13–14 (1972) at 433 and the cases therein cited.

Finally, even if the bank did not furnish appellant a copy of the statement described in § 12–106 of the Commercial Law Article, such failure did not provide appellant with a defense to the bank's action. That statement is, by the terms of § 12–106(b), required to be given to the "borrower"; and the latter term is defined in § 12–101(b) as a "person who borrows money under this subtitle." We do not find that appellant's status as an accommodation maker falls within that definition. Furthermore, § 12–114 provides a criminal penalty for failure to furnish such a statement when it is required, but the statute does not address itself to civil remedies.

Judgment reversed; case remanded for a new trial; costs to be paid by appellee.

Problem

Minor had a check for $2,000 payable to him. He indorsed it over to A as the price of an automobile he purchased from A. A few days later Minor decided to rescind the transaction with A. Under the law of the state the Minor can rescind. In the meantime, A had transferred the check to Y. It appears that A is insolvent and will not be able to return to Minor the $2,000. Minor asks the drawer of the check to stop payment thereon and drawer does so. Can Minor recover back the check from Y? Can drawer defend against Y that the Minor has rescinded the transaction in which Minor indorsed the check over to A? Can Y recover against Minor on Minor's indorsement of the check? In addition to OR 3–305, R 3–305(a)(1)(i), see OR 3–207, R 3–102.

Note

There are very few cases in which a party successfully avoids liability because of "fraud in the factum." There are a few more cases in which parties have avoided liability to holders in due course because of illegality in the underlying transaction. In some states usury makes the transaction void, in some states an obligation of a corporation not licensed to do business in the state is void, and in many states a check given for a gambling debt is void. It is surprising to learn that even in Nevada checks given for gambling debts are void. See *Sandler v. Eighth Judicial Dist. Court,* 96 Nev. 622, 614 P.2d 10 (1980).

F. POLICY JUSTIFICATION FOR THE HOLDER–IN–DUE–COURSE CONCEPT

The HDC concept represents a legislative decision regarding the relative rights of innocent parties when the circumstances dictate that a loss must be borne by one of them. Between the innocent drawer of a check who has received faulty goods from the payee and the innocent transferee of the check, the Code provides that the transferee, in most cases, will be able to enforce the check against the drawer. That result maintains notwithstanding any injustice suffered by the drawer at the hands of the seller of the faulty goods.

Because the justification for the doctrine is founded upon market considerations, it is necessary to consider the elements of HDC status and the benefits which flow from recognizing such favored transactors in terms of the market in negotiable instruments. While it would be inaccurate to conclude that the only societal interest to be considered is efficiency, the cash-substitute nature of paper-based payment media and resultant need for efficiency cannot be ignored.

The elements of HDC status established in OR and R 3–302 provide only half the calculus; the benefits of due course status can only be realized if the instrument is negotiable. Therefore, the OR and R 3–104 elements of negotiability must be satisfied in addition to the elements of HDC status in 3–302 before the commercial interest in the expeditious flow of payment and credit instruments will preempt common law contract and assignment principles. The consequences of that conjunction for the commercial law student, practitioner, and reviewing court should be manifest: In testing the facts of the particular case against the several elements of negotiability and HDC status the courts have a series of opportunities to balance the equities of the particular case against market integrity considerations. Consider the remarks of Grant Gilmore, a noted commercial law scholar and one of the Code drafters.

GILMORE, THE COMMERCIAL DOCTRINE OF GOOD FAITH PURCHASE

63 Yale L.J. 1057 (1954).

The triumph of the good faith purchaser has been one of the most dramatic episodes in our legal history. In his several guises, he serves a commercial function: he is protected not because of his praiseworthy character, but to the end that commercial transactions may be engaged in without elaborate investigation of property rights and in reliance on the possession of property by one who offers it for sale or to secure a loan. As the doctrine strikes roots in one or another field, the "good faith" component tends to atrophy and the commercial purchaser is protected with little more than lip service paid to his "bona fides."

* * *

The good faith purchase idea takes on an extra dimension of complexity when intangibles and not goods are concerned. Goods have an ascertainable location in space and time. If they are in Connecticut it is obvious, even to the legal mind, that they are not in New York. If A, the owner, sells goods to B, then A, except for claims based on breach of warranty, has nothing further to do with them. Nor has anyone ever doubted that goods can be sold. Even if, theoretically, goods can be made the subject of the sort of future interests which make up so much of our real property law, they have never in fact been so burdened.

* * *

The development of the law of good faith purchase in this field [negotiable instruments] has * * * had to take account of burdensome complexities which were not met with in the relatively simple case of goods. It has been necessary to work out a number of subordinate propositions in addition to the basic one that the purchaser in good faith and for value gets "title" or "good title" or even "perfect title." It is this network of good faith purchase rules that we mean when we describe paper as "negotiable."

* * *

Few generalizations have been more often repeated, or by generations of lawyers more devoutly believed, than this: negotiability is a matter rather of form than substance. It is bred in the bone of every lawyer that an instrument to be negotiable must be "a courier without luggage."

* * *

[T]he cherished belief in the sacrosanct nature of formal requisites serves, as do most legal principles, a useful function. The problem is what types of paper shall be declared negotiable so that purchasers may put on the nearly invincible armor of the holder in due course. The policy in favor of protecting the good faith purchaser does not run beyond the frontiers of commercial usage. Beyond those confines every reason of policy dictates the opposite approach. The formal requisites are the professional rules with which professionals are or ought to be familiar. As to instruments which are amateur productions outside any concept of the ordinary course of business, or new types which are just coming into professional use, it is wiser to err by being unduly restrictive than by being over liberal. The formal requisites serve as a useful exclusionary device and as a brake on a too rapid acceptance of emerging trends.

Compare Professor Gilmore's position some time later.

GILMORE, THE GOOD FAITH PURCHASE IDEA AND THE UNIFORM COMMERCIAL CODE: CONFESSIONS OF A REPENTANT DRAFTSMAN

15 Ga.L.Rev. 605 (1981).

More than twenty-five years ago, I wrote a lengthy article which I called "The Commercial Doctrine of Good Faith Purchase." The article summarized, quite accurately, what we all then believed to be the truth of the matter as we had learned the truth from Karl Llewellyn. Rereading the article today, my thought is that it contained a great many elegant descriptions of the trees; what it missed was the forest.

* * *

The good faith purchaser of bills and notes—who was renamed "holder in due course" a hundred years later—arrived with Lord Mansfield and his colleagues. In an incredibly short time, as such things go in the law, it was established that the purchaser of a bill or note who had given value in good faith and without notice in the ordinary course of his business held the instrument free of any outstanding equities of ownership as well as of defenses, such as lack of consideration or fraud, that might have tainted the original transaction. The purchaser was put under no duty of inquiry as to the previous history of the bill or note that came into his hands.

* * *

The moral of the story, as we saw it, was that whenever any kind of property came into the market—that is, became the subject of a large volume of transactions either of outright sale or of transfer for security—then that kind of property sooner or later acquired some or all of the attributes of negotiability: commercial property must be freely transferable—no restraints on alienation can be tolerated; the good faith purchaser for value, at least from the time the property comes into his possession, holds it free both of equities of ownership and of contract defenses; no adverse claims can prevail over the title acquired by good faith purchase. We believed that the process was irreversible: the attributes of negotiability, once acquired, could never be lost.

* * *

In the case of the negotiable instrument construct, the answers appear to be clear. In the late eighteenth century, mercantile bills of exchange and bank notes, a sort of unofficial currency which the merchants and bankers had invented, served as an indispensable supplement to the official currencies, which were in short supply. Without these bills and notes, the primitive banking system could not possibly have coped with the enormously increased number of transactions that followed the industrial revolution. This commercial paper typically passed from hand to hand in a long series of transfers, ending up in the hands of strangers who knew nothing about the original transaction or about earlier transfers of the bill or note and had no way of finding out about them. The need to protect the strangers who bought the paper in the market, even at the cost of doing harm to the obligors and earlier holders, was the compelling reason that led the courts to elaborate the good faith purchaser, or holder in due course, idea in negotiable instruments law.

After the middle of the nineteenth century, currency reforms and modern uses of bank credit made this mercantile currency unnecessary and obsolete. Mercantile paper, to the extent that it remained in use, no longer circulated in anything that could be described as a market; the strangers who had once bought the paper had by 1900 become an extinct species. There are clear indications in the late nineteenth-century case law that the courts—responding to the new situation, as courts, for reasons that escape us, always do—had set about dismantling the structure of the pre-1850 law of negotiable instruments. That discernible trend was interrupted by the codification of the pre-1850 law in the Negotiable Instruments Law (N.I.L.), which was strongly supported by the bankers and their allies and was enacted within the space of a few years throughout the country.

* * *

If, in the 1940's, we had paid any attention to what the courts had been doing for fifty or seventy-five years past, we might have come up with something like this: the good faith purchase idea was an intuitive judicial response to economic conditions that ceased to exist after 1850 or thereabouts. During the second half of the nineteenth century, the courts, losing their enthusiasm for the good faith purchase idea, began cutting back instead of further expanding it.

* * *

I shall not go into any detail about article 3 of the Code, which deals with negotiable instruments, renamed commercial paper. I once commented that article 3 is the N.I.L. doubled in spades—negotiability in excelsis—and went on to say that the article gravely reviews each of the pressure points that had emerged in the N.I.L. case law and resolves the issue in favor of negotiability and the holder in due course. The most outrageous thing about article 3, a statute drafted in the 1940's, is that there is no reference, in text or comment, to the then rapidly developing body of case law holding that finance companies and banks to which consumer notes were negotiated could not hold the notes free of the consumer's contract defenses because of their close connection with the dealer-sellers. That omission has been remedied by an intricate network of state and federal statutes and regulations, but it should never have been tolerated in the first place.

G. NEGOTIABILITY IN THE CONSUMER CONTEXT

de la FUENTE v. HOME SAVINGS ASS'N

Texas Court of Civil Appeals, 1984.
669 S.W.2d 137.

KENNEDY, JUSTICE.

This is an appeal from a suit on a note brought by appellee, Home Savings, against appellants, Pedro and Paula de la Fuente. The transaction underlying the note was the sale of materials and services for the installation of aluminum siding for the de la Fuentes' home. We reverse and render judgment for appellants.

Trial was to the court, and findings of fact and conclusions of law were filed. The court's findings of fact are summarized as follows. In late April or early May of 1978, Roberto Gonzales, a representative of Aluminum Industries, Inc., visited the de la Fuente home to sell them aluminum siding. As a result, on May 3, 1978, the de la Fuentes executed, in their residence, a number of documents, including a contract and promissory note for improvements to their home. The contract granted a first lien on appellants' home. The total contract amount was $9,138.24, with 96 monthly installments of $95.19 and an annual percentage rate of 12%. The contract included a trust deed to Aluminum Industries which granted a first lien on the de la Fuentes' residence. Aluminum Industries, Inc. is no longer in existence.

Appellants, by their fourth, sixth and seventh points of error, complain of violations of the Texas Consumer Credit Code, Tex.Rev.Civ. Stat.Ann. art. 5069, et seq. (Vernon 1971).

By their fourth point of error, appellants assert that the trial court erred in concluding that the lien taken in the transaction was not unlawful and, therefore, there was no violation of the Texas Consumer Credit Code. The version of art. 5069–6.05 of the Texas Consumer Credit Code in effect on May 3, 1978 read:

> Art. 6.95 Prohibited Provisions
>
> No retail installment contract * * * shall:
>
> (7) Provide for or grant a first lien upon real estate to secure such obligation, except, (a) such lien as is created by law upon the recording of an abstract of judgment or (b) such lien as is provided for or granted by a contract or series of contracts for the sale or construction and sale of a structure to be used as a residence so long as the time price differential does not exceed an annual percentage rate of 10 percent. Act of May 4, 1977; ch. 104, section 1, 1977 Tex.Gen.Laws, Local and Spec. 212 *amended* by Act of May 8, 1981, ch. 111, section 18, 1981 Tex.Gen.Laws, Local and Spec. 284. See Tex.Rev.Civ.Stat.Ann. art. 5069–6.05 (Vernon Supp.1984).

The trial court, in the findings of fact, found that the contract for Labor and Materials and Trust Deed granted a first lien on appellants' residence. We agree. See *Jim Walter Homes v. Chapa,* 614 S.W.2d 838 (Tex.Civ.App.—Corpus Christi 1981, writ ref'd n.r.e.). The contract and Trust Deed clearly grant a lien, and both the credit report filled out by Robert Gonzales, the salesman, and the undisputed testimony of Pedro de la Fuente show that there was no lien on the appellants' home at the time of the transaction. However, even if we did not agree with this finding, it was not challenged and is binding upon the appellate court. The retail installment contract signed by the de la Fuentes is in violation of the Texas Consumer Credit Code, art. 5069–6.05 in that the contract provided for a first lien on the de la Fuentes' home.

Appellee asserts that, even if the contract is in violation of the Credit Code, appellee is not liable because of its status as a holder in due course under Tex.Bus. & Com.Code Ann. section 3.302 [R 3–302] (Vernon 1968). The trial court found in its conclusions of law both that appellee, as an assignee of the contract, is derivatively liable for all claims against the contract and that appellee is not liable to appellants on the counterclaim because of its status as a holder in due course of appellants' note. We agree that an obligor may assert against the assignee the defenses he could have asserted against the assignor. However, we disagree that appellee was entitled to the protection of a holder in due course of a negotiable instrument, because (1) the holder in due course doctrine has been abolished in consumer credit transactions by FTC regulation; and, (2) the appellee did not conform to the notice requirements of the Texas Credit Code so as to cut off the rights of action and defenses of the buyer. The note in question contained a notice in bold face type which reads in part:

NOTICE

> ANY HOLDER OF THIS CONSUMER CREDIT CONTRACT IS SUBJECT TO ALL CLAIMS AND DEFENSES WHICH THE DEBTOR COULD ASSERT AGAINST THE SELLER OF GOODS OR SERVICES OBTAINED PURSUANT HERETO OR WITH THE PROCEEDS HEREOF. * * *

This FTC Rule, subjecting the holder of the note to the claims and defenses of the debtor, is in direct conflict with the doctrine of the holder in due course. The Federal Courts have stated, without so holding, that the effect of this FTC Rule is to abolish the holder in due course doctrine. *Federal Trade Commission v. Winters National Bank & Trust Co.*, 601 F.2d 395, 397 (6th Cir.1979).

The FTC, in its Statement of Basis and Purposes specifically named the holder in due course doctrine as the evil addressed by 16 C.F.R. section 433.2 "[A] consumer's duty to pay for goods and services must not be separated from a seller's duty to perform as promised * * *" 40 Fed.Reg. 53,506, 53,523 (November 18, 1975). The FTC intended the Rule to compel creditors to either absorb the cost of the seller's misconduct or return them to sellers. 40 F.R. at 53,523. The FTC "reach[ed] a determination that it constitutes an unfair and deceptive practice to use contractual boiler plate to separate a buyer's duty to pay from a seller's duty to perform." 40 F.R. at 53,524. The effect of this Rule is to "give the courts the authority to examine the equities in an underlying sale, and it will prevent sellers from foreclosing judicial review of their conduct. Seller and creditors will be responsible for seller misconduct." 40 F.R. at 43,524 (emphasis added) [sic]. It was clearly the intention of the FTC Rule to have the holder of the paper bear the losses occasioned by the actions of the seller; therefore, the benefits of the holder in due course doctrine under Tex.Bus. & Com. Code Ann. Section 3.302 [R 3–302] are not available when the notice required by the FTC in 16 C.F.R. section 433.2 is placed on a consumer credit contract.

In addition, the holder of a note subject to the Credit Code has an independent duty to ensure that the retail installment contract conforms to the statutory requirements of the Credit Code. Art. 5069–6.97 of the Credit Code provides in part:

> No right of action or defense of a buyer arising out of a retail installment transaction which would be cut off by negotiation, shall be cut off by negotiation of the retail installment contract or retail charge agreement to any third party unless such holder acquires the contract relying in good faith upon a certificate of completion or certificate of satisfaction, if required by the provisions of Article 6.06; and *such holder gives notice of the negotiation to the buyer* as provided in this Article, and within thirty days of the mailing of such notice receives no written notice from the buyer of any facts giving rise to any claim or defense of the buyer. (Emphasis added)

See Tex.Rev.Civ.Stat.Ann. art. 5069–8.01 (Vernon Supp.1984); *Horn v. Nationwide Financial Corp.*, 574 S.W.2d 218 (Tex.Civ.App.—San Antonio 1978, writ ref'd n.r.e.) (interpreting art. 5069–7.07(b) to impose this duty).

We find that appellee is liable under the Texas Consumer Credit Code as a "person who violates this Subtitle * * * by (ii) committing any act or practice prohibited by this Subtitle. * * *" Tex.Rev.Civ. Stat.Ann. art. 5069–8.01(b) (Vernon Supp.1984). Appellee is therefore liable to appellant under art. 5069–8.01(b) for an amount equal to twice the time price differential or interest contracted for, charged, or received but not to exceed $4,000 in a transaction in which the amount financed is in excess of $5,000 and reasonable attorneys' fees fixed by the court. Appellants' fourth point of error is sustained.

* * *

Appellants, by their fifth point of error, complain of a violation of the Home Solicitation Sales Act in that the obligation was assigned within five days of its execution. The trial court found that this transaction met all the requirements of and is governed by the Home Solicitation Sales Act. Tex.Rev.Civ.Stat.Ann. art. 5069–13.01 et seq. (Vernon Supp.1984). The Home Solicitation Sales Act provides:

> Violations
>
> (a) It shall constitute a deceptive trade practice and a violation of this Act for any merchant to: * * *
>
> (6) negotiate, transfer, sell, or assign any note or other evidence of indebtedness to a finance company or other third party prior to midnight of the fifth business day following the day the contract was signed or the goods or services were purchased; * * *
>
> (b) Any sale or contract entered into in a home solicitation transaction in violation of this Act as set out in Subsection (a) of this section is void and unenforceable.
>
> (c) Any merchant who violates a provision of this Act is liable to the consumer for any actual damages suffered by the consumer as a result of the violation, attorneys' fees reasonable in relation to

the amount of work done, and court costs. Tex.Rev.Civ.Stat.Ann. art. 5069–13.03 (Vernon Supp.1983).

Plaintiff's original petition and plaintiff's first amended original petition both contained the following provisions:

II

On *May 3, 1978,* Defendants and Aluminum Industries, Inc. executed a written contract in Hidalgo County, Texas for labor and materials and trust deed for home improvements to be made on Defendants' home, in Pharr, Texas, according to plans and specifications set out in the agreement and in which Defendants agreed to pay the total sum of 9,138.24 to Aluminum Industries, Inc. or its assigns in consideration, said sum to be paid in installments according to the following schedule: no cash down and the balance to be payable in 96 equal successive monthly installments of $95.19 each. * * *

VI

On *May 3, 1978,* Aluminum Industries, Inc. for value received, assigned, transferred and set over to Gulf Republic Service Corporation of Houston, Texas, the aforementioned Retail Installment Contract, and the Note together with all its right, title, and interest in and to the Consumer goods and other property described in the contract.

VII

On July 6, 1978, Gulf Republic Service Corporation for value received, assigned, transferred and set over to Home Savings Association of Houston, Texas, the aforementioned Retail Installment Contract, and the Note together with all its right, title, and interest in and to the consumer goods and other property described in the contract."

Gulf Republic Service Corporation was at the relevant time a wholly owned subsidiary of Home Savings Association of Houston, Texas.

* * *

[A] violation of the Home Solicitation Sales Act was admitted on the face of appellee's petition. At no time did appellee move to amend. We find, therefore, that there was a violation of the Home Solicitation Sales Act in that the note was assigned to a third party on the same day that it was executed. The contract is void and unenforceable. Tex.Rev.Civ.Stat.Ann. art. 5069–13.03(b) (Vernon Supp.1984). Under the Home Solicitation Sales Act, it is not necessary to find that Roberto Gonzales was an agent or employee of Aluminum Industries, Inc. in order to find that the contract is void and unenforceable by any assignee. Appellants' fifth point of error is sustained.

Appellants, by their first, second and third points of error, complain of the amount of the judgment against them.

We hold that the trial court erred in finding that appellants were in default in the amount of $5,800, the original amount of the contract, since it is undisputed that appellants made a payment of $1,142.28.

Appellants' first point of error is sustained.

Because of our disposition of the other points of error, we need not address appellant's points of error numbers two and three.

Appellee, in its brief, raises the issue of the amount of attorney's fees to be awarded appellants. The trial court found that appellants had incurred attorney's fees in the amount of $3,500. Appellees contend that attorney's fees should not be awarded because appellants did not show the hours devoted to each particular cause of action or defense. *Bray v. Curtis,* 544 S.W.2d 816 (Tex.Civ.App.—Corpus Christi 1976, writ ref'd n.r.e.). However, more recent cases have applied the rule that, where recovery is had on each cause of action or where the causes of action are so intertwined as to be more or less inseparable, the total amount of attorney's fees may be awarded, if the attorney's fees are authorized by the causes upon which recovery is had.

Appellants' defense to appellee's action was the assertion of various violations of statutes. This was also the substance of their cross-claims. In their cross-claims, appellants alleged ten causes of action: two violations of the Home Solicitation Sales Act, three violations of the Deceptive Trade Practices Act, four violations of the Texas Consumer Credit Code, and one action in common-law fraud. Recovery is granted on one violation of the Home Solicitation Sales Act and two violations of the Texas Consumer Credit Code. The Deceptive Trade Practice and fraud actions were not pursued in either the trial court or on appeal. We hold that because recovery was had on a substantial number of appellants' causes of action and because the causes of action are more or less inseparable, all requiring proof of the same facts, that the total amount of attorney's fees can be awarded.

It is, therefore, necessary to determine if attorney's fees are awarded under the relevant statutes. The Home Solicitation Sales Act provides: "Any merchant who violates a provision of this Act is liable to the consumer for * * * attorney's fees * * *" Tex.Rev.Civ.Stat.Ann. art. 5069–13.03(c) (Vernon Supp.1984). "Merchant" is defined as "a party to a consumer transaction other than a consumer." Tex.Rev.Civ. Stat.Ann. art. 5069–13.01(4) (Vernon Supp.1984). A party to the contract is the one who has the right to bring an action to enforce the contract.

Alternatively, as a matter of policy, we would hold appellee liable for attorney's fees under the Home Solicitation Sales Act. First, the trial court, in its findings of fact, found that forms for both the retail installment contract and the contract for labor and trust deed were provided to Aluminum Industries by Home Savings Association. Second, the contract was promptly assigned to Home Savings' wholly owned subsidiary. We find that this assignment is the very evil which the statute was intended to prevent. The Home Solicitation Sales Act "was designed to protect residential occupants from high pressure door-to-door salesmen and to allow a 'cooling off' period in which a contract thus negotiated might be rescinded." [Citations omitted.] Assignees of home solicitation contracts must be held responsible for the acts of their assignors; otherwise, we are faced with the prospect of unscrupulous salesmen pressuring consumers into contract, assigning the benefit of the contract for cash, and disappearing. The assignee would be able to collect without risk, when the assignor could not do so. Both as a matter of statutory interpretation and a matter of policy, we find that appellee is responsible for reasonable attorney's fees under the Home Solicitation Sales Act.

As noted above, we also find that appellee is responsible for reasonable attorney's fees under the Consumer Credit Code. Tex.Rev. Cit.Stat.Ann. art. 5069–8.01(a) and (b) (Vernon Supp.1984).

Appellee raises by cross-point that the trial court erred in not finding that appellee was a member of a Federal Home Loan Bank and, as such, that it may avail itself of the protections given by 15 U.S.C.A. § 57a(f)(3). Appellee did not point out what these protections might be, and upon examination of the cited statutory provision, we cannot ascertain what they are.

Appellee's cross-point is overruled.

We REVERSE the judgment of the trial court and RENDER judgment that appellee take nothing and that the contract, the subject of this suit, is null and void and that appellants recover against appellee, Home Savings, in the amount of $4,000 plus attorney's fees of $3,500 as found by the trial court. Costs are adjudged against appellee.

Note

1. *De la Fuente* illustrates the variety of defensive (as well as offensive) weapons available to the consumer/maker of a promissory note. The protections are provided both by the FTC holder in due course rule and by state consumer protection measures. Do such enactments inure to the benefit of all consumers or do careful consumers in effect subsidize the education of the less careful by paying the increased loan costs engendered by the protection regime? So long as the interest rate charged is based in part upon the holder's risk when he takes negotiable paper we might reasonably expect that interest rates would be increased to compensate the financers of consumer transactions for the risks they must assume when buying consumer paper. What arguments would support that type of subsidization?

In that regard, consider this excerpt from an article which appeared prior to the promulgation of the FTC "preservation of consumers' claims and defenses rule."

> A *priori,* the elimination of creditors' freedom from consumer claims and defenses means that those creditors will be unable to collect some obligations they might otherwise collect. Facing such a prospect, financers have several options. They might, for instance, calculate as best they can their prospective lost revenues, adjust their rates—

upward—accordingly, and continue financing consumer transactions as before. Or they might decide that the increased risk makes it unprofitable to deal in consumer paper when there are safer profits to be made investing in, say, pork bellies or soy bean futures. Or they might attempt some combination of these: slightly higher rates with a more discriminating selection of participating dealers. Theoretically, too, they might insist on better quality control and improved sales practices to minimize the instance of consumer dissatisfaction, or larger dealer reserve accounts to shunt losses back to the retailers.

Any one of these responses can produce effects superficially disadvantageous to consumers—higher credit rates, reduced availability of credit, higher prices. Assuming the maintenance of an economic policy that would assure the consuming public maximum credit at minimum cost, the withdrawal of holder in due course protection from financers must entail some compromise with that policy. The proper question, then, is not whether the withdrawal will be cost-free, but whether the costs are, on balance, reasonably tolerable.

Most discussions slough over the possibility of significant countereffects from the abolition of holder in due course. It is asserted, for example, that automobile financing in Pennsylvania has continued unabated since 1937 without the crutch of the holder in due course, and that those states which have enacted such prohibitions have seen little effect on credit costs or availability. One commentator experienced in the credit industry has said that in a "reputable" market the holder in due course rule is "statistically unnecessary." An economist claimed that the effects of the original Uniform Consumer Credit Code provisions on the consumer credit market was not likely to be substantial. It is difficult to quarrel with these judgments in the face of the obviously continuing growth of consumer credit nationally, at the same time when many states are curtailing use of the holder in due course device. But from other quarters come contrary assertions that the death of holder in due course may spell the death of small merchants, or seriously undercut the utility and acceptability of bank credit cards.

Some less dogmatic voices can be heard. A study on the first year's experience under a Connecticut statute eliminating negotiability in door-to-door sales found a marked reduction in institutional financing of such sales, a shift to repurchase agreements, a cutback in incentive payments to dealers, and increased screening of dealers and inspection of their work. From the dealers' perspective there was some noticeable difficulty in getting financing, some resort to direct lending arrangements, and changes in marketing practices, such as greater reliance on cash sales and wealthier customers.

The National Commission on Consumer Finance conducted a Collection Practices and Creditors' Remedies Survey which, with other data, produced conclusions similar to those just described. Where holder in due course was prohibited there was an "observable reduction" in the availability of credit. This was true not only for finance companies which traditionally deal with high risk credit consumers, but also for the market as a whole. The Commission surmised that this was because the rationing of credit by the finance companies "would probably force out of the market many retailers serving marginal risk consumers unable to obtain credit from general market retailers," thus decreasing the overall supply of credit beyond that withdrawn by the finance companies themselves.

The conclusion that abolition of holder in due course has contributed to a constriction of the money market cannot be disproved. Indeed, some confirmation of it has come to this author in correspondence with creditor attorneys who have handled—and lost—recent holder in due course cases, and who note that after the adverse decision either their clients or the originating dealers withdrew from that consumer credit market. This diminished availability may be a temporary adjustment to the onslaught of anti-holder-in-due-course legislation. The National Commission itself doubted whether the repercussions would be as significant as some predicted. But if the consequences to the credit supply are to be kept minimal, it will be because creditors are willing and able to pass on the new risks to dealers in the first instance and ultimately to the consuming public. In this regard, the Commission noted that its recommendations for restrictions on creditor remedies were "inextricably interwoven" with other recommendations it made concerning rates and availability. These recommendations generally called for "realistic" rate ceilings—as proposed in the Uniform Consumer Credit Code—and broad-scale encouragement of entry into the consumer credit market through such means as relaxation of licensing requirements and possible federal chartering of financial institutions.

The most likely prognosis, it seems, is that universal abolition of holder in due course will produce instinctively careful reactions from financers—some initial curtailment of their dealings in consumer paper followed by a gradual reopening of their coffers at higher rates and with more stringent controls over participating merchants.

Whether the impact will be felt more in the cost of credit or in its availability will depend in large measure on whether the additional risks of nonrecovery can be distributed to all consumer debtors. It is often assumed that increased costs can always be "passed through" to consumers, but the assumption may be unfounded for many retail creditors or financers who find themselves bound by rate ceilings on one side and competitive pressure on the other. So, before presuming too much, one must be satisfied that consumer creditors can fairly be charged not only with the risk of increased losses but also with the resulting burden of distribution.

Ralph J. Rohner, *Holder in Due Course in Consumer Transactions: Requiem, Revival, or Reformation?*, 60 Cornell L.Rev. 503, 534–538 (1975). For a thorough discussion of the HDC doctrine in the consumer finance context, see Ray D. Henson & Alphonse M. Squillante, *The Role of the Holder in Due Course Doctrine in Consumer Credit Transactions*, 26 Hastings L.J. 427 (1974).

2. The Federal Trade Commission Holder-in-Due-Course Regulations, 16 C.F.R. Part 433, became effective May 14th, 1976. The Regulations themselves operate directly only against the seller. They make it an unfair or deceptive practice for a seller of goods or services to (a) take from a consumer a note or other promise to pay for the goods that fails to contain the legend required by 16 C.F.R. § 433.2 or (b) accept the proceeds of a purchase money loan unless the lender includes the legend in the loan agreement. While the rule operates directly only against the seller, the legend in the note or contract assigned or in the loan documents in a purchase money loan creates a contractual agreement that defenses the consumer has against the dealer can be asserted against the transferee in the case of a note or other agreement to pay given by the consumer to the merchant, or against the purchase money lender, in the case of a purchase money loan.

It is fairly common for consumer buyers of large ticket items, particularly automobiles, to make an arrangement with their bank for the finance of the purchase before they commence shopping. The arrangement will often include an agreement that the bank will have a security interest in the item purchased to secure the loan. While under U.C.C. Article 9 that transaction would be a purchase money loan, it is not necessarily such under the FTC Rule. Generally, if a borrower borrows money and uses it to buy bad goods or services, the borrower must repay the loan anyway. Borrower received good money, and generally lenders are not required to see that borrowers spend money wisely or well.

The FTC purchase money loan rule is intended rather to prevent the opportunities for circumvention of the FTC rule that would exist if it could be avoided by arranging for a third party to lend to the customer rather than taking an assignment of the seller's right to be paid under the sales contract. See the definition of "purchase money loan," "contract," and "business arrangement" in 16 C.F.R. § 433.1.

Notice that the FTC rule applies only to sales of goods or services. It does not apply to sales of real estate or to sales of securities. Also it applies only to *sales* of goods, not to *leases.*

Many states (including Texas as the *de la Fuente* case shows) have adopted various state consumer credit protection statutes for the violation of which a transferee of a consumer credit contract may have affirmative liability to the consumer. Also, some state statutes deny holder-in-due-course status to transferees of certain real estate sales promissory notes. For example, the Uniform Consumer Credit Code, enacted in twelve states, prohibits the taking of negotiable instruments other than current checks in consumer transactions, which are defined to include sales of real estate if the interest charge is greater than 12%. See U.C.C.C. §§ 3–307, 1–301(12). The U.C.C.C. prohibition also applies to consumer leases. U.C.C.C. § 3–307.

3. *The Federal Credit Card Rules.*

12 C.F.R. § 226.12(c). Right of cardholder to assert claims or defenses against card issuer [24]—(1) General Rule. When a person who

24. This paragraph does not apply to the use of a check guarantee card or a debit card in connection with an overdraft credit plan, or to a check guarantee card

honors a credit card fails to resolve satisfactorily a dispute as to property or services purchased with the credit card in a consumer credit transaction, the cardholder may assert against the card issuer all claims (other than tort claims) and defenses arising out of the transaction and relating to the failure to resolve the dispute. The cardholder may withhold payment up to the amount of credit outstanding for the property or services that gave rise to the dispute and any finance or other charges imposed on that amount.[25]

(2) Adverse credit reports prohibited. If, in accordance with paragraph (c)(1) of this section, the cardholder withholds payment of the amount of credit outstanding for the disputed transaction, the card issuer shall not report that amount as delinquent until the dispute is settled or judgment is rendered.

(3) Limitations. The rights stated in paragraphs (c)(1) and (2) of this section apply only if:

(i) The cardholder has made a good faith attempt to resolve the dispute with the person honoring the credit card; and

(ii) The amount of credit extended to obtain the property or services that result in the assertion of the claim or defense by the cardholder exceeds $50, and the disputed transaction occurred in the same state as the cardholder's current designated address or, if not within the same state, within 100 miles from that address.[26]

used in connection with cash advance checks.

25. The amount of the claim or defense that the cardholder may assert shall not exceed the amount of credit outstanding for the disputed transaction at the time the cardholder first notifies the card issuer or the person honoring the credit card of the existence of the claim or defense. To determine the amount of credit outstanding for purposes of this section, payments and other credits shall be applied to: (1) Late charges in the order of entry to the account; then to (2) finance charges in the order of entry to the account; and then to (3) any other debits in the order of entry to the account. If more than one item is included in a single extension of credit, credits are to be distributed pro rata according to prices and applicable taxes.

26. The limitations stated in paragraph (c)(3)(ii) of this section shall not apply when the person honoring the credit card: (1) Is the same person as the card issuer; (2) is controlled by the card issuer directly or indirectly; (3) is under the direct or indirect control of a third person that also directly or indirectly controls the card issuer; (4) controls the card issuer directly or indirectly; (5) is a franchised dealer in the card issuer's products or services; or (6) has obtained the order for the disputed transaction through a mail solicitation made or participated in by the card issuer.

Chapter 3

CONTRACT LIABILITY*

A. INTRODUCTION

This chapter deals with the liability of makers, acceptors, drawers, and indorsers and with the special rules applicable to persons who sign negotiable instruments as sureties. It also considers events that result in the discharge of the liability of persons who have signed negotiable instruments.

In Chapter 2 you learned that, except as against a holder in due course, a person liable on an instrument can assert any defense that would be available in an action on a simple contract, except that rights of setoff arising out of unrelated transactions may not be available as against holders, though they would be available as against ordinary assignees. In this chapter, therefore, we will not consider the availability of ordinary contract defenses to the liability Article 3 imposes on parties to instruments. Rather we consider here the extent of liability and the conditions thereto imposed by Article 3.

In addition to the contract liability discussed in this chapter, transferors of commercial paper have warranty liability. While that liability might be described as "contractual," the warranties for the most part are warranties against prior forgery, embezzlement, or fraud and are covered in Chapter 4.

B. AGENT LIABILITY: FORM OF SIGNATURE

The following two cases deal with the circumstances under which an agent is personally liable on an instrument that the agent signs on behalf of her principal. That question is dealt with in OR 3–403 and R 3–402.

* Throughout this text, the designation "OR" refers to an Article in its original form; "R" denotes a revised Article. E.g., OR 3–303 refers to Original Article 3; R 3–303 refers to Revised Article 3.

WURZBURG BROTHERS, INC. v. COLEMAN

Alabama Supreme Court, 1981.
404 So.2d 334.

FAULKNER, J.

The issue on appeal is the effect of a signature on a note by an agent who does not indicate his representative capacity. James H. Coleman, defendant, is the president and 25% shareholder of Coleman American Moving Services, Inc., (Coleman American). Coleman American is a publicly owned Delaware corporation, with several subsidiaries in the south and west. Mr. Coleman is on the board of directors of each corporation and was convicted of securities fraud for activities arising out of his positions with Coleman American. The plaintiff, Wurzburg Brothers, Inc., (Wurzburg) sold supplies to Coleman American on an open account. Coleman American became behind on its payments and issued several checks which were returned to Wurzburg for insufficient funds. The credit manager of Wurzburg feared that Coleman American would become insolvent. On November 14, 1979, the credit manager and the president of Wurzburg procured a note from Coleman to secure the debt. The note stated that "Coleman American Moving Services, Inc. promises to pay" $44,419.68. The note was signed "James H. Coleman." The note did not indicate that Mr. Coleman signed in his representative capacity as president of Coleman American. Mr. Coleman controlled the drafting of the note. The credit manager of the plaintiff corporation testified that Wurzburg intended that Mr. Coleman personally guarantee the debt of Coleman American. The defendant contends, however, that he signed as representative of Coleman American and that the debt is not his, but that of the corporation. Coleman American defaulted on the payment for the supplies sold to it on open account. Coleman American filed a petition of bankruptcy in the United States Bankruptcy Court for the District of Kansas.

The plaintiff brought an action on the note against James Coleman. After a hearing ore tenus, the trial judge entered a judgment in favor of the defendant, Mr. Coleman. Wurzburg now appeals. We reverse.

This action presents two basic issues. First, whether parol evidence is admissible by Coleman as the signer of a note to disestablish his liability on the note. Second, assuming that parol evidence is admissible, did Coleman satisfactorily rebut the presumption raised by Code 1975, § 7–3–403(2)(b) [R 3–402(b)(2)], that he is personally liable on the note. The construction of § 7–3–403(2) [R 3–402(b)] is a question of first impression in Alabama.

Code 1975 § 7–3–403 codifies § 3–403 [R 3–402] of the Uniform Commercial Code.

* * *

The issue of whether parol evidence is admissible to disestablish the signer's liability depends on which provision of Code 1975, § 7–3–

403(2) [R 3–402(b)] applies. Under § 7–3–403(2)(a) [R 3–402(b)(1)], parol evidence is inadmissible to nullify the signer's liability. But, under § 7–3–403(2)(b) [R 3–402(b)(2)], parol evidence is admissible between the immediate parties to the instrument. In turn, the determination of whether Code 1975, § 7–3–403(2)(a) [R 3–402(b)(2)] or § 7–3–403(2)(b) [R 3–402(b)(2)] is applicable depends on whether § 7–3–403(2) authorizes examination of the entire face of the instrument, or the signature only, to see if the person represented is named.

The purpose of Code 1975, § 7–3–403 [R 3–402] is to encourage certainty and definiteness in the law of commercial paper. See *Rotuba Extruders, Inc. v. Ceppos,* 46 N.Y.2d 223, 413 N.Y.S.2d 141, 385 N.E.2d 1068 (1978). The taker of a negotiable instrument should be able "to tell at a glance whose obligation they hold." *Id.* (quoting J. White & R. Summers, *Uniform Commercial Code,* at 13–2 (1972)). While there is authority that only the form of the signature may be examined to determine whether there is ambiguity, see *St. Regis Paper Co. v. Wicklund,* 23 Wash.App. 527, 597 P.2d 926 (1979), the language of § 7–3–403 indicates otherwise. The statute permits admission of parol evidence *between the immediate parties* "if the *instrument* names the person represented but does not show that the representative signed in a representative capacity" (emphasis added). The statute does not say that "if the signature names the person represented" parol evidence is admissible. The language of the section indicates that the entire face of the instrument may be given attention when discovering who is liable on the instrument. This interpretation of Code 1975, § 7–3–403 [R 3–402], is not inconsistent with the goal of the law of commercial paper to foster certainty and definiteness. Examination of the face of the negotiable instrument is not an undue burden to place on a holder of the instrument. We hold that under Code 1975, § 7–3–403 [R 3–402], the face of the instrument must put a person on notice as to who is liable on the instrument. If the face of the note names the person represented but does not show the signer's representative capacity, or vice versa, parol evidence is admissible between the immediate parties to the instrument under § 7–3–403(2)(b) [R 3–402(b)(2)]. Therefore, the trial judge did not err by admitting parol evidence to determine the intent of the parties.

Although parol evidence is admissible under § 7–3–403(2)(b), the burden remains on the signer of the instrument to disestablish liability. See *Byrd Cos. v. Tolbert,* 286 Ala. 465, 241 So.2d 840 (1971); *Fanning v. Hembree Oil Co.,* 246 Ark. 825, 434 S.W.2d 822 (1968). The trial court found that the note was evidence of a corporate liability and not the personal obligation of Mr. Coleman. Although the trial judge, who heard the testimony ore tenus, is due great deference, see *Smith v. McNaughton,* 378 So.2d 703 (Ala.1979), the presumption of correctness does not apply when the trial court applied erroneous principles of law. The trial judge relied on 19 Am.Jur.2d Corporations § 1346 (1964), which states that when a corporation is named in the body of a contract, it is a contract of the corporation. "[T]he signature in the name of the officer with or without an affix designating his representative capacity does not render it his personal contract." *Id.* This statement is contrary to the law under Code 1975, § 7–3–403(2)(b) [R 3–402(b)(2)], which provides that the signer is liable unless he or she can show that personal liability of the signer was not the intent of the parties.

This court finds that Mr. Coleman did not meet the burden imposed by § 7–3–403(2) [R 3–402(b)] of disestablishing his liability. The only evidence that Coleman did not personally guarantee the debt of the corporation is his bare allegation that he did not intend to be bound. In order to meet the burden of proof under § 7–3–403(2)(b) [R 3–402(b)(2)], the evidence must be more than the mere self serving allegation of the signer's subjective intent to sign in a representative capacity. See *Rotuba Extruders, Inc. v. Ceppos,* 46 N.Y.2d 223, 413 N.Y.S.2d 141, 385 N.E.2d 1068 (1978). This is particularly true when the allegations are made by a person who has recently been convicted of securities fraud and fined $15,000. The evidence shows that the credit manager and the president of Wurzburg Brothers flew to Dothan to procure Mr. Coleman's signature guaranteeing the debt of the corporation. The credit manager testified that he feared that Coleman–American would become insolvent and sought to secure the debt. The defendant is a 25% shareholder of Coleman–American and is president of the parent corporation. He is on the board of directors of all subsidiaries of Coleman American. Coleman has been in such a position of authority for almost twenty years, and is an experienced businessman who should know the proper method of signing a contract for his corporation. Mr. Coleman had charge of making out the note and could easily have indicated if he wished to sign in a representative capacity. Under these circumstances, it hardly seems unfair or contrary to the intention of the parties to hold a person of Coleman's business acumen liable on the debt. [Citations omitted.]

The judgment of the trial court is reversed and the cause remanded.

Reversed and remanded.

TORBERT, C.J., ALMON, EMBRY and ADAMS, JJ., concur.

VALLEY NATIONAL BANK, SUNNYMEAD v. COOK

Arizona Court of Appeals, 1983.
136 Ariz. 232, 665 P.2d 576.

CORCORAN, P.J.

The issue raised in this appeal is whether an individual who signs a check without indicating her representative capacity is personally liable on the obligation evidenced by the check when the check has the name of the corporate principal printed on it. We adopt the minority rule and hold that the individual is not personally liable. J. White &

R. Summers, *Handbook of the Law Under the Uniform Commercial Code* § 13–4 (2d ed. 1980).

On October 21, 1977, appellee J.M. Cook (Cook), the treasurer of Arizona Auto Auction and R.V. Center, Inc., (Arizona Auto Auction, Inc.) issued three corporate checks to Central Motors Company. Central Motors deposited these checks in its corporate account which was held by appellant Valley National Bank, Sunnymead, a California corporation (Bank). The Bank then sent each of these checks for payment to Arizona Auto Auction, Inc.'s drawee bank, First National Bank of Arizona. However, a stop payment order had been put on these checks and the First National Bank dishonored each of the checks. The checks were returned to the Bank, and the account of Central Motors was charged back for the amount of the checks which totaled $9,795. The Bank was unable to recover this amount from Central Motors. The Bank demanded payment from Arizona Auto Auction, Inc., but the demand was not honored. On March 27, 1978, the Bank commenced suit against Arizona Auto Auction, Inc., and J.M. Cook and her spouse.

The case was tried to the court on August 1, 1979. After trial, the court found that the Bank was a holder in due course and that the Arizona Auto Auction, Inc., was obligated as drawer for the face amount of the checks, $9,795. However, the judgment provided that Cook was not personally liable on the checks and awarded her attorney fees as a prevailing party against the Bank. Arizona Auto Auction, Inc., does not appeal from the judgment against it. However, the Bank appeals from that portion of the judgment which is in favor of Cook and her husband as to liability and the award of attorneys' fees.

The question of whether Cook signed in her individual or representative capacity is governed by § 3–403 [R 3–402] of the Uniform Commercial Code (UCC) as adopted in this state.

* * *

The Bank argues that this section conclusively establishes Cook's personal liability on the checks. We do not agree. Admittedly, the checks fail to specifically show the office held by Cook. However, we do not find that this fact conclusively establishes liability since A.R.S. § 44–2540(B)(2) imposes personal liability on an agent who signs his or her own name to an instrument only "if the instrument * * * does not show that the representative signed in a representative capacity." Thus, we must look to the entire instrument for evidence of the capacity of the signer. *Southeastern Financial Corp. v. Smith,* 397 F.Supp. 649 (N.D.Ala.1975), rev'd on other grounds 542 F.2d 278 (5th Cir.1976); *Pollin v. Mindy Mfg. Co., Inc.,* 211 Pa.Super. 87, 236 A.2d 542 (1967).

The checks are in evidence and are boldly imprinted at the top "Arizona Auto Auction, Inc." and also "Arizona Auto Auction, Inc." is imprinted above a signature line appearing at the lower right-hand corner. Under the imprinted name of the corporate defendant appears the signature of appellee Cook without any designation of office or capacity on each of the checks before us on appeal. Appellee Cook did not endorse the checks on the back. The record does not reflect appellee Cook made any personal guaranty of these checks or any other corporate obligation. By way of example, we reproduce one of these checks:

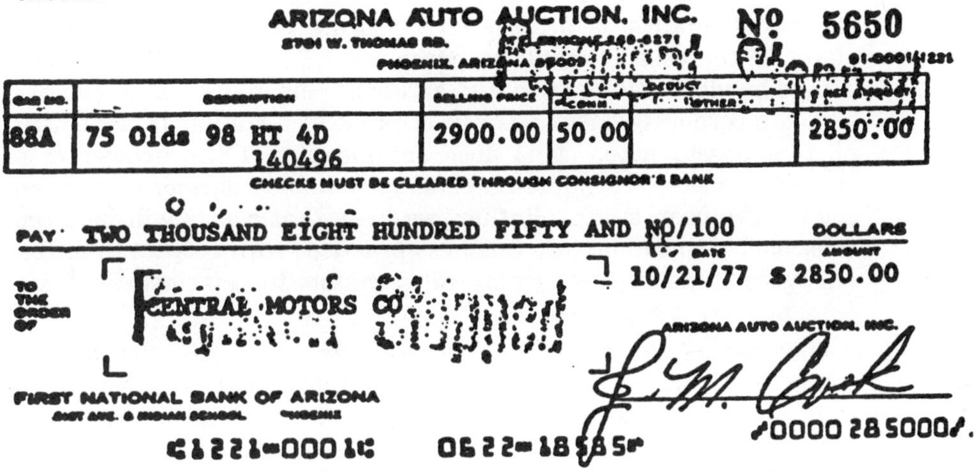

ARIZONA AUTO AUCTION, INC. № 5650

88A	75 Olds 98 HT 4D 140496	2900.00	50.00		2850.00

CHECKS MUST BE CLEARED THROUGH CONSIGNOR'S BANK

PAY TWO THOUSAND EIGHT HUNDRED FIFTY AND NO/100 DOLLARS

10/21/77 $ 2850.00

TO THE ORDER OF CENTRAL MOTORS CO

ARIZONA AUTO AUCTION, INC.

FIRST NATIONAL BANK OF ARIZONA

The Superior Court of Pennsylvania was confronted with a similar situation in *Pollin v. Mindy Mfg. Co., Inc., supra.* There the court denied recovery by a third party endorsee against one who affixed his signature to a payroll check directly beneath the printed corporate name without indicating his representative capacity. In *Pollin* the checks were boldly imprinted at the top with the corporate name, address, and appropriate check number. The printed name of the drawee bank appeared in the lower lefthand corner of the instrument and the corporate name was imprinted in the lower righthand corner. Directly beneath the corporate name were two blank lines. The defendant-appellant had signed the top line without any designation of office or capacity. Pointing out that the code imposes liability on the individual only when the instrument controverts any showing of representative capacity, the court considered the instrument in its entirety. The court in *Pollin* held that disclosure on the face of the instrument that the checks were payable from a special payroll account of the corporation over which the appellant had no control as an individual negated any contention that appellant intended to make the instrument his own order to pay money to the payee.

The difference in outcome in the *Pollin* case and the cases cited by the Bank in which corporate agents were held liable for failing to show a corporate title reflects the *Pollin* court's emphasis on *business expectations,* an emphasis which is proper and entirely consistent with the spirit of UCC § 3-403 [R 3-402]. J. White & R. Summers, *Handbook of the Law Under the Uniform Commercial Code* § 13-4 at 494-95 (2d ed.

1980). In determining what these expectations might be, it is important to draw a distinction between a check and a note:

> The payee of a corporate check with the corporate name imprinted on its face probably expects less from the individual drawer than the payee of a corporate note may, where both the corporate name and the maker's name may be either handwritten or typewritten. Further, it is common for creditors to demand the individual promise of officers on corporate promissory notes, specially in the case of small corporations. Thus, we think a court should be more reluctant to find an agent personally liable who has signed a corporate check than in the case of a similar indorsement of a corporate note. This does not mean that the drawer of a corporate check will never be personally liable; indeed, more than a few have been stuck. Rather, we hope that courts will be more conscious of differences in business practices with respect to different types of instruments when they evaluate the extrinsic evidence presented by the parties.

Id. at 495; see e.g. *St. Croix Engineering Corp. v. McLay,* 304 N.W.2d 912 (Minn.1981), and *Pollin, supra.* Thus, while it may be common for creditors of small corporations to demand that corporate officers personally obligate themselves on corporate notes, it would be most unusual to demand the individual obligation of an officer on corporate checks.

The fact that common business expectations may not be consistent with a strict reading of UCC § 3–403(2), as that section relates to corporate checks, as opposed to notes, is exemplified by the record before us. Regarding the checks, a branch manager employed by the Bank, testified during trial as follows:

> **Q.** Would it be fair to say that when a bank receives an instrument that designates at the top a name of a corporation designated by Inc., that it would deal with that item at all times as a corporate instrument?
>
> **A.** That is correct.
>
> **Q.** And in the custom and usage of banking practices that would be considered a corporate instrument, would it not?
>
> **A.** Yes.
>
> * * *.
>
> **Q.** And you receiving those instruments assumed, did you not, that Mrs. Cook was writing that instrument as a representative of the corporation, did you not?
>
> **A.** I would assume that she would have the authority to sign on that account.
>
> **Q.** And having that authority, you presume that she was writing that for and on behalf of the corporation; is that not correct?
>
> **A.** I would assume so, to pay these funds.

Q. You didn't expect Mrs. Cook to individually pay these funds out of her pocket, did you? You expected the corporation to do it, did you not?

A. I expected these funds to come from the account number coded at the bottom of this particular check.

Q. And as far as you know, that account number was the account of the Arizona Auto Auction Incorporated, is that not correct?

A. That is correct.

Q. You were not misled by the fact that she wrote on the instrument "J.M. Cook" were you?

A. No.

This testimony is consistent with the common business and banking expectation that where a corporate name is printed on a check any accompanying signatures relating to the corporate drawer will be the signatures of officers authorized by the bylaws or corporate resolutions to sign the instrument in a representative capacity without regard to whether there is a specific reference to the representative capacity. This is especially clear where, as here, the check is drawn against a corporate checking account.

In this case the checks clearly show the name of the corporation in two places and the money was payable from the account of Arizona Auto Auction, Inc., over which Cook as an individual had no control. Considering the instruments as a whole, we conclude under these circumstances that they sufficiently disclose that Cook signed them in a representative and not an individual capacity.

Our conclusion is further supported by the actions of the Bank which accepted the checks as that of the corporate defendant, Arizona Auto Auction, Inc. In its complaint it so avers. As the court in *Pollin* stated:

> On that basis it proceeded against the corporate defendant and secured a judgment. That judgment was predicated on a proper execution of the instrument by that defendant which required the signature of its representative. Therefore it accepted appellant's signature as that representative. In fact, in his complaint against appellant he avers the checks were those of the corporation.
>
> Having secured a judgment on that basis against the corporate defendant, we are at a loss to see how he may now contend that appellant's signature was on his individual behalf and not in a representative capacity. It must be one or the other. It cannot be both.

211 Pa.Super. at 93, 236 A.2d at 545; *Viajes Iberia, S.A. v. Dougherty*, 87 S.D. 591, 212 N.W.2d 656, 658 (1973).

The only objection made by the Bank on appeal regarding the award of attorneys' fees is predicated upon the assumption that this court reverses the judgment in favor of appellees Cook. Since we affirm the judgment, we also affirm the award of attorneys' fees. A.R.S. § 12–341.01. Appellees Cook have requested attorneys' fees on appeal. *Fousel v. Ted Walker Mobile Homes, Inc.,* 124 Ariz. 126, 130, 602 P.2d 507, 511 (App.1979). We will consider the issue of attorneys' fees on appeal in accordance with rule 21, Rules of Civil Appellate Procedure.

The judgment of the trial court and the award of attorneys' fees are affirmed.

OGG and FROEB, JJ., concur.

Note

1. In the *Wurzburg* case, the trial court applied the usual contract rule that, if a corporation is named in the body of a contract, an agent of the corporation who signs the contract is not personally liable on the contract, even though the contract does not show that the agent signed only as agent. Under that rule if, for example, a corporate order form is used to purchase 10,000 widgets, the person who signs the order using only his or her individual name is not personally liable on the order even though the agency status is not shown on the form. The appellate court says that rule is not applicable to negotiable instruments. Why should the rule be different as to notes in which a corporation is named as the maker in the body of the note? See the justification suggested in the *Valley National* case. Do you agree that the general contract rule should apply to corporate checks but not to corporate notes?

2. The *Wurzburg* court says that to determine whether the signer has signed only in a representative capacity, the whole instrument, rather than the signature line alone, must be examined. However, it concludes, apparently, that an individual signing an ordinary corporate note is personally liable unless the signature line indicates agency status. As the court notes, under original 3–403 the question was whether *the instrument* showed that the person signed in a representative capacity. Under revised 3–402, however, the question, except as to checks, is whether *the form of the signature* shows representative capacity. See R 3–402(b) and (c).

3. It is clear, is it not, that in the Wurzburg case Coleman American is also liable so that the single signature binds both the corporation and the individual signer? On this point see R 3–402(a) and (b) which state that result. Even though that result is not specifically stated in original Article 3, it is regularly reached in the corporate note situation.

C. LIABILITY OF MAKERS, ACCEPTORS, DRAWERS, INDORSERS, AND DRAWEES

Some of the procedural and substantive differences between the liability of a party to a negotiable instrument and the liability of a party to a simple contract were discussed in the note, supra, at page 53. That note dealt with differences in burden of proof between an action on a negotiable instrument and an action on a simple contract and with the lesser ability of a party to a negotiable instrument to assert defenses arising out of separate transactions. You should re-read that note. In this section, we deal with the specific liability which parties to instruments have as a result of the capacity in which they have signed the instrument.

1. Liability of Makers, Drawers of Drafts on Themselves, and Acceptors

The three above parties are dealt with together here because they have the same liability. It is a simple liability: They must pay the instrument according to its terms. See R 3–409, 3–412, 3–413, 3–105; OR 3–410, 3–413, 3–118(a).

NEWARK STEEL DRUM CO., INC. v. PENN CREST OIL GREASE CORP.

New York Supreme Court, 1967.
4 U.C.C.Rep.Serv. 316.

CRISONA, J.

Plaintiff moves for summary judgment against both defendants pursuant to CPLR 3213.

This is an action by plaintiff, Newark Steel Drum Company, Inc., which alleges that it is a holder in due course of a trade acceptance in the amount of $10,395.50 made by defendant Globe Steel Drum Corp. (hereinafter "Globe") on September 2, 1966 and duly accepted by defendant Penn Crest Oil & Grease Corp. (hereinafter "Penn Crest") and thereafter endorsed by Globe to plaintiff. Plaintiff further alleges that the trade acceptance arose out of the sale of steel drums from Globe to Penn Crest and, by its terms, requires Penn Crest to pay Globe the principal amount. Plaintiff states that at maturity it presented the trade acceptance to Penn Crest, but payment was not made and that the trade acceptance was "protested for nonpayment, and notice of said presentment, demand and non-payment and protest was duly given to the defendant" Penn Crest and the defendant Globe.

In opposition Penn Crest contends inter alia * * * (2) that the trade acceptance made by Globe was never accepted by Penn Crest and (3) that plaintiff is not a holder in due course of the trade acceptance.

* * *

The basis of Penn Crest's second contention is that it never accepted the instrument because it signed as buyer and not as acceptor. "A *trade acceptance* is a draft with a definite maturity date on its face drawn by the seller of goods on the purchaser for the price and accepted by the purchaser." (Whitney, *The Law of Modern Commercial Practices* 2d ed., § 320.) The instrument in question provides:

"TRADE ACCEPTANCE
No. 9/2
To Penn Crest Oil & Grease Corp. 20–59 Borden Ave.

On December 15, 1966 Pay to the order of Globe Steel Drum Corp. Ten thousand three hundred ninety five and 50/100 Dollars ($10,395 50/100). The transaction which gives rise to this instrument is the purchase of goods by the acceptor from the drawer. The drawee may accept this bill payable at any bank, banker or trust company in the United States which such drawee may designate.

Accepted at Lg Island City	)	
Payable at Chemical Bank & Trust Co. Bank	)	Globe Steel Drum Corp.
Bank Location Steinway St. & B'way L I City	)	
Buyer's Signature Michael Sand	)	By Morris Shapiro Treas."
By Agent or Officer Pres	)	

Section 3–410 [R 3–409] of the Uniform Commercial Code, which defines acceptance, states inter alia that acceptance is the "drawee's signed engagement to honor the draft as presented" and that "[i]t must be written on the draft and may consist of his signature alone." The instrument in question contained the necessary elements of acceptance, i.e., the statement that the instrument was accepted and the buyer's signature. The notes to § 3–410 [R 3–409] confirm that the signature alone is sufficient and that the word acceptance need not be written across the draft. Official comment 4 to § 3–410 [R 3–409] states:

> 4. Subsection (1) states the generally recognized rule that the mere signature of the drawee on the instrument is a sufficient acceptance. Customarily the signature is written vertically across the face of the instrument; but since the drawee has no reason to sign for any other purpose his signature in any other place, even on the back of the instrument, is sufficient. It need not be accompanied by such words as "Accepted," "Certified," or "Good." It must not, however, bear any words indicating an intent to refuse to honor the bill; and nothing in this provision is intended to change such decisions as *Norton v. Knapp,* 64 Iowa 112, 19 NW 867 (1884), holding that the drawee's signature accompanied by the words "Kiss my foot" is not an acceptance.

The forms of trade acceptance contained in leading texts are almost identical to the instrument in question. (See Ogden, *The Law of Negotiable Instruments,* 5th ed., § 98, and Whitney, *supra,* § 320.)

The basis of Penn Crest's third contention that plaintiff is not the holder in due course of the trade acceptance is that after Penn Crest received the drums and prior to the endorsement of the instrument by Globe the drums proved defective, and Globe was informed of the defects, and at the time plaintiff took the instrument from Globe plaintiff knew of the defects and of Penn Crest's defense of failure of consideration. Penn Crest states that Morris Shapiro signed the subject trade acceptance as an officer of Globe. Penn Crest submits a second trade acceptance drawn on plaintiff and accepted by Penn Crest on June 21, 1966, and signed for *plaintiff* by Morris Shapiro and contends that this is the same Morris Shapiro who signed the subject trade acceptance for Globe and, therefore, plaintiff, through Morris Shapiro, had knowledge of Penn Crest's defense when it took the instrument. Penn Crest further contends that plaintiff knew of the defense when it took the instrument because the principals of plaintiff and Globe are related.

Plaintiff states that Morris Shapiro has never been its officer, but merely signed the second trade acceptance under the corporate name, Newark Steel Drum Company, Inc., as a matter of convenience of the parties.

The subject trade acceptance is a negotiable instrument. (Britton, *Handbook of the Law of Bills and Notes,* § 13, see Note 2; 41 New York Jurisprudence, p. 203, and Uniform Commercial Code, § 3–104 [R 3–104].) If plaintiff is a holder in due course of the trade acceptance, it takes the instrument free of the defense which Penn Crest could assert against Globe (Uniform Commercial Code, § 3–305 [R 3–305, 3–306]). To be a holder in due course plaintiff must have taken the instrument for value, in good faith, and without knowledge of Penn Crest's defense (Uniform Commercial Code, § 3–302 [R3–302]). Section 3–304(7) [non-uniform] of the Code further defines notice. That section states inter alia:

> (7) In any event, to constitute notice of a claim or defense, the purchaser must have knowledge of the claim or defense or knowledge of such facts that his action in taking the instrument amounts to bad faith.

Under the circumstances there are questions of fact presented as to whether plaintiff, at the time it took the trade acceptance, had knowledge of Penn Crest's defense or had knowledge of such facts that its action in taking the instrument amounted to bad faith. (See also Uniform Commercial Code, § 3–418 [R 3–418].) Accordingly, the motion for summary judgment as against Penn Crest is denied.

The motion for summary judgment as against Globe is granted since Globe asserts no defenses against plaintiff. (See Uniform Commercial Code, § 3–413 [R 3–413].)

Note

1. *The use of trade acceptances.* The *Newark Steel Drum* case illustrates the way in which "trade acceptances" are used. They are still in common use among medium size businesses and are often used in the sale of agricultural commodities. So far as the liability of the buyer is concerned, the same result could be achieved by having the buyer sign a promissory note. However, the trade acceptance has the advantage that the drawer of the draft may be able to induce drawer's bank to advance money on the strength of the draft before it has been accepted since, if the buyer-drawee does not accept, the bank can recover against the drawer on drawer's contract liability. (See the discussion, infra, page 128.) Of course,

seller's bank might be induced to loan money to the seller before the buyer signs a promissory note on the promise of the seller that, once the note is signed, it will be transferred to the bank, but that transaction requires more documentation than merely taking the trade acceptance. As this note suggests, it is common for a seller's bank to "discount" the trade acceptance before the drawee has accepted. In that case, the bank often sends the draft through banking channels to a bank in drawee's city for presentment to the drawee for acceptance.

2. *Certified checks and cashier's checks.* Sellers, particularly in real estate transactions, will frequently decline to accept the buyer's personal check because of the possibility that it will be drawn on insufficient funds. Use of cash in such transactions, however, would be inconvenient and risky. Such sellers, therefore, will ask for a check on which a bank has become liable. A drawee bank can become liable by accepting the check. Such a check is in common parlance and in Article 3 called a certified check. (OR 3–411, R 3–409). Rather than certifying the customer's check, the bank may choose to satisfy the customer's need for a bank obligation by issuing its own check drawn on itself. Such a check is known as a cashier's check. (R 3–104(g). In both cases, the liability of the bank is the same as that of any acceptor or any drawer of a draft drawn on the drawer.

Persons who secure certification of checks or purchase cashier's checks sometimes wish to prevent the bank from paying the check to the holder and will assert that they have a right to stop payment or have a right to intervene in a law suit between the bank and the holder to assert a defense against the holder. Whether a customer can demand that a bank stop payment of a certified or cashier's check is dealt with on pages 318–335 of the casebook, and the ability of the person securing certification or purchasing a cashier's check to assert defenses against the holder is considered on pages 326–335.

2. *Liability of Drawers*

A drawer of a draft, including a check, is not primarily liable on the instrument. Although the drawee/payor bank will incur no liability to the party presenting an item if the drawee refuses to pay (OR 3–409, R 3–408), the holder of a draft must present the instrument for payment to the drawee before demand to pay may be made on the drawer. The drawer contractually undertakes to pay the instrument according to its original tenor only upon the drawee's dishonor of the draft, and, under original Article 3, the drawer's receiving notice of the dishonor. OR 3–413, R 3–414. The drawee, then, could be said to have a sort of quasi-primary liability and the drawer only secondary liability. The first case in this section considers the conditions precedent to the drawer's liability on a check.

TEPPER v. CITIZENS FEDERAL SAVINGS & LOAN ASSOCIATION

Florida District Court of Appeals, 1984.
448 So.2d 1138, 38 U.C.C.Rep.Serv. (Callaghan) 528.

FERGUSON, J.

The sole question presented is when does the statute of limitations begin to run against a drawer in an action for wrongful dishonor of a check—on the date of issuance of the check or the date of presentment and dishonor?

Rose Tepper (appellant) was adjudicated an incompetent in December, 1982. On examination of her personal effects, a court-appointed guardian discovered a check for the sum of $6,068, dated January 4, 1974. The check was drawn to Rose Tepper by Citizens Federal Savings and Loan Association against its account with Jefferson National Bank.

On December 20, 1982, appellant's representative presented the check to the drawee bank, Jefferson National (not a party to this action), which refused payment. The representative then advised the drawer, Citizens Federal (appellee), of the dishonor. Citizens Federal orally notified appellant's representative that it would neither honor nor refund the instrument. The guardian instituted this action against the drawer on July 12, 1983.

The trial court dismissed the guardian's complaint on appellee's motion, holding that "the statute of limitations began to run on the date of issuance of the check herein sued upon, [so the] action is barred by the applicable five-year statute of limitations." We reverse upon a holding that the statute of limitations begins to run against a drawer of a check on the date of presentment and dishonor.

Although there seems to be a dearth of Florida case law on the issue presented, appellant has found all the law necessary to a correct resolution. The decision here is based upon an application of clear statutes and is supported by several treatises.

A draft is a three-party instrument whereby the drawer orders the drawee to pay money to the payee. See J. White and R. Summers, *Uniform Commercial Code* § 13–1 (2d ed. 1980). A draft is also called a check when the drawee is a bank and the instrument is payable on demand. § 673–104(2)(b) [R 3–104(f)], Fla.Stat. (1983). A drawee is not liable on the instrument until there has been an acceptance. § 673.409 [R 3–408]. The drawee may, by accepting in writing on the instrument, agree to honor it as presented. § 673.410 [R 3–409]. By contrast, a drawee may reject the instrument, as by stamping insufficient funds on a check where the drawer's deposited funds are less than the amount of the instrument. The act of accepting the instrument renders the drawee primarily liable as an acceptor. See § 673.414(1) [R 3–413(a)]. Because there are no conditions precedent to its liability, a cause of action accrues against an acceptor in the case of a demand instrument on the date of the instrument or date of issue. § 673.122(1)(b)1 [see comment 1 to R 3–118].

The drawer, on the other hand, is only secondarily liable on the instrument, in that there are conditions precedent to liability. W. Hawkland, *Commercial Paper* 52 (2d ed. 1979). The normal conditions precedent include presentment to the drawee, dishonor, and notice of dishonor. *Id.;* see § 673.501 [R 3–414, 3–502]. Therefore, a cause of action against the drawer of a draft accrues only upon demand following dishonor of the instrument. § 673.122(3) [see comment 1 to R 3–118]. Notice of dishonor constitutes a demand. *Id.* This latter section is clearly dispositive of the issue presented, as a cause of action against the drawer herein, Citizens Federal, thus did not accrue until appellant's representative received notice of dishonor from the drawee, Jefferson National Bank.

Florida case authority for the proposition that the statute of limitations begins to run against an issuing bank on a *cashier's check* at the moment of issuance, *Atlantic National Bank of West Palm Beach v. Havens,* 45 So.2d 342 (Fla.1950), is distinguishable. A cashier's check is a check on which the issuing bank acts as both the drawer and the drawee. Its own act of issuance renders the bank a drawee who has accepted the draft; thus the issuing bank becomes primarily liable as an acceptor. J. White and R. Summers, *Uniform Commercial Code* § 17–5 (2d ed. 1980). Presentment of a negotiable instrument is not necessary in order to establish liability against parties who are primarily liable. In such a case the statute of limitations begins to run on a demand instrument at the moment of issuance. W. Hawkland, *Commercial Paper* 42–43 (2d ed. 1979). As to parties secondarily liable, however, such as the drawer herein, there is no instant liability and thus no cause of action until demand following presentment and dishonor. H. Bailey, *Brady on Bank Checks* § 4.12 (5th ed. 1979).

The distinction between a cashier's check where the issuing bank is primarily liable and other drafts, where the drawer is secondarily liable, is stated:

> [U]nder the Code, cause of action against a certifying bank or a bank issuing a cashier's check accrues on the date of the check (or date of issue if the check is undated). This means that the statute of limitations begins to run at that time and suit against the bank will be barred after the statute of limitations has run. But a cause of action against a drawer of a check does not accrue until demand following dishonor. This theoretically means that the time for bringing action against the drawer may be deferred indefinitely if there is no presentment for payment.

H. Bailey, *Brady on Bank Checks* § 4.122 (5th ed. 1979).

Under Florida law an action may not be deferred indefinitely in all instances; instead, a drawer will be discharged from its liability if presentment is unreasonably delayed and the drawee bank becomes insolvent during the delay. § 673.502(1)(b) [R 3–414(f)]; see also *Robinson v. Brunson,* 383 So.2d 964 (Fla. 2d DCA 1980).

In that appellee herein was the drawer of the instrument which is the subject of this action, and therefore only secondarily liable, a cause of action did not accrue against it until after demand following presentment and dishonor on December 20, 1982. The action for wrongful dishonor of the instrument was commenced timely.

Reversed and remanded.

Note

1. As the case points out, presentment to the drawee is a condition of the drawer's liability. However, delay in presentment discharges the drawer only in the cases specified in original 3–502(1)(b) supplemented by original 3–503(2)(a) and in revised 3–414(f). Both original and revised Article 3 state essentially the same rule: if a holder does not present a check to the drawee bank or initiate bank collection within a specified time the drawer is discharged if (1), after the expiration of the time, the bank fails thereby depriving the drawer of funds kept with the bank to pay the check and (2) the drawer assigns to the holder the drawer's rights against the bank.

There are two slight differences between original and revised Article 3 on this point. Under revised Article 3, the specified time for presentment or initiation of bank collection is 30 days from the instrument's date; under original Article 3 the specified time is a reasonable time (which is presumptively 30 days) from the instrument's date or issue. Also, under original Article 3, the rules just discussed apply to drafts other than checks. That is, apparently, a drawer who draws a draft on a person other than a bank could claim a discharge if she maintained funds with the drawee which were lost due to insolvency after the expiration of the time for presentment. Under revised Article 3, the discharge for delay provisions apply only to checks.

The effect of the revision is to provide certainty by fixing a specific time for presentment and starting that time from a certain date, rather than stating only a presumption as to what is a reasonable time for presentment and starting that time from either date or issue. (The day of issue will likely not be easily provable.)

2. The rule as to discharge of drawers on checks has little practical effect since the Federal Deposit Insurance Corporation insures deposits up to $100,000. Presumably, therefore, only if the checking account is larger than $100,000 would the insolvency of the bank deprive the drawer of funds maintained to pay the check. Further, the FDIC has in fact often protected depositors for amounts above $100,000 on the principle that some banks are too large to permit to fail.

3. The statute of limitations aspects of Tepper are changed by revised 3–118. See R 3–118(d). See also R 3–118(c) on ordinary checks.

Problem

Client calls you in a panic. He relates that his wallet has just been stolen and in the wallet he had two checks. The first was a check for

$10,000 from his brokerage firm payable to him. The second was a cashier's check for $25,000 which he had just purchased. The cashier's check is payable to his mother in law. Neither was indorsed by the payee. What are client's rights? What will you tell him to do. See OR 3–805, R 3–309 and R 3–312. See *Scharz v. Twin City Bank,* 201 Kan. 539, 441 P.2d 897 (1968). See also OR 3–603, R 3–602.

3. Liability of Indorsers

The ordinary assignor does not guarantee that the obligor will perform. Therefore, the fact that the obligor fails to perform does not, by itself, give the assignee a claim against the assignor unless the assignor has expressly agreed that it will perform if the obligor does not. See Restatement of Contracts, 2d § 333. However, the transferror of commercial paper who indorses does, by statute, incur an obligation to pay if the maker or drawee does not pay. But, the duty of the indorser to pay arises only if the holder complies with the statutory rules as to presentment and notice of dishonor.

The following two cases deal with the presentment and notice of dishonor rules.

BRANNONS NUMBER SEVEN, INC. v. PHELPS

Oklahoma Court of Appeals, 1983.
665 P.2d 860.

MEANS, JUDGE.

This is an appeal by the defendant, Robert Phelps, from an order of the trial court which granted summary judgment in favor of the plaintiff, Brannons Number Seven.

The issues involved are (1) whether Brannons, as the holder of two insufficient payroll checks, was required to give notice of dishonor to Phelps as the endorser, and (2) whether a disputed notice of dishonor is a substantial material fact precluding the granting of summary judgment.

We answer both questions in the affirmative and reverse.

The basic facts are not in dispute. Phelps was in the employment of Jet Service Company. Jet issued two payroll checks to Phelps in the amounts of $454.49 and $350.05. Brannons, a grocery store, cashed the two checks for Phelps. Phelps had endorsed the two checks, placing his telephone number on the back of each check, below his endorsement. Phelps received the proceeds from the checks. Upon presentment by Brannons to the drawee bank, notice of dishonor due to insufficient funds in the drawer's account was given to Brannons.

Brannons, by way of affidavit attached to its motion for summary judgment, states that it "requested Robert Phelps to pay Plaintiff [Brannons]" the sums of the two checks. Attached to Phelps' response to Brannons' motion for summary judgment is his affidavit which states that Brannons never requested him to pay the sums of the checks "by either verbal or written demand." Again in Phelps' answers to Brannons' request for admissions, Phelps denied that Brannons requested him to pay the sums of the checks.

The trial court granted plaintiff Brannons' summary judgment for the sum of $804.64, plus attorney's fees and costs.

I

The requirement of notice of dishonor to an endorser is clear.

Title 12A O.S.1981 § 3–501(2)(a) [See R 3–503(a)], states that unless notice is excused under § 3–511 [R 3–504]:

> (a) notice of any dishonor is necessary to charge any endorser; (emphasis added) [1]

The contractual duties and liabilities of an endorser and holder when an uncertified check passes between the parties are found in 12A O.S.1981 § 3–414(1) [See R 3–415]:

> Unless the endorsement otherwise specifies (as by such words as 'without recourse') every endorser engages that *upon dishonor and any necessary notice of dishonor* and protest he will pay the instrument according to its tenor at the time of his endorsement to the holder or to any subsequent endorser who takes it up, even though the endorser who takes it up was not obligated to do so. (emphasis added)

The holder's rights are stated in 12A O.S.1981 § 3–507(2) [See R 3–414].

> *Subject to any necessary notice of dishonor* * * * the holder has upon dishonor an immediate right of recourse against the drawers and endorsers. (emphasis added)

An endorser's liability is contingent and does not become fixed unless and until the holder complies with the requirement of notice of dishonor. This notice is an element of Brannons' cause of action and Brannons thus has the burden of proving that it gave notice.

II

The affidavits, briefs and exhibits to the pleadings relied upon by the trial judge in granting summary judgment present a substantial controversy as to a material fact as to whether notice of dishonor of the checks was given to the endorser Phelps. Assuming arguendo, that requesting payment by Phelps of the checks in question constituted notice of dishonor, Phelps denies that such a request occurred. This presents a question of fact to be proved by Brannons to the satisfaction of the trier of facts before recovery is permissible.

Reversed and remanded for trial on the issue of notice of the dishonor.

1. Uniform Commercial Code Comment 2, 12A O.S.A.1963 § 3–501, relating to this provision, states in part:

> the words "Necessary to charge" are retained from the original Act. They mean that the necessary proceeding is a condition precedent to any right of action against the drawer or indorser.

BACON, P.J., and BOYDSTON, J., concur.

Problem

Indorser indorsed check over to Grocery Store on January 15th. On February 15th, Indorser was notified by Grocery Store that the check had been dishonored. Under original Article 3, what facts do you need to know to determine whether the notification on February 15th is timely so that Indorser is liable to Grocery Store. See OR 3–414, 3–502, 3–503(2)(b), 3–508.

If the notification is not timely, see OR 3–511(1) and (2)(b) and (c) under which Grocery might be excused from the duty to give notice.

Revised Article 3 provides much more lenient rules as to presentment and notice of dishonor as against indorsers of checks. See R 3–415(a), (c), and (e); 3–502(b)(1); 3–503(a) and (c). As you see from the sections just cited, in the problem above under revised Article 3 the indorser would be liable even though Grocery Store waited for 30 days to deposit the check and then waited 30 days after it learned of the dishonor to give notice of dishonor to the indorser. Given the time necessary for the check to go through the banking system to the drawee bank, for the dishonored check to come back to the depositary bank, and for that bank to notify Grocery Store, indorser may be liable even though she does not receive notice of dishonor until 70 or more days after she indorsed the check to Grocery Store. Is that too long a period to keep the indorser on the hook?

Most checks are probably deposited directly into the payee's checking account. In such cases, the payee's indorser liability is not important to the bank, since under Article 4 (and the deposit agreement with its customer) the bank has a right to charge back the check against its depositor's account upon learning that the check has been dishonored. See chapter 6, infra.

HANE v. EXTEN

Maryland Court of Appeals, 1969.
255 Md. 668, 259 A.2d 290, 7 U.C.C.Rep.Serv. (Callaghan) 34.

SINGLEY, J.

John B. Hane is the assignee of the note of Theta Electronic Laboratories, Inc. (Theta) in the stated amount of $15,377.07, with interest at six per cent per annum. The note was dated 10 August 1964; stipulated that the first monthly payment of $320.47 would be due five months from date, or on 10 January 1965; and that "In the event of the failure to pay the interest or principal, as the same becomes due on this Note the entire debt represented hereby shall at the end of thirty (30) days become due and demandable. * * *" The note was assigned without recourse to Hane by George B. and Marguerite F. Thomson, the original payees, on 26 November 1965. A default having occurred in the making of the monthly payments, Hane took judgments by confession in the Circuit Court for Montgomery County on 7 June 1967 against Theta and three individuals, Gerald M. Exten, Emil L. O'Neil, and James W. Hane, and their wives, who had endorsed Theta's note. On motion of the Extens, the judgment was vacated as to them and the case came on for trial on the merits before the court without a jury. From a judgment for the Extens for costs, Hane has appealed.

This case raises the familiar question: Must Hane show that the Extens were given notice of presentment and dishonor before he can hold them on their endorsement?

The court below, in finding for the Extens, relied on the provisions of Uniform Commercial Code (the U.C.C.), Maryland Code (1957, 1664 Repl.Vol.) Art. 95B § 3–414(1) [See R 3–415] of the U.C.C. provides:

> Unless the indorsement otherwise specifies (as by such words as "without recourse") every indorser engages that upon dishonor and any necessary notice of dishonor and protest he will pay the instrument according to its tenor at the time of his indorsement to the holder or to any subsequent indorser who takes it up, even though the indorser who takes it up is not obligated to do so.

Section 3–501(1)(b) [R 3–415] provides that "Presentment for payment is necessary to charge any indorser" and § 3–501(2)(a) [R 3–415] that "Notice of any dishonor is necessary to charge any indorser," in each case subject, however, to the provisions of § 3–511 [R 3–504] which recite the circumstances under which notice of dishonor may be waived or excused, none of which is here present. Section 3–502(1)(a) [R 3–415(e)] makes it clear that unless presentment or notice of dishonor is waived or excused, unreasonable delay will discharge an indorser. See 1 Hawkland, *A Transactional Guide to the Uniform Commercial Code* (1964) § 206 at 945–97.

There was testimony from which the trier of facts could find as he did that presentment and notice of dishonor were unduly delayed.

It is clear that Hane held the note from November, 1965, until some time in April 1967 before he made demand for payment. U.C.C. § 3–503(1)(d) [see comment to R 3–502] provides that "Where an instrument is accelerated presentment for payment is due within a reasonable time after the acceleration." "Reasonable time" is not defined in § 3–503 [see comment to R 3–502], except that § 3–503(2) [see comment to R 3–502] provides, "A reasonable time for presentment is determined by the nature of the instrument, any usage of banking or trade and the facts of the particular case," but § 1–204(2) characterizes it: "What is a reasonable time for taking any action depends on the nature, purposes and circumstances of such action."

Reasonableness is primarily a question for the fact finder. *Vandenberg v. Siter,* 204 Pa.Super. 392, 204 A.2d 494 (1964); 11 Am.Jur.2d Bills and Notes § 754 (1963); 1 *Anderson's Uniform Commercial Code,* Commentary, § 1–204:3 (1961) at 40. We see no reason to disturb the lower court's finding that Hane's delay of almost 18 months in presenting the note "was unreasonable from any viewpoint." See Maryland Rule 886a.

As regards notice of dishonor, § 3–508(2) [See R 3–503] requires that notice be given by persons other than banks "before midnight of the third business day after dishonor." Exten, called as an adverse witness by Hane, testified that his first notice that the note had not been paid was the entry of the confessed judgment on 7 June 1967. Hane's brother testified that demand had been made about 15 April 1967. He was uncertain as to when he had given Exten notice of dishonor, but finally conceded that it was "within a week." The lower court found that the ambiguity of this testimony, coupled with Exten's denial that he had received any notice before 7 June fell short of meeting the three day notice requirement of the U.C.C. The date of giving notice of dishonor is a question of fact, solely for determination by the trier of facts. *First Pennsylvania Banking & Trust Co. v. DeLise,* 186 Pa.Super. 398, 142 A.2d 401 (1958). We cannot say that the court erred in its finding.

In the absence of evidence that presentment and notice of dishonor were waived or excused, Hane's unreasonable delay discharged the Extens, § 3–502(1)(a) [R 3–415(e)].

Hane would have us hold that presentment and notice of dishonor were impliedly excused under § 3–511(2)(b) [R 3–504(a)(ii), (iv) and (v); 3–504(b)] because Exten himself had dishonored the note or had no reason to expect that the note would be paid. Hane finds support for this theory in testimony that payment had been demanded of Theta, the obligor, in behalf of the Thomsons, the payees, in February or March of 1965, at a time when Exten was president of Theta, an office from which he was removed in April or May of 1965. The court below rejected this contention on the ground that there was no evidence that Exten dishonored the note in his individual capacity.

There is an even more persuasive reason which negates the contention that Exten had reason to expect that the note would not be paid. Hane's brother, called as a witness by Hane, testified on cross examination that on 26 November 1965, the balance due on the note was $13,154.94. While the manner in which $2,222.13 had been paid was unexplained, it would appear that at least six monthly payments of $320.47 had been met, with the result that payments were current for the period when Exten was president. As Exten testified:

> This particular note was paid down to something like $13,000 under my management, and it was pursuant to my discharge that no further payments were made.

In the face of this Hane offered no proof that Exten, in his capacity as president of Theta, knew or should have known that the note would not be paid. An indorser's knowledge of the maker's insolvency, standing alone, will not excuse the giving of notice of dishonor. *Plitt v. Grim,* 220 Md. 632, 638, 155 A.2d 672 (1959). There is not even a suggestion that Exten may have consented to an extension of a time for payment. *Leonard v. Union Trust Co.,* 140 Md. 192, 117 A. 318 (1922).

Hane makes much of the fact that he is a holder in due course. We doubt that he was, since there is some evidence that he took the note with notice that it was overdue, § 3–302(1)(c) [R 3–302(a)(2)]. He testified that he assumed that the face amount of $15,377.07 was unpaid when he took the note in November, 1965, when, by the terms of the note, 11 monthly payments should have been made. He apparently held to this belief to the end, since he caused judgment to be confessed for the full amount of the note. In addition, Judge Mathias in the trial below asked him whether he had been able to read the note and realize that some payments were past due. Hane responded affirmatively. Whether Hane was or was not a holder in due course has no relevance to the issue here presented. In either case timely presentment and notice of dishonor were required to hold the Extens. Whether Hane was or was not a holder in due course is of no significance unless there was a defense which could have been asserted against the payee. *Brock v. Adams* 79 N.M. 17, 439 P.2d 234 (1968); *Persson v. McCormick,* 412 P.2d 619 (Okla.1966); and § 3–305.

Judgment affirmed, costs to be paid by appellant.

MAKEL TEXTILES, INC. v. DOLLY ORIGINALS, INC.

New York Supreme Court, 1967.
4 U.C.C.Rep.Serv. 95.

[Defendants Nathan Goldberg and Fred Kushner were indorsers of a note on which Dolly Originals, Inc., was maker. They both defended that there had been no presentment or notice of dishonor.]

SPIEGEL, J. * * *

From all the evidence adduced upon the trial of this action, it appears that the defendant Nathan Goldberg was the president and principal officer of the defendant Dolly Originals, Inc. As such president, he executed the promissory notes and signed the corporate checks hereinabove mentioned. The promissory notes were also endorsed by him as an individual. By virtue of his active participation in the affairs of Dolly Originals, Inc., it is obvious that the defendant Nathan Goldberg well knew that the notes could not be and were not paid from corporate funds. Under these circumstances the obligation to serve Goldberg with notice of dishonor and non-payment must be deemed unnecessary, at least impliedly, within the meaning of the Uniform

Commercial Code. Plaintiff's failure to present the notes for payment and give the said defendant notice of non-payment could not and did not injure nor prejudice his rights in any way. Formal notice of presentment and dishonor to Mr. Goldberg would be merely a useless gesture of advising him of a fact with which he was most familiar (UCC §§ 3–507, 3–511 [R 3–502, R 3–504]; J.W. O'Bannon Co. v. Curran, 129 App.Div. 90; William S. Chemical Co. v. Root, 152 N.Y.S. 368; Nemser v. Goldman, 145 N.Y.S.2d 841).

The defendant Fred Kushner was an endorser only, on each of the two notes for $5,000 (Pl.Exs. 2A and 2B) above mentioned. As to said defendant Kushner, the record is void of any testimony, or proof of notice of presentment and dishonor as required under the Uniform Commercial Code. Nor is there any evidence of any activity or participation in the affairs of the corporation so as to excuse presentment or notice of dishonor.

Accordingly, the defendant Fred Kushner may have judgment against the plaintiff dismissing the complaint, and the plaintiff may have judgment against the defendant Nathan Goldberg in the sum of $8,000 with interest thereon from May 12, 1965.

Note

1. *Waiver of presentment and notice of dishonor.* There are only a handful of reported cases in which the indorser of a negotiable note claims discharge because of a failure of the holder to properly present or give notice of dishonor. The paucity of such cases is no doubt the result of the fact that nearly all negotiable notes contain a provision similar to the following: "Each party to this note waives presentment, notice of dishonor, and all other demands or notices and assents to any extension of the time of payment." Under OR 3–511(6) and R 3–504(a)(iii) and (b)(i) such a provision is binding on indorsers. Also, even if the note itself does not contain a waiver, waivers could be written above or below the signature of an indorser.

If there is a waiver of presentment and notice of dishonor, the indorser's liability becomes the same as that of the maker. That is, there are no conditions to the indorser's liability and the holder, rather than asking the maker to pay, can make immediate demand on the indorser.

2. *Original Article 3 presentment rules: their justification.* As *Hane* indicates, under original Article 3, a failure to make presentment (demand for payment—OR 3–504) on the maker or drawee within the times specified in the statute, or a failure to give notice of dishonor within three days after learning of the dishonor discharges an indorser unless presentment and notice of dishonor are excused. In the case of a note payable on a specified day, OR 3–503(1)(c) requires that presentment be made on that day. If, for example, the holder of a note due on March 15th, 1991, failed to make demand on the maker on that day, any indorsers on the note would be discharged from liability unless presentment was excused. If presentment was made, notice of dishonor by March 18th would be necessary to hold the indorser. See OR 3–508.

The original Article 3 rules as to time of presentment for instruments not due on a specified date are somewhat flexible but nevertheless failure to present within the proper time discharges an indorser. See OR 3–502 and 3–503.

The reason for making prompt presentment and notice of dishonor a condition of the liability of indorsers, while not doing so as to drawers, rests on the differences in their positions. Until a draft has been paid, a drawer has not discharged the obligation for which the draft was given. The drawer has, in effect, given up nothing until the draft is paid. However, an indorser is typically in a net zero position after the transfer of an instrument. He received value when he took the instrument and gave value by transferring the instrument. Therefore, if the indorser now has to pay the instrument, the indorser will be a net loser unless he can recover against the drawer, maker, or other prior parties. The presentment and notice requirements are calculated to give the indorser prompt notice so that he can immediately proceed against the drawer, maker, or prior indorsers.

Those reasons for imposing liability on indorsers only if there is prompt presentment and notice of dishonor are rational. However, as already noted, they have little actual effect because of waivers in negotiable notes and because as to checks deposited by the payee in a bank, the bank has a right of chargeback not dependent on indorser liability. Further, the rule of original Article 3 that presentment of a note due on a specified date has to be made on that date is totally out of step with modern practice. Today the essentially universal expectation is that the holder does not have to seek out the maker of such a note, but, that, to the contrary, the maker will undertake to make payment to the holder, often by mail.

Revised Article 3 makes substantial changes in the presentment and notice of dishonor rules. In summary, the new rules are:

1. **Presentment.** Presentment is not necessary for a note payable on a specified date unless the note is payable at or through a bank. (R 3–502(a)(3)). Since presentment is not necessary, such a note is dishonored if it is not paid on the date. (R 3–502(a)(3)). In other cases presentment is necessary (R 3–502(a)(3)), but a delay in presentment of an instrument other than a check does not discharge an indorser. That is, an indorser cannot be sued unless there is first a presentment to the maker or drawee, but, no matter how long the holder delays presentment, once presentment is made and there is a dishonor, an indorser is liable so long as the statute of limitations has not yet run. (R 3–415). In the case of a check, failure to present for initial bank collection within 30 days after the indorsement discharges the indorser. (R 3–415(e)).

2. **Notice of Dishonor.** However long presentment is delayed, once the instrument is dishonored, the indorser's liability is discharged unless (1) as to instruments handled for collection by banks, notice of dishonor is given by a collecting bank by its midnight deadline, and by others within 30 days of the time they receive notice of dishonor, and (2) as to other instruments, notice of dishonor is given within "30 days following the day on which dishonor occurs." See R 3–503 for a full statement of the rules as to notice of dishonor.

Problem

On March 15, 1993, Client approaches you with a $10,000 negotiable note she has just taken from her safety deposit box. The note is dated August 1, 1980, shows a due date of February 15, 1993, is payable to Marge Hoots, and is signed by Jim Jones. Jones is somewhere in Laos. However, Hoots, who indorsed the note over to Client is in town and solvent. Client received the note from Hoots for value in June, 1983. For reasons not relevant to this problem, she had ignored the existence of the note until the day she appears in your office. Under revised Article 3, can Client recover from Hoots on the note? If so, what steps should be taken to assure liability? See R 3–415, 3–502, 3–504, 3–503.

Under original Article 3, Hoots clearly would not be liable since notice of dishonor was not given within 3 days of February 15. Even if presentment were excused because Jones was in Laos in 1993, the note would have been dishonored and, assuming that Hoots could have been found, notice of dishonor was not excused. See OR 3–507(1)(b) and 3–508(2).

EXCURSUS: ACCOMMODATION PARTY CONTRACT LIABILITY

1. The Contract of Guaranty

As several of the cases that have appeared up to this point in the book demonstrate, it is a common commercial practice to engage the obligation of one party to pay the debt of (become a surety for) another if that other does not pay.

A common non-commercial paper example is the surety company that agrees to complete a building or pay subcontractors and suppliers if the building contractor defaults on either obligation. Another common situation is that of the shareholder of a closely held corporation who personally promises to pay a particular debt of the corporation if the corporation itself does not pay. In suretyship law, the person whose debt the surety promises to pay is called the principal debtor and will be so designated hereafter in this note. The person to whom the obligation is owed is the "creditor."

There are a number of situations in which the law treats one person as surety for another even though there is no agreement between the two that one shall serve as surety for the other. An example of such a non-consensual surety is the ordinary indorser-transferor of a negotiable instrument who becomes, in effect, a surety for all those who were liable on the note when he indorsed it.

Consensual sureties often make their promise to stand behind the debt of another by signing on a negotiable instrument with the principal debtor. While the draftsmen of the Commercial Code did not codify the law of suretyship, they did include several sections in Article 3 which contain some rules of suretyship law applicable to signers of negotiable instruments. These sections in original Article 3 are 3–415, 3–416, and 3–606. In revised Article 3, the sections are 3–419 and 3–605.

The Code describes the consensual surety on commercial paper as an "accommodation party." Original 3–414(1) states "An accommodation party is one who signs the instrument in any capacity for the purpose of lending his name to another party to it." Revised 3–419(a) also describes the surety as an accommodation party, though the definition is somewhat different.

An accommodation party may sign either as maker, one of several co-makers, or as an indorser or acceptor or even as drawer (though an accommodation drawer would be unusual). For example, if Sam has agreed to become an accommodation party on a note which John will give to Bank in return for a Bank loan to John, Sam and John might sign as co-makers, or John might sign as maker with Sam indorsing on the back. Occasionally, in such a case, Sam will sign as maker a note made payable either to John or to Bank and John will indorse the note on the back. However Sam signs, if the Bank makes the loan to John, Sam is an accommodation party or surety. In this note, we will briefly cover some of the basic law of suretyship and its relationship to negotiable instruments law and the accommodation party.

2. Contract Formation

a. Statute of Frauds

Among the contracts required to be in writing by the original English statute of frauds was a "promise to answer for the debt, default or miscarriage of another." Most states presently have statutes with the same or similar language which requires suretyship contracts to be in writing. Under these statutes, the so-called main purpose doctrine has developed under which the contract of the claimed surety is enforceable, though oral, if his "main purpose" was not to serve as surety for another but to serve some independent purpose of his own. See 2 A. Corbin, Contracts, §§ 366–370. The main purpose rule, however, has no importance for statute of frauds purposes in commercial paper suretyship law since the ordinary statute of frauds rules do not apply to commercial paper. The accommodation party is liable on a negotiable instrument in the capacity in which he signs and no writing other than his signature on the negotiable instrument is necessary to make him liable. OR 3–415(2), R 3–419(b).

b. Consideration

Generally a suretyship contract, like any contract, requires consideration to be enforceable. The consideration may, however, flow from the creditor to the principal debtor, or from the principal debtor or the creditor to the surety. If the creditor agrees to extend credit to the debtor if the surety will guarantee the debt, the extension of credit is sufficient consideration for the surety's promise: There is no requirement that separate consideration move to the surety. Many sureties, like the father who signs a note to enable his son to get a loan, derive no financial or material benefit themselves from the suretyship.

U.C.C. § 1–201(44) provides that a person gives value for rights if he acquires them as "security for or in total or partial satisfaction of a pre-existing claim." Under this definition of value, a promise by a debtor to give additional security for an existing debt is binding without any new consideration from the creditor. Also, Article 3 provides that for holder in due course purposes a person gives value for a negotiable instrument to the extent that he takes it "in payment of or as security for an antecedent claim against any person * * *." See OR 3–303; see also R 3–303(a)(3). Similarly, OR 3–415 provides that "when the instrument has been taken for value before it is due the accommodation party is liable in the capacity in which he has signed even though the taker knows of the accommodation." That section, in language which is not as clear as one might hope, is "intended to change occasional decisions holding that there is no sufficient consideration where an accommodation party signs a note after it is in the hands of a holder who has given value." Comment 3 to OR 3–415. Revised 3–419(b) more clearly states "The obligation of an accommodation party may be enforced * * * whether or not the accommodation party receives consideration for the accommodation." Therefore, consistent with the general U.C.C. rule as to promise of additional security for an antecedent debt, an accommodation party is liable on the note even though he signs after the note has already been delivered to the holder and even though the holder gives no additional value in return for the signature of the accommodation party.

3. Rights of the Surety Against the Principal Debtor

As between the principal debtor and the surety, obviously the principal debtor is the one who should pay the debt. As Revised 3–419(e) says "[a]n accommodation party who pays the instrument is entitled to reimbursement from the accommodated party and is entitled to enforce the instrument against the accommodated party." See also OR 3–415(5).

The law gives the surety various rights aimed at assisting the surety in placing ultimate duty of payment on the principal debtor. These rights are cataloged below.

a. Right of Exoneration

A surety who has become such with the assent of the principal debtor has the right to bring suit to compel the principal debtor to pay the debt. Presumably, this right of exoneration is fully available to the accommodation party on commercial paper.

b. Right to Reimbursement and Subrogation

If the surety does pay the debt, he has the right to be repaid by the principal debtor. However, there is generally neither a right of reimbursement against the principal debtor if the surety paid with knowledge that the principal debtor had a defense against the creditor, nor a right of reimbursement against a principal debtor who would not be liable to the creditor because of a lack of capacity or because of a discharge in insolvency proceedings. Presumably the statement in revised 3–419(e) that the surety is entitled to reimbursement from the principal debtor is not intended to change the common law, which denies reimbursement if the surety paid with knowledge of a defense available to the principal debtor.

In aid of the right to reimbursement the surety has the right to be subrogated to the rights of the creditor against the principal debtor. If, for example, the creditor holds a security interest in property of the principal debtor to secure the debt for which the surety is liable, the surety, if he pays the debt, is subrogated to the rights of the creditor under the security interest. Among the subrogation rights of the surety who signs a negotiable instrument with the principal debtor is the right to sue *on the instrument.* See OR 3–415(5) and R 3–419(e).

4. Right to Contribution From Co–Sureties

Frequently, several persons will become co-sureties for an obligation. Contribution is the right of a surety who has paid the debt to require his co-sureties to pay a pro-rata part of the debt. The amount a co-surety will be required to contribute will usually be determined by the number of solvent sureties subject to the jurisdiction of the court. Suppose, for example, that five co-sureties have agreed to be liable on a $3,000 debt that surety A has paid. Suppose further that sureties B, C, and D are subject to the jurisdiction of the court but that surety D is insolvent and unable to pay any part of the debt. B and C will each be required to contribute $1,000 to A. Of course, when there is more than one surety for the debt, they are not necessarily co-sureties. The second surety may have promised only "I will pay if principal debtor and first surety do not pay," and third surety may have promised only "I will pay if principal debtor and first and second surety do not pay" and so on. If that is the nature of the promises, there is, of course, no right of contribution among the sureties and, if third surety pays he can recover against either principal debtor or first or second surety. Where there is more than one surety on a negotiable instrument, whether there is a right of contribution among sureties will depend, of course, on whether they intended to be co-sureties or whether each is a surety for the principal debtor and other prior sureties. Original 3–414(2) states a presumption that applies where sureties indorse a negotiable note. "Unless they otherwise agree indorsers are liable to one another in the order in which they indorse, which is presumed to be the order in which their signatures appear on the instrument." In the case law, the presumption is regularly overcome by proof that indorsers intended to be co-sureties. Original 3–414(2) is not continued in revised Article 3; the Comment to R 3–415 says that OR 3–414(2) is omitted "because it is superfluous." Presumably, the omission does not in any way change the law. See, however, revised 3–116(a) which may be an impediment to a showing that a surety who signed at the same time as other sureties did not intend to be a co-surety.

5. Defenses to Liability

a. Defenses Arising Out of the Contract Between the Creditor and the Principal Debtor (Derivative Defenses)

The issue discussed here is the extent to which the surety is given the benefit of defenses that the principal debtor would have against the creditor. Common sense would tell us that the surety cannot defend that his principal did not have capacity to contract or that his principal has been discharged in bankruptcy. It is just those risks that lead the creditor to require a surety in the first place.

Failure of consideration (non-performance by the creditor) on the other hand should be and is a defense to the surety. It would seem, also, that other contract defenses such as fraud or partial breach should be a defense to the surety. However, some courts have held that such defenses to liability may not be raised. Original 3–306(d) presents a possible additional impediment to assertion by the surety of principal's contract defenses against the creditor or holder. Generally under that section, a party on a negotiable instrument cannot defend that the holder breached the contract (with some third party) under which the holder acquired the instrument. For example, if Maker gives a $2500 note to Payee who then transfers it to Holder in return for a 1986 Ardvark 6 automobile, when Holder sues Maker on the note, Maker cannot defend that the Ardvark was defective. The contract law is generally the same: An obligor cannot raise as a defense against an assignee breach by the assignee of his contract with the assignor.

The rule is, it would seem, proper in assignment or transferor situations. In the Ardvark example, the breach of contract claim of Payee is his own claim and he should be entitled to recover damages for Holder's breach. However, there is no reason why Maker should be able to avoid paying his debt because of a breach of contract between other parties.

But OR 3–306(d) is not limited to assignment or transfer situations. It states that except for claims arising out of theft or payment inconsistent with a restrictive indorsement, "The claim of a third party to the instrument is not otherwise available as a defense to any party liable thereon unless the third party himself defends the action for such party."

That language, read literally, would suggest that a surety cannot raise defenses of his principal debtor against the creditor unless the principal debtor is joined in the action. The surety-principal debtor-holder (creditor) relationship is, however, so different from the ordinary maker-payee-transferee situation that courts may be convinced (1) that sureties should be able to raise defenses of the principal debtor against the creditor and (2) that the draftsmen of OR 3–306(d) did not intend that section to deal with defenses of sureties. In addition, Professor (now Judge) Peters has argued that, since the creditor has an obligation to do nothing to increase the surety's risk, and since a breach by the creditor of his contract with the principal debtor surely increases the risk that the principal debtor will not pay, breach of the contract by the creditor is not a derivative defense for the surety but his own defense. If that argument is accepted, then, of course, OR 3–306(d) placing restrictions on the right of a party to assert defenses of third parties would not be applicable. See Ellen Peters, *Suretyship Under Article 3 of the UCC,* 77 Yale L.J. 833 at 865 (1968).

In Revised Article 3, the accommodation party is specifically given the right to assert any defense which the principal debtor could have asserted "except the defenses of discharge in insolvency proceedings, infancy, and lack of legal capacity." R 3–305(d).

b. Defenses Based Upon Suretyship Status

Generally the creditor must act with due regard to the surety's position and not in such a way as to make it less likely that the surety will receive reimbursement if the surety has to pay. This basic principle has resolved itself into a number of fairly specific common law rules. Sections OR 3–606 and R 3–605 also deal with defenses based on suretyship status. In the following part of this note we consider both the common law rules and the Article 3 rules. After the note, several cases further explore discharge under the Article 3 rules.

(i) Discharge of the Principal Debtor

Under general suretyship law release of the principal debtor by the creditor discharges the surety unless the surety assents or unless the creditor specifically reserves his rights against the surety. An express reservation of rights against the surety is effective because, it is said, a release of the principal debtor in such circumstances does not terminate the surety's right of reimbursement or subrogation. Therefore if the surety has to pay, he can proceed against the principal debtor even though the creditor could not. In other words, the release with reservation of rights against the surety is not viewed as a total discharge of the obligation but as a mere promise by the creditor that it will not itself sue the principal debtor. On the other hand, a discharge without reservation of rights is viewed as a total discharge which also terminates any rights of the surety to reimbursement or subrogation and therefore also releases the surety from his obligation to the creditor. The rationale just stated may appear to be artificial but the rules are well fixed, and original Article 3 restates them for Uniform Commercial Code sureties, including ordinary indorsers, in OR 3–606.

Revised Article 3, however, in 3–605(b) provides: "Discharge, under Section 3–604, of the obligation of a party to pay an instrument does not discharge the obligation of an indorser or accommodation party having a right of recourse against the discharged party." Therefore, under revised Article 3, it is no longer necessary for a creditor to reserve rights against the surety when the creditor releases the principal debtor. As the comment to R 3–605 points out, under OR 3–606, a holder who released the principal debtor could retain rights against the surety merely by expressly stating that the rights were being reserved. There was no requirement that the surety be notified of the reservation. See Comment 3 to R 3–605 which states the rationale for the revised Article 3 rule.

Discharge of the principal debtor by the running of the statute of limitations against the principal debtor is usually held to discharge the surety, but a few courts have reached a contrary result. Nothing in Article 3 deals with his issue so that courts probably would apply whatever rule they apply in cases not involving negotiable instruments.

(ii) Modification of Contracts, Extension of Time

The traditional view has been that any modification by the principal debtor and the creditor of their contract will discharge the surety unless the surety assents or unless the creditor specifically reserves his rights against the surety. However, some courts have held that a modification does not discharge the surety unless the modification is material. Some courts have further held that a modification does not discharge the surety unless it increases his risk. For example, many extensions of time for payment to principal debtors clearly do not increase the surety's risk and courts that discharge the surety only if the risk is increased would not treat the surety as discharged in such a case.

Original Article 3, however, discharges the surety when an extension is granted without regard to materiality or increased risk. See OR 3–606(1)(a): "The holder discharges any party to the instrument to the extent that he agrees to suspend the right to enforce the instrument." Original Article 3 does not deal with contract modifications other than extensions of time and it is not clear whether in that case courts will apply their pre-Code law, reason by analogy from § 3–606, or say that no other modification discharges the surety, though the last result seems unlikely.

Under revised Article 3, however, an extension of time to the principal debtor discharges a surety only to the extent the surety proves that the extension of time caused loss to the surety with respect to the right of recourse. R 3–605(c). Revised Article 3 also deals with modifications of the principal debtor's obligation other than extensions of time and provides that material modifications discharge the surety unless the person enforcing the instrument proves that the loss to the surety from the modification was less than the amount of the right of recourse.

(iii) Impairment of Collateral

A failure of the creditor to take reasonable steps to protect his rights in collateral will discharge the surety to the extent of the value of the collateral lost. For example, the failure to properly perfect a security interest with a resulting loss in priority will discharge the surety to the extent of the loss incurred. This rule is made specifically applicable to the negotiable instrument surety by OR 3–606(1)(b) and R 3–605(f).

(iv) Right to Require the Creditor to Proceed Against Principal Debtor

In about half the states a surety in some circumstances has the right to demand that the creditor bring suit against the debtor so that the surety will not be required to perform. In most of those states the rule is established by statute, but in a few, by judicial decision.

The Illinois statute is set out below:

Illinois Revised Stat. Ch. 132, Sec. 1

Surety May Compel Diligence By Creditor

When any person as surety for another for the payment of money, or the performance of any other contract in writing, apprehends that his principal is likely to become insolvent or to remove from the state, without discharging the contract, if a right of action has accrued on the contract, he may, by writing, require the creditor forthwith to sue upon the same; and unless such creditor shall within a reasonable time, and with due diligence, commence suit thereon, and prosecute the same to final judgment and execution, the surety shall be discharged; but no such discharge shall in any case affect the rights of the creditor against the principal debtor.

The last case in which the Illinois statute was applied to an accommodation party on a negotiable instrument seems to be *Wurster v. Albrecht,* 237 Ill.App. 284 (1925). In that case it was assumed that the act would apply to discharge an accommodation party on a negotiable instrument if the holder did not, on demand, bring suit against the principal debtor in the circumstances stated by the statute. However, the court held that accommodation parties were not discharged by the holder's failure to bring suit when it appeared that, at all times after the demand and up until suit against the accommodation parties, the principal debtor was insolvent and without assets so that a suit against him would not have helped the sureties.

It is arguable that OR 3–415(2) which states that an accommodation party is "* * * liable in the capacity in which he has signed * * *" and R 3–419(b) which states the same rule mean that an accommodation party is liable according to the rules of Article 3 and that other non-Code rules conditioning liability on other acts by the holder no longer apply. That is, since those sections state that sureties will pay with only the conditions to liability stated in the Code, accommodation parties are liable according to those rules and no others.

The student of commercial transactions can best understand the surety cases by recognizing that the guarantor is something of a favorite of the courts. While it might be difficult to reconcile many of the cases that result in abrogation of the guaranty undertaking, creditors who take guaranties should be aware that courts are often not reluctant to excuse the guarantor from performance of the guaranty obligation, unless counsel for the creditor seeking to enforce the guaranty can convince the court that avoiding the guaranty would profoundly frustrate the expectations of the commercial community. Though there may be a measure of hyperbole in that assertion, it encourages the type of vigilance on the part of creditors' counsel that is indispensable in the guaranty context. See Peter A. Alces, The Efficacy of Guaranty Contracts in Sophisticated Commercial Transactions, 61 N.C.L.Rev. 655 (1983) and the sources cited therein for a further discussion of suretyship defenses.

In the context of negotiable instruments any discharge of a surety is a personal defense and therefore unavailable against a holder in due course who is unaware of the discharge.

6. Forms of Guaranty

Commercial attorneys have become quite familiar with the standard (and even the exotic) defenses asserted by sureties and have attempted to preclude their assertion by terms of the long form guaranty (not within Article 3) as well as by the language accompanying the form of guaranty on negotiable instruments. A typical form guaranty that might appear on a negotiable instrument is reproduced below.

> For value received, the undersigned (who, if two or more in number, shall be jointly and severally obligated hereunder) hereby unconditionally guarantee(s) the payment of the Note on the reverse side hereof and all extensions or renewals thereof, and all expenses (including reasonable attorneys' fees and legal expenses) incurred in the collection thereof, the enforcement of rights under any security therefor and the enforcement hereof, and waive(s) presentment, demand, notice of dishonor, protest, and all other notices whatsoever, and agree(s) that the holder of said Note may from time to time, at its sole discretion, extend or renew said Note for one or more periods (whether or not longer than the original period of said Note) and grant any releases, compromises or indulgences with respect to said Note or any extension or renewal thereof or any security therefor or to any obligor thereunder or hereunder, all without notice to any of the undersigned and without affecting the obligations of the undersigned hereunder.

How might you adjust the terms of that form in order to best protect the interest of (i) a creditor client, (ii) a guarantor client?

FITHIAN v. JAMAR

Maryland Court of Appeal, 1979.
286 Md. 161, 410 A.2d 569.

COLE, J. The dispute in this case involves the rights and liabilities of co-makers of a note in a suit among themselves, where none of the disputants is a holder of the note. We granted certiorari to consider two questions, which simply stated are:

1. Whether a co-maker of a note was also an accommodation maker of the note and thus not liable to the party accommodated;

2. Whether the agreement of one co-maker to assume another co-maker's obligation on a note constitutes a defense to the latter when sued for contribution by the former.

In 1967 Walter Fithian (Walter) and Richard Jamar (Richard), who were employed as printers at Baltimore Business Forms, decided to form a partnership to carry on their own printing business. They applied to the People's Bank of Chestertown, Maryland (Bank) for an $11,000 business loan to enable them to purchase some equipment. The Bank agreed to lend the money to Walter and Richard only if Walter's wife, Connie, Richard's wife, Janet, and Walter's parents, Walter William (Bill) and Mildred Fithian would co-sign the note. The Executive Vice–President of the Bank explained that the additional signatures were required to make the Bank more secure. The note, which authorized confession of judgment in the event of default, was signed on its face in the bottom right-hand corner by these six parties. The monies loaned were deposited in Walter and Richard's business checking account and were used to purchase printing equipment.

By 1969, Walter and Richard were encountering business problems. They spoke with Frank Hogans (Hogans) and Gerald Bos (Bos) (who were interested in joining the business) about forming a corporation to be called J–F Printing Co., Inc. and refinancing the note so that it (the note) could become a corporate rather than an individual obligation. The business continued to falter and on March 23, 1972 Walter, Richard, Hogans and Bos met and entered into a written agreement in their individual capacities whereby Richard was to take over management and ownership of the business in exchange for his assumption of liability for the company's outstanding obligations, one of which is the note in question in this case. The agreement also provided that should Richard default in the performance of those obligations, Walter, Hogans, and Bos would have the right to terminate the agreement and resume ownership of the business.

Pursuant to the agreement Richard assumed control of the business but was unable to make any further payments on the note. Consequently, the Executive Vice–President of the Bank requested that Bill and Mildred Fithian pay the note in full. They did and the Bank assigned the note to them for whatever disposition they might choose. Bill demanded that Richard indemnify him for the total amount Bill paid on the note.

Receiving no satisfaction from Richard, Bill and Mildred sought judicial relief. On November 10, 1976, a confessed judgment against Richard and Janet of $8,953.95, the balance on the note paid by Bill and Mildred, with interest from January 18, 1974, court costs, and attorney's fees of $472.70, was entered in the Circuit Court for Kent County. Richard and Janet filed a motion to vacate the judgment, which the circuit court granted and ordered a hearing on the merits. Prior to trial, Richard and Janet filed a third party claim against Walter and Connie averring that as co-makers of the note, Walter and Connie were liable to Richard and Janet for any judgment that Bill and Mildred might recover against Richard and Janet. Walter and Connie counterclaimed contending that the agreement barred Richard's recovery.

The matter was brought to trial on August 25, 1977 before the circuit court, sitting without a jury. The court found that the J–F Printing Company, Inc. was never a de jure corporation and that those who attempted to act under that name were merely acting in their individual capacities; that the March 23, 1972 agreement was not material to the determination of the case; that Bill and Mildred were accommodation makers for Richard, Janet, Walter and Connie and were entitled to collect from any one of the four.

Final judgment was entered on September 6, 1977 for Bill and Mildred against Richard and Janet in the amount of $8,953.95, the principal sum due, plus $2,288.95, representing interest from January 18, 1974 to August 25, 1977. The court denied Bill and Mildred's claim for collection fees specified in the note and also entered a judgment for

Richard and Janet on Walter and Connie's counterclaim. In the third party claim of Richard and Janet against Walter and Connie, judgment was entered for Richard and Janet in the amount of $5,621.45, fifty percent of the total judgment. The costs of the case were to be divided equally between Richard and Janet and Walter and Connie.

Bill and Mildred Fithian filed a timely appeal to the Court of Special Appeals, complaining of the circuit court's adverse ruling as to the collection fees. Walter and Connie took their own appeal, challenging the lower court's findings concerning both Connie's status in relation to the note and the materiality of the March, 1972 agreement. These appeals were consolidated for oral argument in that court.

In an unreported per curiam decision filed on April 7, 1978, Fithian v. Jamar, No. 946, Sept. Term, 1977, the Court of Special Appeals affirmed the circuit court in part and reversed in part. The Court of Special Appeals reversed on the issue of collection fees, ruling that there was a "valid and enforcible contract right of Bill and Mildred to the payment of collection costs * * * "; the Court of Special Appeals affirmed the circuit court's finding that Connie Fithian was a co-maker of the note, and not an accommodation party. The Court of Special Appeals also affirmed the trial court's finding that the March, 1972 agreement was not material to the case because it was "a private agreement between only two (2) of the six (6) makers of the note."

Walter and Connie (appellants) requested review of these rulings in this Court, and we granted their petition for certiorari on June 21, 1978 to consider the two questions presented: whether Connie Fithian was an accommodation maker of the note and thus not liable to the party accommodated; and whether the March, 1972 agreement constitutes a defense to Richard and Janet's (appellees) third party claim against Walter and Connie.

Our disposition of the questioned rulings requires us to reverse and remand. The error which occurred in the court below was caused in part by a failure to fully analyze the individual rights and obligations of Connie, Walter, Janet and Richard. Therefore, in the discussion which follows, in addition to examining the two questions presented, we will clarify the resulting rights and obligations of these parties.

RICHARD V. CONNIE

Since there is no dispute that Connie signed the note, the answer to the first question depends on her purpose in doing so. This is made clear by Maryland Code (1975), § 3–415(1) [R 3–419(a)] of the Commercial Law Article which provides that an accommodation party is "one who signs the instrument in any capacity for the purpose of lending his name to another party to it." The undisputed evidence as presented by the Executive Vice–President of the Bank was to the effect that the wives' signatures were required before the Bank would make the loan to Walter and Richard. Such practices are common among lending institutions which recognize that

> "[o]ne with money to lend, goods to sell or services to render may have doubts about a prospective debtor's ability to pay. In such cases he is likely to demand more assurance than the debtor's bare promise of payment. The prospective creditor can reduce his risk by requiring some sort of security. One form of security is the Article 9 security interest in the debtor's goods. Another type of security takes the form of joining a third person on the debtor's obligation." [J. White and R. Summers, Uniform Commercial Code § 13–12, at 425 (1972)].

It is readily apparent, therefore, that Connie lent her name to facilitate the loan transaction. As such she lent her name to two parties to the instrument, Richard and Walter, to enable them to receive a *joint* loan for the purchase of equipment for their printing business, thereby giving the Bank the added assurance of having another party to the obligation. Connie signed as an accommodation party as to both Walter and Richard.

Nor is there any merit in the argument advanced by Richard that Connie must be either a co-maker or an accommodation party, that she cannot be both. The actual language of § 3–415(1) [R 3–419(a)] indicates that an accommodation party also signs in a particular capacity, as maker, acceptor or indorser of an instrument. The Official Comment 1 to § 3–415 [R 3–419] explains that

> "[s]ubsection (1) recognizes that an accommodation party is always a surety (which includes a guarantor), and it is his only distinguishing feature. He differs from other sureties only in that his liability is on the instrument and he is a surety for another party to it. His obligation is therefore determined by the capacity in which he signs. An accommodation maker or acceptor is bound on the instrument without any resort to his principal, while an accommodation indorser may be liable only after presentment, notice of dishonor and protest."

Moreover, § 3–415(2) [R 3–419(b)] refers specifically to the liability of an accommodation party "in the capacity in which he signed." It follows, therefore, that the fact that Connie was a co-maker of the note does not preclude her from also being an accommodation party.

Section 3–415(5) [R 3–419(e)] of the Commercial Law Article states that "an accommodation party is not liable to the party accommodated"; thus, Connie is not liable to Richard. Our predecessors, prior to Maryland's adoption of the Uniform Commercial Code, explained the reasons for this proposition in Crothers v. National Bank, 158 Md. 587, 593, 149 A. 270 (1930):

> "Since the accommodating party lends his credit by request to the party accommodated upon the assumption that the latter will discharge the debt when due, it is an implied term of this agreement that the party accommodated cannot acquire any right of action against the accommodating party."

* * * It is clear to us that the signatures of both wives were required to effect this joint business venture and thus Connie's signature was as much an accommodation to Richard as it was to Walter. We hold that Connie was an accommodation maker and that she cannot be liable to Richard, the party accommodated. The Court of Special Appeals erroneously held to the contrary.

JANET V. CONNIE

The preceding discussion of Connie's status demonstrates that each of the four parties, Walter, Connie, Richard, and Janet, has certain rights and obligations with respect to this note which are not affected by his or her marital status. The court below erred in not fully analyzing these separate rights and obligations. It follows that our finding that Connie has no liability to Richard in no way changes any obligation she may have to Janet. Janet, as well as Connie, is a co-accommodation maker on this note.

The question is therefore whether one co-accommodation maker who pays more than her proportionate share of the debt has a right of contribution against another co-accommodation maker. The Uniform Commercial Code contains no provision expressly dealing with the right of an accommodation party to contribution from another accommodation party. However, the Code does provide that the principles of the common law remain applicable "[u]nless displaced by the particular provisions" of the Code. Maryland Code (1975), § 1–103 of the Commercial Law Article.

That an accommodation maker has a right of contribution from a co-accommodation maker is a settled principle of the law. The Restatement of Security provides

> "A surety who in the performance of his own obligation discharges more than his proportionate share of the principal's duty is entitled to contribution from a co-surety." [Restatement of Security § 149 (1941)].

* * *

Accordingly Janet has a right of contribution against Connie. But this right to contribution is an inchoate claim which does not ripen into being unless and until Janet pays more than her proportionate share to Bill and Mildred. Cotham and Maldonado v. Board, 260 Md. 556, 556–67, 273 A.2d 115 (1971). Judgment can be entered on behalf of Janet against Connie, but it must be fashioned so that it may not be enforced until Janet proves she actually paid more than her proportionate share to Bill and Mildred.[1]

1. A surety who is called upon to pay more than his proportionate share of the debt has a right of contribution from his co-sureties in an amount not to exceed each co-surety's proportionate share of the debt. See Schindel v. Danzer, 161 Md. 384, 157 A. 283 (1931); 72 C.J.S. Principal and Surety § 369 (1951). Here the note was signed by four sureties (Bill, Mildred, Connie and Janet); Janet's proportionate share of indebtedness to her co-sureties is 25% of the debt.

RICHARD v. WALTER

We now turn to the second question as to whether the March, 1972 agreement by which Richard assumed full liability on the note constitutes a defense to Richard and Janet's third party claim that Walter and Connie reimburse them for fifty percent of the primary judgment granted to Bill and Mildred against Richard and Janet. In the circuit court Bill and Mildred Fithian, having paid the instrument to the Bank, successfully exercised their right of recourse on the note under § 3–415(5) [R 3–419(e)] of the Commercial Law Article which provides that "[a]n accommodation party is not liable to the party accommodated, and if he pays the instrument has a right of recourse against such party." In discussing this general principle of suretyship law Professors White and Summers explain that

> "[a]s between the surety and the debtor, it is clear that the debtor has the primary obligation to pay the debt. Since the creditor is entitled to only one performance and the debtor receives the benefit of the transaction, the surety's obligation is undertaken with the expectation that the debtor will meet his commitment to the creditor. Thus if the surety is made to pay his principal's debt, he has the right to recover from the principal." [J. White and R. Summers, Uniform Commercial Code, § 13–12, at 426 (1972) (footnote omitted)].

This court has adhered to the principle that if an accommodation party pays the note to the holder, he has a right of recourse against the party accommodated. Fuhrman v. Fuhrman, 115 Md. 436, 80 A. 1082 (1911).

Similarly, it is axiomatic that one joint obligor may ordinarily claim contribution from a co-obligor after having discharged their mutual obligation. However, this principle is not controlling in the instant case. While the courts below ruled that Walter and Connie must reimburse Richard and Janet for one-half the judgment against them and discounted the significance of the 1972 agreement on this question, we believe that under both statutory and common law principles the 1972 agreement is material to the decision of this case and plays a substantial role in our determination of whether Walter was properly required to pay contribution to Richard. Because neither Connie nor Janet were parties to the agreement, their rights and obligations are not affected.

In the first place, § 3–601(2) [R 3–601(a)] of the Commercial Law Article and the Official Comments thereto specifically recognize the possibility of discharge by act or agreement of a party who is otherwise liable on an instrument. Section 3–601(2) [R 3–601(a)] reads: "Any party is also discharged from his liability on an instrument to another party by any other act or agreement with such party which would discharge his simple contract for the payment of money." Official Comment 2 to § 3–601 [R 3–601] reads in pertinent part that

> "[s]o far as the discharge of any one party is concerned a negotiable instrument differs from any other contract only in the

special rules arising out of its character to which paragraphs (a) to (i) of subsection (1) are an index, and in the effect of the discharge against a subsequent holder in due course (Section 3–602) [R 3–601(b)]. *Subsection (2) therefore retains from the original Section 119(4) the provision for discharge by 'any other act which will discharge a simple contract for the payment of money,' and specifically recognizes the possibility of a discharge by agreement.*

"*The discharge of any party is a defense available to that party as provided in sections on rights of those who are and are not holders* in due course (Sections 3–305 and 3–306) [R 3–305 and 3–306]. He has the burden of establishing the defense (Section 3–307) [R 3–308]." [emphasis supplied].

While this court has not addressed this precise issue under § 3–601(2) [R 3–601(a)], two recent decisions of other jurisdictions do acknowledge that under § 3–601 [R 3–601], liability of a party on a negotiable instrument may be discharged by a written agreement. Several other courts have endorsed the proposition that co-makers of an instrument may vary their obligations between themselves. Still other courts have held that parol evidence of a special agreement between co-obligors is admissible where liability to a payee is not at issue.

Applying these principles to the present case, we believe that the 1972 agreement operated to modify the liabilities of Richard and Walter on the note between themselves. We accept the trial court's finding based on the record before it that the partnership between Richard and Walter never was converted into a duly constituted corporation and that the parties conducted the business in their individual capacities rather than as directors of a corporation. Thus, the agreement expressed the intentions of these individuals as between themselves, and as such reflects the transfer of all of the assets and liabilities of the business to Richard in return for his promise to keep the other interested parties, Walter, Hogans and Bos, free from any responsibility for payment of any and all of the business debts, including the note in question. The only safety valve for the transferring individuals was their right upon their own decision to terminate the agreement if Richard demonstrated an inability or unwillingness to keep his promise. Richard and Janet in their briefs concede that the evidence of this agreement is "arguably material" but contend that it is "not highly probative." We disagree. The language of the agreement shows that Richard specifically consented to take responsibility for the obligations of the printing business, including the $11,000 note to the Bank: * * *

By this agreement, which was not terminated when Richard defaulted on payment of the loan in subsequent years, Walter and Richard agreed that Richard alone was to henceforth bear responsibility for the note. Thus the document's operative effect was to discharge Walter from any obligation on the note as to Richard. Thus the trial court should have entered judgment for Walter on his counterclaim against Richard for indemnification. In other words, by the agreement, Richard gave up his right to claim contribution from his joint obligor, Walter. Therefore, the Court of Special Appeals below erred in affirming judgment for Richard against Walter.

JANET V. WALTER

That the 1972 agreement serves as a defense by Walter against Richard in no way serves to insulate Walter against Janet. Janet's status as an accommodation maker is unaffected by the agreement. As an accommodation maker, Janet has a right to look to any principal, including Walter for any amounts she actually pays. Maryland Code (1975), § 3–415 [R 3–419] of the Commercial Law Article. Janet's status as Richard's wife does not affect her status as an accommodation maker. She is entitled to judgment from either principal when she actually pays any amount of the debt.

In summary, Richard is not entitled to judgment against Walter because of the agreement. Rather, Walter is entitled to indemnification from Richard for any amount Walter is forced to pay. Richard is not entitled to judgment against Connie because an accommodation party is not liable to the party accommodated. Janet is entitled to contribution from her co-surety, Connie, the judgment being unenforceable unless and until Janet proves she actually has paid more than her proportionate share of the debt to Bill and Mildred. Similarly, Janet as a surety is entitled to judgment against Walter as a principal for any amount of the debt for which Janet proves payment.[3]

Judgment of the court of special appeals reversed; remanded to that court with instructions to reverse the judgment of the circuit court for Kent County and to remand to that court with instructions to enter appropriate judgments consistent with the views expressed herein. Costs to be paid by the appellee, Richard F. Jamar.

Note

In footnote one, the court states that Janet's share of the indebtedness is 25% and that, if she pays more than that she can recover proportionately from Connie. However, Bill and Mildred have a judgment against Janet for the full amount of the debt and Janet did not appeal from that judgment. Is it possible that Janet and Connie were primary sureties and Bill and Mildred were secondary sureties? That is, is it possible that Janet and Connie agreed that if Bill and Mildred had to pay they would fully reimburse Bill and Mildred? If so, could that be shown? See OR 3–414(2) and the discussion, supra, page 143. See also R 3–116 and R 3–419.

Why does Richard's agreement to assume Walter's responsibility on the note not affect Connie's right to a judgment against Walter?

3. Whether Bill and Mildred were entitled to judgment in the full amount of the debt against Janet we do not decide because Janet did not appeal from that judgment.

Problems

1. A negotiable note payable to First Bank for $10,000 is signed by Jerry Iguess. On the back of the note the following appears: "The undersigned guarantee to the First Bank, its successors, indorsers or assigns, the punctual payment at maturity of said loan. /s/ Tom Daigle, David Chaisson, Marlene Daigle." Marlene Daigle is Tom Daigle's wife. The three had signed because Iguess asked Daigle and Chaisson to sign and the bank said that it must also have Marlene Daigle's signature. The bank did not make presentment of the note to Iguess or give notice of dishonor to the three persons who signed on the back. Nevertheless, on demand of the Bank, Tom Daigle paid the amount due ($12,000) on the note. Based on the above facts alone, to what extent can Daigle recover from Chaisson? See OR 3–416(1). Observe that OR 3–416(1) is not continued in revised Article 3. Does that mean that under revised Article 3, Daigle paid a debt that he need not have paid? See R 3–419(c). See also OR 3–118(e), OR 3–414, R 3–116. Cf. *Daigle v. Chaisson,* 396 So.2d 573 (La.App.1981).

2. Arthur and John agree to enter into a partnership selling automobile parts. Under the partnership agreement, Arthur is to contribute to the partnership a store building that he owns and John is to contribute $75,000. Arthur is to be the manager of the enterprise for which he will receive a salary of $50,000 per year. John needs to borrow $50,000 of the $75,000 he will contribute. John, therefore, applies at First Bank for a loan of $50,000. John tells the loan officer that he needs the money to contribute to a partnership with Arthur. The loan officer says that the bank will make the loan only if Arthur also signs the note. Arthur does sign.

As between John and Arthur, is Arthur a surety? Compare OR 3–415(1) with R 3–419(a). Hint: as between John and Arthur, who has ultimate liability for payment of the $50,000? Examine R 3–419(a). Is it clear to you that Arthur is not "a direct beneficiary of the value given for the instrument"? The use of the "direct beneficiary" test may be unfortunate: one could easily conclude that Arthur is a direct beneficiary. The real test is whether as between Arthur and John, John is the one who is obligated to pay the debt. Of course, unless the bank knows that, it can assume that both Arthur and John are equally liable, and Arthur would have, as against bank, only defenses that a co-maker would have. See OR 3–606 and R 3–605(h).

3. X Corporation owed Smith $10,000. It gave Smith a negotiable promissory note payable to Smith for $10,000. Smith asked his bank to buy the note, but the bank refused to do so unless the note was guaranteed by the sole shareholder of X Corporation, Jones. Smith then went back to Jones, told him that the bank had refused to buy the note without Jones' guarantee and asked Jones to sign the note as a co-maker. Jones did so. Smith then sold the note to the bank. The corporation became insolvent and did not pay. Bank made a demand on Jones for payment and he paid. Jones now sues Smith, claiming that as between Jones and Smith, Smith is

primarily liable. What result? This problem is suggested by Gibbs Oil Company v. Collentro & Collentro, 6 U.C.C.Rep.Serv. 361 (Mass.App.Div. 1968).

D. DISCHARGE

An indorser's liability is conditional upon compliance with any applicable presentment rules and upon proper notice of dishonor; we might say that failure to comply with those rules is a discharging event. In fact, OR 3–601(1)(i) says just that. However, in this Section of the casebook we deal with the discharging events specified in the substantive sections of Part 6 of Article 3. That Part deals with acts of a liable party or the holder (in revised Article 3 the "person entitled to enforce", R 3–301) that discharge the obligation.

1. *Payment*

CHENOWITH v. BANK OF DARDANELLE

Arkansas Supreme Court, 1967.
243 Ark. 310, 419 S.W.2d 792.

HARRIS, CHIEF JUSTICE.

Four checks in the amounts of $3,800.00, $3,000.00 (these checks being dated January 13, 1966), $1,242.55 and $155.00 (these checks being dated January 14, 1966) were drawn on the Citizens Bank of Pottsville by Glen D. Chenowith, appellant herein, made payable to Homer Parham. These checks were all deposited in the Bank of Dardanelle by Parham, where he had an account, and were forwarded on to the correspondent bank in Little Rock. When they reached the Pottsville Bank, this bank refused payment, noting insufficient funds on the two larger checks, and "Bank closed for examination" on the two smaller ones. The correspondent bank notified the Bank of Dardanelle by wire or telephone call that the checks were being returned. Thereupon, the Bank of Dardanelle, appellee herein examined Parham's balance, and found that he had on deposit in excess of $6,800.00; a hold order of $6,800.00 was placed on Parham's account so that when the unpaid checks were returned to Dardanelle, they would be covered.[3] In the meantime, Parham wrote a check to Chenowith, drawn on the Bank of Dardanelle, for $6,800.00, and this check was presented for payment in the Dardanelle Bank *after* the bank had been notified that the $3,800.00 and $3,000.00 checks had been turned down, but before those checks were actually forwarded to the Dardanelle bank. When this $6,800.00 check was presented, the bookkeeper at the Bank of Dardanelle mistakenly believed that the purpose of the $6,800.00 hold order was to cover this $6,800.00 check, and, under this belief, the hold order was removed and the $6,800.00 check was paid. When the two checks

3. The two smaller checks are not affected by the controlling statute in this litigation, and will be treated separately in this opinion.

(already turned down by the Pottsville bank) arrived at the Dardanelle bank, there were no funds in Parham's account to chargeback. A bank employee, not knowing that the hold order had been removed, and that Parham no longer had sufficient funds on deposit to cover a chargeback, mailed both checks to Parham with a notice advising the latter that the two unpaid checks would be charged back against his account. The bank was unable to collect the $6,800.00, and accordingly instituted suit in the Pope County Circuit Court against Parham and Chenowith for the amount of the four checks. At the conclusion of appellee's evidence, appellants moved for a directed verdict, and this motion was denied. At the conclusion of all the evidence, the court again denied a motion for directed verdict, and the case was submitted to the jury. The jury returned a verdict of $4,098.70 against Chenowith, and a like amount against Parham. From the judgment entered in accordance with this verdict, Chenowith brings this appeal. Parham does not appeal from the judgment rendered against him. Three points are alleged for reversal, but since Point 2 controls the litigation, there is no need to discuss the other contentions. Appellant's Point 2 alleges that the court erred in refusing to give a directed verdict for the appellant, at least insofar as the $3,000.00 and $3,800.00 checks are concerned.

This case is governed by the provisions of the Uniform Commercial Code. Ark.Stat.Ann. § 85–3–603 [See R 3–602] (Add.1961), *inter alia,* provides as follows:

> (1) The liability of any party is discharged to the extent of his payment or satisfaction to the holder even though it is made with knowledge of a claim of another person to the instrument unless prior to such payment or satisfaction the person making the claim either supplies indemnity deemed adequate by the party seeking the discharge or enjoins payment or satisfaction by order of a court of competent jurisdiction in an action in which the adverse claimant and the holder are parties. This subsection does not, however, result in the discharge of the liability
>
> (a) of a party who in bad faith pays or satisfies a holder who acquired the instrument by theft or who (unless having the rights of a holder in due course) holds through one who so acquired it.

Parham testified that he was notified by John Hamilton, Vice–President of the Dardanelle bank by phone call that the Chenowith checks were not good, and that something would have to be done about them. Parham stated that he would have to get in touch with Chenowith. Hamilton advised that he (Parham) had around $18,000.00 in the bank, and the banker requested that he be allowed to deduct these bad checks from that amount. Parham approved this procedure, and subsequently received the two checks in the mail. A few days later, Hamilton called back, and told him to come over to the bank. Parham complied with the request. He found Hamilton somewhat upset, the latter stating that the bank examiners would be in, wanting Parham to sign a "paper"; Parham signed a note for something over $11,000.00.[4] Parham and Chenowith went back the next day, and according to the former, Hamilton informed him that the amount wasn't as much as originally thought, and had him sign a new note. This note was in the amount of $8,847.55, and included the four checks here involved upon which payment had been refused. Parham insisted that the notes were signed at Hamilton's request. The banker, however, testified to the contrary, i.e., he said that the suggestion had been made by Parham. Hamilton stated that Parham said, "I sure don't want the bank to be in any jam on my account, and I don't want the bank to lose on this. Just let me sign something to take care of it. Just let me sign a note." Whereupon, Hamilton prepared a demand note, which Parham signed. According to the banker, the note was not even filed; he simply "pitched" it into a box. When asked what the note was for, Hamilton replied, "Nothing whatever. It was never recorded in our books at all. The note was not carried through the bank in any way." The purpose of obtaining the note is never made clear, though it certainly would appear that it could only have been for the purpose of placing the bank in a position to, at some time in the future, collect its money for the checks that had not been paid. The testimony does not reflect that Hamilton even asked Parham for the checks. Chenowith was present when Parham signed the note.

The note was signed on January 25, and Chenowith testified that, on January 28, he settled the checks with Parham; at that time, Parham returned the checks to appellant. The settlement was reached largely on the basis of the fact that each man owed the other different sums of money for various transactions, and Chenowith stated that, after all credits had been allowed by each, Parham owed him $272.00. Parham's testimony is not at all clear. He first said that they had not settled; he subsequently said that their accounts were settled within a few hundred dollars, not more than $300.00, and if Chenowith said $272.00, that amount was probably correct.

Appellant contended that his liability was discharged under the provisions of § 85–3–603 [R 3–602], heretofore quoted, since he fully satisfied the amount of these checks with the holder (Parham). The Circuit Judge however, denied the motion for directed verdict, because Chenowith was with Parham at the bank when Hamilton advised that the checks were unpaid. This ruling was erroneous. It will be noted that the statute says that the liability of the party is discharged "even though it is made with knowledge of a claim of another person to the instrument," unless the claimant (the bank) supplies indemnity deemed adequate by the party seeking the discharge (Chenowith) or enjoins payment or satisfaction by court order in an action which the adverse claimant (Chenowith) and the holder (Parham) are parties. No indemnity was supplied, nor did the bank, in filing its suit, seek an injunction,

4. There were other checks upon which payment had been refused, besides the four involved in this litigation.

as provided by the statute. It is also asserted by appellee that Chenowith and Parham were acting in bad faith, i.e., they knew the checks had not been paid at the time they made this settlement. Appellee, in its brief, asserts that Parham was nothing more than a bailee, and his conduct amounted to a conversion of the checks "to his own use or a larceny by bailee, and accepting them with knowledge of the circumstances, Chenowith participated in the conversion or larceny and was nothing more than an accessory thereto."

Under the statute, Chenowith would not have been discharged from liability if he paid or satisfied a holder "who acquired the instrument by theft or who holds through one who so acquired it," but the commissioners' comment with reference to Subsection (1) makes clear that the question of good or bad faith has nothing to do with liability. That comment is as follows:

> Subsection (1) changes the law by eliminating the requirement of the original Section 88 that the payment be made in good faith and without notice that the title of the holder is defective.

Of course, Parham did not steal the check, and it might also be mentioned that the complaint does not charge that Chenowith and Parham entered into a conspiracy to defraud the bank.

Appellee also argues, as a matter of supporting its judgment, that Chenowith and Parham had not completely settled their financial transactions with each other (this contention being made on the basis of Parham's testimony), and since they had not fully settled, Chenowith's liability had not been discharged. We disagree. Whether the entire indebtedness between the men had been settled is immaterial here, for it is admitted that the checks had been turned over to Chenowith by Parham, who had become the holder, having been sent the checks by the bank. Thus, Chenowith had settled *this* indebtedness with Parham.

Of course, the checks were sent back to Parham by the bank through error, but, under the quoted section of the Commercial code, this is of no aid.

As to the two smaller checks, we think without going into detail, that the appellant is liable. Succinctly, this conclusion is reached because these checks, though not paid, were not returned by the bank to Parham, and appellee accordingly remained the holder of those checks. Being the holder, it had a right to proceed against Chenowith.

In accordance with the reasoning herein set out, we hold that the court erred in not directing a verdict for appellant on the $3,800.00 and $3,000.00 checks, and the judgment is reversed to that extent. There was no error in that part of the judgment covering the $1,242.55 and $155.00 checks. The cause is therefore remanded to the Circuit Court, with instructions to enter a judgment not inconsistent with this opinion.

Note

1. It would be worthwhile to diagram the relationship among the parties to the litigation in *Chenowith* before trying to sort out the arguments of the several transactors concerned. Then, consider who among the parties to the transactions was most negligent, in the common law tort sense. Does OR 3–603 vindicate the result you would reach by applying that negligence analysis?

2. Note that an OR 3–603 or OR 3–602 discharge is a personal defense to liability on a negotiable instrument. Therefore, a holder in due course without knowledge of the discharge may still enforce the paper against the "discharged" party. OR 3–602, R 3–601(b).

3. Should the promissory note signed by Parham alter the rights of the parties under the Code? How could it? Consider the testimony of Hamilton concerning the note.

GROOVER v. PETERS

Georgia Supreme Court, 1973.
231 Ga. 531, 202 S.E.2d 413.

JORDAN, JUSTICE.

This is an appeal from a ruling in Fulton Superior Court ordering C.W. Groover to deliver up an original deed to secure debt, to Erick Peters in order that it might be marked satisfied and therefore canceled as a cloud upon Peters' title.

On August 1, 1964, Peters, appellee here, executed a note and deed to secure debt on property owned by him to Ralph Norwood for consideration of $1,000, payable on or before July 1, 1965. Nine days later Norwood made a written transfer and assignment of said note and deed to appellant "for value received." On June 11, 1965, prior to the due date, appellee paid Norwood $800, and received a settlement receipt upon which was written "Note in full on above addressed property." Appellant, Groover, had no notice of the payment by appellee. On November 23, 1966, appellant filed the assignment and deed to secure debt for record. Due to conflicting contentions as to when appellee received actual notice of the assignment the parties stipulated that it was not before the date of filing, November 23, 1966, and not after August of 1968, when appellee claims he received actual notice. Norwood made two payments to appellant on the indebtedness totaling $250, and appellant claims he is entitled to the other $750 before delivering up the deed. The trial court found that the $800 payment to Norwood was valid as against appellant and ruled accordingly. It is from this ruling that appellant appeals. *Held:*

The maker of a negotiable note and security deed must determine at the time of payment whether the payee is the holder of the instrument or the authorized agent of the holder in order to protect himself against liability for double payment. If the original grantee has assigned the instrument to another, who is a holder in due course, the burden rests with the maker to determine same and pay only the holder or his authorized agent. See Wilcox, Gibbs & Company v. Aultman, 64 Ga. 544; Walton Guano Company v. McCall, 111 Ga. 114, 36 S.E. 469; Bank Of The University v. Tuck, 96 Ga. 456, 465, 23 S.E. 467. There is no evidence in the record which even indicates that Norwood was the agent of the appellant.

The long and short of the matter is that the borrower must be as careful in repaying the debt as the lender presumptively was in making the loan.

Judgment reversed.

All the Justices concur.

ALUMINUM COMPANY OF AMERICA v. HOME CAN MANUFACTURING CORP.

Illinois Appellate Court, 1985.
134 Ill.App.3d 676, 89 Ill.Dec. 500, 480 N.E.2d 1243.

HARTMAN, JUSTICE:

Defendant, Richard A. Keefe, incorrectly named in the pleadings as Richard Keefe, Sr. (hereinafter referred to as "defendant"), appeals from a judgment of the circuit court finding him secondarily liable on a note executed by codefendant Home Can Manufacturing Corporation ("Home Can") and awarding plaintiff, Aluminum Company of America, also known as ALCOA, $16,248.61 plus $8,361.77 in interest, or a total of $24,610.38.[1] Defendant's primary argument on appeal is that he was discharged from liability as a guarantor of the note by the subsequent making of six installment notes without his consent also payable to plaintiff for the same debt, which were executed by Home Can and guaranteed by defendant's son Richard I. Keefe.

Count II of plaintiff's amended complaint, the count upon which the circuit court found defendant liable, alleged the following: (1) on April 21, 1977, and again on May 10, 1977, Home Can ordered certain aluminum stock from plaintiff which was delivered and accepted on December 19, 1977, and June 6, 1978, at a total cost of $18,248.61; (2) on October 9, 1978, defendant as officer and agent of Home Can executed a note for $18,248.61 payable by Home Can to plaintiff on December 11, 1978, with interest at 12 percent per annum; (3) defendant "acting in his individual capacity, personally endorsed the reverse [side] of the October 9, 1978, Note * * * and thereby promised to pay ALCOA the amount of the Note according to its terms and effect in the event that Home Can did not pay the amount of the Note"; (4) Home

1. A default judgment was entered against codefendants Home Can Manufacturing Corporation and Richard I. Keefe, improperly named in the pleadings as Richard Keefe, Jr. They subsequently entered into bankruptcy proceedings and are not parties to this appeal.

Can paid only $2,000 of the principal due; and (5) despite presentment and demand for payment defendant had not paid the balance of $16,248.61 plus interest. A copy of the front and reverse side of the note as attached to the complaint are reproduced below.

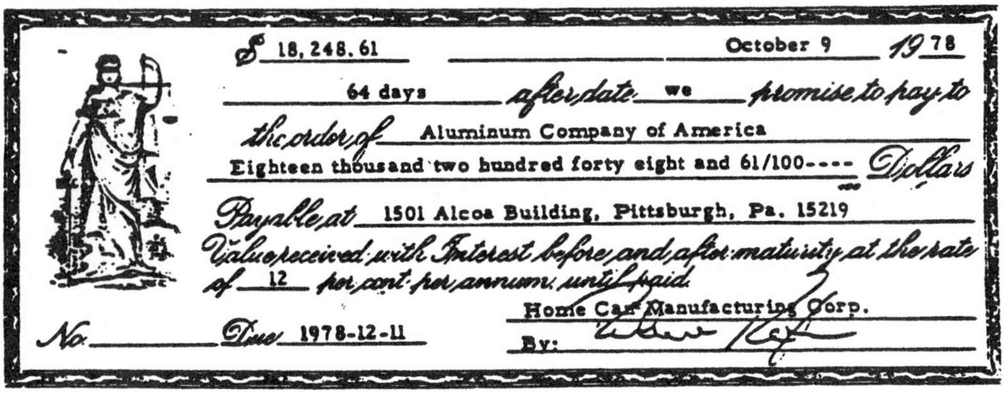

$ 18,248.61 October 9 1978

64 days after date we promise to pay to

the order of Aluminum Company of America

Eighteen thousand two hundred forty eight and 61/100---- Dollars

Payable at 1501 Alcoa Building, Pittsburgh, Pa. 15219

Value received with Interest before and after maturity at the rate of 12 per cent per annum until paid.

Home Can Manufacturing Corp.

No. Due 1978-12-11 By:

Also appended to the complaint were copies of the six installment notes. Each of those notes is dated December 12, 1978; they total $18,248.61, bear interest at an annual rate of 12 percent and mature on the first of every month from April through September 1979. The parties do not dispute that the installment notes were executed on behalf of Home Can by Richard I. Keefe acting as its officer and agent. Nor is it disputed that the reverse side of each of the installment notes has the words "PAYMENT GUARANTEED" typed on it, ostensibly followed by Richard I. Keefe's signature. * * *

In his amended answer to plaintiff's amended complaint defendant: * * * (3) claimed that plaintiff had agreed to accept the installment notes and the first payment of $2,000 in lieu of and as payment for the October 9, 1978 note, as a result of which there was a novation of that note.

* * *

The only evidence concerning the issue of novation was introduced by the defense during direct examination of defendant. Defendant testified that the six installment notes dated December 12, 1978 were actually delivered by plaintiff's attorney to Richard I. Keefe, and executed by him, in April 1979. Defense counsel inquired of defendant on two occasions as to the purpose of the six installment notes. Defendant answered as follows:

> "A The purpose was to rearrange and take care of the first note and replace it with a series of six notes.
>
> * * * * * *
>
> "A They replaced the original note, they paid off the original note of $18,000 and made a series of notes out of the original note."

Defendant was then asked whether he had agreed in writing to the extension of the October 9, 1978 note, to which he replied that he had not. Plaintiff did not cross-examine defendant on his testimony concerning the purpose of the installment notes and did not introduce any rebuttal evidence on that issue.

The circuit court found that * * * the conditions supporting a novation had not been satisfied. The court thereupon entered judgment against defendant and in favor of plaintiff for the balance due on Home Can's account plus accrued interest. In his post-trial motion defendant attempted to raise as a new defense theory that he was an accommodation party under the note of October 9, 1978, and that he was discharged from liability on the note by an agreement between plaintiff and Home Can to extend the time for payment of the note without his consent and without plaintiff reserving its right to proceed against defendant. The trial court denied the post-trial motion and defendant has appealed.

On appeal defendant has presented three theories in support of his contention that he was discharged from liability on the note of October 9, 1978, by the subsequent making of the six installment notes at plaintiff's behest for the same debt but with a different guarantor. First, defendant claims he was discharged from liability on the note under section 3–802(1) [R 3–310(a), (b)] of the Uniform Commercial Code. (Ill.Rev.Stat.1983, ch. 26, par. 3–802(1) [R 3–310(a), (b)] ("UCC").) Second, under common law, defendant argues that the installment notes were given in "payment" of the original note, which extinguished that note and discharged its obligors, rather than in "renewal" of the original note which would have merely postponed the time for payment. Third, defendant asserts that he was discharged from liability under section 3–606(1)(a) [See R 3–605(c)] of the UCC (Ill.Rev.Stat.1983, ch. 26, par. 3–606(1)(a)) [R 3–605(c)] because plaintiff, without his consent, agreed to suspend the right to enforce the note against him.

I

The portion of section 3–606(1)(a) [R 3–605(c)] of the UCC relied upon by defendant provides, in part:

> "(1) The holder discharges any party to the instrument to the extent that without such party's consent the holder

(a) without express reservation of rights * * * agrees to suspend the right to enforce against such person the instrument or collateral or otherwise discharges such person * * *."

This section, however, pertains to an extension of time to pay the obligation granted to the principal debtor. (Ill.Ann.Stat., ch. 26, par. 3–606(1)(a), Illinois Code Comment, at 410 (Smith–Hurd 1963).) As stated above, the question whether plaintiff ever agreed to give Home Can an extension of time to pay the October 9, 1978 note was not an issue at the trial and is not properly before this court on appeal.

II

Defendant's reliance on section 3–802(1) [R 3–310(a), (b)] of the UCC (Ill.Rev.Stat.1983, ch. 26, par. 3–802(1)) is also misplaced. Defendant argues in his brief that section 3–802(1) [R 3–310(a), (b)] discharges an obligor when the obligee takes a subsequent negotiable instrument drawn or made to his order on which there is no recourse or express reservation against the original obligor. This contention is premised upon the language in section 3–802(1)(a) [R 3–310(a), (c)] which by its terms applies only "if a bank is drawer, maker or acceptor of an instrument," which is not the situation in this lawsuit. Section 3–802(1)(b) [R 3–310(b), (c)] states that "in any other case [where an instrument has been taken for an underlying obligation] the obligation is suspended pro tanto until the instrument is due * * *." Section 3–802(1)(b) [R 3–310(b), (c)] is a codification of the Illinois common law holding that a note given by a debtor for a precedent debt will not be held to extinguish the debt in the absence of an agreement to that effect, but will be considered as conditional payment or collateral security or as an acknowledgment or memorandum of the amount ascertained to be due. (*Keller v. North American Life Insurance Co.* (1921), 301 Ill. 198, 204, 133 N.E. 726. This provision does not support the proposition for which it is cited by defendant in his brief, but rather merely clarifies that by signing the October 9, 1978 note, Home Can did not extinguish its liability on the underlying obligation based on its account stated with plaintiff.

III

Illinois case law concerning the effect on the guarantor when the primary debtor gives a new note for an indebtedness evidenced by a prior note has been recently summarized in *Corn Belt Bank v. Lincoln Savings and Loan Association* (1983), 119 Ill.App.3d 238, 247–48, 74 Ill.Dec. 648, 456 N.E.2d 150. There the appellate court stated:

"A general rule has developed that if a new note is taken for the same indebtedness evidenced by a prior note, a guarantor on the prior note is discharged if the new note constitutes a valid agreement supported by consideration extending the time for payment on the old note. (38 C.J.S. *Guaranty* sec. 75a (1943); see *Schuman v. Arsht* (1928), 249 Ill.App. 562; *cf. White v. Walker* (1863), 31 Ill. 422.) However, when the new note is not based on valid consideration flowing to the payee, the extension of time purportedly provided for in the new note does not operate as a valid extension of the time for payment of the debt and does not operate to discharge the guarantor. *Mitchell v. Peterson* (1981), 97 Ill.App.3d 363 [52 Ill.Dec. 817] 422 N.E.2d 1026; 38 C.J.S. *Guaranty* sec. 75b (1943); *Lee v. Pioneer State Bank* (1981), 97 Ill.App.3d 97 [53 Ill.Dec. 26] 423 N.E.2d 218.

"Application of the foregoing rule of discharge depends not only upon whether the new notes are supported by consideration flowing to the payee of the old notes, but also upon the related question of whether the new notes were intended to discharge the old notes or merely to operate as security for those notes. In *Weger v. Robinson Nash Motor Co.* (1930), 340 Ill. 81, 172 N.E. 7, the supreme court held that the question of whether new notes are intended as a satisfaction of a previous note discharging the guarantor of that note is basically a question of fact."

The elements of novation are a previous valid obligation, a subsequent agreement by all of the parties to the new contract, the extinguishment of the old contract and the validity of the new contract. (*Greenbaum & Browne, Ltd. v. Braun* (1980), 88 Ill.App.3d 210, 213, 43 Ill.Dec. 303, 410 N.E.2d 303.) The intention of the parties to extinguish a debt is not presumed. The party asserting discharge or novation has the burden of proving novation by a preponderance of the evidence. *Greenbaum & Browne, Ltd. v. Braun,* 88 Ill.App.3d 210, 213, 43 Ill.Dec. 303, 410 N.E.2d 303; *Faith v. Martoccio* (1974), 21 Ill.App.3d 999, 1004, 316 N.E.2d 164.

In this case, the parties do not dispute the validity of the note of October 9, 1978, or of the six installment notes subsequently executed for the same indebtedness. Consideration for the installment notes was imputed, and no additional consideration for those notes was required. (Ill.Rev.Stat.1983, ch. 26, par. 3–408) [R 3–303(b)]. The question is whether the parties agreed to extinguish the original note by executing the installment notes. The only evidence on that issue was defendant's uncontroverted testimony that the installment notes were intended to pay off and replace the original note.

In general it is the duty of the trier of fact to assess the credibility of the witnesses and the weight to be given to their testimony. Nonetheless, unimpeached testimony may not be arbitrarily or capriciously rejected. Where the testimony of a witness is neither contradicted, either by positive testimony or by circumstances, nor inherently improbable, and the witness has not been impeached, that testimony may not be disregarded by the trier of fact. *People ex rel. Brown v. Baker* (1981), 88 Ill.2d 81, 85, 58 Ill.Dec. 875, 430 N.E.2d 1126.

At the close of the trial, the circuit court ruled that the evidence was insufficient to prove a novation of the note; however, defendant's uncontradicted testimony was sufficient to establish an agreement by the parties to replace or discharge the original note. Accordingly, the circuit court's ruling on that affirmative defense and its finding in favor of plaintiff were improper and must be reversed.

For the reasons set forth above the judgment of the circuit court is reversed.

Reversed.

Note

In *First Pennsylvania Bank v. Triester,* 251 Pa.Super. 372, 380 A.2d 826 (1977), defendant and one Mercer had signed a note for $60,000 payable to plaintiff. Three months later, defendant and Mercer gave plaintiff a second note for the same debt. Mercer gave defendant a hold harmless agreement on the second note. Plaintiff sued defendant on the first note and defendant, apparently fearful that the hold harmless agreement would not apply to liability on the first note, asserted that the second note had discharged the first note. The court cited OR 3–802 and said:

> "* * * [When] an obligee takes a negotiable instrument which is tendered in payment of a promise to pay money, the obligor is not discharged on the underlying promise of payment until the second instrument itself is paid; once the second instrument is due, the first instrument is revived. The failure to pay on the second instrument gives rise to an action on either instrument."

The court then held that to overcome that rule, the defendant had to introduce evidence that it was the plaintiff's intention that taking the second note discharged liability on the first note.

What result in the *ALCOA* case if defendant had the burden of proof imposed on the defendant in *First Pennsylvania?*

As *First Pennsylvania* indicates, the "underlying obligation" to which OR 3–802 and R 3–310 refer may be a first negotiable instrument. In such a case, there are two underlying obligations: the debt for which the first note was given (in *ALCOA* the price of goods delivered) and the first note.

The note in the *ALCOA* case did not contain on its front a statement that all parties to the note agree that the holder may grant extensions or take renewal notes. Such provisions are common in promissory notes and it is surprising that the ALCOA note did not contain such a provision.

In the absence of such a provision, the extension of time given in the second note itself discharged the defendant, if he was an accommodation indorser, since ALCOA did not expressly reserve its rights against defendant when it extended the time. See OR 3–606. Since defendant surely was an accommodation indorser (we cannot believe that he was really the principal debtor and the company was the surety), defendant's lawyer had a slam dunk defense but did not realize it until it was too late. Perhaps the judges decided to save him from a possible malpractice claim by stretching the facts. Or do you think it was appropriate to accept the defendant's characterization of the second note as "payment" of the first note? Did the defendant's testimony show that the intention of the parties had been to enter into a novation in which father was discharged when son signed the second note as accommodation party? A difficulty with that conclusion is that defendant was not a party to the second transaction: How can he testify as to what his son and ALCOA intended?

The lawyers for ALCOA were from one of the largest firms in Chicago. They probably knew that defendant had a clear defense which defendant's lawyer had not raised. Did they have any obligation to call that to anyone's attention?

The comments of the court in the first few paragraphs of Part III of the opinion may seem somewhat unclear. They relate to the proposition that an extension of time to the principal debtor made without the consent of, and without reservation of rights against, the surety discharges the surety. However, merely delaying to bring suit against the principal debtor is not treated as an extension of time and similarly, according to the court, a promise to forebear which is not legally enforceable is not treated as a discharging extension. However, under R 3–605 an agreement to extend time, whether or not supported by consideration, may discharge a surety. We deal with extension of time as a discharging event supra, at page 146.

Problem

Jill owed John $1,000,000. She secured a cashiers check from Y Bank payable to John and delivered it to him. John accepted the check and deposited it in his bank. Before the check was presented to Y Bank, Y Bank failed. Does Jill still owe John the $1,000,000? Would she still owe John $1,000,000 if the cashiers check had been payable to her and she had indorsed it over to John? See OR 3–802, R 3–310.

Suppose when Jill indorsed the check she had written below her name "without recourse." See OR 3–414, R 3–415.

2. *Cancellation or Surrender*

J.J. SCHAEFER LIVESTOCK HAULING, INC. v. GRETNA STATE BANK

Nebraska Supreme Court, 1988.
229 Neb. 580, 428 N.W.2d 185.

[Gretna State Bank held the checking account of Parks and Parks Auction Company (P & P). P & P took goods on consignment for auction and after an auction remitted sales proceeds to the owners of items sold. Pending remittance, the funds were deposited in the P & P checking account in Gretna. P & P owed some $167,000, represented by two negotiable notes, to Gretna. Gretna charged the notes to P & P's checking account, stamped the notes "Paid" and returned them to P & P. Plaintiffs, owners of property sold by P & P, brought suit against Gretna claiming that the funds in P & P's account were held in trust for them and was not available for setoff against P & P's debt to Gretna. Summary judgment was issued against Gretna on plaintiff's claim and Gretna paid out $198,000 to plaintiff. Gretna asserted in a third-party action that it was entitled to reinstate the notes as against P & P and the estate of a deceased P & P principal who had guaranteed the notes.]

HASTINGS, C.J. * * *

* * *

DISCHARGE OF THE NOTES

It is undisputed that the two promissory notes were stamped "PAID" and returned to P & P. In case No. 87–113 the district court found that the marking of the words "Paid 9/19/84" on the promissory notes in the amounts of $115,000 and $50,000 and returning them to the maker constituted a discharge of the debt under the Uniform Commercial Code. The court further found that because the notes were discharged, the guaranties executed by Patricia Parks and Charles Parks were likewise discharged.

Specifically, Neb.U.C.C. § 3–605 [See R 3–604] (Reissue 1980) provides:

* * *

The plain language of § 3–605(1)(b) [R 3–604(a)(ii)] is controlling here and provides that an instrument may be discharged by a written renunciation "*or by surrender of the instrument to the party to be discharged.*" (Emphasis supplied.) The statute provides that this result will occur even if such action is taken "*without consideration.*" (Emphasis supplied.)

The bank points to Neb.U.C.C. § 1–103 (Reissue 1980) to note that the law of mistake should supplement § 3–605 [R 3–604] regarding discharge. It refers us to Guaranty Bank & Trust Co. v. Dowling, 4 Conn.App. 376, 494 A.2d 1216 (1985), where a note was erroneously canceled and surrendered. After the mistake was pointed out to the plaintiff bank, it restored the funds to the partnership account in which the defendant had an interest. The court concluded that the marking of "paid in full" was a mistake, as the money had been taken out of the wrong account. The cancellation of the negotiable instrument thus had no effect and was unintentional, as it was made by mistake. The bank "would not have surrendered the note if it did not, in good faith, believe it had, in fact, been paid." Id. at 380, 494 A.2d at 1219. If the bank is somehow arguing a lack of consideration as the basis for the alleged mistake, its position is clearly untenable, as § 3–605 [R 3–604] covers failure of consideration.

Other courts have ruled that whether a court chooses to consider the stamping of a note "paid" as a cancellation of the instrument under § 3–605(1)(a) [R 3–604(a)(i)] or as a renunciation of rights under § 3–605(1)(b) [R 3–604(a)(ii)], the discharge must be made intentionally and not as a result of mistake. See, Gibraltar Sav. Ass'n v. Watson, 624 S.W.2d 650 (Tex.App.1981) (clerical error); First Galesburg Nat'l Bk. & Tr. v. Martin, 58 Ill.App.3d 113, 373 N.E.2d 1075 (1978) (note was marked "paid" and returned to defendants through a clerical error—writing off defendants' account as a bad debt as a matter of internal accounting procedure). A clerical error should be contrasted to the actions of a bank president and vice president. Further, Dowling may be contrasted in that the bank there immediately returned the funds to the account.

Rather, surrender of the notes canceled the obligations. Additional authority for this proposition is found in the case of Peterson v. Crown Financial Corp., 661 F.2d 287 (3d Cir.1981). At the district court level, it was resolved that an original note that was canceled and returned to Peterson was discharged although the renewal note failed to incorporate interest on the original note. The court of appeals for the third circuit agreed, finding the reasoning of the district court persuasive, that

> "parties such as Crown, which deal regularly in negotiable instruments, 'ought to be held, as a matter of law, to an understanding of the implications which normal business practice assigns to "intentionally cancelling [an] instrument" * * *' 476 F.Supp. at 1159. The court thus held that subjective intent not to discharge was irrelevant; mere intent to cancel was sufficient."

661 F.2d at 290.

The court of appeals focused on the relationship between an instrument and the debt it represents under both common-law principles and the U.C.C.:

> "[A] negotiable instrument is regarded as the debt itself. This conception is due, in part, to the similarity, in form and function, of commercial paper to that of government currencies and bank notes. The unitary concept of a debt fused into the written evidence of it, leads readily to the further concept that destruction of the physical res itself by its owner destroys the legal relations which it induces. Consideration is thus not necessary. Cancellation then becomes a sort of constructive tearing up of the instrument."

661 F.2d at 290.

The result that the notes are discharged is consistent with the precode case decided in Nebraska of In re Estate of Mathews, 134 Neb. 607, 279 N.W. 301 (1938). The record showed that five notes returned to the president and owner of a corporation were marked "paid." "This indicates an intent on the part of the bank to treat the obligations represented by the notes as satisfied." Id. at 611, 279 N.W. at 303. The liability of all the parties to the negotiable instrument was extinguished as a matter of law. There was no claim of fraud or mistake.

The normal scenario remains that stamping the notes "paid" and delivering them to the defendant are sufficient to discharge the notes. "Statutory law makes cancellation or holding by the principal debtor after maturity a discharge of the instrument." Bryant v. Bowles, 108 N.H. 315, 318, 234 A.2d 534, 536 (1967). There is a strong presumption that a written instrument correctly expresses the intention of the parties to it. Ridenour v. Farm Bureau Ins. Co., 221 Neb. 353, 377 N.W.2d 101 (1985). The bank's officers were experienced in the banking business and certainly must have known the effects of issuing paid notes.

Even viewing the evidence most favorably to the bank, as this matter was disposed of on summary judgment, we hold that the promissory notes have been discharged as a matter of law. The personal guaranties are also thus discharged.

* * *

Affirmed.

Problem

Drawer drew a check payable to Jones. The check now bears on the back the following indorsements:

Thomas Jones
Bill France
John Able
Peter Fratcher

Bill Paine, the holder of the check, drew three lines through the name of Bill France, a friend of his. Who is liable on the check? See OR 3–606, R 3–605.

3. Suretyship Defenses: Discharge by Release of Prior Party or by Impairment of Collateral

MATTHEWS V. SALEEN

Colorado Supreme Court, 1991.
812 P.2d 1186.

[Plaintiffs, limited partners in Eaton Associates, indorsed a note for $700,000 on which Eaton was maker. The note was secured by a mortgage on certain property. The payee transferred the note to Illinois Mutual. Eaton sold the property involved to the Saleens who assumed the debt; the Saleens then sold the property to Technical Equities which in turn assumed the debt. As a part of the latter transaction, Illinois Mutual released the Saleens from liability on the debt, but the release agreement provided: "The terms and conditions of this agreement shall in no way prejudice the rights of the holder to pursue its rights and remedies against the original or prior parties to the promissory note or deed of trust."

A subsequent grantee who assumed the debt defaulted, Illinois Mutual foreclosed, and after the foreclosure demanded that the plaintiffs pay the deficiency (the amount by which the foreclosure proceeds failed to pay the debt). Plaintiffs paid and now bring suit against the Saleens. The trial judge granted the Saleens summary judgment. Plaintiffs appeal.]

ROTHENBERG, J. * * *

II.

RELATIONSHIP BETWEEN INDIVIDUAL PLAINTIFFS AND SALEENS

A grantee who assumes and agrees to pay an existing encumbrance upon receiving title to real property becomes a principal and the grantor becomes a surety. Ruther v. Thomas, 43 Colo.App. 435, 604 P.2d 703 (1979). Thus, when Eaton Associates sold the real estate to the Saleens and the Saleens assumed Illinois Mutual's note, the Saleens became the principal obligor on the note and deed of trust, and the limited partnership became a surety. The individual plaintiffs remained guarantors. Similarly, when the Saleens sold the property, Technical Equities became the principal obligor, and the Saleens became sureties. At the time of the default, Girard was the principal obligor and all the past owners were sureties.

III.

DISCHARGE OF SURETY

Section 4–3–606 [R 3–605] C.R.S., of the Uniform Commercial Code addresses the circumstances under which a surety is discharged. * * *

In sum, if a creditor or holder (Illinois Mutual) discharges a principal obligor (the Saleens) without reserving its rights against the surety (the individual plaintiffs), or without obtaining the surety's consent to remain liable, the release also discharges the surety. See Fisher v. Denver National Bank, 22 Colo. 373, 45 P. 440 (1896). See also Security National Bank v. Continental Insurance Co., 586 F.Supp. 139 (D.Kan.1982).

IV.

RESERVATION OF RIGHTS

All parties agree that Illinois Mutual discharged the Saleens in the assumption agreement. However, the individual plaintiffs claim that inasmuch as Illinois Mutual expressly reserved its rights against them in the assumption agreement, the individual plaintiffs remained liable on their obligation to Illinois Mutual. Similarly, they claim that the Saleens' obligation to the individual plaintiffs remained intact. We agree with the individual plaintiffs that the Saleens' obligation to them was not altered by the assumption agreement.

At common law, it was recognized that when a party entitled to payment granted an extension of time for payment to the principal obligor or made other such concessions which impaired the collateral, without first obtaining the surety's consent, the surety was released. The rationale for this rule was that the payee's action impaired the surety's rights and therefore the surety was discharged from any further obligation.

Under § 4–3–606(2) [see R 3–605(b)], C.R.S., a creditor may release a principal debtor but expressly reserve its right to proceed against a surety, and in such circumstances, the surety is not discharged by the release. See McAllister v. People, 28 Colo. 156, 63 P. 308 (1900) (surety was not discharged where the obligee expressly reserved its remedy against the surety by taking a judgment against him). See also Security National Bank v. Continental Insurance Co., supra.

Of importance here is that this code section contains no requirement that the party against whom the rights are reserved (here, the individual plaintiffs) receive notice of the reservation or consent to it. In W. Hawkland, J. Leary, R. Alderman, Uniform Commercial Code Series § 3–606:07 (1990), the rationale behind the UCC's provision for express reservation of rights is explained:

> "A holder can release, grant an extension to or otherwise discharge a person without discharging a party who has a right or recourse against such person if the holder expressly reserves his rights against the party seeking the discharge. By releasing or discharging a person or granting him an extension, the holder cannot maintain an action against that person. *But by expressly reserving his rights the holder preserves all of his rights as against the party as to whom the rights were reserved.* For instance, if the holder grants the maker an extension while reserving his rights against the indorser, the holder may sue the indorser on the instrument. The indorser against whom the rights are reserved may proceed as if the release, discharge or extension did not exist. He is permitted to pay the instrument on the original date due. After payment, he is entitled to all of the holder's rights of recourse against all other parties as if no release, discharge or extension had occurred.
>
> * * *
>
> "At the time this section was drafted, sentiment was expressed concerning the unfairness to the party released or granted the extension of permitting the holder to expressly reserve his rights against the other parties. Banking interests successfully convinced the drafters to retain the provision. The banks argued that it was standard practice among banks to reserve rights against the indorser when granting an extension to a maker since it was often hard to locate the indorser to obtain his consent.
>
> * * *
>
> "*There is no requirement that the party as against whom the rights are reserved receive notice of reservation.* A provision in an earlier draft providing for such notice to the party was deleted * * *." (emphasis added)

In the instant case, the trial court understandably relied on [pre-code Colorado law] and ruled that Illinois Mutual's express reservation of rights "had no effect" because "it diminishes the individual plaintiffs' security without their consent." We also presume that the trial court's interpretation of § 4–3–606(2), C.R.S., was based on the official comment accompanying that section which states:

"Subsection (2), which is new, states the generally accepted rule as to the effect of such an express reservation of rights *which to be effective must be accompanied by notification to any party against whom rights are so reserved (subsection (3))....*" (emphasis added)

Section 3-606(3) of the 1952 official text of the Uniform Commercial Code did indeed require the creditor to give notice to the surety when the creditor expressly reserved his rights against the surety. That subsection stated:

> "An express reservation of rights is not effective as such as against any party whom the holder does not use due diligence to notify within ten days after the reservation."

However, subsection (3) was deleted from the 1958 official text in response to criticism, and it was never adopted in Colorado. See J. White & R. Summers, Uniform Commercial Code § 13-15 n. 140 (2d ed. 1980). Thus, the comment to § 4-3-606(2), C.R.S., is misleading because it alludes to a requirement of notice and refers to the nonexistent subsection (3).[a]

* * *

* * * We conclude that, insofar as the comment to § 4-3-606(2), C.R.S., refers to notification and a subsection (3), that portion of the comment should be disregarded. Applying that principle to the instant case, we hold that notice to the individual plaintiffs and the individual plaintiffs' consent to Illinois Mutual's reservation of rights was not required by § 4-3-606(2). * * *

V.

CONCLUSION

In sum, we conclude that Illinois Mutual's express reservation of rights was effective. Thus, any obligation which was previously owed by the Saleens to the individual plaintiffs remained intact and the trial court erred in granting summary judgment in favor of the Saleens. In view of our ruling here, we need not consider plaintiffs' additional contentions.

The judgment is reversed, and the cause is remanded for further proceedings consistent with this opinion. Because we are unable to determine from the record before us the exact nature or extent of the individual plaintiffs' right to contribution from the Saleens or the Saleens' right to contribution from third-party defendants, the cause is remanded to the trial court for determination of those issues. On remand, the trial court may determine that additional new parties and amendment of the pleadings are necessary.

Note

The rules of OR 3-606 applied in the *Matthews* case seem questionable in two respects: First if the person granting the extension or discharging

a. The comment referred to was deleted from the official code in 1966. [Ed.]

the principal debtor failed to get the consent of, or reserve rights against, the surety, the surety is discharged without regard to whether the discharge or extension actually harmed the surety. Often an extension will actually benefit the surety because the principal debtor will be able to pay at the end of an extension even though she would not have been able to pay at the original maturity date. Therefore, it might be appropriate to conclude that an extension of time discharges the surety only when the extension has harmed the surety. It is harder to imagine cases in which a discharge of the principal debtor benefits the surety but it may be that there are cases in which a discharge of the principal debtor in return for receiving a partial payment does in fact benefit the surety.

The second objection is that it seems unfair to the surety for the surety to remain liable on the contract even though the holder has not notified the surety of an extension of time or discharge. Since the surety will have rights against the principal debtor if the surety has to pay, a strong argument can be made that the surety should be notified of any discharge or extension so that the surety can decide whether to pay the debt immediately and proceed against the principal debtor. It is also somewhat odd that the purely formal step of reserving rights against the surety is necessary to preserve the rights even though that reservation does not have to be communicated to the surety.

In any event, it is safe to say that extensions and discharges of principal debtors usually do not discharge sureties or indorsers because (1) most promissory notes contain a clause by which all parties to the note including indorsers agree to remain bound not withstanding extensions of time or discharge of prior parties and (2) holders can reserve rights against sureties including ordinary indorsers.

Revised 3–605 makes interesting changes in the discharge rules. First, under R 3–605(b) a discharge of a party obligated to pay never discharges an indorser or accommodation party. Second, under R 3–605(c), extensions of time without the consent of the surety discharge the surety only to the extent that she can establish loss with respect to her right of recourse. That is, the surety will have to show that had the extension not been given, the debt would have been paid or the surety would have had access to reimbursement which she does not have because of the extension. In spite of the fact that an argument can be made that a surety ought to be told that the holder is extending time to, or discharging, the principal debtor, R 3–605 does not require that notice be given.

The most interesting change made by the revision is the adoption of the position that a discharge of the principal debtor does not discharge a surety. That may not be a major change after all because the holder under original Article 3 merely has to expressly reserve rights against the surety to prevent discharge. On the other hand, the total lack of discharge for a release, but discharge for an extension of time to the extent of harm to the surety presents an odd juxtaposition of results. For a discussion of the revised Article 3 rules by the Reporter for the Restatement of Suretyship, 2d, see Neil B. Cohen, *Suretyship Principles in the New Article 3: Clarifications and Substantive Changes*, 42 Ala.L.Rev. 595 (1991).

CRIMMINS v. LOWRY

Texas Supreme Court, 1985.
691 S.W.2d 582.

CAMPBELL, J. Carl E. Crimmins sued James M. Lowry to recover the unpaid principal and interest due on a promissory note. Lowry contends he is discharged because Crimmins unjustifiably impaired the collateral given for the note. Following a nonjury trial, the trial court rendered judgment for Crimmins. Lowry appealed, and the court of appeals reversed the trial court judgment and remanded the cause to the trial court for a new trial. 665 S.W.2d 230. We reverse the judgment of the court of appeals and affirm the judgment of the trial court.

In April 1977, Lowry joined Donald F. McNiel as McNiel's law partner in Stephenville, Texas. On September 24, McNiel and Lowry executed a promissory note payable to Crimmins for eleven thousand dollars at ten percent interest. The note was signed: "McNiel and Lowry (typewritten name) By James M. Lowry (signed name) By Donald F. McNiel, II (signed name)." McNiel and Lowry signed a security agreement and a financing statement giving Crimmins a security interest in the furniture, library and office machines of the partnership.

McNiel and Crimmins were good friends. McNiel had incurred substantial debts, and asked Crimmins not to file the financing statement. Lowry neither knew of, nor consented to, this agreement.

On March 18, 1978, McNiel and Lowry orally dissolved the partnership. Neither McNiel nor Lowry made any agreement with Crimmins on payment of the debt.

Crimmins filed the financing statement on August 26, 1980. McNiel continued to make payments on the note until September 18. McNiel filed a petition in bankruptcy shortly afterwards. The bankruptcy court declared Crimmins' security interest a void preferential transfer because he had not filed the financing statement more than ninety days before McNiel filed for bankruptcy.

Our question is whether a comaker on a promissory note may claim the defense of impairment of collateral. The court of appeals in this case held the defense applicable. However, two courts of appeals have held the defense does not apply to a comaker. Pan American Bank v. Nowland, 650 S.W.2d 879 (Tex.App.—San Antonio 1983, writ ref'd n.r.e.); Hooper v. Ryan, 581 S.W.2d 237 (Tex.Civ.App.—Waco 1979, no writ).

A split of authority exists in other jurisdictions on this question. Cases holding that a comaker is not discharged include: Commerce Union Board v. May, 503 S.W.2d 112 (Tenn.1973); Wohlhuter v. St. Charles Lumber & Fuel Co., 62 Ill.2d 16, 338 N.E.2d 179 (1975); Peoples Bank of Point Pleasant v. Pied Piper Retreat, Inc., 209 S.E.2d 573

(W.Va.1974); Smiley v. Wheeler, 602 P.2d 209 (Okl.1979); Oregon Bank v. Baardson, 256 Or. 454, 473 P.2d 1015 (1970). Cases holding that a comaker is discharged include: Beneficial Fin. Co. v. Husner, 82 Misc.2d 550, 369 N.Y.S.2d 975 (1975); Rushton v. U.M. & M. Credit Corp., 245 Ark. 703, 434 S.W.2d 81 (1968); Southwest Florida Prod. Credit Ass'n v. Schirow, 388 So.2d 338 (Fla. 4 DCA 1980).

The Texas Business & Commerce Code provides:

> "(a) The holder discharges *any party* to the instrument to the extent that without such party's consent the holder * * *
>
> "(2) Unjustifiably impairs any collateral for the instrument given by or on behalf of the party or any person against whom he has a right of recourse." (emphasis added).

Tex.Bus. & Com.Code Ann. § 3.606(a)(2) [R 3–605(e), (f)] (Vernon 1968).

The question is whether the words "any party" should be construed to include comakers. Lowry argues that the term "any party" means any party including comakers. The plain meaning of the phrase "any party" is broad enough to include comakers. A fundamental rule controlling the construction of a statute is to determine, if possible, the intent of the legislature as expressed in the language of that statute. However, legislative intent is the law itself, and must be enforced if determined although it may not be consistent with the strict letter of the statute. State v. Dyer, 145 Tex. 586, 200 S.W.2d 813 (1947). Because the plain meaning of the statute supports Lowry's construction of the statute, his construction is correct unless the legislative history of the act reveals that the legislature intended not to provide this defense to comakers.

To determine legislative intent this court must examine "the old law, the evil, and the remedy." Tex.Rev.Civ.Stat.Ann. art. 10, § 6 (Vernon 1969). The Texas Business and Commerce Code contains the Texas version of the Uniform Commercial Code. Before the Texas Legislature enacted the Business and Commerce Code, the Texas version of the Uniform Negotiable Instruments Law, Tex.Rev.Civ.Stat. art. 5948 (repealed 1965), was the law of commercial paper.

Section 120 of the Uniform Negotiable Instruments Law listed five acts by a holder that would discharge a party "secondarily liable." Section 192 of the Uniform Negotiable Instruments Law provided:

> "The person 'primarily' liable on an instrument is the person who by the terms of the instrument is absolutely required to pay the same. All other parties are secondarily liable."

5 U.L.A. § 192 (1943). The Texas version contained the same provisions as the Uniform Negotiable Instruments Law. Tex.Rev.Civ.Stat. art. 5948, §§ 120, 192 (repealed 1965).

The Texas version of the UCC provision on discharge of parties is Tex.Bus. & Com.Code Ann. § 3.606 [R 3-605] (Vernon 1968). Section 3.606 [R 3-605] carries forward several of the acts which constituted a discharge under section 120 of the Negotiable Instruments Act. Section 3.606(1)(b) [R 3-605(e)], however, had no counterpart in the Negotiable Instruments Act.

The Uniform Commercial Code Comment to § 3–606 [R 3-605] explains the substitution of the phrase "any party" for the phrase "primarily liable" as follows:

> "The words 'any party to the instrument' remove any uncertainty arising under the original section. [Section 120 Uniform Negotiable Instruments Law.] The suretyship defenses here provided are not limited to parties who are 'secondarily liable,' but are available to *any party who is in the position of a surety, having a right of recourse either on the instrument or dehors it, including an accommodation maker or acceptor known to the holder to be so.*" (emphasis added).

Tex.Bus. & Com.Code Ann. § 3.606 [R 3-605] comment 1 (Vernon 1968). The Official Comment explains the addition of section 3.606(1)(b) [R 3-605(e)] as follows:

> "Paragraph (b) of subsection (1) is new. The suretyship defense stated has been generally recognized as available to indorsers or accommodation parties."

Tex.Bus. & Com.Code Ann. § 3.606 comment 5 (Vernon 1968).

The legislative history indicates that the drafters of the UCC intended § 3.606 [R 3-605] to apply to all parties "in the position of a surety." According to the Official Comment, a party "in the position of a surety" is a party who has a right of recourse. Thus, the question of whether the drafters intended a comaker to be entitled to invoke the suretyship defenses depends upon whether a comaker is a party in the position of a surety.

A surety is a party who promises to answer for the debt of another. Tolbert v. Standard Accident Insurance Co., 148 Tex. 235, 223 S.W.2d 617 (1949). Because the surety promises to pay the debt of another, equity confers the right of subrogation. If the surety or party in the position of a surety pays the debt of the principal, the surety is subrogated to all of the rights, remedies, equities, and securities of the creditor. The surety can bring an action on the debt itself against his principal and foreclose on collateral given as security for the note. Fox v. Kroeger, 35 S.W.2d 679 (Tex.1931). The defenses in § 3.606 [R 3-605] protect the surety's right to sue on the note and foreclose the collateral. Clark, Suretyship in the Uniform Commercial Code, 46 Tex.L.Rev. 453, 457 (1968). A party has a "right of recourse" if he possesses a right of subrogation. See J. White and R. Summers, Handbook of the Law Under the Uniform Commercial Code §§ 13–16 and n. 145 (2d ed. 1980).

A comaker occupies a hybrid status. A comaker is in the position of a surety to the extent that he promises to answer for the portion of the debt that benefited his fellow comaker but is not a surety for the portion of the debt for which he personally benefited.

A comaker, being in the position of a surety, has a potential right of recourse against his fellow comakers. One comaker, if prejudiced by action against him alone, has a right to contribution from the other comakers for the excess of his pro rata share. Reed v. Buck, 370 S.W.2d 867 (Tex.1963). Moreover, upon payment or satisfaction, the comaker assumes the rights of a transferee of the note. Tex.Bus. & Com.Code § 3.603(b) (Vernon 1968). As a constructive transferee of the note, the comaker is subrogated to the rights of the creditor and may sue on the instrument and foreclose the collateral to the extent of his right of contribution. Tex.Bus. & Com.Code Ann. § 3.201(a) [R 3-203(b)] & (b) [R 3-204(c)] (Vernon 1968). We hold this right of subrogation is a "right of recourse" that entitles a comaker to claim the suretyship defenses in § 3.606 [R 3-606].

Having determined that § 3.606 [R 3-605] applies to comakers, we must now determine the extent to which a comaker is discharged. The Official Comment indicates that the drafters intended § 3.606 [R 3-605] to protect a surety's right of recourse. A comaker has only a partial right of recourse. The legislature could not have intended to completely discharge a party with only a partial right of recourse. We hold that the drafters of the Uniform Commercial Code intended § 3.606 [R 3-605] to discharge a comaker only to the extent of his right of recourse against his fellow comaker. See J. White and R. Summers, Handbook of the Law Under the Uniform Commercial Code § 13–14, n. 125 (2d ed. 1980). The opinion in Pan American Bank v. Nowland, 650 S.W.2d 879 (Tex.App.—San Antonio 1983, writ ref'd n.r.e.) and Hooper v. Ryan, 581 S.W.2d 237 (Tex.Civ.App.—Waco 1979, no writ) are disapproved to the extent that they conflict with this opinion.

We must now determine the extent to which Lowry is discharged. When the note was executed, McNiel and Lowry were partners and shared the loan proceeds equally. Tex.Rev.Civ.Stat.Ann. art. 6132b § 18(1)(b) (Vernon 1970). Lowry, therefore, had a right of recourse against McNiel for one-half of the debt. Here, Lowry lost his right of recourse because of McNiel's discharge in bankruptcy.

The note was for $11,000 and only $5,685 principal was paid; less than one-half of the note was unpaid. Lowry is discharged for that part of the debt for which he was a surety. The defenses in § 3.606 [R 3-605] are affirmative defenses. Lowry had the burden to prove what part of the remaining debt represents his surety liability. There is no evidence of the amount paid by the partnership for which Lowry should be credited. Therefore, the trial court did not err in awarding Crimmins judgment for the unpaid balance of the note.

The judgment of the court of appeals is reversed and the judgment of the trial court is affirmed.

RAY, J., concurring. I concur with the result reached by the court in this cause. In fact, I agree with the rule announced in the court's opinion on how Tex.Bus. & Comm.Code § 3.606(a)(2) [R 3-605(e)] (Vernon 1968) applies to comakers. However, I find it unfortunate that this cause must be decided on this basis.

Upon the oral presentation of this cause, Lowry raised for the first time the argument that Tex.Bus. & Comm.Code § 3.415 [R 3–419] (Vernon 1968) allows a party who appears to be a comaker to demonstrate that he is actually an accommodation party. Indeed, § 3.415(c) [See 3–605(h)] provides:

> "As against a holder in due course and without notice of the accommodation oral proof of the accommodation is not admissible to give the accommodation party the benefit of discharges dependent on his character as such. *In other cases the accommodation character may be shown by oral proof.*" (emphasis added).

Since Crimmins did not negotiate the note, he is not a holder in due course. Tex.Bus. & Comm.Code § 3.302 [R 3-302] (Vernon 1968). Thus, § 3.415(c) provides Lowry with a mechanism to prove that he is not a comaker, but only an accommodation party to the note. If he is an accommodation party, then Lowry will be entitled to the full discharge made available by the impairment of collateral defense in § 3.606(a)(2) [R 3-605(e)].

In determining whether a party is a comaker or an accommodation party, the threshold question is: did the party receive a direct benefit from the execution of the instrument? See Dalton v. George B. Hatley Co., 634 S.W.2d 374, 378 (Tex.App.—Austin 1982, no writ); 2 R. Anderson, Uniform Commercial Code § 3.415:9 (2d ed. 1971). If a party does not retain any benefit from the note's execution, then that party is likely to be regarded as an accommodation party. Id. At oral argument, Lowry pointed out that upon the dissolution of the partnership, he did not keep any of the office equipment that secured the note. Also, Lowry called attention to the fact that he did not receive any of the proceeds of the sale of this equipment at the liquidation of McNiel's bankruptcy. Thus, Lowry now makes a good argument that he is only an accommodation party to the note.

The problem is that Lowry bears the burden of proving his status as an accommodation party. See Caldwell v. Stevenson, 567 S.W.2d 278, 280 (Tex.Civ.App.—Austin 1978, no writ); 4 W. Hawkland & L. Lawrence, U.C.C. Series § 3.415:03 (1984). At trial, however, Lowry did not request any findings of fact on this matter. Also, he did not present this argument before the court of appeals. Thus, he is precluded from raising this argument at this stage in the litigation. Consequently, I concur with the result reached by the court.

JUSTICES SPEARS and KILGARLIN join in this concurring opinion.

Note

There is some confusion regarding the use of the term "co-maker." When A and B sign as makers of a note, one of them may intend to sign as surety for the debt of the other, or they may intend as among themselves to be equally liable. If they intend to be equally liable, they are often referred to as "co-makers" and that is the terminology used in the *Crimmins* case. However, as to third parties, one can say that in both cases A and B are ("co-makers") since, whether or not one is a surety for the other, they have joint and several liability as makers. See OR 3–415(2), 3–118(e); R 3–419(b); 3–116(a). In the business world the surety "co-maker" is often referred to as a "co-signer."

Revised 3–605(f) clearly adopts the position of the *Crimmins* case as to whether impairment of collateral can be asserted as a defense by a co-maker.

See R 3–605(g) regarding acts that constitute impairment of collateral.

4. *Discharge by Alteration*

BUSINESS BANK v. PLANK v. UNITED FINANCIAL BANKING COS., INC.

United States District Court, Eastern District of Virginia, 1989.
710 F.Supp. 619.

ELLIS, DISTRICT JUDGE. Among the host of issues raised in this diversity land development dispute is a Uniform Commercial Code question addressed, but not explained in Virginia. The question involves the application of Virginia Code § 8.3–407(2)(a) [See R 3–407(b)] (1964). That section, inter alia, provides that a maker of a note is discharged from his obligation where there is an alteration of the note "by the holder which is both fraudulent and material * * * " Id. The question presented is whether the fraud required must be actual rather than merely constructive. This question arose in the context of a jury instruction offered by the defendants, the makers of the note, which would have permitted the jury to consider constructive as well as actual fraud. The court rejected this proffered instruction and states here its reasons for concluding that only actual fraud will suffice to meet the requirements of § 8.3–407(2)(a) [R 3-407(b)].

BACKGROUND

This case arises out of a failed venture to develop several hundred acres of land in Loudoun County. On January 28, 1988, plaintiff, the Business Bank ("the Bank"), issued a letter of credit in the amount of $200,000 in favor of Leesburg Estate II Associates, one of the participants in the land development venture. On that same day, as collateral for the issuance of the letter of credit, the defendants, William Plank and William Nottingham, executed a $200,000 commercial note in favor of the Bank. The note was to be payable on demand in the event the $200,000 was drawn down on the letter of credit. Also, the note was to bear interest from the time the money was drawn down on the letter of credit at the prime rate of the Chase Manhattan Bank in New York.

The note was prepared using the Bank's pre-printed form. Included on the form are numerous blanks to be filled in with the particulars of a transaction. At the time the defendants executed the note, many of the blanks on the form had not been completed. Among the uncompleted blanks was the portion of the pre-printed form that included a "cognovit," or confession of judgment, provision. Specifically, when the defendants executed the note, the spaces for identifying the attorneys in fact and the name of the court had not been filled in. These and other blanks on the form were filled in by one of the Bank's employees on instruction of the Bank's president. The Bank's president testified that she assumed she had authority from the defendants for completing the form and filling in these blanks. Defendants hotly contest this, claiming instead that the alterations were unconsented to, material and fraudulent. On the issue of fraud, the defendants argue that constructive fraud is adequate to satisfy the fraud requirement of § 8.3–407(2)(a) [R 3-407(b)] because Virginia recognizes constructive fraud as a species of actionable fraud. See e.g. Nationwide Ins. Co. v. Patterson, 331 S.E.2d 490 (Va.1985); see also 8B Michie's Jurisprudence, Fraud and Deceit § 3 (1977).

Analysis

Virginia Code § 8.3–407(2)(a) is derived from various sections of the Uniform Negotiable Instruments Law and is essentially identical to provisions in force in virtually every state. It provides for discharging the maker's obligation on a note where there has been an "alteration by the holder which is fraudulent and material." No specific definition of "fraudulent" is provided in the statute. The only Virginia decision on point, Avocet Development Corp. v. McLean Bank, 364 S.E.2d 757 (Va.1988), indicates, but does not explain, that constructive fraud will not suffice under § 8.3–407 [R 3-407]. While some authority from other jurisdictions reaches the opposite conclusion, the majority does not. Moreover, the structure and purpose of this provision make clear that only actual fraud will suffice to discharge the obligation on a note that has been materially altered without the consent of the obligor.

Compelling support for requiring actual fraud in connection with § 8.3–407(2)(a) is furnished by (2)(b) [See R 3–407(b).]. That subsection provides that alterations that are not material or fraudulent do not warrant discharging the maker; rather, in those circumstances, the altered note "may be enforced according to its original tenor, or as to incomplete instruments according to the authority given." In other words, subsection 2(b) establishes that an obligor on a note is not discharged where the alteration, whether or not material, results from careless or innocent misrepresentation, i.e., constructive fraud. Thus, construing subsection (2)(a) to include constructive fraud is wholly inconsistent with the existence and effect of (2)(b). Put another way, the drafters' purpose in enacting (2)(b) would be frustrated by construing (2)(a) to include constructive fraud. Material alterations resulting from less than actual fraud would then, contrary to (2)(b), result in discharges rather than enforcement in accordance with the note's original tenor. Only an actual fraud requirement accords with the overall purpose of the entire alteration provision in § 8.3–407 [R 3-407].

The Virginia Code's Official Comment implicitly recognizes this by referring to "fraudulent purpose."

Representative of the majority of decisions on this point is Bank of Ripley v. Sadler, 671 S.W.2d 454 (Tenn.1984). There a bank was awarded judgment for the balance due on a note in part because no actual fraud was found in the bank's action in extending the note and raising the interest rate. In the words of that court, "the majority rule requires actual fraud or dishonesty before there will be a discharge." Id. at 459. Another court put the point as follows:

> " 'fraudulent' requires a dishonest and deceitful purpose to acquire more than one was entitled to under the note assigned by the maker rather than a misguided purpose."

Thomas v. Osborne, 13 Wash.App. 371, 536 P.2d 8 (1975). Hutcheson v. Herron, 131 Ill.App.2d 409, 266 N.E.2d 449 (1970) is apparently to the contrary. There, the court found that fraud requires only that the alteration attempted to impose an obligation on the maker additional to the obligation assumed when the instrument was signed. Apparently, no deceitful intent was required. This minority decision is unpersuasive; it does not come squarely to grips with the issue.

For the reasons stated above, this court concludes, with Bank of Ripley, that "the alteration by the holder must involve some type of actual fraud, dishonesty or deceit to support a finding of 'fraudulent.' " Bank of Ripley, 671 S.W.2d at 459. And, in Virginia, of course, the fraud must be proved by clear and convincing evidence. The instructions will so provide.

It is so ordered.

Problem

A delivers 10,000 bushels of wheat to B, and B gives A a note for $25,000 with interest at 8%. Interest rates rise and A without authority erases the 8% and inserts 10%. A knows that B did not authorize the change but "felt the change was fair." Is the alteration fraudulent and material? If so, does B get the wheat for free? See OR 3–802(1)(b). Does the rule of OR 3–802(1)(b) continue under revised Article 3? See R 3–310(b)(3); OR & R 3-407.

Restatement of Contracts 2d, § 286(1) reads: "If one to whom a duty is owed under a contract alters a writing that is an integrated agreement or that satisfies the Statute of Frauds with respect to that contract, the duty is discharged if the alteration is fraudulent and material."

Do you think it appropriate for B to get the wheat free because of A's alteration of the note? The Introductory Note to the topic of alteration in the Restatement remarks that because of the forfeiture that results from discharge of the obligation if the promisee has already performed, in the future the effect of alteration may be limited, but that § 286 states the present law.

Note

Article 3 and "non-negotiable instruments". The Article 3 provisions, including the provisions discussed in this chapter, apply only to instruments which are negotiable *with one exception.* Original 3–805 provides that the rules of Article 3 apply to an instrument which is otherwise negotiable but is not payable to order or to bearer, except that there can be no holder in due course of such an instrument. Therefore, under original Article 3, if a promissory note reads:

"May 1, 1992

I hereby promise to pay to Tom Smith $10,000 on December, 1992.

/s/ Joe Jackson"

and Tom Smith indorses the note to William Thomas, Smith has Article 3 indorser liability. That is, subject to the Article 3 presentment and notice of dishonor rules, Smith has to pay if Jackson does not. Similarly, all the other rules of Article 3 apply to the instrument except those relating to holders in due course.

Original 3–805 is not continued in revised Article 3. Therefore, under revised Article 3, Smith would not have indorser liability, but only the liability of an assignor of an ordinary contract right. However, it is possible that a court might decide that as a common law matter, by analogy to the Article 3 rules, an indorser of such an instrument does guarantee payment. Similarly, a court might apply other Article 3 rules to such an instrument by analogy. Recall that under R 3–104(c), a check is negotiable even though it is not payable to order or to bearer. Therefore, all the rules of Article 3, including the holder in due course rules, apply to such a check under the revision. See comment 2 to R 3–104.

Chapter 4

FORGERY, ALTERATION, AND OTHER FRAUD: WARRANTY, CONVERSION, AND NEGLIGENCE*

A. INTRODUCTION

In this chapter we deal with the issue of who must take the loss caused by wrongdoing with respect to a negotiable instrument. The wrongdoing may involve either: (1) forgery of a signature, (2) fraudulent alteration, (3) use inconsistent with a restrictive indorsement, or (4) misappropriation of negotiable instruments or their proceeds by an employee or fiduciary.

We will find that familiar ideas and principles from other areas of law, particularly warranty, conversion, and negligence, modified to fit the commercial paper situation, come into play.

It is common to say that the underlying principle of the Article 3 and 4 liability rules is that the loss should be imposed on the party best able to prevent the loss.[1] However, it is not always clear who the best loss avoider is. Therefore, while the stated principle may be helpful, there are several more specific principles that may serve as a better general guide to the specific relevant Article 3 and 4 provisions. A basic liability rule, imposed by the warranty and conversion provisions, is that the person who took the instrument from the wrongdoer takes the loss. If that person is unavailable or cannot respond to a judgment, then the next transferee, and so on, takes the loss. There are several exceptions to those rules. First, a person whose negligence caused the loss may have to bear it. Second, an employer may have to take the

* Throughout this text, the designation "OR" refers to an Article in its original form; "R" denotes a revised Article. E.g., OR 3–303 refers to Original Article 3; R 3–303 refers to Revised Article 3.

1. See Donald J. Rapson, *Loss Allocation in Forgery and Fraud Cases: Significant Changes under Revised Articles 3 and 4*, 42 Ala.L.Rev. 435 (1991) text at and notes 1 and 2, page 435.

loss with respect to wrongdoing by certain of her employees. Third, a drawee that pays over a forged drawer's signature may not be able to recover the money from the person to whom payment was made. If you keep in mind this skeletal statement as to liability rules, it may help you to follow the detailed coverage which follows.

B. WARRANTY LIABILITY (RECOVERY UPSTREAM)

Problem

Smith forged the name of Jones as drawer on a $5,000 check payable to Smith. Smith then indorsed the check and transferred it to Able as the price of an automobile which Able sold to Smith. Able then transferred the check, without indorsement, to Baker in payment of a debt of $5,000 which Able owed Baker. Baker deposited the check in his bank, but when it was presented to the drawee bank, drawee discovered the forgery and returned the check. Can Baker recover $5,000 from Able? OR 3–417(2); R 3–416.

Suppose that it appears that Jones was insolvent and, even if the check had been genuine, could not have paid it. Could Baker recover from Able?

Further suppose that Able, before he transferred the check to Baker, had heard that Jones was in bankruptcy? Could Baker recover from Able?

In all the above hypotheticals, how does Able's liability change if Able had indorsed the check before transferring it to Baker?

Observe that the first three warranties stated in OR 3–417(2) and R 3–416(a) are "without fault" warranties and apply even though the fraud is that of a prior party and even though the transferror is totally innocent in the transaction. The last two warranties, which do not relate to possible fraud of prior parties, may be characterized as "fault" warranties, since the transferror should have disclosed the things of which he was aware that might diminish the ability of the transferee to collect the note.

If the transferror breaches the warranty that he has no knowledge of a defense good against him, can the transferee rescind the transaction and recover back from the transferror the consideration paid? Compare OR 3–417(2) with R 3–416(b). Notice that if the transferee is a holder in due course, she will be able to recover from prior parties free of a defense that is good against the transferror.

In *Price v. Neal,* 3 Burr. 1354, 97 Eng. Rep. 871 (1762), King's Bench held that a drawee that paid drafts with forged drawers' signatures could not recover the amount paid from a presenter of the drafts who had taken them "innocently and bona fide, without the least privity or suspicion of the said forgeries * * * and paid the whole value [of the drafts]."

The present status of the rule in *Price v. Neal* can be gleaned from reading OR 3–418, 3–417(1)(b), and 4–207(1)(b), R 3–418, 3–417, and 4–208, the comments to those sections, and the following case and notes.

AETNA LIFE AND CASUALTY CO. v. HAMPTON STATE BANK

Texas Court of Civil Appeals, 1973.
497 S.W.2d 80.

GUITTARD, JUSTICE.

Hampton State Bank sued Aetna Life and Casualty Company on an insurance contract called a "banker's blanket bond" for a loss resulting from a forged check. Aetna answered that no insured loss occurred, since Hampton forwarded the check through banking channels to the drawee, Northwest National Bank, and after Northwest paid the check, Hampton asked Northwest to send it back and voluntarily refunded the payment. In order to determine whether an insured loss occurred, we must decide whether Hampton was legally required to make this repayment. We hold that repayment was not required and, consequently, that the loss was not insured.

The facts are undisputed and are stated in the trial court's findings of fact. The check in question was drawn on an account in Northwest National Bank in the name of Pizza Inn, Inc. Check forms furnished by Northwest to Pizza Inn, Inc. were stolen and one of these forms was filled in with the amount of $4,000 payable to the order of "Pizza Inn, Inc., # 32." This name was fictitious, since no "Pizza Inn, Inc. # 32" existed. The signature of F.J. Spillman, president of Pizza Inn, Inc., was forged to the check in a credible likeness of the signature of that officer on file with Northwest. The forged check was endorsed "Pizza Inn, Inc. # 32 For Deposited Only, Account No. (Op1275 5) Ronnie Couch," and was deposited in an account opened under that number in the name of "Pizza Inn, Inc. No. 32" in Hampton State Bank. Hampton credited this account with $4,000, endorsed the check "Pay Any Bank P.E.G.," which in banking parlance means "prior endorsements guaranteed," and forwarded it for collection through banking channels to Northwest, which ran the check through its computer and, in accordance with its practice, compared the signature with the signature of F.J. Spillman on file, failed to discover the forgery, and paid Hampton for the check.

About twenty-two days later Hampton advised Northwest that the $4,000 check was forged, and that it intended to make a claim against its bonding company for it, and requested Northwest to return it. Accordingly, Northwest returned the check through banking channels to Hampton, which accepted it and repaid the $4,000 to Northwest.

The trial court found that when Hampton requested return of the check it knew all the facts and was fully aware of any right which it may have had to claim that Northwest by accepting and paying the check could not recover the $4,000 from it. Hampton paid out $3,953.10 from the fictitious account before discovering the forgery, and the trial court found that it suffered a loss in that amount.

By the terms of its bond, Aetna agreed to indemnify Hampton and hold it harmless against certain losses, including "any loss through FORGERY ... of, on or in any checks. * * *"

The trial court rendered judgment for Hampton for the amount of the loss. The court found and concluded that Hampton breached its warranty of the endorsement in that the endorsement was forged, and that Hampton was not a holder in due course.

Our first question is whether Hampton breached its warranty of title under Tex.Bus. & Comm.Code Ann. § 4.207 [R 4–208] (1968), which, as here pertinent, provides:

> (a) Each * * * collecting bank who obtains payment * * * of an item * * * warrants to the payor bank * * * that
>
> (1) he has a good title to the item or is authorized to obtain payment * * * on behalf of one who has a good title * * *.

Hampton contends that since the purported endorsement of the payee, "Pizza Inn, Inc. # 32," as well as the signature of the drawer, was forged, the forged endorsement is inoperative under § 3.404(a) [R 3–403(a)]:

Any unauthorized signature is wholly inoperative as that of the person whose name is signed * * *.

Hampton argues that it acquired no title by the forged endorsement, and, therefore, was liable to Northwest for breach of warranty under § 4.207 [R 4-208].

Aetna contends that the endorsement was not inoperative, and that Hampton did not breach its warranty because anyone, even a forger, can effectively endorse the name of a fictitious payee in view of § 3.405 [R 3–404], which provides:

> (a) An indorsement by any person in the name of a named payee is effective if * * *
>
> (2) a person signing as or on behalf of a maker or drawer intends the payee to have no interest in the instrument * * *.

We conclude that Aetna's interpretation of the Code is correct. The person who forged the check may not have been a "drawer" for all purposes, but he signed "as or on behalf of" the drawer, within § 3.405 [R 3–404]. Obviously he "intended the payee to have no interest" in the check because the payee was fictitious. Since, under this section, anyone is authorized to endorse on behalf of a person not intended to have any interest in the instrument, the endorsement in the name of "Pizza Inn, Inc. # 32" was effective to pass title to Hampton. It may seem odd to speak of a warranty of title to a forged check, but that is exactly what we have here. Title to a check does not necessarily mean the right to collect it from the drawer, since the drawer may have a good defense. A person (other than the drawee bank) who has paid value for a forged check has title to the spurious instrument which enables him to recover against his transferor under § 3.417(b)(2) [R 3–416(a)(1), (2)] and against prior endorsers under § 3.414 [R 3–415]. A warranty of title is nothing more than an assurance that no one has better title to the check than the warrantor, and therefore, that no one is in a position to claim title as against the warrantee, as the payee or other owner of a genuine check could do if his endorsement were forged. On payment of the check to Hampton, Northwest's loss could not be said to have resulted from any breach of Hampton's warranty of title because no person whose name appeared to be endorsed on the check has asserted any claim of title based on lack of a genuine endorsement. Northwest's loss was rather the result of paying out its money on a check to which its own depositor's name was forged.

Hampton also argues that it was liable to Northwest on its express warranty, "P.E.G.," meaning "prior endorsements guaranteed," although it does not enlighten us as to what this express warranty adds to the warranty of title implied under § 4.207 [R 4–208] above quoted. The comment by the commissioners who drafted the Uniform Commercial Code explains that § 4.207 [R 4–208] "is intended to give the effect presently obtained in bank collections by the words 'prior indorsements guaranteed' in collection transfers and presentments between banks." Uniform Commercial Code § 4.207, Comment 2. A warranty of endorsements serves only to warrant the title as against the claim of any person whose name appears as an endorser. Therefore, this express warranty would have afforded no additional ground for Northwest to recover its payment from Hampton.

Hampton's argument that its warranty of the endorsement "contributed" to Northwest's loss in paying the forged check and that Northwest was entitled to rely on Hampton's warranty as assurance of the genuineness of the check is equivalent to an assertion that Hampton's warranty of the endorsement amounted also to a warranty of genuineness of the drawer's signature. Adoption of such a rule would expand the warranty beyond that provided in § 4.207 [R 4–208], and would be contrary to the better-reasoned decisions before the Code.

Hampton relies on *First Nat'l Bank of Winnsboro v. First Nat'l Bank of Quitman,* 299 S.W. 856 (Tex.Comm'n App.1927), *aff'd First Nat'l Bank of Quitman v. Wood County,* 294 S.W. 324 (Tex.Civ.App., Texarkana 1927), in which the Commission of Appeals held that a payor bank could recover from a collecting bank money paid out on a forged check made payable to an existing person whose endorsement was also forged. The collecting bank had stamped the check "All prior endorsements guaranteed." The stated ground of the decision was that the action of the collecting bank in accepting the forged endorsement and putting it in circulation with a guarantee of integrity "contributed" to the payment of the forged check. This holding seems to be based on negligence of the collecting bank, since the principal authority cited is *Rouvant v. San Antonio Nat'l Bank,* 63 Tex. 610 (1885), which allowed recovery by a drawee bank against an endorser in a case where the endorser's negligence in dealing with a forger contributed to the loss. The Supreme Court did not adopt the *Quitman* opinion, but only the judgment, which was sustainable on the negligence theory adopted by the Court of Civil Appeals.

In our opinion, whatever authority *Quitman* may have had was eliminated by enactment of the Uniform Commercial Code. A different decision would now be required under § 3.418 [R 3-418], which provides:

> Except for recovery of bank payments as provided in the chapter on Bank Deposits and Collections (Chapter 4) and except for liability for breach of warranty on presentment under the preceding section, payment or acceptance of any instrument is final in favor of a holder in due course, or a person who has in good faith changed his position in reliance on the payment.

According to the commissioners who drafted the Code, this section follows the rule of *Price v. Neal,* 3 Burr. 1354, 97 Eng. Reprint 871 (1762) and makes payment of a forged check by the drawee bank final in the sense that the bank cannot recover back the payment. Uniform Commercial Code § 3–418 [R 3-418], Comment 1. The commissioners explain further that this section rejects decisions permitting recovery on the basis of negligence of the holder in taking the instrument unless the negligence amounts to lack of good faith. *Id.,* Comment 4. The Code sweeps away all exceptions to the *Price v. Neal* rule and substitutes the more definite standard of good faith for the standard of ordinary care, which has produced confusion and uncertainty. J. Brady, *Bank Checks* 469 (4th ed. H. Bailey 1969). Consequently, we find no merit in Hampton's argument, based on such pre-code cases as *First Nat'l Bank of Quitman v. Wood County,* 294 S.W. 324 (Tex.Civ. App., Texarkana 1927), aff'd *First Nat'l Bank of Winnsboro v. First Nat'l Bank of Quitman,* 299 S.W. 856 (Tex.Comm'n App., 1927), and *First State Bank of Bellaire v. Citizens National Bank,* 407 S.W.2d 365 (Tex.Civ.App., Houston 1966, no writ), that Hampton had a common-law liability to Northwest for negligence in failing to observe the prevailing banking practice of requiring a corporate resolution before permitting withdrawal from an account opened in a corporate name. Under § 3.418 [R 3-418], common-law liability is excluded and the controlling question is whether payment of the check by Northwest to Hampton was "final."

We recognize that the rule of finality as stated in § 3.418 [R 3-418] expressly excepts liability for breach of warranty, but Hampton was not liable for breach of warranty for reasons already given. Hampton also argues that payment of the check was not final because under § 3.418 [R 3-418], payment is final only "in favor of a holder in due course, or a person who has in good faith changed his position in reliance upon the payment" and the trial court found that Hampton was not a holder in due course. Aetna attacks this finding as without support in the evidence. We conclude that Aetna's contention is well taken, since the burden was on Hampton to prove that it was not a holder in due course, and it has failed to carry that burden.

Ordinarily when a defense to the instrument is shown, the burden of proof on the holder-in-due-course issue is on "the person claiming the rights of a holder in due course," as provided in § 3.307(c) [R 3–308(b)], but Aetna is not in that position here, since it is simply resisting Hampton's suit on the bond. Hampton has the negative burden to prove that it was not a holder in due course because one of the elements necessary to its recovery on the bond is that it was not a holder in due course when it sent the check to Northwest for payment.

The effect of the trial court's finding that Hampton was not a holder in due course must be determined in the light of the definition of "holder in due course" in § 3.302 [R 3-302]. Under subdivision (a) of that section, a holder in due course is one who takes the instrument (1) for value, (2) in good faith and (3) without notice of any defense. Consequently, the trial court's finding implies a more particular finding in one or more of the following respects: (1) that Hampton did not take the check for value or (2) that Hampton did not take the check in good faith, or (3) that Hampton took the check with notice of the defense of forgery. We find no evidence to support a finding in Hampton's favor in any of these respects.

Hampton's status as a holder for value is established to the extent of the withdrawals of $3,953.10 from the fictitious account. Section 4.209 [R 4–211] provides that a bank "has given value to the extent that it has a security interest in the item," and § 4.208 [R 4–210] provides that a bank has such a security interest in an item deposited "to the extent to which credit given for the item has been withdrawn or applied." The effect of these sections is that a collecting bank does not become a holder for value simply by crediting the account of the depositor, but may become such a holder by paying funds out of the account. J. Brady, *supra,* § 4.6. * * *

Neither do we find any evidence to support Hampton's claim that it did not take the check in good faith or its claim that it took the check with notice of the defense of forgery. In this respect, as in other aspects of this case, Hampton's posture is unusual. In order to recover against Aetna it must establish that it was liable to reimburse Northwest for the payment it received from Northwest on the forged check. In order to establish liability to Northwest it must show that it was not a holder in due course, and in order to show that it was not a holder in due course it asserts its own lack of good faith in taking the check. It insists that in accepting the check for deposit and permitting withdrawals against the account without obtaining sufficient identification and a proper corporate resolution, it was guilty of gross negligence equivalent to lack of good faith.

We do not agree that Hampton has presented evidence tending to establish its own lack of good faith. The record contains no evidence of the circumstances under which the check was received or the withdrawals permitted. * * * Thus Hampton is left without any evidence to support the assertion of its own gross negligence.

Moreover, we cannot accept Hampton's argument that failure to exercise ordinary care or even gross negligence is equivalent to lack of good faith. "Good faith" is defined in § 1.201(19) [R 3–103(a)(4)] as "honesty in fact in the conduct or transaction concerned." "Honesty" in this case would mean accepting the $4,000 check for deposit and permitting withdrawal of funds from the fictitious account without any reason to believe that the check was forged. This record fails to show any lack of honesty in this respect, since it contains no evidence tending to show that Hampton's employee who handled the transaction connived with the forger or had any reason to believe that the check was not genuine. Therefore, there is no evidence to support any implied finding that Hampton did not take the check in good faith or that it took the check with notice of any defense against it.

For the reasons stated we hold that the payment by Northwest was "final" within § 3.418 [R 3-418] and that Hampton was not liable to return it. It follows that Hampton has failed to establish that it sustained a "loss through forgery" within the coverage of the bond.

The judgment of the district court is reversed and judgment is here rendered that Hampton take nothing by this suit.

Note

1. *Price v. Neal and payees.* In *First National City Bank v. Altman,* 3 U.C.C.Rep.Serv. 815 (1966), wrongdoer forged the drawer's name on a check and made it payable to Altman, a dealer in diamonds. Altman accepted the check in payment for some diamonds that were delivered to the wrongdoer. The court held that the issue was whether Altman had in good faith changed position in reliance on payment of the check. See OR 3–418. It did not consider whether Altman might have been a holder in due course for the purposes of OR 3–418.

Should the court have held that Altman could have recovered if he met the tests for holding in due course? Did the fact that he was the payee on the check preclude finding that he was a holder in due course? See OR 3–302. Probably the court did not consider the possibility that Altman should be treated as a holder in due course because holder in due course issues generally arise only when a *transferee* of a negotiable instrument claims to take free of defenses or claims of a prior party.

Notice the language in R 3–418(c). Under that language, Altman does not need to prove that he is a holder in due course, but only that he took the instrument for value and in good faith. Note the failure to include the holder-in-due course requirement that the taker must take without notice of claims or defenses. Can you imagine a case in which a person took with notice of a claim or defense but nevertheless acted in good faith under the revised Article 3 definition of good faith? If you can, is it appropriate to allow the person with notice who acted in good faith to keep the money?

2. *Application of the rule of OR and R 3–418 to situations other than forged drawer's signature.*

Both original and revised 3–418 apply also to the drawee which pays an overdraft check, a no-account check, or a check as to which there was a valid stop order.

Revised 3–418(c) does not apply to payment of an overdraft or no-account check: rather R 3–418(b) does. It is not clear whether application of the general law of mistake and restitution would lead to a different result than would be reached under subsection (c). The following excerpt from Marion W. Benfield, *The New Payments Code and the Abolition of Holder in Due Course Status as to Consumer Checks*, 40 Wash. & Lee L.Rev. 11 (1983), 20–21, deals with the analogous issue of whether a mistaken payment to an assignee can be recovered back.

"In several cases obligors have been able to recover, on mistake theory, payments made to assignees where, when the obligor made the payment, the assignor had breached the contract with the obligor but the obligor had not yet learned of the breach.[31] On the other hand, several other cases have held that an assignee is no different than any other transferee of money and is not obligated to return money collected under the assignment even though he could not have recovered the money in an action against the obligor. Some of those courts reason that if the obligor had paid the money directly to the assignor who had then paid a creditor with the money, the obligor clearly could not recover the money from the creditor and that the result should not change merely because the creditor has an assignment and the obligor makes payment directly to the creditor as assignee.[32] In other cases the courts have said that an obligor may recover payments made to an assignee only on an unjust enrichment theory and that the assignee is not unjustly enriched by receiving payment of a claim for which the assignee has already given value.[33] Palmer points out that the weakness in that argument is that if the obligor had not paid, the assignee's position as good faith purchaser for value would not have enabled the assignee to recover free of the obligor's defense.[34] However, the Restatement of Restitution provides that an assignee of a non-negotiable instrument who paid value therefor and has received payment from the obligor is under no duty to make restitution to the obligor although the obligor had a defense to payment, if the transferee made no misrepresentation and had no notice of the defense."[35]

31. Munson v. De Tamble Motors Co., 88 Conn. 415, 91 A. 531 (1914); J.I. Case Credit Corp. v. Andreason, 90 Idaho 12, 408 P.2d 165 (1965). *See* 4 A. CORBIN, CONTRACTS § 895 (1951).

32. Midtown Bank of Miami v. Travelers Indem. Co., 366 F.2d 459 (5th Cir.1966); California Bank v. U.S. Fidelity & Guar. Co., 129 F.2d 751 (9th Cir.1942).

33. See the cases discussed in 3 G. Palmer, Law of Restitution § 16.7 (1978). Apparently very few cases exist; Palmer cites less than 10.

34. *Id.*

35. Restatement of Restitution § 14(2) (1937).

GIRARD BANK v. MOUNT HOLLY STATE BANK

United States District Court, District of New Jersey, 1979.
474 F.Supp. 1225.

BROTMAN, DISTRICT JUDGE.

* * *

I. FACTUAL AND PROCEDURAL BACKGROUND

Certain facts are not disputed by the litigants. On August 4, 1977, third-party defendant Penn Mutual Life Insurance Company issued its check numbered 377406, dated August 4, for $28,269.54 to a Morris Lefkowitz of New York City, as a return of a policy premium. The check was drawn on Penn Mutual's account at plaintiff Girard Bank in Philadelphia. The check, prepared and signed in Philadelphia, was to be sent by mail to Penn Mutual's agency in New York for distribution to Mr. Lefkowitz.

On August 5, third-party defendant Darlene Payung deposited the check in her account at Mount Holly State Bank of Mount Holly, New Jersey, the defendant and third-party plaintiff. The check bore a forgery of Mr. Lefkowitz's signature as an indorsement; the origin of the forgery is disputed. Ms. Payung also added her signature as an indorsement when she deposited the check. Mount Holly transferred the check through normal banking channels to Central Penn National Bank of Philadelphia, which then presented it for payment to the drawee and payor, Girard. Mount Holly, the depository and a collecting bank, recovered the full amount of the check from Central Penn.

The facts surrounding the discovery of the forgery are disputed but much of the evidence submitted for these summary judgment motions is uncontroverted. According to a Penn Mutual official, its New York agency first alerted the Philadelphia office that the check had not been received by a telephone call on August 19; the agency had become aware about August 11 that the check might be missing. Deposition of Ronald M. Sherlock at 74–75. Mr. Sherlock further states that both Girard and Mount Holly were notified that the check was missing on the 19th. *Id.* at 74–75, 86.

John Hall, executive vice president of Mount Holly, has indicated in his deposition that Mr. Sherlock indeed notified Mount Holly on the morning of the 19th, enabling the bank to freeze the remaining $5600 in Ms. Payung's account. Deposition of Hall at 8–9. Most of the proceeds had already been withdrawn by Ms. Payung. *Id.* at 13–14.

Mr. Sherlock of Penn Mutual also discussed the check with a Girard Bank officer on August 25, the same day that Mr. Lefkowitz signed an affidavit swearing that the indorsement was forged. Deposition of Sherlock at 86; Plaintiff's Exhibit B. That telephone conversation was confirmed by letter dated August 26 from Penn Mutual to Girard. Affidavit of Robert Torzone and Accompanying Exhibit A.

It is not certain how the check was stolen and forged. Mount Holly maintains that several checks had been stolen by Penn Mutual employees prior to August 4, and that the company knew of the problem and unreasonably failed to take proper security measures. The defendant further contends that it can prove at trial that the Lefkowitz check, which was deposited at Mount Holly the day after it was drawn, was stolen by a Penn Mutual employee.

Girard has sued Mount Holly to recover on the latter's presentment warranty which it alleges was breached by the forged check. Jurisdiction is based on diversity of citizenship, 28 USC § 1332(a). Mount Holly has filed third-party complaints against Ms. Payung and Penn Mutual, while the two third-party defendants have cross-claimed against each other. Girard now seeks summary judgment against Penn Mutual for the full amount of the check, and Penn Mutual has asked for summary judgment dismissing Mount Holly's third-party claim against it. The claims by and against Ms. Payung are not at issue here.

II. Drawee's § 4–207 [R 4–208] Claim

Choice of Law

Neither party disputes that New Jersey law applies to Girard's claim against Mount Holly. This court must follow the choice of law rule of New Jersey in determining what state's substantive law should apply. *Klaxon Co. v. Stentor Electric Manufacturing Co.,* 313 U.S. 487 (1941). Section 4–102(2) [R 4–102(b)] of the Uniform Commercial Code, as codified in New Jersey, N.J.Stat. 12A:4–102(2) [R 4–102(b)], states in pertinent part:

> (2) The liability of a bank for action or non-action with respect to any item handled by it for purposes of presentment, payment or collection is governed by the law of the place where the bank is located.

The term "liability" in the statute is most logically construed to mean the legal liability of the collecting bank, Mount Holly, on its presentment warranty, rather than the actual loss to the drawee bank, Girard, if its warranty claim is unsuccessful. This construction is supported by Official Comment 2c. Accordingly, the law of New Jersey, where Mount Holly is located, will apply to Girard's claim.

B. Presentment Warranty

Girard seeks recovery for Mount Holly's breach of its presentment warranty under N.J.Stat. 12A:4–207(1)(a) [R 4–208(a)(1)]. (Further citation to the Code will omit the codification title N.J.Stat. 12A, and titles in other states where an enactment of the Code is construed.) That statute provides in pertinent part:

> § 4–207. Warranties of Customer and Collecting Bank on Transfer or Presentment of Items; Time for Claims.
>
> (1) Each customer or collecting bank who obtains payment or acceptance of an item and each prior customer and collecting bank

warrants to the payor bank or other payor who in good faith pays or accepts the item that

(a) he has a good title to the item or is authorized to obtain payment or acceptance on behalf of one who has a good title; * * *

The forged indorsement prevented Mount Holly, the depository and collecting bank, from obtaining good title to the check, and Mount Holly therefore breached its warranty. See § 3–417 [R 3-417]; Comment 3; § 4–207 [R 4-208], Comment 1; J. White & R. Summers, *Uniform Commercial Code* 510 & n 37 (1972).[2] The overriding scheme of the Code is to place liability on the person who takes from the forger, which is often the depository bank. The rationale is that this party is normally in the best position to detect the forgery and prevent the fraud. This has long been the policy of negotiable instruments law.

This policy is reflected throughout Articles 3 and 4 of the Code. Various sections indicate that a check bearing a forged indorsement is not "properly payable" within the terms of § 4–401(1) [R 4-401(a)]. That section indicates that, absent cognizable negligence on the part of the drawer, the drawee bank may not charge the drawer for a check that is not "properly payable." However, the drawee which has paid the check may seek recovery against prior banks in the collection chain for breach of presentment warranty under § 4–207 [R 4–208]. The depository bank may also sue the prior transferring party under a similar warranty provided in § 3–417 [R 3-417]. In the instant case, Mount Holly, if found liable to Girard, may be able to shift the loss back to the prior transferor, Ms. Payung. However, it is often the case that a depository bank will be unable to recover from a prior party and will ultimately bear the loss.

While the Code essentially presumes that the depository bank (or prior party) was negligent in accepting the check and should be held liable, that bank can sometimes shift the loss to the drawer or drawee if those parties were negligent. Mount Holly does not deny the applicability of § 4–207 [R 4–208] here, but raises various negligence defenses under several Code provisions.

C. § 4–207(4) [R 4–208(e)] Defense

Mount Holly first contends that it is relieved of liability on its warranty by subsection (4) [R 4-208(e)] of § 4–207 [R 4-208], which states:

(4) Unless a claim for breach of warranty under this section is made within a reasonable time after the person claiming learns of the breach, the person liable is discharged to the extent of any loss caused by the delay in making claim.

2. The forged indorsement of Mr. Lefkowitz's name in blank does not convert the check into a valid bearer instrument which could allow Ms. Payung to pass good title. See §§ 3–202 [R 3-201], 3–401(1) [R 3-401(a)]; White & Summers, *supra* at 459.

Mount Holly argues that there is a genuine issue of material fact precluding summary judgment as to whether Girard asserted its claim within a reasonable time.

While reasonableness has been held to present a fact question, *Phoenix Assurance Co. v. Davis,* 126 N.J.Super. 379, 391, 314 A.2d 615, 622 (Law Div.1974), the court finds there is nothing in the record to show that Mount Holly suffered a loss as the result of any delay by Girard in making its claim against Mount Holly. Mount Holly's vice president stated in his deposition that the bank was notified of a problem the morning of August 19, and immediately froze the remaining proceeds of the check. Uncontroverted evidence also indicates that Girard was first notified of the problem on August 19. Therefore any delay in Girard's noticing Mount Holly could not possibly have caused any loss since all proceeds of the check were frozen the same day Girard first learned it had a claim against Mount Holly. There is no factual issue here, and this defense can be precluded as a matter of law. See *Twellman v. Lindell Trust Co.,* 534 S.W.2d 83, 99 (Mo.App.1976).

* * *

Note

The two prior cases and the introductory problem indicate, quite straightforwardly, the operation of the warranty provisions. What determines whether the Article 3 or the Article 4 warranties apply? How do the warranties in Article 3 and in Article 4 differ?

SAVINGS BANKS TRUST CO. v. FEDERAL RESERVE BANK

United States District Court, Southern District of New York, 1984.
577 F.Supp. 964 aff'd, 738 F.2d 573 (2d Cir.1984).

PER CURIAM:

The present case arose out of the theft of a signed but otherwise incomplete teller's check drawn on an account maintained by Franklin Savings Bank with the plaintiff, Savings Banks Trust Company ("Savings"). Savings received a written stop payment order with respect to the check in question from Franklin. Persons not involved in the present litigation completed the check and proceeded to deposit it in a North Carolina bank. The check came into possession of the defendant Federal Reserve Bank of New York through ordinary collection channels and was presented to Savings for payment. Savings failed to dishonor the check or to apprise the defendant of an intention to dishonor within the time specified by the Thrift Institution Collection Arrangement and New York Uniform Commercial Code Section 4–212 [R 4–214] (McKinney 1964). Defendant thereupon debited Savings' account in the amount of the check and Savings brought the present action to recover the amount in question.

Savings' action against the Federal Reserve Bank is based on a claim that it breached the presenter's warranty of no material alterations in the check in question as provided by New York Uniform Commercial Code § 4–207(1)(c) [R 4–208(a)(2)] (McKinney 1964). However, Section 4–207 [R 4-208] accords such a warranty only to a "payor bank * * * who in good faith pays or accepts the item."

Savings argues that the requisite "good faith" exists even when a party has sound reason to be suspicious so long as it does not have actual guilty knowledge. However, knowledge and disregard of suspicious circumstances are sufficient to vitiate an assertion of good faith where negotiable instruments are concerned. *In Re Legel Braswell Government Securities Corp.,* 695 F.2d 506 (11th Cir.1983); *Otten v. Marasco,* 235 F.Supp. 794 (S.D.N.Y.1964), *aff'd* 353 F.2d 563 (2d Cir. 1965). See also H. Bailey, *Brady on Bank Checks* § 8.5 (1984 Cum. Supp. No. 1).

Since receipt of the stop order by Savings imparted knowledge of suspicious circumstances sufficient to bar an action under Section 4–207, we affirm.

Note

1. Do you agree that the stop order gave notice of suspicious circumstances and that payment with that notice was bad faith? Why would a bank pay over a stop order? Intentionally? If the stop order information had been improperly entered into the computer so that the computer failed to put the check on the "stop payment" list and the check was, therefore, paid, would the drawee be guilty of bad faith under original Articles 3 and 4? Under the revised articles? The original warranty provisions do not state specifically whether negligence of the drawee is sufficient to preclude it from asserting a warranty claim against a prior party. But the statutory reference to good faith would suggest that the negligent drawee can still recover on a warranty claim. In *Hartford Accident & Indemnity Co. v. First Pennsylvania Bank,* 859 F.2d 295 (3d Cir.1988), the court held that negligence of the drawee did not preclude a warranty recovery. Subsection (b) of R 3–417 and R 4–208 specifically state that the right to assert a breach of warranty claim is not affected by the drawee's failure to exercise ordinary care in making payment.

2. As the principal case illustrates, unauthorized completion of a negotiable instrument constitutes a material alteration. See OR 3–407(1)(b) and R 3–407(a).

3. When an accepted instrument, including a certified check, has been materially altered, the extent of the liability of the drawee is determined by reference to the time at which the alteration occurred. See OR 3–417(1)(c)(iii) and (iv) and OR 4–207(1)(c)(iii) and (iv). The language of those subsections is consistent with OR 3–407(2) and (3). See comment 4 to R 3–417. Consider a case in which A draws a check in the amount of $1,000 and has it certified by the drawee. She then mails the check to the payee, who alters the amount of the check to read $10,000. The payee properly indorses the item and deposits it in his account at Depositary Bank (D). When D forwards the check through the Federal Reserve System it arrives

at the drawee/acceptor, which promptly pays it in the altered amount, $10,000. After A notices that the item has been paid in the wrong amount, she notifies the drawee. When the drawee puts the check back up through the collection stream, what amount, if any, will the drawee be able to recover from the presenter of the item and for what amount, if any, can the drawee charge A's account? Work your answer through original and revised 3–407 as well as through the apposite warranty provisions.

DRAFTING EXERCISE

Although a substantial number of cases concern the warranty of good title in the context of the check collection process, the warranty flows with the transfer or presentment of all negotiable instruments. That includes, of course, the promissory notes that accompany sophisticated commercial financing transactions. Consider the warranties from the standpoint of the creditor/holder. Would you want to add to or rephrase the warranties? After all, the warranties are implied and not expressly made part of a negotiable instrument. How might you want to adjust the warranties to better serve the interests of a bank or commercial finance company that would take and present promissory notes in the ordinary course of business? Might any of the adjustments impair the negotiability of the instrument?

MELLON NAT'L BANK & TRUST CO. v. MERCHANTS BANK OF NEW YORK

United States District Court, Southern District of New York, 1972.
15 U.C.C.Rep.Serv. (Callaghan) 691.

MacMahon, District Judge.

This is a diversity action in which plaintiff, Mellon National Bank & Trust Company, seeks to recover $10,355.00 for breach of warranties that checks which plaintiff received from defendant and paid had not been materially altered. Defendant, Merchants Bank of New York, brings a claim over against the party which altered the checks in question, Racon Corporation, and the drawer of the checks, Westinghouse Air Brake Company (Wabco).

Plaintiff moves, pursuant to Rule 56, Fed.R.Civ.P., for summary judgment against defendant. Third party defendant Wabco also moves for summary judgment dismissing the complaint against it.

The basic facts are undisputed. On January 9, 1969, Wabco drew a check upon plaintiff bank to the order of Racon Corporation in the amount of $928.62. Racon raised the amount on the check to $9,283.62 before depositing it with defendant bank. On February 7, 1969, Wabco drew another check to the order of Racon in the amount of $7.51, and that check was raised to $6,667.51 before being deposited with defendant.

The checks were forwarded to plaintiff, which paid them and debited Wabco's account by the altered amount. When the alterations were discovered, Racon repaid to Wabco $4,660.00 of the difference between the checks as drawn and as altered, and plaintiff reimbursed Wabco for the remaining $10,355.00. Plaintiff then brought this action for breach of the collecting bank's warranty.

We consider, first, plaintiff's motion for summary judgment. Plaintiff maintains that defendant is statutorily liable to it under §§ 3–417(2)(c) [R 3–417(a)(2)] and 4–207(1)(c) [R 4–208(a)(2)] of the New York Uniform Commercial Code, under which a collecting bank warrants to a payor bank that any checks it forwards to that bank have not been materially altered. Although defendant does not refute its liability as a collecting bank under the Code, it claims that plaintiff is precluded from recovering against it on three grounds:

First, it is asserted that plaintiff had a defense under § 3–406 [R 3–406] of the Code against reimbursing its customer, Wabco, based on Wabco's alleged negligence in drawing the checks and that plaintiff cannot waive that defense against its customer and go against the collecting bank on a warranty claim.

It has long been held in New York that the negligence of a drawer of a check is no defense to a collecting bank's liability on its warranty to the payor bank because there is no privity between the drawer and the collecting bank and because the drawer owes the collecting bank no duty of vigilance. Thus, a payor bank could waive a defense based on negligence that it might have against its customer and choose instead to reimburse the customer and recover from the collecting bank for breach of warranty.

Defendant contends that this rule was changed by subsection 4–406(5) [See R 4–208(c)] of the Uniform Commercial Code, which provides:

> If under this section a payor bank has a valid defense against a claim of a customer upon or resulting from payment of an item and waives or fails upon request to assert the defense the bank may not assert against any collecting bank or other prior party presenting or transferring the item a claim based upon the unauthorized signature or alteration giving rise to the customer's claim.

Defendant's reliance in the present case on this subsection of the Code is unfounded. Section 4–406 [R 4–406] is intended to encourage bank customers to examine their cancelled checks promptly for forgeries or alterations. To effect that goal, it creates for a payor bank a defense against reimbursing a customer for an altered check based on that customer's failure to report the alteration within a reasonable time after receipt of its bank statement. The waiver subsection upon which defendant relies clearly indicates that it refers to the waiver of the defense created by § 4–406 [R 4–208(c)] and not of the defense based on a customer's negligent drawing of a check created by § 3–406 [R 3–406]. Official Comment 7 to § 4–406 specifically states:

> Although the principle of subsection (5) might well be applied to other types of claims of customers against banks and defenses to these claims, the rule of the subsection is limited to defenses of a payor bank under this section. No present need is known to give the rule wider effect.

The history of the New York Uniform Commercial Code reinforces the view that the waiver subsection was meant to be a limited one. In an early official draft of the Code, a similar provision was included under § 4–207 [R 4–207, 4–208], the warranty section, and was thus applicable to a waiver of defenses based both on delay in reporting alterations and negligence in preparing checks. However, in the adopted version of the Code, the provision was moved to § 4–406 [R 4–208(c)] and the phrase limiting it to that section was added. No comparable provision was included in § 3–406 [R 3–406].

Defendant points to a Comment to § 4–406, which says that subsection (5) is intended to reject the holding of *Fallick v. Amalgamated Bank of New York, supra,* to the effect that a payor bank could waive defenses against customers based on both negligent preparation of checks and delay in reporting alterations. We think that the language of the Code provision and the Comment shows that the Fallick decision was rejected only insofar as it allowed a waiver of the defense based on delay in reporting alterations.

Defendant also points to *Canadian Imperial Bank of Commerce v. Federal Reserve Bank of New York,* 316 N.Y.S.2d 507 (1970), which held that subsection 4–406(5) [R 4–208(c)] is applicable to defenses arising under § 3–406 [R 3–406]. Federal courts must give weight to lower state court decisions in determining the law of that state, but such a ruling is not a binding determination of the state's law. In view of our analysis of § 4–406 [R 4–208(c)] of the Code, we cannot accept the conclusion of the Canadian Imperial case, since we do not feel that the Court of Appeals of New York would reach such a result.

Consequently, we reject defendant's contention that subsection 4–406(5) [R 4–208(c)] of the Code precludes plaintiff from recovering on the warranty claim because plaintiff waived a defense based on negligence that it allegedly had against reimbursing Wabco. Since Wabco's alleged negligence in preparing the checks is not material to defendant's liability for breach of warranty, the unresolved issue of that negligence does not prevent us from deciding the present motion for summary judgment on the merits.

Defendant's second claim is based on its allegation that plaintiff and Wabco negligently failed to notify it promptly about the alteration of the January check. Defendant claims that their negligence resulted in its accepting the February check and that, thus, plaintiff cannot recover on the warranty on the February check.

Defendant fails to establish that there is any real issue of negligence here. It does not offer any evidence to refute Wabco's statement that it did not receive its January bank statement or discover the first alteration until after the February check had been honored by the banks. The mere allegation by defendant's attorney that Wabco should have received its January statement on the 1st of February is certainly not sufficient to create a genuine issue of fact about whether there was any negligence which delayed defendant's learning about the first altered check.

Defendant's third claim is that plaintiff has already elected its remedy and is thus precluded from suing on the warranty claim. An election of remedies occurs only when a litigant chooses between different inconsistent remedies on a single cause of action. We think it clear that in the present case plaintiff has not made such a choice. We reject defendant's contention that Wabco's negotiations with Racon after discovery of the alterations and Racon's partial repayment of the money constitutes plaintiff's election of a remedy that is inconsistent with its warranty claim. We also reject defendant's contention that the negotiations between Wabco and Racon created a new agreement to which defendant was not a party and thus destroyed defendant's liability on its warranty. The warranty liability of a collecting bank is not affected by a drawer's efforts to recover its losses from altered checks.

We conclude, therefore, that defendant is liable to plaintiff under the Uniform Commercial Code, and since there are no genuine issues of fact material to that liability which require a trial, summary judgment for plaintiff is granted.

We turn, now, to the motion by the third party defendant, Wabco, for summary judgment dismissing the complaint against it. Defendant's claim over against Wabco is based on its contention that Wabco was negligent in drawing the checks and thus substantially contributed to their alteration. Wabco maintains that there is no basis by which it may be held liable to defendant and that, even if there were, it was not negligent in drawing the checks.

As we mentioned above, there is no privity between a drawer and a collecting bank, and the drawer owes the collecting bank no duty of vigilance. It is the rule in New York, therefore, that there is no liability of a drawer to a collecting bank. The drawer of a check is not a party to a collecting bank's warranty against material alteration and is, therefore, not liable to the collecting bank if it must pay for breach of that warranty.

Although it is not clear from defendant's papers on what basis it considers Wabco liable to it, defendant appears to rely on § 3–406 [R 3–406] of the Uniform Commercial Code, which precludes the drawer of a check, whose negligence substantially contributes to the material alteration of that check, from asserting the alteration against a holder in due course, a drawee or other payor who pays the instrument in good faith.

We think defendant's reliance of § 3–406 [R 3–406] is misplaced. That section makes the negligent drawer of a check liable on the instrument only to specific parties, and defendant, which acted solely as a collecting bank, is not one of those parties. Section 3–406 [R 3–406] creates no other liability as to the drawer, and Official Comment 5 [Comment 1 to R 3–406] notes that: "This section does not make the negligent party liable in tort for damages resulting from the alteration." Thus, we reject defendant's claim that § 3–406 [R 3–406] has created a statutory liability of a drawer of a check to a collecting bank that is not a holder in due course. Consequently, defendant's claim over should be dismissed for failure to state a claim upon which relief may be granted.

Accordingly, plaintiff's motion for summary judgment is granted, and third party defendant Wabco's motion to dismiss the claim against it is also granted.

GIRARD BANK v. MOUNT HOLLY STATE BANK

United States District Court, District of New Jersey, 1979.
474 F.Supp. 1225 (D.C.N.J.1979).

[The facts and a portion of the opinion are set out, supra, page 195. In an omitted part of the opinion, the court held that Mount Holly, the depositary bank, could not defend that Girard, the drawee bank had a 3–406 [R 3–406] defense which it could have asserted against Penn Mutual, the drawer. The following portion of the opinion deals with whether Mount Holly has a direct negligence action against Penn Mutual.]

Brotman, District Judge

* * *

B. Existence of a Cause of Action

1. Under § 3–406

Mount Holly first contends that § 3–406 [R 3–406] implicitly creates a cause of action against the drawer. Reliance on this section is misplaced. Mount Holly is not a drawee, payor or holder in due course. See White & Summers, supra at 541–54 n. 42. Furthermore, Comment 5 to § 3–406 [Comment 1 to R 3–406] states: "This section does not make the negligent party liable in tort for damages resulting from the alteration." In the Mellon Bank case, cited above, the depository bank also attempted to bring a third-party claim based on § 3–406 [R 3–406] against the allegedly negligent drawer, but the court dismissed the claim for the same reasons stated here. A similar view is expressed in Whaley, supra at 21.

2. *Under Common Law*

While it is clear that no provision of the Code provides a cause of action by the depository bank against the drawer for its negligence, this omission cannot be read as an intent by the legislature to preclude such an action based on common law principles. Indeed, § 1–103 of the Code provides:

"§ 1–103. Supplementary General Principles of Law Applicable.

"Unless displaced by the particular provisions of this Act, the principles of law and equity, including the law merchant and the law relative to capacity to contract, principal and agent, estoppel, fraud, misrepresentation, duress, coercion, mistake, bankruptcy, or other validating or invalidating cause shall supplement its provisions."

The New Jersey Supreme Court has indicated its general policy in construing statutes:

"In reading and interpreting a statute, primary regard must be given to the fundamental purpose for which the legislation was enacted. Where a literal rendering will lead to a result not in accord with the essential purpose and design of the act, the spirit of the law will control the letter. This doctrine permeates our case law."

New Jersey Builders, Owners and Managers Association v. Blair, 60 N.J. 330, 338, 298 A.2d 855, 859 (1972).

Here a cause of action would further the Code policy favoring deterrence of the actor best able to prevent the fraud. Courts should be hesitant to improvise new remedies outside the already intricate scheme of Articles 3 and 4. However, this new cause of action would not interfere with that scheme but extend its principles to a situation not specifically foreseen by the drafters. The Code cannot be read to preclude a common law action.

Plaintiff asserts that such an action should be based on ordinary negligence principles, as it alleges Penn Mutual's unreasonable failure to supervise its employees and check processing procedures has now resulted in an injury to Mount Holly. The New Jersey courts have never published an opinion discussing this type of claim, so the case must be approached as one of first impression.

The one recent case in another jurisdiction deciding whether there is a common law cause of action by a depository bank against a drawer is the Mellon Bank decision. There the depository bank also asserted a claim against the drawer based on common law, but the court held that such a claim would not be recognized. The judge relied on two pre-Code New York state court opinions, one of which had been affirmed by the Court of Appeals.

A closely analogous situation is where a drawer attempts to sue a depository bank, another claim not specifically provided for in the Code.

The courts have disagreed on this issue. Courts finding there can be no common law-based action have also relied on pre-Code decisions barring such claims. These courts have also indicated that such a claim would circumvent the §§ 3–406 [R 3–406] and 4–406 [R 4–406] defenses by the drawee against the drawer.

Unlike in these cases and in the Mellon Bank case, here no New Jersey pre-Code case covers the situation. Also, allowance of a cause of action would not circumvent any Code defenses; rather it would allow a defense based on § 3–406 [R 3–406] which could not otherwise be raised because of the actions of the drawee.

A recent decision by the New York Court of Appeals allowing a drawer-depository bank suit stressed the need to shift liability to the negligent party. The court stated:

> "It is basic to the law of commercial paper that as between innocent parties any loss should ultimately be placed on the party which could most easily have prevented that loss."

Underpinning & Foundation Constructors, Inc. v. Chase Manhattan Bank, 46 N.Y.2d 459, — N.E.2d —, 414 N.Y.S.2d 298, 302.

Here, too, a negligence action could allow the loss to be shifted to the party which was in the best position to have prevented the forgery. Such a policy is implicit in §§ 3–405 [R 3–404, 3–405], 3–406 [R 3–406] and 4–406 [R 4–406]. While this situation is not encompassed by § 3–405 [R 3–404, 3–405] and subsections (1) and (4) of § 4–406 [R 4–406], it is within the ambit of § 3–406 [R 3–406]. However, because of the rigid limitation written into § 4–406(5) [R 4–208(c)], the policy behind § 3–406 [R 3–406] can be thwarted when the drawee decides not to sue its negligent customer.

Creation of a cause of action by the depository bank against the drawer would bridge this gap in the Code provisions, and allow relevant deterrence and compensatory policies, indorsed by the legislature through enactment of the Code, to reach this situation. The court therefore concludes that if the New Jersey Supreme Court were faced with the issue, it would, to paraphrase the Blair case, look to the "essential purpose and design," of the Code and create an interstitial cause of action for negligence by the depository bank against the drawer. Accordingly, the court holds that the law of New Jersey recognizes Mount Holly's claim against Penn Mutual.

C. Parameters of the Cause of Action

As this action, though based on common law negligence, is a creature of the policies implicit in the Code, its shape should also derive from those policies. Since this action is designed to bridge a gap in the Code provisions, it should not extend to situations which the Code directly addresses. In accordance with these two principles, the holding here is limited in the following ways.

First, the depository bank may not sue the drawer directly for the types of negligence that are covered by subsections (1) and (4) of § 4–

406 [R 4–406(a), (b), (c), and (f)]; those types of negligence may only be addressed by the depository bank asserting an estoppel against the drawee bank under subsection (5) [R 4–208(c)]. The only types of negligence that are cognizable under the new action are those otherwise covered by § 3–406 [R 3–406] where the drawer sues the drawee. The negligence must substantially contribute to the forgery. See Gast v. American Casualty Co. of Reading, Pa., 99 N.J.Super. 538, 542–44, 240 A.2d 682, 684–86 (App.Div. 1968); Whaley, supra at 22–24, 34–38. Certainly this would cover the alleged failure of Penn Mutual to adequately supervise those employees having access to prepared checks. Whether it would also cover any delay by Penn Mutual in reporting the forgery where such a delay allowed a wrongdoer to withdraw funds need not be reached here since it is not clear if Mount Holly has charged that Penn Mutual was so negligent. Neither does the court rule on whether this cause of action extends to situations involving forged drawer's signatures or material alterations.

This cause of action would not be appropriate until the depository bank is adjudged or has admitted liability on a presentment warranty. Of course, such a judgment has been entered here. The court also believes a second prerequisite is appropriate to the special facts of this case. Since Mount Holly's prior transferor, Ms. Payung, has been sued by Mount Holly and has appeared in this court, and since she is charged with forging the Lefkowitz indorsement, the court believes that the claim against her should be tried before the claim against Penn Mutual. The first priority of the law should be to shift liability to the forger where that is possible. Therefore Mount Holly's claim against Penn Mutual is stayed pending a final disposition of its claim against Ms. Payung. If, after a good faith attempt to litigate the claim and collect a judgment, recovery is insufficient, then the stay of the claim against Penn Mutual will be lifted and the action will proceed to trial. If full recovery is had from Ms. Payung, the claim against Penn Mutual will be barred.[14]

Finally, if the claim against the drawer is allowed to proceed, the drawer may raise the depository bank's own negligence in accepting the check as a defense barring the bank's recovery. Use of contributory negligence here parallels the requirement in § 3–406 [R 3–406] that a drawee must act in accordance with reasonable commercial standards, and the restriction in § 3–419(3) [See R 3–420(c)] that the depository bank which acts in accordance with such standards cannot be sued for conversion. This also parallels subsection (3) of § 4–406 [R 4–406(e)], which bars a drawee from raising the drawer's subsection (1) [R 4–406(c)] negligence where the drawee failed to use ordinary care in paying the item.

14. If Ms. Payung took the check from the forger, as she alleges, then she can attempt to sue that party if she is found liable. She might also attempt to pursue a common law negligence claim against the drawer, although the court does not now reach the question of whether such a transferor may sue the drawer.

The court finds support for inclusion of a contributory negligence defense from the fact that the outcome of litigation is similar under Code provisions governing the drawer-drawee suit. In that type of claim, the drawer will win where both drawer and drawee are negligent—just as a contributory negligence defense will absolve the negligent drawer in the cause of action here by the depository bank.

Another parallel is to the New Jersey Appellate Division's recent use of the "last clear chance" doctrine to dismiss a common law negligence claim by a drawer against a depository bank where the drawee bank had the opportunity to prevent an erroneous overpayment on a check. In the instant case it might be found that Mount Holly had the last opportunity to prevent the forgery by not accepting or crediting the check.

However, the parallel to other situations is not perfect. Where both the depository bank and the drawer are negligent, but the drawee is not, the outcome will still depend on whether the drawee raises the drawer's negligence and fails to credit its customer. If the drawee successfully does this, it will not need to sue the depository bank and that bank's negligence will not create liability. But, as was noted above, the drawee will often fail to dispute its customer's claim, preferring to sue the depository or collecting bank where there is no § 4–406(5) [R 4–208(c)] estoppel. The new cause of action created here is, of course, designed to alleviate this gap in the Code. However, if a contributory negligence defense can be asserted against a direct negligence claim, then the depository bank's own negligence will put the loss on the bank, and its liability will still have been caused by the drawee's failure to raise its customer's negligence.

Yet another factor should be noted in connection with the instance where both drawer and depository bank are negligent. Where the drawee successfully asserts the drawer's negligence, the liability may still be shifted to the depository bank if the jurisdiction allows the drawer to then sue the depository bank directly but does not allow the depository bank to raise a § 3–406 [R 3–406] drawer negligence defense to the claim. In that jurisdiction it would thus not matter whether the drawee chose to assert drawer negligence since the liability would eventually fall on the depository bank regardless, and the outcome would also not differ where the depository bank is barred from its own claim because of its own negligence. In addition, even where the depository bank has a § 3–406 [R 3–406] defense to the drawer's claim, where both parties are negligent the bank would still be liable as a result of a drawer's action if the drawer can preclude the bank's § 3–406 [R 3–406] defense by asserting the bank's failure to adhere to reasonable commercial standards. * * *

All this would place the liability on the depository bank where both it and the drawer are negligent, as allowance of a contributory negligence defense in the cause of action in the instant case will do. The court approves this outcome since it believes deterrence of the parties taking from forgers is a higher priority than deterrence of negligent drawers. A better solution might be a comparative negligence system, but this court will leave such a radical step to the New Jersey legislature or supreme court.[16] This limited negligence cause of action may alter the result in only a few situations, but the court feels the sound principles behind various Code provisions will be served by allowing such a claim by the depository bank against the drawer.

D. CONCLUSION

Third-party defendant Penn Mutual has supported its summary judgment motion solely with the legal argument that there can be no claim by third-party plaintiff Mount Holly against it. Since the court holds that Mount Holly may base an action on common law negligence, Penn Mutual's summary judgment motion is denied. For the reason indicated, this claim is stayed pending disposition of Mount Holly's claim against Darlene Payung.

Note

Under revised 3–417(c) and revised 4–208(c) a prior party sued by the drawee for breach of warranty can defend that the indorsement or alteration was effective under R 3–404 or R 3–405 or that the drawer is precluded from asserting it under R 3–406 or R 4–406. Therefore, the result on that issue in *Mellon* and *Mount Holly* is changed.

Both *Mellon* and *Mount Holly* hold that a depositary bank has no direct right under OR 3–406 against a negligent drawer. In *Mellon,* the court does not go beyond that conclusion with the unfortunate result that the depositary bank will suffer the loss even though drawer was guilty of OR 3–406 negligence. In *Mount Holly,* the court concludes that a common law negligence action is available to the depositary bank.

However, a more careful analysis suggests that in both cases the depositary banks might have recovered against the drawers *under OR 3–406.* It is true that the comments to OR 3–406 state that the section does not support a negligence-based cause of action against the person against whom a preclusion under the section can be asserted. However, that is because such a cause of action is not needed to properly shift the loss to the negligent person. Under OR 3–406, a drawer whose negligence substantially contributes to the making of a forged signature is precluded from asserting the forgery against a holder in due course. A depositary bank can certainly be a holder in due course if it meets the ordinary requirements.

If Mount Holly or Merchant's Bank were holders in due course and the checks in question had been dishonored on presentment, they could have brought suit against the drawers on drawers' ordinary drawer liability. And, if the drawers' negligence substantially contributed to the alteration or forgery, the drawers would be precluded from asserting alteration or

16. The California Supreme Court has indicated in a brief dictum that comparative negligence may be used for § 4–406 [R 4–406] defenses in actions by the drawer against the depository bank. Sun 'n Sand, Inc. v. United Cal. Bank, 21 Cal.3d 671, 148 Cal.Rptr. 329, 582 P.2d 920, 939 (1978). See also 582 P.2d at 945 n 4 (Clark, J., concurring and dissenting).

forgery as a defense. Where, as in the two cases, the depositary bank has to refund the payment to the drawee because of an asserted breach of warranty, the depositary bank should be able to argue that, since they had to return the amount of the checks to the drawer, the checks have not been paid and they can maintain a suit on the checks as if they had been dishonored on original presentment.

Under original 3–406 a suit by depositary bank on drawer's ordinary drawer liability would be more favorable to Mount Holly than the negligence action crafted by the court, since ordinary negligence would not prevent the depositary bank from recovery as a holder in due course.

Under revised Article 3, the preclusion of 3–406 applies in favor of a person who in good faith pays the instrument or takes it for value or for collection, and, as just argued, would support a direct suit by the depositary bank against the drawer if a check is dishonored on presentment. But, under revised 3–406, if the depositary bank is negligent but acts in good faith, comparative negligence rules apply.

Because under revised Articles 3 and 4 the depositary bank can defend in a warranty action that drawer's negligence contributed to the making of the forgery or alteration, it is less important that the depositary bank also have a direct action against the drawer if the check has been paid. However, there may be situations in which the depositary bank prefers not to raise its R 3–417(c) or R 4–208(c) defenses against a warranty claim by the drawee bank. If it does not raise the defense, the question will arise whether it may bring a direct suit against the drawer under R 3–406, 3–404, 3–405, or 4–406. What do you think about that issue?

C. CONVERSION LIABILITY (RECOVERY DOWNSTREAM)

1. *Forged Indorsements*

A negotiable instrument is property and the law of conversion applies to negotiable instruments just as it applies to a television set or watch. As in the case of tangible personal property, a transferee of a negotiable instrument from a thief is liable in conversion to the true owner even though the transferee is innocent of any wrongdoing. In the case of ordinary property, even a bona fide purchaser for value from a thief is guilty of conversion. However, a holder in due course of commercial paper takes free of claims of prior parties and is, of course, not liable in conversion. If, however, a necessary indorsement is forged, as we learned in Chapter 2, any subsequent transferee cannot be a holder, and, therefore, cannot be a holder in due course. Such a transferee will be liable in conversion to the owner of the instrument, even though the transferee acts in good faith, unless a Code rule provides protection. In addition to the common law rules of conversion, OR 3–419 and R 3–420 state additional rules applicable to negotiable instruments. The following cases and notes explore the conversion rules.

DENN v. FIRST STATE BANK OF SPRING LAKE PARK

Minnesota Supreme Court, 1982.
316 N.W.2d 532.

WAHL, JUSTICE. This appeal raises the issue of whether a depositary bank which collected and paid out on two checks bearing forged indorsements is absolved from liability to the payee of the checks under Minn.Stat. § 336.3–419(3) [See R 3–420(c)] (1980) when it acted in good faith and in accordance with reasonable commercial standards. We hold that it is.

The facts are straightforward. Plaintiff Edward Denn, the sole shareholder of Advance Foam of Minnesota, brought an action against the First State Bank of Spring Lake Park (Spring Lake) and Northfield National Bank (Northfield) for conversion of two checks paid over a forged indorsement. Both checks were drawn on Northfield by Blesener Roofing and Insulation and were issued to Advance Foam. The first check, dated July 7, 1978, was in the amount of $5,004.67. The second check, dated August 5, 1978, was in the amount of $2,468.38.

Dennis Carlson, a former employee of Advance Foam, deposited the checks to an account which he had opened at Spring Lake on March 29, 1978. He and his wife were joint owners of that account, which was titled "Dennis Carlson/Advanced Foam Account." Carlson indorsed the checks "Advanced Foam/Dennis Carlson" before depositing them.

Spring Lake gave Carlson provisional credit and then presented the checks to drawee Northfield, which paid them. Once Northfield had paid the checks, Spring Lake allowed Carlson to withdraw the money from the account. On September 5, 1978, Denn executed an Affidavit of Forgery in which he stated that he had not received the proceeds of the checks in question, but the affidavit reached Northfield too late to prevent payment.

After Denn brought his conversion action against the two banks, Spring Lake cross-claimed against Northfield on the ground of failure to comply with proper banking procedures and initiated a third-party complaint against Carlson. Plaintiff then also asserted a claim against Carlson, and Northfield cross-claimed against Spring Lake, alleging that Spring Lake had breached the presentment warranties imposed on a collecting bank by Minn.Stat. § 336.4–207 [R 4–208] (1980). The trial court granted Northfield's motion for summary judgment on its cross-claim against Spring Lake, after which Denn dismissed without prejudice his cause of action against Northfield.

The court submitted the remaining issues to a jury which found that (1) Spring Lake had acted in accordance with reasonable commercial standards in accepting for deposit the two checks in question, (2) Denn and Carlson were not business partners, (3) Carlson did not have the authority to indorse and deposit the two checks, (4) the check proceeds were not used in furtherance of the Denn business, (5) Denn had been negligent in the use of his corporate name, and (6) Denn's negligence did not contribute to the making of the indorsement at issue.

The court found Carlson liable to Denn in the amount of the forged checks and denied Denn's claim against Spring Lake. The court held, in effect, that Minn.Stat. § 336.3–419(3) [R 3–420(c)] absolves from liability in conversion a depositary bank which acts in good faith and in accordance with reasonable commercial standards. Since the depositary bank is ultimately liable on the presentment warranties of Minn. Stat. § 336.4–207 [R 4–208], the effect of the trial court's decision is to require the rightful payee of a check to bring his conversion action against the drawee bank, which will then proceed against the depositary bank. Denn appeals from the trial court's decision in this regard and argues that he should be allowed to collect directly from Spring Lake, the depositary bank.

Appellant's position would be unassailable at common law. A payee was allowed to bring his conversion suit directly against the depositary bank. Moler v. State Bank of Bigelow, 176 Minn. 449, 223 N.W. 780 (1929). The depositary bank was liable to the true owner of the check because the first party to take from a forger was ultimately liable on his indorsement. F. Kessler, Forged Instruments, 47 Yale LJ 863 (1938). In Minnesota, this result obtained prior to the adoption of the U.C.C. whether the bank cashed the check or gave the forger provisional credit. Rosacker v. Commercial State Bank, 191 Minn. 553, 254 N.W. 824 (1934).

The Minnesota legislature adopted the Uniform Commercial Code (UCC) in 1965. Although the Code contemplates actions in conversion,[3] there is no provision which expressly governs suits by a payee against a depositary bank. Spring Lake does not claim that the UCC prohibits Denn from bringing this action. It does claim, however, to be absolved from liability to Denn by § 336.3–419(3) [R 3–420(c)], which provides:

> "Subject to the provisions of this Act concerning restrictive indorsements a representative, including a depositary or collecting bank, who has in good faith and in accordance with the reasonable commercial standards applicable to the business of such representative dealt with an instrument or its proceeds on behalf of one who was not the true owner is not liable in conversion or otherwise to the true owner beyond the amount of any proceeds remaining in his hands."

Spring Lake claims it is free of liability to Denn because it (1) was acting in a representative capacity, (2) was acting in good faith and in

3. The Uniform Commercial Code provides that, "An instrument is converted when it is paid on a forged endorsement." Minn.Stat. § 336.3–419(1)(c) [R 3–420(a)] (1980). Denn's conversion claim arose when Northfield paid Spring Lake over Carlson's forged indorsement.

accordance with reasonable commercial standards, and (3) did not retain any "proceeds" of the forged instruments.

There is considerable controversy among the courts and legal commentators over the question of when a bank is acting in a representative capacity. The Code itself defines a representative simply as "an agent, an officer of a corporation or association, and a trustee, executor or administrator of an estate, or any other person empowered to act for another." Minn.Stat. § 336.1–201(35) (1980). At common law such an agent is "liable in conversion when he disposes of goods for his principal, even though the agent has acted in good faith and no longer exercises control over the converted goods." Cooper v. Union Bank: California Protects the True Owner Against a Forged Indorsement Despite Uniform Commercial Code Section 3–419(3), 25 Hastings L.J. 715, 719 (1974). There was a common-law exemption from such liability, however, for a broker who dealt with stolen negotiable bonds on behalf of his principal. Id.; First National Bank v. Goldberg, 340 Pa. 337, 17 A.2d 377 (1941).

Did the Code drafters intend merely to codify the existing exemption for brokers, or did they intend also to exempt from liability depositary and collecting banks dealing with order instruments in the normal check collection process? To resolve this question we turn to the history of U.C.C. § 3–419(3) [R 3–420(c)] and its comments.

The "representative exception" was first included in the May 1949 draft, which stated that "A representative who in good faith has dealt with an instrument or its proceeds is not liable for conversion even though his principal was not the owner of the instrument." Payee v. Depositary Bank: What is the UCC Defense to Handling Checks Bearing Forged Indorsements? 45 U.Colo.L.Rev. 281, 308 (1974) (quoting ALI & National Conference of Commissioners on Uniform State Laws, Uniform Commercial Code § 3–427 (May 1949 Draft)). Under "Purposes of Section," the drafters went on to state that the intent of the section is "to adopt the rule of decisions which have held that a *broker* who *sells* a negotiable instrument for his principal * * * is not liable for conversion of the instrument." Id. at 309 (citing Official Comment) (emphasis added). It is quite likely that the drafters of the 1949 version of the Code meant to exempt from liability only those brokers who had been exempt at common law.

However, in 1951 the drafters added to § 3–419(3) [R 3–420(c)] the phrase "including a depositary or collecting bank." Id. The fact that this crucial phrase was added to the Code and was not part of the original version supports the idea that the 1951 drafters intended specifically to exempt depositary and collecting banks from liability. In 1952, the drafters added Comment 5, which also included a reference to depositary banks. Id. Comment 5 states:

> "Subsection (3), which is new, is intended to adopt the rule of decisions which has held that a representative such as a broker or depositary bank, who deals with a negotiable instrument for his

> principal in good faith is not liable to the true owner for conversion of the instrument or otherwise, except that he may be compelled to turn over to the true owner the instrument itself or any proceeds of the instrument remaining in his hands."

Minn.Stat.Ann. § 336.3–419 [R 3–420], at 471 (West 1966). The fact that the phrase "such as a broker or *depositary bank*" is used to describe representative strongly suggests that the drafters intended to expand the scope of the common-law exception for brokers.[4]

Comment 6 to § 3–419(3) [R 3–420(c)] further supports the idea that the drafters intended to offer defenses to a depositary bank which took from a forger. Comment 6 states:

> "The provisions of this section are not intended to eliminate any liability on warranties of presentment and transfer (Section 3–417) [R 3–416, 3–417]. Thus a collecting bank might be liable to a drawee bank which had been subject to liability under this section, even though the collecting bank might not be liable directly to the owner of the instrument."

Id. Since, at common law, a collecting bank which took from a forger would have been liable to the true payee, the suggestion here that such a bank "might not be liable" implies that the bank now has some defenses by which it may absolve itself from its common-law liability.

Several courts have interpreted "representative" not to include a depositary or collecting bank. The Pennsylvania Court of Common Pleas, in Ervin v. Dauphin Deposit Trust Co., 84 Dauph. 280, 38 Pa.D. & C.2d 473, 3 U.C.C.Rep. 311 (1965), reasoned that the legislature could not have intended to exempt collecting and depositary banks from their common-law liability to the true payee because such an exception would lead to an unreasonable result. Id. at 287, 38 Pa.D. & C.2d at 483, 3 U.C.C.Rep. at 318–19. It would seem to limit the liability of the collecting bank "in the face of other sections of the code which place the ultimate liability on the check cashing bank when the payee's name is forged * * * because of the check cashing bank's warranties on the indorsements." Id. at 287, 38 Pa.D. & C.2d at 483, 3 U.C.C.Rep. at 319.

The California Supreme Court has reached the same results primarily because of the absence of Code comment on such a major change from the common law: "Had such substantial and controversial deviation from prior law been intended, moreover, it could be expected that

4. At least one commentator believes that the bankers, who presumably urged the addition of the phrase "including a depositary or collecting bank," intended to relieve such banks from liability only when they were acting in the capacity of a broker:

"Unfortunately, the drafters of the Code did not leave this provision in a separate section where it belongs. When it was incorporated as a subsection under Section 3–419 [R 3–420], its meaning was inevitably intermingled with the notion of handling checks bearing forged indorsements. It is probable that the drafters never foresaw the way in which its meaning would get expanded." Payee v. Depositary Bank: What is the UCC Defense to Handling Checks Bearing Forged Indorsements?, 45 U.Colo.L.Rev. 281, 311 (1974).

the official commentary to § 3419 [R 3–420] would have so stated and would have included extensive explanation of the reasons for the change." Cooper v. Union Bank, 9 Cal.3d 371, 382, 107 Cal.Rptr. 1, 9–10, 507 P.2d 609, 617 (1973). Similarly, the District Court of the Northern District of Texas has concluded simply that § 3–419(3) [R 3–420(c)] does not contemplate the normal check collection process. Tubin v. Rabin, 389 F.Supp. 787 (N.D.Tex.1974).

The arguments of the Ervin and Cooper courts are persuasive, but we are compelled to reach an opposite conclusion. We can ignore neither the plain language of the statute which expressly includes depositary and collecting banks in its description of representatives nor the comments which appear to exclude such banks from liability.

Professor Stanley V. Kinyon, in his comment to the Minnesota version of the Code, noted that § 336.3–419(3) [R 3–420(c)] applies to collecting banks and went on to distinguish Moler from Rosacker. The Moler decision "is *not* within the rule of this subsection and will not be changed" because the bank acted as a purchaser in cashing the check and not as a representative or collecting bank. MinnStatAnn § 336.3–419(3) [R 3–420(c)] (1966), p 468 (emphasis in original). However, the Rosacker decision would be changed by the U.C.C. because the bank, acting in a representative capacity, credited the forger's account and permitted withdrawals from it. Id. at 469. Appellant offers us no authority for ignoring this comment, which the legislature has left in its original form since its adoption.

Professor Allan Fransworth's analysis parallels that of Kinyon: "The depositary bank would be liable under the Code if it cashed checks, but it would not be liable if it took them for collection and gave a provisional credit. If it cashed them, then it is not a representative, but is purchasing the checks." Farnsworth & Leary, UCC Brief No. 10: Forgery and Alteration of Checks, 14 PracLaw, No. 3, 75, 79 (1968).

The facts of this case are similar to those of Rosacker. In allowing Carlson to deposit the Advance Foam checks in his account and then presenting the checks to Northfield for payment, Spring Lake was acting as Carlson's representative. Spring Lake is, therefore, absolved of liability to Denn unless it has failed to act in good faith and in accordance with reasonable commercial standards or has retained any proceeds of the checks.

The trial court found on the jury's special verdict that Spring Lake had acted in good faith and in accordance with reasonable commercial standards. Denn did not contest testimony to this effect at trial. Rather, he urges this court, as a matter of law, to find, as did the Court of Appeals of Washington, that a bank is not acting in accordance with reasonable commercial standards when it accepts for deposit to a personal account checks which are payable to a corporation. Von Gohren v. Pacific National Bank, 8 Wash.App. 245, 505 P.2d 467 (1973). This we decline to do absent proof that the bank would know either that these checks were payable to a corporation or that Carlson was depositing them in an individual account. Denn has failed to show that the facts of this case fall within the Von Gohren rule.

The California Supreme Court rested its decision in the Cooper case on the theory that, even though the depositary bank had paid over money to the forger, it had not turned over the "proceeds" of the checks. With reference to the law of constructive trusts, which allows a claimant to trace funds which are rightfully his, the court concludes that "the banks retain the proceeds of the instruments even though amounts set forth in the instruments, in the banks' own money, were remitted to [the forger]." 9 Cal.3d at 379, 107 Cal.Rptr. at 7, 507 P.2d at 615.

The Florida Court of Appeals, faced with this "proceeds" rationale in Jackson Vitrified China Co. v. People's American Bank, 388 So.2d 1059 (Fla.Dist.Ct.App.1980), could find no evidence that the drafters of the Code intended such a strained construction. Nor can we. "To the extent that a distinction is drawn regarding the time of payment vis a vis the time of collection, such a distinction is artificial; to the extent that no distinction is made, the provision is rendered nugatory." Id. at 1061.

Furthermore, it is the law of this state that, when the depositary bank had disbursed the amount it had received from the drawee bank, it had "paid out the entire proceeds of the check." Soderlin v. Marquette National Bank, 214 Minn. 408, 412, 8 N.W.2d 331, 332 (1943). Minnesota thus favors the less mechanistic "balance sheet" view of proceeds, with the result in this case that, because Spring Lake has paid out the total amount to the forger, it no longer holds proceeds of the checks and is not liable to Denn.

There are strong policy arguments in Denn's favor. It is judicially efficient to allow the true payee to proceed directly against a collecting bank. The collecting bank will bear the ultimate loss in most cases. If the payee must sue the drawee bank, the drawee bank will sue the collecting bank on the warranties of Minn.Stat. § 336.4–207 [R 4–208] as Northfield did in this case. Therefore, "a suit by the owner-payee against the depositary bank avoids an additional suit and thus resolves the entire dispute in a more economical manner." J. White & R. Summers, Uniform Commercial Code 590 (2d ed. 1980). Collecting banks are also more convenient defendants. While the forged checks may be drawn on several different banks, the forger often cashes or deposits them all at the same bank, or at banks in the same geographical area. Both the payee and the judicial system suffer when the payee is required to sue the drawee banks in a number of jurisdictions to recover on a forged indorsement. The Michigan Court of Appeals relied on this policy consideration when it held that "3–419(3) [R 3–420(c)] provides no defense for the collecting bank in a suit by the true owner of the instrument in this type of fact situation." Sheriff–Goslin Co. v. Cawood, 91 Mich.App. 204, 210, 283 N.W.2d 691, 694 (1979). The court was concerned about the number of suits that would result if it did not allow a payee's direct action against a depositary bank.

We reluctantly conclude, however, that to deny a collecting bank the defenses of § 336.3–419(3) in Denn's case is to ignore the clear intent of our legislature. As the Florida Court of Appeals so well stated, where the choice is "between following what appears to be bad law, or 'adapting' that law to what we perceive to be commercial reality, * * * [o]ur role commands adherence to lawful legislative decree." Jackson, 388 So.2d at 1063. The authority for changing the plain meaning of Minn.Stat. § 336.3–419(3) lies with the Minnesota legislature. Although the people of Minnesota would benefit by a change which would hold a depositary bank directly liable to the true payee of a check which it has paid over a forged indorsement, we hold that Minn.Stat. § 336.3–419(3), as it was passed by the legislature in 1965, provides defenses which absolve the depositary bank of such liability.

Affirmed.

Note

1. As the court points out, First State Bank, which dealt with the wrongdoer Carlson, must ultimately take the loss. The only question is whether First State is liable directly to Denn if he chooses to assert a claim against First State, or whether Denn can only assert a claim against the drawee bank which must then go against First State. The drawee bank's liability to Denn is also in conversion. See OR 3–419(1); R 3–420(a).

Judge Wahl criticizes the rule of OR 3–419(3) but concludes that the court must follow it. Revised 3–420(c) changes the rule so that the owner of the check can sue a depositary bank in conversion. The owner cannot, however, sue an intermediary bank, even though an intermediary bank would have warranty liability to the drawee bank.

2. A check paid over a forged indorsement is not properly chargeable to the customer's account. See OR and R 4–401 and comment 1 to R 4–401. * * * "An item containing a forged drawer's signature or a forged indorsement is not properly payable." Therefore, alternatively to making a claim against the drawee or First State Bank, Denn might just ask the drawer to issue another check. The drawer could then demand that the drawee recredit drawer's account for the amount of the stolen check. Further, since the check has not been paid (see OR 3–603; R 3–602), Denn could sue the drawer on the check (See OR 3–804; R 3–309) or, under original Article 3, possibly on the underlying obligation (see OR 3–802). Revised 3–310(b)(4) (second sentence) limits the payee of a stolen check to a suit on the check. See comment 4 to R 3–110.

Under revised Article 3, therefore, Denn could sue either depositary bank, drawee bank, or drawer. Whomever he decides to assert a claim against, the ultimate loss falls on depositary bank.

3. We have discussed the Denn case assuming that Denn does not take the loss because the wrongdoing was that of his employee. As we

shall see shortly, under revised Article 3, Denn probably would take the loss as employer of a wrongdoing responsible employee (see R 3–405).

4. The main theme in this chapter is allocation of the loss from forgery, alteration, or other fraudulent conduct. However, we noted in the discussion of warranty liability that several of the warranties do not relate to fraudulent conduct. Similarly, a drawee may have conversion liability not because of any lack of title in the person presenting the instrument, but because the drawee delays in returning the instrument. Original 3–419(1)(a) imposes liability on a drawee if the drawee refuses to return on demand an instrument presented to the drawee for acceptance, and (1)(c) imposes liability on any person if an instrument delivered to the person for payment is not either paid or returned on demand. If, for example, a draft is drawn on buyer's bank by the seller of goods and presented to the bank for payment, the bank, on demand of the seller, must either pay or return the draft. If the bank does not do so, it is liable in conversion. The seller is entitled to have the draft back as evidence of the fact that buyer has not paid.

Revised 3–420 does not continue the specific rules of OR 3–419(1)(a) and (b). Rather it provides that the law applicable to conversion of personal property applies to instruments. The comment states that it is better to allow the general law of conversion to determine when, under the circumstances, the presenter's right to possession has been denied. It is not clear whether leaving the matter to general conversion law will lead to different results, but it certainly leaves the court free to engage in common law development. Restatement of Torts, § 237 states: "One in possession of a chattel as bailee or otherwise who, on demand, refuses without proper qualification to surrender it to another entitled to its immediate possession, is subject to liability for its conversion." However, section 238 provides a limited exemption from liability for failure to deliver immediately if "the circumstances are such that the demand for immediate surrender is unreasonable."

Conversion liability for failure, on demand, to pay or return negotiable instruments has limited importance for banks since under OR and R 4–302, a bank has absolute liability, except as to documentary drafts, if it fails to pay or return items by its midnight deadline.

STONE & WEBSTER ENG'G CORP. v. FIRST NAT'L BANK

Massachusetts Supreme Judicial Court, 1962.
345 Mass. 1, 184 N.E.2d 358.

WILKINS, CHIEF JUSTICE.

In this action of contract or tort in four counts for the same cause of action a demurrer to the declaration was sustained, and the plaintiff, described in the writ as having a usual place of business in Boston, appealed. G.L. (Ter.Ed.) c. 231, § 96. The questions argued concern the rights of the drawer against a collecting bank which "cashed" checks for an individual who had forged the payee's indorsement on the checks, which were never delivered to the payee.

In the first count, which is in contract, the plaintiff alleges that between January 1, 1960, and May 15, 1960, it was indebted at various times to Westinghouse Electric Corporation (Westinghouse) for goods and services furnished to it by Westinghouse; that in order to pay the indebtedness the plaintiff drew three checks within that period on its checking account in The First National Bank of Boston (First National) payable to Westinghouse in the total amount of $64,755.44; that before delivery of the checks to Westinghouse an employee of the plaintiff in possession of the checks forged the indorsement of Westinghouse and presented the checks to the defendant; that the defendant "cashed" the checks and delivered the proceeds to the plaintiff's employee who devoted the proceeds to his own use; that the defendant forwarded the checks to First National and received from First National the full amounts thereof; and that First National charged the account of the plaintiff with the full amounts of the checks and has refused to recredit the plaintiff's checking account; wherefore the defendant owes the plaintiff $64,755.44 with interest.

Count 2, also in contract, is on an account annexed for money owed, namely $64,755.44, the proceeds of checks of the plaintiff "cashed" by the defendant on forged indorsements between January 1, 1960, and May 15, 1960.

Counts 3 and 4 in tort are respectively for conversion of the checks and for negligence in "cashing" the checks with forged indorsements.

By order, copies of the three checks were filed in court. The checks are respectively dated at Rowe in this Commonwealth on January 5, March 8, and May 9, 1960. Their respective amounts are $36,982.86, $10,416.58, and $17,355. They are payable to the order of "Westinghouse Electric Corporation, 10 High Street, Boston." The first two checks are indorsed in typewriting, "For Deposit Only: Westinghouse Electric Corporation By: Mr. O.D. Costine, Treasury Representative" followed by an ink signature "O.D. Costine." The third check is indorsed in typewriting, "Westinghouse Electric Corporation By: [Sgd.] O.D. Costine Treasury Representative." All three checks also bear the indorsement by rubber stamp, "Pay to the order of any bank, banker or trust co. prior indorsements guaranteed * * * [date] [1] The First National Bank & Trust Co. Greenfield, Mass."

The demurrer, in so far as it has been argued, is to each count for failure to state a cause of action.

* * *

1. Count 1, the plaintiff contends, is for money had and received. We shall so regard it. "An action for money had and received lies to

1. The respective dates are January 13, March 9, and May 11, 1960. Each check bears the stamped indorsement of the Federal Reserve Bank of Boston and on its face the paid stamp of The First National Bank of Boston.

recover money which should not in justice be retained by the defendant, and which in equity and good conscience should be paid to the plaintiff."

The defendant has no money in its hands which belongs to the plaintiff. The latter had no right in the proceeds of its own check payable to Westinghouse. Not being a holder or an agent for a holder, it could not have presented a check to the drawee for payment. Uniform Commercial Code, enacted by St.1957, c. 765, § 1, G.L. c. 106, §§ 3–504(1) [R 3–501(a)], 1–201(20). See Am. Law Inst. Uniform Commercial Code, 1958 Official Text with comments, § 3–419, comment 2: "A negotiable instrument is the property of the holder." See also Restatement 2d: Torts, Tent. draft no. 3, 1958, § 241A. The plaintiff contends that "First National paid or credited the proceeds of the checks to the defendant and charged the account of the plaintiff, and consequently, the plaintiff was deprived of a credit, and the defendant received funds or a credit which 'in equity and good conscience' belonged to the plaintiff."

In our opinion this argument is a non sequitur. The plaintiff as a depositor in First National was merely in a contractual relationship of creditor and debtor. The amounts the defendant received from First National to cover the checks "cashed" were the bank's funds and not the plaintiff's. The Uniform Commercial Code does not purport to change the relationship. See G.L. c. 106, §§ 1–103, 4–401 to 4–407 [R 4–401 to 4–407], Section 3–409(1) [R 3–408] provides: "A check or other draft does not of itself operate as an assignment of any funds in the hands of the drawee available for its payment, and the drawee is not liable on the instrument until he accepts it." This is the same as our prior law, which the Code repealed. See, formerly, G.L. c. 107, §§ 150, 212. Whether the plaintiff was rightfully deprived of a credit is a matter between it and the drawee, First National.

If we treat the first count as seeking to base a cause of action for money had and received upon a waiver of the tort of conversion—a matter which it is not clear is argued—the result will be the same. In this aspect the question presented is whether a drawer has a right of action for conversion against a collecting bank which handles its checks in the bank collection process. Unless there be such a right, there is no tort which can be waived.

The plaintiff relies upon the Uniform Commercial Code, G.L. c. 106, § 3–419 [R 3–420], which provides, "(1) An instrument is converted when * * * (c) it is paid on a forged indorsement." This, however, could not apply to the defendant, which is not a "payor bank," defined in the Code, § 4–105(b) [R 4–105(3)], as "a bank by which an item is payable as drawn or accepted." See *Am.Law Inst. Uniform Commercial Code,* 1958 Official Text with comments, § 4–105, comments 1–3; G.L. c. 106, §§ 4–401 [R 4–401], 4–213 [R 4–215], 3–102(b) [R 3–103(a)(6)].

A conversion provision of the Uniform Commercial Code which might have some bearing on this case is § 3–419(3) [See R 3–420(c)].

This section implicitly recognizes that, subject to defences, including the one stated in it, a collecting bank, defined in the Code, § 4–105(d) [R 4–105(5)], may be liable in conversion. In the case at bar the forged indorsements were "wholly inoperative" as the signatures of the payee, Code §§ 3–404(1) [R 3–403(a)], 1–201(43), and equally so both as to the restrictive indorsements for deposits, see § 3–205(c) [R 3–206], and as to the indorsement in blank, see § 3–204(2) [R 3–205(b)]. When the forger transferred the checks to the collecting bank, no negotiation under § 3–202(1) [R 3–201(a)] occurred, because there was lacking the necessary indorsement of the payee. For the same reason, the collecting bank could not become a "holder" as defined in § 1–201(20), and so could not become a holder in due course under § 3–302(1) [R 3–302(a)]. Accordingly, we assume that the collecting bank may be liable in conversion to a proper party, subject to defences, including that in § 3–419(3) [R 3–420(c)]. But there is no explicit provision in the Code purporting to determine to whom the collecting bank may be liable, and consequently, the drawer's right to enforce such a liability must be found elsewhere. Therefore, we conclude that the case must be decided on our own law, which, on the issue we are discussing, has been left untouched by the Uniform Commercial Code in any specific section.

In this Commonwealth there are two cases (decided in 1913 and 1914) the results in which embrace a ruling that there was a conversion, but in neither was the question discussed and, for aught that appears, in each the ruling seems to have been assumed without conscious appreciation of the issue here considered.

The authorities are hopelessly divided. We think that the preferable view is that there is no right of action.

* * *

We state what appears to us to be the proper analysis. Had the checks been delivered to the payee Westinghouse, the defendant might have been liable for conversion to the payee. The checks, if delivered, in the hands of the payee would have been valuable property which could have been transferred for value or presented for payment; and, had a check been dishonored, the payee would have had a right of recourse against the drawer on the instrument under § 3–413(2) [R 3–414(b)]. Here the plaintiff drawer of the checks, which were never delivered to the payee had no valuable rights in them. Since, as we have seen, it did not have the right of a payee or subsequent holder to present them to the drawee for payment, the value of its rights was limited to the physical paper on which they were written, and was not measured by their payable amounts.

The enactment of the Uniform Commercial Code opens the road for the adoption of what seems the preferable view. An action by the drawer against the collecting bank might have some theoretical appeal as avoiding circuity of action. It would have been in the interest of speedy and complete justice had the case been tried with the action by the drawer against the drawee and with an action by the drawee against the collecting bank. So one might ask: If the drawee is liable to the drawer and the collecting bank is liable to the drawee, why not let the drawer sue the collecting bank direct? We believe that the answer lies in the applicable defences set up in the Code.[4]

The drawer can insist that the drawee recredit his account with the amount of any unauthorized payment. Such was our common law. This is, in effect, retained by the Code §§ 4–401(1) [R 4–401(a)],[5] 4–406(4) [R 4–406(f)]. But the drawee has defences based upon the drawer's substantial negligence, if "contributing," or upon his duty to discover and report unauthorized signatures and alterations. §§ 3–406 [R 3–406], 4–406 [R 4–406]. As to unauthorized indorsements, see § 4–406(4) [R 4–406(f)]. Then, if the drawee has a valid defence which it waives or fails upon request to assert, the drawee may not assert against the collecting bank or other prior party presenting or transferring the check a claim which is based on the forged indorsement. § 4–406(5) [R 4–208(c)]. See *Am.Law Inst. Uniform Commercial Code,* Official Text with comments, § 4–406, comment 6, which shows that there was no intent to change the prior law as to negligence of a customer. If the drawee recredits the drawer's account and is not precluded by § 4–406(5) [R 4–208(c)], it may claim against the presenting bank on the relevant warranties in §§ 3–417 [R 3–416, 3–417] and 4–207 [R 4–208], and each transferee has rights against his transferor under those sections.

If the drawer's rights are limited to requiring the drawee to recredit his account, the drawee will have the defences noted above and perhaps others; and the collecting bank or banks will have the defences in § 4–207(4) [R 4–108(e)] and § 4–406(5) [See R 4–208(c)], and perhaps others. If the drawer is allowed in the present case to sue the collecting bank, the assertion of the defences, for all practical purposes, would be difficult. The possibilities of such a result would tend to compel resort to litigation in every case involving a forgery of commercial paper. It is a result to be avoided.

The demurrer to count 1 was rightly sustained.

* * *

The demurrer [also] was rightly sustained as to count 3.

4. Count 4 alleges that "on divers dates between January 1, 1960, and May 15, 1960, the defendant by reason of its negligence in cashing checks with forged indorsements thereon damaged the plaintiff in the full amount of said checks, to wit $64,755.44. Wherefore, the plaintiff prays judgment against the defendant in the sum of $64,755.44, with interest." From the checks, we observe that, wholly apart from any duty on the part of the defendant toward the plaintiff (compare *Me-*

4. Cases where a payee has acquired rights in an instrument may stand on a different footing.

5. "As against its customer, a bank may charge against his account any item which is otherwise properly payable from that account * * *."

chanics Nat. Bank v. Worcester County Trust Co., 341 Mass. 465, 473–474, 170 N.E.2d 476), there is no allegation of legal damage. When the defendant "cashed" checks with its own funds, no legal harm befell the plaintiff. From what we have said in respect of counts 1 and 3, there would be difficulty in making such an allegation. The harm which befell the plaintiff was the charging of its account by the drawee bank. As has been noted above, the drawer has a cause of action, possibly subject to defences, against that bank. It does not appear that this right is impaired.

There was no error in sustaining the demurrer to count 4.

Order sustaining demurrer affirmed.

Note

1. While a drawer who brings a breach of warranty action must contend with the language of OR 3–417 and 4–207 or R 3–416, 3–417, 4–207 and 4–208, the same drawer may, as the principal case suggests, have different rights when she brings a conversion action. How did the court describe the nature of the drawer's ownership interest in a check made payable to someone other than the drawer?

2. In order to follow the court's conclusions regarding the circuity of action issue, it is worthwhile to diagram the relationships among the parties and the flow of the checks through the collection process. Be sure you are able to follow why the use of conversion theory to avoid circuity of action might compromise the drawee/payor's position. Do contemporary rules of civil procedure suggest a better approach? The New York Court of Appeals in *Underpinning & Foundation Constructors, Inc. v. Chase Manhattan Bank,* 46 N.Y.2d 459, 414 N.Y.S.2d 298, 386 N.E.2d 1319 (1979) held that a drawer may bring an action against a depositary bank which pays an item in violation of the "for deposit only" restrictive indorsement. But in *Sun 'N Sand, Inc. v. United California Bank,* 21 Cal.3d 671, 148 Cal.Rptr. 329, 582 P.2d 920 (1978), the California Supreme Court held that the negligence preclusions in OR 4–406 could be asserted defensively by a depositary bank resisting a drawer's direct action (for breach of warranty).

As noted in Stone & Webster, some courts have allowed a drawer to recover against a depositary bank on conversion theory. A few other courts have allowed the drawer to sue the depositary bank for breach of warranty. Under OR 3–417 the presentment warranties run to a person who pays and under OR 4–207 the warranty runs to "the payor bank or other payor." In a well-known California case, *Sun 'N Sand, Inc. v. United California Bank, supra,* the court held that a drawer of a check was an "other payor" under 4–207 and could maintain suit against the depositary bank under that section.

Revised Article 3 adopts the position of Stone & Webster. The last sentence of R 3–420(a) reads: "An action for conversion of an instrument may not be brought by (i) the issuer or acceptor of the instrument or (ii) a payee or indorsee who did not receive delivery of the instrument either directly or through delivery to an agent or co-payee." Similarly, revised 3–417 and 4–208 provide that warranties run to a drawer only when a dishonored draft is presented to the drawer for payment. Comment 2 to R 3–417 states that the result in *Sun 'N Sand* is rejected.

2. *Restrictive Indorsements*

LA JUNTA STATE BANK v. TRAVIS

Colorado Supreme Court, 1986.
727 P.2d 48.

KIRSHBAUM, J. The respondents, personal representatives of the estate of Katherine A. Warnock, deceased, filed this action against the petitioner, La Junta State Bank (the Bank), seeking recovery of the amount of a cashier's check they alleged had been wrongfully deposited by the Bank. After a bench trial, the trial court entered judgment in favor of the Bank. The Court of Appeals reversed the trial court's judgment. Travis v. La Junta State Bank, 694 P.2d 350 (Colo.App. 1984). We granted certiorari to review the Court of Appeals' decision, and now reverse that judgment.

I

On or about November 15, 1979, Warnock purchased a cashier's check in the amount of $53,541.93 payable to her order and drawn on the Pueblo Bank and Trust Company. At some time between November 15, 1979, and November 30, 1979, Warnock indorsed "Katherine Warnock" on the reverse side of the check and Warnock's attorney, Jerry Quick, wrote the words "deposit only" under Warnock's indorsement. On November 30, 1979, Quick or one of his employees deposited the check into the Marquez Trust account, an account maintained at the Bank by Quick. Warnock did not at any time maintain an account with the Bank. The Bank collected the amount of the check from the Pueblo Bank and Trust Company.

Warnock died on November 10, 1981. One of the respondents subsequently conducted an examination of Warnock's personal papers and found no record of a receipt for the sum of $53,541.93. On June 24, 1982, the respondents made demand on the Bank for payment of that amount. No funds remained in the Marquez Trust account at that time, and no evidence was introduced at trial regarding disbursement of funds from that account.

When the Bank refused their demand, the respondents filed an action seeking recovery of the sum of $53,541.93 on grounds of conversion, negligence, breach of implied contract, and money had and received. The respondents contended that the words "deposit only" were placed on the check by Quick for the benefit of Warnock. Alternatively, they argued that the Bank had a duty either to deposit the item into an account for Warnock or to undertake further investigation of the indorsement before crediting the sum to any account other than an account for Warnock.

The trial court determined that Warnock had indorsed the check in blank and delivered it to Quick, that the check therefore became bearer paper upon Warnock's indorsement, and that the check was negotiable by delivery alone. The trial court then concluded that the respondents failed to establish any legal interest in the check or its proceeds and, therefore, lacked standing to recover on their claims. It also concluded that the respondents failed to prove they had suffered damages.

On appeal, the majority of a divided Court of Appeals panel concluded that Quick's addition of the words "deposit only" below Warnock's signature created a restrictive indorsement and that, because the Bank failed to treat the instrument accordingly, it was liable to the respondents for the full amount of the check.

II

* * *

An indorsement may * * * become qualified or restrictive as the result of the addition of certain language to a blank or special indorsement. Section 4–3–205 [R 3–206] provides the following definition of a restrictive indorsement:

> "An indorsement is restrictive which either:
>
> (a) Is conditional; or
>
> (b) Purports to prohibit further transfer of the instrument; or
>
> (c) Includes the words 'for collection', 'for deposit', 'pay any bank', or like terms signifying a purpose of deposit or collection; or
>
> (d) Otherwise states that it is for the benefit or use of the indorser or of another person."

Subsections 4–3–206(2) and (3) [See R 3–206(c)] contain the following provisions relating to "for deposit" restrictive indorsements:

> "(2) An intermediary bank, or a payor bank which is not the depositary bank, is neither given notice nor otherwise affected by a restrictive indorsement of any person except the bank's immediate transferor or the person presenting for payment.
>
> (3) Except for an intermediary bank, any transferee under an indorsement which is conditional or includes the words 'for collection', 'for deposit', 'pay any bank', or like terms * * * must pay or apply any value given by him for or on the security of the instrument consistently with the indorsement and to the extent that he does so he becomes a holder for value. In addition, such transferee is a holder in due course if he otherwise complies with the requirements of section 4–3–302 [R 3–302] on what constitutes a holder in due course."

These provisions require a depositary bank or other taker of an instrument containing a "for deposit" restrictive indorsement to apply the value evidenced by the instrument in accordance with the indorser's direction. Rutherford v. Darwin, 95 N.M. 340, 622 P.2d 245 (Ct.App.

1980); Underpinning & Foundation Constructors, Inc. v. Chase Manhattan Bank, 46 N.Y.2d 459, 414 N.Y.S.2d 298, 386 N.E.2d 1319 (1979); see also J. White and R. Summers, supra, § 13–10, at 513–15.

III

The foregoing summary of relevant Code provisions is helpful in assessing the effect of Quick's addition of the words "deposit only" to Warnock's indorsement and in determining the Bank's responsibilities upon taking the check. It is undisputed that when Warnock purchased the check it was negotiable order paper in her hands. See §§ 4–3–104(1)(d), –110(1) [R 3–104, –110]. The trial court concluded that when Warnock indorsed the check in blank and delivered it to Quick, it was converted from order paper to bearer paper, negotiable by delivery alone until specially indorsed. § 4–3–204(2) [R 3–205(b)]. The trial court also concluded that Quick's addition of "deposit only" below Warnock's signature did not convert Warnock's blank indorsement into a special indorsement. See § 4–3–204(3) [R 3–205(c)].

Implicit in the trial court's conclusions is the assumption that Quick added the words "deposit only" to the check at some time after Warnock's indorsement thereof. This implicit finding is supported by the stipulation of facts and the evidence disclosed by the record.[3] Therefore, we also conclude that when Warnock indorsed the check in blank and delivered it to Quick, Quick became a holder of the instrument in bearer form with the right to transfer or negotiate it by delivery alone.[4] §§ 4–3–301 [see comment to R 3–301], –204(2) [R 3–205(b)].

The respondents argue that, assuming Quick was initially a holder of a check in bearer form, his act of affixing the words "deposit only" to the check deprived him of that status, destroyed the negotiability of the check and converted Warnock's blank indorsement into a restrictive indorsement. This argument is untenable.

Quick, as holder of an instrument, was not authorized by any Code provision to convert his transferor's blank indorsement into a restrictive one. Cf. § 4–3–204(3) [R 3–205(c)] ("The holder may convert a blank indorsement into a special indorsement by writing over the

3. The trial court's determination that Quick wrote "deposit only" on the check after Warnock had signed it finds analogous support in § 4–3–414(2) [R 3–415(a)]. That provision, dealing with an indorser's contract of liability, states that "indorsers are liable to one another in the order in which they indorse, which is presumed to be the order in which their signatures appear on the instrument." Id. While we are mindful that Quick's writing of "deposit only" on the check did not constitute his signature, we are persuaded that the order in which Warnock's and Quick's writing appears on the check is indicative of the sequential order in which they affixed their respective writing to it.

4. The respondents have never directly questioned the trial court's finding that Warnock delivered the check to Quick. The stipulation of facts and the evidence presented at trial do not make clear the manner in which Quick obtained possession of the check. This factor does not, however, alter our analysis; once Quick obtained possession of the check he was a holder of bearer paper, and whether or not the owner thereof, he had the right to transfer or negotiate the check. See 5 R. Anderson, Anderson on the Uniform Commercial Code, § 3–202:42 (1984).

signature of the indorser in blank any contract consistent with the character of the indorsement."). Furthermore, the respondents incorrectly assume that a blank indorsement and a restrictive indorsement create mutually exclusive methods for negotiation. As U.C.C. § 3–206 official comment 5 (1978) indicates, "indorsements 'for collection' or 'for deposit' may be either special or blank." See also J. White and R. Summers, supra, § 13–10, at 504 ("a special or a blank indorsement may also be a 'restrictive indorsement' "). A single indorsement, therefore, may be both in blank and restrictive. See Spielman v. Manufacturers Hanover Trust Co., 60 N.Y.2d 221, 469 N.Y.S.2d 69, 456 N.E.2d 1192 (1983). The nonrestrictive character of Warnock's indorsement was determined when she affixed her signature to the check.

The respondents suggest that cases decided under the prior Negotiable Instruments Law, C.R.S. 1963 95–1–1 to 95–4–7, support their argument that Quick's addition of words of restriction destroyed his ability to negotiate the check. See Barnes v. Cherry Creek National Bank of Denver, 163 Colo. 414, 431 P.2d 471 (1967) (under Negotiable Instruments Law a restrictive indorsement destroys negotiability). Section 4–3–206(1) [R 3–206(a)] of the Code expressly provides that "[n]o restrictive indorsement prevents further transfer or negotiation of the instrument." See U.C.C. § 3–206 [R 3–206] official comment 1 ("[s]ubsection (1) [of section 3–206] * * * appl[ies] to all four classes of restrictive indorsements defined in [s]ection 3–205") [omitted in revised Article 3]. By adopting the Code the General Assembly changed the effect of a restrictive indorsement on a negotiable instrument. See People v. Marques, 184 Colo. 262, 520 P.2d 113 (1974). Therefore, the cases relied upon by the respondents do not answer the question presented here.

The respondents' assertion that Quick's addition of the restrictive language to the check was for Warnock's benefit is not supported by evidence in the record. Section 4–3–202(2) [R 3–204(a)] states that "[a]n indorsement must be written by or on behalf of the holder. * * *" Although an authorized agent can indorse an instrument on behalf of a principal, § 4–3–403(1) [R 3–402(a)] the respondents presented no evidence that Quick wrote "deposit only" on behalf of Warnock, and no such inference can be drawn from the fact that Quick was Warnock's attorney at all pertinent times. The record contains no evidence suggesting why Warnock purchased the check or how Quick acquired it. The evidence presented at trial simply failed to support the respondents' theory.

The majority of the Court of Appeals panel determined that Quick's conduct altered the status of the check, converting it "back to non-bearer paper," and also "made the indorsement restrictive." Travis v. La Junta State Bank, 694 P.2d at 351. Whether a negotiable instrument is order or bearer paper in the hands of a particular possessor is determined by the face of the instrument or the last indorsement thereon. As a result of Warnock's indorsement in blank, Quick became a holder of the check in bearer form and the check was negotiable by delivery alone. Contrary to the conclusion of the majority of the Court of Appeals panel, Quick's addition of the words "deposit only" to the check neither changed Warnock's blank indorsement into a special indorsement, thereby converting the bearer paper to order paper, nor altered the effect of her blank indorsement. * * *

IV

The fact that Quick was a holder of bearer paper does not end the inquiry into the propriety of the Bank's conduct. Section 4–3–206(3) [R 3–206(b), (c), and (e)] of the Code requires a depositary bank, upon being presented with a negotiable instrument containing an indorsement which includes the words "for deposit" or like terms, to "pay or apply any value given by him for or on the security of the instrument consistently with the indorsement. * * *" This obligation affords protection to payees or indorsers who indorse items "for deposit" in the belief that such indorsement will guard against further negotiation of the instrument to a holder in due course by a finder or a thief. See U.C.C. § 4–205 official comment 2; J. White and R. Summers, supra § 13–10, at 515. The duty to examine a restrictive indorsement and follow its directions may require a bank to refuse to deposit an item in a particular account if such conduct would be inconsistent with the restrictive indorsement, or to investigate rather than accept an item as a matter of course.

On November 30, 1979, the Bank received a cashier's check in the amount of $53,541.93, payable to Warnock and inscribed "Katherine Warnock, deposit only," accompanied by a deposit slip for an account maintained by Quick. In spite of the fact that the check appeared to contain a restrictive indorsement by a payee who did not have an account with the Bank, the Bank neither refused to deposit the check nor inquired into the circumstances surrounding what appeared to be a restrictive indorsement.

The Bank and amicus Colorado Bankers Association argue that because Quick's writing of "deposit only" on the check created a restrictive indorsement by Quick, the Bank was authorized by § 4–4–205(1) [R 4–205(1)], 2 C.R.S. (1973), to supply any necessary missing information to complete his indorsement. Section 4–4–205(1) [R 4–205(1)] states:

> "A depositary bank which has taken an item for collection may supply any indorsement of the customer which is necessary to title unless the item contains the words "payee's indorsement required" or the like. In the absence of such a requirement a statement placed on the item by the depositary bank to the effect that the item was deposited by a customer or credited to his account is effective as the customer's indorsement."

This provision is not applicable to the circumstances of this case.

Although § 4–4–205(1) [R 4–205(1)] authorizes a depositary bank to place a statement [6] on its customer's check which is effective as the customer's indorsement, no such statement was placed on the check by the Bank. Moreover, we do not believe § 4-4-205(1) [R 4-205(1)] permits a depositary bank to evade its duty to act consistently with restrictive indorsements imposed by § 4-3-206(3) [R 3-206(b), (c), and (e)].

Section 4-4-205(2) [R 4-205], in a nearly verbatim restatement of § 4-3-206(2) [R 3-206(c)(4) and (d)], provides that "[a]n intermediary bank, or payor bank which is not a depositary bank, is neither given notice nor otherwise affected by a restrictive indorsement of any person except the bank's immediate transferor." The clear import of both § 4-4-205(2) and § 4-3-206(2) [R 3-206(c)(4) and (d)] is that while intermediary banks and nondepositary payor banks may ignore all restrictive indorsements except those of the bank's immediate transferor, depositary banks may not so ignore restrictive indorsements. See U.C.C. § 4-205 official comment 2. The Code's forceful restatement of a depositary bank's responsibility with regard to restrictive indorsements supports the conclusion that a depositary bank may not invoke its authority to supply a customer's missing indorsement to escape the consequences of its failure to comply with the directions of what objectively appears to be a restrictive indorsement of another. Cf. Perini Corp. v. First National Bank of Habersham County, 553 F.2d 398 (5th Cir.1977) (authority to add missing indorsement under U.C.C. § 4-205(1) [R 4-205(1)] does not immunize bank from liability under its warranty of title). A contrary conclusion would severely weaken the Code's protection of restrictive indorsers.

In this case the Bank, as a depositary bank, received a check containing what appeared to be a restrictive indorsement by Katherine Warnock. The record does not reveal who actually delivered the check and the deposit slip to the Bank. Thus, at the moment it received the restrictively indorsed check, the Bank appeared to owe a duty to Warnock to either comply with the directions of the indorsement or to inquire further concerning the transaction because of the simultaneous receipt of a deposit slip directing deposit of the check into an account other than Warnock's. However, because the check was bearer paper when Quick received it, he was free to direct its deposit in any manner he elected. Any inquiry by the Bank would have revealed that, although the language inscribed on the instrument appeared to constitute a restrictive indorsement by Katherine Warnock, the words "deposit only" had been added by Quick on his own behalf; the indorsement was in fact a restrictive indorsement by Quick; and the Bank owed a duty to Quick on November 30, 1979, to honor his restrictive indorsement. Under the particular circumstances of this case, the

6. Such a statement, applied in stamp form by what is commonly called a § 4-205 [R 4-205] stamp, generally provides the following, or language to like effect:

"CREDIT TO THE ACCOUNT OF THE WITHIN NAMED PAYEE
In Accordance with Payee's Instruction
Absence of Endorsement Guaranteed"

Bank in fact owed no duty to Warnock and the respondents are entitled to no damages.

V

For the foregoing reasons, the judgment of the Court of Appeals is reversed. The case is remanded to that court with directions to reinstate the judgment of the trial court.

Note

As the case indicates, a common way for a payee of a check to protect against theft after indorsement is to indorse

"For deposit only

Payee"

In that case, any subsequent taker is liable in conversion to the indorser if the check is not credited to the account of the indorser or the indorser does not otherwise receive the funds. The original Article 3 section dealing with the issue, 3–206, is not well-drafted and addresses the issue in a back-handed way. Subsection (3) provides that a transferee other than an intermediary bank "must pay or apply any value given by him for or on the security of the instrument consistently with the indorsement and to the extent that he does so he becomes a holder for value * * *." The section, therefore, does not directly state transferee's liability if the transferee does not apply the value given for the instrument consistently with the indorsement. However, the clear implication, and the holding of many cases, is that payment inconsistent with the restrictive indorsement makes the taker liable in conversion to the restrictive indorser. Revised 3–206(c) is much better drafted. Read that section now.

Would the result in the *La Junta* case have been different if Quick had written "For deposit only" above the signature of Ms. Warnock, rather than below it? Would the analysis have been different if he had signed his own name as he wrote for deposit only? Since the check was indorsed in blank, but restrictively, it seems that the court correctly assumes that the depositary bank became a holder of the instrument.

The court notes that a restrictive indorsement could be either blank or special. If Ms. Warnock had written "for deposit only in La Junta Nat. Bank", the indorsement would have been a special indorsement and only La Junta could further transfer the check. If the indorsement is "for deposit" but blank, the proceeds still must be credited to the restrictive indorser, but could be properly accepted by any bank in which the indorser had a deposit account.

The analysis of the court, if not the result, is subject to question. The court suggests that the bank had a duty to inquire as to the appropriateness of the deposit to Quick's account since the check seemed to be indorsed for deposit by Ms. Warnock. But, says the court, if inquiry had been made, the bank would have discovered that the indorsement had been made by Quick. The difficulty with that line of analysis is that if the bank had a duty to inquire, it must be because the form of the indorsement put it on notice of a possible claim by Ms. Warnock. If it was on notice of a possible claim of Ms. Warnock, it was not a holder in due course, and, if it was not a holder in due course, it is subject to the claim of prior parties, and should be subject to conversion liability for acting inconsistently with Warnock's rights. Further, if there is a duty of inquiry, perhaps it should not be sufficient to inquire only of Quick, rather than of Warnock as well.

However, while the court's analysis can be criticized, the result may be appropriate. Perhaps it is fair to conclude that the Bank was entitled to assume that the "For deposit" indorsement had been written by Quick. Because the check was already indorsed in blank, his indorsement was not necessary to transfer title of the check to Bank. (However, your editors believe that it would be very unusual for a depositor of a check indorsed to him to place a "for deposit" indorsement on the check without also signing his own name. In fact, as in the Warnock case, such conduct at least raises a question as to whether the deposit should be to the credit of the person who has signed above the "for deposit" indorsement, or to the credit of the person who presents the check to the bank.)

Since Warnock indorsed, and since any intermediate collecting bank and a drawee bank that is not the depositary bank are not liable for paying inconsistently with a restrictive indorsement, the drawee bank in *La Junta* has properly paid to defendant depositary bank. (OR 3–206(2), 4–205(2), R 3–206(c)(4)). Therefore, Warnock's estate cannot make a claim against the drawee bank.

In *Rutherford v. Darwin,* 95 N.M. 340, 622 P.2d 245 (1980), Darwin was general manager of two partnerships, Rancho Village Partners and the Settlement. He indorsed a check payable to Rancho, "Deposit to the account of Rancho Village Partners," took the check to defendant First National Bank in Albuquerque where both partnerships had an account, and filled out a deposit slip showing a deposit to the account of the Settlement. The bank credited the check to the Settlement account. The court, over a dissent, held that the bank was liable to Rancho Village for failing to give value consistently with the indorsement, even though Darwin had full power to handle the check and could have stricken the indorsement, indorsed the check in blank, and deposited it in the Settlement account. The court stated the issue as whether the person making the deposit could "waive" a restrictive indorsement and concluded that he could not.

D. IMPOSTERS

COVINGTON v. PENN SQUARE NATIONAL BANK

Oklahoma Court of Appeals, 1975.
545 P.2d 824, 17 UCC Rep.Sav. 1048.

REYNOLDS, J. This is a suit against two banks to recover the amount of a cashier's check obtained from plaintiff by fraud and paid in contravention of a stop order. The case was submitted to the trial court on pleadings, admissions and interrogatories. The plaintiff appeals summary judgment for the defendant banks.

In November of 1972 one James F. Beaird, Jr. contacted the plaintiffs to sell them an oil lease. He represented himself to be an employee of Western Geophysical Company of Houston, Texas, and showed the plaintiffs a map which purported to show the location of eight test well holes located on the leased property along with purported logs of the eight holes showing oil sand. The plaintiffs placed a telephone call to Western Geophysical and asked if James Beaird was an employee. They were told that a man with the name of James "Baird" (spelled B-a-i-r-d) was in charge of data processing. When asked how his name was spelled, James Beaird said that his name was spelled with an "i".

On November 16, 1972, plaintiffs purchased a cashier's check from defendant Boulder Bank in Tulsa in the amount of $6,400.00 payable to James Baird. They delivered it to James Beaird as consideration of the lease. The next day the check was cashed by defendant Penn Square National Bank in Oklahoma City. Beaird told the cashier, whom he had known for five years, that his name was misspelled on the check. On request of the cashier he endorsed the check twice, James Baird and James F. Beaird, Jr.

On November 18 and 19 the plaintiffs became suspicious, and on investigation learned that James Beaird was not the same James Baird who was employed by Western Geophysical and that no oil exploration had been done on the lease which they had purchased. On Monday morning, November 20th, plaintiffs requested the Boulder Bank to stop payment on the cashier's check. The bank agreed to do so in return for plaintiffs' promise to hold Boulder harmless. It stamped "payment stopped" on the check and returned it to Penn Square. Penn Square again demanded payment. Boulder concluded that it could not legally stop payment and forwarded to Penn Square the amount of the check.

Suit was filed by plaintiffs against both banks in March of 1973. In August of 1974 the defendants filed a Joint Motion for Summary Judgment. The trial court sustained the motion.

On appeal, it is contended by appellants that the payee of the cashier's check was one James Baird, an employee of Western Geophysical Company of Houston, Texas, but that the payment by Penn Square Bank was to one James F. Beaird, Jr., who is a different individual; that the payment to Beaird resulted from a forged indorsement. Therefore, Penn Square Bank is liable for the loss since it indorsed the check with all prior indorsements guaranteed, and Boulder Bank is liable as it violated its agreement to refuse payment on the check.

Statutory language and case law unmistakably place the burden of loss from a forged instrument on the party who deals with the forger. A bank is obliged to pay only according to the customer's order.

* * *

The Uniform Commercial Code, 12A O.S.1971, § 3–404(1) [See R 3–403(a)] . . . states:

> "Any unauthorized signature is wholly inoperative as that of the person whose name is signed unless he ratifies it or is precluded from denying it; . . ."

An unauthorized signature is defined in 12A O.S.1971, § 1–201(43) as "... one made without actual, implied or apparent authority and includes a forgery."

This rule is designed to protect bank customers from financial loss incurred through forgeries of lost or stolen checks. The rule is not rigid, however, because it has exceptions. One of these exceptions is carved out by 12A O.S.1971, § 3–405(1)(a) [See R 3–404(a)] which states the imposter rule:

> "(1) An indorsement by any person in the name of the named payee is effective if
>
> "(a) an imposter by the use of the mails or otherwise has induced the maker or drawer to issue the instrument to him or his confederate in the name of the payee; or * * *"

The policy underlying this rule is that the person who is taken in by an imposter or a dishonest employee should bear the burden of loss rather than a collecting bank. * * *

The cases previously decided concerning forgeries on certified checks are not in point with the case at bar. In this fact situation, James F. Beaird, Jr. dealt directly with the plaintiffs. They were induced by him to purchase the check. The check was purchased by the plaintiffs as consideration for the oil lease and presented to him personally.

The imposter rule was stated in Schweitzer v. Bank of America N.T. & S.A., 42 Cal.App.2d 536, 109 P.2d 441.

> "* * * (W)here a check is delivered to an imposter as payee and the drawer believes that the imposter is the person upon whose endorsement it will be paid, the endorsement by such imposter in the name which he is using to impersonate another is not a forgery * * * If a buyer is deceived as to the true name of the individual with whom he deals, but at the same time he intends to purchase from the man who commits the deception, he there identifies the seller by sight and hearing."

On a motion for summary judgment, "* * * (T)he court shall render judgment if it appears that there is no substantial controversy as to any material fact and that any party is entitled to judgment as a matter of law." 12 O.S.Supp.1974, ch. 2, App., Rule 13.

This court finds no substantial controversy as to the material facts.

Affirmed.

ROMANG, P.J., and BOX, J., concur.

Note

Would the result be different if plaintiffs had made the check out to Western Geophysical Company rather than to James Baird? Compare OR 3–405(1)(a) and Comment 2 with R 3–404(a) and Comment 1.

Would the result be different if James Beaird had claimed to be Jim Weathers, a representative of Western Geophysical, had been given a check payable to Weathers, and had opened an account in that name into which he deposited the check? (Does the similarity of names in the case make any difference to the result?)

E. NEGLIGENCE, EMPLOYEE FRAUD

KOERNER & LAMBERT v. ALLSTATE INSURANCE CO.

Louisiana Court of Appeal, 1979.
374 So.2d 179.

SAMUEL, JUDGE. Plaintiff, a professional law corporation, filed two law suits, which were later consolidated, against Allstate Insurance Company and other defendants to recover the respective sums of $2,190 and $3,389, representing drafts drawn by Allstate on Deposit Guaranty National Bank, Jackson, Mississippi. Plaintiff had deposited the drafts for collection and, after collection, had disbursed the amounts to various creditors of its client, Paul H. Boucher, d/b/a Marina–Rama, and to itself for professional services rendered. Unknown to plaintiff, the signatures of two of the payees on these drafts had been unauthorized or forged, and Allstate eventually took action, as outlined below, which caused plaintiff's bank to debit its account for $5,579, the total of the two drafts. Defendants answered, denying liability.

After a trial on the merits, judgments were rendered in favor of plaintiff and against Allstate in the amount of $2,190 in one case and $3,389 in the other, together with appropriate interest. The judgments dismissed the suits as to all other defendants. Allstate has appealed.

The record shows that Burnell Robinson and George Driscoll owned boats which were damaged in separate incidents. Coincidentally, both men were insured by Allstate and each independently selected Marina–Rama to perform the necessary repairs.

The owner of Marina–Rama, Paul H. Boucher, submitted repair estimates to Allstate, which furnished two drafts to Boucher. The first, dated August 5, 1976, was in the amount of $2,190 and made payable to the order of Burnell Robinson in full payment of repairs to be done on the Robinson vessel. The second, dated August 11, 1976, was in the amount of $3,389 and made payable to the order of George Driscoll and Marina–Rama for repairs to be done on the Driscoll vessel.

Allstate did not notify either Robinson or Driscoll of the delivery of the drafts to Boucher, nor did it subsequently verify that the signatures on the drafts were actually those of Robinson and Driscoll. Neither Robinson nor Driscoll signed the drafts nor did either have any knowledge of their existence.

Driscoll's signature was forged on his draft, and Robinson's brother was tricked into signing Robinson's name on the other draft after being led to believe it constituted a work authorization. Boucher never repaired the vessels.

Plaintiff represented Boucher in a contemplated bankruptcy proceeding and, in an effort to avoid bankruptcy, Boucher gave the drafts to plaintiff for payment to his creditors. During the month of August, 1976, plaintiff deposited the drafts in its notarial account at the Whitney National Bank in New Orleans for collection and requested of Whitney that it notify plaintiff when the funds were collected and deposited in its account. Only after plaintiff received such notice, also during the month of August, 1976, did it actually disburse the funds in question. As above set forth, disbursement was made to Boucher's creditors and plaintiff retained some of the funds for professional services rendered.

There is no question that plaintiff was entirely free from fault in the transaction; it had no knowledge whatever that signatures on the drafts given it by its client were unauthorized or forged.

More than five months after issuance of the drafts, Robinson contacted Allstate regarding payment for the repairs to his boat. At this time Allstate first notified Robinson that the draft had been given to Boucher. On January 27, 1977, after all checks written by plaintiff had cleared, Allstate obtained a forged signature affidavit from Robinson. Later Driscoll also contacted Allstate regarding payment for repair to his boat, and he was then notified the draft had been given to Boucher. Driscoll also executed a forged signature affidavit.

Allstate presented the affidavits to Deposit Guaranty National Bank, which made demand for collection on Whitney. Pursuant to this demand, Whitney paid Guaranty National $5,579 and debited plaintiff's notarial account for that amount. These lawsuits ensued.

In holding for plaintiff, the trial judge emphasized defendant delivered the drafts only to Boucher and honored them when presented. Only after a fraud was discovered more than five months later did Allstate take any action at all and then only to recover the amounts paid as above set forth. We repeat for emphasis that Allstate failed to notify their insured the drafts in their names had been given to Boucher.

Revised Statute 10:3–406 [R 3–406] provides as follows:

> "Any person who by his negligence substantially contributes to a material alteration of the instrument or to the making of an unauthorized signature *is precluded* from asserting the alteration or lack of authority against a holder in due course or against a drawee or other payor who pays the instrument in good faith and

in accordance with the reasonable commercial standards of the drawee's or payor's business." LSA–RS 10:3–406. (Emphasis added).

The question of negligence is one of fact for the trial court's determination. The record contains sufficient evidence for the trial judge to have concluded that Allstate was guilty of negligence by entrusting the drafts to Marina–Rama without notifying its insureds or otherwise taking some action to verify the signature of each payee on the drafts and that such negligence substantially contributed to the unauthorized and forged signatures. The record does not justify a reversal by this court of the trial judge's finding of fact in this regard.

Defendant argues that in spite of this finding of negligence, plaintiff violated the warranties of good title, authorized signature, lack of material alteration, etc., imputed to one who obtains payment or acceptance of a negotiable instrument from one who acts in good faith. We do not agree with the argument.

Louisiana law on commercial paper is the result of the legislature's adoption of portions of the Uniform Commercial Code by Act 92 of 1974. It is generally regarded by scholars of the Uniform Commercial Code that the question of negligence cuts across the issue of warranty, since the wording of R.S. 10:3–406 [R 3–406], quoted above, clearly states that one whose negligence contributes to an unauthorized signature (here also a forgery) "is precluded from asserting the alteration or lack of authority against a holder in due course * * *" This statutory provision is regarded as an estoppel against the negligent party from asserting the question of warranty under R.S. 10:3–417 [R 3–416, 3–417].

For plaintiff to be a holder in due course, it must have taken the instruments (1) for value, (2) in good faith, and (3) without notice that they were overdue, dishonored, or subject to any defense or claim of any person. Plaintiff clearly took the drafts from its client in good faith and without notice of any defects. Moreover, since it received the drafts with the understanding that a part of the proceeds thereof were to be appropriated to a fee balance owed it by its client, it also took the drafts for value. We consequently conclude plaintiff was a holder in due course insofar as R.S. 10:3–406 [R 3–406] and 3–417 [R 3–416, 3–417] are concerned.

Having concluded in this case plaintiff was a holder in due course, and having adopted the trial court's conclusion that defendant was guilty of substantially contributing negligence under the above quoted R.S. 10:3–406 [R 3–406], it necessarily follows that Allstate is precluded or estopped from asserting the unauthorized signature and forgery against the plaintiff.

For the reasons assigned, the judgments appealed from are affirmed.

Affirmed.

Problems

1. Reed Company's treasurer inadvertently left three blank checks in the company's check writing machine while the machine was being serviced by Bluett Computer Services. The Bluett employee doing the servicing completed the checks in the amount of $3,000 each and made them payable to himself. The machine automatically signed the checks. The employee then indorsed the checks and deposited them in his bank. The drawee bank had agreed with Reed that it would exercise ordinary care to avoid paying machine-signed checks for more than $1,000. The bank's computers were programmed to read a symbol on machine signed checks, but, because of a computer failure, the checks were paid. Can Reed demand that drawee bank recredit the Reed account with the amount of the three checks? See OR and R 3–406. Would the result be different if, to the bank's knowledge, the computer had not been reading the machine-signed check symbol for three weeks before the checks in question were presented? Does the result depend on whether the depositary bank has given value for the checks? See OR 4–208, 4–209, R 4–210, 4–211, stating when a depositary bank gives value for HDC purposes.

2. Arena Auto Auction owed $5,000 to Tom Pluckett of Elgin, Illinois. Arena had in the past also done business with a Tom Pluckett of Dothan, Alabama. Arena's secretary inadvertently mailed a $5,000 check to the Alabama Pluckett to whom Arena owed no money. Alabama Pluckett indorsed the check and deposited it in his bank account. The check was paid on presentment. Was the check properly chargeable to Arena's account? (1) Was the indorsement of Alabama Tom Pluckett a forgery? (2) If so, is Arena precluded from asserting the forgery? See OR and R 3–406 and see comment 1 to R 3–110 and Comment 3 to R 3–406. See also *Park State Bank v. Arena Auto Auction,* 59 Ill.App.2d 235, 207 N.E.2d 158 (1965).

E.F. HUTTON & CO., INC. v. CITY NAT'L BANK

California Court of Appeals, 1983.
149 Cal.App.3d 60, 196 Cal.Rptr. 614.

FAINER, JUSTICE.

Plaintiff E.F. Hutton & Co., Inc. (Hutton) appeals from a judgment of dismissal entered after the trial court sustained general demurrers of defendant City National Bank (City Bank) to plaintiff's second amended complaint. The minute order sustaining the demurrer stated that the court's order was made "* * * per points and authorities in moving papers * * * [and the demurrers were sustained] *without leave to amend.*" (Emphasis added.)

Plaintiff, as a drawer of eighteen checks totalling $638,598.00, sought recovery from defendant City Bank, a collecting bank, for losses it sustained when one of plaintiff's employees obtained the eighteen checks made payable to various named individual payees, forged the payees' indorsements, presented the checks with the forged indorsements to the defendant City Bank who collected the amount of the checks from plaintiff's drawee bank or banks and then deposited the check funds in the employee's personal account at defendant City Bank. Plaintiff's theory of recovery against defendant City Bank was for negligence, breach of the warranty obligations imposed by sections 3417 [R 3–416, 3–417] and 4207 [R 4–208] of the California Uniform Commercial Code, and a common count.

In *Allied Concord Financial Corp. v. Bank of America* (1969) 275 Cal.App.2d 1, 80 Cal.Rptr. 622, it was held that a drawer, such as plaintiff Hutton, had a direct cause of action against a collecting bank, such as defendant City Bank, on the theory that the drawer was a third party beneficiary of the implied presentment warranties of section 4207 [R 4–208] owed by the collecting bank to the drawee bank.

This right was reaffirmed by our Supreme Court in *Sun 'N Sand, Inc. v. United California Bank* (1978) 21 Cal.3d 671, 148 Cal.Rptr. 329, 582 P.2d 920, in which the court discussed the theories of recovery available to the drawer, including negligence and breach of warranty. The pleadings of plaintiff Hutton are reviewed with the holding of *Sun 'N Sand* as a guide.

First, as to plaintiff's negligence cause of action, the following is alleged: Plaintiff's employee, one Hamaoui, maintained an account in the Beverly Hills office of defendant City Bank. Defendant City Bank knew or should have known Hamaoui was "an employee and fiduciary" of plaintiff. Eighteen checks, totalling $638,598.00, were drawn by plaintiff payable to eighteen different named individual payees. The smallest check sum was $10,000.00, the largest, $81,598.00. The amount of each check was properly made payable to each payee. The funds drawn rightfully belonged to each named payee. Over a period of approximately one year, Hamaoui presented these checks to defendant City Bank for collection and for credit to Hamaoui's personal account at defendant City Bank. Each check contained a forged indorsement of the named payee. It was foreseeable to defendant City Bank that plaintiff would be injured by any negligence of defendant City Bank in accepting said checks for collection from plaintiff's drawee bank or banks; therefore, defendant City Bank owed plaintiff a duty to act with care in handling these checks. Defendant City Bank and its employees knew or should have known that each check was irregular and that further inquiry was required. The checks were handled for collection by defendant City Bank for credit to Hamaoui's account without any reasonable attempt to verify the indorsements or Hamaoui's authority to deposit the proceeds in his personal account. Defendant City Bank breached its duty of due care in failing to take reasonable steps to ascertain the genuineness of the check indorsements and was "grossly negligent" in failing to follow reasonable commercial banking standards. Finally, as a proximate cause of this negligence, plaintiff was damaged in the sum of $638,598.00.

Negligence is a tort, a theory for imposing liability on a defendant for injuries incurred by a plaintiff. "Negligence, * * *, is conduct that falls below a standard established by law for the protection of others against unreasonable risk of harm. The standard of conduct applicable to a particular defendant can be expressed in terms of defendant's duty to plaintiff or to people generally." (California Tort Guide (Cont.Ed. Bar 1979) General Principles, § 1.2, p. 2.) Civil Code section 1714, subdivision (a) embodies a fundamental standard of conduct and states that a person is responsible for injury occasioned to another by the person's want of ordinary care or skill in management of his property or person.

Actionable negligence has three elements: a legal duty to use due care, breach of that duty, and a proximate or legal causal connection between the breach and plaintiff's injuries. (*United States Liab. Ins. Co. v. Haidinger–Hayes, Inc.* (1970) 1 Cal.3d 586, 594, 83 Cal.Rptr. 418, 463 P.2d 770.)

In *Sun 'N Sand, Inc. v. United California Bank, supra,* 21 Cal.3d 671, 692–696, 148 Cal.Rptr. 329, 582 P.2d 920, our Supreme Court held that a drawer could state a cause of action against a collecting bank for negligence and that a bank cannot rely upon mere possession of an instrument, e.g., a check, by an agent or employee of drawer as a sufficient representation to create apparent authority to negotiate the check in the favor of the employee or agent. The court reasoned that a duty to exercise reasonable care depends upon foreseeability of the risk of loss or injury to the drawer by the conduct of the collecting bank.

In the situation where a collecting bank is presented with one or more checks of a significant amount by a person the bank knows or should know is an employee of the drawer and the employee will receive the check proceeds, then sufficiently suspicious circumstances are present to alert the collecting bank that a fraud may be perpetrated on the drawer-employer. Given these factors, *Sun 'N Sand* says a duty of due care is imposed on the collecting bank.

In *Sun 'N Sand,* the Supreme Court was dealing with a variation of the situation of an employer-drawer suing a collecting bank to recover funds embezzled by a dishonest employee through the manipulation of company checks. In discussing the negligence cause of action by the drawer, the high court said the collecting bank "* * * should have appreciated the indicia of misappropriation * * * [which] is, of course nothing other than a determination that * * * [the drawer/employer's] loss was reasonably foreseeable. * * * We are not persuaded that commerce will be impeded by a duty of inquiry in the context that we should depart from the fundamental principle that actors are liable for reasonably foreseeable issues occasioned by their conduct * * *. We hold simply that the bank cannot ignore the danger signals inherent in such an attempted negotiation. There must be objective indicia from which the bank could reasonably conclude that the party presenting the check is authorized to transact in the manner proposed. In the absence of such indicia the bank pays at its peril." (*Id.,* at pp. 695–696, 148 Cal.Rptr. 329, 582 P.2d 920.)

The *Sun 'N Sand* court limited the duty to those situations in which the "* * * checks, not insignificant in amount, are drawn payable to the order of a bank and are presented to the payee bank by a third party seeking to negotiate the checks for his own benefit." (*Id.*, at p. 695, 148 Cal.Rptr. 392, 582 P.2d 920.) The Supreme Court's narrowing of the scope of a collecting bank's duty of inquiry to checks drawn to the order of a bank was merely an application of the *Sun 'N Sand* facts to the rule that the collecting bank has a general duty and obligation, based on foreseeability of risk to a drawer, to exercise reasonable care. In *Joffe v. United California Bank, supra,* 141 Cal. App.3d 541, 190 Cal.Rptr. 443, the check was payable to an "escrow account" of a bank but the indorsed check was presented to the collecting bank by a third party, who was not the designated payee and was not identified as the authorized representative. The Joffe court held that there was insufficient objective indicia from which the collecting bank could reasonably conclude that the person presenting the check was authorized to negotiate it for said person's benefit. (*Id.*, at p. 556, 190 Cal.Rptr. 443.) The *Joffe* decision did not limit the negligence cause of action only to the situation where the check or checks are drawn payable to the order of a bank, and neither do we.

In our instant case, the checks, either in the aggregate or individually, were for a substantial amount, payable to individual payees at another bank, with inadequate indicia on the face of the checks (as pleaded) regarding the authorization of Hamaoui (who, it appeared, was to benefit from each transaction) to negotiate the instruments. Under the circumstances, it must be concluded that the risk to the drawer plaintiff was sufficiently foreseeable to impose a duty on defendant City Bank, the collecting bank, not to ignore the danger signals inherent in the forged negotiations by Hamaoui. The defendant bank proceeded at its peril when it failed to take reasonable steps to investigate Hamaoui's authority to negotiate the checks and to deposit the collected check funds in his personal account.

The plaintiff's allegations, in its negligence claim, state facts of duty and of a breach of that duty proximately causing its loss or injury. The plaintiff, therefore, has alleged facts sufficient to state a cause of action for negligence unless, as claimed by defendant City Bank, the provisions of section 3405, subdivision (1)(c) [See R 3–404(b)] are a necessary element of a negligence cause of action by a drawer against a collecting bank based upon the actions of drawer's dishonest employee in forging indorsements on checks payable to a named individual payee and then negotiating the check to the employee's benefit. Section 3405, subdivision (1)(c) [R 3–404(b)] provides that "* * * [a]n agent or employee of the maker or drawer has supplied him with the name of the payee intending the latter to have no such interest * * *." This Uniform Commercial Code provision is often referred to or called the "padded payroll" preclusion.

As background for this code section, a drawee bank or a collecting bank, under most circumstances, is liable if it pays on a forged indorsement. "This is because it is bound to pay only in accordance with the * * * [drawer's] order * * *. [A] forged indorsement is no indorsement at all, and when the bank pays on it, it is paying in violation of the * * * [drawer's] order. [Citations omitted.]" (2 Witkin, *Summary of Cal. Law,* (8th ed.) Negotiable Instruments, § 144, p. 1397.) One of the exceptions to this principle is the "padded payroll" preclusion (section 3405, subd. (1)(c)) [R 3–404(b)], which states that the forged indorsement is deemed effective if an employee of the drawer has supplied the drawer with the name of the payee when the employee intends to dishonestly benefit from the transaction. What this means is that the employee's fraudulent indorsement permits title to pass as if no forgery had ever occurred; the employer, having drawn the check cannot ordinarily assert the forgery to recover from the collecting bank. The rationale for the rule is a balancing of losses and " * * * the loss should fall upon the employer rather than upon the subsequent holder or drawee * * * [because] the employer is normally in a better position to prevent such forgeries by reasonable care in the selection or supervision of his employees, or, if he is not, is at least in a better position to cover the loss by fidelity insurance; and that the costs of such insurance is properly an expense of his business rather than of the business of the holder or drawee." (See Cal.Code Comment, West's Ann.U.Com. Code (1964 ed.) § 3405, pp. 287–288.) We hold, however, that the collecting bank may bear liability for loss if it has culpably contributed to the forgery's success.

It is argued that this padded payroll exclusion applied to tort action including negligent claims. We disagree. Section 1103 states that the principles of law and equity shall supplement the code unless displaced by particular provisions of the Uniform Commercial Code. No provision of the Uniform Commercial Code displaces common law negligence recovery. (See *Joffe v. United California Bank, supra,* 141 Cal.App.3d 541, 557–558, 190 Cal.Rptr. 443.) Section 3405, subdivision (1)(c) is "not applicable in * * * [a negligence cause of action.] Moreover, * * * [the section does] not create a loss distributive scheme which would shield depositary * * * [or collecting] banks under fact patterns similar to that alleged in the * * * [plaintiff Hutton's] complaint. (See *Sun 'N Sand, Inc. v. United California Bank, supra,* 21 Cal.3d at p. 696 [, 148 Cal.Rptr. 329, 582 P.2d 920]; *Fireman's Fund Ins. Co. v. Security Pacific Nat. Bank,* 85 Cal.App.3d at p. 813 [, 149 Cal.Rptr. 883].)" (*Joffe v. United California Bank, supra,* 141 Cal.App.3d 541, 190 Cal.Rptr. 443.)

Our Supreme Court specifically has held that the padded payroll section did not apply and does not bar the drawer from pursuing its remedies in tort. (*Sun 'N Sand, Inc. v. United California Bank, supra,* 21 Cal.3d 671, 696, 148 Cal.Rptr. 329, 582 P.2d 920.) The court stated that the application of the padded payroll provision "derives from the premise that the employer/drawer is better able to prevent the success of such fraud than the bank * * *." (*Ibid.*) The court then said that when the balance of the equities between a drawer-employer and a collecting bank do not exist due to circumstances surrounding a transaction, the padded payroll section can not be applied. (*Ibid.*) *When the collecting bank is confronted with obviously suspicious circumstances and could have reasonably foreseen the plaintiff's loss, the padded payroll provisions of the California Uniform Commercial Code cannot be invoked and the defendant became subject to general negligence liability.* (*Id.*, at p. 696, 148 Cal.Rptr. 329, 582 P.2d 920.) [Emphasis supplied by court.]

The plaintiff has alleged facts sufficient to state a cause of action for negligence. The padded payroll exclusion is not applicable to the elements of plaintiff-drawer's negligence cause of action against defendant City Bank. If not applicable, then it is certainly not a necessary or essential allegation for plaintiff's negligence cause of action. The trial court erred in sustaining defendant's demurrer to plaintiff's "First Cause of Action" for negligence.[6]

Second, as to plaintiff's breach of warranty claim against defendant City Bank, the following is alleged: Plaintiff incorporated most of the negligence allegations into the warranty count and alleged that by reason of the forged indorsements, defendant City Bank breached its warranty obligations under sections 3417 [R 3–416, 3–417] and 4207 [R 4–207, 4–208]. Plaintiff also alleges it was damaged in the sum of $638,598.00 as the result of defendant's breach of warranties, that defendant City Bank, disregarding reasonable commercial banking practice, acted in bad faith, and was guilty of gross negligence. Finally, plaintiff alleges that defendant is estopped to assert the padded payroll defense of section 3405 [R 3–404] because of defendant's gross negligence.

The *Sun 'N Sand* court, in analyzing the statutory scheme for pleading and proving a breach of the implied presentment warranties of section 4207 [R 4–208], said that the good title warranty is concerned only with the validity of indorsement, and if the dishonest employee's behavior comes within section 3405, subdivision (1)(c) [R 3–404(b)], there is no breach of warranty claim. The Supreme Court concluded that the warranty of good title " * * * involves a very limited inquiry: does the instrument presented contain all necessary indorsements, are such indorsements genuine or otherwise effective?" *Sun 'N Sand, Inc. v. United California Bank, supra,* 21 Cal.3d 671, 687, 148 Cal.Rptr. 329, 582 P.2d 920. We conclude that the *Sun 'N Sand* holding requires the drawer, suing the collecting bank for damages for a breach of warranty of title, to allege ultimate facts that the forged indorsements were not genuine or otherwise effective.

As plaintiff Hutton has alleged that the checks were presented to defendant City Bank with forged indorsements, plaintiff-drawer cannot

6. Nothing in this decision prevents the defendant City Bank from pleading and asserting the affirmative defense to plaintiff's negligence cause of action of comparative negligence first announced in *Li v. Yellow Cab Co.* (1975) 13 Cal.3d 804, 119 Cal.Rptr. 858, 532 P.2d 1226 and refined by the progeny of *Li.* This defense may include the negligence of plaintiff in permitting a padded payroll situation under appropriate circumstances.

allege facts sufficient to state a cause of action for damages for a breach of an implied presentment warranty for good title against defendant City Bank unless plaintiff alleges ultimate facts that the eighteen checks presented to defendant City Bank did not contain all necessary indorsements and that the indorsements were not genuine or otherwise effective. In order to do this, plaintiff must allege facts either negating the padded payroll exclusion or that defendant City Bank culpably contributed to the success of the dishonest employee, Hamaoui. Plaintiff has not done this and its breach of implied warranty for good title cause of action is defective.

The demurrer to plaintiff's breach of warranty count was properly sustained.

Plaintiff contends that the padded payroll preclusion of section 3405, subdivision (1)(c) [R 3–404(b)] is an affirmative defense and does not have to be prematurely pleaded in its complaint. Under most circumstances this is true. The plaintiff, of course, is not required to plead negative facts to anticipate a defense. There are exceptions to this rule. (See 3 Witkin, *Cal. Procedure* (2d ed. 1971) Pleadings, §§ 313, 314, pp. 1983–1984.) Such an exception exists when our Supreme Court says that it exists. In *Sun 'N Sand,* the Supreme Court, in fixing pleading guidelines for a breach of an implied warranty of good title cause of action by a drawer against a collecting bank based on a forged indorsement by an employee of the drawer, held that the drawer-plaintiff must plead that the checks contained indorsements that were not valid or effective. (*Sun 'N Sand, Inc. v. United California Bank, supra,* 21 Cal.3d 671, 687, 148 Cal.Rptr. 329, 582 P.2d 920.) These pleading requirements, necessary to allege facts sufficient to state a cause of action, are couched in conclusionary terms. The plaintiff must, however, plead ultimate facts (Code Civ.Proc., § 425.10, subd. (a); 3 Witkin, *Cal. Procedure* (2d ed. 1971) Pleadings, §§ 268–285, pp. 1939–1960) and, in its second count, plaintiff must plead ultimate facts in its breach of warranty cause of action to negate the padded employee preclusion of section 3405, subdivision (1)(c) [R 3–404(b)] once plaintiff alleges facts of forged indorsements by one of its employees of plaintiff's checks naming individual payee or an excuse based on defendant's culpability.

If plaintiff cannot plead such facts under the circumstances of this case, plaintiff cannot plead a cause of action for breach of implied warranties of good title. At the present stage of proceeding, applying the applicable substantive law, it is not clear whether plaintiff can cure the breach of warranty pleading defects. (See *Minsky v. Los Angeles* (1974) 11 Cal.3d 113, 118, 113 Cal.Rptr. 102, 520 P.2d 726.) This is not a case where plaintiff has been given repeated chances to state a cause of action for a breach of warranty and the amended pleading remains demurrable. This is a situation where an honest dispute existed as to whether our Supreme Court, in *Sun 'N Sand,* had made the effectiveness and validity of the indorsements under section 3405 [R 3–404] an element of plaintiff's cause of action for breach of warranty of good title. The proper interpretation of the *Sun 'N Sand* decision is that plaintiff Hutton can either plead facts showing that the padded payroll section is not present in its breach of warranty cause of action or that the preclusions of section 3405, subdivision (1)(c) [R 3–404(b)] are not applicable because of the misconduct or culpability of defendant City Bank.

We do not know any of the factual details of the case at bar. If the checks were properly made out to customers of plaintiff Hutton upon proper authorization of an employee, but that employee or some other employee thereafter improperly took the checks and forged the names of the customer-payees, then the padded payroll preclusion is not applicable as the element lacking is the embezzling employee supplying the names of the payees with the intent that they have no interest in the checks. (Anderson, *Uniform Commercial Code* (Cum.Supp.1970–1974) Commercial Paper, § 3–405:5.2, p. 866.) It is entirely possible that plaintiff Hutton can allege such facts.

The padded payroll section is not an absolute defense. A collecting bank or any other person seeking to use this section must comply with the standards of conduct imposed by the Uniform Commercial Code. These standards are violated if the bank did not act in good faith in handling the transaction (see § 1203), had knowledge of the employee's breach of fiduciary duty (§ 3304, subd. (2) [see R 3–307]; *Sun 'N Sand Inc. v. United California Bank, supra,* 21 Cal.3d 671, 148 Cal.Rptr. 329, 582 P.2d 920, [this notice section " * * * seems to contemplate that notice derives * * * from affirmative indications that an improper party is attempting to procure payment." (*Id.* at p. 690, 148 Cal.Rptr. 329, 582 P.2d 920.)]) or acted with objective notice of an impropriety in the transaction. (§ 3304; *Sun 'N Sand,* 21 Cal.3d at p. 689–690, 148 Cal.Rptr. 329, 582 P.2d 920.) In addition to these defenses to the padded payroll section, the plaintiff can plead negligence of the collecting bank in handling the transactions under the general legal principles of the duty imposed upon the bank to act with reasonable care and the trier of fact can consider the balancing of equities in the loss distribution scheme. (*Sun 'N Sand, Inc. v. United California Bank, supra,* 21 Cal.3d 671, 696, 148 Cal.Rptr. 329, 582 P.2d 920.)

Finally, we note that plaintiff has alleged in general conclusionary terms that the defendant City Bank was guilty of bad faith and it disregarded reasonable commercial bank practices in the breach of warranty cause of action. We do not know if plaintiff Hutton, in alleging "bad faith" on the part of City Bank, is claiming that defendant bank failed to act "in good faith" as defined by section 1203, which is defined by section 1201, subdivision (19) to mean " * * * honesty in fact in the conduct or transaction concerned" or if plaintiff is claiming defendant acted in "bad faith" under the broader common law principle of contract law that here is an implied covenant of good faith and fair dealing in every transaction that neither party will do anything which will injure the right of the other. (1 Witkin, *Summary of Cal. Law* (8th ed.) Contracts, § 576, p. 493.)

The principles of "good faith" in the Uniform Commercial Code and in the common law are basic principles running throughout all commercial transactions including those governed by the Uniform Commercial Code.

Courts of other jurisdictions have acknowledged that the good faith requirement extends to those who assert the padded payroll preclusion.

Pleading and proving that lack of good faith under section 1203 will be difficult because plaintiff must show that the defendant City Bank failed to act "honestly" in the transactions. Courts have often expanded this requirement that the defendant bank merely have a subjective awareness of wrongdoing to lack "good faith." A recent New Jersey court, *Kraftsman Container v. United Counties Trust* (1979) 169 N.J.Super. 488, 404 A.2d 1288, in holding that a bank paying checks in bad faith, cannot claim protection of section 3405 [R 3–404], said, "Effective indorsements do not relieve the bank from liability if there is proof of a course of dealing so irregular in nature that the bank is shown to have violated its own policies and to have failed to act according to the standard of honesty-in-fact." This concept of "good faith" seems to be consistent with the fact claims of plaintiff Hutton.

Pleading and proving a breach of City Bank's implied covenant of good faith and fair dealing would seem to be less burdensome to plaintiff because this "bad faith" concept is so much broader than the Uniform Commercial Code "good faith" provision.

Plaintiff Hutton should be given an opportunity to plead its breach of warranty cause of action consistent with the guideline set forth in this opinion.

The demurrer to the common count cause of action was sustained without leave to amend because the demurrers to the negligence and breach of warranty causes of action were sustained. As the negligence cause of action was sufficient and plaintiff will be given an opportunity to amend its breach of warranty cause of action, the trial court erred in sustaining the general demurrer to the common count cause of action. (See *Neal v. Bank of America* (1949) 93 Cal.App.2d 678, 681, 209 P.2d 825.)

In summary, construing the allegations of the negligence cause of action liberally in favor of the pleader (*Joffe v. United California Bank, supra,* 141 Cal.App.3d 541, 550, 190 Cal.Rptr. 443), plaintiff Hutton has alleged facts sufficient to state a cause of action for negligence and in its common count. The trial court erred in its rulings sustaining the general demurrers as to these causes of action. As to the plaintiff's breach of warranty cause of action, the trial court abused its discretion in sustaining the demurrer without leave to amend because there exists a reasonable possibility that the pleading defects can be cured by amendment. (*LaSala v. American Sav. & Loan Assn.* (1971) 5 Cal.3d 864, 876, 97 Cal.Rptr. 849, 489 P.2d 1113.)

The judgment is reversed. The matter is remanded to the trial court to proceed in a manner consistent with this opinion.

SPENCER, P.J., concurs.

L. THAXTON HANSON, ASSOCIATE JUSTICE, dissenting.

I respectfully dissent.

* * *

THE NEGLIGENCE THEORY

Plaintiff alleged in its first cause of action that CNB, as the collecting bank, owed it a duty to use due care in collecting the checks and depositing them in Hamaoui's account, a duty CNB breached by processing the checks "without making any reasonable attempt to verify the endorsements thereon or defendant Hamaoui's authority to cash or deposit each and every check referenced above." Plaintiff further alleged that CNB breached its duty of due care because "it failed to take reasonable steps available to it to ascertain the genuineness of the endorsements on the said checks * * *" and "failed to follow reasonable commercial banking standards."

The requirements for stating a cause of action for negligence in California are well established, and need only be referred to briefly here. "Actionable negligence involves a legal duty to use due care, a breach of such legal duty, and the breach as the proximate or legal cause of the resulting injury." (*United States Liab. Ins. Co. v. Haidinger–Hayes, Inc.* (1970) 1 Cal.3d 586, 594, 83 Cal.Rptr. 418, 463 P.2d 770.) While Civil Code section 1714, subdivision (a) declares that "Every one is responsible, not only for the result of his willful acts, but also for an injury occasioned to another by his want of ordinary care or skill in the management of his property or person, * * *" the question of determining the existence of a duty giving rise to liability is one of law and fact, involving social policy decisions as well as assessment of the foreseeability of harm. (*Weirum v. RKO General, Inc.* (1975) 15 Cal.3d 40, 49, 123 Cal.Rptr. 468, 539 P.2d 36.)

A recent California Supreme Court case declined to define the precise scope of the duty owed by a collecting bank to a drawer relative to forged endorsements. (*Sun 'n Sand, Inc. v. United California Bank* (1978) 21 Cal.3d 671, 693, 148 Cal.Rptr. 329, 582 P.2d 920.) The analysis utilized in *Sun 'n Sand, supra,* however, is of assistance here. In *Sun 'n Sand,* a suit by a drawer against the collecting bank, UCB, the facts were that plaintiff, too, had a faithless employee, who presented small checks payable to UCB to the drawer for signature; UCB collected these checks (substantially altered upward) and in some manner was persuaded to deposit the funds so collected in the UCB account of the drawer's embezzling employee. While the decision declined to adopt a general holding on the scope of duty owed by a collecting bank to a drawer in California, it did determine that "a bank presented with checks payable to itself by one who proposes to deposit such checks in his personal account ' "is put upon inquiry and if it fail to make it, pays at its peril." ' " (21 Cal.3d 694, 148 Cal.Rptr. 329, 582 P.2d 920; emphasis added.) In other words, the harm was, under these circumstances, foreseeable.

Sun 'n Sand did not hold that a collecting bank proceeding on forged endorsements always breaches a duty of care owed to the drawer. The negligence perceived in the *Sun 'n Sand* opinion was the defendant bank's collection of paper payable to itself and the deposit of the proceeds of such a collection to the account of the drawer's employee's account without further inquiry.

The rationale of *Sun 'n Sand* is extended a step further in *Joffe v. United California Bank* (1983) 141 Cal.App.3d 541, 190 Cal.Rptr. 443, wherein the check was payable to the escrow department of the bank. The implication of these holdings is that such commercial paper is not regular on its face, that its designation of the collecting bank (or a part thereof) as payee puts the bank on notice that a crime may be involved.

In the case at bench, the pleader, Hutton, characterizes the checks as irregular not because there was anything unusual about them per se, but because they turned out to carry forged endorsements. The payees were not the collecting bank or any bank. The payees were individuals who appeared to have endorsed the checks. I am unaware of any California statutory or decisional law which declares, as a general principle, the rule that a drawer has a cause of action for negligence against a collecting bank which accepts as valid endorsements which turn out to be forged. Nor has New York, except where some circumstance independent of the forgery should have alerted the collecting bank to the type of "suspicious circumstances" warranting further inquiry.

In my view the fact that Hamaoui was known to defendant CNB as an employee of plaintiff in maintaining his personal checking account with CNB is not a sufficiently "suspicious circumstance" of a nature which would trigger a duty on the part of CNB to investigate further the validity of the endorsements or Hamaoui's authority to possess such checks. Nor should the possibility that one particular teller received the checks from Hamaoui, on behalf of the defendant, for collection purposes, affect the result either; there were no direct allegations of complicity in Hamaoui's scheme on the part of any CNB employee, except an allegation, made on information and belief, that said unidentified employee "knew or should have known that the nature of each of the said checks was irregular and that further inquiry by defendant Bank was required."

What we have here is a situation where there was nothing on the face of the checks or on the endorsements thereon which would have alerted the collecting bank, CNB, to any unusual or suspicious circumstances. There was no foreseeable harm. In my view such paper must be assessed as it itself appears to the collecting bank. The reason for this is that, as amicus curiae, the California Banking Association suggest, to hold otherwise would create an intolerable burden on collecting banks as a practical matter; banks process great amounts of endorsed commercial paper in a very short period of time, paper which appears valid on its face. It has long been the rule that they need not inquire further in the absence of "suspicious circumstances" which were not extant here—or were certainly not so pleaded. I would not extend *Sun 'n Sand* beyond the limited holding of the California Supreme Court in that case. That is what the majority opinion, as I read it, is attempting to do.

* * *

Note

Most courts hold under original Article 3 that the preclusions of 3–405 apply even though the transferee or drawee has been negligent. See e.g. *Western Casualty & Surety Co. v. Citizens Bank,* 676 F.2d 1344 (10th Cir.1982); *Merrill Lynch, Pierce, Fenner & Smith v. Chemical Bank,* 57 N.Y.2d 439, 456 N.Y.S.2d 742, 442 N.E.2d 1253 (1982). However, under revised Article 3 (R 3–404(d)), if the transferee or payee "fails to exercise ordinary care in taking the instrument and that failure substantially contributes to loss resulting from the payment of the instrument, the person bearing the loss may recover from the person failing to exercise ordinary care to the extent the failure to exercise ordinary care contributed to the loss." Also, R 3–404 continues the rule of OR 3–405 that, in order to have the benefit of the section, a transferee or payee must take or pay in good faith.

The new definition of good faith and the due care provision of R 3–404(d) present interesting possibilities. Suppose that in the Hutton case it appears that Hamaoui always dealt with the same teller, that he often brought her a small box of chocolate when he made large deposits, and that she did not report the gifts to superiors. Would that suggest a failure to observe "reasonable commercial standards of fair dealing." Might reasonable commercial standards of fair dealing require banks to instruct tellers not to accept gifts from depositors or to report such gifts to their supervisors? If not, might a bank fail to exercise ordinary care if it did not so instruct tellers? Might the teller, in any event, have failed to exercise ordinary care by not reporting to her superiors the gifts of candy? Might she have been negligent in not calling attention of superiors to the nature and size of the checks being deposited? If the bank is found to be negligent, how does the finder of fact determine "the extent [to which] the failure to exercise ordinary care contributed to the loss"? Should a comparative fault test be used? Since the employer's liability in the case is essentially "no-fault" liability, it is difficult to use comparative fault principles. However, in the products liability area, many courts do in fact apply comparative fault principles as between a defendant who is liable without negligence under warranty or strict tort and a negligent plaintiff. (See e.g. *Sandford v. Chevrolet Div. of General Motors,* 292 Or. 590, 642 P.2d 624 (1982); *Fiske v. MacGregor, Div. of Brunswick,* 464 A.2d 719 (R.I.1983).)

However, the language of R 3–404(d) seems to suggest that the issue is causation in fact rather than comparative fault. How would causation in fact be determined? See comment 4 to R 3–405 and particularly the last sentence thereof. In spite of the causation in fact tilt of the language, fact finders may in effect treat the issue as one of comparative fault.

TRUST COMPANY BANK OF AUGUSTA N.A. v. HENDERSON

Court of Appeals of Georgia, 1987.
185 Ga.App. 367, 364 S.E.2d 289.

SOGNIER, JUDGE.

James S. Henderson instituted action against Trust Company Bank of Augusta N.A. to recover funds allegedly misappropriated from Henderson's business by an employee and converted by the bank when it allowed the employee to endorse in blank checks made payable to the business, and cash them or deposit them to a personal checking account. The case was tried by a jury and at the close of the evidence, the trial court directed a verdict in favor of Henderson as to the checks cashed by the bank, in the amount of $5,239, and denied the bank's motion for a directed verdict as to Henderson's claim for attorney fees and liability for the proceeds of the checks deposited in the employee's personal checking account. These issues were submitted to the jury, which returned a verdict for Henderson for $66,161, representing the amount of the deposited checks, plus interest, and for attorney fees, which the parties stipulated were $12,500. The trial court entered judgment accordingly, and the bank appeals.

The record reveals that appellee owned and operated a Ramada Inn in Augusta, Georgia. In the fall of 1984, appellee hired Thomas Muia for the position of general manager of the inn. It was part of Muia's responsibility as general manager to handle personnel, purchasing, and daily supervision of operations, including depositing operating revenues of the business into one of Ramada Inn's two bank accounts: the regular account, or the special account used to pay such items as musician fees, liquor bills, and other hotel expenses which were not charged. He was specifically authorized by appellee to endorse all checks either with a rubber stamp provided for that purpose, or by running them through the hotel's cash register, both of which provided a restrictive endorsement for deposit to the Ramada Inn's accounts. Muia had authority to write checks on the special account, but not on the regular account. In connection with his banking duties, Muia was introduced by appellee to the personnel at appellant's branch handling the Ramada Inn accounts and soon thereafter opened a personal checking account.

In February of 1985, Muia deposited to his personal account three checks made payable to Ramada Inn which he had endorsed by hand, in blank, both on behalf of the Ramada Inn and himself, and also containing his personal account number. Thereafter, from June through November, 1985, Muia made deposits to his personal account consisting of charge reimbursement checks from American Express Travel Related Services Company, Inc., all made payable to Ramada Inn and all endorsed in blank on behalf of Ramada Inn by Muia. Some also bore Muia's endorsement or account number. On one occasion, a teller questioned her supervisor regarding a Ramada Inn check Muia sought to deposit into his personal account, and was told it was proper. Other transactions typically were not questioned. One transaction was a "split deposit," in which some cash was disbursed and the remainder deposited; one American Express check was cashed by Muia with the approval of appellant's branch manager, rather than deposited to his personal account. The total amount of the checks either cashed or deposited was over $71,000.

1. Appellant contends the trial court erred by denying its motion for directed verdict with regard to its liability for the proceeds of the checks deposited to Muia's personal account because OCGA § 7–1–352(a) protects the bank from liability to appellant. OCGA § 7–1–352(a) provides that "[w]henever any agent, administrator, executor, guardian, trustee, either express or implied, or other fiduciary, whether bona fide or mala fide, shall deposit any money in any bank to his credit as an individual, or as such agent, trustee, or other fiduciary, whether the name of the person or corporation for whom he is acting or purporting to act be given or not, such bank shall be authorized to pay the amount of such deposit, or any part thereof, upon the order of such agent, administrator, executor, guardian, trustee, or other fiduciary, signed with the name in which such deposit was entered, without being accountable in any way to the principal, cestui que trust, or other person or corporation who may be entitled to or interested in the amount so deposited." We do not agree that OCGA § 7–1–352(a) is the statute which governs this case. As this court pointed out in *Bank South v. Grand Lodge, etc.,* 174 Ga.App. 777, 780, 331 S.E.2d 629 (1985), the legislative history of OCGA § 7–1–352(a), resting in common law adhered to by this State for almost a century, indicates that the statute means simply that " '[w]hen a trustee [or agent or other fiduciary] deposits money in a bank, the bank has a right to assume that the money so deposited will be applied by the trustee [or agent or other fiduciary] to the proper purposes under the trust, and acting under this assumption it may lawfully pay the checks drawn by the person depositing the money, whether signed in his representative capacity or not.' " Had Muia deposited the checks in question in the case sub judice into the Ramada Inn special account (on which he had been authorized to write checks), and then proceeded unlawfully to enrich himself by writing checks on that account made payable to himself, we could agree with appellant that the bank would be protected by OCGA § 7–1–352(a). However, such is not the case. The record indicates that appellee's claim against the bank is based on the bank's acceptance for deposit into Muia's personal checking account of checks made payable to Ramada Inn.

Contrary to appellant's argument, *National Factor, etc., Corp. v. State Bank of Cochran,* 224 Ga. 535, 163 S.E.2d 817 (1968), is inapposite.

Rather than supporting the claim made by the appellant, that case supports the distinction we draw here. In *National Factor,* the plaintiff sought to recover from the bank which paid checks drawn by one who had diverted the plaintiff's funds to the embezzler's account. Thus Code Ann. § 13–2042, the predecessor of OCGA § 7–1–352, was appropriately relied on there. The facts in *National Factor,* supra, are further distinguishable from those here as the embezzler there was the proprietor and operator of a closely held family business, and there was far less reason for the bank to be aware that anything untoward was taking place.

In the case at bar, Muia's endorsements on the checks deposited into his personal account were "forged" because, with intent to defraud, he knowingly signed and presented the checks so as to give the appearance of authority from appellee, which he did not have. See OCGA § 16–9–2(a).

By accepting the checks for deposit into Muia's personal account, the bank converted appellee's funds. OCGA § 11–3–419(1)(c) [R 3–420(a)]. OCGA § 11–3–419(3) [R 3–420(c)] would provide an exception to the bank's liability for conversion had the bank acted "in good faith and in accordance with the reasonable commercial standards" applicable to the banking business. However, good faith and commercial reasonableness are separate requirements, both of which must be met to support the defense. While appellant may have acted in good faith, it was for the jury to decide whether its acceptance of the checks for deposit into Muia's personal checking account was consistent with reasonable commercial standards. " 'In *E.L. Von Gohren v. Pacific National Bank of Washington,* * * * the court held as a matter of law that a bank which accepted checks made payable to a corporation for deposit into the *personal account* of the bookkeeper could not have acted in a commercially reasonable manner.' " *National Bank of Ga. v. Refrigerated Transport Co.,* 147 Ga.App. 240, 244, 248 S.E.2d 496 (1978). "In a case involving similar circumstances * * * this court held that ' "[t]he indorsements were irregular enough on their face to raise some question as to their validity; and certainly when the checks were offered for deposit into the * * * account of one not the payee, [the bank] had a duty to inquire to ascertain the authority of [the depositor] to indorse and deposit [the payee's] checks. [The bank] could not escape its duty of inquiry by relying on the word of its customer, [the depositor], [Cits.]." ' " *Thornton & Co. v. Gwinnett Bank, etc., Co.,* 151 Ga.App. 641, 647, 260 S.E.2d 765 (1979).

In the case at bar, the endorsements were unusual for checks made out to the Ramada Inn, in that the customary rubber stamp, containing a restrictive endorsement, was not present, nor had the checks been run through the Ramada Inn's cash register, which also provided a restrictive endorsement. This was an "irregularity" such as the jury could have concluded should have put the bank on notice and activated the bank's duty to make inquiry, particularly because here, as in *Thornton,* supra, the checks were being deposited into the depositor's personal account. In fact, this irregularity *was* brought to the bank's attention when one of its tellers questioned the propriety of depositing a check made out to the Ramada Inn, and endorsed in blank by Muia, to Muia's personal account. We do not hold that the bank could not, as a matter of law, have asserted the § 11–3–419(3) [R 3–420(c)] defense, but that the matter was properly submitted to the jury. "On appeal, the evidence must be construed to uphold the jury's verdict, and the sole question for determination is whether there is any evidence to authorize the verdict. [Cits.]" *Gold Kist Peanuts v. Alberson,* 178 Ga.App. 253, 254(1), 342 S.E.2d 694 (1986). As the evidence would have authorized the jury to find that the bank did not act in a commercially reasonable manner, the bank is liable to appellee for conversion, and we affirm the jury's verdict.

2. Appellant enumerates two errors which concern the trial court's instructions to the jury.

(a) Appellant argues the trial court erred by failing to charge the jury that "[i]f you should find that Mr. Muia was authorized by actual or apparent authority to endorse checks payable to Ramada Inn, the payment of these checks would not constitute payment over a forged endorsement." However, as stated in Division 1 above, Muia's testimony admitting he endorsed the American Express Travel checks so as to have them deposited in his personal account established that Muia's endorsement of these checks was a forgery and thus, by accepting them and crediting the proceeds to Muia's personal account, appellant committed conversion under OCGA § 11–3–419(1)(c) [R 3–420(a)]. Therefore, the charge requested by appellant was not applicable to the jury's inquiry (that is, whether or not appellant was liable in conversion because it acted in good faith and in accordance with reasonable commercial standards under OCGA § 11–3–419(3) [R 3–420(c)]), and the failure to so charge the jury was not error. See generally *Atkinson v. Allstate Ins. Co.,* 182 Ga.App. 50(2), 354 S.E.2d 866 (1987).

(b) Appellant also argues the trial court, by giving appellee's request to charge number 10, erroneously required the jury to find that Muia had authority both to endorse the checks and to deposit them into his personal account before they could find Muia was acting under apparent authority. Aside from the fact that Muia's actions in endorsing the checks constituted a forgery and thus his authority to endorse the checks was not in issue, appellant has misread the charge as given. The charge required the jury to find Muia had the authority both to endorse and to deposit the checks in order to find that "Muia had apparent authority *to act as he did.*" (Emphasis supplied.) The charge thus addressed evidentiary questions rather than questions of law under OCGA § 11–1–201(43). Being predicated on some evidence adduced at trial, it follows that the trial court did not err by so charging.
* * *

4. In appellant's final enumeration of error, it asserts the trial court erred by denying its motion for a directed verdict as to the issue

of attorney fees. OCGA § 13–6–11 provides that "[t]he expenses of litigation generally shall not be allowed as a part of the damages; but where the plaintiff has specially pleaded and has made prayer therefor and where the defendant has acted in bad faith in making the contract, has been stubbornly litigious, or has caused the plaintiff unnecessary trouble and expense, the jury may allow them." This section may be applied to suits in both contract and tort. *Jones v. Spindel,* 122 Ga.App. 390, 391(3), 177 S.E.2d 187 (1970).

We agree with appellant that there is no issue of "bad faith" here. (See Division 1.) While issues of stubborn litigiousness are normally for the jury, if there is a *bona fide* controversy, there can be no stubborn litigiousness as a matter of law. *Woodson v. Burton,* 241 Ga. 130, 131–132(4), 243 S.E.2d 885 (1978). While the record does reflect that with respect to the amounts *cashed,* rather than deposited into Muia's account, appellant first admitted liability but then insisted on litigating this issue, the total amount of funds in this category was a minimal portion of the total liability—less than $5,300 out of a total amount of over $71,000 plus interest. Even assuming, *arguendo,* that appellant was unnecessarily litigious with respect to that one issue, we do not find it sufficient to support the award of attorney fees. We therefore affirm with direction that the $12,500 awarded as attorney fees be written off.

Judgment affirmed with direction.

DEEN and BANKE, P.JJ., and POPE and BEASLEY, JJ., concur.

MCMURRAY, P.J., and CARLEY and BENHAM, JJ., dissent.

BIRDSONG, C.J., disqualified.

MCMURRAY, PRESIDING JUDGE, dissenting.

As I construe the facts of the case sub judice, Mr. Muia's responsibilities, as general manager of plaintiff's Ramada Inn facility, included the acquisition and termination of personnel, purchasing food, beverages and other supplies and supervising the daily operations of the business. Mr. Muia was also responsible for depositing operating revenues of the business into Ramada Inn's accounts at the Trust Company Bank of Augusta, N.A. (the bank). In this capacity, Mr. Muia was authorized by plaintiff to endorse all checks and he was instructed by plaintiff to endorse the checks with a "rubber stamp" or "by running the checks through the [hotel's] cash register." (Both the "rubber stamp" and the cash register contained a restrictive endorsement.) While Mr. Muia was not authorized to execute checks on Ramada Inn's regular checking account, he did have express authority to execute checks on a special checking account used by Ramada Inn to pay musicians, purchase liquor and acquire other supplies and services that could not be charged by the hotel.

Upon Mr. Muia's employment, the plaintiff brought him to the bank and introduced him to the bank's branch manager as " 'the new general manager of the Ramada Inn here in Augusta.' " Soon thereafter, Mr. Muia opened a personal checking account at the bank.

In conducting Ramada Inn's financial transactions, Mr. Muia visited the bank "[j]ust about every day." He became familiar with the bank's employees and often invited the bank's tellers to "come to the Ramada Inn for happy hour * * *."

On February 15, 1985, Mr. Muia presented for deposit into his personal account three checks made payable to Ramada Inn and drawn on the accounts of Champion International Corporation, Cain & Bultman, Inc., and Southern Wood Piedmont Company. The bank deposited the checks into Mr. Muia's personal account. These checks were endorsed in blank on behalf of Ramada Inn and also contained the endorsement of Thomas Muia and his personal account number.

From June 20, 1985, through November 1985 Mr. Muia deposited into his personal account several checks made payable to Ramada Inn and drawn on the account of American Express Travel Related Services Company, Inc. (American Express Travel). One of these transactions was a "split deposit" where Mr. Muia received $1,750 in cash and the balance of the deposit was deposited into his personal account. With regard to the remaining American Express Travel deposits, the proceeds from the checks were deposited directly into Mr. Muia's personal account. The bank cashed a check for Mr. Muia drawn by American Express Travel to Ramada Inn, dated September 6, 1985, in the amount of $3,485.52. This transaction was approved by the bank's branch manager, Ms. Laurel Bradshaw. (The total amount of Ramada Inn checks cashed by Mr. Muia or deposited into his personal account is $71,397.29.)

All of the American Express Travel checks were endorsed on behalf of Ramada Inn and some of the checks bore the additional endorsement of Mr. Muia or contained Mr. Muia's personal account number. The American Express Travel check that was dated September 6, 1985, and was cashed for Mr. Muia by the bank contained the following endorsement: "Ramada Inn Thomas Muia G.M."

Ms. Kay Ross, a teller employed by the bank, inquired of her "supervisor" regarding a Ramada Inn check deposited by Mr. Muia into his personal checking account. She was informed "[t]hat it was fine because of the fact that Thomas Muia did business for the Ramada Inn, and this was for the Ramada Inn." Ms. Ross accepted the deposit and several similar deposits thereafter. Other tellers who accepted deposits from Mr. Muia did not inquire of his authority to make such deposits as they relied on his position as general manager to perfect banking transactions on behalf of Ramada Inn.

The bank contends the trial court erred in failing to grant its motion for directed verdict with regard to the proceeds of the checks deposited directly to Mr. Muia's personal account. In support of this contention the bank relies on OCGA § 7–1–352(a), which provides as follows: "Whenever any agent, administrator, executor, guardian, trustee, either express or implied, or other fiduciary, whether bona fide or mala fide, *shall deposit any money in any bank to his credit as an individual,* or as such agent, trustee, or other fiduciary, whether the name of the person or corporation for whom he is acting or purporting to act be given or not, *such bank shall be authorized to pay the amount of such deposit, or any part thereof,* upon the order of such agent, administrator, executor, guardian, trustee, or other fiduciary, signed with the name in which such deposit was entered, *without being accountable in any way to the principal,* cestui que trust, or other person or corporation who may be entitled to or interested in the amount so deposited." (Emphasis supplied.)

In *Trust Co. of Ga. v. Nationwide Moving, etc., Co.,* 235 Ga. 229, 219 S.E.2d 162, "the Supreme Court stated: 'It is clear that the statute is designed to protect a bank from liability where an agent or fiduciary misappropriates funds of the owner in breach of his agency or trust without the bank's knowledge. The bank is not required to scrutinize every check written by a fiduciary or agent to see if the check is written in compliance with the agent's authority.' p. 230 [219 S.E.2d 162]." *Flo–Control v. Northeast Bank,* 150 Ga.App. 880, 882, 258 S.E.2d 695. It appears this rule applies equally where an agent or fiduciary endorses a check and deposits the proceeds thereof to an account other than that of his principal. See *National Factor, etc., Corp. v. State Bank of Cochran,* 224 Ga. 535, 536(1), 163 S.E.2d 817. However, application of this rule is not unbridled.

"In *National NuGrape Co. v. Citizens & Southern Nat. Bk.,* 94 Ga.App. 5, 14 (93 S.E.2d 381), (certiorari denied), the Court of Appeals, after quoting Code § 13–2042 [formerly Ga.Code Ann. § 41A–1605 and now OCGA § 7–1–352], stated: 'To charge a bank with notice that a depositor is acting in violation of his trust so as to render it liable for the amount paid out on his check or order *to one other than the bank itself,* the circumstances must be such as to raise a presumption of knowledge that the depositor is acting dishonestly, or adequate notice to the bank may come from circumstances which reasonably support the *sole inference* that a breach of trust is intended. Michie, Banks & Banking, Vol. 5A, p. 161; Am.Jur. 376, § 522; *Bischoff v. Yorkville Bank,* 218 N.Y. 106 (112 N.E. 759, LRA 1916F, 1059). Judge Sibley speaking for the court in *Atlanta & St. A.B.R. Co. v. Barnes,* 95 F2d 273, stated as to such cases: "The penalty thus visited ought to be supported by the mala fides of a fraudulent intent, or by a negligence so great as to show wilful ignorance. Simple neglect to inquire about circumstances which ought to have excited attention is not enough, just as it is not enough to prove a want of good faith in purchasing negotiable paper * * *. Commercial transactions are not put within the strict fetters of constructive notice." ' " *National Factor, etc., Corp. v. State Bank of Cochran,* 224 Ga. 535, 539, 163 S.E.2d 817, supra.

Under circumstances similar to those of the case sub judice, the Supreme Court in *National Factor* accepted the above quoted rule and held, "that the circumstances must be such as to raise a presumption of knowledge that the party is acting dishonestly, or adequate notice to the bank may come from circumstances which reasonably support the sole inference that a breach of trust is intended." *National Factor, etc., Corp. v. State Bank of Cochran,* 224 Ga. 535, 539, 163 S.E.2d 817, supra. From this rule, it follows that plaintiff in the case sub judice carries a heavy burden of showing that the bank was aware of Mr. Muia's alleged misappropriation of funds. In this regard, Mr. Muia deposited 19 checks made payable to Ramada Inn directly into his personal account. In a "split deposit" transaction, Muia received a substantial amount of cash from the proceeds of a Ramada Inn check, which was made a part of that transaction; and, the bank cashed for Mr. Muia a check made payable to Ramada Inn for over $3,400. These facts raise the question of the scope of Mr. Muia's actual, apparent and implied authority as general manager to handle Ramada Inn's financial transactions.

"We do not hold that a general manager can never have the authority or inherent agency power to arrange for the handling of corporate [or business] funds. See, e.g., *Fidelity & Deposit Co. v. Merchants Nat. Bank,* 223 Ia. 446 (273 N.W. 141) (1937). * * * The scope of a general manager's power depends on his duties and responsibilities and his actual authority. See *Raleigh & G.R. Co. v. Pullman Co.,* 122 Ga. 700 (50 S.E. 1008) (1905), and *Knowles v. Rome Tribune Co.,* 127 Ga. 90 (56 S.E. 109)." *Trust Co. of Ga. v. Nationwide Moving, etc., Co.,* 235 Ga. 229, 232, 233, 219 S.E.2d 162, supra.

In the case sub judice, in my view plaintiff's statement to the bank's branch manager that Mr. Muia was the "new general manager of the Ramada Inn * * *," combined with plaintiff's authorization allowing Mr. Muia to endorse checks and deposit funds into Ramada Inn's regular checking account and withdraw funds from Ramada Inn's special checking account, was sufficient to support the bank's conclusion that Mr. Muia had wide authority to conduct Ramada Inn's financial transactions. This conclusion is further supported by evidence indicating that Mr. Muia had authority to bind plaintiff for services rendered and products supplied to Ramada Inn by vendors and service personnel. This view is in line with the weight of authority in other jurisdictions "to the effect that a bank is not charged with notice of misappropriation by an agent or fiduciary, because of the mere fact that the latter deposited to his individual account a check or note payable to or indorsed by him in his fiduciary capacity." 57 A.L.R. 925, 930, § III. See also supplementing annotations in 64 A.L.R. 1404, § III; 106 A.L.R. 836, § III; and 115 A.L.R. 648, § III.

Consequently, in the case sub judice, with the bank's specific denial that it had knowledge of the misappropriation by Muia of funds belonging to plaintiff, this court should conclude that the facts and circumstances relied upon by plaintiff to show knowledge by the bank of conversion of funds by Mr. Muia do not make an issue of fact for the jury. The trial court erred in allowing this matter to go to the jury and in failing to grant the bank's motion for directed verdict as to its liability for the checks deposited into Mr. Muia's personal account.

I, therefore, respectfully dissent. I am authorized to state that Judge Carley and Judge Benham join in this dissent.

Note

1. The specific point on which the dissent and the majority disagree is whether the blank hand written indorsements by Muia were forgeries. If Muia had apparent authority to indorse checks in blank, the indorsement is effective. See OR and R 1–201(43) and see OR 3–403 and comment 1 thereto and R 3–402. On that point, which of the positions is more convincing to you? There are at least two other cases holding that an agent with power to restrictively indorse checks payable to his principal did not have real or apparent authority to indorse the checks in blank and deposit them into his personal account. *Mott Grain Co. v. First Nat'l Bank & Trust,* 259 N.W.2d 667 (N.D.1977); *Pargas, Inc. v. Estate of Taylor,* 416 So.2d 1358 (La.App.1982).

2. Under the Georgia statute cited in the case, if Muia had apparent authority to indorse the checks, the bank, so long as it acted in good faith, would not be liable to Henderson for allowing Muia to deposit the checks into his account and then use the money for his own purposes. The Uniform Fiduciaries Act, adopted in some 23 states, also, in its Section 9, protects a bank which in good faith allows a fiduciary to deposit checks payable to his principal or to him as fiduciary into the fiduciary's personal account. Original Article 3 addresses the issue of the liability of parties dealing with fiduciaries only briefly. Original 3–304(2) states "The purchaser has notice of a claim against the instrument when he has knowledge that a fiduciary has negotiated the instrument in payment of or as security for his own debt or in any transaction for his own benefit or otherwise in breach of duty." Comment 5 to OR 3–304 states in part: "The purchaser may pay cash into the hands of the fiduciary without notice of any breach of the obligation [of the fiduciary]." Neither the statutory language nor the comment specifically covers deposit by the fiduciary into his personal account, though allowing deposit to his account might be viewed as analogous to payment of cash to the fiduciary.

Revised 3–307 contains an elaborate provision on the liability to the principal of persons who deal with a fiduciary who is committing a breach of trust. Subsection (b)(2) of that section reverses the rule of Uniform Fiduciaries Act, Section 9 (and the Georgia statute referred to in the Trust Company Bank case). Section 3–307 imposes on the depositary bank that knows it is dealing with a fiduciary the risk that the fiduciary which deposits instruments payable to the principal or to the fiduciary as such into the fiduciary's personal account will then embezzle the funds.

Therefore, under revised Article 3, the bank in the case would lose whether or not Muia's indorsement was a forgery. If the indorsement is a forgery, the bank loses under conversion principles (R 3–420). If the indorsement is not a forgery, then 3–307(b)(2) would apply. Under that section, bank would have notice of the breach of fiduciary duty, and would again be liable to Henderson on conversion theory since it dealt with the instrument on behalf of one not the true owner with notice of the claim of the true owner.

BENFIELD & ALCES, BANK LIABILITY FOR FIDUCIARY FRAUD

42 Ala.L.Rev. 475, pages 519–525.

a. Credit of Check to Fiduciary's Personal Account.—Revised section 3–307 makes one major change from the rules under the U.F.A. Under the U.F.A., a bank can permit a fiduciary to deposit fiduciary funds to the personal account of the fiduciary and then allow the fiduciary to withdraw the funds without incurring liability to the beneficiary, unless the transferee is acting in bad faith.[279] However, under revised section 3–307, a depositary is on notice of breach of fiduciary duty if the depositary allows the fiduciary to deposit to an account other than one for the benefit of the beneficiary: (a) an instrument payable to the beneficiary or the fiduciary as such, or (b) an instrument drawn by the beneficiary or the fiduciary and payable to the depositary.[280] There is, therefore, automatic liability if a bank allows a fiduciary to deposit items of the types just described in the fiduciary's personal account and the fiduciary then uses the funds for non-fiduciary purposes.[281]

The U.F.A. rule is based upon the assumption that a fiduciary will properly apply fiduciary funds and that knowledge by a depositary bank that a fiduciary has deposited fiduciary funds in her personal checking account is not knowledge or notice of a present or intended future misappropriation. On the other hand, revised Article 3 treats a deposit by a fiduciary in her personal account as, in effect, a suspicious circumstance imposing on the depositary bank the risk that the deposit is part of a scheme to misappropriate funds.[282]

While revised section 3–307 departs from the U.F.A. regarding the liability of banks that accept deposits from fiduciaries for the personal account of the fiduciary,[283] the revised Article 3 provisions are consistent with many, but not all, recent cases.[284] The comments to revised

279. Unif. Fiduciaries Act § 9, 7A U.L.A. 417 (1985). Section 9 provides that a bank is not liable to the beneficiary for allowing a fiduciary to deposit fiduciary funds (either checks payable to the beneficiary or fiduciary or drawn by the fiduciary) into the fiduciary's personal account, nor is it liable for allowing the fiduciary to subsequently withdraw such funds, unless it has knowledge of the misappropriation or knows such facts that its allowance of the withdrawal is bad faith. Section 9 does not specifically refer to checks made payable to the depositary bank, but its language is sufficiently broad to cover checks payable to the beneficiary, to the fiduciary, and to the bank. See Sugarhouse Fin. Co. v. Zions First Nat'l Bank, 21 Utah 2d 68, 440 P.2d 869 (1968).

280. *See* U.C.C. § 3–307(b) (1990).

281. *Id.* § 3–307(b)(2) & (4).

282. *Id.* § 3–307 comment 3 ("[I]t is not normal for an instrument payable to the * * * fiduciary, as such, to be used for the personal benefit of the fiduciary.").

283. *Id.*

284. *See infra* notes 292–312 and accompanying text.

section 3–307 accurately state that the matter is one on which the courts are divided.[285] Nearly all the recent cases involve disloyal employees rather than trustees of trusts or estates.[286]

A common form of employee misconduct involves taking a check payable to the employer, placing the indorsement of the employer thereon, and depositing the check in the employee's personal account. Under former Article 3, if the employee has no real or apparent authority to indorse the check, the indorsement is a forgery.[287] Subject to the possible limitation imposed by former subsection 3–419(3),[288] and to possible liability of the employer under former section 3–406,[289] the bank that takes the check from the employee is liable in conversion to the employer for interfering with the employer's rights in the check. On the other hand, if the employee had authority to indorse the check, no forgery is involved and the depositary bank will take free of the claim of the employer if the bank is a holder in due course.

In recent years, however, courts have generally found that banks were not holders in due course when they accepted for deposit into an employee's personal account checks payable to an employer. In spite of the fact that the official comment to former subsection 3–304(2) stated that "the purchaser may pay cash into the hands of the fiduciary without notice of any breach of the obligation [of the fiduciary to the beneficiary]," [293] several courts have held that depositing the check into

285. U.C.C. § 3–307 comment 3 (1990) ("there is a split of authority").

286. *See id.* § 3–404 comment 3.

287. *See* U.C.C. § 3–405(1)(b) ("a person signing as or on behalf of a maker or drawer" will provide the transferee with an effective indorsement) & comment 3 (1989).

288. Under former subsection 3–419(3), a representative, including a depositary bank who dealt in good faith with an item on behalf of a person who was not the true owner, would not be liable to the true owner beyond the amount of the proceeds of the item still in the hands of the representative when it learned of the true owner's interest. *See* U.C.C. § 3–419(3) (1989). However, since, in the case posited, the depositary bank would be liable to subsequent parties, including the payee bank, for breach of the warranty of title, many courts have refused to give effect to former section 3–419(3), and have instead held that depositary banks may be liable to the true owners even though the banks permitted complete withdrawal of all the account funds by wrongdoers. *See* J. White & R. Summers, Uniform Commercial Code 668 (3d ed. 1988). Revised Article 3 does not provide the protection that former subsection 3–419(3) furnished depositary banks. *See* U.C.C. § 3–420(c) (1990) ("A representative, *other than a depositary bank,* that has in good faith dealt with an instrument or its proceeds on behalf of one who was not the person entitled to enforce the instrument is not liable in conversion to that person beyond the amount of any proceeds that it has not paid out." (emphasis added)).

289. Under former section 3–406, a person whose negligence substantially contributed to the making of an unauthorized signature was precluded from asserting the forgery against a holder in due course or a drawee or other payor who had paid the instrument in good faith and in accordance with the reasonable commercial standards of the drawee's or payor's business. U.C.C. § 3–406 (1989). An employer that was itself negligent, as in failing to discover that an employee had been previously guilty of embezzlement, would be barred from asserting the forgery. *See* Commercial Credit Equip. Corp. v. First Ala. Bank, 636 F.2d 1051 (5th Cir. Unit B 1981) (where the employee was a known embezzler).

293. U.C.C. § 3–304 comment 5 (1989); *see also id.* § 3–304(2) ("The purchaser has notice of a claim against the instrument when he has knowledge that a fiduciary has negotiated the instrument in payment of or as security for his own debt or in any transaction for his own benefit or otherwise in breach of duty.").

the account of the employee was a transaction for the benefit of the employee-fiduciary under former subsection 3–304(2); therefore, the depositary bank had notice of the claim of the employer.[294] * * *

In states, however, that have adopted section 9 of the U.F.A., the courts should hold that, unless a bank is guilty of bad faith or has knowledge of a misappropriation, a bank does not become liable to the beneficiary merely by allowing the fiduciary to deposit a check payable to the principal or the fiduciary as such into the personal account of the fiduciary.[296] A case so holding is *Johnson v. Citizens National Bank,*[297] decided by the Illinois Court of Appeals in 1975.

Many fiduciaries are not employees. As to nonemployee fiduciaries, two recent cases took opposing positions concerning the question whether a bank that accepts a check payable to the fiduciary as such for deposit into the fiduciary's personal account is liable if the fiduciary subsequently misappropriates the funds. The first involved a father who deposited in his personal account a check payable to him as trustee for his minor son. The New York Court of Appeals held the depositary not liable.[298] In contrast, the Washington Supreme Court held in a case involving a father-guardian who deposited guardianship funds in his personal account that the bank was liable.[299] In the New York case, the court said that there is no requirement that a check payable to a fiduciary be deposited to a fiduciary account and that, in general, a bank may assume that a person acting as fiduciary will apply trust funds for trust purposes.[300] In the Washington decision, the court followed an earlier Washington case involving an embezzling employee and held that a bank that allowed a check payable to a father as guardian of his minor son to be deposited to the father's personal account was on notice that the father was breaching his fiduciary duty.[301]

Another common situation in the reported cases is that of a bank which takes a check payable to the bank from a person other than the drawer, and credits the check to the account of the person presenting the check or otherwise allows the presenter to control the disposition of the proceeds of the check. The presenter may or may not be an

294. *See, e.g.,* Waukon Auto Supply v. Farmers & Merchants Sav. Bank, 440 N.W.2d 844 (Iowa 1989); Mott Grain Co. v. First Nat'l Bank & Trust, 259 N.W.2d 667 (N.D.1977); Pargas, Inc. v. Estate of Taylor, 416 So.2d 1358 (La.Ct.App.1982); Von Gohren v. Pacific Nat'l Bank, 8 Wash.App. 245, 505 P.2d 467 (1973). In *Mott,* the court also found that the indorsement was a forgery since the wrongdoer only had authority to indorse for deposit into the account of the company, even though the wrongdoer did have authority to draw checks on the account. *Mott,* 259 N.W.2d at 669–70. In *Pargas,* the court held that an employee who has authority to indorse checks only for deposit to the account of his employer commits forgery when the employee indorses and deposits in his personal account. *Pargas,* 416 So.2d at 1363.

296. *See* Unif. Fiduciaries Act § 9, 7A U.L.A. 417 (1985).

297. 30 Ill.App.3d 1066, 334 N.E.2d 295 (1975).

298. *In re* Knox, 64 N.Y.2d 434, 477 N.E.2d 448, 64 N.Y.2d 434 (1985).

299. Smith v. Olympic Bank, 103 Wash.2d 418, 693 P.2d 92 (1985).

300. *In re* Knox, 64 N.Y.2d at 436, 477 N.E.2d at 449, 488 N.Y.S.2d at 148.

301. *Smith,* 103 Wash.2d at 420, 693 P.2d at 94.

employee of the drawer and may or may not be a fiduciary of the drawer. Here, too, the cases have split, some imposing liability if the presenter is acting inconsistently with the intent of the drawer [302] and others holding that a bank can be a holder in due course of a check so deposited if it takes in good faith and without notice of claims or defenses.[303] (As a holder in due course the bank takes free of the claim by the beneficiary that the fiduciary wrongfully deposited the check.[304]) Of course, it is implicit in the second line of cases that the mere fact that a check is payable to the bank and presented by one other than the drawer is not sufficient to put the bank on notice of a claim or defense of the drawer. The decisions usually make that point expressly.[305]

Most of the cases that impose liability on a bank if the presenter of the check had no authority from the drawer to negotiate the check do not focus upon whether the presenter was an employee or fiduciary of the drawer. Rather, the result is based on a categorical rule that a bank which takes a check payable to the bank, itself, from one other than the drawer is bound to apply the check according to the wishes of the drawer. For example, in *Douglass v. Wones,*[306] the court first noted that prior Illinois cases had held that the payee of a check, who took the item in payment of the debt of a presenter other than the drawer, could be a holder in due course. Therefore, the payee could take free of a claim by the drawer that the presenter had misappropriated the check.[307] *Douglass* then held that a different rule applies to a bank.[308] The *Douglass* court reasoned that:

> "[W]hen [a bank] is named as the payee of a check by a party not indebted to the bank, such bank will be presumed to have accepted the same subject to the directions of the drawer, and not to the directions of a stranger to the paper who happens to present it." [309]

302. *See, e.g.,* Bank of S. Md. v. Robertson's Crab House, 39 Md.App. 707, 389 A.2d 388 (1978). In *Robertson's Crab House,* the bank was held liable for applying proceeds of the corporation's checks to an employee's account without using ordinary care to establish the employee's authorization. The court held that the bank was negligent as a matter of law where the bookkeeper of plaintiff Robertson deposited checks into the tax escrow account of plaintiff at defendant bank, but also deposited portions of some of these checks, and all of others, into his own account or the tax accounts of other business for which he was also bookkeeper. *See also* PWA Farms v. North Platte State Bank, 220 Neb. 516, 371 N.W.2d 102 (1985); Douglass v. Wones, 120 Ill.App.3d 36, 458 N.E.2d 514 (1983). *See generally* Spaulding & Sherwood, *The Wayward Corporate Check: Notice of Diversion under the U.C.C.,* 18 Cath.U.L.Rev. 127, 145–47 (1968).

303. *See, e.g.,* G.D.F. Enters. v. Nye, 37 Ohio St.3d 205, 525 N.E.2d 10 (1988); St. Stephen's Evangelical Lutheran Church v. Seaway Nat'l Bank, 38 Ill.App.3d 1021, 350 N.E.2d 128 (1976); Richardson Co. v. First Nat'l Bank, 504 S.W.2d 812 (Tex.Civ.App. 1974).

304. U.C.C. 3–305 (1989).

305. *See, e.g.,* St. Stephen's Evangelical Lutheran Church v. Seaway Nat'l Bank, 38 Ill.App.3d 1021, 350 N.E.2d 128 (1976); Richardson Co. v. First Nat'l Bank, 504 S.W.2d 812 (Tex.Civ.App.1974).

306. 120 Ill.App.3d 36, 458 N.E.2d 514 (1983).

307. *Douglass,* 120 Ill.App.3d at 45, 458 N.E.2d at 522.

308. *Id.*

309. *Id.* at 46, 458 N.E.2d at 522 (quoting Milano v. Sheridan Trust & Sav. Bank, 242 Ill.App. 362, 369 (1926)). *See infra* notes 352–62 and accompanying text. *See also, e.g.,* Bank of S. Md. v. Robertson's Crab House, 39 Md.App. 707, 714–16, 389 A.2d 388, 393–94 (1978) (stating a similar

Other courts have expressed the same idea by saying that a bank cannot treat a check payable to itself as a bearer instrument; that is, the bank cannot assume that the person presenting the item is the owner or is authorized to control disposition of the item.[310] As noted above, the rule, as stated in *Douglass* and similar cases, is not limited to fiduciaries.[311] In fact, in the case of fiduciaries, if the particular state has adopted the U.F.A., a different result is mandated if the fiduciary deposits, into the fiduciary's personal account, a check drawn by the beneficiary and payable to the bank.[312]

Problems

Jack Kates was the office manager of R & R Enterprises. He was a 25 year employee who had the implicit trust of his employers and rightfully so. Jack had no authority to sign or indorse checks. He did, however, regularly prepare checks to be signed by the company treasurer. He also prepared deposit slips for checks received by R & R. In May, 1992, his wife of 30 years became seriously ill and needed very expensive treatment which was not covered by his health insurance. From May to October, 1992, he engaged in the following fraudulent activity:

1. Knowing that the treasurer often signed checks prepared by Kates without looking at the payee or amount, Kates prepared a check for $10,000 drawn on Southern Bank and payable to First Bank. After the treasurer signed the check, Kates took the check to First Bank and used it as payment on a $15,000 debt which Kates owed the Bank. The check was paid by Southern when First Bank presented it through the clearing house.

(a) Was the check properly payable so that R & R cannot require that Southern re-credit its account?

(b) Can R & R recover the amount of the check from First Bank.

See R 3–404, 3–307 and OR 3–405. See also the excerpt from Marion W. Benfield Jr. & Peter A. Alces, Bank Liability for Fiduciary Fraud, supra, and see *Travelers Indemnity Co. v. American Express Co.,* 559 F.Supp. 452 (S.D.N.Y.1983).

2. Kates forged the signature of the treasurer as drawer on a check for $10,000 payable to the Mayo Clinic. When the check was presented to

rule). *See generally* 5A Michie on Banks and Banking § 183 (1983); 9 C.J.S., *Banks & Banking* § 340 (1938).

310. *See, e.g.,* Sun 'N Sand, Inc. v. United Cal. Bank, 21 Cal.3d 671, 582 P.2d 920, 935–36, 148 Cal.Rptr. 329, 344–45 (1978).

311. *See infra* notes 301–09 and accompanying text.

312. Unif. Fiduciaries Act § 9, 7A U.L.A. 417 (1985) (dealing generally with checks drawn by the fiduciary, checks payable to the fiduciary as such, and checks payable to the beneficiary and indorsed by the fiduciary). Section 9 contains a catch-all provision that covers deposit of checks payable to the bank, viz: "or otherwise makes a deposit of funds held by him as fiduciary." *Id.* In the described cases, the bank may accept the deposit into the personal account of the fiduciary and pay the funds out on the personal check of the fiduciary without being liable to the beneficiary unless the bank pays with actual knowledge of fiduciary wrongdoing or acts in bad faith. *See also* Unif. Fiduciaries Act § 8, 7A U.L.A. 415 (1985) (check drawn by the fiduciary and payable to the depositary bank) * * *. Illinois has adopted the U.F.A., but the court in *Douglass* did not refer to it.

the drawee bank, Southern, it discovered the apparent forgery and returned the check to Mayo. Can Mayo recover from R & R?

3. Kates stole a check for $15,000 payable to R & R, indorsed the check in the name of R & R, and transferred the check to the Mayo Clinic in payment of a part of his wife's medical expenses. Before the check was presented to the drawee bank, the fraud was discovered and R & R induced the drawer to stop payment on the check. Can Mayo recover from the drawer on the check? Can Mayo recover the amount of the check from R & R? Would the result in this problem be different if Kates had actual authority to indorse checks for R & R? See OR 3–304(2); R 3–307.

4. Kates stole a check for $5,000 payable to R & R, indorsed the check in the name of R & R, added his own name, and deposited the check in his checking account in Southeastern Bank. Southeastern secured payment of the check and Kates has withdrawn the amount involved. Is Southeastern liable in conversion to R & R? Would the result be different if Kates had authority to indorse R & R checks?

5. R & R used a check writing machine for checks under $1,000. Kates had no authority to instruct the computer as to such checks: that was done by the treasurer's personal secretary. However, Kates gained access to the computer and instructed it to issue 3 checks for $950 each to Jim Jones, at Kates's address. Kates took the checks, indorsed Jones's name, then his own, and deposited the checks one at a time, several days apart, in First Bank. The checks were paid by the drawee, Southern. Is First Bank liable to Southern for breach of warranty? OR 3–405; R 3–404, R 3–110(b).

K & K MANUFACTURING, INC. v. UNION BANK

Arizona Court of Appeals, 1981.
129 Ariz. 7, 628 P.2d 44.

HATHAWAY, CHIEF JUDGE.

In this case we must apply articles three and four of the Uniform Commercial Code to determine who should bear the risk of loss when a dishonest employee forges her employer's name as drawer on a number of checks on his business and personal checking accounts, then appropriates the proceeds for her personal use.

Appellant Bill J. Knight is the president and majority stockholder of both K & K Manufacturing, Inc. and Knight Foundry & Manufacturing, Inc. Knight Foundry employed about 80 people at the time of trial, while K & K Manufacturing, which was formed to accomplish the contracting, buying and selling for the foundry business, employed only two persons when the events which form the basis of this action occurred. These two employees were Knight and a bookkeeper, Eleanor Garza. The bookkeeper's duties at K & K Mfg. were very broad, including picking up the company mail and Knight's personal mail from a common post office box, preparing checks for Knight's signature to pay both company and personal bills and making entries in a cash disbursement journal reflecting the expenses for which the checks were written. Most importantly, it was her responsibility to reconcile the monthly statements prepared and sent by appellee Union Bank, where Knight kept both his business checking and savings accounts. No one shared these duties with Miss Garza.

Between March 1977 and January 1978, Miss Garza forged Knight's signature on some 66 separate checks drawn on his personal or business accounts at Union Bank. The majority of these checks were made payable to her. The total amount of the forgeries on the K & K Mfg. account was $49,859.31. The total on Knight's personal account was $11,350. The bank paid each such check and Miss Garza received or was credited with the proceeds.

We need not concentrate on the details of the fraud, except to comment that it proved to be effective for nearly one year. Miss Garza assured that the disbursement journal balanced by overstating legitimate expenditures, forging checks to herself for the difference, and later showing the forged check as "void." Upon receipt of appellee's monthly statement and cancelled checks, she removed and concealed the bad checks. The proceeds from most of the forgeries were deposited directly into her personal account rather than taken in cash. She usually presented the bad checks to the bank tellers with numerous authorized checks, and spread her banking transactions among several tellers so that no one teller knew the extent of her business.

Eventually, an in-house audit showed the discrepancies in the 1977 disbursements. Appellants brought this action against appellee for breach of contract, seeking repayment of the funds the bank paid out in checks with unauthorized signatures. After a court trial, judgment was entered in favor of appellant Knight for $5,500, representing the amount paid out of his personal account on forged checks from March 28 to May 20, 1977. This figure included eight forged checks paid by the bank prior to the mailing of its monthly statement containing a record of the payments and the checks themselves to Knight on May 6, plus a 14–day period. Since no forged checks on the K & K Mfg. account were paid prior to May 20, judgment was entered for appellee against it. In addition, the trial court made findings of fact and conclusions of law. Both Knight and K & K Mfg. had appealed.

Appellants contend that findings 13, 14 and 15 are not supported by the evidence. They argue the record shows their actions were not negligent and that the bank's practice and procedures were negligent as a matter of law. The disputed findings are as follows:

> 13. Defendant bank [appellee] paid all the checks in good faith and in accordance with reasonable commercial standards.
>
> 14. Defendant bank did not fail to exercise ordinary care in paying the checks.

15. The plaintiffs [appellants] did not exercise reasonable care and promptness to examine the bank statements and cancelled checks in order to discover the forgeries.

Our duty begins and ends with the inquiry of whether the trial court had before it evidence which reasonably supports its actions, viewed in a light most favorable to sustaining the findings. *United Bank v. Mesa N.O. Nelson Co.,* 121 Ariz. 438, 590 P.2d 1384 (1979). We will not weight conflicting evidence or set aside the trial court's findings unless they are clearly erroneous. *Id.* The determination of which actions are commercially reasonable and what constitutes ordinary care on the part of the bank, as well as reasonable care and promptness on the part of the depositor, are questions of fact for the trier of fact. See *West Penn. Administration, Inc. v. Union National Bank,* 233 Pa.Super. 311, 335 A.2d 725 (1975).

The concept of which party bears the loss in a forgery situation such as the one presented here is addressed in articles three and four of the Uniform Commercial Code, covering commercial paper and bank deposits and collections. * * *

* * *

[UCC Sections 3–406 [R 3–406] and 4–406 [R 4–406]] * * * impose a duty on the depositor to check his monthly statement for unauthorized signatures or alterations on checks. If a depositor fails to do so, after the first forged check and statement relating thereto is sent to him, plus a reasonable period not exceeding 14 days, he is precluded from asserting the unauthorized signature or alteration against the bank. UCC § 4–406, comment 3 [comment 1 and 2 to R 4–406]. The burden of proof of depositor's negligence is on the bank. Even if the bank succeeds in establishing the depositor's negligence, if the customer establishes that the bank failed to exercise ordinary care in paying the bad checks, the preclusion rule of ARS § 44–2632(B) does not apply. UCC § 4–406, comment 4.

We first address the issue of whether appellee met its burden of proof of showing that appellants "substantially contributed" to the forgeries or failed to exercise "reasonable care and promptness" in examining the monthly statements. The record shows that appellants trusted Miss Garza completely with both writing checks and reconciling the monthly statements. No spot checks were made by Knight or the controller at Knight Foundry, both of whom had access to the banking records. Knight was informed by a bank officer that his personal account was overdrawn on 12 occasions in 1977, yet did nothing to discover the reasons therefor. Knight testified he was aware Miss Garza's work was often inaccurate as well as tardy in 1977 and 1978.

Appellants argue they were not negligent in relying on a previously honest employee, citing *Jackson v. First National Bank,* 55 Tenn. App. 545, 403 S.W.2d 109 (1966). We decline to follow *Jackson,* which held, contrary to the bulk of authority, that since a defalcating financial secretary had been a longtime faithful and trusted member of the church he cheated, the church could not be found negligent. Misplaced confidence in an employee will not excuse a depositor from the duty of notifying the bank of alterations on items from the depositor's account. We adopt the majority view that the depositor is chargeable with the knowledge of all facts a reasonable and prudent examination of his bank account would have disclosed if made by an honest employee. The trial court's finding number 15 is amply supported by the evidence.

Secondly, we turn to the question of whether appellants met their burden of proof of demonstrating appellee did not exercise ordinary care in paying the bad checks, and did not act in good faith and in accordance with reasonable commercial standards. There appears to be no dispute regarding the good faith of appellee in paying the forgeries. The issue is whether its method of ascertaining unauthorized signatures on its depositor's checks met the standard of care under the circumstances.

Implied in the debtor/creditor relationship between a bank and its checking account depositor is the contractual undertaking on the part of the bank that it will only discharge its obligations to the depositor upon his authorized signature. *Hennesy Equipment Sales Co. v. Valley National Bank,* 25 Ariz.App. 285, 543 P.2d 123 (1975). The mere fact that bank has paid a forged check does not mean the bank has breached its duty of ordinary care, however. See Comment, 12 Ariz.L.Rev. 417, 425 (1970).

At trial, an operations officer for appellee testified as to the methods employed during the period the forgeries occurred to discover unauthorized signatures on depositor's checks. She testified that checks were organized so that a bundle from the same account could be compared with the authorized signature on the bank's signature card. A staff of five filing clerks handled an average of approximately 1,000 checks each per hour in this manner. She testified it was common for a file clerk to become familiar with the drawer's signature in large accounts such as appellants'. An official of a large Arizona bank testified that tellers and file clerks are not trained to be handwriting experts. He testified that in his opinion, because most large banks have completely abandoned physical comparison of checks with the signature card, the system employed by appellee was better than the norm of the banking community in Southern Arizona.

In view of this and other evidence, we conclude that there was sufficient evidence to support findings 13 and 14 and the judgment entered below. Similar methods of comparing drawer's signatures have been upheld as constituting ordinary care and being within reasonable commercial standards across the country. Appellant Knight and his controller admitted the forgeries were quite good. Appellants also argue that because the bank tellers recognized Miss Garza was cashing large checks made to herself and her boyfriend and that she was driving an expensive sports car, they had a further duty to check the validity of the drawer's signature. This evidence was balanced by testimony that Miss Garza thoroughly explained the reasons for the large checks as increased salary, bonuses, and payment of Knight's expenses while he was out of town. Knight and Miss Garza were in the bank together on a regular basis and the tellers knew Miss Garza was authorized to handle large amounts of Knight's money. See *Cooper v. Union Bank,* 9 Cal.3d 123, 371, 507 P.2d 609, 107 Cal.Rptr. 1 (1973).

Finally, there was evidence that some K & K Mfg. checks were forged with a rubber stamp facsimile of Knight's signature, which was only authorized for uses with the Knight Foundry Account. Appellants argue appellee fell below the standard of ordinary care in honoring these checks. The trial court personally examined appellee's expert witness on this subject. There was testimony that if facsimile signatures appear "all of a sudden" on the checks, the depositor may be contacted, but there was sufficient evidence that the piecemeal use of the stamp here, which was at times authorized by appellants, was not such that appellee should be held to bring it to their attention. The finding of fact that appellee's acts, including those regarding the facsimile signature did not fall below ordinary care or reasonable commercial standards was not clearly erroneous.

Affirmed.

Note

In the case, in spite of Knight's and K & K's failure to have reasonable procedures in place for examination of returned checks for forgery or alteration, Knight recovers $5,500. Why? Under OR and R 4–406, what would Union Bank have had to show to avoid liability for that $5,500?

Observe that the 14 day period of OR 4–406(2)(b) has been expanded to 30 days by R 4–406(d)(2).

Revised 4–406 accommodates the practice of many credit unions and possibly some banks of not returning paid checks to the customer. The last sentence of subsection (a) provides "The statement of account provides sufficient information if the item is described by item number, amount, and date of payment." Subsection (b) requires a bank that does not return checks to maintain the capacity to furnish legible copies of the items for seven years after their receipt. (Banks generally make photocopies of all checks as a part of the payment process.)

WILDER BINDING CO. v. OAK PARK TRUST & SAVINGS BANK

Illinois Supreme Court, 1990.
135 Ill.2d 121, 142 Ill.Dec. 192, 552 N.E.2d 783.

[From December 1983 to June 1984, plaintiff's bookkeeper forged the name of D.S. McCarrell, who was authorized to sign checks for plaintiff, on 42 checks which she made payable to herself. Each check was for less than $1000. Returned checks and bank statements were examined by the bookkeeper. Therefore, the forgeries were not discovered until July 1984. Defendant bank did not examine signatures on checks for less than $1000. Plaintiff claims that bank's failure to examine signatures is negligence as a matter of law and that, therefore, even though plaintiff was negligent in failing to have someone other than the bookkeeper examine returned checks, under OR 4–406(3) the loss falls on the bank.

Defendant gave an affidavit stating that (1) defendant processed an average of between 8,000 and 11,000 checks per day and that 650 to 750 of those checks were written for more than $1000; (2) defendant maintained a staff of five full-time employees and additional part-time employees to manually verify the signatures of checks for more than $1000, and (3) defendant and at least four other banks in the Chicago area utilized check sorting machines to separate checks "drawn for less than the designated amount from checks drawn for the designated amount or more" and did not examine signatures on checks for less than the designated amount.

The trial court held that defendant's conduct was negligent as a matter of law and gave summary judgment for plaintiff. The appellate court, over a dissent, affirmed. The Supreme Court granted leave to appeal. The Illinois Public Action Council filed an amicus brief in support of the plaintiff. The American Banker's Association, the Illinois Banker's Association, and the Chicago Clearing House filed amicus briefs in support of the defendant.]

MORAN, CHIEF JUSTICE. * * *

Plaintiff contends that the appellate court did not err in affirming the circuit court's entry of summary judgment. Its contention is based on its belief that no genuine issue as to any material fact exists and, accordingly, that it is entitled to summary judgment. It argues that defendant's admitted use of automated check-sorting equipment and automatic payment of checks drawn for less than $1,000 without manual verification of the signatures on those checks conclusively establishes, as a matter of law, defendant's failure to exercise ordinary care under the section.

Notwithstanding its admissions, defendant argues that its use of automated check-sorting equipment and automatic payment of checks drawn for less than $1,000 without manual verification of the signatures on those checks constitutes the prima facie exercise of ordinary care. Defendant's argument is based on § 4–103(3) [R 4–103(c)] of the Commercial Code, which provides in pertinent part:

> "[I]n the absence of special instructions, *action or nonaction consistent * * * with a general banking usage* not disapproved by this Article, *prima facie constitutes the exercise of ordinary care.*" (Emphasis added.) Ill.Rev.Stat., 1985, ch. 26, par. 4–103(3).

The term *general banking usage* "is not defined but *should be taken to mean a general usage common to banks in the area concerned.*"

(Emphasis added.) (Ill.Ann.Stat., ch. 26, par. 4–103, Uniform Commercial Code Comment, at 441 (Smith–Hurd 1963).) Additionally,

> "[w]here the adjective 'general' is used, the intention is to require a usage broader than a mere practice between two or three banks but it is not intended to require anything as broad as a country-wide usage. *A usage followed generally throughout* a state, a substantial portion of a state, a *metropolitan area or the like would certainly be sufficient.*" (Emphasis added.) (Ill.Ann.Stat., ch. 26, par. 4–103, Uniform Commercial Code Comment, at 441 (Smith–Hurd 1963).)

Therefore, defendant concludes that its use of automated check-sorting equipment and automatic payment of checks drawn for less than $1,000 without manual verification of the signatures on those checks constitutes the prima facie exercise of ordinary care. Defendant's conclusion is based on Visconti's counteraffidavit, which indicates that more than two or three banks in the metropolitan Chicago area also use automated check-sorting equipment and automatically pay checks drawn for less than a designated amount without manually verifying the signatures on those checks.

In affirming the circuit court's entry of summary judgment, the appellate majority relied primarily on the case of Medford Irrigation District v. Western Bank (1984), 66 Or.App. 589, 676 P.2d 329. In Medford, a majority of the Oregon Court of Appeals held that, as a matter of law, Western Bank failed to exercise ordinary care pursuant to the Oregon Commercial Code when it used automated check-sorting equipment and automatically paid checks drawn for less than $5,000 without manually verifying the signatures on those checks. (Medford, 66 Or.App. at 593, 676 P.2d at 332.) The dissent expressed the opinion that the question regarding whether a bank exercised ordinary care in the payment of checks is one of fact which should be answered by the trier of fact. Medford, 66 Or.App. at 598, 676 P.2d at 335 (Van Hoomissen, J., dissenting).

Like the Medford dissent and the dissent in this case, several other courts have held that the question of whether a bank exercised ordinary care in paying a check presents a genuine issue of material fact which should be answered by the trier of fact and, therefore, summary judgment should not be entered. See also 7 R. Anderson, Uniform Commercial Code § 4–406:12 (3d ed. 1985).) We agree with the rationale of these cases. * * *

After carefully reviewing the record, including both defendant's admissions and Visconti's counteraffidavit, we believe that a genuine issue of material fact exists regarding whether defendant exercised ordinary care in paying checks under the section. Therefore, it should be left up to the trier of fact to determine whether defendant's use of automated check-sorting equipment and automatic payment of checks drawn for less than $1,000 without manual verification of signatures on those checks is "consistent with general banking usage" and, accordingly, "*prima facie* constitutes the exercise of ordinary care." As such, we hold that the appellate court erred in affirming the circuit court's entry of summary judgment in favor of plaintiff.

JUSTICE CALVO, dissenting: * * *

* * * Defendant's automatic payment of all checks drawn for less than $1,000, without manual verification of the signatures on those checks, conclusively established defendant's failure to exercise ordinary care under the Code. Complete absence of review accompanied by an absence of a *system* for review, in my view, constitutes, as a matter of law, lack of ordinary care.

* * *

The Code does not define "ordinary care." (Ill.Ann.Stat., ch. 26, par. 4–103, Uniform Commercial Code Comment, at 440 (Smith–Hurd 1963).) Instead, for purposes of the Code, ordinary care is "used with its normal tort meaning and not in any special sense relating to bank collections." (Ill.Ann.Stat., ch. 26, par. 4–103, Uniform Commercial Code Comment, at 440 (Smith–Hurd 1963).) Under § 4–103(3) [R 4–103(c)] of the Code, however, action or inaction by a bank which is consistent with general banking usage "prima facie constitutes the exercise of ordinary care." (Ill.Rev.Stat.1983, ch. 26, par. 4–103(3) [R 4–103(c)].) Nevertheless, customers can:

> "prescribe other standards and where there may be no direct supervision or control of clearing houses or banking usages by official supervisory authorities, the confirmation of ordinary care by compliance with these standards is prima facie only, thus conferring on the courts the ultimate power to determine ordinary care in any case where it should appear desirable to do so. The prima facie rule does, however, impose on the party contesting the standards to establish that they are unreasonable, arbitrary or unfair." (Ill.Ann.Stat., ch. 26, par. 4–103, Uniform Commercial Code Comment, at 441 (Smith–Hurd 1963).)

Consequently, while proof of compliance with general banking usage can provide the bank with prima facie evidence of ordinary care, a customer can rebut this evidence with proof that the bank's standards are unreasonable, arbitrary or unfair.

* * *

Even if defendant "established conformity with local standards," defendant "is not automatically exonerated." (Hanover Insurance Cos. v. Brotherhood State Bank (D.Kan.1979), 482 F.Supp. 501, 506.) The industry standard may be considered as evidence of compliance with ordinary care, but such evidence is not conclusive. " 'Even an entire industry, by adopting such careless methods to save time, effort or money, cannot be permitted to set its own uncontrolled standard.' " (Hanover, 482 F.Supp. at 506, quoting W. Prosser, Law of Torts 167 (4th ed. 1971).) * * *

"Mere technological innovations, an increased workload and a desire to save time, money and effort do not relieve the bank of its responsibility to exercise ordinary care." (Hanover, 482 F.Supp. at 509.) We should not permit an industry to set standards which thereby insulate it from liability.

Defendant claims it does not lack procedures to discover forgeries; rather, it has one such procedure. That procedure involves sending bank statements and cancelled checks to customers monthly. In this way, customers, who are in the best position to do so, can detect forgeries once they review the statements. Defendant's argument has absolutely no merit. Customers already have a duty to examine their bank statements under §§ 4–406(1) [R 4–406(c)] and 4–406(2) [R 4–406(d)]. Defendant cannot abdicate its duty of ordinary care under § 4–406(3) [R 4–406(e)] to plaintiff. Defendant is, in effect, relying on its customers' duty of review to fulfill its own duty of ordinary care. I cannot sanction such a result. The result I reach in no way lessens a customer's responsibility to promptly examine bank statements. I simply conclude that a bank cannot use its customers' duty to discharge its own duty of care.

While in some circumstances, the decision as to what amounts to ordinary care may be an issue of fact, the situation before this court does not present such an instance. The affidavits and admissions before the circuit court indicated defendant's system of clearing checks precluded any review of the checks and forgeries here in question. Defendant's affidavit revealed that out of 8,000 to 11,000 checks processed per day, an average of 650 to 750 of the checks are written for more than $1,000. Defendant's automatic check-sorting equipment separates these 650 to 750 checks from the other checks for manual review. Thus, defendant verifies the signatures on about 7% of the checks processed. Defendant does not verify the signatures on approximately 93% of all checks. Automatic preclusion from review of 93% of all checks processed based solely on the amount of the check does not present a genuine issue as to any material fact.

* * *

My decision does not mean defendant would have to manually review the signatures on all of the checks which cross defendant's threshold prior to payment. Nevertheless, every check crossing defendant's threshold should be subject to some *probability* of examination. For example, the court in Rhode Island Hospital Trust National Bank v. Zapata Corp. (1st Cir.1988), 848 F.2d 291, 294 found the bank exercised ordinary care when the bank (1) examined signatures on every check for more than $1,000; (2) examined signatures on checks between $100 and $1,000, if the bank had reason to suspect a problem (e.g., if a check was drawn on an account with insufficient funds); and (3) examined signatures on a randomly chosen 1% of all other checks between $100 and $1,000. In Rhode Island, though the bank did not review every check, the bank's system subjected virtually every check to the potential for sight review prior to payment. I cannot say the procedure in Rhode Island would conclusively constitute ordinary care. The facts of Rhode Island played a significant role in that decision and I cannot at this time determine whether the $100 threshold or the 1% level would be appropriate. Nevertheless, Rhode Island provides an example of a system of review. * * *

Defendant asserts the appellate court's holding is contrary to the policy behind § 4–406 [R 4–406] because sight review of checks does not necessarily detect forgeries. Defendant also contends that the Code does not require banks to know the genuineness of a customer's signature on a check. Moreover, defendant points out banks have no statutory duty to perform any specific review procedure, including sight review.

First, I am not requiring a bank to guaranty the signatures on all of the checks it sight reviews. In other words, if a bank institutes sight review, it is not automatically liable for any forgeries it may fail to detect. The Code only requires banks to exercise *ordinary* care; that is, to exercise the degree of care which would "reasonably relate to the detection of unauthorized signatures." Medford, 66 Or.App. at 593, 76 P.2d at 332.

Second, the Code only allows banks to pay checks with authorized (nonforged) signatures (Ill.Rev.Stat.1983, ch. 26, pars. 3–404 [R 3–403], 1–201(43)) and checks which are "properly payable" (Ill.Rev.Stat.1983, ch. 26, par. 4–401(1) [R 4–401(a)]). Moreover, defendant required plaintiff to sign and have on file signature cards. Consequently, while the Code does not expressly require banks to sight review checks, banks are required to know their customers' signatures. How banks choose to fulfill their duty is up to them as long as they exercise ordinary care. As I have indicated, defendant did not exercise such care.

In summary, it is of little consequence that four other banks in the area use the same procedures as defendant. We should not permit an industry to establish a standard which relieves it of its duty of care to a large segment of its customers. Defendant has no procedure to review the signatures on checks drawn for less than $1,000, even though it has a duty to plaintiff. Where a duty is owed and none is given, the only reasonable conclusion is the one reached by the circuit and appellate courts.

JUSTICE CLARK joins in this dissent.

Note

Under revised Article 3 would Oak Park Trust be entitled to summary judgment on the issue whether it was negligent in its handling of checks presented to it for payment? See R 4–406, 3–103(a)(7).

Revised 3–406 and 4–406 apply comparative negligence rules when both the drawer and the drawee are negligent. The new rules are always more favorable to banks than the original Article 3 rules since under original Article 3 the bank always lost if both the bank and the customer were negligent. Original Article 3 was drafted before the general move in tort law from contributory negligence rules (any negligence on the part of plaintiff defeats recovery) to comparative negligence rules. Therefore, one can say that revised Article 3 is merely adopting the latest tort thinking. However, as the following materials suggest, it might be argued that the original Article 3 rules are preferable in the bank-customer relationship.

PUTNAM ROLLING LADDER CO., INC. v. MANUFACTURERS HANOVER TRUST CO.

New York Supreme Court, 1989.
74 N.Y.2d 340, 547 N.Y.S.2d 611, 546 N.E.2d 904.

[The trial court found that both customer and bank had been negligent under OR 3–406 and 4–406 as to forgeries by an employee of customer and applied comparative negligence rules to apportion liability between the two. Appeal.]

KAYE, JUDGE * * *

COMPARATIVE NEGLIGENCE

While the Appellate Division erred in reversing the trial court on proof of due care, that error cannot be rectified simply by reinstating the trial court judgment, which applied comparative negligence principles and divided the loss.

The importation of comparative negligence into the UCC—which was drafted before widespread acceptance of comparative fault—is not without its advocates (noted in, 1 White and Summers, op. cit., § 16–7, fn. 6 at 809), but has generally been rejected by both courts and commentators (id.). We agree. As one court stated in addressing this issue, "the balancing of rights under the UCC represents the ultimate distillation of a painstaking process of evolution, pursuant to which the risk of loss in commercial matters has been attempted to be adjusted in a fair and equitable manner." (Five Towns Coll. v. Citibank, 108 A.D.2d 420, 429–30; see also, United States Fid. and Guar. Co. v. The Fed. Reserve Bank, 620 F.Supp. 361.) It is not for the courts to unsettle the UCC's carefully drawn balance by introducing comparative fault principles drawn from tort law.

Moreover, the UCC serves an important objective not shared by the law of torts (see, by analogy, Board of Education v. Sargent, 71 N.Y.2d 21, 29). Unlike tort law, the UCC has the objective of promoting certainty and predictability in commercial transactions. By prospectively establishing rules of liability that are generally based not on actual fault but on allocating responsibility to the party best able to prevent the loss by the exercise of care, the UCC not only guides commercial behavior but also increases certainty in the marketplace and efficiency in dispute resolution. These ends would not be furthered by the introduction of the sort of fact inquiries necessitated by comparative negligence.

In that plaintiff adduced sufficient evidence of the bank's lack of ordinary care in paying the 37 forged checks (thereby avoiding preclusion under UCC 4–406[2] [R.4–406(d)] for its own negligence), and the bank offered no evidence whatever of general rules or usage, judgment should have been awarded to plaintiff in the undisputed amount of its loss.

Accordingly, the Appellate Division order should be reversed, with costs, and judgment granted for plaintiff in the amount of $43,737.02, with interest from December 9, 1980.

RUBIN, EFFICIENCY, EQUITY AND THE PROPOSED REVISION OF ARTICLES 3 AND 4

42 Ala.L.Rev. 551 at 569–570 (1991).

But the most serious problem with the fault principle that Article 3 embodies, and that the revision perpetuates, is the enormous cost of its effectuation. Determining fault requires a complex, fact-based adjudication that will rapidly devour the amount at issue in all but the largest cases. The reporters were aware of this problem. While they never abandoned the fault principle, they did propose that the loss simply be divided in half in situations where both parties were negligent. Even this modest effort to reduce loss imposition costs troubled the banking industry, and the provisions were dropped. Instead, sections 3–405 and 3–406 now contain a comparative negligence provision to deal with cases where both parties are at fault. This is even worse, of course; with the contributory negligence or dual contributory negligence of the existing law, only the fact of negligence must be established. Under the revision the precise amount of negligence becomes important, so every fact is relevant, and the agonizingly expensive process of discovery and trial can go on even longer.

This is a market failure of its own, a market failure generated by the structure of the legal system. It means that consumers can virtually never enforce their rights against a bank because it will simply be too expensive to do so. What makes this particularly serious is that consumers almost always end up with the loss if there is a dispute. The bank is holding the consumer's money, and can simply debit the account for the amount in question. This power, virtually unique among businesses, means that the consumer must generally initiate the lawsuit. Since the suit cannot be economically pursued, the consumer has to "lump it." The result is inefficient because the consumer is not necessarily the party who should bear the loss, even according to the rather limited precaution-based rules of Article 3, and certainly not according to more general principles of economic efficiency that include loss spreading. But the only thing that is more inefficient than failing to bring suit is bringing it; then the loss may be allocated in accordance with economic efficiency, but the expense of allocating it will outweigh any allocational advantage.

Note

Do you agree with the criticisms by the New York court and Professor Rubin of comparative fault in the bank-customer context? Professor Rubin is speaking only of consumers: that is ordinary family or personal account holders. Is comparative fault more justified in the case of commercial bank customers? Very little reported litigation involves consumer bank customers, probably because the amounts typically involved do not justify a law suit, or at least do not justify an appeal.

The Federal Reserve Board's Regulation CC governing check collection adopts a comparative negligence rule. 12 CFR 229.38(c). The Reg. CC negligence rules will not often have effect outside the banking system, though bank liability for negligence under Reg. CC 229.38(a) does run to bank customers. Regulation CC is discussed in Chapter 6.

Problem

Following are the facts from *Garnac Grain Co. v. Boatmen's Bank & Trust Co. of Kansas City,* 694 F.Supp. 1389 (W.D.Mo.1988). Mrs. Millison embezzled more than two million dollars from her employer, Garnac Grain Co., Inc., from 1976 to 1982. Garnac had hired her in 1973 while she was in a halfway house in Kansas City, Missouri. She had just been released from a Federal Prison in West Virginia after serving time for interstate transportation of forged and altered bank checks. She told Garnac that she had been imprisoned for possession of marijuana. She also had a prior conviction for embezzlement from an employer. Garnac did not learn of her prior convictions until after they discovered her embezzlement from it.

At Garnac, Mrs. Millison processed invoices from barge companies for sums Garnac owed them for carrying grain. Her dealings with the invoices gave her the opportunity to embezzle. Mrs. Millison used two different fraudulent schemes. Under the first scheme, she forged Garnac's signature on checks for the amount due on barge company invoices, but made the checks payable to her husband, L.R. Millison, signed his name as indorser, and deposited the checks in the joint account which she and her husband maintained at Oskaloosa Bank. When bank statements with the forged checks were returned to Garnac, she took the forged checks out and replaced them with checks payable to the correct payees.

Under the second scheme, Mrs. Millison took genuine checks payable to different barge companies, typed on the payee line "or L.R. Millison," indorsed the checks in her husband's name, and again deposited the checks in their joint account at Oskaloosa Bank. When bank statements were returned to Garnac, Mrs. Millison removed the altered checks, obliterated her husband's name as payee and his apparent indorsement on the back, and returned the checks to the file.

The checks deposited in Oskaloosa ranged in amounts from $3,600 to $77,800. There were 38 different corporate payees "or L.R. Millison." The Oskaloosa tellers knew when they took the deposits that both Mr. and Mrs. Millison worked for Garnac.

All the checks were drawn on Boatmen's Bank and were paid by it. An expert witness testified that he believed that both Oskaloosa and Boatmen's were negligent. Surely Garnac was also negligent.

Now consider the following issues under revised Article 3.

1. At the moment, Garnac has suffered all the loss since its account has been charged and Boatmen's refuses to re-credit the account. Can Garnac bring a direct action against Oskaloosa to recover based on Oskaloosa's negligence? Remember that under R 3–420 "an issuer" cannot bring an action in conversion. Also note that under R 3–406 preclusion from asserting a forged payee's signature would mean that a conversion action would not lie, but under R 3–420 a conversion action is not available anyway. (Comment 4 to R 3–406 refers to a conversion action against a depositary bank by a payee whose indorsement has been forged. The comments do not discuss the claim of a drawer against a negligent depositary bank when an employee has forged the indorsement of a payee who never received the check.) Does the denial to Garnac of a conversion action against Oskaloosa suggest that Garnac has no direct right against Oskaloosa? Comment 1 to R 3–420, in explaining the denial of a conversion action to a drawer, states: "The drawer has an adequate remedy against the payor bank for re-credit of the drawer's account for unauthorized payment of the check."

Perhaps courts will in fact give a drawer in a case like Garnac a direct action in negligence against the depositary bank. If so, however, the negligence action should lie whether or not the drawer is negligent. The result would then be that there is no direct action for non-negligent conversion, but there would be an action for negligently taking the instrument.

Any direct negligence action is complicated by the fact that the drawee bank, Boatmen's, was also likely negligent. How should that be taken account of in the suit between Garnac and Oskaloosa? Does it make a difference whether or not Boatmen's is joined in the suit?

2. Suppose that Boatmen's re-credits Garnac's account in full and asserts a breach of warranty claim against Oskaloosa. Under R 4–207(c), Oskaloosa can defend that the indorsement is effective under R 3–404 or 3–405 or that the drawer is precluded from asserting the unauthorized indorsement or alteration under R 3–406 or 4–406. How does Oskaloosa's negligence affect that defense?

3. Suppose a court finds that on the facts, Oskaloosa was not only negligent, but also failed to act in good faith. How does that affect the outcome of a direct suit by Garnac against Oskaloosa or of a warranty action by Boatmen's against Oskaloosa?

Chapter 5

BANK-CUSTOMER RELATIONS*

A. INTRODUCTION

This chapter deals with three important duties of a bank to its customer: first, the duty to pay only "properly payable" items, second the duty not to wrongfully dishonor items, and third, the duty to honor stop payment orders. These three duties have in common that they may be unrelated to any forgery, alteration, or third party fraud. Also, they do not relate to a bank's duties as a collecting bank. While other relationships between the bank and its customer might be dealt with here, we believe it is pedagogically more sound to deal with them in other chapters. Duties of collecting banks, including the depositary bank, are dealt with in Chapter 6, and the rights and duties of the bank and its customer in forgery, alteration, or fraud cases are dealt with in Chapter 4.

B. OBLIGATION TO PAY ONLY "PROPERLY PAYABLE" ITEMS

COLUMBIAN PEANUT COMPANY v. FROSTEG

United States Court of Appeals, Fifth Circuit, 1973.
472 F.2d 476.

RIVES, CIRCUIT JUDGE. In July 1970, Columbian Peanut Company (Columbian) entered into a written contract with Frosteg and his wholly-owned corporation, Pelham Peanut Company, by which Frosteg, on a commission basis, was to purchase and store peanuts for Columbian during the 1970 crop season in the peanut growing area of southwest Georgia. During the 1969 crop season a similar arrangement had existed between Columbian and Frosteg. The manner, time and quantity of the purchases were left to Frosteg's discretion.

* Throughout this text, the designation "OR" refers to an Article in its original form; "R" denotes a revised Article. E.g., OR 3–303 refers to Original Article 3; R 3–303 refers to Revised Article 3.

Carrying out that agreement, Columbian turned over to Frosteg several hundred blank checks signed by Columbian and drawn on five banks (including Farmers Bank of Pelham, but not including Bank of Camilla) located in rural southwest Georgia. Frosteg usually left the blank checks at Columbian's office in Pelham, Georgia, and hired two of Columbian's employees, Mrs. Charlene Lawhorne and Mrs. Sue Strickland, to work during their off-duty hours computing the totals of each day's purchases and writing on each Columbian check the appropriate amount and the name of the respective grower-payee. The checks would then be given to Frosteg or one of his other employees. Some of the named payees actually received their checks. In a number of other instances, to keep current the bank balances of Frosteg and Pelham Peanut Company, Frosteg forged the signatures of the payees and then deposited the checks usually to the credit of Pelham Peanut Company. Frosteg would then issue to the grower a Pelham Peanut Company check in the same amount as the Columbian check. This fraudulent practice was long continued apparently without discovery, and certainly without complaint. During the preceding peanut season of 1969, Frosteg had so endorsed some 93 checks payable to various payees, totaling $139,291.99. The fraud was apparently not discovered until Pelham Peanut Company's checks began "bouncing" in the latter part of September, 1970. The growers named as payees in 37 of the Columbian checks, totaling $55,645.33, fraudulently endorsed by Frosteg and cashed by the Bank of Camilla, and the growers named in 2 of the checks, totaling $2,020.63, fraudulently endorsed by Frosteg and cashed by Farmers Bank of Pelham, were not paid by either Frosteg or his corporation. Shortly before his fraud was discovered, Frosteg borrowed $20,000.00 from Farmers Bank of Pelham and assigned as security commissions claimed to be due him. Columbian accepted the assignment.

Columbian had received the peanuts purchased, or peanuts of like quantity and quality, and Columbian ultimately paid the agreed purchase price to each of the unpaid growers. Columbian then brought this suit asserting a right to reimbursement. Frosteg and Pelham Peanut Company did not answer or defend, but unfortunately they are insolvent. Both Bank of Camilla and Farmers Bank of Pelham answered at length. Farmers Bank of Pelham also cross-claimed on Columbian's acceptance of Frosteg's assignment of his commissions.

The liability vel non of the banks for payment on the forged endorsements of Columbian's checks turns largely on an oral agreement of Columbian with each of the banks. Columbian never made any deposit with the Bank of Camilla. It did carry a deposit in the Farmers Bank of Pelham but the checks here involved were not to be charged against that deposit. Columbian's oral agreement with each bank and with other banks in that area was to the effect that the bank would pay its checks to growers for peanut purchases as presented; at the end of each banking day the bank would tally or total the checks and either mail or present them to Columbian's office in Pelham;

Columbian would then give the bank its check drawn on the First National Bank of Atlanta for the total amount of that day's checks; as compensation for the use of the bank's money and for its services, Columbian would pay to the bank a fee of 1/8 of 1% of the total amount of Columbian's checks so handled.

The case was tried to a jury. The district court reserved ruling on the Bank of Camilla's motion for directed verdict. The jury returned a verdict against the Bank of Camilla for $23,624.10, an admittedly inadequate amount if Columbian should have any recovery. The jury returned a verdict for $20,000.00 in favor of the Farmers Bank of Pelham on its cross-claim.

On post-trial motions, the district court held that Columbian is not entitled to recover against either bank. It entered judgment notwithstanding the verdict for the Bank of Camilla, and also granted the alternative motion of the Bank of Camilla for a new trial in the event the judgment n.o.v. should be set aside or reversed on appeal. The district court denied Columbian's motion for new trial as against Farmers Bank of Pelham and also denied Columbian's motion for a partial new trial against the Bank of Camilla. Columbian appeals from the judgments entered against it on the post-trial motions.

We hold that the district court erred in ruling as a matter of law that Columbian is not entitled to recover against the banks on its claims that they wrongfully paid Columbian's checks bearing forged endorsements, but that the district court did not err in denying Columbian's motion for new trial with respect to Farmers Bank of Pelham's cross-claim against Columbian.

I.

Columbian's Claims that the Banks Wrongfully Paid Columbian's Checks Bearing Forged Endorsements

A. *Responsibility as between Drawer of Check and Bank*

In its memorandum opinion on the post-trial motions, the district court said:

> "In considering the question here presented it is important to keep in mind that the relationship of bank and depositor did not exist in this case because Columbian never had an account at The Bank of Camilla. Therefore, the principle of law regarding the responsibility of a bank to its customers has no application here * * *."

Concededly the question is a difficult one, and no case has been found where the precise relationship existed as that between Columbian and the banks in this case. Nonetheless, we are persuaded that each bank's oral contract, based on agreed consideration to pay Columbian's checks as presented, placed upon the bank the same responsibilities and liabilities as if the checks had been paid from a general deposit of money by Columbian in the bank. In the latter case the law has been long established in Georgia that:

> "Where one deposits money in a bank on general deposit, the bank immediately becomes the debtor of the depositor for the money deposited, and undertakes, impliedly, to pay that money either to the depositor or to some person to whom he directs it paid; and, in order to discharge itself from this liability to the depositor, the bank must pay the money to the depositor, or as directed by him. The liability cannot be discharged in any other way. In the present case Burke, the depositor, drew a check in favor of Mrs. Knapp for a certain amount of money, and the bank did not pay the money to her or to her order, but paid the money to Knapp, upon a forged indorsement. How does the bank discharge its indebtedness to Burke? It has not paid the money to Burke, or to the person to whom he directed it to be paid, or to her order; and it is only in these ways that the bank can be discharged of its liability."

Atlanta Nat. Bank v. Burke, Ga.1888, 7 S.E. 738, 739. * * *

The Burke case is also in accord with the law generally prevailing in other states:

> "Ordinarily, as between the drawer of a check and the bank upon which it is drawn, the latter is bound at its peril to determine the genuineness of the indorsements upon which it is paid; it cannot, if the drawer is free from negligence or conduct warranting his estoppel, charge against the drawer's account a check payable to a named payee or his order and paid upon a forged indorsement."

10 Am.Jur.2d, Banks § 623, p. 587. See also 9 C.J.S., Banks & Banking § 356 c, p. 734, et seq.

* * *

Apart from questions of negligence or other conduct of the drawer operating to preclude him, these strict rules of responsibility of the bank apply despite the fact that the person who forged the endorsement was an agent or employee of the drawer. First National Bank v. Guaranty Life Ins. Co., Ga.App.1962, 164 S.E. 242; cases collected in Ann. 39 A.L.R.2d at 648.

The Uniform Commercial Code adopted by the Georgia Legislature, effective January 1, 1964, left applicable the general principles of law not particularly displaced, Georgia Code Ann. 109A–1–103.

Specifically, Georgia Code Ann. 109A–4–102(2) [See R 4–102(b)] provides that:

> "(2) The liability of a bank for action or nonaction with respect to any item handled by it for purposes of presentment, payment or collection is governed by the law of the place where the bank is located."

Section 109A–4–104 [R 4–104(a)(1), (5) and (9)] contains the following pertinent definitions:

"(g) 'Item' means any instrument for the payment of money even though it is not negotiable but does not include money."

"(a) 'Account' means any account with a bank and includes a checking, time, interest or savings account."

"(e) 'Customer' means any person having an account with a bank or for whom a bank has agreed to collect items and includes a bank carrying an account with another bank."

We think that Columbian was a "customer" of the bank within the foregoing definition for either of two reasons. (1) Columbian had an "account" with the bank, though the account was tallied daily. By statute (§ 109A–4–104(a) [R 4–104(a)(1)]) " 'account' *means any* account with a bank and *includes*" the usual accounts. [Emphasis added.] "Account" is not limited to the accounts specifically named. (2) The bank had agreed to collect "items" for Columbian. For a consideration the bank agreed to cash and collect Columbian's checks. Those checks were clearly "items" as defined in the Act (§ 109A–4–104(g) [R 4–104(a)(9)]).

True, the "customer" owes certain duties to discover and report unauthorized signatures or alterations as specifically provided by Georgia Code Ann. 109A–4–406 [R 4–406]. Columbian did not and does not ask that judgment be rendered by the court in its favor but simply that it be accorded a trial by jury. For that reason, it would be premature for us to discuss the duties of the customer further than to observe that Columbian is not barred by the one-year limitation prescribed by section 109A–4–406(4)(b) [R 4–406(f)]:

"(4) Without regard to care or lack of care of either the customer or the bank

* * *

"(b) a customer who does not within one year from the time the statement and items are made available to the customer (subsection (1)) discover and report any alteration on the back of the item or any unauthorized indorsement is precluded from asserting against the bank such alteration or unauthorized indorsement."

Thus Columbian falls within the strict letter of the Uniform Commercial Code as a "customer" of the bank.

Of more importance, the considerations of policy which impose a strict measure of responsibility upon a bank arising from the contract either of the drawer bank or of an intermediate bank would seem to apply also in favor of Columbian as the drawer of a check paid by a bank pursuant to a contract, even though the contract is not that of a general depositor. The bank's opportunity to determine whether an endorsement is genuine is usually better than the opportunity of the drawer of the check. The bank is also in better position to protect itself by insurance. Under usual commercial practices, such policy considerations place a strict responsibility upon a bank which contracts to cash a drawer's checks.

We conclude that the district court erred in ruling that "the principle of law regarding the responsibility of a bank to its customer has no application here."

Note

1. It has long been the rule that, unless the customer's negligence contributes to the loss, a bank cannot charge to the customer's account a check paid over a forged drawer's signature or a forged indorsement. That rule is so firmly fixed in American law that original Article 4 did not state it. Original 4–401 merely states "As against its customer, a bank may charge against his account any item which is otherwise properly payable even though the charge creates an overdraft." The following sentence was added to revised 4–401(a): "An item is properly payable if it is authorized by the customer and is in accordance with any agreement between the customer and bank." That language clearly covers a forged drawer's signature, but does not so clearly cover a forged indorsement. Nevertheless, the rule certainly continues to be that, as between the bank and its customer, the bank takes the loss on forged indorsements unless the customer's negligence has contributed to the loss.

2. While many writers have criticized Article 4 for being unduly favorable to banks, it is not obvious that, as between the bank and its customer, the loss on forged indorsements should fall on the bank. The court in the Columbian case asserts as justification for the rule that (1) the bank has a better chance to discover the forged indorsement, and (2) in any event the bank can insure against the loss. As to the first justification, in many, probably most, cases the drawee bank does not take from the forger, but through the bank collection process and in fact has little chance to discover a forged indorsement. Perhaps the second justification is a sound one, but the bank customer could also insure. Of course, under the Code scheme, the person who dealt with the forger, if that person is solvent, will ultimately take the loss. (See the discussion at page 186). Often, however, that person will be the depositary bank. The total effect of the rules as to liability for forged indorsements commonly is, therefore, to put the loss on the banking system (and on all customers) rather than on the individual customer who draws a check that is subsequently transferred after a forged payee's indorsement. That policy is at least questionable. In England the rule as to bank liability for forged indorsements is different. There if the drawee bank pays in good faith and in the ordinary course of business the check is properly chargeable to the customer's account. See 4 Halsbury's Laws of England, 4th Ed. § 452 (1973).

3. On the particular facts of the Columbian case, where the forged indorsement was by an agent of the drawer, Revised 3–405 would probably impose the loss on Columbian. See the discussion at page 234ff.

4. The traditional rule has been that a bank is liable to its customer for paying a postdated check before its date. See e.g. *Siegel v. New England Merchants Nat. Bank,* 386 Mass. 672, 437 N.E.2d 218 (1982). That rule imposes substantial risk on banks under modern electronic processing

procedures since the date of the check is not magnetically encoded and drawee banks usually do not visually examine checks. Revised 4–401(c) requires a customer to notify the bank if a postdated check has been drawn.

ISAAC v. AMERICAN HERITAGE BANK & TRUST CO.

Colorado Supreme Court, 1984.
675 P.2d 742.

DUBOFSKY, JUSTICE.

We granted certiorari to review the judgment of the Court of Appeals in *American Heritage Bank and Trust Co. v. Isaac,* 636 P.2d 1296 (Colo.App.1981), which held that a bank customer may not recover for his bank's improper payment of a draft unless the customer proves that the bank's action caused his loss. We affirm the judgment of the Court of Appeals.

James B. Isaac (Isaac), defendant-petitioner, and Mikle Sadler (Sadler) formed a partnership, Cash Cattle Co., to buy and sell cattle. On June 30, 1977, the partners executed a $102,000 note payable to American Heritage Bank and Trust Company (Bank), plaintiff-respondent. The proceeds of the note were credited to the partnership account in the Bank and were to be used to purchase cattle. The partners also signed an authorization which permitted the Bank "to accept and pay checks or drafts drawn upon any or all bank accounts * * * *standing in the name* of said copartnership * * *." (Emphasis added.) The partnership name used in the authorization was "Cash Cattle Co.," and the authorization was to remain in effect unless amended in writing by both partners.

Sadler was the managing partner. He authorized all the transactions of the partnership in buying and selling cattle. Drafts drawn on the partnership and payable through the Bank were used to purchase the cattle. Whenever a draft was delivered to the Bank for payment, the Bank would telephone Sadler and receive his express approval before paying the draft. Isaac was the non-operating partner. He received the monthly bank statements, and the Bank relied on his financial statement when it made the loan to the partnership.

In January 1978, Sadler, his wife and another person had Articles of Incorporation filed with the Secretary of State of Texas for a corporation named "Cash Cattle Company." There is no evidence that this corporation ever functioned. Shortly after these Articles were filed, the Bank was presented over several days with four drafts drawn on "Cash Cattle Company, Inc." in the total amount of $85,430.30. In accordance with its usual practice, the Bank contacted Sadler, and he approved the payment of these drafts from the Cash Cattle Co. partnership account. It is unclear whether the Bank advised Sadler of the "Inc." reference or merely told him the amount of the drafts and to whom they were to be paid. In March, 1978, the partners executed another note to the Bank in the amount of $59,501.06.

On June 9, 1978, the Bank brought suit on the promissory notes, which were in default. Isaac claimed in defense that the Bank had caused him loss in the amount of the four drafts drawn on Cash Cattle Company, Inc., but paid from the Cash Cattle Co. partnership account. He asserted that the partnership records revealed that 180 cattle, worth approximately $90,000, were unaccounted for, and that the payment of the "Inc." drafts caused this loss. Isaac also made various cross-claims against Sadler for mismanagement and fraud. The Bank argued that the partnership suffered no loss from the payment of the "Inc." drafts because the cattle purchased with the "Inc." drafts were invoiced on the partnership records.

Sadler defaulted at trial. The district court entered judgment against Sadler and Isaac in the amount of $103,195.07, representing unpaid principal and interest on the notes, and $6,600 stipulated attorney fees. In addition, the court ruled that the bank improperly charged against the partnership account the drafts drawn on Cash Cattle Company, Inc., because payment was made without the consent and authority of Isaac. Therefore, the court allowed Isaac a set-off of $85,430.30. In the district court's opinion, Sadler used the money for his own purposes. The court also held that Isaac did not prove his cross-claims against Sadler.

The Court of Appeals agreed that the Bank failed to exercise ordinary care in debiting the drafts drawn on Cash Cattle Company, Inc. However, the Court of appeals reversed Isaac's set-off because there was insufficient evidence in the record to establish that the payment of the "Inc." drafts proximately caused Isaac's loss.

On certiorari review, Isaac argues that the Court of Appeals improperly substituted itself as a finder of fact; that the Bank is liable for improperly paying the "Inc." drafts under both negligence and contract principles; that when a bank charges an item not properly payable against an account, the customer is entitled to have the account recredited without a showing of proximate cause; and that the Court of Appeals erred in affirming the district court's award of attorney fees. We disagree and hold that Isaac failed to carry his ultimate burden of proving that he suffered a loss as a result of the Bank's improper actions. Therefore, we affirm the judgment of the Court of Appeals.

I

The issue before us is how liability is established when a bank charges against a customer's account an item that is not properly payable.[1] The majority opinion of the Court of Appeals emphasizes

1. Both the district court and the Court of Appeals ruled that the Bank did not exercise ordinary care when it charged the drafts drawn on Cash Cattle Company, Inc. against the partnership account of Cash Cattle Co. We think the question of ordinary care is a close one, but because the Bank did not file a cross-petition for certio-

commonlaw negligence principles. We think the better approach is through the Uniform Commercial Code (U.C.C.), codified in Colorado at sections 4–1–101, et seq., C.R.S. and 1982 Supp. Article 4 of the Code governs bank deposits and collections and provides the framework for analysis.

The U.C.C. does not state specifically the customer's remedy for his bank's improper payment of a draft, but the customer's right to demand that the bank recredit his account may be implied [sic] from section 4–4–401(1) [R 4–401(a)], C.R.S., which provides:

> As against its customer, a bank may charge against his account any item which is otherwise properly payable from that account. * * *

The negative implication that a bank may not charge against an account an item that is not properly payable is clear. In such a case the customer may demand that his account be recredited. In most cases a customer demand is all that should be necessary. The question thus raised is whether a customer has an absolute right to recrediting, or whether the bank may assert defenses. The facts of this case demonstrate that a bank should not be required to automatically recredit its customer's account in all circumstances.

The district court and the Court of Appeals held that the Bank's improper payment of the "Inc." drafts was a failure to exercise due care. Section 4–4–103(5) [R 4–103(e)], C.R.S., establishes the amount a customer may recover when a bank improperly handles an item:

> The measure of damages for failure to exercise ordinary care in handling an item is the amount of the item reduced by an amount which could not have been realized by the use of ordinary care. * * *

Comment 6 to section 4–4–103 [R 4–103] provides additional guidance:

> Of course, it continues to be necessary under subsection (5) [(e)] as it has been under ordinary common law principles that, before the damage rule of the subsection becomes operative, liability of the bank and some loss to the customer or owner must be established.

This language indicates that the customer must establish that he suffered a loss resulting from the bank's action. We agree.

One of the basic principles of law is that a party may not recover damages if he has not suffered an injury. "To warrant the recovery of damages, there must be both a right of action for a wrong inflicted by the defendant and damage resulting to the plaintiff therefrom. Wrong without damage, or damage without wrong, does not constitute a cause of action." 22 Am.Jur.2d Damages § 2 (1965). It is fundamental that the claimant must also establish that the loss was caused by the party

rari on this issue, we assume for purposes of this opinion that the draft was not properly payable.

being sued. "[B]efore damages can be awarded to a claimant he must establish that the damages he seeks are traceable to and are the direct result of the wrong sought to be redressed." *Runiks v. Peterson,* 155 Colo. 44, 45, 392 P.2d 590, 590 (1964).

We note, however, that the Supreme Court of Ohio, in *Cincinnati Insurance Co. v. First National Bank of Akron,* 63 Ohio St.2d 220, 407 N.E.2d 519 (1980), held that U.C.C. § 4–103(5) [R 4–103(e)] does not apply to situations where a bank charges an item not properly payable. *Cincinnati Insurance* involved the payment of checks lacking necessary endorsements. The court said: "The trial court's * * * reliance on [U.C.C. § 4–103(5) [R 4–103(e)]] was misplaced. That section's specific reference to 'ordinary care' manifests an intent that it relate only to a negligence-type action and not one based on the duty imposed upon the bank under [U.C.C. § 4–401 [R 4–401]] to only pay 'properly payable' items of its customer." 407 N.E.2d at 523. It is unclear what the court meant by a "negligence-type action." [3] We believe that bank payment of an item not properly payable may be characterized as negligence because a contract may be breached by a failure to exercise ordinary care. See *Cosmopolitan Homes, Inc. v. Weller,* 663 P.2d 1041 (Colo. 1983); W. Prosser, *The Law of Torts* § 92 at 616–18 (4th ed. 1971).

Relying on *Cincinnati Insurance,* Isaac asserts that by improperly paying an item a bank breaches its contract with its customer and, therefore, the bank must recredit the customer's account without regard to whether the customer has suffered a loss. While it is true that an improper payment is a breach of contract, the asserted remedy of recrediting an account is not required by contract principles. In order to recover more than nominal damages for breach of contract a plaintiff must prove that he suffered a loss resulting from the defendant's actions. See J. Calamari & J. Perillo, *Contracts* § 14–4 (2d ed. 1977).

In *Ford Motor Credit Co. v. United States Automobile Ass'n,* 11 U.C.C. Rep.Serv. 361 (N.Y.Civ.Ct.1972), a case cited approvingly by the Ohio Supreme Court in *Cincinnati Insurance,* the court held: "It is axiomatic in banking relations that a bank may pay a check and debit its customer's account only as directed by the customer. Failure to pay as directed renders the bank *strictly liable for any loss sustained.*" *Id.* at 363 (citations omitted) (emphasis supplied). Strict liability in this context does not excuse the customer from establishing a causal loss; instead, the bank's liability may be established without proving fault of the bank. See generally W. Prosser, Torts § 75 (1971). We conclude that a bank customer must establish loss resulting from the bank's action before he is entitled to have his account recredited.

3. In *G & R Corp. v. American Security & Trust Co.,* 523 F.2d 1164, 1170–71 (D.C.Cir.1975), the United States Court of Appeals for the District of Columbia described the U.C.C. as incorporating traditional tort principles into common law contract actions.

While a customer must show loss in the context of an action such as the one before us, this is not a substantial burden. The U.C.C. implicitly forbids a bank's charging of an item not properly payable against its customer's account. Normally, the customer need only demand that the bank recredit his account.[4] Similarly, a customer establishes his loss for purposes of a prima facie case merely by showing that the improper payment was charged to his account.

If, however, the customer suffered no loss as a result of the bank's improper payment, he would be unjustly enriched by recovering the amount of the item from the bank. Therefore, the bank may come forward with evidence establishing that the customer did not suffer a loss. The bank has the burden of going forward at this point. Once a bank produces such evidence, the ultimate burden of proof of loss is on the customer. This is in keeping with the general principles discussed above that an injured party must prove his injury. Additionally, the customer is in the best position to establish his loss, and should bear the burden. This result is analogous to the U.C.C. requirement that a customer bear the burden of "establishing the fact and amount of loss resulting from the payment of an item contrary to a binding stop payment order." Section 4–4–403(3) [R 4–403(c)], C.R.S. 1973. *Cf., Siegel v. New England Merchants Nat. Bank,* 386 Mass. 672, 437 N.E.2d 218 (1982).

The rule we adopt here is similar to the rule adopted by other courts in cases where a bank has paid an item over the valid stop payment order of its customer. In *Thomas v. Marine Midland Tinkers National Bank,* 86 Misc.2d 284, 381 N.Y.S.2d 797 (N.Y.Civ.Ct.1976), the court rejected defendant bank's argument that plaintiff had failed to prove the prima facie case since no evidence was introduced to negate the ultimate right of the payee to the proceeds of the stopped check. The court held: "[I]f the bank fails to meet its burden with legally sufficient proof of non loss, the customer has proven a prima facie case and is entitled to judgment. Where the burden of going forward is met by the bank, the customer must sustain the ultimate burden of proof on the issue of loss."

In *Cooper v. Stock Yards Bank of Oklahoma City,* 644 P.2d 123 (Okl.App.1981), a bookkeeper, without proper authorization, signed checks on the company account to pay company creditors. The owner of the company, the customer of the bank, brought suit to recover the amount of all the checks signed by the bookkeeper. The Oklahoma court denied recovery, holding that the customer had failed to prove that he was damaged by the wrongful payment of the checks. "It is elementary that a party may not recover for a breach of duty unless he also proves he was damaged by the breach," *Id.* at 125. The court emphasized that the bank had offered uncontroverted evidence that all

4. In the case before us, Isaac made no complaint about improper payment and did not request recrediting of the partnership account until he filed his answer and counterclaims to the Bank's action on the unpaid notes on September 11, 1978.

checks signed by the bookkeeper went to pay legitimate debts of the company.

We now turn to whether Isaac, as representative of Cash Cattle Co. partnership, carried the burden of proving that the partnership suffered a loss as a result of the Bank's improper payment. Because the partnership, not Isaac, was the Bank's customer, a loss to the partnership must be shown. Isaac established a prima facie case by showing that the Bank charged the "Inc." drafts against the partnership account. Additionally, Isaac presented evidence that Sadler filed Articles of Incorporation in Texas for a corporation named "Cash Cattle Company" shortly before the "Inc." drafts were presented to the bank. The partnership records indicate that the partnership purchased 180 more cattle, worth approximately $90,000, than it sold. Isaac argues that the discrepancy was caused by the payment of the "Inc." drafts in the amount of $85,430.30.

The record further indicates that the Bank met its burden of coming forward with evidence establishing that its actions did not cause a loss to the customer. The Bank pointed out that the four "Inc." drafts list the particular cattle that were purchased by the drafts. The drafts correspond exactly with invoices in the partnership records for purchases of cattle from the payee of the four drafts. These invoices were used by Sadler to approve the payment of drafts by the Bank. It is instructive to note that the four "Inc." drafts purchased 321 cattle, while Isaac claims the loss of 180 cattle. When questioned whether he knew what happened to the 180 cattle, Isaac responded that he did not. Our review of the record establishes that the partnership did not carry its burden of proving that the Bank's improper payment resulted in a loss to the partnership.

The district court, however, found that Sadler used the money from the drafts for his own purposes, an implication that the partnership suffered a loss. The only evidence which might indicate that Sadler used these funds for his own purposes is that Sadler filed Articles of Incorporation in Texas shortly before the drafts were paid, and that the partnership cannot account for 180 cattle. The inference presumably is that Sadler used the funds from the "Inc." drafts to purchase 180 cattle for his corporation, a corporation that was never shown to have operated.

Although the factual findings of a trial court are not to be disturbed upon appeal unless clearly erroneous and not supported by the record, *Gebhardt v. Gebhardt,* 198 Colo. 28, 30, 595 P.2d 1048, 1050 (1979), the district court's inferential finding here is clearly erroneous in light of the uncontroverted documentary evidence that the Bank paid the "Inc." drafts to the payee of the drafts for 321 cattle, a purchase clearly invoiced on the records of the partnership. Whatever happened to the 180 cattle, Isaac did not prove that their loss was caused by the Bank's action of paying the "Inc." drafts.[5]

5. In this case the Bank might also have avoided liability by relying on section 4–4–407 [R 4–407] * * *. If the payee on the four disputed drafts actually sent cattle

The Court of Appeals held that the evidence did not establish that the Bank's action was the proximate cause of the partnership's loss. We hold that in this context a customer need only show that the bank's action was a cause of loss. Section 4–4–103(5) [R 4–103(e)]. * * *

The judgment is affirmed.

KIRSHBAUM, J., does not participate.

Notes

(1) How does the *Isaac* court characterize the customer's action? Is payment of an item not properly payable a tort or breach of contract? Could it be both?

(2) Section OR 4–103(5) [R 4–103(e)], cited in *Isaac*, establishes the measure of damages when a bank fails to exercise ordinary care with regard to an item. The comment accompanying the section explains that the subsection "sets forth the rule for determining the measure of damages which, under subsection (1), cannot be limited by agreement." OR 4–103, comment 6. Subsection (1) refers to agreements used by a bank to attempt to limit "responsibility for its own lack of good faith or failure to exercise ordinary care." The deposit account agreement would cover those issues with regard to which banks might try to limit liability, such as payment of an item not properly payable or collection of items deposited. The *Isaac* opinion quotes a portion of comment 6 to the effect that "some loss to the customer * * * must be established" before damages are recoverable. But that language may not modify all of subsection OR 4–103(5) or R 4–103(e) as the court suggests. Indeed, the damage "limitation" described in the comment applies to situations in which "it is established that some part or all of the item could not have been collected even by the use of ordinary care."

C. WRONGFUL DISHONOR

NORTHSHORE BANK v. PALMER

Texas Court of Civil Appeals, 1975.
525 S.W.2d 718.

BROWN, J. James T. Palmer (Palmer or appellee) brought suit against Northshore Bank (Bank or appellant) for the wrongful dishonor of several checks. Trial was to a jury which answered special issues paraphrased as follows: (1) That someone other than Palmer endorsed his name on a $275 check; (2) That thereafter, Bank intentionally refused payment of checks written by Palmer; (3) That the bank attempted to collect an overdraft resulting from the chargeback against

to the partnership under these drafts, the Bank would be subrogated to its rights against the partnership.

The Bank's right to subrogation is not an exclusive remedy. Comment 5 to 4–4–407 provides in part: "The spelling out of the affirmative rights of the bank in this section does not destroy other existing rights (Section 1–103)."

the account of the $275 check and insufficient check fund charges resulting from its dishonor of Palmer's checks after it knew or should have known that the endorsement was a forgery; (4) That Palmer had suffered actual damages of $2,000; (5) That Palmer was entitled to punitive damages of $3,500; and (6) That the dishonor of the checks was not a result of a mistake. A Tex.R.Civ.P. 301 motion for judgment notwithstanding the verdict or in the alternative to disregard the answer to special issues four and five was filed by the Bank. The trial court overruled this motion and entered judgment for Palmer for $5,500.

Liability for the wrongful dishonor of an item is governed by Tex.Bus. & Com.Code § 4.402 [See R 4–402(b)] (UCC 1968) which provides:

> "A payor bank is liable to its customer for damages proximately caused by the wrongful dishonor of an item. When the dishonor occurs through mistake liability is limited to actual damages proved. If so proximately caused and proved damages may include damages for an arrest or prosecution of the customer or other consequential damages. Whether any consequential damages are proximately caused by the wrongful dishonor is a question of fact to be determined in each case."

Appellant attacks the submission and answers to the special issues on damages. Its attack on the actual damages contends that the trial court erred in overruling its Rule 301 motion. The answer to special issue number four is attacked on a factual sufficiency basis as well. In connection with this issue the jury was instructed as follows:

> "In connection with this issue you are instructed that you may take into consideration for finding actual damages the sum of money, if any, not repaid to James T. Palmer by Northshore Bank after Northshore Bank charged the check, payable in the amount of $275.00, dated October 18, 1971, marked as Pltf's. Ex. 1 against his account, the damage to the credit and reputation of James T. Palmer, if any, mental anguish suffered by James T. Palmer, if any, the time lost by James T. Palmer from his employment and schooling, if any, on the occasion or occasions in question."

Appellant did not object to the instruction. Tex.R.Civ.P. 274. The gist of its argument with regard to the 301 motion is that the "actual damages" were established conclusively as to two of the elements: (1) the sum of money not repaid to Palmer after the charge-back and (2) the loss of time from employment and schooling. The Bank claims there was no evidence as to mental anguish or damage to credit and reputation. Given the lack of objection to the instruction in this case, loss of credit and mental anguish were properly considered here as "consequential" damages.

There was testimony by Palmer that he had lost approximately one week of time from school and work. At the time the Bank dishonored the checks, Palmer was in the process of becoming certified as a pipe welder. There was oral and documentary evidence as to the approximate salary he was making at that time. There was also testimony by an officer of the bank as well as bank records to show that in addition to the charge-back of the $275 forged instrument, Palmer was charged $15 for checks drawn on insufficient funds. This was supplemented by evidence of humiliation, embarrassment and of having been turned down for credit for the first time in his life. Given this evidence, the trial court did not err in overruling the Rule 301 motion. Further, after reviewing the entire record under appropriate standards, we believe that there was factually sufficient evidence to support the jury's finding on actual damages.

Appellant cites State Nat. Bank of Iowa Park, Tex. v. Rogers, 89 S.W.2d 825 (Tex.Civ.App.—Fort Worth 1935, no writ), as authority for the proposition that a depositor may not recover exemplary damages for wrongful dishonor. This case was decided before the enactment of § 4.402 [R 4–402(b)], supra, and is not applicable. The authors of the code did not attempt to specify whether the bank's liability sounds in contract or tort. See Comment 2 to § 4.402, supra. We think that the liability is "statutory" and more in the nature of tort than contract. The jury did not find that the dishonors were the result of a "mistake" which would have limited appellee to recovery of his *actual* damages only. In the instant case, unlike State Nat. Bank of Iowa Park, Tex. v. Rogers, supra, actual damages were established. Gustason v. Northeast National Bank, 486 S.W.2d 596 (Tex.Civ.App.—Fort Worth 1972, no writ), seems to be the only Texas case decided since the Legislature enacted § 4.402 [R 4–402(b)], supra. Although mental anguish and exemplary damages were not involved in the case, the court by way of dicta cited 8 Tex.Jur.2d Banks § 261 to the effect that:

> "[d]amages may be recovered for loss of time, money, and credit, provided a foundation for such recovery is laid by the pleadings, but not otherwise. But exemplary damages based on malice or damages for mental suffering are not recoverable."

In addition to this statement being dicta, the case is distinguishable on at least two grounds. First, the court did not consider the full impact of § 4.402 [R 4–402(b)] since the court merely sustained an attack on a summary judgment in favor of the bank and the allowable elements of damages were not before it. Second, all of appellant's attacks here are based upon claimed evidentiary deficiencies and not upon any improper elements being submitted to the jury. No objections to the issues were made on the basis that the issues submitted elements of damages which were not recoverable under the statute. The jury found, and appellant does not attack the finding, that the acts of dishonoring the checks were done intentionally. While there was no issue regarding a lack of good faith, appellant did not object to the lack of submission of such an issue. Tex.R.Civ.P. 274. The jury was instructed with regard to exemplary damages as follows:

> "In connection with this issue you are instructed that punitive damages may be recovered only where there has been oppressive conduct or a reckless or malicious disregard of the rights of another. Punitive damages are intended as a warning and an example to prevent the defendant and others from the commission of like offenses and wrongs. In a legal sense an unlawful act done willfully and purposely is, as against that person, malicious."

The issue of malice or reckless disregard of Palmer's rights, if supported in the evidence, must be deemed found in his favor. Tex.R.Civ.P. 279.

A forger had secured a number of printed checks of one Marvel Fikes and proceeded to include Palmer as one of his victims. A person showed up at the Bank seeking to cash the $275 check payable to Palmer. The teller ascertained that Palmer had an account with the Bank and paid out the money. She could not testify as to whether this person was or was not Palmer. Some four or five days later, the check was returned by the bank on which it was drawn because the signature was not like the signature of Fikes which it had on file. The checks written by Palmer, which are in question here, had already been paid by the Bank, when the situation with respect to the forgery became known to it. The officer in charge immediately charged Palmer's account with the forged check despite his protestations that his endorsement was a forgery. When he went to see the Bank officer to deny endorsement and receipt of the proceeds of the forged check, the officer called over a uniformed guard. Even though the checks had been cleared for payment and were covered by sufficient funds when presented, the Bank recalled them and returned them marked "paid in error" or "account closed." Palmer immediately reported the forgery to the police, contacted the bank on which the forged Fikes check was drawn, and contacted Mr. and Mrs. Fikes. He then underwent the embarrassment of calling on each of the payees of the dishonored checks. The Bank never relented. They charged appellee $5 for each check they considered drawn on "insufficient funds". Additionally, after all of the claims of Palmer were known to the Bank officer having charge of the matter, the Bank placed the claimed balance due in the hands of a collection agency, where it rests today. The Bank never has paid Palmer the $275 which under the jury's findings is wrongfully charged to his account. Under the Bank's own evidence, each step it took was deliberate and intentional and done with a knowledge of Palmer's claim of right. The exemplary damages found by the jury are reasonably related to the amount of actual damages found and are fully justified under the evidence. We overrule appellant's points attacking special issue number five and the answer of the jury thereto.

The case is affirmed.

IN RE GERI ZAHN, INC.

United States Bankruptcy Court, Southern District of Florida, 1991.
135 B.R. 912.

A. JAY CRISTOL, BANKRUPTCY JUDGE. This cause came before the court on April 11, 1991 on remand from the United States District Court. The district court remanded the case for a determination and recommendation as to the damages awarded the Trustee (plaintiff) for the defendant's First American Bank & Trust Company (FABT) violation of Florida Statutes §§ 674.402 [R 4–402(b)] and 673.407 [R 3–407] and acts of common law fraud. The facts are as follows:

Barnett Bank loaned Just Clothes Corporation (Debtor) $150,000 consisting of a $100,000 promissory note and a $50,000 revolving line of credit. By offering lower rates, FABT persuaded the Zahns, the principals of the Debtor, to transfer these loans to FABT and, in turn, FABT would loan the Debtor $150,000.

On October 29, 1985, FABT sent a letter to the Zahns delineating the terms of the loan. The total amount of the loan was to be $150,000.00, with $100,000 to be applied as a capital loan to repay Barnett Bank and $50,000 to be used as a revolving line of credit and deposited in the Debtor's account with FABT. FABT proposed to hold as collateral for the loan a $25,000 C.D. in the name of Geri Zahn; a $50,000 C.D. in the name of Nathan Vlock; and a life insurance policy in the name of Jason Zahn, with a cash surrender value of $20,000.

The Zahns agreed to accept FABT's loan on the understanding that the funds from the revolving line of credit would be made available immediately. The Zahns explained they were going on a buying trip for the Debtor in December and needed the funds from the line of credit. Based on that understanding, the Zahns executed the loan papers on November 26, 1985.

Unbeknownst to the Zahns, however, FABT did not fund the line of credit on November 26, 1985. In fact, FABT would not fund the revolving line of credit until January 8, 1986.

* * *

Meanwhile, in December, 1985, the Zahns went to New York on a buying trip and purchased merchandise from several wholesale merchants. They paid with checks drawn on their FABT account. By January, 1986, FABT had dishonored a series of those checks totalling over $50,000.

Approximately one year later, the Debtors filed a petition for relief under Chapter 11 of the Bankruptcy Code. In October, 1988, the case was converted to Chapter 7 and the plaintiff subsequently commenced this adversary proceeding. Plaintiff's complaint against FABT alleged common law fraud, wrongful dishonor of checks, and interference with an advantageous business relationship.

On July 13, 1989, this court entered Findings of Fact and Conclusions of Law as follows:

"1. FABT engaged in common law fraud by intentionally misrepresenting the terms of the loan to the Debtor, thereby persuading the Debtor to transfer its loans from Barnett Bank;

* * *

"3. FABT wrongfully dishonored the Debtor's checks, in violation of Florida Statutes § 674.4–402 [R 4–402(b)], ruining the Debtor's business reputation and forcing the Debtor into bankruptcy; and

"4. FABT owed damages in the amount of $349,000."

On July 21, 1989, FABT appealed to the United States District Court. On April 16, 1990, Federal Deposit Insurance Corporation (defendant), as receiver for FABT, was substituted as defendant.

On December 14, 1990, the district court entered an order and memorandum opinion adopting this court's findings, but remanded the case for further findings on the amount of damages owed plaintiff, both compensatory and punitive.

Conclusions of Law

Under Florida law, a "payor bank is liable to its customer for damages proximately caused by the wrongful dishonor of an item." Fla.Stat. § 674.4–402 [R 4–402(b)]. Defendant contends that it is not liable to the Debtor because FABT dishonored only 12 checks, of which a maximum of 5 were payable to the sellers of merchandise in New York. Accordingly, defendant argues FABT's wrongful dishonor was not the proximate cause of the Debtor's bankruptcy. However, this court does not find "proximate cause" to be the issue here on remand inasmuch as the July 13, 1989 Findings of Facts and Conclusions of Law found that FABT's wrongful dishonor was the proximate cause of the Debtor's bankruptcy and the district court adopted this finding. Moreover, in its remand order, the district court agreed that FABT was responsible for the damages the Debtor incurred when it wrongfully refused to honor the checks presented.

The issue the district court remanded is the exact amount of damages owed plaintiff given FABT's wrongful dishonor which caused the Debtor's bankruptcy.[1] The plaintiff requests this court calculate

1. Arguably, the plaintiff need not even show proximate cause to receive substantial damages. Elizarraras v. Bank of El Paso, 631 F.2d 366 (5th Cir.1980). In Elizarraras, the Fifth Circuit held that where the wrongful dishonor is intentional, as in the instant case, the common law trader rule applies. Id. at 377. Under the trader rule, a plaintiff can recover substantial damages due to a loss of credit on a showing of "business size, past income, prospects, and need and past use of credit." Id. See also White & Summers, Uniform Commercial Code 892 (3d ed. 1988). Nevertheless, other courts believe that the U.C.C. rejects the trader rule, even in the case of mistake. See, e.g., Raymer v. Bay State National Bank 384 Mass. 310, 424 N.E.2d 515 (1981). These courts cite Comment 3 to U.C.C. § 4–402. However, because we believe that plaintiff proved that FABT's wrongful dishonor was the proximate

damages by adding up the value of the Debtor's assets at the time of the filing of Debtor's Chapter 11 petition. * * *

One court has upheld the plaintiff's formula for damages. In Murdaugh Volkswagen v. First Nat'l Bank of South Carolina, 801 F.2d 719 (4th Cir.1986), a bank's wrongful dishonor of checks forced a car dealership into bankruptcy. The lower court measured damages by adding up the value of the dealership's assets at the time it filed bankruptcy. The United States Court of Appeals for the Fourth Circuit upheld this formula for damages on the grounds that it was "not unreasonable." Murdaugh Volkswagen, 801 F.2d at 727, n. 8. * * *

A more accurate formula for damages would compare the value of the Debtor before the wrongful dishonor of checks to the value of the Debtor after the wrongful dishonor of checks, which is effectively the value of the Debtor after bankruptcy. Stated as a formula: Damages = V1 (value of Debtor prior to the wrongful dishonor) minus V2 (value of Debtor after the wrongful dishonor).

Calculating V2 is a relatively simple matter. V2 is typically a negative value, equal to the amount of debt remaining following liquidation of the Debtor's assets. In a Chapter 7 case, creditors seize the Debtor's assets to satisfy the debts the Debtor owes them. Generally, however, the liquidated assets are insufficient to satisfy all of the debts. Therefore, because a corporation's debts are not discharged, all that remains of a corporation following a Chapter 7 is debt.

In the instant case, at the time of the Chapter 7, the Debtor had debts of approximately $308,308.00. The value of the liquidated assets was approximately $8,849.00. Therefore, the value of the Debtor following the Chapter 7 liquidation was ($299,459.00). The creditors owed this amount are likewise victims of the bank's wrongful conduct.

To calculate V1, the court must rely on financial statements, submitted as plaintiff's Exhibit J, which reveal the Debtor's assets, liabilities, and earnings as of April 30, 1985. Given the figures in the plaintiff's exhibit, the best, albeit imperfect, valuation formula for calculating V1 is the "sum of assets" technique. The formula under this technique is:

Value = Current Assets − Current Liabilities + Tangible Assets + Intangible Assets

This formula is based on the assumption that each of these elements can be individually valued and their sum represents the value of the enterprise. Smith, Corporate Valuation, A Business and Ethical Guide, 90 (1988).

As of April 30, 1985, Debtor's current assets were $296,435. Current liabilities were $144,276. Tangible assets of the Debtor, factoring in depreciation, were $20,590.

cause of the Debtor's bankruptcy, we do not address the issue of whether the trader rule applies.

The financial statements submitted by plaintiff make no mention of the value of Debtor's intangible assets. The court could estimate a value for intangible assets, but it has no expertise for so doing. Alternatively, the court could assign a value of 0 to the intangible assets of the Debtor since plaintiff, who has the burden of coming forward with evidence of damages, failed to provide figures for intangible assets. Assuming the value of intangible assets is 0, V1 = $296,435 − $144,276 + $20,590 + 0 = $172,749. Therefore, actual damages = $172,749 − ($299,459.00) = $472,208.00.

The second issue before the court is whether the Plaintiff is entitled to punitive damages. Many courts analyzing U.C.C. § 4–402 [R 4–402(b)], which Florida Statute § 674.4–402 [R 4–402(b)] codifies, have held that a plaintiff is entitled to punitive damages where the wrongful dishonor of checks is morally culpable, violative of public policy, or motivated by malice. Furthermore, the Florida Supreme Court, in First Interstate Development v. Ablanedo, 511 So.2d 536, 539 (1987), citing its prior opinion in Winn & Lovett Grocery Co. v. Archer, 126 Fla. 308, 171 So. 214 (1936), held that "punitive damages are appropriate for any tortious conduct accomplished through fraud." The rationale for the award of punitive damages is that the defendant acts "willfully * * * [and] with a wanton disregard of the rights of others." Ablanedo, 511 So.2d at 539.

In the instant case, FABT knowingly misrepresented terms of the loan to lure the Debtor to switch its banking from Barnett Bank. Furthermore, FABT knew that the Debtor needed access to the revolving line of credit to purchase merchandise on the buying trip to New York, yet failed to timely fund the line of credit and dishonored checks written by the Debtor. These actions are morally culpable, indicate a wanton disregard of the rights of the Debtor, and culminated in the Debtor's destruction. It is thus within the discretion of the court to award punitive damages in the instant case.

To determine the amount of punitive damages the court may award, plaintiff contends Florida Statute § 768.73(1)(a) should control. Florida Statute § 768.73 states that "in any civil action based on * * * misconduct in commercial transactions * * * punitive damages shall not exceed three times the amount of compensatory damages." However, § 768.73 only applies to causes of action arising after July 1, 1986. Fla.Stat. § 768.71(2). The cause of action in the instant case arose in December of 1985, when FABT wrongfully dishonored the Debtor's checks. Therefore, § 768.73(1)(a) does not apply to the instant case.

Prior to July 1, 1986, the rule in Florida was that the amount of punitive damages awarded should be based on the wrong committed by the defendant and "need not bear any reasonable relation to the compensatory damages awarded." Lassitter v. Internat'l Union of Operating Engineers, Local No. 675, 349 So.2d 622 (Fla.1976). The rationale was that punitive damages were designed to punish the defendant and to deter such future wrongdoing, and were thus unrelated to compensatory damages. Lassitter, 349 So.2d at 626. It appears then it is within the court's discretion to award punitive damages in an amount this court determines to be commensurate with FABT's wrongdoing.

Although the court believes it is within its discretion to award punitive damages in excess of an amount equal to three times the compensatory damages, the court feels a punitive damage award in the amount of $100,000 is sufficient.

Accordingly, it is Ordered that judgment is entered in favor of plaintiff against defendant in the total amount of $572,208.00. A final judgment will be entered in accordance with this order.

Note

In footnote one in the *Zahn* case, the court points out that some courts hold that original 4–402 preserves the trader rule if the dishonor is other than the result of mistake. Under the trader rule, applied by many courts prior to the adoption of the Code, a person in trade is presumed injured by a wrongful dishonor and can recover "moderate or temperate" damages without proof of harm. Revised 4–402, say the comments to that section, is reworded to avoid the possible implication that the trader rule continues. Compare OR with R 4–402.

AGOSTINO v. MONTICELLO GREENHOUSES, INC.

New York Court of Appeals, 1990.
166 A.D.2d 471, 560 N.Y.S.2d 690.

[First National Bank of Highland was one of the defendants. Plaintiff was president of Mid–Valley Garden Center, Inc., which maintained a checking account at defendant bank. Because of a dispute between plaintiff and defendant about whether Mid–Valley owed the bank reimbursement for certain attorney's fees, the bank dishonored a corporate check drawn by plaintiff even though there were sufficient funds in the account to pay the check. The payee of the check swore out a criminal complaint charging plaintiff with issuing a bad check. Plaintiff was arrested, arraigned and held for eight hours until he furnished $500 bail. The charges were later dismissed. Plaintiff claims that he is a customer of the bank and is entitled to recover damages for the injury he personally suffered as a result of the wrongful dishonor. The trial court dismissed his claim against the bank on the ground that he was not a customer under 4–402 [R 4–402(b)].]

MEMORANDUM BY THE COURT * * *

The plaintiff contends that he has standing in his individual capacity to maintain an action against the defendant First National Bank of Highland (hereinafter the bank) pursuant to UCC § 4–402, for wrongful dishonor of a check. He claims that he is qualified to bring the action because he was a "customer" within the meaning of that statute. We disagree. The record indicates that, at all material times, a corporation known as Mid-Valley Garden Center, Inc. (hereinafter Mid-Valley), of which the plaintiff was president, had a checking account with the bank. The check which the bank dishonored was drawn on that account. UCC § 4-402 [R 4-402(b)] provides that "[a] payor bank is liable to *its customer* for damages proximately caused by the wrongful dishonor of an item" (emphasis supplied). The term "customer" is defined in UCC § 4-104 [R 4-104(a)(5)] as "any person having an account with a bank or for whom a bank has agreed to collect items". While such authority as exists in this state is sparse and unclear * * * there are numerous decisions in other jurisdictions which construe UCC § 4-104 [R 4-104(a)(5)] and § 4-402 [R 4-402(b)] as precluding a corporate officer from bringing a wrongful dishonor suit in an individual capacity, where the corporation, not the corporate officer, is the "person having an account with [the] bank." Exceptions exist, permitting a corporate officer to maintain such an action, individually, when there is a "close intertwinement of [the corporate officer] and [the] company" or where "the bank treated [the officer] and the corporate depositor as one entity" 1 White and Summers, Uniform Commercial Code § 18-4, at 891-892). Since there is no evidence in the record that such conditions existed in the case before us, we conclude that the plaintiff lacks standing to maintain an action pursuant to UCC § 4-402 [R 4-402(b)].

However, we agree with the plaintiff that the court erred in failing to reinstate his negligence cause of action against the bank. At all material times, the bank held a mortgage on premises owned by Mid-Valley. As a result of fire damage to those premises in July 1980 an insurance carrier issued a settlement check of $39,000 payable to Mid-Valley, to the bank, and to the plaintiff's adjuster. A dispute arose between the bank and the plaintiff over the plaintiff's refusal to pay $2,000 in legal fees asserted against him by the bank's attorney. As a result, the bank placed a "hold" of $2,000 on Mid-Valley's account into which the settlement check had been deposited. Significantly, the plaintiff and the bank are at odds over whether the plaintiff, pending settlement of the dispute, consented to the "hold".

On December 12, 1980, before the fee dispute was settled, the plaintiff, in his corporate capacity, wrote a check to the defendant Monticello Greenhouses, Inc. (hereinafter Monticello), drawn on Mid-Valley's account. The bank processed the check on December 17, 1980, and returned it unpaid. * * *

The plaintiff has properly pleaded a cause of action sounding in negligence against the bank, asserting that it owed him a duty to take reasonable care not to cause him loss and injury by what he claims is improper repudiation of the corporate check. It would be incongruous to deny the plaintiff the right to bring a negligence action against the bank, considering that as a corporate officer he may be taken into custody and held criminally liable for allegedly issuing a bad check drawn on a corporate account while, at the same time, holding that he had no standing to bring a statutory cause of action to recover damages for wrongful dishonor under UCC § 4–402 [R 4–402(b)] because he is not a "customer" within the meaning of that provision. Moreover, the UCC does not, either in language, spirit, or intent, proscribe such a cause of action sounding in negligence. Indeed, the Code impliedly permits it by providing that the principles of law and equity "shall supplement its provisions" (UCC § 1–103).

The resolution of this cause of action cannot be determined summarily on this record. There are disputes of fact, including whether the plaintiff did or did not agree to the "hold" on the Mid–Valley account, and the extent to which the plaintiff was notified of the dishonor.

We have examined the parties' remaining contentions and find them to be without merit.

[The case was remanded to the trial court.]

Note

In *Parrett v. Platte Valley State Bank & Trust Co.*, 236 Neb. 139, 459 N.W.2d 371 (1990), Parrett was president of P & P Machinery. Parrett drew a corporate check payable to Nelson. The defendant bank dishonored the check even though the corporation had sufficient funds to pay it. Parrett was charged with felony theft in South Dakota and was extradited to South Dakota to stand trial. The trial commenced but, at trial, the charges were dismissed. Parrett then brought suit against Platte Valley for the damages he sustained. The trial court held that Parrett was not a customer of the bank and sustained a demurrer by the bank. On appeal, reversed.

> "* * * [W]e find that Parrett was a 'customer' of the bank within the meaning of § 4–402 [R 4–402(b)] and that Parrett's petition does state a cause of action for the banks' wrongful dishonor of the P & P Machinery check signed by Parrett. As reflected by Parrett's petition, the parties' business relationship, which included Parrett's personal guarantee for P & P Machinery's obligations to the bank, was such that it was foreseeable that dishonoring the corporation's check would reflect directly on Parrett. This is borne out by the fact that a criminal charge based on the dishonored check was brought against Parrett * * * Since the consequences of the dishonor fell upon Parrett, it would elevate form over substance to say that he was not the bank's 'customer' * * *. This is not to say that in every case a corporate officer has a wrongful dishonor action against the depositary action against the depository bank on which the corporation's check has been drawn and later dishonored * * *"

See the comment to R 4–402 for the position of revised Article 4 on whether a drawer of a corporate or partnership check is a "customer" with the right to bring a wrongful dishonor action.

D. THE "RIGHT" TO STOP PAYMENT

1. *Sufficiency of the Stop Payment Request*

CAPITAL BANK v. SCHULER

Florida Court of Appeals, 1982.
421 So.2d 633.

DANIEL S. PEARSON, JUDGE.

Mrs. Schuler drew check no. 102, payable to one Charles Mouyos in the amount of $700, on her checking account at Capital Bank. Believing that this check was lost, Schuler cashed another check in the amount of $750 and gave Mouyos $700 in cash. Unbeknownst to Schuler, Mouyos had deposited the $700 check in his account at another bank. The check, having run its course through normal banking channels, arrived at Capital Bank at a time when Schuler had insufficient funds in her account to cover it. Accordingly, the check was stamped "insufficient funds" and returned to the Federal Reserve Bank of Miami, the last endorser.

Eleven days later, Schuler placed a stop-payment order on the $700 check she had issued to Mouyos. On the stop-payment form provided by Capital, Schuler specified the correct account number, check number, and payee. She placed a question mark in the space provided for the date of the check. She wrote—incorrectly and, as will be seen, significantly—that the amount of the check as to which she sought to stop payment was $750.

About ten days after Schuler wrote the stop-payment order, check no. 102 was presented to Capital Bank for payment and, there then being sufficient funds in Schuler's account, paid by Capital. The next day, a Capital Bank clerk, while in the process of hand sorting checks for filing and return to the last endorser, noticed the stop-payment order for check no. 102 and, failing to notice that the check had been paid, stamped the check "Payment Stopped." Schuler's account was then erroneously credited $700 and the check forwarded to the Federal Reserve Bank.[1] Months later, due to an unexplained delay in the system, the Federal Reserve Bank returned check no. 102 to Capital. Capital Bank, recognizing that it paid the check, debited Schuler's account $700, reversing the erroneous credit. This debit created an overdraft in Schuler's account of $379.68. Capital sued to collect this debt. Schuler counterclaimed for the wrongful payment of a check over a stop-payment order, abuse of process, and gross negligence in breach of contract. The jury rejected the bank's claim and awarded Schuler damages of $15,320.32. Capital appeals from the judgment entered thereon.

1. The Bank is not accused of negligence resulting from the obviously futile act of its clerk stamping "Payment Stopped" on a check that has been paid and thereafter sending the check to the Federal Reserve Bank.

The Bank contends that it was entitled to a directed verdict on its claim and Schuler's counterclaim. It says that, as a matter of law, it could rightfully make payment despite the stop-payment order since the order failed to describe the check with certainty as required by [non-uniform] Section 674.403(1), Florida Statutes (1977), and was, therefore, neither valid nor binding.[3] Because we conclude that the Bank is correct in this contention and neither waived the protection afforded it by the statute nor was estopped by its conduct from relying on the statute, we do not reach the Bank's other grounds for reversal which go to the extent and nature of damages awarded Schuler.

I

Section 4–403 [See R 4–403(a)] of the Uniform Commercial Code (1978) provides:

> A customer may by order to his bank stop payment of any item payable for his account but the order must be received at such time and in such manner as to afford the bank a reasonable opportunity to act on it prior to any action by the bank with respect to the item. * * *

The code provision, unlike Section 674.403(1) [R 4–403(a)], Florida Statutes (1977), does not separately address how the check is to be described, that question being subsumed in the broader phrase that the stop-payment order must be made "in such manner as to afford the bank a reasonable opportunity to act on it."[4] A 1965 report of the Uniform Commercial Code Committee, *Report On Variations To Code In Adopting States,* Report # 2 of the Permanent Editorial Board for the U.C.C. (West 1965), indicates that the Code's framers intended to place no greater burden on the depositor in describing the check than that which is found in the Code. In its report the committee examined modifications to the Code made in California (requiring, as Florida, that

3. Section 674.403(1), Florida Statutes (1977), governing stop-payment orders, reads:

> (1) A customer, or any customer if there is more than one, or any person authorized to sign checks or make withdrawals on or from an account, may stop payment of any item payable, for or drawn against such customer's or customers' account *but the same shall not be effective and the bank may disregard the same unless the order* is in writing, is signed by such customer or authorized person, *describes with certainty the item on which payment is to be stopped, and is served upon and received by an officer of the bank* at the banking-house during regular banking hours and *in such time and in such manner as to afford the bank a reasonable opportunity to act on it* prior to the happening of any of the events described in § 674.303 [R 4–303], and in any event no bank shall be responsible or liable for failure to comply with any such order on the day the same is served upon or received by such bank unless such omission or failure to comply with the same on the day received resulted from the willful and intentional disregard of such order. (emphasis supplied [by court]).

4. Forty-four states and the Virgin Islands have adopted Section 4–403 [R 4–403] U.C.C. (1978) as written. In addition to Florida, four states (Arizona, California, Nevada and Texas) require that the check be described with "certainty." See, respectively, Ariz.Rev.Stat.Ann. § 44–2629 (1967); Cal.Com.Code § 4403 (West 1964); Nev.Rev.Stat. § 104.4403 (1979); Tex. Bus. & Com.Code Ann. § 4–403 (Vernon 1968). Utah and the District of Columbia require that the check be "specifically" described. Utah Code Ann. § 70A–4–403 (1980); D.C.Code Ann. § 28:4–403 Supp. VII 1980).

the check be described with "certainty") and the District of Columbia (requiring that the check be "specifically described") and rejected each version as going beyond the "fixed policy" represented by the Code provision. It is apparent, then, that the policy of the Code is not that the check be specifically described or described with certainty, but only that the description be such as to afford the bank "a reasonable opportunity to act on it." In this respect, the Code effected no significant change in the existing common law respecting stop-payment orders, under which the duty of the customer was to describe the item with "reasonable accuracy." See, e.g., Hawkland, *Stop Payment Orders Under the Uniform Commercial Code,* 3 U.C.C.L.J. 103 (1970). Thus it is that in states which have adopted the Code as written, common law cases construing "reasonable accuracy" may be looked to to determine whether under the Code provision the check was described "in such manner as to afford the bank a reasonable opportunity to act on it." See *Sherrill v. Frank Morris Pontiac–Buick–GMC, Inc.,* 366 So.2d 251 (Ala.1978).

But, as we have said, Florida has not adopted the Code provision as written. Instead, our legislature saw fit to require that the stop-payment order shall not be effective and may be disregarded unless it "describes with certainty the item on which payment is to be stopped." Fundamental rules of statutory construction require that where a statute materially changes the language of the uniform act upon which it is patterned, we must presume that the legislature intended the change to have meaning.

Certainty is defined as freedom from any doubt; a sure thing, belief in which is based on thorough examination of all evidence. *American Heritage Dictionary of the English Language* 220 (1979). Thus, the requirement of "certainty" found in Section 674.403(1) [R 4–403(a)] does not permit us to say "close enough" and judicially make "certainty" the equivalent of "reasonable accuracy" or judicially muddle the clear and unequivocal meaning of the word by adding the antecedent "reasonable." [5] We must instead conclude that our legislature in enacting Section 674.403(1) [R 4–403(a)] intended to place a greater burden on the depositor in describing the check in a stop-payment order than that which existed at common law and that which exists in the Uniform Commercial Code.[6] We must further conclude that the instant stop-

5. "Certain is often preceded by more or most or terms such as fairly and reasonably, even though by definition certain is seemingly absolute in most of its senses." American Heritage Dictionary 220 (1979). The rejection of the "certainty" requirement found in the like California statute, see Report On Variations To Code In Adopting States, *supra,* demonstrates the substantial nature of our legislative change.

6. This is not to suggest that Schuler's stop-payment order necessarily satisfied the less stringent "reasonable accuracy" test, or provided the bank with a "reasonable opportunity" to act on it. Compare *Elsie Rodriguez Fashions, Inc. v. Chase Manhattan Bank,* 23 U.C.C.Rep. 133 (N.Y.Sup.1978) (ten-cent difference between amount on stop-payment order and amount on check reasonably accurate); *Thomas v. Marine Midland Tinkers National Bank,* 86 Misc.2d 284, 381 N.Y.S.2d 797 (N.Y.Civ.Ct.1976) (single digit mistake in check number afforded bank reasonable opportunity to act); *Kentucky–Farmers*

payment order being in error as to the amount of the check failed to describe it with certainty and was neither effective nor binding. Cf. *Rimberg v. Union Trust Co. of the District of Columbia,* 12 U.C.C.R.S. 527 (D.C.Sup.Ct.1973) ($250 check described as $235 on stop-payment order was not specifically described as required by D.C. statute).

In arriving at these conclusions, we do not overlook the fact that Section 674.403(1) [R 4–403(a)] contains the code language that the order must be served upon and received by the bank "in such manner as to afford the bank a reasonable opportunity to act on it." By including both this language and the antecedent certainty requirement, the Florida Legislature has, in our view, determined that a bank cannot be deemed to have a reasonable opportunity to act on a stop-payment order unless the item is described with certainty. If the description of the item is uncertain, the opportunity afforded the bank to act is not reasonable.

But even if, arguendo, we were to read the "reasonable opportunity" clause of the statute as qualifying the "certainty" requirement, rather than the converse, we would still be compelled to conclude that under the circumstances of the present case the bank was not afforded a reasonable opportunity to act on the stop-payment order.

The undisputed evidence in the present case reveals that the computerized systems used by Florida banks require that the first bank to get a check write the amount of the check as the key feature of identification. When a customer stops payment, the computer is given the description of the check in terms of the amount. If the customer is mistaken as to the amount, the computer will not be able to effectuate the stop order. This process is designed to provide the most efficient service to the greatest number of customers at the least cost.

Thus, whether or not an uncertain description of the date, check number or name of payee would nonetheless afford the bank a reasonable opportunity to act on the order, it is undisputed that the amount of the check is critical, and an error in this regard will mean that the bank has no reasonable opportunity to act on the order.

Bank v. Staton, 314 Ky. 313, 235 S.W.2d 767 (1951) (correct date, number and name of payee, but wrong amount, reasonably accurate); *Shude v. American State Bank,* 263 Mich. 519, 248 N.W. 886 (1933) (incorrect date insignificant where bank erroneously placed hold on wrong account); *Levine v. Bank of United States,* 132 Misc. 130, 229 N.Y.S. 108 (N.Y.Mun.Ct.1928) (payee described as "Harold Orkand" reasonably accurate description of check payable to "H. Orkand") with *Sherill v. Frank Morris Pontiac–Buick–GMC, Inc., supra* (misstatement of date and first name of payee and omission of check number not reasonably accurate, although amount of check correct); *John H. Mahon Co. v. Huntington National Bank,* 62 Ohio App. 261, 23 N.E.2d 638 (1939) (jury finding that erroneous check number not reasonably accurate upheld); *A. Sidney Davison Coal Co. v. National Park Bank,* 201 A.D. 309, 194 N.Y.S. 220 (1922) ($15,000 as amount of draft on stop-payment order not reasonably accurate to describe $17,000 check); *Mitchell v. Security Bank,* 85 Misc. 360, 147 N.Y.S. 470 (Sup.Ct.App. Term 1914) (wrong date, payee, and amount, but proper check number, not reasonably accurate); *Western Union Telegraph Co. v. Louissell,* 11 Ala.App. 563, 66 So. 839 (1914), *cert. denied,* 191 Ala. 665, 67 So. 1019 (1915) (stop payment describing payee as "James F. Manison" not reasonably accurate description of draft payable to "James J. Manson").

> [T]he kind of information that is needed by the bank often will depend on its size, its technology, and the like and that therefore the resolution of specific fact situations under one set of circumstances may not be valid for another.

Hawkland, *supra,* at 117. Where, then, the bank has adopted a procedure for flagging checks pursuant to stop orders, the reasonableness of which is not challenged, that procedure is a factor, if not the controlling factor, in determining whether the bank was afforded a reasonable opportunity to act.

> To a certain extent, the validity of stop orders should depend on the procedures that the drawer uses to identify stopped checks and on the reasonableness of such procedures. An incorrect check number is no cause for complaint by a bank that examines checks solely by the name of the payee, but it would be to a bank that hunts for stopped checks principally by reference to check numbers.

J. White & R. Summers, *Uniform Commercial Code* § 17–5, at 680 (2d ed. 1980). If the amount of the check triggers the computer in flagging the check as having a stop-payment order outstanding, then whatever else may be uncertain, the amount must not be.

> [I]f the stop is entered into a computer the "manner" in which the depositor gives it [the stop order] must be precise. Thus, one would assume the depositor has to give at least the correct dollar amount, and perhaps also the correct check number, for the computer to do its thing.

Quinn's *Uniform Commercial Code Commentary and Digest,* 1982 Cum. Supp. # 1, 84–61 (1982).

> Where a customer has written many checks in the same amount the computer will retrieve all of these items if one is stopped, but at that point hand sorting is possible. If, on the other hand, the customer is mistaken as to the amount, this kind of hand sorting is not possible, and there is every reason to believe that his countermand is ineffective.

Hawkland, *supra,* at 118.

II

Our holding that Schuler's stop-payment order was, as a matter of law, ineffective does not end our inquiry. Schuler asserts that the bank was estopped to claim this ineffectiveness as a defense to her damage counterclaim. Since the statute requiring certainty of description is intended for the benefit of the bank, clearly the bank may be estopped to claim the statute's benefit.

The only act of the bank which arguably could have misled Schuler into believing that the amount stated in the stop-payment order did not have to be correct was the bank's acceptance of the order with a question mark in the blank provided for the date of the check. Were it the bank's position that lack of certainty as to the date of the check rendered the stop order ineffective, an argument that Schuler was misled by the bank's acceptance of the order into believing that the date of the check was inconsequential to the bank would be compelling. See, e.g., *Rimberg v. Union Trust Co. of the District of Columbia, supra* (where depositor informed bank teller that she was uncertain whether the amount of the check was $235 or $250 and teller told her to complete the stop order without informing depositor of the importance of the amount or suggesting that she prepare stop orders for each amount, court held that depositor was actively led to believe that stop order was effective regardless of the correctness of amount, and bank had waived statute's requirement that check be specifically described). But the argument that the bank's acceptance of the order misled Schuler into believing that the amount of the check was inconsequential requires that we attribute to the bank's action the singular meaning that no information on the stop order was important to it. The bank's action, however, was certainly equally susceptible of the meaning that only the date of the check was inconsequential to it. Since there is nothing in the bank's acceptance of the order or any other conduct which unquestionably and unambiguously points to the former meaning, the estoppel argument must fail.[7] *Enstrom v. Dunning, supra.* See *Jarrard v. Associates Discount Corp.*, 99 So.2d 272 (Fla.1957) (facts necessary to constitute an estoppel cannot be taken by argument or inference, nor supplied by intendment).

Accordingly, the judgment entered in favor of Schuler on her counterclaim is reversed with directions to enter judgment in favor of Capital Bank on both its claim and counterclaim.

Reversed with directions.

PARR v. SECURITY NAT'L BANK

Oklahoma Court of Appeals, 1984.
680 P.2d 648.

REYNOLDS, JUDGE.

We are called upon to decide whether Security National Bank had a reasonable opportunity to stop payment on a check when the description received was exact in all respects except for a single digit error in the check amount. This issue has not been decided by an Oklahoma court.

Parr wrote check number 949 to Champlin Oil. She dated and mailed it September 14, 1981. The amount of the check was $972.96. On September 15, 1981, Parr ordered payment stopped by telephone. Parr gave the bank her account number, the check number, the date, the payee and the amount of the check. A 50 cent error was made in

7. Indeed, the evidence reveals that had Schuler given the bank any inkling that she was unsure of the amount, she would have been advised to close her account, since the stop order would not have worked.

identifying the amount of the check. Parr went to the bank on September 16th or 17th and executed a written stop order dated September 14, 1981. The written stop order was also in error. Security National paid check number 949 on September 17, 1981.

Parr brought suit against Security National seeking recovery for the amount of the check, 12% interest on that amount, reasonable attorney's fees and costs. Security National defended by showing their computers were programmed to stop payment only if the reported amount of the check were correct. They argued Parr's 50 cent error relieved them of liability. Timeliness of notice was not at issue.

Section 4–403(1) [See R 4–403(a)] of the Uniform Commercial Code, 12A O.S. 1981 § 4–403(1), contains the applicable law on stop payment orders:

> A customer may by order to his bank stop payment of any item payable for his account but the order must be received at such time and in such manner as to afford the bank a reasonable opportunity to act on it prior to any action by the bank with respect to the item described in Section 4–303 [R 4–303].

It is appropriate to examine the purpose of this section before construing it.[1] The policy underlying § 4–403 is found in Comment 2 [R 4–403 comment 1] following the section:

> The position taken by this section is that stopping payment is a service which depositors expect and are entitled to receive from banks notwithstanding its difficulty, inconvenience and expense. The inevitable occasional losses through failure to stop should be borne by the banks as a cost of the business of banking.

Security National contends that whether a stop payment order has been received "in such manner as to afford the bank a reasonable opportunity to act" should be determined *after* examining how the defendant bank handles stop orders. This interpretation has found favor among highly respected legal authorities,[2] but not among the majority of courts that have addressed this issue.[3]

1. 12A O.S. 1981 § 1–102(1): "This Act shall be liberally construed and applied to promote its underlying purposes and policies." Comment 1 following § 1–102 states:

> The Act should be construed in accordance with its underlying purposes and policies. The text of each section should be read in the light of the purpose and policy of the rule or principle in question, as also of the Act as a whole, and the application of the language should be construed narrowly or broadly, as the case may be, in conformity with the purposes and policies involved.

2. White & Summers, *Handbook of the Law Under the Uniform Commercial Code* § 17–5, at 679–80 (2nd ed. 1980); Hawkland, *Stop Payment Orders Under the Uniform Commercial Code,* 3 UCC L.J. 103, 117–18 (1970); Roberts and Mann, *A Proposal for Regulating Banks' Use of Exculpatory Clauses in Stop Payment Orders,* 84 Com.L.J. 183, 187–188 (1979).

3. See e.g., *Sherrill v. Frank Morris Pontiac–Buick–GMC, Inc.,* 366 So.2d 251 (Ala.1979); *Delano v. Putnam Trust Co.,* 33 UCC Rep. 635 (Conn.Super.Ct.1981); *Pokras v. National Bank of North America,* 30 UCC Rep. 1089 (N.Y.App.Term.1981); *Elsie Rodriguez Fashions, Inc. v. Chase Manhattan Bank,* 23 UCC Rep. 133 (N.Y.Sup.Ct. 1978); *Thomas v. Marine Midland Tinkers Nat'l Bank,* 86 Misc.2d 284, 381 N.Y.S.2d 797 (N.Y.City Civ.Ct.1976); *FJS Electronics, Inc. v. Fidelity Bank,* 288 Pa.Super.

Both groups acknowledge § 4–403(1) [R 4–403(a)] has not changed the common law rule that a stop payment order must identify the check with "reasonable accuracy."[4] It is from this premise that courts have determined whether the description is reasonably accurate without consideration of the defendant/bank's computer program. In *Elsie Rodriguez Fashions, Inc. v. Chase Manhattan Bank,* 23 UCC Rep. 133 (N.Y.Sup.Ct.1978), the customer gave the bank the correct payee, check number and date but made a 10 cent error in the amount of the check. The court determined the check had been described with sufficient accuracy to allow the bank to stop payment. The opinion makes no mention of the bank's computer program. In accord with this approach on similar facts are the New York cases of *Pokras v. National Bank of North America,* 30 UCC Rep. 1089 (N.Y.App.Term.1981), and *Thomas v. Marine Midland Tinkers National Bank,* 86 Misc.2d 284, 381 N.Y.S.2d 797 (N.Y.City Civ.Ct.1976). A different result was reached by a New York court where the customer was told by the bank the stop order would not be effective unless she provided the exact amount of the check. *Poullier v. Noacua Motors, Inc.,* 108 Misc.2d 913, 439 N.Y.S.2d 85 (N.Y.Sup.1981). Security National does not contend they gave notice to Parr that any discrepancy in the check amount would prevent compliance with her stop payment order.

In *Delano v. Putnam Trust Co.,* 33 UCC Rep. 635 (Conn.Super.Ct.1981), a single digit error in the amount of $100.00 did not prevent recovery where customer supplied bank with the correct check number, date, payee, and account number of the check. The bank's computer program required an exact match of check amount before it would stop payment. Court held bank had received sufficient information to allow it a "reasonable opportunity to act" on the stop payment order. Court stated the bank had a duty to inform its customer of the need for precision in reporting the amount before it could rely on customer's error to relieve it of liability.

The Supreme Court of Alabama denied customer's recovery in *Sherill v. Frank Morris Pontiac–Buick–GMC, Inc.,* 366 So.2d 251 (Ala. 1979). Customer gave bank three descriptive elements of the check: check amount, payee and date. The check was not numbered. Two of the three pieces of information were incorrect. Court determined the check was not described with reasonable accuracy, therefore the bank was not afforded a "reasonable opportunity to act" on the stop payment order.

138, 431 A.2d 326 (1981). But see, *Midgen v. Chase Manhattan Bank, N.A.,* 32 UCC Rep. 937 (N.Y.Civ.Ct.1981) (finding for customer on grounds that bank was negligent in failing to program its computer to avoid payment where reported amount of check was in error by only ⅔ of one percent of actual check amount).

4. See notes 1 and 2, *supra.* See also *Capital Bank v. Schuler,* 421 So.2d 633, 635 (Fla.App.1982). This is not so in states like California and Florida whose legislatures added to § 4–403(1) [R 4–403(a)] the requirement that the item be described "with certainty." See Cal.Com.Code § 4–403(1) (West 1964); Fla.Stat. § 674.4–403(1) (1966); See also D.C.Code § 28:4–403(1) (1967).

In *FJS Electronics, Inc. v. Fidelity Bank,* 288 Pa.Super. 138, 431 A.2d 326 (1981), Court allowed customer to prevail even though its 50 cent error in check amount prevented bank's computer from acting on stop payment order. The bank asserted § 4–403 [R 4–403] "should be read to require compliance with the procedures of a particular bank, regardless of what they are and regardless of whether the customer has been made aware of them." *Id.* 431 A.2d at 328. Court determined that the drafter's policy stated in Comment 2 to § 4–403 [R 4–403 comment 1] precluded such an interpretation. They reasoned:

> Fidelity made a choice when it elected to employ a technique which searched for stopped checks by amount alone. It evidently found benefits to this technique which outweighed the risk that an item might be inaccurately described in a stop order. This is precisely the type of inevitable loss which was contemplated by the code drafters and addressed by the comment quoted above. The focus of § 4–403 is the service which may be expected by the *customer,* and a customer may expect a check to be stopped after the bank is given reasonable notice. A bank's decision to reduce operating costs by using a system which increases the risk that checks as to which there is an outstanding stop payment order will be paid invites liability when such items are paid.

We find this analysis, as well as that in *Delano, supra,* persuasive. We hold Parr described her check with reasonable accuracy, and Security National had a reasonable opportunity to act on the stop payment order.

We are aware of the burden this may place on Oklahoma banks. However, the industry has two alternatives to avoid liability if banking procedures necessitate an exact description of an item: (1) notify the customer at the time a stop order is given, or (2) seek a legislative amendment to § 4–403 [R 4–403].

We recognize Parr received the benefit of having her debt paid to Champlin Oil and will recover from Security National for failure to stop payment. To avoid this possibility of unjust enrichment, § 4–407(b) [R 4–407(2)] subrogates the payor bank [Security National] to the rights of the payee [Champlin] against the maker [Parr]. In such a suit, an award of attorney's fees and costs to Security National would be proper under 12 O.S. 1981 § 936, as Champlin would have been suing Parr on an open account if Security National had stopped payment on the check.

Trial court is REVERSED and this cause REMANDED for award of $972.96 plus reasonable attorney's fees and costs consistent with this opinion.

Reversed and remanded.

YOUNG, P.J., and ROBINSON, J. concur.

Note

1. Could a bank include language in its account agreement to effect the result achieved by the Florida version of OR 4–403? See the Roberts and Mann article cited in footnote 2 of the *Parr* decision, citing *Thomas v. First Nat'l Bank,* 376 Pa. 181, 101 A.2d 910 (1954); *Op. Att'y Gen. Utah,* 3 U.C.C.Rep.Serv. (Callaghan) 115 (1966).

Compare the version of U.C.C. § 4–103(1) in a 1951 draft of the Code:

> (1) Affected parties may by general or special agreement agree as to what constitutes proper handling or otherwise vary the effect of provisions of this Article except that no agreement can * * *
>
> (d) limit a bank's obligation on a written order to stop payment signed by the customer.

Uniform Commercial Code § 4–103 (Spring 1951, Proposed Final Draft No. 2) reprinted in 12 Uniform Commercial Code: Drafts 160–61 (E. Kelley ed. 1984), *and* comment 8 to current OR 4–403 (comment 7 to R 4–403),

> A payment in violation of an effective direction to stop payment is an improper payment, even though it is made by mistake or ignorance. Any agreement to the contrary is invalid under Section 4–103(1) if in paying the item over the stop payment order the bank has failed to exercise ordinary care.

with original 4–103(1) and revised 4–103(a).

> The effect of the provisions of this Article may be varied by agreement except that no agreement can disclaim a bank's responsibility for its own lack of good faith or failure to exercise ordinary care or can limit the measure of damages for such lack or failure; but the parties may by agreement determine the standards by which such responsibility is to be measured if such standards are not manifestly unreasonable.

In light of the foregoing, how would you advise a bank client regarding the enforceability of an account agreement that provided the following concerning stop payment orders?

Stop Payment Order

> If you write a check which has not yet cleared, any authorized signer on the account may be able to prevent it from being paid by coming into the office of account and completing a proper and timely Stop Payment Order.
>
> If you furnish us with the date, the check number, the exact amount of the check, and the name of the payee, we can arrange to stop payment on the check when it is presented for payment. We will not be responsible for orders if we do not have a reasonable opportunity to act on them before final payment of the items. Please note that the correct check number, the exact amount of the check and other information must be stated in order for us to stop payment. If you give us any incorrect information, we will not be responsible for our failure to stop payment on the check.

We are not obligated to accept verbal stop payment orders. If we elect to honor a verbal order, it will be enforced only if you sign a written stop payment order and the office of account receives it during normal banking hours within three banking days.

You may not stop payment on checks guaranteed by our Check Guarantee Card.

There is a per-check charge for each stop payment order requested. Each order will remain in effect for 6 months. If the check is still outstanding after that time, another stop payment order may be requested for an additional fee (see Schedule for amount). Anyone holding the check, including the Bank, may be entitled to enforce payment against you despite the stop payment order. You also agree to indemnify, defend and hold us harmless from all costs (except attorneys' fees), actions, damages, claims and demands related to or arising from our action in stopping payment on the check.

If we inadvertently pay any check over a correct, valid and timely stop payment order, we will recredit your account for the amount of the loss you prove has occurred. You agree to assign to us all of your rights against the payee and/or any other holder of your check. You also agree to cooperate fully with us in any legal actions that we subsequently take against such persons.

You may not stop payment on electronic point of sale transactions, cashier's checks, certified checks, official checks, money orders, checks designated "escrow checks," or checks or payments guaranteed by [this] bank (e.g., because of a dispute with the payee or for similar reasons). If such items are lost, stolen or destroyed, we may, in our sole discretion, stop payment on the items if you and/or the payee sign a Stop Payment Request. You may also be required to purchase a surety bond or lost instrument bond for up to twice the amount of the instrument to protect us against claims made by others.

Rules Governing First Interstate Deposit Accounts, 10–11 (effective January 1985) (emphasis in original). Consider the section 1–201(3) definition of "agreement."

2. Section 425 of the U.N.P.C. contained a subsection that provided with some specificity a thorough catalog of the information that a customer would have to provide the drawee in order to issue a binding stop order:

(9) Any direction to an account institution to stop or reverse payment of an order must at least accurately identify,

(a) the account number on which such order is drawn;

(b) the dollar amount (not cents) of the order except where a draw order is prearranged;

(c) the payee of the order;

(d) the drawer or person on whose behalf the stop or reversal is directed; and

(e) the date, within one (1) calendar week, of initiation of the order.

Problem

Sally had the transmission in her automobile repaired at a cost of around $1500.00. She paid the garage, Ace Garage, Inc., by check. She immediately left in the automobile to visit her brother 2,000 miles away. After five hours on the road, her car stalled, and she discovered that Ace had failed to properly seal the transmission so that all the fluid leaked out. The transmission was destroyed. Sally called her bank to stop payment on the check to Ace. She was told that the bank could not stop payment unless she provided the exact amount of the check or the check number. She did not have her checkbook with her on the trip and was not sure about the check number or amount. She did know that the amount was between $1500 and $1600 dollars; she thought about $1545 and some cents. She had no idea about the check number. The person in the bank she spoke with suggested that she direct it to close the account. However, she had just mailed at least five checks to other creditors which had not yet cleared, so she chose not to close the account. Rather she insisted that, since she did know the date and the payee of the check, the bank had an obligation to stop it. The bank disagreed and refused to accept the stop order.

By the time Sally returned home two weeks later, the check had been cashed, Ace Garage had been closed, and the principals of the Garage have disappeared. Sally filed suit against the bank to recover the amount ($1547.35) of the check. The bank asserts that she did not describe the check with reasonable certainty. It appears that the bank does not ordinarily visually examine checks under $10,000 and that its computer processing system is programmed to process stop orders by either check number or amount. The bank charges $15.00 for stop orders. If you were the judge how would you decide the case?

In a marked up version of Article 4 showing the changes made by the 1990 amendments, an explanatory comment to 4–403 includes this sentence: "In describing the item, the customer, in the absence of a contrary agreement, must meet the standard of what information allows the bank under the technology then existing to identify the item with reasonable certainty." (See page 1115 of West, 1992 Selected Commercial Statutes.) That comment, however, does not appear in the comment to revised 4–403 in the permanent text.

2. *Customer's Rights on Failure of Bank to Honor a Stop Payment Order; Bank's Right of Subrogation*

SOUTHEAST FIRST NATIONAL BANK OF SATELLITE BEACH v. ATLANTIC TELEC, INC.

Florida Court of Appeals, 1980.
389 So.2d 1032.

SHARP, J.

Southeast First National Bank of Satellite Beach appeals from a judgment against it for $13,000.00 in favor of Atlantic Telec, Inc. The bank also appeals the trial court's dismissal of the bank's third party complaint against Genesis Two–Atlantic Limited for lack of personal jurisdiction. We affirm the $13,000.00 judgment against the bank but we reverse the dismissal of the complaint against Genesis.

Atlantic brought suit against the bank because the bank failed to stop payment on a $13,000.00 check drawn by Atlantic on its account payable to Genesis. The stop payment order was oral, contrary to § 674.403(1) [nonuniform],[2] but the bank does not appeal the determination that it wrongfully failed to stop payment. It argues that Atlantic failed to show it had a right to stop payment on the check, and therefore Atlantic suffered no actual loss.

Simply because a bank pays a check over a stop payment order does not entitle the customer to recover damages against the bank, but it does establish a prima facie case for the customer. The bank must present evidence to show absence of loss, or the right of the payee of the check to receive payment. Then the customer must sustain the ultimate burden to show why there was a defense to payment of the item.

The parties agree for purposes of this appeal that Atlantic established a prima facie case. The bank then proved that the check was given by Atlantic to Genesis pursuant to a contract between the parties. Atlantic agreed to purchase a "soil inoculant" from Genesis, for resale to large farm operators in central Florida, and Genesis agreed to provide various sales assistance and technical help. The $13,000 check was in part payment of Atlantic's obligations under the contract to Genesis.

Atlantic then had the burden of going forward to show why it had the right to stop payment on the check. We believe the record shows it carried that burden. It presented testimony to show that Genesis breached its contract with Atlantic by failing to provide the technical information and sales assistance to Atlantic, as required under the contract. Although the payee of a check may be a holder in due course, Genesis did not take the check for value in view of the breach of contract and failure of consideration testimony, and the check, like the

2. § 674.403(1), Fla.Stat. (1979), provides: "A customer * * * may stop payment on any item payable, for or drawn against such customer's or customers' account but the same shall not be effective and the bank may disregard the same unless the order is in writing * * *" See *Florida Nat. Bank at Coral Gables v. Dental,* 210 So.2d 241 (Fla.3d DCA 1968).

underlying contract for which it was given, could be defeated by such defenses.

* * *

Affirmed in part; reversed in part and remanded.

ORFINGER, J., concurs.

FRANK D. UPCHURCH, JR., J., concurs without participation in oral argument.

Note

1. If there are two or more joint holders of an account, that is, multiple people with the authority to draw checks against the account, may A stop payment of a check drawn by B? See Comment, *Cambridge Trust Co. v. Carney: Overdraft Liability of Account Cosignatories,* 28 Me.L.Rev. 254 (1976). Bank practices in this regard are not uniform. Some banks will permit any customer on an account to countermand a payment order while others will only accept a stop order from the party who drew the particular item in issue. See R 4–403(a).

2. Bank customers stop payment of an item either because (1) the check was lost or stolen, or (2) the customer has a dispute with the payee of the check and wants to retain the leverage described by the venerable legal maxim, "possession is nine tenths of the law." When should a customer be required to pay a stop payment order fee to the drawee bank? Should the reason for stopping payment matter? Whatever your answer to that question, try to explain your analysis of the issue to the teller at your bank when you go in to contest the $10 charge that appears on your periodic statement for stopping payment. Compare Op.Mich.Att'y Gen. No. 5867 (1981) (bank may not charge customer a fee on stop payment order), reprinted in 30 U.C.C.Rep.Serv. (Callaghan) 1626 (1981), with Op.Att'y Gen. No. 5947 (1981) (bank may contract with customer for fee on stop payment order), reprinted in 33 U.C.C.Rep.Serv. (Callaghan) 1445 (1981). For an exhaustive treatment of several stop payment issues, see Thomas A. Mittelsteadt, *The Stop Payment Right in an Electronic Payment Environment: An Analysis of the Transition Problems Involved when Integrating a Traditional Right Into New Value Transfer Systems,* 17 New Eng.L.Rev. 355 (1982).

SIEGEL v. NEW ENGLAND MERCHANTS NATIONAL BANK

Massachusetts Supreme Judicial Court, 1982.
386 Mass. 672, 437 N.E.2d 218.

HENNESSEY, C.J. We are called upon to define the respective rights of a bank and its depositor when the bank has paid a post-dated check before maturity and deducted the amount of the check from the depositor's account. Applying the Uniform Commercial Code, G.L. c. 106, we conclude that the bank must recredit the depositor's account, but may then assert against the depositor any rights acquired by prior holders on either the instrument or the transaction from which it arose.

In the course of this opinion, we shall describe the parties' responsibilities of proof with respect to the bank's subrogation claim. We remand for a further hearing on the question of subrogation.

The plaintiff's decedent, David Siegel, maintained a checking account with the defendant, New England Merchants National Bank. On September 14, 1973, Siegel drew and delivered a $20,000 check to Peter Peters, post-dated November 14, 1973. Peters immediately deposited the check in his own bank, which forwarded it for collection. The defendant bank overlooked the date on the check, and, on September 17, paid the item and charged it against Siegel's account. Siegel discovered the error in late September when another of his checks was returned for insufficient funds. He informed the bank that the check to Peters was post-dated November 14, and asked the bank to stop payment of the check. Later, he requested that the bank return the $20,000 to him.

When the bank refused to restore the $20,000, Siegel brought this action for wrongful debit of his account. The bank denied liability, raised defenses of waiver, estoppel, and ratification, and filed counterclaims asserting rights on the instrument and rights of subrogation. Two banks in the collecting chain became parties, one permitted to intervene as a party defendant and the other impleaded by the bank. The bank also impleaded Peters, the payee, who filed a suggestion of bankruptcy. The case was later dismissed as against the two collecting banks.

After a trial, jury-waived, the judge found that the check was post-dated by agreement between Peters and Siegel, without fraudulent purpose, and that Siegel had acted with reasonable speed to inform the bank of the error. He also found that Peters had paid no money to Siegel since receiving the check. The judge ruled that (1) the check was a negotiable instrument; (2) the check was not payable until November 14; (3) the bank was negligent in paying it before that date; (4) the bank had no right to debit Siegel's account; (5) Siegel had not waived his rights or ratified the bank's action and was not estopped from demanding the $20,000; and (6) the wrongful debit caused Siegel a loss of $20,000. He also rejected the bank's counterclaims as having no merit. He then entered judgments for Siegel against the bank in the amount of $20,000, for Siegel on the bank's counterclaims, and for the bank against Peters for $20,000.[3] The bank appealed, and we transferred the case to this court on our own motion. We vacate the judgment and remand the case for further consideration of the bank's subrogation claims.

1. Wrongful Debit and Subrogation

The parties agree that the bank should not have paid the check when Peters presented it on September 14, and had no right at that

3. The judge ruled that Peters's debt to the bank was not dischargeable in bankruptcy, so that the bankruptcy proceeding against Peters did not bar entry of judgment for the bank against him. Peters has not appealed, and this ruling is not at issue.

time to charge it against Siegel's account. G.L. c. 106, §§ 3–114 [R 3–113], 4–401 [R 4–401]. Their differences center instead on whether the bank's wrongful action caused Siegel any loss, so as to entitle him to damages. Siegel contends, and the judge ruled, that his loss must be $20,000 because that amount was debited from his account. The bank contends that there was no loss, because Siegel drew the check with the intention that it eventually be paid, and the bank could rightfully have charged it against his account on November 14. We believe that the drafters of the code anticipated disputes such as this, and provided a logical system for their resolution.

We begin with G.L. c. 106, § 4–401(1) [R 4–401(a)], which governs bookkeeping between depositor and bank. A bank may charge any "properly payable" item against its depositor's account.[4] Implicitly, the bank may not charge items, such as post-dated checks, that are not properly payable. If the charge is unauthorized, it follows that the depositor has a valid claim to the amount of the charge by virtue of the account itself.

As the bank points out, the depositor's realization of this claim may produce unjust enrichment. Even when an item is not properly payable, due to prematurity or a stop payment order, the bank's payment may discharge a legal obligation of the depositor, or create a right in the depositor's favor against the payee. See G.L. c. 106, §§ 3–601(1)(a) [R 3–601(a)], 3–603(1) [R 3–602(a)], 3–802(1)(b) [R 3–310(b)]; J. White & R. Summers, Uniform Commercial Code 542 (2d ed. 1980). If the depositor were permitted to retain such benefits, and recover the amount of the check as well, he would profit at the bank's expense. Therefore, § 4–407 [R 4–407] provides that upon payment, the bank is "subrogated" to any rights prior holders may have had against the drawer-depositor, on either the check or the initial underlying transaction, and to any rights the drawer may have against the payee or other holders. G.L. c. 106, 4–407.

Thus, the code fixes the rights of the bank and the depositor by a two part adjustment. The depositor has a claim against the bank for the amount improperly debited from its account, and the bank has a claim against the depositor based on subrogation to the rights of the payee and other holders. The bank may assert its subrogation rights defensively when its depositor brings an action for wrongful debit. See Universal C.I.T. Credit Corp. v. Guaranty Bank & Trust Co., supra at 794–795.

Here, the bank asserted a subrogation claim based on the rights of Peters, the payee. Neither party, however, introduced evidence concerning Peters's rights against Siegel. A question then arises as to what matters each party was obligated to prove in order to prevail.

4. General Laws c. 106, § 4–401(1) [R 4–401(a)], as appearing in St.1957, c. 765, § 1, provides in full that "[a]s against its customer, a bank may charge against his account any item which is otherwise properly payable from that account even though the charge creates an overdraft."

Section 4–403(3) [R 4–403(c)] of the code provides that when the problem is one of improper payment over a stop order, the "burden of establishing the fact and amount of loss * * * is on the customer." G.L. c. 106, § 4–403(3) [R 4–403(c)]. Here, of course, the bank's liability is for premature payment rather than for payment over a stop order. Nevertheless, these two forms of improper payment have in common the problem of unjust enrichment, and we believe that § 4–403(3) [R 4–403(c)] is a source of useful analogy.

The rule of § 4–403(3) [R 4–403(c)], that a depositor must prove his loss, may at first seem at odds with our earlier conclusion that § 4–401(1) [R 4–401(a)] provides the depositor with a claim against the bank in the amount of the check, leaving the bank with recourse through subrogation under § 4–407 [R 4–407]. We believe, however, that § 4–403(3) [R 4–403(c)] was intended to operate within the process of credit and subrogation established by §§ 4–401(1) [R 4–401(a)] and 4–407 [R 4–407]. See G.L. c. 106, § 4–403, comment 8 [R 4–403, comment 7]. When a bank pays an item improperly, the depositor loses his ability to exercise any right he had to withhold payment of the check. His "loss," in other words, is equivalent to his rights and defenses against the parties to whose rights the bank is subrogated—the other party to the initial transaction and other holders of the instrument. Section 4–403(3) simply protects the bank against the need to prove events familiar to the depositor, and far removed from the bank, before it can realize its subrogation rights. The depositor, who participated in the initial transaction, knows whether the payee was entitled to eventual payment and whether any defenses arose. Therefore, § 4–403(3) [R 4–403(c)] requires that he, rather than the bank, prove these matters * * *.

This view of the three relevant sections of the code suggests a fair allocation of the burden of proof. The bank, which has departed from authorized bookkeeping, must acknowledge a credit to the depositor's account. It must then assert its subrogation rights, and in doing so must identify the status of the parties in whose place it claims. If the bank's subrogation claims are based on the check, this would entail proof that the third party subrogor was a holder, or perhaps a holder in due course. This responsibility falls reasonably upon the bank, because it has received the check from the most recent holder and is in at least as good a position as the depositor to trace its history.

The depositor must then prove any facts that might demonstrate a loss. He must establish defenses good against a holder or holder in due course, as the case may be. See G.L. c. 106, §§ 3–305, 3–306 [R 3–305]. If the initial transaction is at issue, he must prove either that he did not incur a liability to the other party, or that he has a defense to liability. Thus the bank, if it asserts rights based on the transaction, need not make out a claim on the part of its subrogor against the depositor. Responsibility in this area rests entirely with the depositor, who participated in the transaction and is aware of its details. Further, the depositor must establish any consequential loss.[8]

A further hearing is necessary to determine the question of subrogation in the present case. The judge ruled that the check was a negotiable instrument, see G.L. c. 106, § 3–114(1) [See comment to R 3–113], and the evidence at trial fairly indicated that Peters was a holder. See G.L. c. 106, § 1–201(20). Thus the burden, under the rules we have set out, was upon Siegel to prove a defense good against a holder of the instrument. However, the trial record makes clear that neither the parties nor the judge was proceeding with these rules in mind. Indeed, the judge excluded, at the bank's strenuous request, evidence offered by Siegel concerning the transaction between Siegel and Peters. We believe, therefore, that Siegel's executrix should have an opportunity to present evidence that Siegel suffered a loss.

2. Other Claims and Defenses

Several other arguments offered by the bank to escape or counteract its liability can be disposed of quickly. First, the bank asserts a claim against Siegel in its own right, contending that it is a holder in due course of the check. This argument is without merit because the check has been finally paid and is not in the bank's possession. See G.L. c. 106, §§ 3–603(1) [R 3–602(a) and (b)], 3–601(3)(a) [omitted from revision]; J. White & R. Summers, supra at 536, 661. But see Roland v. Republic Nat'l Bank, 463 S.W.2d 747, 749–750 (Tex.Civ.App.1971).

The bank also argues that the judge erred in rejecting its affirmative defenses of waiver, estoppel, and ratification. In support of these defenses, the bank argues that Siegel did not make a timely complaint about the debit from his account. The judge found, however, that Siegel "took action within a reasonable amount of time to inform the Bank of its wrongful action," and this finding has support in the evidence. See Mass.R.Civ.P. 52(a), 365 Mass. 816 (1975). The bank also points out that Siegel did not return the check to the bank. There is no indication in the code, however, that a depositor must return a cancelled item to the bank before he is entitled to credit for an improper debit under § 4–401(1) [R 4–401(a)]. Finally, the bank contends that Siegel should have renewed his stop payment order when it expired in April, 1974. See G.L. c. 106, § 4–403(2) [R 4–403(b)]. The order,

8. Several courts have harmonized § 4–403(3) [R 4–403(c)] with §§ 4–401(1) [R 4–401(a)] and 4–407 [R 4–407] in terms of shifting burdens of production and persuasion. "Simply because a bank pays a check over a stop payment order does not entitle the customer to recover damages against the bank, but it does establish a prima facie case for the customer. The bank must present evidence to show absence of loss, or the right of the payee of the check to receive payment. Then the customer must sustain the ultimate burden to show why there was a defense to payment of the item." Southeast First Nat'l Bank v. Atlantic Telec, Inc., 389 So.2d 1032, 1033 (Fla.Dist.Ct.App.1980). Mitchell v. Republic Bank & Trust Co., 35 N.C.App. 101, 104 (1978). Thomas v. Marine Midland Tinkers Nat'l Bank, 86 Misc.2d 284, 290–291 (N.Y.Sup.Ct.1976). Although our analysis will often have the same result as that of the cited cases, it may in some cases give greater force to § 4–403(3) [R 4–403(c)].

however, was not the basis of Siegel's claim, and in any event the check had already been paid.

In sum, Siegel had a valid claim against the bank for premature payment in the amount of the item paid, but the bank was entitled to assert the rights of prior holders on the check and on the transaction from which it arose. We vacate the judgment and remand for a further hearing to determine those rights. At the hearing, the bank must establish the status of its subrogor. Siegel's executrix must establish any defenses to liability on the instrument as well as the absence of rights or presence of defenses on the underlying transaction.

So ordered.

Problems

1. Jim Jackson operated a small jewelry store. He has more debts than money. He decided to delay paying the rent on his store building for a month so that he could make the installment payment on his car. He wrote a check for $700.00 to the automobile finance company. The next day, however, his landlord told him that he would be evicted unless he paid his rent by the 15th of the month. Jackson thereupon called the bank, asked it to stop payment on the check to the finance company, and gave it the proper information. He then wrote a check to the landlord. The bank inadvertently failed to honor the stop order and paid the finance company check. Payment of that check reduced the balance in his account below the amount of the rent check and it was dishonored. Jackson was evicted. He claims that he has suffered loss of at least $50,000 because of the disruption of his business.

Bank claims that it has no liability because it does not have to recredit his account until he establishes "the fact and amount of loss" and that he cannot do so since the check written to the finance company paid a real debt of Jackson. Is the bank's position sound? See James J. White & Robert S. Summers, Uniform Commercial Code, Student Edition, 3d, § 18–6 (1988).

2. Jim Jones contracted with Long Construction Company for a total renovation of the master bath in Jones's home at a contract price of $25,000. The price was due upon completion of the work. Long finished and Jones gave him a check for the price. The next day Jones discovered a number of defects in the work. He gave the drawee bank a stop order on the check. The bank without excuse failed to honor the stop order. What are bank's subrogation rights?

3. Customer's Attempt to Stop Payment of Bank Checks

DZIURAK v. CHASE MANHATTAN BANK

Supreme Court of New York, 1976.
88 Misc.2d 641, 388 N.Y.S.2d 496.

DEMATTEO, J.

Despite the court's exhaustive search and the commendable cooperation of counsel, the court, surprisingly, is unable to find a New York reported case like the one at bar.

Plaintiff seeks to recover the sum of $17,000.00 by reason of defendant's refusal to honor a "stop payment" order on its cashier's check.

The parties have waived trial by jury and their right to submit requests for finding of facts which the court finds as follows (Sec. 4213 CPLR):

* * *

Prior to June 15, 1973, plaintiff (Dziurak), without his own attorney, orally agreed with one Mario Staveris (Staveris) that for $22,000.00 Dziurak would receive original-issue stock equivalent to a one-third interest in a corporate restaurant of which Staveris was President. The entire proceeds were to be deposited in the corporate account to be used solely for corporate purposes.

After having paid Staveris $5,000.00, Dziurak on (Friday) June 15, 1973, requested defendant's branch to remove $17,000.00 from his savings account of $18,000.00 therein and to issue an official bank check in said amount to Staveris. Following a conversation with the branch manager relating to the above agreement, Dziurak heeded the manager's advice to have the bank check payable to Dziurak's order rather than to Staveris' order. The check was drawn by the defendant on itself. Dziurak then signed the check in blank and delivered it to Staveris.

Dziurak learned that Staveris violated their agreement by depositing the check to Staveris' individual savings account in the Green Point Savings Bank. Immediately, and during the afternoon banking hours of June 21, 1973, Dziurak and then Irving Cook, the attorney Dziurak had summoned for help, stated to the branch manager that Staveris had swindled Dziurak and they ordered him to stop payment on the check. The manager conceded the bank check had been received in the morning delivery and as yet had not been paid, but under advice of bank counsel, and expressly for lack of a court order, rejected plaintiff's stop-payment request.

The check shows that it was deposited by Staveris in the Green Point Savings Bank on June 18, 1973, was then forwarded to Chemical Bank for collection, and was received by defendant's main office official check processing unit from Chemical via the New York Clearing House Exchanges on June 20, 1973. The check was then forwarded to Chase's branch office, the drawer of the check, which received and paid it to Staveris on June 21, 1973.

Dziurak then sued Staveris and others in this court, alleging fraud. After a plenary trial Dziurak, on November 12, 1973, recovered a judgment against Staveris in the amount of $22,955.00. No appeal has been taken therefrom and execution thereon was returned wholly unsatisfied on December 24, 1973, after which plaintiff commenced this action.

Against this factual background the issue appears to be: Was the order to defendant by Dziurak to stop payment on its cashier's check valid?

Defendant contends that the answer to this is in the negative. It relies, inter alia, upon a host of citations wherein judicial discourse is engaged in to create an aura of eternal precedent concerning the nature of a cashier's check. The instrument in question is continually referred to as the equivalent of cash. It assumes the mere issuance of a check by the drawee bank gives rise to an executed sale of credit, not subject to rescission or countermand. In *Rosenbaum v. First Nat'l City Bank* (13 A.D.2d 100 [1961]), a pre-code case,[1] the instrument was defended in the following terms:

> The requirements of stability in commerce and banking dictate that the obligations of a bank on its cashier's checks be not lightly avoided.

Within that class of citations, the payee is a bona fide retailer, and the check is drawn to his order as a third party. *Malphrus v. Home Savings Bank* (254 N.Y.S.2d 980) is a case unduly applied by defendant to the one at bar. There, the purchaser gave to the plaintiff, as payee, a teller's check, drawn by defendant, her savings bank, in part payment for a secondhand automobile. At the purchaser's request the bank stopped payment.[2] Although the bank asserted that, as a "customer," it had a right to stop payment under § 4–403 [R 4–403] of the Code, the court granted summary judgment to the payee. Under § 3–802(1)(a) [R 3–310(a)] the buyer's underlying obligation to the plaintiff seller is pro tanto discharged whenever a bank is "drawer, maker or accepter" of the instrument given in payment without reservation of recourse against the buyer. Therefore, to permit the bank to withhold payment under § 4–403 [R 4–403], would leave the seller with no enforceable rights against the underlying obligor (the actual consumer) or anyone else. Since the Code is promulgated to protect a genuine transaction involving a quid pro quo between the remitter and payee, the premise of the *Malphrus* decision that § 3–802 [R 3–310(a)] discharges the remitter, is sound.

Defendant then argues that *Kaufman v. Chase Manhattan Bank* (370 F.Supp. 276) decidedly represents the rule of law in its favor.

1. All sections cited are under the Uniform Commercial Code adopted by New York in 1962, effective September 27, 1964. All underlining [italicizing] is [the court's] for emphasis.

2. In most instances relating to teller's checks and other bank instruments, it is the remitter or purchaser and not the bank that has an interest in stopping payment. In many cases the bank satisfies its depositors by acceding to their request to stop payment. In the case of a teller's check, for example, the remitter has no apparent right to stop payment under § 4–403 [R 4–403]; it can be argued that he is not a customer of the drawee bank which is charged with the payment of the item. A bank instrument drawn on another bank gives the drawer the right to stop payment. Under § 4–104(1)(e) [R 4–104(a)(5)] "Customer" is defined to include "A bank carrying an account with another bank" and under § 4–403 [R 4–403], a customer may stop payment on any instrument payable for his account. However, if the drawer stops payment, it remains liable on the instrument.

Kaufman obviously enlarges upon the traits of a cashier's check into a sweeping generic rule of public policy. It rehashes the timeworn maxim of labeling the cashier's check as a primary obligation of a bank, equivalent to cash, its issuance constituting acceptance by the issuer. Kaufman reiterates verbatim the maxim of law asserted in *National Newark & Essex Bank v. Giordano* (268 A.2d 327) at page 329:

> * * * To allow the bank to stop payment on such an instrument would be inconsistent with the representations it makes in issuing the check. Such a rule would undermine the public confidence in the bank and its checks and thereby deprive the cashier's check of the essential incident which makes it useful. People would no longer be willing to accept it as a substitute for cash if they could not be sure that there would be no difficulty in converting it into cash.

The defendant adopts the intransigent position that unless Dziurak obtained injunctive relief, he was doomed the moment he gave the check to Staveris, even though Staveris gave no value.

* * *

Whereas, the dictum in *T.P.O. v. Federal Deposit Insurance Corp.* (487 F.2d 13 [1973]) represents a much more valid approach in characterizing the cashier's check as one of limited value in the emporium. It affirms the position taken by the authors of Willier and Hart in *Bender's Uniform Commercial Code Reporter Digest,* volume 60 thereof at 2–1194:

> A bank may draw a cashier's check either on itself or another bank. When drawn on another bank, the check is governed by the same rules as any other check; when—as here—drawn by the bank on itself, the check is effective as a note under Section 3–118(a) [R 3–104(e), 3–103(a)(6)] with the bank as maker. Thus the court erred in referring to the instrument as a draft which had been accepted * * *

Circuit Judge Weis, speaking for the court in T.P.O. (*supra*), continued at page 136 thereof:

> In any event, while a cashier's check is equivalent to a negotiable note of a bank, *it is not the same as cash as has been loosely asserted, and the cases discussing this particular type of instrument must be carefully analyzed* * * *.

To say that a cashier's check is the equivalent of cash appears to be irreconcilable with § 4–104(1)(g) [R 4–104(a)(9)] which defines "Item" as "any instrument for the payment of money * * * but does not include money." Thus, one may argue that a cashier's check is not money and therefore not cash. We embrace the practical view that until paid by a bank in due course a check is not absolute payment (3 Anderson, U.C.C., 2d ed., p. 144).

Undoubtedly, the Code intends to protect the bank customer's use of instruments for the payment of money when its states, in relevant part, at § 4–403 [R 4–403]:

> (1) A customer may by order to his bank stop payment of any item payable for his account.[4]

A liberal interpretation by the court is intended as suggested in the following official comments to the section as well as by others.

> (2) The position taken by this section is that stopping payment is a service which depositors expect and are entitled to receive from banks notwithstanding its difficulty, inconvenience and expense. The inevitable occasional losses through failure to stop should be borne by the banks as a cost of the business of banking. [See R 4–403 comment 1].
>
> Absent "* * * certification of a check or other acceptance * * *" (official comment 5) "* * * the right to stop payment is not limited to checks, and extends to any item payable by any bank." (official comment 4).

"Customer" is defined as "any person having an account with a bank or for whom a bank has agreed to collect items" (§ 4–104(1)(e) [R 4–104(a)(5)]); and "account" is "any account with a bank and includes checking, time, interest or savings account" (§ 4–104(1)(a) [R 4–104(a)(1)]). Again, "item" means "any instrument for the payment of money * * * but does not include money" (§ 4–104(1)(g) [R 4–104(a)(9)]).

The depositor is the prime, dominating influence mainly responsible for the growth and development of the banking system. The influx of his funds serves as a conduit to the source from which business loans are poured into the mainstream of American Capitalism. The Code seeks to shelter this essential, economic entity, fundamental to the survival of the Banking Industry.

While we are aware of foreign case law to the contrary,[6] the obvious broad scope of the statute and the logic of the official comments clearly manifest that Dziurak is a customer and the cashier's check an item payable for his account.

With this salutary intendment for the bank customer in mind we question as tenuous defendant's contention that the item had already been accepted upon the act of issuance under § 3–410(1) [R 3–409(a)], and therefore no stop payment order could be valued under § 4–303(a)(1) [R 4–303(a)(1)].

4. The section goes beyond the prior NIL rule that the drawer of a personal check has the right to stop payment. It gives the "customer" of a bank a right to stop payment on "any item payable for his account." Incontrovertibly, a cashier's check is an instrument for the payment of money and is an "item" under § 4–104(1)(g) [R 4–104(a)(9)].

6. E.g., *Wertz v. Richardson Heights Bank & Trust*, 495 S.W.2d 572, 91 B.L.J. 177, Texas 1973, holds that a cashier's check is payable for the bank's account.

We have already noted some challenges to this oft-repeated argument. What, in reality, do we have here? Dziurak had paid the defendant for the cashier's check from his savings account in defendant's branch; hence, at the time of issuance, the check represented Dziurak's proceeds. Defendant undertook an absolute obligation to dispose the same and give an account for their disposition. If the unsophisticated Dziurak is denied the right to stop payment once he negotiates it, it would be less than fair if the risk of instantaneous, irrevocable loss should not be made unmistakably clear to him. If, and so it seems, "acceptance" equates finality, the issuing bank should be held to strict compliance of § 3–410 [R 3–409], especially since the statute fails to express or imply that a cashier's check is accepted, upon issuance. "The drawee's signed engagement to honor the draft as presented * * * must be written on the draft, and may consist of his signature alone." Here, this is lacking. The check was signed by the bank once and where the drawer normally signs. Our attention is invited to official comment 4 of § 3–410 [comment 2 to R 3–409], " * * * the mere signature of the drawee on the instrument is a sufficient acceptance. Customarily the signature is written vertically across the face of the instrument, but *since the drawee has no reason to sign for any other purpose* his signature in any other place * * * of the instrument is sufficient." Thus, the statute and official comment make clear that the drawee's signature must appear for the sole reason and for no other purpose but to accept the instrument. Moreover, § 3–104(1) [R 3–104(a)] provides that "any writing to be a negotiable instrument within this Article must (a) be signed by the maker or drawer." We hold that the cashier's check was a completed negotiable instrument by reason of defendant's signature as drawer. To judicially hold that when a bank wears two hats, its one signature affixed where the drawer normally signs, fulfills two purposes, that of drawer and drawee, and thereby, ipso jure, transforms a cashier's check into an "accepted" check is, in light of statutory silence and the official comments, tantamount to judicial wrenching of the legislative arm.

Whereas, the cashier's check herein is equivalent to a note by reason of § 3–118(a) [R 3–104(e), R 3–103(a)(6)] " * * * A draft drawn on the drawer is effective as a note."

While we agree to a considerable extent with the defendant with the warranted significance the courts have attached to the use of a cashier's check (and to bank instruments generally) in promoting economic stability, we are of the opinion that they are universal favorites because they cannot be dishonored for insufficient funds.

Absent the inviolability of a certified check or "accepted" draft, it is critical to the basic issue in the use of other instruments to consider the parties to the instrument and the underlying quid pro quo as the instrument travels the negotiation route—no less than the courts cited by the defendant have done. There are factual disparities in this case from the others the defendant cites. For example, plaintiff is defendant's customer and payee on the check. He gave it to one [Staveris] who gave no value for it. Therefore, Staveris is not entitled to the statutory benefits of a holder in due course. No innocent person or genuine transaction is involved. The discharge of an underlying obligation under § 3–802 [R 3–310] is lacking.

Moreover, by withholding payment no innocent person would suffer. In addition, the defendant, as a stakeholder, could easily insulate itself from any difficulty and without any loss and with dispatch.[8] Instead, by paying Staveris, defendant chose to get involved, and enabled Staveris and, with him, to literally squeeze Dziurak to his financial extinction.

With respect to defendant's request that plaintiff obtain injunctive relief as a condition to stopping payment, since no action was then pending, plaintiff could not enjoin "payment by order of a court in an action in which the adverse claimant (Dziurak) and the holder (Staveris) are parties." (§ 3–603[1] [R 3–602(a)].)

Undoubtedly, any attempt by plaintiff to supply "indemnity deemed adequate" to defendant (which defendant had not requested), would prove fruitless since plaintiff's stop-order was given during the imminence of bank closing hours. We believe that if adequate security is to be furnished, that adequate time be furnished within which to provide that security, particularly if there is no wrongdoing on the part of the adverse claimant. Also, since the bank manager had proffered [sic] Dziurak to have the check payable to his order, in heeding the advice, Dziurak apparently relied on the manager's trustworthiness and his concern as well as the bank manager's sophistication with bank instruments. Because of the bank-customer relationship in the above circumstances, it would appear that if the bank manager wanted or expected security from Dziurak that there was an obligation on the manager to demand the same and thus alert Dziurak to furnish the security. In not requesting the security, defendant is deemed to have waived the provision that was for its benefit. We allude to section 1006 CPLR wherein, without a court order or security, defendant could have withheld payment and insulated itself in interpleader.

We touch now on defendant's next contention. Even assuming, arguendo, plaintiff was covered by a binding stop order in accordance with § 4–403(1) [R 4–403(a)], defendant now postulates that plaintiff's rescission comes too late, as provided by statute. Section 4–303 [R 4–303] absolves a bank when the stop order is received and a reasonable time for the bank to act thereon expires after the bank has accepted or certified; paid; settled for; completed posting; or became accountable

8. The common law doctrines of adverse claim and jus tertii which enabled a party who is obligated on a [sic] instrument to raise a defense based upon the rights of a third person have been perpetuated by the Code so that the drawee is spared the necessity of deciding the merits of a customer's adverse claim at the peril of double liability (§§ 3–306 [R 3–306], 3–603 [R 3–602]). Moreover, under CPLR §§ 1006 (interpleader) and 2601, the defendant comes within the definition of a stakeholder and it can easily insulate itself without difficulty or expense against the exposure of multiple liability.

for the item. This court finds none of these defenses to be valid. Defendant had ample time to "return the item or send notice of dishonor" before "its midnight deadline" (§§ 4–302[a]; 3–508[2] [R 3–503(c)]; 4–104[1][h] [R 4–104(a)(10)]; see, also *Tusso v. Security Nat'l Bank,* 76 Misc.2d 12.

Defendant's last contention, that by suing Staveris plaintiff elected his remedies, is untenable, in view of the requirements of § 4–403(3) [R 4–403(c)] which puts the burden on the customer to prove the loss and amount thereof before any recovery can be had against his bank for paying an item contrary to a binding stop payment order.

Dziurak, the customer, was not given the protection by the bank he enriched which it was obliged to give, "nonwithstanding [sic] its difficulty, inconvenience or expense." It seems eminently fair that a bank that can insulate itself without "difficulty, inconvenience or expense" be held to walk a tightrope. Had the defendant honored the stop payment order so that a reasonable opportunity would be given to Dziurak to protect his funds against a dishonest holder, a lasting harm would have been avoided. Had this occurred, it is doubtful our economy would have suffered a trickle or a cashier's check would lose whatever glamour it now possesses and thus come into disuse.

Perhaps the role of the cashier's check in promoting economic stability has been overplayed, vis-a-vis the ordinary check. Do we abolish the latter because it lacks "sacrosanct" qualities? Economic stability, world-wide, would be naught without it. The evidence is overwhelming that this is so because drawers of ordinary checks promote their self-interest by honoring their obligations. What we are trying to say is: Adverse claims are relatively few. When they seek to arrest thieves, commerce flows smoothly. One who claims that a holder has given no value and has committed fraud and therefore is not entitled to his proceeds, should be given the opportunity to willingly expend his money, effort and time to prove it in court.

In sum, stripped of the jargonistic mumbo jumbo which conflicting statutory and case law and legal scholars have brought to the legal arena involving cashier's checks, it is crystal clear that at this juncture of our case, because of defendant's behavior, Dziurak lost his money, the defendant lost Dziurak as a customer, and Staveris—well, as for him, he was lucky he was given a cashier's check and not an ordinary check, for his fraud paid off. To us, this is not ratio legis.

Defendant's motions to dismiss, hereinbefore reserved, are denied.

The court finds plaintiff's case satisfactorily establishes the fact and amount of his loss. Judgment for plaintiff in the sum of $17,000.00 together with interest from June 21, 1973.

Settle judgment.

DZIURAK v. CHASE MANHATTAN BANK

New York Supreme Court, Appellate Division, 1977.
58 A.D.2d 103, 396 N.Y.S.2d 414,
aff'd, 44 N.Y.2d 776, 406 N.Y.S.2d 30, 377 N.E.2d 474 (1978).

COHALAN, J.P.

The sole question on this appeal is whether a bank depositor to whom an "official bank check" has been issued (and by him endorsed to the order of a third party), can legally stop payment thereon, in the absence of a court order or an indemnification bond. An official bank check is commonly referred to as a "cashier's check." Trial Term held it could be stopped. We disagree.

* * *

[Appellate Division's elaboration of the facts developed at the trial:] Dziurak paid Staveris $5,000 down. He then went to the [defendant/appellant] Bank and, through the assistant manager, arranged for the proper withdrawal. He asked for a "check" to be drawn to the order of Staveris. Monaco, the assistant manager, advised him to have the check drawn to himself as payee. A further bit of advice by Monaco was for Dziurak to go to his attorney, who would instruct him how to endorse the check.

The $17,000 was transferred to the Bank's coffers and Dziurak's savings account was debited accordingly. A cashier's check was then issued to the order of "Francis A. Dziurak."

Plaintiff ignored the suggestion that he consult with his attorney. Instead, he wrote on the back of the instrument "Francis Dziurak. Pay to order Mario Staveris" and delivered the item to Staveris. The latter, instead of depositing the check into the corporate restaurant account, deposited it in his own savings account.

Before he learned of Staveris' perfidy and before the cashier's check had cleared, Dziurak belatedly sought the advice of a local attorney. Very properly, the attorney advised him to try to stop payment on the cashier's check.

Back went Dziurak to the Bank. He saw Monaco and asked him if the check had cleared. It had not, but had arrived at the Bank that morning.

While plaintiff was with him, Monaco telephoned the Bank's attorneys and was advised that the check could not be stopped, absent a court order. He so advised the plaintiff and while Dziurak was still with him he telephoned the plaintiff's attorney to advise him to the same effect. The attorney said he was aware that a court order could effectively produce a stop of the payment.

This action was started against the Bank after judgment was first taken against Staveris, and after execution was returned unsatisfied.

As to the law, the controlling statutes are contained in several sections of the Uniform Commercial Code (hereafter U.C.C.) which, in turn, are fleshed out in reported decisions of nisi prius and appellate courts.

We begin with subdivision (1) of § 4–403 [R 4–403] of the U.C.C. ("Customer's Right to Stop Payment; Burden of Proof of Loss"):

> A customer may by order to his bank stop payment of *any item payable for his account* but the order must be received at such time and in such manner as to afford the bank a reasonable opportunity to act on it prior to any action by the bank with respect to the item described in § 4–303 [R 4–303] (emphasis supplied).

As to this section (4–403 [R 4–403]) we part company with Trial Term, which held that the $17,000 represented by the cashier's check was actually Dziurak's money and not that of the Bank. As noted in *Wertz v. Richardson Heights Bank & Trust* (495 S.W.2d 572, 574 [Tex.]):

> A cashier's check is not one payable for the customer's account, but rather for the bank's account. It is the bank which is obligated on the check.
>
> The reference in § 4–403 [R 4–403] more properly fits the situation where the depositor, as drawer, issues his own check on his own bank, as drawee. Such a check can be stopped if reasonable notice is given.
>
> A cashier's check is of a very different character. It is the primary obligation of the bank which issues it (citation omitted) and constitutes its written promise to pay upon demand (citation omitted). It has been said that a cashier's check is a bill of exchange drawn by a bank upon itself, accepted in advance by the very act of issuance (Matter of Bank of United States [O'Neill], 243 App.Div. 287, 291).

This exposition of the law has been followed consistently.

No decisions holding to the contrary have been unearthed.

But to go on. Subdivision (1) of § 4–303 [R 4–303(a)] of the U.C.C. ("When Items Subject to * * * Stop–Order") states, in part:

> Any * * * stop-order received by * * * a payor bank, whether or not effective under other rules of law to terminate * * * the bank's right or duty to pay an item * * * comes too late to so terminate * * * if the * * * stop-order * * * is received * * * and a reasonable time for the bank to act thereon expires * * * after the bank has done any one of the following:
>
> (a) accepted or certified the item.

The next section to consider is 3–410 [See R 3–409] ("Definition and Operation of Acceptance"):

> (1) Acceptance is the drawee's signed engagement to honor the draft as presented. It must be written on the draft, and may

consist of his signature alone. It becomes operative when completed by delivery or notification.

At this point we can refer back to annotation 5 in the Official Comment under § 4–403 of the U.C.C. (McKinney's Cons.Laws of N.Y., Book 62, Part 2, p. 611):

> There is no right to stop payment after certification of a check or other acceptance of a draft, and this is true no matter who procures the certification. See Sections 3–411 [R 3–409] and 4–303 [R 4–303]. The acceptance is the drawee's own engagement to pay, and he is not required to impair his credit by refusing payment for the convenience of the drawer.

Thus, the Bank's one signature on the instrument constitutes both a drawing and an acceptance and makes the Bank a drawer and a drawee. (See *Matter of Bank of United States* [O'Neill] *supra*).

In the recitation of the facts, mention was made that the local attorney for the plaintiff remarked to Monaco that he was aware that a court order (presumably one of a court of competent jurisdiction) could have acted as a "stop payment" order. The statute providing for such an order is § 3–603 [R 3–602(b)] of the U.C.C. It is headnoted "Payment or Satisfaction" and, pertinently, reads:

> (1) The liability of any party is discharged to the extent of his payment * * * to the holder even though it is made with knowledge of a claim of another person to the instrument unless prior to such payment * * * *the person making the claim either supplies indemnity deemed adequate by the party seeking the discharge* or enjoins payment or satisfaction by order of a court of competent jurisdiction in an action in which the adverse claimant and the holder are parties (emphasis supplied).

The fact that the attorney for the plaintiff was aware that a court order could effect a stop payment presupposes that he also knew he could file an indemnity bond to protect the Bank, since both options are included in subdivision (1) of § 3–603 [R 3–602] of the U.C.C.

Viewed in retrospect, the Bank, as a practical matter, could quite safely have stopped payment on its cashier's check and, by interpleader, have paid the money into court. Staveris could not have established himself as a holder in due course (see U.C.C. § 3–302 [R 3–302]). But, if the Legislature laid upon a bank the onus of questioning the reason for the issuance of all cashier's checks it would destroy the efficacy of such instruments, which, for all practical purposes, are treated as the equivalent of cash (*Goshen Nat. Bank v. State of New York,* 141 N.Y. 379, 387).

To do justice to the Bank, it is only fair to observe that the entire brouhaha was occasioned by the intransigence of Dziurak. Had he followed the advice of Monaco to consult his own attorney, the situation in which the parties are now involved would have been averted. It was well said in *National Safe Deposit Savings & Trust Co. v. Hibbs* (229

U.S. 391, 394, wherein the doctrine of equitable estoppel was invoked for dismissing the complaint) and cited with approval in *Bunge Corp. v. Manufacturers Hanover Trust Co.* (31 N.Y.2d 223, 230):

> That where one of two innocent persons must suffer by the acts of a third, he who has enabled such third person to occasion the loss must sustain it.

Dziurak provoked the issue; Dziurak should shoulder the blame.

There is a profusion of cases to the effect that a cashier's check, once issued and in the possession of a third party, cannot legally be stopped except as provided by statute (see U.C.C., § 3–603 [R 3–602]). One of the leading cases of recent vintage is *Kaufman v. Chase Manhattan Bank, Nat. Assn.,* 370 F.Supp. 276.

There, in an opinion by Chief Judge Edelstein, plaintiff Kaufman was granted summary judgment. In that case the bank, at the request of a depositor drew a cashier's check to plaintiff as payee. When it was presented for payment the bank refused to honor it. Chief Judge Edelstein wrote that (p. 278)

> A cashier's check * * * is a check drawn by the bank on itself, payable to another person, and issued by an authorized officer of the bank. The bank, therefore, becomes both the drawer and the drawee; and the check becomes a promise by the bank to draw the amount of the check from its own resources and to pay the check upon demand. Thus, the issuance of the cashier's check constitutes an acceptance by the issuing bank; and the cashier's check becomes the primary obligation of the bank.

A reference to subdivision (1) of § 3–410 [R 3–409(a)] of the U.C.C. was contained in a footnote to the opinion with respect to acceptance upon issuance.

Contrary to Trial Term's opinion, the statute makes no distinction between a cashier's check presented for payment by a payee or one presented by an endorsee of the payee. It [sic] engages to pay on demand to the person who presents the check unless he falls within either of the categories listed in subdivision (1) of § 3–603 [R 3–602(a) and (b)] of the U.C.C. (theft or restrictive endorsement).

From all that has been stated, and harsh as it may appear, it follows that the judgment must be reversed and the complaint dismissed, with costs.

Whether future remedies are available to persons situated as is the plaintiff at bar must be left to the discretion of the State Legislature.

All concur.

BANK OF NEW YORK v. WELZ

New York Court of Appeals, 1983.
118 Misc.2d 645, 460 N.Y.S.2d 867.

SEYMOUR SCHWARTZ, J.

Plaintiff, The Bank of New York ("BONY") moves pursuant to CPLR 3212 for summary judgment against defendants The Greater New York Savings Bank ("GNYSB") and Robert Welz. GNYSB cross moves pursuant to CPLR 3212 for summary judgment against BONY or in the alternative for summary judgment against third party defendant Anne Welz.

The facts are undisputed. On April 23, 1981, Anne Welz purchased a teller's check from GNYSB drawn to BONY. The check was drawn on GNYSB's account with Manufacturer's Hanover Trust ("MHT"). Anne Welz tendered $1,900 to GNYSB but through GNYSB's error she received a teller's check in the amount of $19,000. Ms. Welz delivered the teller's check to her husband, defendant Robert Welz, who on April 24 brought it to BONY to purchase shares of Dreyfus Liquid Assets. Because BONY was the named payee on the teller's check, it was not necessary for Mr. or Ms. Welz to endorse it.

On April 24 GNYSB recognized its error and issued a stop payment order to its drawee bank MHT. BONY did not send the check to MHT for collection until May 26. In the interim BONY allowed Mr. Welz to redeem his Dreyfus Liquid Assets shares purchased with the $19,000 check. Mr. Welz also received additional funds of $9,966.16 from BONY to which he was not entitled.

BONY and GNYSB argue that as between themselves, the other is liable for the loss.

BONY contends that New York does not permit a teller's check to be stopped by a drawer bank.

GNYSB contends that the loss was caused by BONY waiting more than one month before presenting the check to MHT, the drawee bank. GNYSB also contends that BONY permitted Mr. Welz to redeem his Dreyfus shares seven days after it received the check in violation of the understanding with Dreyfus permitting redemption only after fifteen days from its receipt.

If GNYSB is not entitled to stop payment, BONY's delay in presenting the check and its rapid redemption of Robert Welz's Dreyfus shares would not relieve GNYSB from liability to BONY. Therefore, the court will first address the question whether a teller's check may be stopped in these circumstances.

UCC § 4–403 [R 4–403] provides that "[a] customer may by order to his bank stop payment of any item payable to his account * * *" As defined in UCC § 4–104(e) [R 4–104(a)(5)] " 'Customer' * * * includes a bank carrying an account with another bank." Here, GNYSB carried an account with MHT and is therefore entitled to stop payment on teller's checks.

The Code distinguishes between teller's checks (drawn by a bank on an account carried with another bank) and cashier's checks (drawn by a bank where the bank is both drawer and drawee). A cashier's check is accepted in advance by the act of issuance, *Taboada v. Bank of Babylon,* 95 Misc.2d 1000, and once a check is accepted, which occurs when a bank issues a cashier's or certified check, it cannot stop payment even on its customer's order. *Id.*

While the Code allows a teller's check to be stopped, New York courts nevertheless have frequently imposed liability on the drawer bank where it has stopped payment. See e.g. *Meckler v. Highland Falls Sav. & Loan Assn.,* 64 Misc.2d 407; *Malphrus v. Home Savings Bank of City of Albany,* 44 Misc.2d 705. In those cases, the courts dealt with the effect of UCC § 3–802(1) [R 3–310(a)] which provides that an "obligation is pro tanto discharged if a bank is drawer * * * and there is no recourse on the instrument against the underlying obligor." Thus, where a party accepts a check where the bank is the drawer (a teller's check), the party (the underlying obligor) giving it in payment is discharged if he does not endorse the teller's check.

The effect of UCC § 3–802(1) [R 3–310(a)] is that when Mr. Welz gave BONY the teller's check he became discharged on the underlying obligation to pay for the Dreyfus Liquid Assets. Thus, as payee, BONY's only remaining recourse is against GNYSB which stopped payment.

In *Malphrus, supra,* the court was concerned with this result and limited a bank's right to stop a teller's check to cases "where the bank issuing the teller's check is an actual party to a transaction." *Id.* at 707. Here GNYSB is not a party to the Dreyfus transaction.

A teller's check may also be stopped where it is endorsed to a third party who sues on the instrument. *Fur Fantastic v. Kearns,* 104 Misc.2d 1030. There the teller's check was made payable to the purchaser of the check, who endorsed it to the plaintiff as payment for services. Unlike the instant case and *Malphrus,* the teller's check in *Fur Fantastic* did not discharge the underlying obligation because the purchaser of the check, the underlying obligor, was an endorser and so there was recourse on the instrument against him, making UCC § 3–802(1) [R 3–310(a)] inapplicable.

Limiting a bank's right to stop payment on a teller's check to instances where the payee is a party to the transaction with the bank, or where the payee endorses the check to a third party is unnecessary. See Note, *Personal Money Orders and Tellers Checks: Mavericks Under the UCC,* 68 Col.L.Rev. 524, 542. A payee such as BONY has a cause of action against the drawer (GNYSB) on the instrument even if the drawer stops payment. UCC § 3–413 [R 3–414]. Moreover, a payee who has not dealt directly with the drawer may take the instrument as a holder in due course free from all defenses of any party to the instrument with whom the holder has not dealt with certain exceptions not relevant here. See UCC § 3–305 [R 3–305, 3–306].

In other words, the Code permits stop payment of a teller's check but the stop payment does not automatically preclude recovery on the instrument. Defenses may be raised by the endorser where an instrument is endorsed to a third party. Where the payee is a party to the transaction, defenses may be raised to recover on the instrument against the drawer. But where the payee is the holder in due course a stop payment does not permit defenses to be raised because such a payee has exchanged the underlying obligation for the instrument and must be protected.

GNYSB argues that BONY is not a holder in due course because of its failure to present the instrument for payment for more than a month after it was received. The argument lacks merit. UCC § 3–302(1)(b) [R 3–302(a)] provides that good faith requires honesty only. It does not require the exercise of due care. *Industrial National Bank v. Leo's Used Car Exchange, Inc.*, 362 Mass. 797, 291 N.E.2d 603 (1973).

None of the defenses available against a holder in due course (UCC § 3–305 [R 3–305]) are applicable here. Therefore, summary judgment is granted to BONY against GNYSB. Robert Welz is discharged from his obligation to pay BONY the amount of the teller's check. BONY is granted summary judgment on default against Robert Welz in the amount of $9,966.16.

GNYSB's cross motion for summary judgment against BONY is denied. Its alternative motion for summary judgment against Anne Welz is granted on default in the amount of $17,100.

Note

1. There are two related but different questions which arise in situations such as that confronted by Dziurak. The first is that dealt with in the cases: whether the drawer-issuer of the check is obligated to stop it on the request of the remitter. The second opinion holds that the issue is governed by OR 3–603 (R 3–602) of the Code. The second question is whether, if the drawer-issuer had refused to pay and had been sued by the payee, it could raise the defense of its customer? (The bank has no defense of its own since it has been paid for the check.) That issue is governed by OR 3–306 and R 3–305. Read those sections. What is the answer to the second question?

2. What advice would you offer someone in Dziurak's position with regard to the form of commercial paper he should use to pay for a one-third interest in a restaurant?

3. Read OR 3–603(1). What should constitute "indemnity deemed adequate by the party seeking the discharge"? Compare U.N.P.C. § 153, which uses the language "reasonable indemnity deemed adequate by the party seeking the discharge." Do you see any significant difference between the two formulations? Also consider § 1–203. See also R 3–602(b)(1).

4. In the *Dziurak* cases, which opinion, trial term or appellate division, offers a more convincing analysis of the "public (commercial) policies" evoked by an attempt to stop payment of a cashier's check? The New York Clearing House Association filed an amicus curiae brief in support of the appellant bank's position. Why would bank interests resist the countermand of a cashier's check?

5. Professor Lawrence concludes his analysis of remittance items with a proposal:

> Bank checks can potentially serve two important functions in the economy. Primarily, bank checks can be utilized as cash substitutes, offering the finality of payment in cash while at the same time insulating the transacting parties from the risk of loss. Additionally, bank checks serve as the personal checks of banks. The Uniform Commercial Code totally ignores these two distinct roles of bank checks and therefore should be revised.
>
> Since it is impossible for a single instrument to serve the conflicting roles of cash equivalent and personal check, the Code should explicitly assign one role to each instrument. Cashier's checks should be clearly defined as cash equivalents, and teller's checks should continue to serve as the personal checks of banks.

Lary Lawrence, *Making Cashier's Checks and Other Bank Checks Cost–Effective: A Plea for Revision of Articles 3 and 4 of the Uniform Commercial Code,* 62 Minn.L.Rev. 275, 340 (1980). Professor Shupack has observed:

> All commentators agree that cashier's checks should be cash equivalents, but none has asked what cash equivalence means. If we assume that the parties to transactions used cashier's checks because they are cash equivalents, then we should analyze each such transaction to see what would have happened if cash had in fact been used. The rules governing the capacity of a payor to recall a cash payment ought to provide an analogy for judging the capacity of a remitter to a cashier's check.
>
> Let us apply a cash equivalence test to the case of Mr. Dziurak. What would have happened had he paid for the newly issued stock with a suitcase filled with $17,000 in small bills, instead of with a cashier's check? Dziurak would have been entitled to the imposition of a constructive trust or an equitable lien on the funds. Dziurak's major problem would have been finding the funds after the transfer.
>
> Assume Mr. Staveris, the gentleman who defrauded Dziurak, took the suitcase and placed it in a safety deposit box. A well-pleaded complaint alleging fraud, could (and would) have persuaded a court to enjoin Staveris from removing the suitcase or its contents from the jurisdiction. The court would also enjoin the bank from permitting Staveris or his agent to remove the suitcase. If Staveris had deposited the small bills in his own account, a well-pleaded complaint alleging fraud could convince a court to freeze Staveris's account. If the account mingles these credits with other funds belonging to Staveris, a number of extreme legal fictions would support Dziurak's claim that

the credits commingled in the account represented credits "traceable" to his money.

Only if Staveris had taken action rendering the funds impossible to identify by use of the tracing rules would Dziurak lack a remedy against the funds themselves. The fund's loss of identity reduces Dziurak to the less satisfactory position of being Staveris's general creditor. All the commentators assume, but never state, that the law should give a cashier's check the same treatment as a dissipated fund, that is, a fund not recoverable in specie by a defrauded remitter. They never explain why that must be. Insofar as the cashier's check represents a claim to funds, the law can still identify it as a discrete entity. In that sense, identifiable cash in the suitcase represents a closer analogy to a cashier's check than to untraceable cash.

Paul M. Shupack, *Cashier's Checks, Certified Checks, and True Cash Equivalence,* 6 Cardozo L.Rev. 477 (1985). U.N.P.C. § 425 provides:

Except as provided in subsection (8), any individual shall have the same right to stop or reverse payment on a draw order drawn on the individual's behalf or accepted by an account institution as would a consumer drawer if the consumer drawer had drawn the order. Such right shall be exercised by a direction to the account institution which has drawn or accepted the order within the time limits specified by subsections (1) and (2). If such account institution has drawn the order on another account institution, it shall before midnight of the business day on which it receives the direction to stop or reverse direct such payor account institution, in accordance with the direction it has received and shall recredit the individual's account for the amount of the order or return to the person any consideration, up to the amount of the order, it received for drawing the order. No drawee or payor account institution on an order so stopped or reversed by such person shall have any further obligation to any funds claimant. Any individual who stops or reverses an order under this subsection assumes the obligation of the drawer on the order, and the individual's underlying obligation, if discharged under Section 801 when the order was transmitted, is reinstated.

Neither an account institution nor any other person may stop or reverse payment on a draw order which,

(a) an account institution has reduced to writing and on which it has assumed the obligations of the drawer or on which an account institution is an accommodation party or acceptor;

(b) is issued in tangible form by the account institution to the person from whom it receives consideration for the order, or is endorsed or accepted in tangible form by the account institution; and

(c) bears prominently on its face the legend that the order is not subject to stop or reversal and should be treated as cash, for any reason other than loss or a claim that the order is unauthorized. Any party so requesting an account institution to stop or reverse such an order shall either provide indemnity reasonably acceptable to the account institution or enjoin payment of the order by judgment of a court of competent jurisdiction in an action in which the account institution is a party.

The § 425(8)(c) legend requirement was included by the U.N.P.C. drafters at the suggestion of consumer representatives. If an exception to the stop payment restriction exists for lost or stolen instruments, are cashier's checks that satisfy the § 425(8) requirement really cash equivalents? If Dziurak came into your office before he tried to stop payment and U.N.P.C. § 425 were the law in your jurisdiction, what would you advise him to do? What ethical considerations might temper your advice?

The countermand of remittance items has been the source of considerable case law "development," see, e.g., Moon Over the Mountain, Ltd. v. Marine Midland Bank, 87 Misc.2d 918, 386 N.Y.S.2d 974 (Civ.Ct.1976) (bank refused to stop payment of cashier's check notwithstanding remitter's execution of affidavit of loss); Malphrus v. Home Savings Bank, 44 Misc.2d 705, 254 N.Y.S.2d 980 (Albany Co.1965) (teller's check drawn at request of customer cannot be stopped). The commentators have also given this issue at least as much attention as it is due, see Richard G. Bell, *The Payor Bank and Its Customer: An Analysis of Recent Cases,* 6 U.Tol.L.Rev. 110 (1974); David J. Benson, *Stop Payment of Cashier's Checks and Bank Drafts Under the Uniform Commercial Code,* 2 Ohio N.U.L.Rev. 445 (1975).

It has always been clear that as a matter of the Article 3 rules, cashier's checks and teller's checks are treated the same as any other checks. The drawer may stop payment of teller's checks or decline to pay cashier's checks, but holders in due course can recover free of any defenses that the drawer may have. And, of course, even non-holders in due course can recover against the drawer unless the drawer has a defense. Also, as noted in the cases, under both OR 3–306 and R 3–305, a drawer cannot assert as a defense the claim of a third party unless the third party is joined in the suit.

However, a number of writers have suggested that holders of cashier's and teller's checks should have an absolute right to recover on them, so that they are, in effect, just like cash. As noted earlier, a few courts have agreed with that conclusion. Revised Article 3 does not change the basic law. However R 3–411 encourages banks to pay cashier's or teller's checks even though their customer, the purchaser of the check, has asked them not to pay. It does so through imposing consequential damages in certain cases on a bank that refuses to pay such checks. Read that section.

How effective do you expect that section to be in stiffening a bank's resistance to a customer who asks the bank not to pay a cashier's check he had purchased?

Chapter 6

BANK DEPOSITS AND COLLECTIONS*

A. INTRODUCTION

This chapter examines the law governing the check collection system, which handles the more than 50 billion checks or "items" written each year. The movement of a check, a draft payable on demand and drawn on a bank, can be complex. The check collection process varies depending on the policies of the banks involved, the states in which the banks are located, and the terms of any special agreements between a bank and its customers.

This introduction traces the path of a check once it leaves the drawer's hands. Throughout the discussion, special attention is paid to the rules and regulations that banks must follow when processing checks. Specifically, the focus is on Article 4 of the Uniform Commercial Code and Federal Reserve Board Regulations J and CC. Understanding the interrelationship among the three bodies of law is essential to appreciating the purposes and effects of each.

Article 4 of the Code governs bank deposits and collections generally and defines the rights and obligations among the participants in the bank collection system. It applies to the entire banking system, not just to banks that are members of the Federal Reserve System. The U.C.C. is state law and the provisions of Article 4 are, therefore, preempted by Federal Reserve Board regulations by operation of the Supremacy Clause of the U.S. Constitution. Consequently, when there is a conflict between Article 4 and Regulation J or CC, the federal regulations override the U.C.C. provisions. The 1990 amendments to Article 4 were designed to reconcile the state and federal law. However, since these amendments have not been adopted in all 50 states, the original Article 4 provisions retain currency.

* Throughout this text, the designation "OR" refers to an Article in its original form; "R" denotes a revised Article. E.g., OR 3–303 refers to Original Article 3; R 3–303 refers to Revised Article 3.

Regulation J governs the collection of checks handled through the Federal Reserve Banks (FRBs). Its scope is therefore narrower than that of U.C.C. Article 4. Prior to 1972, Regulation J, for the most part, mirrored the original Article 4. The 1972 amendments to Regulation J significantly altered its effects and in several instances brought it into direct conflict with the provisions of original Article 4. FRBs and collecting and paying banks, using the services of FRBs, are required to comply with both Article 4 and Regulation J, though in the case of a conflict, the provisions of Regulation J prevail. The main purpose of Regulation J is to move up the deadline for a payor bank to make final settlement for a check with an FRB, in order to expedite collection. It imposes a shorter deadline on the payor bank than Article 4 requires, and banks using FRBs to clear their checks must be sure that they have complied with the stricter Regulation J deadline.

Regulation CC was enacted to form a more comprehensive and coherent set of rules to govern the check collection system. It was promulgated on September 1, 1988, pursuant to the Expedited Funds Availability Act (E.F.A.A.), passed by Congress and signed into law by President Reagan in 1987. The E.F.A.A. made expedited availability of deposited funds a matter of federal statute and encouraged the Federal Reserve Board to explore ways to make the check return process more efficient. The Board responded with Regulation CC, which necessarily incorporated the strict availability schedules set forth in the E.F.A.A. and completely overhauled the check return process. The effect of Regulation CC is to make funds represented by checks available to business and consumer depositors more quickly, while accelerating the process by which depositary banks are notified of dishonored checks. Consequently, depositaries are not exposed to too great a risk by having to make funds available more expeditiously. They should learn of a check's dishonor before they are required to make its proceeds available for withdrawal by the depositor. Regulation CC is meant to supplement Article 4 of the U.C.C. with regard to some matters and to completely replace it with regard to others. Unlike Regulation J, it applies to the entire banking system, not just to situations in which an FRB is involved. Consequently, all banks must comply with the requirements of Regulation CC even when Article 4 would dictate otherwise.

A Day In the Life of a Check

When you write a check at a store as payment for goods or services, you are issuing a negotiable instrument in the form of a "draft." According to revised 3–104, a check is a draft which is an "unconditional * * * order to pay a fixed amount of money, * * * payable on demand and drawn on a bank." Your check is a draft payable on demand to the store. It may take several days for the money to be debited from your account; this is one instance of "float." You retain the funds, at least for a couple of days, after acquiring the goods or services. There are many different types of float that can arise during the check collection process. The nature and duration of the float will depend on several factors, many of which are the object of Regulation CC provisions.

Once the check has been received by the cashier at the store, it will be placed in the cash drawer. At the end of the day, the check will be assembled with all of the other checks received by the store that day and taken to the store's bank as one bulk deposit. A teller will "post" the deposit to the store's account. The posting of the deposit immediately records that a deposit has been made, although a deposit made after the close of the banking day may not be posted until the next banking day. "Banking day," as defined by R 4–104(a)(3) (OR 4–104(1)(c)) and § 229.2(g) of Regulation CC, is the part of a day on which a bank is open for substantially all of its banking activities. Revised 4–108 (OR 4–107) and § 229.19(a) of Regulation CC both allow banks to fix a cut-off hour of 2:00 p.m. or later as the close of their banking day for receipt of deposits at bank locations. Any deposits made after this established deadline can be recorded as having been made at the beginning of the next banking day.

Once posted, the funds may not be available for withdrawal for up to five days, depending on the policies of the bank and the location of the banks on which the checks were drawn. Funds availability is now governed by the E.F.A.A. and Subpart B of Regulation CC.

Under OR 4–213(4)(a) banks were allowed to hold funds for "a reasonable time to learn that the settlement is final" before making the deposited funds available to the depositor. This meant that banks could withhold the funds represented by deposited items until they were reasonably certain that the deposited checks would be honored by the payor banks. Banks do not actually receive notice from the payor banks that checks have been honored, and the return process for dishonored checks, pre-Regulation CC, was notoriously slow. Depositary banks, therefore, felt justified in withholding the proceeds of deposited checks for a substantial time (as long as fifteen business days in some cases) in case notice of dishonor was indeed forthcoming.

Subpart B of Regulation CC completely changes the rules for funds availability as they existed under original Article 4. It calls for different categories of checks to be made available by a specified number of "business days" following the "banking day" of deposit. In order to grasp when funds must actually be made available, it is important to appreciate the distinction that Regulation CC draws between banking days and business days. As previously noted, a banking day is a day on which a particular bank is open for carrying out the vast majority of its banking functions. A business day is any day except Saturdays, Sundays, and legal holidays. Therefore, if a particular bank only provides drive-thru service on Wednesdays, Wednesdays would not be considered banking days for the bank, although they are certainly business days.

For purposes of determining when a deposit is made or when a bank must take a certain action, the funds availability provisions of

Regulation CC focus on the banking day of a particular bank. However, when counting days in order to determine when funds must be made available, the number of business days is relevant. Therefore, if Wednesdays are not banking days for a bank they will still be counted when determining how quickly funds must be made available, although a deposit made on a Wednesday would not be posted until Thursday morning.

Section 229.10 of Regulation CC mandates next day availability for certain "low risk" types of checks, such as cashier's checks, treasury checks, and "on-us" checks (when the drawee and depositary bank are the same). Any deposits subject to this section must be made available to the depositor on the business day following the banking day of deposit if the deposit is made in person to an employee of the bank. If the deposit is not made in person, i.e., a deposit made at an automated teller machine (ATM), the funds must be made available on the second business day following the banking day of deposit.

Section 229.12 of Regulation CC fixes the availability schedule for checks that fall outside the low risk category covered by section 229.10. For these, availability depends on whether the check is classified as "local" or "non-local." A check is considered local if it is payable through a bank located in the same Federal Reserve check processing region as the depositary bank. If it is drawn on a bank located outside the check processing region of the depositary bank, then it is considered a non-local check. For local checks, the funds must be made available by the second business day following the banking day of deposit. If the check is deemed non-local, the funds must be made available by the fifth business day following the banking day of deposit. Of course, banks can opt to give faster availability to their customers if they so choose. Regulation CC merely defines the outside limits of the holds that may be imposed by depositary banks.

These sections of Regulation CC completely obviate the open-ended standard found in OR 4–213(4)(a). The 1990 amendments to Article 4 modified this section, renumbered 4–215(e)(1), to reflect the fact that changes in the U.C.C. were mandated by the time schedules required by Regulation CC. The new section provides that a bank may withhold funds until the bank has had a "reasonable time to receive return of the item and the item has not been received within that time." Since Subpart C of Regulation CC (discussed below) speeds up the amount of time it takes to learn of dishonor of a check, the "reasonable" period for a bank to withhold funds is substantially reduced.

Sections 229.15 through 229.18 of Regulation CC describe the disclosures that banks must now make to their current and prospective customers regarding the banks' funds availability policy. Banks must post reminder disclosures in branch lobbies, at ATMs, and on preprinted deposit slips. In addition, banks are required to make separate disclosures when a special hold is being imposed or when case-by-case holds may be necessary. Article 4 of the U.C.C. contains no provisions requiring these types of disclosures.

The check that is the subject of this introduction will most likely be drawn on a local bank. This means that the deposited funds must be available for withdrawal by the second business day following the banking day of deposit. Since a banking day generally ends at 2:00 p.m., any deposits made after 2:00 p.m. will be recorded as having been received on the next banking day. If the store makes its deposit at 12:30 p.m. on Monday, then the funds must be available for withdrawal by Wednesday morning. If the store makes its deposit at 3:00 p.m. on Monday, the funds will not have to be made available until Thursday morning, because the deposit will be recorded as having been made on the morning of the Tuesday banking day.

The store's bank is now concerned with getting the money for each check from the many banks on which they are drawn. Depending on the bank, all of the checks deposited may be sent at the end of the day to a central processing location or main branch of the bank within the state. Many banks send the checks through an intermediary branch for initial processing before they go to the main branch. Assume that the store's bank uses an intermediary branch for initial processing.

Once the intermediary receives the checks from the store's bank and from the other branches of the bank that use this branch for the initial processing, the branch employees will begin the tasks of "inscribing" and "proving" the checks. Inscribing involves encoding each check with the amount for which it is written using "Magnetic Ink Character Recognition" (MICR). This encoding is accomplished by a machine that responds to an operator who types in the amount of the check on a number pad. The MICR-encoded amount appears in the right field, lower right-hand corner of the check. The pre-printed checks are already encoded with numbers that represent the drawee bank's name, branch location, and customer account number. Having all of this information encoded on the check in this way enables the checks to be processed by computer from this point forward.

The checks from each branch must also "prove." Proving may be done by a computer that reads the MICR number or may be accomplished simultaneously as the operator enters the amount of the check on the encoding machine. In order for a branch's batch of checks to prove, the total amount on the deposit slips that accompanied each customer's deposit must match the total amount of all of the checks. The deposit slips represent a "debit," or liability, for the bank and the total amount of the checks represents a "credit," or asset, for the bank. These amounts must balance.

The last thing that the intermediary branch will probably do is stamp or "indorse" the back of each check with the bank's nine-digit routing number, the name of the bank, the date, and the place that the check is processed. Indorsement of the check by each bank that is involved in its processing helps facilitate the prompt return of a dishonored check to the original depositary institution as well as error resolution.

Section 229.35 of Regulation CC greatly supplements the almost non-existent indorsement standards found in OR and R 4–206. Rather than the "any agreed method that identifies the transferor bank" language of the U.C.C., Regulation CC, in both section 229.35 and Appendix D, sets out a rigid and uniform system that accomplishes clear identification of the check as it travels through the processing system. In order to comply with the new rules in Subpart C of Regulation CC (discussed below), which governs the process by which dishonored checks are returned, the indorsements on the back of the checks must be clear and readable. The returning bank must be able to identify the original depositary bank and all the intermediary banks that handled the check during its forward collection, a task that was often difficult when the U.C.C.'s lenient indorsement standard was all that banks had to observe.

The checks will now be sent to the bank's main branch for further processing. Once received there, the checks will be fed into machines—"reader-sorter" computers—that read the MICR numbers and sort the checks according to the location of the bank on which the check is drawn. The checks will probably be divided into "on us" checks, checks drawn on one of the bank's own branches; checks drawn on other local banks; checks drawn on other in-state, non-local banks; and checks drawn on out-of-state banks. Inevitably some of the checks will be rejected by the machine as unreadable and will have to be processed by hand.

The reader-sorter will print out all of the information read off the checks. It will also compare the debit totals (the deposit slips) with the credit totals (the check amounts) for each batch of checks which is run through the machine. Any discrepancies between these numbers will, if all goes well, be accounted for by the amounts of the "non-machinables." This proves the checks once again.

In this example, assume that the store's bank is a member of the Federal Reserve System (the Fed) and that all clearing functions are performed for the store's bank by the Federal Reserve Banks. Although this type of arrangement is by far the most prevalent, many banks are not members of the Fed and use correspondent banks or separate clearinghouse banks to process their checks. Some banks use the Fed's processing procedures without being members and then accomplish their clearing of accounts with other banks through separate arrangements. The next step in this check's processing is to get it ready to go to the appropriate branch of the Fed.

Before sending checks to the Fed, the store's bank must prepare "cash letters." These are developed from the information obtained from the sorted checks. Cash letters indicate how much money is owed to the store's bank from all of the banks on which the different checks are drawn. In effect, these cash letters represent a claim against the accounts held by other banks. Once the letters are prepared, the checks are put into special boxes, supplied by the Fed, for shipment. Depending on the categories of bank locations that the checks fall into (local, in-state, out-of-state, etc.), they are shipped to the appropriate branch of the Fed.

When the checks leave the possession of the main branch of the depositary bank, they carry with them several warranties made by that bank for the benefit of the Fed and all subsequent collecting banks. These warranties are found in both Regulation J and U.C.C. Article 4.

Section 210.5(a)(2) of Regulation J provides that a sender of an item warrants to the FRB that the sender has good title and that the item has not been materially altered. Original and revised 4–207 provide that a sender makes these same warranties to any collecting bank or customer. In addition, R 4–207(a)(5) (OR 4–207(2)(e)) provides a warranty that the sender has no knowledge of any insolvency proceeding against the maker, acceptor, or drawer of an item. That warranty is not found in Regulation J.

Both § 210.5(a)(3) of Regulation J and R 4–207 similarly describe the remedies available to a collecting bank when the warranties are breached by the sender. Both require the sending bank to indemnify each FRB or collecting bank for expenses incurred as a result of the breach of warranty. Section 210.5(a)(3) of Regulation J specifically allows an FRB to recover attorney's fees. Original and R 4–207 refer more generally to recoverable "expenses" associated with the loss and do not specifically authorize attorney's fees. However, the official comment to R 4–207 provides that attorney's fees are not necessarily excluded as part of the recoverable "expenses" permitted by this section (by referring the reader to the official comment to R 3–416 which covers transfer warranties for negotiable instruments generally). The ambiguity is intended to leave the question of attorney's fees to other state law (see e.g. *Guaranty Bank & Trust Co. v. Federal Reserve Bank of Kansas City,* 454 F.Supp. 488 (W.D.Okl.1977)).

Section 210.6(a)(2) of Regulation J allows an FRB to rely on the routing number that appears in any form, including magnetic ink, on a check, for purposes of transfer (among collecting banks) or presentment (to drawee/payor). When acting in reliance on this number, the FRB is not responsible for any delay resulting from an incorrect routing designation. This protection used to only be implicit in Article 4, but in 1990, R 4–209 was added, providing "encoding warranties." Under R 4–209(a), a person or bank that encodes information on an item warrants to any collecting or payor bank that the information is correctly encoded. Consequently, as under Regulation J, a collecting bank may rely on the encoded information and will not be held liable for any delay resulting from erroneous information. In addition, R 4–209 allows a collecting bank to recover for any loss suffered as a result of breach of this warranty by the sender.

At this point in the check's journey, it is probably sometime in the early evening of the day that the check was deposited at the store's bank. The sooner the checks get to the Fed, the better. Original and revised 4–202 require all banks handling an item to take the necessary action (in this case sending it on for presentment) by midnight of the banking day following the banking day of receipt. However, it is in the depositary bank's interest to get the checks to the appropriate branch of the Fed on the night of the day of receipt. By doing this, the bank will get an extra day's use of the funds represented by the cash letters. The bank's account with the Fed is credited immediately with the amount of the cash letter sent by the bank. This is important because all member banks are required to keep a certain percentage of their total deposits in cash in their vaults or on deposit with the Fed. Having an extra day's use of the amount of the cash letter will either help the bank meet its reserve requirements or provide excess reserves that can then be loaned, at a price, to other banks that are having trouble meeting their reserve requirements ("Fed Funds").

While the checks are en route to the Fed, the main branch has probably sent each branch a magnetic tape containing all of the information read off the checks deposited at that branch. The store's branch will then merge this tape with a computerized ledger of the branch's accounts. This will credit each account with the amount of the deposit made earlier that day. The credit to the account does not mean that the funds are immediately available. The funds only need be made available for withdrawal by the store in compliance with rules of Regulation CC.

Competition among banks for customer's business often forces banks to give depositors credit the day after the deposit is made for checks drawn on local banks. Before Regulation CC, some banks denied customers access to funds even after the bank had in fact received credit for the deposit by the Fed or payment from the drawee bank. Float existed because the bank would have use of the customers' deposits for a period before the depositors were allowed to withdraw it.

As noted above, usually a customer who receives credit for a deposit the next day is not obtaining a float at the expense of the bank: the bank was given immediate credit by the Fed for its cash letter and so the bank had use of the funds the day after the deposit was made as long as there were no delays in getting the checks to the Fed. If, for some reason, a shipment to the Fed was delayed, the customer may have use of his funds before the bank gets Fed credit and, therefore, be the recipient of a day or two of float at the bank's expense.

Later in the evening of the same day that the store made its deposit, the checks are received at the different branches of the Fed. They are "proved" once again against the cash letters sent by the banks and then stamped with the Fed's indorsement. The Fed has now accepted the cash letters and it will credit the reserve account of each of the depositing banks. At this point, the amount of the checks is owed to the Fed by each of the banks on which the checks are drawn because the depositing banks have already received credit for the deposit.

If the store's checking account with the depositary bank is an interest bearing account, the deposit will begin earning interest as soon as the bank receives credit from the Fed for its cash letter. This is because section 229.14 of Regulation CC requires that depositary banks begin paying interest on deposits in interest bearing accounts on the banking day that the bank receives credit from the Fed for the deposit. Again, this is a subject not dealt with by Article 4.

The checks are then sorted according to the individual banks on which they are drawn and the total amount owed to the Fed by each drawee bank is determined. Generally, a bank will settle with the Fed for the amount of the checks drawn against it by allowing the Fed to debit its reserve account held with the Fed. This may mean borrowing Fed Funds from other banks with excess reserves in order to keep the required amount of funds on deposit. By crediting the reserve accounts of depositing banks and then debiting the reserve accounts of drawee banks, the Fed has performed its clearinghouse function. If the drawee bank is not a member with reserves on deposit, it has to make a remittance for the amount of the checks drawn against it.

Settlement by the drawee bank must be made in compliance with the rules provided by Article 4 of the U.C.C. and Regulation J. Section 210.9 of Regulation J, as amended in 1972, is the part of the regulation that seeks to reduce the amount of float in the bank collection process. The provision regulates the time and manner of settlement for cash items by drawee banks. It imposes a new deadline on drawee banks that was not present in original Article 4 and is not present in revised Article 4.

Original and revised 4–302 state that a drawee bank becomes accountable for an item if it has not settled for it by midnight of the banking day of receipt. Under section 210.9 of amended Regulation J, a drawee bank is accountable for an item at the close of the drawee bank's banking day on the banking day the item was received. This means that the drawee bank must settle with the FRB for the amount of the item by the end of the banking day on which it receives it. When settling for items, drawee banks must make sure that they satisfy the time requirements of Regulation J, even though Article 4 does not require the same expedience.

Normally, a drawee bank will settle for an item by a debit to its reserve account with the Fed, but this is not always the case. Under OR 4–211, a drawee bank is allowed to settle for an item with a collecting bank using a draft remittance drawn on another bank. Section 210.9(a)(1) of Regulation J changes this by requiring that remittance, other than debit to an FRB account, be made in cash unless the FRB agrees to accept another form of remittance.

This discrepancy between Regulation J and the U.C.C. generated much litigation over whether Regulation J overrode Article 4 and to whom the new rules should apply (see, e.g., *Community Bank v. Federal Reserve Bank of San Francisco,* infra page 350). Regulation J prevailed because of OR 4–103, which allows the Fed to vary the U.C.C. bank collection rules. The 1990 amendments to U.C.C. Article 4 bring the state law into conformity with Regulation J. Revised 4–213 requires that settlement be made in cash or by credit to an account with the Fed, unless the Fed specifically authorizes remittance by another means.

The checks are now sent to the individual banks on which they are drawn. The FRB also makes some warranties when it sends items on to the drawee banks or other collecting banks. Again, these warranties are imposed by Article 4 and Regulation J.

Pursuant to section 210.6(b) of Regulation J, the FRB warrants that checks forwarded by the Fed contain no forged indorsements and have not been materially altered. These are the same warranties that OR and R 4–207 impose on all collecting banks. In addition, under R 4–208(a)(3) (OR 4–206(2)(b)), a transferor warrants that it has no knowledge of a forged drawer's signature. This warranty is not found in Regulation J.

Article 4 and Regulation J also provide standards of care that must be observed by the FRB when handling an item, as well as the possible liability to which an FRB might be exposed if something were to go wrong. Section 210.6(a)(1) of Regulation J provides that an FRB acts "only as an agent or sub-agent of the owner with respect to an item" and that the agency relationship terminates when the FRB receives payment for the item. In addition, FRBs are required to use ordinary care and to act in good faith when handling an item. However, because of the agency relationship, unless an FRB fails to use ordinary care or to act in good faith, it cannot be held liable for the item or its proceeds unless there is a breach of warranty. As a result, risk of loss is on the sender unless the FRB has been negligent, acted in bad faith, or breached a warranty. The U.C.C. provisions on these topics are similar. Original and revised 4–201 also make a collecting bank an agent or sub-agent with regard to the owner of an item. Original and revised 4–202 require that a collecting bank use ordinary care in its handling of the item as agent for the owner.

Before 1986, section 210.6 of Regulation J was in conflict with OR 4–202. The federal law insulated an FRB from negligence liability to a nonbank sender (usually the owner) of an item. This often left a nonbank sender completely without recourse when an FRB handled an item negligently (see *Childs v. Federal Reserve Bank,* 719 F.2d 812 (5th Cir. 1983)). In response to litigation, the language of section 210.6 was amended to make the FRB liable to the owner, the sender, or a prior collecting bank. Consequently, Regulation J and Article 4 are now consistent on this point.

When the drawee banks receive the checks from the FRB they have probably already settled with the Fed by having their Reserve account debited. They must now debit the individual drawer's accounts. This will most likely occur two to five days after the check was deposited, depending on the locations of the drawee and depositary banks. There is float involved at this end also. When the store customer wrote the check she became immediately accountable to the store for the amount of the check. However, she has use of the funds until the amount of the check is actually debited from her balance. Of course, she still must make sure that there are sufficient funds in her account to cover the check by the time it is received by her bank or her check will be dishonored and she may have to pay a penalty.

If the drawee bank discovers that the drawer has insufficient funds in her account, and chooses not to pay the check, the drawee bank must return the item to the Fed or the depositary bank within the Article 4, Regulation J, and Regulation CC time limits. Regulation CC has the most to say on this subject and it overrides several of the provisions of both Article 4 and Regulation J.

When the E.F.A.A. was enacted by Congress in 1987, it did not require that the Federal Reserve Board enact new standards for faster return of dishonored checks. However, Congress strongly encouraged the Board to take such action in order to complement the new funds availability schedules of the E.F.A.A. Subpart C of Regulation CC is the Board's response. It decreases the amount of time it takes for a returned check to make it back to the depositary bank. By speeding up the return process, Regulation CC provides protection to depositary banks. This protection is necessary because depositary banks now have to meet the stricter time requirements for making funds available to depositors under Subpart B of Regulation CC. With Subpart C of Regulation CC in effect, depositary banks should receive notice of dishonor before they are required to place the funds at the disposal of their depositors.

Original and revised 4–301 and 4–302 and section 210.12 of Regulation J require that a drawee bank send a dishonored check back through its chain of indorsements by midnight of the banking day following the day the item is received. Both Article 4 and Regulation J are concerned only with the time when the returning bank actually dispatches the dishonored check back up the collection chain.

Regulation CC shifts the focus to the time of receipt by the depositary bank. Sections 229.30 and 229.31 outline the responsibilities of the returning bank and call for the check to be returned in an "expeditious manner." Whether or not a bank has sent a check back in an expeditious manner is determined by two tests. Satisfaction of either test means that the returning bank has fulfilled the expeditious return requirement.

The "two-day/four-day" test is satisfied if the drawee bank returns a local check to the depositary bank by 4:00 pm on the second business day following the banking day of deposit (by the fourth business day if the check is non-local). The "forward collection" test is satisfied if the drawee bank returns the check by a means as fast as a similar bank would use for the forward collection of the check. The drawee bank and all intermediary banks are required to meet this expeditious return standard by satisfying one of those two tests when handling a dishonored item.

Under Article 4 there is no duty imposed on a drawee bank to give early notification to a depositary bank that an item has been dishonored. Regulations J and CC do require such notice. Section 210.12 of Regulation J requires wire notice of dishonor for checks over $2,500 to be sent to the depositary bank by midnight of the third day following presentment. This provision of Regulation J has been supplemented by Section 229.33 of Regulation CC under which the duty to give notice of dishonor applies to all checks over $2,500 (rather than the Regulation J standards which only affected checks in the Fed system) and the deadline has been adjusted so that notice must be received by the depositary bank by 4:00 pm on the second business day following presentment.

Regulation CC also has a substantial impact on the path a dishonored check will follow on its way back to the depositary bank. Pre–Regulation CC, as a check made its way through the forward collection process, each collecting bank would receive a provisional settlement for the item. Then, if the check was dishonored, it would have to be sent back along the same chain of banks that it traveled on its trip forward so that each bank could revoke its provisional credit. Because this often caused the return process to be unnecessarily slow, Regulation CC § 229.36(d) makes settlement in the forward collection process final instead of provisional. This means that a returning bank does not receive credit for a dishonored check by a revocation of the previous provisional settlement. Instead the returning bank settles with a prior collecting bank with another final settlement. In other words, there is final settlement by each bank on the forward trip and final settlement by each bank on the return trip.

This eliminates the need for the returned check to follow the same path that it did during forward collection. The purpose of this section is to encourage a returning bank to skip steps in the collection chain in order to speed up the return process. Section 229.31 of Regulation CC also authorizes direct return of an item to the depositary institution, i.e. completely skipping the intermediary banks that handled the check in its forward collection. This section overrides revised 4–214, which calls for an item to be returned by having each bank send it back to its transferor and receive a charge-back against the provisional credit it should have received on the forward collection trip. In original 4–212(2) there is an optional provision that states can adopt allowing for direct return. Revised Article 4 eliminates this optional section and instead chooses simply to recognize the pre-emptive nature of the new provisions of Regulation CC. The Official Comment 4 to revised 4–214 of the U.C.C. acknowledges that Regulation CC overrides this section, by allowing direct return and making settlement final during forward collection, and states that these U.C.C. provisions apply only to non-check items.

If all requirements for returning checks are met, the drawee bank should receive settlement from the Fed for the amount of the dishonored check, probably by means of a credit to its Federal Reserve account. The depositary bank will have to settle with the Fed for the amount of the dishonored check and will most likely do so by having its reserve account debited. Once notice of dishonor reaches the depositary bank, the depositary will debit the depositor's account for the amount of the check, if it has already credited the check to the account. Pursuant to OR and R 4–202, the depositary bank has a duty to notify the depositor that the check has been dishonored by midnight of the day following the day the bank received the returned check.

If the check that you wrote to the store is returned to the store due to insufficient funds in your account, the store may try redepositing in the hope that you have remedied the problem with your account. This can become extremely costly because both the store and your bank will probably charge $15–$20 each time the check is returned. For this reason, it is important to keep track of your account balance and not to rely for too long on the "float" that you received immediately after you wrote the check.

The materials in this chapter focus on the conflicts and problems that can arise at different stages during the check collection process and the interplay between Article 4, as adopted by different states, and federal regulation. The chapter is organized into four broad topics: the role of the Federal Reserve, including the operation of Regulation J, as compared with U.C.C. Article 4; funds availability issues under Article 4 and the impact of Subpart B of Regulation CC; the return process for dishonored checks as addressed by Article 4 and Subpart C of Regulation CC; and, finally, fraud and negligence issues that arise in the check collection system.

B. EVOLUTION OF CHECK COLLECTION AND THE FEDERAL RESERVE SYSTEM

The Federal Reserve System defines the bank collection process, regulating the manner in which checks can be collected and the time in which funds must be made available for withdrawal. The following excerpt describes, summarily, the role of the Federal Reserve in the bank collection process and surveys some of the measures taken by the Fed to expedite collections and support the finality of payments by various media.

THE FEDERAL RESERVE AND THE PAYMENTS MECHANISM: 1983

Excerpted from *Uniform Commercial Code Annual Survey,* 39 Bus.Law. 1315, 1364–66 (1984).

Background

The Federal Reserve, since its inception in 1913, has been a major participant in the nation's payments system. Indeed, the Federal Reserve System was originally established, in part, to respond to the breakdown of the payments system during the panic of 1907.

The Federal Reserve provides a nationwide network for the collection of checks as well as for the settlement of debts involved in the collection process. Depositary institutions may deposit checks (either directly or indirectly through a correspondent) with the Federal Reserve for collection. A depositary institution depositing a check for collection with the Federal Reserve receives provisional [a] credit based upon an availability schedule determined in part by the location of the paying bank. The Federal Reserve may send the check to a subsequent collecting bank, or may itself present it at a place requested by the paying bank under a special collection arrangement with the paying bank, or through a clearinghouse. The paying bank may pay for the check through a debit to its account at the Federal Reserve, in cash, or in any other form of payment acceptable to the Reserve Bank. Federal Reserve check float is created when the Federal Reserve has not received payment from the paying bank when credit is provided to the depositing bank in accordance with the applicable availability schedule.

The Federal Reserve also provides a nationwide network for the collection of items ineligible for processing through normal check collection channels. Such "noncash items" include coupons, bonds, and bankers' acceptances. A depositary institution depositing such a noncash item for collection with the Federal Reserve receives provisional credit based either upon an availability schedule or upon when the Federal Reserve receives payment for the item in actually and finally collected funds.

The Federal Reserve has established a mechanism for the wire transfer of funds between two depositary institutions maintaining accounts with the Federal Reserve. Unlike the collection of checks and noncash items, a wire transfer is finally paid when the Federal Reserve sends the item, or an advice of credit, to the receiving depositary institution.

The Federal Reserve also clears, settles, and delivers electronic payments through the provision of automated clearinghouse services (ACH). Depositary institutions may use the ACH to automatically function recurring credits (for example, salary payments) or debits (for example, mortgage payments) to a customer's account. ACH transactions may be settled against the depositary institutions' accounts with

a. Under Regulation CC, final credit[-ed].

the Federal Reserve. Like check transactions, but unlike wire transfers, ACH transactions may be returned.

In 1980 Congress substantially rewrote the ground rules governing the Federal Reserve's involvement in the nation's payments system. The Monetary Control Act of 1980 (MCA) required the Federal Reserve, for the first time, to provide access to virtually all of its services to all depositary institutions on the same terms and conditions, and to charge for such services. Over the long run, the fees for such services are to be established "on the basis of all direct and indirect costs actually incurred in providing the Federal Reserve services priced," including imputed costs which take into account the taxes and the return on capital that would have been applicable had the services been furnished by a private business firm. Due regard may be given, however, to "competitive factors and the provision of an adequate level of such services nationwide."

Federal Law preempts inconsistent state law, as a matter of constitutional imperative. So how do the actions of the Federal Reserve Board operate with Article 4 of the U.C.C.? The fit between the two is not always perfect, and the courts must determine the parameters of the accommodation. The following case treats the sometimes uneasy tension in terms that may foreshadow a good deal to come as the federal regulators become increasingly aggressive in their promulgation of check collection law.

COMMUNITY BANK v. FEDERAL RESERVE BANK OF SAN FRANCISCO

United States Court of Appeals, Ninth Circuit, 1974.
500 F.2d 282.

SNEED, CIRCUIT JUDGE:

On June 21, 1972, the Board of Governors of the Federal Reserve System unanimously approved changes in Regulation J, 12 C.F.R. 210, which governs the collection of checks and other items by Federal Reserve Banks. Appellant State Banks, who are neither members of nor affiliated with the Federal Reserve System, object to the amendments to Regulation J insofar as they affect nonmember and non-affiliated payor banks.

Briefly stated, the changes in Regulation J affect both the time and manner in which payor banks must settle for demand items presented for collection by Reserve Banks. Prior to the amendments, payor banks became accountable if they failed to settle for demand items before midnight of the banking day of receipt, and settlements made earlier could be revoked prior to the midnight deadline. The amendments to Regulation J advance the settlement time to the close of the banking day of receipt, and only if settlement is made prior to this time may it be revoked before midnight of the banking day of receipt. The amendments also affect the manner in which settlement may be made by eliminating drafts drawn on other banks as permissible forms of settlement.[1]

Appellants attack the amendments to Regulation J on two broad grounds. First, they urge that the changes are inconsistent with the time and manner of settlement provisions contained in the California Commercial Code, which they contend should govern the operations of nonmember banks chartered under the laws of the State of California. Second, they argue that, to the extent that they attempt to bind payor banks which are not members of the Federal Reserve System, the amendments to Regulation J exceed the power conferred on the Board under the Federal Reserve Act.

* * *

I.

Background

Approximately 25 billion checks were collected by banks in 1972; of these, eight billion, or roughly one-third, were handled by Federal Reserve Banks. The Reserve Banks provide check collection services for member banks and affiliated nonmember banks which maintain a certain balance with a Reserve Bank; neither the members nor the affiliated nonmembers, however, are required to use the services of the Reserve Banks to collect checks which have been presented to them.

To handle the increased volume of checks, Federal Reserve and other large banks now use computer-controlled, highspeed electronic sorters which are capable of handling 1000 checks per minute. For this purpose, "Magnetic Ink Character Recognition" (MICR) units are preprinted on each check. The first group of four digits in the MICR number encoded on the bottom of each check designates the Federal Reserve district, territory, and relationship to the local Federal Reserve office.[3] Each of the appellant State Banks encode their checks with a MICR number that begins with "12," which indicates that they are located in the district of the Federal Reserve Bank of San Francisco. The consequence of this is that checks which are drawn on appellants may be presented by a member or affiliated nonmember bank for collection through the Federal Reserve system.

When checks are presented to a Reserve Bank for collection, settlement is made on the basis of a deferred-payment schedule. This schedule is, with one important exception, based on the amount of time usually required for the Reserve Bank to collect items of a similar type. Since checks drawn on banks in the same city may usually be collected

1. Prior to the amendments, the time and manner of settlement provisions of Regulation J and the California Commercial Code were virtually identical.

3. In addition, the numerator of the fraction located on the upper right-hand portion of appellants' checks represents the Federal Reserve routing number.

on the same day, same-day credit is passed to the depositor. Checks drawn on banks in other cities having Federal Reserve offices may usually be collected the following day; accordingly, one-day credit is passed to the depositor. Twoday [sic] credit is passed when the check is drawn on banks located within the same Federal Reserve territory but outside of a Reserve office city. The exception exists because, while three days may be required to collect checks drawn on banks outside of the Reserve territory and not located in an office city,[4] two-day credit is the maximum length of deferment for any check presented to a Reserve Bank for collection.[5] Thus, in this latter situation the Reserve Bank pays for a check on the basis of the deferred-payment schedule one day before that check is actually collected; this effectively generates a one-day, interest-free loan to the bank involved. The total amount of such loans is known as Federal Reserve "float." Aggravating the problem of delay in the process of settlement is the practice of some payor banks to settle by means of drafts drawn on other banks.[6]

To alleviate these problems, the amendments to Regulation J (1) advance the time within which payor banks must settle for checks presented for collection by Reserve Banks, and (2) eliminate the use of bank drafts as permissible forms of settlement by requiring settlement to be in immediately-available funds. The resulting acceleration of the process, in turn, enables the Reserve Bank in some instances to pass earlier credit to the depositor bank. From the vantage point of the Federal Reserve, the changes are particularly desirable in that they tend to reduce the problem of "float."

II.

State Law

We now turn to a consideration of whether the amendments to Regulation J are, as the appellants insist, in conflict with the pertinent provisions of the California Commercial Code.

A. *Time of Settlement*

Two principal California Commercial Code provisions governing the time in which a payor bank must settle when presented with a check for collection are affected by the amendments to Regulation J. Section 4302 [R 4–302] makes a payor bank accountable if it retains an item beyond midnight of the banking day of receipt without settling for it, and Section 4301 [R 4–301] allows the payor banks to revoke a provisional settlement if such revocation is made before the midnight deadline. Section 210.9(a)(1) of the amended Regulation J, however, makes a payor bank accountable if it fails to settle for demand items

4. The three days include: (1) one day to process the item at the Reserve Bank of first receipt and transmit it to the Reserve Bank for the area in which the payor bank is located; (2) one day for the item to be processed by the second Reserve Bank and transmitted to the payor bank; and (3) one additional day to receive the remittance.

5. Federal Reserve Operating Circular No. 1.

6. A draft on the remitting bank itself is not permissible because it would merely substitute for the original item another item on the same payor. California Commercial Code 4211(a) [R 4–213(a)].

before the close of its banking day of receipt, and Section 210.12(a) provides that only if settlement has been made by this time may the payor bank revoke prior to midnight of the banking day of receipt.

Taken this far, Regulation J quite obviously is in conflict with the above provisions of state law. The conflict disappears, however, in light of the flexibility provided in Section 4103 [R 4–103] of the Commercial Code. Subsection (1) of this provision permits variation of the Code's provisions by agreement, and subsection (2) provides that "Federal Reserve regulations and operating letters, clearing house rules, and the like, have the effect of agreements * * * whether or not specifically assented to by all parties interested in the items handled."

Appellants contend that Section 4103(2) [R 4–103(b)] does not operate to make Federal Reserve regulations binding on nonmember, payor banks. We disagree. The legislative history behind the language of subsection (2), which elevates Federal Reserve regulations to the status of agreements, "whether or not specifically assented to by all parties interested in the items handled," makes clear that it may be applicable to non-member payor banks. The California Commercial Code Comment indicates that, under prior California law, clearinghouse rules "did not govern the rights of drawer and payee who were not members of the clearinghouse and who did not contract with express reference to those rules." The reference to the rights of drawers and payees under "prior California law" suggests that the Code had changed this result. That this change effected by the Code is not limited to drawers and payees is indicated by the breadth of the following comment of the Senate Fact Finding Committee: "Subdivision 2 apparently changes the rule insofar as it applies between parties who are not members of the clearinghouse."

The Report of the New York Law Revision Commission contains an even stronger indication that Section 4103(2) [R 4–103(b)] is applicable to nonmember, payor banks which affiliate themselves with the Federal Reserve's check collection process:

> Federal Reserve Regulations and operating letters now operate as "agreements" between the Federal Reserve Banks and banks using the Federal Reserve facilities for collection, and clearinghouse rules now operate of course as agreements among member banks and banks clearing through banks that are members of the clearinghouse association. *They are similarly effective as agreements binding on other banks, and their customers, whenever a claim of agency and subagency can be made out connecting the remote bank, and its customer, with the banks that are parties to the agreement,* and the agency includes, as a term of the agreement binding the remote party, the power to adhere to that agreement on behalf of the remote principal. Explicit agreement is sometimes difficult to spell out, however. Section 4103(2) [R 4–103(b)] postulates an implied assent as a rule of law.

The "claim of agency or subagency" referred to in the Report, which constitutes the necessary predicate for Federal Reserve regulations to be binding on nonmember banks, is readily established by the current voluntary use of MICR members by appellants.

As mentioned above, each of appellants encode their checks with the number "12," which indicates that they are located in the 12th Federal Reserve district. Obviously, if this number is merely removed, appellants' checks cannot be electronically processed. If, however, it is replaced by appropriate symbols, the checks may be electronically processed and collected outside of the Federal Reserve system.

That elimination of the Federal Reserve routing numbers is commercially feasible is demonstrated by the current practices of nonpar banks. Since Reserve Banks are prohibited by statute from paying an exchange fee, 12 U.S.C. 342, checks drawn on nonpar banks cannot be collected through the Federal Reserve system. Nonpar banks replace the Federal Reserve routing number on the lower left-hand portion or their checks with the number "9." This enables the checks of nonpar banks to be electronically processed even though the MICR number begins with a "9" and even though it does not contain a number referring to any Federal Reserve office. A somewhat similar system as an alternative to the use of Federal Reserve routing numbers is available to appellants. The fact that nonmember banks may find it less commercially advantageous than utilizing the Federal Reserve routing number does not militate against this conclusion.

In sum, appellants are not required to include the Federal Reserve routing number on their checks, and so long as they continue to use this number, the "claim of agency or subagency" referred to in the Report of the New York Law Revision Commission exists, and the terms of Regulation J are binding upon them because of the operation of Section 4103(2) [R 4–103(b)].

B. Manner of Settlement

The asserted conflict between the amended Regulation J and Section 4211 [R 4–213] of the California Commercial Code is also nonexistent.

Section 4211 [R 4–213] lists six forms of remittance which "a collecting bank may take in settlement of an item." The first of these, Section 4211(1)(a) [R 4–213(a)], is "a check of the remitting bank or of another bank on any bank except the remitting bank." Section 210.-9(a) of Regulation J, however, provides that settlement shall be affected [sic] in one of three ways: (1) a debit to an account on the books of a Federal Reserve Bank; (2) payment in cash, or (3) at the discretion of the Federal Reserve Bank, any other form of remittance, provided that the proceeds of such payment are available to the Reserve Bank "not later than the close of the banking day for such Federal Reserve Bank on the day on which such item was so received by the paying bank." A check of the payor bank drawn on another bank would not be convertible into proceeds within the time limits set forth in Section 210.9(a) of the amended Regulation J; thus, Section 4211(1)(a) [R 4–213(a)] of the Commercial Code is no longer available as a means of settlement for checks cleared through the Federal Reserve system.

Appellants argue that Section 4211 [R 4–213] treats settlement as a two-way proposition, and that it was designed for the convenience of both the payor and the collecting banks. From this, they conclude that the collecting bank, in this case the Federal Reserve, does not have the option of refusing to accept any of the six forms of settlement listed in Section 4211 [R 4–213].

Those contentions are refuted by the background of and change effected by Section 4211 [R 4–213]. At common law, a collecting bank which accepted anything short of specie in settlement did so at its own risk. As the Uniform Commercial Code Comment makes clear, the purpose of Section 4211 [R 4–213] is to protect the collecting bank if it accept something less than legal tender:

> Subsection (1) states various types of remittance instruments and authorities to charge which may be received by a collecting bank in a settlement for an item, without the collecting bank being responsible if such form of remittance is not itself paid * * *. Since it is not feasible for banks to perform their collection functions except with the use of these provisional remittances, they should not be penalized for acting in the only way they can act.

Thus, the thrust of Section 4211 [R 4–213] is to alleviate the problems of the collecting bank in accepting in settlement various types of remittances. It was not designed to require a collecting bank to accept any one or all mentioned forms of remittances in settlement of items. Collecting banks *may,* with legal safety, accept any one of the mentioned forms. Whether they will accept a given form is a different issue, one to which the amended Regulation J is directed.

Thus, neither the time of settlement nor the manner of settlement provisions of Regulation J are contrary to California law.

III.
Federal Law

Finally, we turn to a consideration of whether the regulation is within the scope of authority conferred on the Board by the Federal Reserve Act. Appellants strongly contend that it is not.

The critical statutory provision dealing with the Federal Reserve's role in the check collection process is 12 U.S.C. 342, which provides:

> Any Federal reserve bank may receive from any of its member banks * * * checks, and drafts, payable upon presentation, and also, for collection, maturing notes and bills; or solely for purposes of exchange or of collection, may receive from other Federal reserve banks deposits of * * * checks upon other Federal reserve banks, and checks and drafts, payable upon presentation within its district * * *; or, solely for the purposes of exchange or of collec-

> tion, may receive from any nonmember bank or trust company deposits of * * * checks and drafts payable upon presentation * * *; Provided, such nonmember bank or trust company maintains with the Federal reserve bank of its district a balance sufficient to offset the items in transit held for its account by the Federal reserve bank; * * *

The authority of Reserve Banks under this section includes the power to collect checks drawn on nonmember banks. The Board is also authorized to promulgate rules and regulations necessary to the performance of its functions.

The appellant State Banks heavily rest their contention on Farmers and Merchants Bank of Monroe v. Federal Reserve Bank of Richmond, 262 U.S. 649, 43 S.Ct. 651, 67 L.Ed. 1157 (1923). The problem in Farmers and Merchants Bank arose because of the practice of many nonmember and nonaffiliated North Carolina State Banks to charge a fee when presented with a check for collection. This practice, also followed by certain banks in other states, is known as "no par clearance," and the Federal Reserve is prohibited by statute from paying such a fee. 12 U.S.C. 342. The Federal Reserve attempted to pressure the State Banks into accepting par clearance by presenting checks drawn on banks following no par practices over the counter for settlement in cash. The common law required that over the counter settlements be in cash. To remove this instrument from the hands of the Reserve, North Carolina enacted legislation providing that, unless the drawer indicated by notation on the face of the check that he required payment in cash, the payor bank was at liberty when the check was presented by a Federal Reserve Bank to pay the check by exchange drawn on its reserve deposits. The statute was thus clearly designed "to relieve state banks from the pressure which * * * Federal Reserve banks were in a position to exert and thus compel submission to par clearance." 262 U.S. at 659, 43 S.Ct. at 655.

The Supreme Court sustained the North Carolina statute, and, for purposes of the present controversy, two points resolved in the opinion are significant. First, the Court rejected the Federal Reserve's argument that the state statute impaired the legitimate functions of the Federal Reserve in the area of check collection. The Court reasoned that, since the Act does not require the Federal Reserve to collect checks drawn on banks which follow no par practices, "no duty or right of the Federal Reserve Bank to collect checks is obstructed by the North Carolina statute which merely gives to the drawee bank the right to pay in the customary exchange draft, where its depositor, has, by the form used in drawing the check, consented that this be done." 262 U.S. at 664, 43 S.Ct. at 657.

There is nothing in this that supports the appellants. The Court only recognized the right of a state to alter the common law rules relating to bank collections. Here we only recognize the right of the Federal Reserve to promulgate rules with respect to check collections in a manner countenanced by applicable state law. Neither the Federal Reserve here nor North Carolina in Farmers and Merchants Bank acted beyond its power.

The Federal Reserve also argued that the North Carolina statute interfered with the duty of the Board to establish a universal system of par clearance and check collection. There can be little question that, if the Federal Reserve correctly perceived its role, the state statute would have been a serious impediment to the exercise of its responsibilities. The Court, however, flatly rejected the argument that the Federal Reserve Board was charged with the responsibility of establishing universal par clearance and collection of checks.

> Congress did not in terms confer upon the Federal Reserve Board or the federal reserve banks a duty to establish universal par clearance and collection of checks; and there is nothing in the original act or in any amendment from which such duty to compel its adoption may be inferred.

262 U.S. at 664, 43 S.Ct. at 657.

Since the amendments to Regulation J do not, in our view, represent an attempt to establish a universal system of check clearance, appellants' reliance on Farmers and Merchants Bank is misplaced. Because the State Banks are not required to use Federal Reserve routing numbers on their checks, and because alternatives exist to the use of such numbers, the system must be characterized as essentially voluntary. Under such circumstances, the amendments to Regulation J cannot be viewed as an attempt by the Board to establish a universal system of check collection. If the amended Regulation J proves too onerous to the State Banks, they are free to remove themselves from the system.

The amendments to Regulation J are both consistent with California law and within the power conferred on the Board by the Federal Reserve Act. The judgment of the district court is, therefore, affirmed.

Note

1. The amendments to Regulation J differed substantially from the original Article 4 provisions governing how and when a payor bank must settle for a cash item.

> Prior to the 1972 amendments, Regulation J was virtually a mirror image of Article 4. Payor banks became accountable under Regulation J only if they failed to act on an item before the midnight deadline and bank drafts were considered permissible remittance instruments for a payor bank. In an effort to cut down on float by accelerating the bank collection process, the 1972 amendments to Regulation J (1) advanced the time within which payor banks must settle for checks presented for collection by Reserve banks, setting a deadline on the day of receipt rather than midnight of the day following receipt and (2) eliminated the use of bank drafts as permissible forms of settlement by requiring

settlement to be made in immediately available funds if the Fed so demanded.

* * *

The *Community Bank* decision underscores the need for banks and bank attorneys to scrutinize Regulation J and Operating Circulars of the various Federal Reserve Banks, in addition to the collection rules of Article 4.

Barkley Clark, The Law of Bank Deposits, Collections and Credit Cards, ¶ 4.09[1], p. 4–84 (3d ed. 1990).

2. The 1990 amendments to Article 4 brought the U.C.C. rules into conformity with Regulation J concerning the type of payment from the drawee bank that a Federal Reserve Bank will accept. Revised 4–213 requires settlement to be made in cash or by credit to a reserve account unless the Reserve Bank's operating circulars allow another form of remittance.

C. FUNDS AVAILABILITY UNDER ARTICLE 4 AND FEDERAL RESERVE REGULATION CC

Federal Reserve Board Regulation CC was designed to respond to the problem of delayed availability, a problem tolerated by the drafters of the uniform commercial law and not redressed by the courts confronted with the occasionally dilatory depositary banks that imposed the risks of the "no news is good news" system on their customers. Before the enactment of Regulation CC, depositary banks had extremely lenient standards for making deposited funds available, and often placed substantial holds on customers' accounts. Consider the response of a New York court to the depositor's frustration in the following case when all there was to govern bank policies were the rules of Article 4.

RAPP v. DIME SAVINGS BANK OF NEW YORK

New York Supreme Court, Appellate Division, 1978.
64 A.D.2d 964, 408 N.Y.S.2d 540.

MEMORANDUM BY THE COURT

* * *

The plaintiffs maintain savings and checking accounts with the defendant, The Dime Savings Bank of New York (hereinafter The Dime). Like most other banks, The Dime has imposed certain time restrictions on when withdrawals may be made against deposits into a patron's checking account. These restrictions essentially provide that the proceeds of a deposit consisting of checks are not available to the depositor for (1) 6 business days for local checks and (2) 15 business days for nonlocal checks. The plaintiffs' complaint alleges, in eight separate causes of action, that the imposition of these time restrictions violates various statutes and common-law doctrines.

It is emphasized that it is not alleged that the proceeds of any particular deposit were ever unreasonably withheld from the plaintiffs. On the contrary, the record unequivocally shows that the proceeds of deposits have always been immediately available to the plaintiffs. This resulted from The Dime's policy of allowing immediate withdrawal when: (1) the deposited check does not exceed $50; or (2) the deposited check is equal to or exceeds $50, but the prior checking balance or savings account balance equals or exceeds the amount of the deposited check. If the savings account balance is relied upon an amount equal to the deposited check is held against withdrawal, but continues to draw interest. Nor is it alleged that time restrictions on the availability of checking account deposits made by check are illegal per se. Rather, the gravamen of the complaint is that the particular time restrictions imposed by The Dime are illegal.

* * *

The first and second causes of action basically allege that The Dime's time restrictions are in violation of article 4 of the Uniform Commercial Code. Citing sections 4–204 [R 4–204] and 4–213 [R 4–215] of the Uniform Commercial Code, Special Term determined that dispositive of the first and second causes of action was the issue of the reasonableness of the time restrictions and that since reasonableness is a question of fact, summary judgment did not lie. However, in the circumstances of this case, the dispositive issue is more properly framed in the context of whether the time restrictions comport with the exercise of ordinary care gauged by general banking usage, as long as such standard is not manifestly unreasonable (see Uniform Commercial Code, § 4–103 [R 4–103]). From this perspective the record unquestionably shows that The Dime has exercised ordinary care in imposing the subject time restrictions and is, therefore, entitled to summary judgment declaring the legality of the said restrictions.

The third and fourth causes of action essentially allege that The Dime engaged in false advertising and fraudulent concealment by advertising that it offered free checking accounts without also advertising its policy of restricting withdrawals for a period of time on deposits made by check. Here, as with the fifth through eighth causes of action, the plaintiffs have failed to set forth an evidentiary showing which raises a triable issue of fact. On the competent evidence before us, it is plain that The Dime has engaged in neither false advertising nor fraudulent concealment. Therefore, The Dime is also entitled to summary judgment on the third and fourth causes of action.

Central to the plaintiffs' complaint is the assertion that the subject time restrictions (6 days on local checks and 15 days on nonlocal checks) are unreasonable. However, it is undisputed that the vast majority of all banks impose some type of time restrictions on when the proceeds of a deposit are available. The basic purpose of such time restrictions is to protect the bank and, indirectly, the bank's depositors, against making payments, via withdrawals, on deposited checks which prove to be uncollectible. Thus, the time restrictions are imposed to give the deposited check time to clear. There is, however, no definite means of determining in advance when a check will clear. Rather, the collecting bank will usually learn that final payment has been made "merely by not learning the opposite within a reasonable time. How much time is 'reasonable' for these purposes will of course depend on the distance the item has to travel and the number of banks through which it must pass * * * and other pertinent facts." Certainly, the specific time that final payment is made on a particular check will vary. But the complaint here is not that payment was unreasonably delayed on a particular check. Rather, the complaint is directed at the general time restrictions which are designed to best secure the bank against making payments on uncollectible checks.

The Dime is a "thrift" institution which is not directly associated with either the Federal Reserve Bank or the New York Clearing House Association. For the most part, these organizations will directly deal only with commercial banks. Since a check may be cleared only through these organizations, it is necessary that The Dime, like most other savings banks, clear its checks through the auspices of a commercial bank.

As described by The Dime's fairly detailed papers, the process for the clearance of a local check is as follows: day one, The Dime forwards the check to a commercial bank; days two through five, the commercial bank routes the check; day six, the checks which have not cleared are returned to The Dime. The four-day routing process is beyond the control of The Dime and may involve several different banks. The routing process for nonlocal checks is more complex, typically involving more intermediary banks, and is consequently lengthier. The Dime has substantiated its position by including photostatic copies of local checks which were returned on the sixth business day as uncollectible.

Rather than disputing by competent evidence The Dime's persuasive showing of the reasonableness of its time restrictions, the plaintiffs have done little more than urge that the restrictions are too long and, therefore, are not reasonable. However, in the circumstances of this case, such conclusory claims are insufficient to raise a substantial question of fact. Furthermore, Special Term erred by relying upon sections 4–204 [R 4–204] and 4–213 [R 4–215] of the Uniform Commercial Code for the proposition that the abstract question of reasonableness is dispositive of the case at bar. Neither of those sections is controlling.

Subdivision (1) of section 4–204 [R 4–204(a)] of the Uniform Commercial Code provides: * * *.

That subdivision concerns the presentment of items between banks and "prescribes the general standards applicable to proper sending or forwarding of items" (Official Comment, Purpose 1, McKinney's Cons. Laws of N.Y., Book 621/2, Part 2, Uniform Commercial Code, § 4–204, p. 557). Other, more specific prescriptions have been promulgated to insure that banking institutions make settlements as quickly as possible. The Dime is subject to these various deadlines, but they are relevant only insofar as they require The Dime to promptly forward checks for clearance. The existence of the 6/15–day time restrictions do not bespeak a failure to comply with the applicable regulations. Nor have the plaintiffs made any evidentiary showing which even casts doubt upon The Dime's full compliance with the various regulations governing the timely presentment of items for settlement.

More relevant, though not determinative, is section 4–213 [R 4–215] of the Uniform Commercial Code which provides, in part:

> "(4) Subject to any right of the bank to apply the credit to an obligation of the customer, credit given by a bank for an item in an account with its customer becomes available for withdrawal as of right
>
> "(a) in any case where the bank has received a provisional settlement for the item, when such settlement becomes final and *the bank has had a reasonable time to learn that the settlement is final.*" (Emphasis supplied.)

The potential factual issue of whether the 6/15–day time restrictions represent a "reasonable time to learn that the settlement is final" has been obviated by operation of section 4–103 [R 4–103] of the Uniform Commercial Code, which provides, in pertinent part:

> "(1) *The effect of the provisions of this Article may be varied by agreement* except that no agreement can disclaim a bank's responsibility for its own lack of good faith or failure to exercise ordinary care or can limit the measure of damages for such lack or failure; *but the parties may by agreement determine the standards by which such responsibility is to be measured if such standards are not manifestly unreasonable.*
>
> "(2) Federal Reserve regulations and operating letters, clearing house rules, and the like, have the effect of agreements under subsection (1), whether or not specifically assented to by all parties interested in items handled.
>
> "(3) Action or non-action approved by this Article or pursuant to Federal Reserve regulations or operating letters constitutes the exercise of ordinary care and, in the absence of special instructions, *action or non-action consistent with* clearing house rules and the like or with a *general banking usage not disapproved by this Article, prima facie constitutes the exercise of ordinary care.*" (Emphasis supplied.)

This section essentially allows the parties to vary any of the provisions of article 4 of the Uniform Commercial Code. As applied to this case, the effect of this section is to functionally define "reasonable time to learn that the settlement is final" in terms of the 6/15–day time restrictions. Pursuant to section 4–103 [R 4–103], the instant time restrictions must be upheld if they have been agreed to and if they are not manifestly unreasonable.

The term "agreement" is given an extremely broad definition in section 1–201 (subd. [3]) of the Uniform Commercial Code, and applies to both direct and indirect agreements. An agreement is merely "the bargain of the parties in fact as found in their language or by implication from other circumstances including course of dealing or usage of trade or course of performance."

In the instant action the applicable agreement concerning time restrictions is evinced by the following "Collection Agreement":

> "Deposits made in cash, including partial deposits of cash, are available on the date received.
>
> "The proceeds of a deposit consisting of checks is *not* available on the date received. Checks should *not* be issued against this deposit until 6 business days clearance time has elapsed for a local check and/or 15 business days on all other checks." (Emphasis in original.)

This Collection Agreement is printed on the reverse side of each of The Dime's checking account deposit slips, the face of which states: "See Over for Collection Agreement." The Collection Agreement is also prominently posted in each of its branch offices that offers checking accounts. In addition, the terms of the Collection Agreement are explained to each patron when a checking account is opened. It is noted that the plaintiffs have not denied being so advised and plaintiff Julius Rapp admitted in a deposition that he was aware of the terms of the Collection Agreement.

The Official Comment to section 4–103 [R 4–103] of the Uniform Commercial Code (Purpose 2) specifically recognizes that "(l)egends on deposit tickets, collection letters and acknowledgments of items, coupled with action by the affected party constituting acceptance, adoption, ratification, estoppel or the like, are agreements if they meet the tests of the definition of 'agreement.' "

The above-quoted Collection Agreement essentially constitutes a term and condition of maintaining a checking account at The Dime. By voluntarily opening a checking account with The Dime, the plaintiffs implicitly agreed to the terms thereof. This agreement was further ratified each time the plaintiffs voluntarily deposited checks into their account. Thus, the 6/15–day time restrictions satisfy the requirements of an agreement and effectively preempt the more ambiguous language of section 4–213 [R 4–215] of the Uniform Commercial Code. The terms of the Collection Agreement must be upheld unless the plaintiffs can demonstrate that the time restrictions are manifestly unreasonable or otherwise inconsistent with the exercise of ordinary care (see Uniform Commercial Code, § 4–103, subd. (1) [R 4–103(a)]). However, the plaintiffs have failed to make any evidentiary showing which raises a material question of fact as to whether the 6/15–day time restrictions depart from the exercise of ordinary care.

As relevant to this case, ordinary care can be measured by the general standards of banking usage (see Uniform Commercial Code, § 4–103, subd. [3] [R 4–103(c)]). The relationship between "general banking usage" and "ordinary care" is elucidated, in part, in Official Comment, Purpose 4, to section 4–103 of the Uniform Commercial Code, as follows:

> "Subsection (3) further provides that, absent special instructions, action or non-action consistent with clearing house rules and the like or with a general banking usage not disapproved by the Article, prima facie constitutes the exercise of ordinary care * * * The term 'general banking usage' is not defined but should be taken to mean a general usage common to banks in the area concerned. See Section 1–205(2). Where the adjective 'general' is used, the intention is to require a usage broader than a mere practice between two or three banks but it is not intended to require anything as broad as a country-wide usage. A usage followed generally throughout a state, a substantial portion of a state, a metropolitan area or the like would certainly be sufficient * * * The prima facie rule does, however, impose on the party contesting the standards to establish that they are unreasonable, arbitrary or unfair."

In support of their general position that the time restrictions are unreasonable, the plaintiffs have compared the time restrictions imposed by The Dime to corresponding restrictions imposed by various commercial banking institutions. It is generally agreed that commercial banks tend to restrict withdrawals against deposits of local checks to 3 business days and impose longer time restrictions (generally 5–10 days) on deposits of nonlocal checks. However, the practices of commercial banking institutions have little bearing on the reasonable practices of a savings bank "thrift" institution in the conduct of its checking accounts. The more appropriate analogy is to the practices of other savings banks, which, like The Dime, must collect checks through commercial banks which are members of the New York Clearing House Association or Federal Reserve Bank.

As part of its extensive evidentiary record made in support of its cross motion for summary judgment, The Dime introduced a table showing the check clearing policies of other local savings banks which offer free checking. The time restrictions for local checks ranged from 5–8 days and the restrictions on nonlocal checks ranged from 8–21 days (with an average of 15 days). This comparison with the practices of other New York City savings banks is undisputed and conclusively establishes that The Dime's time restrictions are fully in accord with general banking usage and therefore comport with the exercise of ordinary care.

* * *

The record clearly shows that no charge is imposed for maintaining a checking account at The Dime. Nor is any minimum balance required to keep the checking account active. This is all that the advertising may fairly be claimed as representing. Furthermore, the time restrictions are well posted and are fully explained to the prospective depositor before the checking account is opened. Thus, nothing is concealed.

Nor may it be inferred that The Dime prospers from the imposition of the time restrictions, except indirectly by protecting itself against making payments on uncollectible checks. Conversely, the plaintiffs have failed to demonstrate how they have been injured. Indeed, even if money in a savings account is held, that money continues to earn interest. Nor may it be claimed that the depositor has lost the use of his money, because there is in actuality no "money" until there has been final payment. Until there is final payment, the collecting bank has a security interest in any payment it may have made (Uniform Commercial Code, § 4–208 [R 4–210]).

The subject advertising is consistent with that of other banks, each of which imposes some period of restriction on withdrawals. The existence of such restrictions is wholly incidental to whether the checking account is free and, therefore, it must be concluded that the third and fourth causes of action are of no merit.

Accordingly, the defendant is entitled to summary judgment as to the first through fourth causes of action as well as the fifth through eighth causes of action.

Note

1. *Rapp* is consistent with the sparse case law treating the impact of Article 4 on the funds availability issue. Though the flexibility of the Code certainly would have provided the courts a means to respond to unreasonable holds within the uniform commercial law regime, the courts' failure to find the statutory basis to assure reasonable funds availability precipitated the federal government's response in the form of the Expedited Funds Availability Act and Regulation CC.

Note that the uniform commercial law legislative process differs dramatically from the regulatory process, both in terms of celerity and in the form and substance of the final product. Revisions of the U.C.C. may take years to formulate and additional years to enact in the states. (It took the better part of two decades for Missouri to finally enact the 1972 amendments to Article 9 of the U.C.C.) Federal regulations may be promulgated and put into force in months. (See Charles H. Koch, Jr., Administrative Law & Practice §§ 1.22, 2.16 (1985, Supp.1992) (describing efficiency, expertise, and fairness benefits of regulatory system).) But perhaps more striking is the tenor of the statutory/regulatory language. Regulation CC, which focuses virtually entirely on the funds availability issue, takes up over a hundred pages of the Code of Federal Regulations and all of Article 4 occupies less than half of that number of printed pages in the West statutory supplement accompanying this casebook. There is a good deal of micro-management in the federal initiative, which is symptomatic of federal consumer protection law generally. While Article 4 still relies to a significant extent on broad statements of collection practices, Reg. CC leaves few gaps in the availability regime.

But the federal regulators did provide the keepers of the uniform commercial law flame a good deal of time to respond to bank customers' frustration with the system. Only after nonuniform state law initiatives began to address the availability issues did the federal government step in with the funds availability legislation. There may be a lesson to be learned from that experience. Section 609(c) of the E.F.A.A. provides the Federal Reserve Board authority to regulate "any aspect of the payment system, including the receipt, payment, collection, or clearing of checks." That is, Congress has empowered the Fed to preempt, and in short order, all of Article 4 of the U.C.C. (and perhaps a good portion of Article 3 as well). There has been for some time heated debate about whether the commercial law should be federal or state legislation. As the revision of Article 3 and the amendments to Article 4 work their way through the state legislatures, the debate is likely to continue, and the lawyers at the Federal Reserve will be paying attention.

2. Subpart B of Federal Reserve Regulation CC governs funds availability in the bank collection system. It incorporates the availability schedules of the EFAA and adopts regulations to implement the Act and to improve the check collection system in general. Consider the introduction provided by the regulators:

FEDERAL RESERVE SYSTEM

12 CFR PARTS 210 and 229

Availability of Funds and Collection of Checks (Regulation CC) and Collection of Checks and Other Items and Transfers of Funds (Regulation J).

OVERVIEW [OF PROPOSED RULES]

Delayed availability—the holds that some banks place on checks deposited into their customers' accounts before the funds may be withdrawn—was a subject of growing concern in the Congress for a number of years. Many argued that the holds placed by many banks were unduly long, and that depositors have a right to prompter access to their funds. Banks that impose holds responded that their availability schedules reflect the time needed for the collection and return of checks dishonored by the paying bank and provide a measure of protection against the risk that the bank could not recover funds from the depositor if those funds had already been withdrawn from the depositor's account.

The Congress concluded that federal legislation was required to address delayed availability practices and passed the Expedited Funds Availability Act (the "Act") (Title VI of the Competitive Equality Banking Act, enacted on August 10, 1987). The Act seeks to ensure prompt availability of funds and to expedite the return of checks; the Board is directed to issue regulations to implement the Act, which becomes effective on September 1, 1988.

The Act includes specific and detailed provisions requiring banks to: (1) make funds available to their customers within specified time frames, (2) pay interest on interest-bearing transaction accounts not later than the day the bank receives provisional credit, and (3) disclose their funds availability policy to their customers. These statutory provisions provide the Board with little flexibility in developing rules to implement the Act's requirements.

The Act requires that cash deposits, wire transfers, and certain check deposits that Congress believes pose little risk to the depositary bank, such as Treasury checks and cashier's checks, be made available for withdrawal by the business day after the day of deposit. The time when the depositary bank must make other check deposits available for withdrawal depends on whether the check is "local" or "nonlocal" to the depositary bank. A local check is a check deposited in a depositary bank that is located in the same Federal Reserve check processing region as the paying bank. A nonlocal check is a check deposited in a different check processing region than the paying bank. There are a total of 48 Federal Reserve check processing offices in the United States, and the territory served by each office constitutes a region.

Under the temporary schedule that becomes effective on September 1, 1988, a depositary bank must make the proceeds of local checks available for withdrawal by the third business day following deposit; that is, the proceeds of local checks deposited on a Monday must be available for withdrawal by the following Thursday. The depositary bank must make the proceeds of nonlocal checks available for withdrawal by the seventh business day following deposit; that is, the proceeds of a Monday deposit must be available for withdrawal by Wednesday of the following week. On September 1, 1990, these time periods are reduced. At that time, proceeds of local and nonlocal checks must be available for withdrawal by the second and fifth business day following deposit, respectively. Special rules are provided for cash withdrawals, deposits at nonproprietary automated teller machines, and deposits made in banks outside the continental United States.

Although the proposed improvements to the check system will accelerate the return of most checks, many checks will not be returned to the depositary bank by the time funds must be made available for withdrawal under the temporary schedule—a number that will increase when the permanent schedule becomes effective. In order to reduce the risk to banks from making funds available to consumers before learning that the check has not been paid, Congress provided several exceptions to the availability schedules. When a bank invokes one of these exceptions, it may extend the hold on its customer's account beyond the statutory schedule. Nevertheless, the Board must establish limits on the additional hold that may be placed on checks subject to these exceptions.

The statute requires banks to disclose their availability policies to their customers and inform their customers that deposited funds may not be available for immediate withdrawal. Banks are required to provide disclosures to new customers prior to opening an account, to existing customers, and to any person upon request. In addition, disclosures are required on preprinted deposit slips, at staffed locations where consumers make deposits, and at automated teller machines. Banks must also provide notice to their customers whenever their availability policies change.

The Act gives the Board authority to make improvements in the check collection and return system in order to shorten the time within which depositary banks learn of the nonpayment of checks, and thereby reduce the number of situations when the bank will be required by law to make funds available to its customers before it learns a check has been dishonored. The Board's authority is broad and general, and extends to checks that are not cleared through the Federal Reserve System. Previously, the Federal Reserve generally had the authority to regulate only those checks it collected.

Upon enactment of the Act, Board staff formed a Steering Committee to develop proposals to implement the law's requirements. The Steering Committee consists of representatives from three Divisions of the Board's staff and three Federal Reserve Banks. In developing these proposals, the Steering Committee considered: (1) costs to the banking industry, businesses, and consumers; (2) the ability of banks to select from several alternative approaches to comply with the Act and the Board's regulation; (3) the ability of the private sector and the Federal Reserve to provide services to expedite the return of unpaid checks; and (4) the extent to which the improvements to the check collection system reduce risk.

In developing the proposals, the Board relied heavily on input from the private sector. The Board staff discussed the proposal with the Consumer Advisory Council and the Return Item Advisory Committee, which is a joint Federal Reserve/banking industry group. In addition, the staff met on over 20 occasions with representatives from consumer groups, banking and corporate trade associations, and individual banks. Two consulting firms were retained to assess the effect of certain aspects of its proposals on the banking industry. Many of the major concepts underlying the proposal have been suggested by the private sector.

The proposed Regulation CC (12 CFR Part 229), Availability of Funds and Collection of Checks, contains three subparts. Subpart A defines terms and provides for administrative enforcement. Subpart B specifies schedules within which banks must make funds available for withdrawal. Subpart B also includes rules regarding exceptions to the schedules, disclosure of funds availability policies, and payment of interest. Subpart C includes rules to expedite the collection and return of checks. These rules cover the means by which the paying and returning banks must return checks to the depositary bank, authorization of direct returns, notification of nonpayment of large-dollar returns by the paying bank, check indorsement standards, and other related changes to the check collection system.

3. Sections 229.10 and 229.12 of Subpart B of Regulation CC, which call for funds to be made available to depositors by the second or fifth business day after deposit, depending on whether they are classified as local or non-local, have completely overturned OR 4–213(4)(a), which allowed the bank to hold the funds until they had reasonable time to learn that settlement was final. Because the check return process was so slow—it could take up to 10–15 days for a depositary bank to learn of a dishonored check—banks felt they were acting reasonably in imposing holds on funds availability of like duration. Indeed, they were acting consistently with the language of Article 4 since they would not know if settlement was final until after the return period had passed without hearing of dishonor.

As noted earlier, Subpart C of Regulation CC requires drawee banks to expedite the return of dishonored checks to the depositary bank. This offers protection to the depositary banks because they should learn of dishonor of a check before they are required to make funds available under the new time schedules imposed by Subpart B of Regulation CC.

In light of these Regulation CC provisions, the 1990 amendments to Article 4 have changed what is considered a "reasonable" amount of time to withhold funds from a depositor. Revised 4–215(e)(1) changes the language to "a reasonable time to receive return of the item and the item has not been received within that time." Because the depositary bank should now receive notice of dishonor much more quickly, due to the provisions of Subpart C, the reasonable period is significantly reduced.

4. The *Rapp* court's analysis of what constitutes ordinary care and reasonableness with regard to holds placed on deposited checks, is still significant in certain instances even with the Regulation CC mandatory availability schedules in effect. Under section 229.13 of Regulation CC, certain types of checks and deposits are excepted from the availability rules of sections 229.10 and 229.12. Additional holds may be placed on checks deposited in new accounts, aggregate deposits of more than $5,000, redeposited checks, checks deposited in accounts on which there have been repeated overdrafts, and checks for which there is reasonable cause to doubt collectability. Section 229.13(h) allows an extended hold of up to four days on these types of items. If a bank wishes to impose an even longer hold, it must establish that a longer period is reasonable under the circumstances. In determining whether an additional hold placed on an excepted deposit is reasonable, courts will likely follow an analysis of banking practices similar to that used by the *Rapp* court.

In addition, only holds imposed by banks to protect themselves against draws on uncollected funds are within the scope of Regulation CC. Holds imposed for other reasons, such as death of the depositor, certification of a check, legal notice of the depositor's bankruptcy, garnishment, and IRS tax levy, are not subject to the Regulation CC provisions. In these cases, the holds must meet the ordinary care standard of general banking usage, required by OR and R 4–103 that is discussed by the *Rapp* court.

5. If the federal regulators decide to leave some commercial paper-bank collection issues to the states and the drafters of uniform commercial law, what subjects would be best reserved for uniform state legislation? What types of legal issues generally are deemed the province of the states?

6. Why are credit card and electronic funds transfer regimes, see Chapter 7, provided by federal law and the check and note law governed by the U.C.C.?

7. The following case confronts some of the financial institution competition issues raised by Reg. CC and reveals the considerations to be balanced. Is there, however, a unitary foundation of Reg. CC, a regulatory *raison d'etre,* that would guide resolution of the particular issue in controversy? See if the court discerns such a principle and then applies it coherently.

CREDIT UNION NATIONAL ASSOCIATION, INC. v. BOARD OF GOVERNORS OF THE FEDERAL RESERVE SYSTEM

United States District Court, District of Columbia 1988.
700 F.Supp. 1152.

GASCH, SENIOR DISTRICT JUDGE.

I. INTRODUCTION

This matter is before the Court on cross-motions for summary judgment. The Board of Governors of the Federal Reserve System (the "Board") has also moved to dismiss the case for lack of standing. The Court has accepted for filing the submission of the American Bankers Association (the "ABA") as amicus curiae. Plaintiffs, Dearborn Federal Credit Union ("Dearborn") and Credit Union National Association, a trade association representing credit unions, challenge one provision of Regulation CC, 53 Fed.Reg. 19,435 (May 27, 1988) (to be codified at 12 C.F.R. § 229.2(z)) ("Regulation CC"), which was promulgated on May 11, 1988, by the Board under the Expedited Funds Availability Act of 1987, 12 U.S.C. §§ 4001–4010 (the "Act"). Plaintiffs contend that the challenged regulation defines "originating depository institution" in a manner that is so substantially different from the statutory definition that it produces a different result from what was intended by Congress.

The case concerns the application of the challenged provision to credit union share drafts with respect to determining whether they are local or nonlocal for purposes of the maximum "check-holds" set forth in the Act. Rather than basing that determination on the location of the credit union on which the share draft is drawn, the Board concluded that the location of the credit union's "payable through" bank would determine whether a share draft was local or nonlocal for purposes of the Act. The Court agreed to hear this matter on an expedited basis, because the challenged regulation will go into effect on September 1, 1988.

II. BACKGROUND

A. The Check Collection System

Traditional checks, as opposed to share drafts, that are deposited or cashed in a bank are processed or cleared through a check collection process. As a general rule, the bank that receives a check for deposit drawn on a different depository institution processes it for payment in one of two ways: (1) it sends the check directly for presentment to the bank on which a check is drawn; or (2) it sends the check through a clearinghouse, a corresponding bank or the Federal Reserve System for presentment to the bank on which the check is drawn. If the bank on which the check is drawn (the "payor" or "drawee" bank) refuses to honor the check for insufficient funds or some other reason, the check will be returned to the bank of first deposit along the same path it followed to be presented.

The check clearing process takes time, particularly when checks deposited are drawn on accounts not located within the depository institution. There is some risk of nonpayment to the depository institution if the funds deposited are made available to its customer before the check has cleared. As a result, some banks have imposed "holds" on checks not drawn on their accounts, making funds available to their depositors only after sufficient time has elapsed for notification that the check has cleared. In the case of those banks that currently impose holds, checks drawn on banks located within the same city as the depository institution are usually made available more promptly than those drawn on nonlocal banks. Some banks currently impose no holds on any of their customers' deposits. Other banks do not impose holds on deposits made to certain customers' accounts, depending on the nature of the customer and their relationship with the bank. The Expedited Funds Availability Act does not require holds to be imposed; it only limits the duration of check holds based on whether the check is local to the depository institution or not.

B. Share Draft Accounts

Credit unions, unlike banks, are cooperative and nonprofit depository institutions, which provide to their members, among other bank-like services, share draft accounts.[1] Share draft accounts are the equivalent of checking accounts, in that they are used by members in the same manner that bank customers employ their checking accounts.[2] Share drafts are drawn on the credit union by a member, payable to a specific payee out of the share draft account maintained by the member of the credit union.

Most credit union share drafts are "payable through" one of five banks nationally ("payable through banks") that specialize in the processing of share drafts. About seventy-five percent of the 6000 credit unions offering share draft accounts use payable through banks for collection and processing. Over 3000 of these credit unions use one of the five national payable through banks. Payable through banks are

1. The statutory definition of "depository institution" includes credit unions. 12 U.S.C. § 4001(12) (adopting the definition provided in the Federal Reserve Act, 12 U.S.C. § 461(b)(1)(A)(iv)).

2. Under the Act, share drafts are covered by the statutory definition of the term "check." 12 U.S.C. § 4001(7).

an efficient and cost effective method of collecting and processing share drafts.

A share draft, although it looks like an ordinary bank check, normally carries both the credit union's name and the name of its payable through bank on its face. See B. Clark, The Law of Bank Deposits, Collections and Credit Cards ¶ 10.9[1](a) (rev. ed. 1981). Usually the routing number of the payable through bank is imprinted with machine readable magnetic ink characters at the bottom of the share draft, providing for expeditious processing. The payable through bank functions as a collecting bank to present the share draft to the credit union as drawee, but is not authorized to pay the item. Id. The payable through bank serves as the credit union's vital link to the Federal Reserve System for collection purposes. Id.

When a share draft is deposited or cashed, it is sent through the check collection system to the payable through bank for presentment to the credit union on which it is drawn. The payable through bank presents the share draft electronically to the credit union on the same day it is received. On the next day, the credit union responds electronically to the payable through bank that it will either honor or dishonor the share draft.[3] If the credit union refuses to pay the share draft, it is sent back through the check collection system to the depository bank.

C. The Expedited Funds Availability Act

The Expedited Funds Availability Act (the "Act") was passed as part of the Competitive Equality Banking Act of 1987, Pub.L. No. 100–86. In the Act, Congress addressed a perceived abuse by depository institutions in delaying their customers' access to funds deposited by check into their accounts. The Act seeks to ensure prompt availability of funds and to expedite the return of checks. The Act creates maximum time periods within which depository institutions must make funds deposited by check available for withdrawal. Under the statutory scheme, the availability of funds depends on whether the check is "local" or "nonlocal."

The Act provides for a transitional period between September 1, 1988 and August 31, 1990, during which time "not more than 2 business days shall intervene between the business day on which funds are deposited in an account at a depository institution by a check drawn on a local originating depository institution and the business day on which such funds are available for withdrawal." 12 U.S.C. § 4002(c)(1).[4] The Act further provides that during the transitional

3. Most share drafts, including those used by members of plaintiff Dearborn Federal, are "truncated" at the payable through bank. Truncation refers to the practice whereby the actual paper share draft is retained by the payable through bank, which is responsible for maintaining a copy of the share draft for the member. B. Clark, supra at ¶ 10.6. The members receive a monthly statement showing which share drafts have been paid, but without return of the actual paper share drafts.

4. The Act defines "local originating depository institution" as "any originating depository institution which is located in the same check processing region as the

period, not more than six business days shall intervene between the date of deposit of a check drawn on a nonlocal originating depository institution and the business day on which such funds are available for withdrawal. 12 U.S.C. § 4002(c)(2).[5] After the transitional period, shorter hold periods of one intervening business day on local checks and four intervening business days on nonlocal checks will be the rule. 12 U.S.C. § 4002(b).

D. The Federal Reserve Board Regulation CC

The Act defines the term "originating depository institution" as the branch of a depository institution on which a check is drawn. 12 U.S.C. § 4001(17). In the challenged regulation, the Board substituted the term "paying bank" [6] for the term "originating depository institution." As a result, the nature of share drafts drawn on credit unions that use payable through banks ("payable through share drafts") will be determined by the location of the payable through bank, rather than the location of the credit union itself.

After the proposed regulation was published, the Board received 72 comments on the definition of "paying bank." Fifty commentors objected to the inclusion of payable through banks within the definition of paying bank.[7] These commentors pointed out, among other things, that the statutory definition of "originating depository institution" was the branch of a depository institution on which a check is drawn. The Board responded that the Act "does not explicitly include payable through or payable at banks." The Board stated that it believed the Act did not specify the treatment of payable through drafts for the purposes of availability, or other purposes. The Board further asserted that the Act does not define the term "drawn." While acknowledging that in a technical sense the institution on which a check is drawn refers to the institution holding the drawer's account, the Board stated that "the term [drawn] can be used more generically to designate the

receiving depository institution." 12 U.S.C. § 4001(13). "Check processing region" refers to the 48 Federal Reserve check processing regions located throughout the country.

5. The Act defines "nonlocal originating depository institutions" as any originating depository institution which is not a local depository institution. 12 U.S.C. § 4001(15).

6. The Board defined "paying bank" as: (1) The bank by which a check is payable, unless the check is payable at or through another bank and is sent to the other bank for payment or collection; (2) The bank at or through which a check is payable and to which it is sent for payment or collection; (3) The bank whose routing number appears on a check in magnetic ink or in fractional form and to which the check is sent for payment or collection; (4) The Federal Reserve Bank or Federal Home Loan Bank by which a check is payable; or (5) The state or unit of general local government on which a check is drawn. 53 Fed.Reg. 19,435 (May 27, 1988) (to be codified at 12 C.F.R. § 229.2(z)).

7. The government states that of the 1,000 comment letters received by the Board on the proposed regulation, only 50 commentors objected to the inclusion of payable through banks within the definition of "paying bank," as if to suggest that the relatively small number of comments on the definition reflects on their merit. Presumably, however, these fifty commentors represented all of the credit unions that made comments on the provision. See 53 Fed.Reg. 19,373 n. 2 (stating that 5% of the 1000 commentors were credit unions).

person to whom a draft is directed and who is requested to pay the amount specified." 53 Fed.Reg. 19,390.

Finding that "depository institution on which a check is drawn" could refer to either the institution at which the customer's funds are held or to the institution through which a draft may be payable, the Board turned to specific examples. Using the example of a credit union share draft, the Board suggested that it is unclear from the terms of the statute which institution Congress intended to be the originating depository institution (the credit union) or its payable through bank. 53 Fed.Reg. 19,391. Concluding that the term was capable on its face of more than one meaning, the Board then turned to the legislative history and purposes of the statute to make its determination. The Board found that credit union share drafts "were intended to be viewed as drawn on the payable through institution for purposes of determining whether they are local or nonlocal checks." Id. The Board stated that its "approach is consistent with the Act's designation of checks as local or nonlocal based on the time required for the collection and return of the checks." Id.

The Board further rationalized its result by stating that there would be an increased risk of check fraud if the location of the credit union itself determined whether the share draft was local or nonlocal. The risk of fraud feared by the Board was based on the fact that drafts sent to the payable through institution for collection routinely would be returned after funds would have to be made available under the availability schedules for local checks in the Act. In response to some comments that the treatment of payable through share drafts as nonlocal checks would reduce the acceptance of these instruments, the Board stated that on balance, it did not "believe this potential for a lower acceptance of credit union share drafts offsets the risks of increased fraud to other banks," concluding that on balance a different approach to the treatment of payable through share drafts was not warranted. 53 Fed.Reg. 19,391.

Another rationale offered by the Board for its treatment of payable through share drafts was expediency. The Board found that to base the nature of the payable through share draft on the location of the credit union would "greatly complicate the tasks of banks taking share drafts for deposit." 53 Fed.Reg. 19,391. This analysis was premised on the universal use of machine-read magnetically encoded routing numbers in processing share drafts. As stated previously, the routing number on payable through share drafts refers to the payable through bank, and not to the credit union itself. The Board concluded that these routing numbers represented the only practicable method for depository institutions to determine whether a share draft is local or nonlocal. Id.

III. Discussion

A. Standing

The Board of Governors of the Federal Reserve System has moved to dismiss on grounds that the plaintiffs lack standing. In order to satisfy the standing requirements of Article III of the Constitution and the Administrative Procedures Act, plaintiffs first must establish an actual or threatened injury that fairly can be traced to the challenged agency action. Wilderness Society v. Griles, 824 F.2d 4, 11 (D.C.Cir. 1987). Second, the injury must be to an interest that arguably is within the zone of interests to be protected or regulated. Id. Third, plaintiffs must show that the injury is likely to be redressed by a decision rendered in favor of the plaintiff. Id.

1. Injury

Plaintiffs assert that they are threatened with injury by the Board's substitution of the term "paying bank" for the term "originating depository institution" used by Congress. As stated previously, Regulation CC allows depository institutions to treat share drafts payable through nonlocal banks as nonlocal items, even if the credit union is local to the depository institution.

For example, plaintiff Dearborn is located in Dearborn, Michigan. All of its share drafts are payable through Chase Manhattan Bank, N.A., located in New York, New York. Under Regulation CC, if a Dearborn member writes a share draft payable to a local merchant, the share draft may be treated by the merchant's depository institution as a nonlocal item. As a result, the merchant's bank may withhold the funds deposited into the merchant's account by a Dearborn share draft for a longer period of time than it would if Dearborn's share draft were treated as a local item. Thus, if the regulation becomes effective in its present form, the share drafts of many credit unions using the specialized national payable through banks may be treated as nonlocal items, even if they are drawn on local credit union accounts, deposited in local banks, and cleared as quickly as local checks.

The credit unions contend that they are threatened with injury by the potential decrease in competitive vitality and potential loss of customers that the regulation's treatment of payable through share drafts will cause. The Court agrees. Plaintiffs face the substantial likelihood of several repercussions from Regulation CC as it stands. As a result of the longer holds allowable on share drafts, the challenged provision will likely cause credit union share drafts to be judged an unacceptable or less favorable form of payment by some people and businesses to whom they are given in payment for goods and services. In turn, some members of credit unions may terminate their share draft accounts and open checking accounts at competing banks and savings and loan associations. Additionally, in the ever-increasing competition between financial institutions, some banks and savings and loan associations will likely distinguish the holds allowable on their checks from those allowable on share drafts in disclosure statements and sales literature, luring credit union members to terminate their share draft accounts and open checking accounts at those competing institutions.

Should Regulation CC remain in effect as promulgated, the credit unions also contend that they will be compelled to make the costly conversion to using local check processing banks or to process their own share drafts in-house, in order to avoid the stigma of the longer holds caused by the use of specialized nonlocal payable through banks. Dearborn's board of directors has already determined that it will convert to in-house processing if Regulation CC is implemented as promulgated. According to plaintiffs, the necessary change in processing of share drafts will produce economic injury and diminish their effectiveness as competitors with banks and other financial institutions. The use of specialized national payable through banks, such as Chase Manhattan Bank, not only provides credit unions with access to the Federal Reserve System, it also provides an economical and expeditious means for processing share drafts.

The Board characterizes plaintiffs' allegations of threatened injury as speculative and hypothetical, stating that it is conjectural to say that the third parties on which the injury depends will react to the challenged regulation in the manner feared by plaintiffs. The Board argues that the repercussions feared by plaintiffs were capable of occurring in equal measure prior to Regulation CC. In the same vein, the thrust of the amicus brief is that in all the fourteen years of share drafts' existence, the discrimination against share drafts feared by plaintiffs has been entirely lawful, but has not occurred.

In order to satisfy the injury requirement of standing, the plaintiffs need make "a credible allegation that plaintiff's course of behavior will be harmed" by the likely actions of third parties caused by this regulation. Griles, supra, 824 F.2d at 12. The Court is required to ascertain whether the response of depository institutions and credit union members will in turn affect the plaintiffs' intended behavior. Id. In this case, the plaintiffs have made a credible allegation that in the rough-and-tumble of competition between financial institutions, there is a sufficient threat of injury flowing from the regulation to credit unions that use nonlocal payable through banks to withstand a standing challenge. The regulation permits banks to treat payable through share drafts as nonlocal items, even though the credit union on which they are drawn is local to the bank. This in turn will permit the banks to impose longer holds on payable through share drafts, making them in all likelihood less desirable forms of payment. Further, in order to remain competitive with local banks, should Regulation CC remain in effect, plaintiff Dearborn has already determined the necessity of converting its share draft processing to an in-house operation, which will cause the nonprofit credit union to spend $300,000 that it otherwise would not have to spend.

The Court holds that the plaintiffs have made out sufficient allegations of threatened injury to withstand the motion to dismiss. The

Board itself has acknowledged the potential for a lower level of acceptability of share drafts as a result of the regulation. See 53 Fed.Reg. 19,391. The potential harm to credit unions that use nonlocal payable through banks exists, in the threat of lost customers and the otherwise unnecessary expense of changing their processing methods. This threat of injury is not "unadorned speculation," Simon v. Eastern Kentucky Welfare Rights Organization, 426 U.S. 26, 44, 96 S.Ct. 1917, 1927, 48 L.Ed.2d 450 (1976). Indeed, plaintiffs face a "realistic danger" of injury as a result of the regulation's implementation. Pennell v. San Jose, ___ U.S. ___, 108 S.Ct. 849, 855, 99 L.Ed.2d 1 (1988).

2. Zone of Interests

Plaintiffs contend that their interests are also within the zone of interests to be protected by the Act. The Board does not challenge this assertion. The ABA suggests, however, that the injury threatened is not arguably within a zone of interests protected or regulated by the statute. The Bankers base their argument on the fact that the Expedited Funds Availability Act is narrow in scope and was consumer-driven in its inception. But the Act was passed as part of the Competitive Equality Banking Act of 1987, which clearly is broad in scope.

The ABA's argument must be rejected. The credit unions and other depository institutions arguably are the "subject of the contested regulatory action." Clarke v. Securities Industry Association, 479 U.S. 388, 107 S.Ct. 750, 757, 93 L.Ed.2d 757 (1987). The credit unions' interests are not "so marginally related to or inconsistent with the purposes implicit in the statute that it cannot reasonably be assumed that Congress intended to permit the suit." Id. The test for standing does not rely on whether the plaintiff was meant to benefit by the statute. No doubt, Congress intended consumers to benefit from the Act. But it is clear that the credit unions are arguably within the zone of interests to be regulated. See American Data Processing Service Organizations v. Camp, 397 U.S. 150, 153, 90 S.Ct. 827, 829, 25 L.Ed.2d 184 (1970).

3. Redressability

The Board contends that the plaintiffs lack standing because there is not a substantial likelihood that the requested relief will redress the plaintiffs' alleged injuries. The Board asserts that a declaration that payable through share drafts drawn on local credit union accounts must be treated as local checks will not necessarily prevent the loss of credit union share draft accounts feared by the credit unions. Instead, the Board suggests that the depository institutions will exercise their right to refuse to accept an item for deposit. See 12 U.S.C. § 4006(c)(2)(A) (stating that no provision of the Act may be construed as affecting a depository institution's right to reject a check for deposit).

Plaintiffs correctly assert that the defendant cannot defeat their standing by arguing that a second and different injury will befall the credit unions if the Court grants them their desired result. Furthermore, the language of the provision preserving banks' right to refuse to accept "a check" for deposit, 12 U.S.C. § 4006(c)(2)(A), suggests that it is designed to protect banks from having to receive noncollectible items. That provision cannot be used by banks to reject an entire class of items, such as all share drafts. Plaintiffs need only demonstrate a substantial likelihood that the threatened injury they allege will be redressed by the relief sought. Duke Power Co. v. Carolina Environmental Study Group, 438 U.S. 59, 75 n. 20, 98 S.Ct. 2620, 2631 n. 20, 57 L.Ed.2d 595 (1978); Greater Tampa Chamber of Commerce v. Goldschmidt, 627 F.2d 258, 265 (D.C.Cir.1980). The challenged regulation permits payable through share drafts to be treated as nonlocal items by banks otherwise local to the credit unions on which they are drawn. There is a substantial likelihood that a ruling that the nature of a payable through share draft must be determined by the location of the credit union on which it was drawn will redress the threatened injuries to the credit unions. For the foregoing reasons, the Court holds that plaintiffs have standing to challenge Regulation CC.

B. The Merits

Turning to the merits of the case, we must begin with a comparison of the language in the Act with the challenged regulation. As stated previously, the time within which funds must be made available depends on whether the deposited check is local or nonlocal to the depository institution. In the Act, Congress defined the "originating depository institution" as the branch of a depository institution on which a check is drawn. 12 U.S.C. § 4001(17). The Board has ignored and abandoned the statutory term, substituting its own term, "paying bank," and giving that term its own definition. As a result, payable through share drafts may be treated as nonlocal items by a depository institution if the payable through bank is nonlocal, even if the credit union itself is local to the depository institution.

* * *

In this case, the plain language of the Act dictates that the location of the institution on which a check is "drawn" determines whether it is local or nonlocal. The Board itself has acknowledged that at least in a technical sense the credit union is the originating depository institution on which a share draft is drawn. 53 Fed.Reg. 19,391. Furthermore, the Board is on the record as having referred to the credit union as the "organization on which a check is drawn" and the payable through bank as the place "where the check is sent for collection." 53 Fed.Reg. 47,113 (Dec. 11, 1987). The Board has now apparently concluded that the term "drawn" contains sufficient ambiguity as to warrant the change in terms. The alleged ambiguity is a fiction. The Board argues that the payable through bank performs many of the functions that might otherwise be performed by the credit union, making the payable through bank eligible for treatment as the institution on which a share draft is drawn. The fact remains, however, that it is the credit union that decides whether to pay or dishonor the share draft; the payable through bank is merely a collecting bank.

Common usage and commercial law provide a useful reference in determining the plain meaning of terms. In this case, both suggest that share drafts are never said to be drawn on or paid by the payable through bank. Under the Uniform Commercial Code, the "drawee" or "payor" institution is the one that holds the drawer's funds and which is requested to pay an item upon proper presentment. See U.C.C. § 4–105 & Official Comment 2 [R 4–105(3) & Comment 4]. As applied to credit union share drafts, the drawee institution is the credit union, which decides whether or not the share draft will be honored. Indeed, the Board does not dispute that the credit union is a drawee institution with regard to its share draft accounts. See 53 Fed.Reg. 19,392. The payable through bank merely serves as a collecting agent, not authorized to pay the item, but only to present the share draft to the credit union. See Section 3–120 [R 4–106(a)] of the Uniform Commercial Code; see also B. Clark, supra, at ¶ 10.9[1][a].

The Board does not dispute that commercial law, as reflected in the UCC, supports the contention that the credit union is a drawee institution. The Board suggests, however, that the creation of the term "paying bank" in the Board's Regulation J, which is not at issue in this case, provides the basis for an alternative meaning of the term "institution on which a check is drawn." Under Regulation J, payable through banks and banks on which checks are drawn are treated the same for purposes of collection. At the outset, the Court notes that the Board first raised this "Regulation J" argument in its papers in this case. Hence, the argument does not merit much credence, as it resembles a post hoc rationalization. Nonetheless, the Court will address the argument.

The Board argues that there is evidence in the structure of the Act that Congress intended to adopt the "federal law" term "paying bank" of Regulation J. It must be noted, however, that although the term "paying bank" had been in existence for seven years at the time that Congress passed the Act, Congress did not choose to adopt the Board's terminology. In the context of credit union share drafts, the Board contends that Congress left a gap in the Act with respect to nondepository institutions that can only be cured by the substitution of "paying bank" as defined by the Board for "originating depository institution" as defined by Congress. The plaintiffs concur that the Act is unclear as to the treatment of drafts drawn on nondepository institutions, such as insurance companies. But plaintiffs are correct that any such gap does not extend to credit union share drafts, for credit unions are clearly depository institutions under the Act. See 12 U.S.C. § 4001(12).

As for common usage, even the dictionary definition relied on by the Board in creating the alleged ambiguity within the term "drawn" supports plaintiffs' contention that the plain meaning of the term involved in this case can only refer to the credit union. Black's Law

Dictionary defines the drawee of a check as "the bank on which it is drawn" and the party "requested to pay the amount of money" stated in the check. Black's Law Dictionary 444 (5th ed. 1979). In the case of a credit union share draft, the institution on which it is drawn and which is requested to pay its stated amount can be none other than the credit union.

IV. CONCLUSION

This case is reminiscent of the United States Supreme Court's recent rejection of the Board's redefinition of statutory terms defined within the Bank Holding Company Act. Board of Governors of the Federal Reserve System v. Dimension Financial Corp., 474 U.S. 361, 106 S.Ct. 681, 88 L.Ed.2d 691 (1986). Dimension concerned "nonbank banks"—institutions that offer services similar to bank services—which much to the Board's dismay were not subject to the Board's regulation. The Board redefined the term "bank" in a manner contrary to the definition in the Bank Holding Act and the intent of Congress. Id. In a similar vein, the Board in this case substituted its own term, "paying bank," in a manner contrary to the Expedited Funds Availability Act and the intent of Congress.

The Court need not inquire into the legislative history of the Expedited Funds Availability Act because the phrase "depository institution on which a check is drawn" is clear and unambiguous. The statutory term universally refers to the institution that decides whether to pay or dishonor the item presented. Congress has directly spoken to the issue at hand, thereby eliminating the need for further inquiry by the Court. The institution on which a share draft is drawn is unquestionably the credit union.

It is equally unnecessary for the Court to accord deference to the Board's substitution of terms and redefinition, as the original term of the statute is clear and unambiguous. As was the case in Dimension, no amount of agency expertise can make the term at issue—"depository institution on which a check is drawn"—mean what the Board would have it mean.

To summarize, the Court finds that the plaintiffs have made credible allegations of a threatened injury fairly traceable to Regulation CC as promulgated. The Court further finds that there is a substantial likelihood that an order favorable to the plaintiffs will redress the threatened injuries. Based upon the foregoing, the Court holds that plaintiffs have standing to challenge Regulation CC. The Court further holds that Regulation CC as promulgated veers dramatically from the clear and unambiguous intent of Congress. In the Act, Congress chose the term "originating depository institution" and gave that term an unambiguous definition. Neither the Court nor the Board can substitute its judgment or its own terms for the judgment and plain language of Congress.

Note

1. In response to *CUNA,* the Federal Reserve Board amended Regulation CC to conform the regulatory definition of "paying bank" in Part B of the Regulation, concerning availability schedules, with the statutory definition, so far as the definition applies to depositary institutions. The pre-*CUNA* definition still applies in Subpart C, the expedited return provisions.

2. Note that the federal regulation provides a definition of a drawee; original Article 4 did not. Revised Article 4 does contain a definition of "drawee," see 4–104(a)(8). Cf. R 3–103, which defines drawee in the same terms as does amended Article 4.

3. Footnote 6 of the *CUNA* decision reproduces the Federal Reserve Board's definition of paying bank; see particularly item (3): "The bank whose routing number appears on a check in magnetic ink or in fractional form and to which the check is sent for payment or collection." Keep that definition in mind as you read the MICR fraud cases later in this chapter.

4. The credit unions complained that merchants would both be aware the credit union drafts payable through a distant bank would be "non-local" and that the items' non-local character would invite prejudice against credit union customers. How would the items' character be discernible and what steps would merchants have to take to accomplish the result feared by the credit unions? And at what cost?

5. The *CUNA* court speculated that

> in the ever-increasing competition between financial institutions, some banks and savings and loan associations will likely distinguish the holds allowable on their checks from those allowable on share drafts in disclosure statements in sales literature, luring credit union members to terminate their share draft accounts and open checking accounts at those competing institutions.

Is that argument convincing? Why didn't competitive pressures encourage banks to advertise their more expeditious funds availability policies prior to Reg. CC? Has the promulgation of Reg. CC encouraged or discouraged such competition and has that result benefitted or harmed consumer interests? Paradoxically, would competitive pressures cause some banks to provide "non-local" share drafts "local" availability?

6. Could banks, as part of the OR and R 4–103 account agreement, contract with their customers to delay availability of credit union share drafts notwithstanding the Fed's adjustment of the "paying bank" definition? If the banks would be disposed to try that, what problem for expedited availability and the check collection system generally does that intimate about the *CUNA* court's conclusion?

7. Note that OR 3–120 and 4–105(b) (and R 4–106) define the payable through bank as a collecting bank; so the OR and R 4–302 midnight deadline would not pertain to the payable through bank's retention of the collection item. Contrast the Reg. CC definition of paying bank, for purposes of Subpart C concerning expedited return, and consider the coordination of the two definitions. Does Reg. CC preempt the U.C.C.'s

midnight deadline? Are the two inconsistent? What are the consequences of the federal/state law interrelation?

Problems

1. IBM maintains an account with a large commercial bank in New York City, into which it deposits checks that it receives as payment from its customers for orders of computer equipment. The bank's policy is to make deposited funds represented by checks available to the depositor in accordance with federal regulation, but no sooner.

(a) Do the funds availability provisions of Subpart B of Regulation CC apply to IBM as a non-consumer depositor? See the Official Commentary to § 229.2(n) of Regulation CC.

(b) Assume IBM makes a deposit of several checks before the end of the banking day on Monday. When must the funds represented by the checks be available for withdrawal by IBM if the deposit consists of:

(1) A U.S. Treasury check for $10,000;

(2) Two local checks totaling $300;

(3) Four non-local checks totaling $9,000.

See Regulation CC §§ 229.10(c)(i), 229.10(c)(vii), 229.12(b), 229.12(c), and 229.13(h).

2. Bank X is a small commercial bank. It is open Monday through Friday. On Thursdays, however, it only provides drive-thru service, which means that many of the in-office services such as loan processing and lock-box access are not available. The cut-off time for the bank's banking day is 2:00 p.m.

(a) Is Thursday considered a "banking day" for Bank X for purposes of Regulation CC funds availability? See Regulation CC § 229.2(f).

(b) Determine when Bank X must make the proceeds of the following deposits available to the depositor for withdrawal. Assume that all of the checks are written for amounts less than $5,000, that there are no legal holidays during the month that the deposits are made, and that all deposits are made in person to an employee of Bank X unless otherwise stated.

(1) a local check deposited on Friday at 4:00 p.m. See Regulation CC § 229.12(b).

(2) a non-local check deposited Wednesday at 3:00 p.m. See Regulation CC § 229.12(c).

(3) a local check made payable to "cash" and deposited on Tuesday at 9:30 a.m.

(4) a certified check made payable to the depositor and deposited in Bank X's ATM machine on Monday at 8:00 a.m., along with the special deposit slip required by Bank X for certified checks. See Regulation CC § 229.10(c)(2).

(5) a U.S. Postal Service money order made payable to the depositor and deposited at 11:30 a.m. on Thursday. See Regulation CC § 229.10(c)(ii).

(6) a check made payable to the depositor, which is drawn on a Visa account with an out-of-state finance company, and deposited at Bank X's ATM machine on Saturday afternoon. See Regulation CC § 229.12(c).

(7) a traveler's check payable through a bank located within Bank X's check processing region and deposited on Wednesday at 10:00 a.m. See Official Commentary to Regulation CC § 229.2(hh), and Regulation CC § 229.12(b).

D. RETURN OF DISHONORED CHECKS UNDER ARTICLE 4 AND FEDERAL REGULATION CC

Before Regulation CC was enacted, Article 4 of the U.C.C., supported by Regulation J, contained the rules for the return of a dishonored check. Under OR 4–302, a drawee bank acts seasonably if it returns the item or sends notice of dishonor before its midnight deadline, midnight of the banking day following the banking day of receipt (as defined in OR 4–104(h) and now in R 4–104(a)(10)). All the drawee bank has to do, in order to avoid liability, is send the item back to its transferor—the institution that presented the item to the drawee bank—before its midnight deadline. Under OR 4–202, the transferor, who is a collecting bank in the forward processing of the item, then has to send the item to its transferor before its midnight deadline. This process continues until the depositary bank finally receives notice of dishonor or return of the dishonored item.

Under OR 4–212 (R 4–214), the depositary bank has the right to charge-back any provisional credit given to the depositor for the dishonored check. Original 4–103(5) (R 4–103(e)) allows damages for failure to use ordinary care in the handling of an item to be the amount of the item. Using this section, depositary banks, and depositors themselves, sometimes attempt to hold a bank strictly liable for the amount of a dishonored check when that bank fails to meet its midnight deadline. Consider the following cases' discussion of the Article 4 rules governing the return of dishonored checks.

PULASKI BANK AND TRUST CO. v. TEXAS AMERICAN BANK/FORT WORTH, N.A.

Texas Court of Appeals, 1988.
759 S.W.2d 723.

THOMAS, JUSTICE.

Appellant, Pulaski Bank and Trust Company, sued Texas American Bank/Fort Worth (TAB/Fort Worth), Texas American Bank/West

Side (TAB/West Side) and Texas American Services, Inc. (TASI), appellees, alleging that they were liable for losses suffered by Pulaski when notice of dishonor of a $150,000 check drawn upon TAB/West Side was not timely relayed to Pulaski. After a nonjury trial, the trial court entered a take-nothing judgment against TAB/West Side and TASI and further entered judgment in favor of Pulaski against TAB/Fort Worth for $8,202.14. In three points of error, Pulaski contends that the trial court erred: 1) in concluding that TAB/West Side was not liable for Pulaski's loss, because as a matter of law TAB/West Side did not timely return the check; 2) in using the wrong measure of damages after imposing liability upon TAB/Fort Worth; and 3) in failing to award attorney's fees to Pulaski. We find no merit in any of Pulaski's points of error, and affirm the trial court's judgment.

STATUTORY FRAMEWORK

This action is governed by chapter 4 of the Uniform Commercial Code. Chapter 4 sets out the method by which a bank in which a check is deposited may be finally paid by the bank upon which the check is drawn. It has been said that chapter 4 provides the "traffic rules" which keep the bank collection process flowing smoothly. Malcolm, How Bank Collection Works—Article 4 of the Uniform Commercial Code, 11 How.L.J. 71, 86 (1965) (hereinafter cited as "How Bank Collection Works"). In order to place the facts of this case in context, we must first set out the framework of chapter 4.

To begin the collection process on a check, the person having possession of the item must transfer it to a bank, but not necessarily the bank through which or upon which the check is drawn. See Annot., 84 A.L.R.3d 1073, 1076 (1978). The first bank to which a check is transferred for collection is called the depositary bank. See § 4.105(1) [R 4–105(2)]; Union Bank of Benton v. First National Bank, 621 F.2d 790, 793 (5th Cir.1980). After the depositary bank has processed the check and entered a provisional credit to the account of its depositor, the bank will transfer the check to another bank which may be the first of many banks that will handle the check before it reaches the bank upon which it is drawn.

The last bank in the chain—the bank by which an item is payable as drawn—is denominated the payor bank. See § 4.105(2) [R 4–105(3)]; Lockhart Savings & Loan Assn. v. RepublicBank Austin, 720 S.W.2d 193, 194 (Tex.App.—Austin 1986, writ ref'd n.r.e.); cf. Hamby Co. v. Seminole State Bank, 652 S.W.2d 939, 941 (Tex.1983) (defining payor bank in case involving documentary draft). The other banks in the chain are intermediary banks and collecting banks. An intermediary bank is any bank to which an item is transferred in the course of collection, except the depositary or payor bank. See § 4.105(3) [R 4–105(4)]; Annot., 84 A.L.R.3d at 1077. A collecting bank is one which handles the check for collection, but not the payor bank. See § 4.105(4) [R 4–105(5)]; Ohio Bell Telephone Co. v. BancOhio National Bank, 1 Ohio Misc.2d 11, 440 N.E.2d 69, 71 (1982). These classifications of banks in the collection process are not exclusive. Thus, it is entirely possible that a depositary bank could also be a collecting bank. See § 4.105(1) [2] & (4) [5]; Annot., 84 A.L.R.3d at 1076 & n. 5.

As the check moves along the chain from the depositary bank to the payor bank, all the banks in the chain enter provisional debits and credits on the account of the bank from which and to which the check is transferred. These provisional credits are termed provisional settlements under chapter 4. See § 4.104(a)(10) [R 4–104(a)(11)]; Lockhart Savings & Loan, 720 S.W.2d at 194. As the check passes from the depositary bank to the payor bank through collecting banks, each collecting bank must act seasonably in forwarding the check. A bank acts seasonably if it acts before its midnight deadline following receipt of the check. See § 4.202(b) [R 4–202(b)]; Wilhelm Foods, Inc. v. National Bank of North America, 388 F.Supp. 1376, 1379 (D.C.N.Y. 1974). The midnight deadline is midnight on the next banking day following the banking day on which the bank receives the check. See § 4.104(a)(8) [R 4–104(a)(10)]; First State Bank of McKinney v. American Bank of Sherman, 732 S.W.2d 404, 405 (Tex.App.—Dallas 1987, no writ).

When the check reaches the payor bank, that bank must decide whether to pay the check or dishonor the check. If the payor bank pays the check, all the provisional settlements among the banks in the collection chain become final. See § 4.213 [R 4–215]; Riggs v. State, 34 Md.App. 324, 367 A.2d 22, 26 n. 5 (1976). If the payor bank decides to dishonor the check, it must return the item or send notice of dishonor to the intermediary bank from which it received the check. The payor bank must take this step before its midnight deadline. See § 4.301 [R 4–301]; North Carolina National Bank v. Harwell, 38 N.C.App. 190, 247 S.E.2d 720, 724 (1978), pet. denied, 296 N.C. 410, 267 S.E.2d 656 (1979). If the payor bank does not return the item or send notice of dishonor before its midnight deadline, the provisional settlements become final. See § 4.213(a)(3) [R 4–215(d)]; Annot., 23 A.L.R.4th 203, 216–18 (1983). Until a check is finally paid, a collecting bank which makes a provisional settlement has the right to charge back the amount of any credit given or to obtain a refund from the bank it credited. See § 4.212 [R 4–214]. The right of charge-back terminates when a settlement becomes final. Id; Regal Tour, Inc. v. European American Bank, 108 Misc.2d 699, 438 N.Y.S.2d 947, 949 (1981).

A payor bank that does not timely return the check or send notice of dishonor becomes liable to the depositary bank for the full amount of the check. See §§ 4.213(a) [R 4–215(a)(3)] & 4.302 [R 4–302]; Hamby Co., 652 S.W.2d at 941; Pecos County State Bank v. El Paso Livestock Auction Co., 586 S.W.2d 183, 187 (Tex.Civ.App.—El Paso 1979, writ ref'd n.r.e.). A collecting bank becomes liable if it fails to use ordinary care in returning items or giving notice of dishonor by its midnight deadline. See § 4.202 [R 4–202]; Citizens Bank, Bentonville v. Chitty, 285 Ark. 55, 684 S.W.2d 814, 816 (1985). In such instances, the collecting bank's liability is measured by the amount of the check reduced by an amount which could not have been realized by the use of ordinary care by the collecting bank. See § 4.103(e) [R 4–103(e)]; Marquette National Bank v. Heritage Pullman Bank & Trust Co., 109 Ill.App.3d 532, 65 Ill.Dec. 178, 181, 440 N.E.2d 1033, 1036 (1982); Whitehall Packing Co. v. First National City Bank, 55 A.D.2d 675, 390 N.Y.S.2d 189, 191 (1976).

FACTUAL BACKGROUND

On February 5, 1985, Laboratory Management, Inc. deposited into its account at Pulaski, a Little Rock, Arkansas bank, a check in the amount of $150,000. The check was made by Fairway Farms, Inc., and was drawn on TAB/West Side, a Fort Worth bank. Lab Management received a provisional credit in the amount of $150,000 at that time. Pulaski immediately transmitted the check for collection to its correspondent bank, Worthen Bank & Trust Company of Little Rock. Immediately upon receiving the check on February 6th, Worthen sent the check for collection to MBank Dallas, Worthen's corresponding bank in Dallas. MBank Dallas, still on February 6th, delivered the check to MBank Fort Worth.

That same day, MBank Fort Worth delivered the check to the Fort Worth Clearinghouse. Since TAB/West Side is not a "clearing member," it could not participate in the exchange of items at the clearinghouse. Therefore, TAB/Fort Worth, a clearing member, received for collection the $150,000 check payable by TAB/West Side. The clearinghouse sent the check to TASI, an off-premises data processing center used by both TAB/Fort Worth and TAB/West Side.

TASI received the check on February 6th. During the computerized processing procedure, the check was sorted into the TAB/West Side reject pocket and was listed on the TAB/West Side rejects list because of insufficient funds in Fairway Farm's account. The rejects list was delivered to TAB/West Side by 8:00 a.m. on February 7th. Barry Smith, the account officer responsible for the Fairway Farms account upon which the $150,000 check was drawn, was notified that there were insufficient funds to cover the check. Smith decided that the check should not be paid and informed the customer service department of TAB/West Side that the check should be returned unpaid. The rejects list was transmitted by courier to TASI between 10:00 a.m. and 11:00 a.m. on February 7th. Thereafter, the check was manually pulled and marked to be returned. The check was then taken to the customer accounting, or bookkeeping, department at TASI. Because of the directions of TAB/West Side that the check should be returned unpaid, the ledger entries previously made were reversed.

The check was then taken to the return item department. The testimony revealed that the return item department represented TAB/Fort Worth in the transaction at this point in time. According to the testimony, once the check was physically pulled and the entries to the general ledgers were reversed, TAB/West Side was "out of the picture." Although it is disputed whether TASI gave MBank Dallas telephone notice of the return on February 7th, it is undisputed that the check was not physically returned to MBank Dallas on February 7th. The check was misrouted by TASI; rather than returning the check to MBank Dallas, TASI sent the check to RepublicBank. After the check was misrouted to RepublicBank, it appears that RepublicBank sent the check to the Federal Reserve Bank of Dallas. On February 14th, TASI received telephone notification from the Federal Reserve Bank that it had the check and was sending it back. The return item department of TASI physically received the check on February 15th, and on that same date telephoned MBank Dallas notifying them of the return of the check. Because of an intervening bank holiday, MBank Dallas did not receive the check itself until February 19th. However, on February 15th, MBank notified Worthen Bank of the return by telephone. MBank sent the check to Worthen on February 19th and Worthen received it on February 21st. Worthen notified Pulaski by telephone on February 22nd that the check was being returned and Pulaski actually received the check from Worthen on February 23rd.

On February 22nd and 23rd, the balance in Lab Management's checking account at Pulaski was $46,036.65. Pulaski did not freeze the account at that time because it considered the return to be late. It was Pulaski's position that since this was a late return, one of the collecting banks would be required to pay the entire amount of the check. Pulaski sent a late return claim to Worthen. Worthen disclaimed responsibility for the late return, and made a late return claim against MBank Dallas. MBank also disclaimed responsibility, and sent a late return claim to TAB/Fort Worth. TAB/Fort Worth also disclaimed responsibility, relying upon telephonic notice to MBank on February 7th. By March 25th, all of the banks in the collection chain had disclaimed, in writing, liability for late return. The Lab Management account was finally frozen and the $150,000 deposit charged back on April 30, 1985. At that time, the account balance was $1,433.99.

If the check had been returned timely by all the banks in the collection chain, Pulaski should have received notification of dishonor on February 12th. By February 12th, Pulaski had paid out $95,761.21 from the Lab Management account. Between February 12th, the date upon which Pulaski should have received notice of dishonor, and February 23rd, the date upon which the check was returned unpaid, Pulaski paid out $8,202.14 from the Lab Management account.

* * *

Liability of TAB/West Side

Pulaski contends in its first point of error that "[t]he trial court should have found as a matter of law that TAB/West Side was liable for Pulaski Bank's loss because it did not timely and adequately revoke settlement and return the check." Pulaski concedes that the U.C.C. does not require TAB/West Side to return directly to Pulaski, but rather requires a return to its immediate transferor before the midnight deadline. See § 4.301 [R 4–301]. Pulaski contends, however, that MBank, not TAB/Fort Worth, was TAB/West Side's transferor.

Pulaski characterizes TAB/Fort Worth as a "mere agent" of TAB/West Side and a "nominal participant" in the check-handling process. Thus, argues Pulaski, a return to TAB/Fort Worth before TAB/West Side's midnight deadline was ineffective to cut off TAB/West Side's liability.

In the alternative, Pulaski contends that, even if TAB/Fort Worth is the transferor bank, we would frustrate the public policy behind the enactment of chapter 4 of the U.C.C. if we held that return and revocation of provisional settlements can be achieved through "mere" book entries at TASI. This presents an issue of first impression in this state, and apparently in all jurisdictions that have adopted the U.C.C. Further, in the event these arguments are unavailing, and we conclude TAB/West Side correctly and timely returned the check to its transferor as required by the U.C.C., Pulaski argues that the return was untimely under the rules of the Fort Worth Clearinghouse and thus, subjects TAB/West Side to liability.

A. TAB/West Side's Midnight Deadline

We must first determine when TAB/West Side's midnight deadline fell. The midnight deadline falls on midnight on the next banking day following the banking day on which TAB/West Side received the check. See § 4.104(a)(8) [R 4–104(a)(10)]. The $150,000 check reached TASI on February 6th. It is undisputed that TASI functions as the data-processing center for both TAB/Fort Worth and TAB/West Side. It is also undisputed that the check remained at TASI February 6th and 7th and that TAB/West Side's decision to dishonor was not made until February 7th. We need not decide yet whether the delivery of the check to TASI was delivery to TAB/West Side directly or to TAB/West Side only through delivery first to TAB/Fort Worth. TAB/West Side and TAB/Fort Worth concede that, in some fashion, TAB/West Side received the check at TASI at some time on February 6th. This Court has held that the midnight deadline calculation begins with the day on which a check is received at an off-premises data-processing center and not the day on which the check or check information is taken to the bank premises from the data-processing center. First State Bank of McKinney, 732 S.W.2d at 406–07.

Thus, we conclude that the midnight deadline time period must be calculated starting with February 6th, the day TAB/West Side "received" the check by presentment to TASI (Whether that presentment was made by MBank or by TAB/Fort Worth will be addressed later). Therefore, TAB/West Side's midnight deadline was midnight of the next banking day. See § 4.104(a)(8) [R 4–104(a)(10)]. By midnight of February 7th, TAB/West Side had to return the check to its transferor bank. We must now determine the identity of that transferor bank.

B. TAB/Fort Worth's Status As TAB/West Side's Transferor Bank

Pulaski argues that TAB/Fort Worth was acting merely as an agent for presentment of the check and not as a collecting bank. The essence of its argument is that TAB/Fort Worth was involved with this check only because the Fort Worth Clearinghouse rules prohibited TAB/West Side from directly clearing the check. Pulaski alludes to the close relationship between TAB/Fort Worth, TAB/West Side and TASI as proof that TAB/Fort Worth was merely acting as agent for TAB/West Side. We are not persuaded by Pulaski's argument.

Pulaski relies in part on clearinghouse rule 2.03, which provides that a clearing member acts as agent or subagent for the bank for which the clearing member sends or receives items. We do not read this rule to change TAB/Fort Worth's status from a collecting bank to a mere agent. Even the U.C.C. provides that collecting banks are agents. See § 4.201 [R 4–201]. Because of the similarity in language of clearinghouse rule 2.03 and section 4.201 [R 4–201] of the U.C.C., we believe that the clearinghouse rule was enacted for the same reason that section 4.201 [R 4–201] was enacted: to end confusion over whether a bank handling an item was a purchaser of the item or merely an agent for collection. See § 4.201 [R 4–201] comment 1. Thus, we conclude that any agency status between TAB/West Side and TAB/Fort Worth does not prevent TAB/Fort Worth from being TAB/West Side's transferor bank.

Pulaski also argues that the corporate relationship between TAB/West Side, TAB/Fort Worth and TASI prevents TAB/Fort Worth from being the transferor bank. TAB/West Side, TAB/Fort Worth and TASI are each separate corporate entities; however, they are all wholly-owned subsidiaries of Texas American Bancshares, Inc. Pulaski argues that this close relationship requires us to view TAB/West Side and TAB/Fort Worth as a single entity, disqualifying TAB/Fort Worth from being TAB/West Side's transferor bank.

We note that Pulaski has asserted no grounds justifying the disregarding of corporate status. Under Texas law, the separate identity of corporations will be observed by the courts, even in instances where one may dominate or control the other, or may even treat it as a mere department, instrumentality or agency of the other. Norton v. Integral Corp., 584 S.W.2d 932, 935 (Tex.Civ.App.—Austin 1979, no writ). The mere fact that a subsidiary is wholly owned by a parent corporation does not justify disregarding the corporate identity of the parent. Texas Oil & Gas Corp. v. Hagen, 683 S.W.2d 24, 28 (Tex.App.—Texarkana 1984, writ granted) (dismissal of writ of error pending approval of settlement agreement). See also Lucas v. Texas Industries, Inc., 696 S.W.2d 372, 374–75 (Tex.1984). We decline to accept Pulaski's argument, unfounded in Texas law, that the joint ownership of TAB/Fort Worth and TAB/West Side prevents TAB/Fort Worth from being TAB/West Side's transferor bank.

* * *

After reviewing the record, we are constrained to hold that there is ample evidence to support the trial court's finding that TAB/Fort Worth was TAB/West Side's transferor with respect to the $150,000 check. TAB/Fort Worth was authorized by Fort Worth Clearinghouse rules to clear checks for TAB/West Side. TAB/West Side, as an associate member, could not have received the check through the clearinghouse from MBank Fort Worth. TAB/Fort Worth, like any collecting bank, stamped the check with its endorsement. Transferor banks carry accounts for the next bank in the collection chain and will debit the account when it passes the check to that bank. In this case, TAB/Fort Worth carries an account for TAB/West Side. After the check was received at TASI and sorted to TAB/West Side, TAB/Fort Worth charged TAB/West Side's account for the amount of the check. After TAB/West Side notified TASI of its decision to dishonor the check, the ledger entries debiting TAB/West Side's account with TAB/Fort Worth were reversed. These actions are consistent with the relationship of transferor-transferee bank.

We hold that there is some evidence to support the trial court's finding. In light of this conclusion, we need not reach the question of whether the contrary proposition is conclusively established. See Holley, 629 S.W.2d at 697.

C. Public Policy

Pulaski argues that one of the underlying policies of chapter 4 of the U.C.C. is speed in the collection process. Pulaski contends that we would frustrate this policy encouraging speed if we approved the "legal fiction" of allowing returns and revocations "within the confines of the same data processing center." Pulaski does not explain why it feels speed in collection would suffer by joint use of a data processing center. Its argument appears to be that a bank could extend its midnight deadline by "pretending" that another bank, which shared the data processing center, was involved in the collection chain. Thus, a bank could effectively double the amount of time that the U.C.C. gives it to act.

Pulaski cites numerous cases from other jurisdictions which it contends support the conclusion that the midnight deadline cannot be extended through joint use of a data processing center by a transferor collecting bank and a transferee payor bank. However, none of the cases cited by Pulaski involved the joint use of a data processing center. The issue in the cases relied upon by Pulaski was when the midnight deadline commenced in a situation where a check was presented at a bank's off-premises data processing center. That issue has already been resolved for this jurisdiction in First State Bank of McKinney, 732 S.W.2d at 406–07. Pulaski has not presented any authority directly on point. Pulaski relies heavily upon Capital City First National Bank v. Lewis State Bank, 341 So.2d 1025 (Fla.App.1977), which it claims is factually similar to the case at bar. Pulaski is correct, in that the payor bank's off-premises data processing center was a collecting bank's computerized proof and transit department. However, the issue in Capital City was when the midnight deadline commenced, not when the check was returned to the transferor bank. Thus, we have been presented with no case authority to support Pulaski's public policy argument.

This court has recognized that speed in the collection process is a policy encouraged by the U.C.C. See First State Bank of McKinney, 732 S.W.2d at 406. There is, however, a competing interest that we must recognize. A bank must be given sufficient time in which to make an informed, intelligent decision whether to pay a check or to dishonor it. The framers of the U.C.C. recognized this time-consuming process: After an item has been received by a bank it goes through a series of processes varying with the type of item that it is. It moves from the teller's window, branch office, or mail desk at which it is received through settlement and proving departments until it is forwarded or presented to a clearing house or another bank, if it is a transit item, or until it reaches the bookkeeping department, if the bank receiving it is the payor bank. In addition, in order that the books of the bank always remain in balance while items are moving through it, the amount of each item is included in lists or proofs of debits or credits several times as it progresses through the bank. The running of proofs, the making of debit and credit entries in subsidiary and general ledgers and the striking of a general balance for each day requires a considerable amount of time. See § 4.107 [R 4–108] comment 1. While we agree with Pulaski that it would be unfair to allow a bank, through use of a sham transferor bank, to double its midnight deadline, it would be equally unfair to halve the time by requiring separate banks to share the same midnight deadline.

The Code recognizes that each bank is entitled to at least twenty-four hours to process a check. See § 4.104(a)(8) [R 4–104(a)(10)]. Even closely-related banks have this right; the U.C.C. provides that each branch or separate office of a bank is to be considered a separate bank for purposes of computing the time in which a bank is to act. See § 4.106 [R 4–107]. Thus in Lawrence v. Bank of America, 163 Cal. App.3d 431, 209 Cal.Rptr. 541 (1985), one branch bank was allowed, after cashing a check, an event which would render payment final if taken by a payor bank, to revoke a provisional settlement on a check drawn on another branch of the bank, even though both branches were linked by a common computer system. The branches, despite the shared computer system, were considered separate entities under section 4.106 [R 4–107].

After weighing the competing interests of the U.C.C., we conclude that TAB/Fort Worth and TAB/West Side must be treated as separate banking entities, each entitled to a separate midnight deadline despite the shared data-processing center. Pulaski argues in its brief: If the judgment is upheld, a payor bank, such as TAB West Side, could effectively emasculate its potential liability under [the U.C.C.] through legal fictions. In essence, a group of banks could each avoid their respective payor bank liabilities and midnight deadlines through the fiction of revocations of settlement and "returns" of checks within the confines of the same data processing center. Taken to a logical extreme, the banks might never be held strictly liable under [the U.C.C.] because of their internal "returns" and "revocations" at the data processing center. The argument is, in the abstract, very persuasive. However, Pulaski offered no evidence at trial to indicate that TAB/West Side used TASI in order to insulate it from liability. As stated previously, the evidence showed that TAB/Fort Worth and TAB/West Side had a true transferor-transferee relationship and were not using TASI to perpetrate a fraud.

D. TAB/West Side's Return of the Check to TAB/Fort Worth Before Its Midnight Deadline

As we noted previously, TAB/West Side's deadline for return of the check was midnight on February 7th. We have also held that the return had to be made to its transferor bank, which was TAB/Fort Worth. We turn now to the evidence to determine if TAB/West Side returned the $150,000 check to TAB/Fort Worth before midnight on February 7th. The evidence shows that TAB/West Side returned the rejects list with no "pay" notation next to the $150,000 check to TASI between 10:00 a.m. and 11:00 a.m. on February 7th. The lack of a "pay" notation informed TASI that TAB/West Side was returning the check unpaid. At TASI, the check was pulled and routed to the customer accounting department where the ledger entries between TAB/West Side and TAB/Fort Worth were reversed. From that department, the check was taken to the return items department. According to a TASI vice-president, the return between TAB/West Side and TAB/Fort Worth was completed when two events occurred: when the item was physically pulled and the ledger entries were reversed. This occurred before midnight on February 7th. We hold, based upon this evidence, that TAB/West Side met its U.C.C. midnight deadline for returning the check to TAB/Fort Worth.

E. The Clearinghouse Rules

Pulaski's final argument is that, even if TAB/West Side timely returned the check under the U.C.C., the return was still untimely under the rules of the Fort Worth Clearinghouse. The U.C.C. provides that chapter 4 may be varied by agreements and that clearinghouse rules have the effect of agreements whether or not specifically assented to by all parties interested in items handled. See § 4.103(a) & (b) [R 4–103(a) and (b)]. Further, section 4.213 [R 4–215], which provides that a payor bank must return an item within a specified time or the settlement becomes final and may not be revoked, sets out the time when the settlement becomes irrevocable and any return is rendered ineffective: when the payor bank has "made a provisional settlement for the item and failed to revoke the settlement in the time and manner permitted by statute, *clearing house rule* or agreement." See § 4.213(a)(3) (emphasis added). In Lockhart Savings & Loan, 720 S.W.2d 193, the Austin court of appeals held that the U.C.C. clearly provides that clearinghouse rules will determine final payment *when a clearinghouse was the vehicle for presentment.* Id. at 195–96. However, we have held that the Fort Worth Clearinghouse was not the vehicle for presentment to TAB/West Side. While the clearinghouse was the vehicle for presentment to TAB/Fort Worth, it was TAB/Fort Worth, and not the clearinghouse, which presented the check to TAB/West Side. Thus, TAB/West Side was not required to meet clearinghouse rules in returning the check to TAB/Fort Worth.

F. Conclusion

We hold that TAB/West Side timely returned the $150,000 check to its transferor bank, TAB/Fort Worth. Accordingly, we conclude that the trial court was correct in finding that TAB/West Side was not liable for damages to Pulaski. Pulaski's first point of error is overruled.

APPLIANCE BUYERS CREDIT CORPORATION v. PROSPECT NATIONAL BANK OF PEORIA

United States Court of Appeals, Seventh Circuit 1983.
708 F.2d 290.

COFFEY, CIRCUIT JUDGE.

This is an appeal from the district court's dismissal of the plaintiff's claim under section 4–212 [R 4–214] of the Uniform Commercial Code on the grounds that the plaintiff failed to establish its damages. Affirmed.

The Appliance Buyers Credit Corporation, a Delaware corporation with its principal place of business in Michigan, is a finance company that provides wholesale "floor-plan financing" to appliance dealers.[1] The corporation makes monthly inspections of participating dealers' inventory to determine whether the dealers are current in their finance payments to Appliance Buyers. During one of Appliance Buyers' monthly inspections of the Nevius Appliance & Furniture inventory it was determined that Nevius had failed to report the sale of certain merchandise to Appliance Buyers and owed $65,736.78. Immediately following the inspection on October 17, 1979 Nevius gave a check to the Appliance Buyers Credit Corporation representative in the amount of $55,736.78 and delivered a $10,000 check to the corporation the next day, October 18, 1979; both checks were drawn on the Corn Belt Bank of Bloomington, Illinois. Appliance Buyers Credit Corporation deposited these two checks on October 18, 1979 with the Prospect National Bank, and Prospect National credited Appliance Buyers' account with a provisional credit. Prospect National processed these two checks through the Chicago Federal Reserve Bank who in turn forwarded the checks to the drawee bank, the Corn Belt Bank of Bloomington. On October 22, 1979, the Corn Belt Bank dishonored the checks due to insufficient funds (NSF) and notified the Federal Reserve Bank of the

1. As a "floor-plan financier," Appliance Buyers finances the inventory of various appliance dealers and maintains a security interest in the merchandise so financed.

dishonor by telephone that day. On the day following, October 23, 1979, the Federal Reserve Bank of Chicago notified Prospect National Bank of the dishonor, by telephone, and returned the dishonored checks to the Prospect National Bank by mail. Prospect National, upon receipt of the NSF checks on October 29, 1979, immediately revoked the provisional credit given to the Appliance Buyers' account and notified Appliance Buyers of the dishonor that same day (October 29th). Appliance Buyers received the dishonored checks through the regular mail on the day following, October 30, 1979, and on the next day, October 31, Nevius Appliance & Furniture filed a voluntary petition for bankruptcy. Appliance Buyers then brought suit to recover the $65,736.78.

The district court dismissed the plaintiff's claim under section 4–202 [R 4–202] of the Uniform Commercial Code (Ill.Rev.Stat. ch. 26 § 4–202) initially finding that Prospect National Bank was negligent in failing to notify the Appliance Buyers Credit Corporation of the dishonor of Nevius' checks by the October 24th midnight deadline, the day it received a telephone notification of the checks' dishonor. 505 F.Supp. 163. However, notwithstanding the fact that Prospect National was negligent in notifying Appliance Buyers of the dishonor, in its order the district court also found that Appliance Buyers failed to establish its damages and therefore was not entitled to recover:

"Because the plaintiff has not demonstrated that it had a reasonable chance to collect all or part of the amount of the checks, the amount plaintiff was actually damaged, if any, as a result of the bank's failure to exercise ordinary care in notification is pure speculation. The court will not indulge in such speculation. [Appliance Buyers] has not produced any evidence that if it had known of the dishonor on October 24, 1979, it might have had a reasonable chance to collect any part of the money represented by the checks that it can't recover in the bankruptcy proceeding. Because the court is unable to determine what an appropriate award of damages would be in this case, if any, none can be awarded." (Footnote and citations omitted). The district court denied the Appliance Buyers Credit Corporation's motion to modify the above quoted court order regarding the corporation's failure to prove its damages: "The court is not convinced, however, that § 4–212 [R 4–214] gives a depositor a complete and automatic windfall if the bank is late in notification of dishonor of deposited and provisionally-credited items, when it is not proved that such lateness made any financial difference to the depositor, or, if so, within reasonable limits, how much difference it made. The court is not willing to adjudicate such an inconsistency of consequences between two sections of the Uniform Commercial Code dealing with the same subject, especially in a case where plaintiff took large checks it had substantial reason to suspect might 'bounce,' and now seeks thereby to saddle its bank with liability thereon after its debtor's bankruptcy." The plaintiff (Appliance Buyers Credit Corp.) appealed.

Appliance Buyers does not "seek review * * * of the trial court's dismissal of [its] section 4–202 [R 4–202] claim," recognizing that "the trier of fact's weighing of the evidence is not an appropriate subject for appellate review in this case." Because there is no challenge to the district court's application of section 4–202 [R 4–202], the question in this case is one of first impression: is a bank strictly liable as the plaintiff contends for the face value of a check under section 4–212 [R 4–214] of the Uniform Commercial Code if, after failing to give the depositor timely notice of the check's dishonor, the bank charges back the depositor's account?

Appliance Buyers Credit Corp. asserts that section 4–212 [R 4–214] makes a bank liable for the face value of a check when the bank breaches its duty to give a depositor timely notice of the check's dishonor, as under section 4–212 [R 4–214] timely notice of dishonor is a pre-condition to the bank's right to charge-back. While it is clear that the drafters of section 4–212 [R 4–214] of the Uniform Commercial Code intended to condition a bank's right to charge-back upon the giving of timely notice of dishonor, section 4–212 [R 4–214] fails to set forth language holding a bank "accountable" for the face value of a dishonored check if and when the bank fails to give timely notice of dishonor.

Ill.Rev.Stat. ch. 26 § 4–212 [R 4–214] provides: * * *

A reading of section 4–212 [R 4–214] reveals that while the section conditions a bank's right to "charge-back" on a timely notice of dishonor, it is silent on the measure of damages a depositor can recover, if any, when the bank breaches its duty of giving a timely notice of dishonor and still charges back the provisionally credited check. In its brief, Appliance Buyers contends that the bank should be held strictly liable for the face value of the dishonored check and for any other damages arising out of the bank's improper charge-back. The plaintiff has failed to supply the court and we have been unable to find any legal support either in the Uniform Commercial Code or case law for Appliance Buyers' unique contention that banks should be held strictly liable for the face value of dishonored checks under section 4–212 [R 4–214]. For example, certain sections of the Uniform Commercial Code such as 4–302(a) [R 4–302(a)(1)], 4–213(1)(d) [R 4–215(a)(3)] and 4–213(3) [R 4–215(d)] do impose liability on a bank for the face value of items in given situations, but we have found no similar obligation under section 4–212 [R 4–214]. The specific language of sections 4–302(a) [R 4–302(1)], 4–213(1)(d) [R 4–215(a)(3)] and 4–213(3) [R 4–215(d)] holds the bank "accountable for the amount of" the item in question. Cases construing these sections hold that the term "accountable" is "the operative term * * * which imposes liability for the face amount of a check * * *." Colorado National Bank v. First National Bank & Trust Co., 459 F.Supp. 1366, 1372 (W.D.Mich.1978). Section 4–212 [R 4–214] does not contain the "operative term" holding a bank "accountable" for the face value of a check if the bank improperly charges back the amount of a provisional credit against the depositor's account. It is obvious that if the drafters of the Uniform Commercial Code had intended to make a bank liable for the face value of a check under section 4–212 [R 4–214], they would have held the bank "accountable" in specific language for the face amount of the check as they have under other Code sections. Because section 4–212 [R 4–214] does not contain any language holding a bank "accountable" for the face value of a dishonored check, nor has our independent research uncovered any case law holding a bank "accountable" under section 4–212 [R 4–214], we hold that the drafters of section 4–212 [R 4–214] did not intend to impose absolute liability on a bank if the bank charged back a dishonored check against the depositor's account after failing to give the depositor timely notice of the check's dishonor.

Because section 4–212 [R 4–214] is silent concerning a depositor's measure of damages arising out of an improper charge-back, we will examine the Code and case law to determine the proper standard to be applied when deciding what Appliance Buyers must establish in order to recover under section 4–212 [R 4–214]. Ill.Rev.Stat. ch. 26 § 4–103(5) [R 4–103(e)], the general damages section of the Uniform Commercial Code, provides: * * * The official comment to section 4–103 [R 4–103] states that "[w]hen it is established that some part or all of the item could not have been collected even by the use of ordinary care the recovery is reduced by the amount which would have been in any event uncollectible." In applying this standard to the instant dispute, the district court ruled that there was serious question as to whether Appliance Buyers could have recovered any of the disputed $65,736.78 even if it had received timely notice of the checks' dishonor, as Nevius Appliance was in severe financial difficulty during the period in question and filed for bankruptcy just nine days after the checks were dishonored. Indeed, the district court found that the "fact of bankruptcy within two weeks of issuance of the first check and other evidence concerning Nevius' [insolvency] during the relevant period * * * raise serious doubt that [Appliance Buyers] could have collected any part of the amount of the checks, even if notified of the checks' dishonor in timely fashion." When evidence at trial demonstrated that "some or all of the item could not have been collected" had Appliance Buyers received timely notice of dishonor, the district court found that under section 4–103 [R 4–103] the burden was on Appliance Buyers to establish "that it had a reasonable chance of collecting something on the checks, before any award of damages caused by [Prospect National's] negligence could be made." We hold the district court was correct in placing the burden on Appliance Buyers to establish their damages and in dismissing the corporation's claim on the grounds that Appliance Buyers failed to prove to the court's satisfaction that they would have been able to recover any funds from Nevius had they in fact received timely notice from the bank.

A depositor bears the burden of establishing its actual damages under section 4–103 [R 4–103] in order to recover damages arising out of the negligence of a bank for failing to give a timely notice under other sections of the Code. It is the Appliance Buyers' position that the bank's failure to give timely notice of dishonor has caused their difficulty in proving damages since Nevius' business records do not reveal whether Appliance Buyers could have recovered a measure of damages from Nevius Appliance by repossessing those items in which Appliance Buyers had a security interest. Thus, under the plaintiff's analysis, the bank must prove the amount Appliance Buyers could not have collected even had the bank given timely notice of dishonor and if it is unable to meet this burden, Prospect National should be held liable for the face value of the checks. However, Appliance Buyers has failed to cite any sections of the Code or case law that do in fact shift the burden of proof from the depositor to the bank to prove the extent of a depositor's loss.

In the absence of "accountability" under other Uniform Commercial Code sections such as section 4–202 [R 4–202], courts have required depositors to prove the extent of their actual damages. For example, in Marcoux v. Van Wyk and the other cases cited herein dealing with untimely notice, courts clearly place the burden on a depositor seeking recovery to prove the amount "they would have had at least a reasonable chance to collect * * *. It is not enough to show that by a fortuitous combination of unlikely events there was a dim hope of collection." Furthermore, the bank will not be held liable "unless there is a clear causal relationship between the bank's actions and the plaintiff's loss." In a similar, pre-Code case, one court held "the burden [is] on the [depositor] not only to prove negligence on the part of the defendant [bank] but also the amount of loss in fact sustained as a result of that negligence. The defendant is not liable unless it is made to appear that collection could have been made, and was not made, because of want of reasonable effort and diligence on defendant's part." A fair reading of the Code and relevant case law reveals that since depositors must prove untimely notice and actual damages as conditions precedent to recovery under section 4–202 [R 4–202], under section 4–212 [R 4–214] depositors must also prove that they received untimely notice as well as the amount of actual damages suffered as a result of the untimely notice.[3]

The only decision that has been cited to the court in support of the Appliance Buyers' position is a case from the Civil Court of the City of New York, Manufacturers Hanover Trust Co. v. Akpan, where the bank sought to recover $2,500 from the defendant/depositor for a check which had been returned to the bank. The court held that the bank could not charge-back the depositor's account under section 4–212 [R 4–214] because the bank had failed to give the depositor timely notice of dishonor by the midnight deadline. The Akpan decision is clearly

3. Contrary to the dissent's assertion, the language of section 4–103 [R 4–103] does not place the burden on the bank to prove what "would have been uncollectible even if timely notice had been given." Rather, if the evidence at trial raises a question that some or all of the item was in any event uncollectible, under section 4–103 [R 4–103] and the cases construing it, the burden remains on the plaintiff/depositor to prove their actual damages. This result is consistent with the time-honored principle of law that a party bringing a claim has the burden of proving their damages to a reasonable degree of certainty. The position advocated by the dissent is apparently based solely on policy considerations.

distinguishable from the instant case in several respects: (1) In Akpan, the bank allowed the depositor to withdraw $2,490 against the $2,500 check provisionally credited to the depositor's account; there is nothing in the record to suggest that Prospect National allowed Appliance Buyers to draw against their provisional credit; (2) The Akpan court found that the depositor had detrimentally relied on the fact that the bank had allowed her to draw against the provisionally credited item; there is no evidence of detrimental reliance in the instant case; and (3) In Akpan the issue of the depositor's damages (i.e. what would have been collected had the bank given timely notice) was not before the court. There, the bank was notified of the check's dishonor on August 19 and yet the bank permitted the depositor to withdraw $2,490 on August 22, a sum the defendant then gave to the maker of the check. It is obvious that had the bank notified the depositor that the $2,500 check had been dishonored on the 19th, the depositor never would have given the $2,490 to the check's maker on the 22nd. Thus, in Akpan there was no doubt but that the depositor was actually damaged by the bank's failure to give timely notice of dishonor and that the damage was the $2,490. In the instant case, the amount of Appliance Buyers' damages is pure speculation. The district court properly found proof was lacking that Appliance Buyers was actually damaged by the bank's untimely notice; on the contrary, the court found there was serious doubt as to whether Appliance Buyers could have collected any money had it received timely notice. Therefore, we hold that Manufacturers Hanover Trust Co. v. Akpan is not controlling in this case.

The district court in its decision noted that when Appliance Buyers accepted Nevius' checks, Appliance Buyers "had substantial reason to suspect [the checks] might 'bounce' * * *." Indeed, testimony was presented at trial that a representative of Appliance Buyers was told by Ken Nevius that he (Nevius) was unsure whether "we have enough money to cover this check." Moreover, one of Appliance Buyers' employees testified that although Nevius Appliance had agreed to make weekly payments on its account to Appliance Buyers, Nevius had not done so in the last month and a half prior to the time they issued the two NSF checks in question. Now, Appliance Buyers is attempting to shift the loss, caused by their own lax financial policy, to Prospect National Bank. Finance companies such as Appliance Buyers Credit Corporation have the obligation to actively police the floor plans of participating dealers and to ensure that dealers are current in their payments. When a finance company fails to develop a sound financial policy and allows dealers to fall behind in their payments, the finance company must bear the burden if the dealers fail to pay their bills when due. It is apparent from the record that having failed in its duty to protect its investments by keeping tighter reins on Nevius' account, absent proof that Prospect National Bank's untimely notice actually damaged the corporation, Appliance Buyers cannot now shift the responsibility for their own negligence to the bank.

We agree with and affirm the district court's decision and hold that in order for the plaintiff in this case to recover for damages arising out of Prospect National Bank's alleged failure to give timely notice of dishonor as required by section 4–212 [R 4–214] of the Uniform Commercial Code, the burden is on the depositor (Appliance Buyers) to establish that Prospect National failed to give timely notice, and the amount of damage Appliance Buyers actually suffered as a result of Prospect National's untimely notice.

Note

1. Consider the *Pulaski Bank* court's treatment of the purchaser v. agent status of a collecting bank. What different results would flow from the two different conclusions? Are they diametrically opposed? Which is more consistent with commercial expectations and negotiable instruments law generally?

2. Are you convinced that the *Pulaski Bank* court dismissed Pulaski's argument premised on the public policy informing the *Capital City First National Bank* decision? How does the court distinguish *Capital City*? Note that the trend of authority on the processing center issue is in line with Capital City. See *Farmers & Merchants Bank v. Bank of America,* 20 Cal.App.3d 939, 98 Cal.Rptr. 381 (1971); *Sass Trucking, Inc. v. Security Bank & Trust Co.,* 737 P.2d 113 (Okla.1987); *First State Bank of McKinney v. American Bank of Sherman,* 732 S.W.2d 404 (Tex.Civ.App.1987).

3. Federal Reserve Regulation CC expressly adopts the result reached in Appliance Buyers Credit Corporation.

> (d) *Charge-back.* This paragraph [§ 229.33(d)] adopts the view of Appliance Buyers Credit Corp. v. Prospect National Bank, that sending a returned check or notice of nonpayment to the depositary bank's customer in a timely manner is not a condition precedent to charge-back to the customer's account by the depositary bank. Draft section 4–212(2) [R 4–214] of the NCCUSL proposal contains a similar provision.

12 C.F.R. § 229.33(d).

Subpart C had a significant impact on the process by which dishonored checks are returned to the depositary institution. The following excerpt, written by Professor Corinne Cooper, describes the operation of the subpart.

EXPEDITED COLLECTION AND RETURN OF CHECKS

Excerpted from *Uniform Commercial Code Annual Survey*
43 Bus.Law. 1305, 1327–34 (1988).

Unless the time it takes to return unpaid checks is substantially reduced, many deposits will be available to customers well in advance of the time the depositary bank learns that the item is being returned. Subpart C of proposed Reg. CC attempts to speed up the return process, so that in most cases depositary banks will learn that checks are being returned unpaid before they must make the funds available to their customers.

The expedited return provisions fall into several categories. They include regulations which specify: the obligations of the payor bank; the obligations of the returning bank; the obligations of the depositary bank; and the uniform indorsement standards for depositary banks. In addition, there are proposed amendments to regulation J to make it consistent with the requirements imposed by proposed regulation CC.

THE OBLIGATIONS OF THE PAYOR BANK

The proposed regulations require the payor bank to return an item as expeditiously as it would present an item for payment. The payor bank would appear to satisfy this obligation if it handles and routes the check at least as fast as it would collect a forward check of similar amount drawn on the depositary bank and received by the payor bank before noon on the banking day following the banking day of presentment of the returned check. If the payor bank's normal method for routing items to the depositary bank is materially slower than that of other similarly situated banks in its community, it would not satisfy the requirements of the proposed regulation.

A payor bank has several options for routing a return item. First, it may return the item to the bank that presented it for payment, as occurs under current law. But this will satisfy the obligation of expeditious return only if the payor bank would normally route forward items through the presenting bank, or if this route is as expeditious as the route that would be used for forward collection. Second, a payor bank may return the item directly to the depositary bank. If it uses this route, it is not necessary to return the item to the branch of first deposit. Third, the payor bank may satisfy its obligation by returning the item to a Federal Reserve Bank, whether or not the Federal Reserve handled the item during the forward collection process. Fourth, the payor bank may return the item to any other returning bank that agrees to handle items pursuant to the requirements of proposed Reg. CC.

Despite its compliance with the requirements of proposed Reg. CC, the payor bank is not relieved of its obligations for timely return under either the U.C.C. or regulation J. However, several provisions permit the payor bank to retain the item longer than is permitted under either the U.C.C. or regulation J.

* * *

The * * * provision permits the payor bank to retain an item beyond the midnight deadline if it will expedite return of the item. The proposed commentary explains:

> Many paying banks do not dispatch their returned checks by courier with the checks that are sent for forward collection if the courier leaves after midnight. Instead, they mail their returns by their midnight deadline in order to meet their legal responsibility

under the U.C.C., but by doing so delay the completion of the return process.

Under this provision, the payor bank will not become accountable for an item that it retains beyond the midnight deadline if the expedited method of delivery would ordinarily result in the returned check's being received by the bank to which it is sent on or before the bank's next banking day following the otherwise applicable time for return, or such later time as would result from the use of highly expeditious means of transportation.

Three provisions in proposed regulation CC also concern notice of return by the payor bank. First, the payor bank must give direct notice of return to the depositary bank for all checks in the amount of $2,500 or more. This is similar to the current requirement of regulation J, but it differs in several important respects. First, under the current version of regulation J, the notice need only be given if the check was presented through the Federal Reserve; under proposed Reg. CC, notice must be given for all checks, regardless of whether they passed through the Federal Reserve during the forward collection process. Second, the time period for giving this notice is shorter by one day under proposed Reg. CC as compared to the current regulation J requirement. Under proposed Reg. CC, the notice must be received by the depositary bank by 4:00 p.m. on the second business day following presentment. The notice must include: the name and routing number of the payor bank; the name of the payees; the amount of the check; the date of the depositary bank's indorsement; the account number of the customer and branch of the depositary bank where the check was deposited; the trace number of the indorsement; the reason for return; and if written, the name and routing number of the depositary bank. The payor bank is not obligated to include any information in this notice that cannot be determined with reasonable certainty from the check itself and the indorsement of the depositary bank. Even if this notice is given, the check must still be returned to the depositary bank.

Second, the payor bank may give notice of return under this provision for checks in amounts less than $2,500. This notice satisfies the payor bank's expeditious return obligation, but the check must be returned in a reasonably prompt manner.

Third, if the physical check is unavailable for return, the payor bank may give notice of return in lieu of returning the item. In this instance, the notice must state that it is a notice in lieu of return.

The payor bank has an additional obligation under the proposed regulations, and that is to respond "promptly" to any inquiry concerning a depositary check, including the verification of amount, payee, whether it has been paid or dishonored, and whether payment has been stopped. The paying bank does not agree to pay the instrument by giving the required information.

The Obligations of the Returning Bank

During the return process, a returning bank occupies the role of the collecting bank during the forward collection process. It is an intermediary, neither a depositary nor a payor bank, but it has obligations concerning the returned instrument.

A returning bank has the same obligations of expeditious return as the payor bank. The returning bank acts in an expeditious manner if it returns a check in the same manner that it would handle a check of similar amount drawn on the depositary bank and received for forward collection at the time it received the return item. Since a collecting bank is obligated to forward a check by the day following the day upon which it receives the item, a returning bank must similarly process a return item overnight. If the bank processes forward collection items more expeditiously, then this more expeditious time limit also applies to return items.

The returning bank may return the check to a collecting bank that presented the check to the returning bank during forward collection, so long as that meets the returning bank's obligation of expeditious return—that is, this route must be just as fast as the route that would be used for collecting a check drawn on the depositary bank. A bank that handled an item during the forward collection process may not refuse to handle the item as a return item. In the alternative, the returning bank may return the check to the depositary bank, to any Federal Reserve Bank, or to any other bank agreeing to act as a returning bank and to comply with the obligation of expeditious return applicable to returning banks. The returning bank may charge the payor bank or prior returning bank for handling a return item. And the returning bank must settle for the return item, as discussed below.

The Qualified Returned Check

One of the methods which will speed the return process is the creation of returned checks that can be handled by the same equipment that handles forward collection checks. By creating machine-readable return items, the returning bank expedites return handling.

The proposed regulations recognize the benefit of this process by extending the returning bank's deadline for returning an item when it creates a machine-readable return item. If the returning bank creates a machine-readable return item, called "qualified returned checks," then the returning bank has an additional business day before it must dispatch the return. However, this additional time is not available if the returning bank returns the item directly to the depositary bank, since creating a machine-readable check does not expedite return in that circumstance.

The Return Warranties, Indorsements, and Settlement

Under the proposed regulations, instruments will not necessarily be traveling the same path back to the depositary bank that they took on the forward collection trip. Instead, checks may be returned directly to the depositary bank, to a Federal Reserve Bank that never handled the item on the forward collection, or to a returning bank that was never a collecting bank. As a result, the check will not necessarily be returned to a party that made a transfer warranty or an indorsement contract during the forward collection.

For this reason, proposed Reg. CC contains three important provisions to adjust the relationships among the parties to the collection and return process. First, the regulation imposes a warranty by the payor and returning banks. Every payor or returning bank that transfers a returned check and receives settlement warrants to any subsequent returning bank, the depositary bank, and the owner of the check: that the bank timely returned the check; that it is authorized to return the check; and that there is no material alteration. Second, the proposed regulation provides that the payor and returning banks make indorsement contracts with regard to the returned instrument and may have the rights of a holder with respect to each returned check.

Third, the proposed regulation reflects the fact that a return process which does not reverse the presentment process results in provisional settlements made when the presentment was becoming final, despite the fact that the instrument was never paid. The regulations deal with repayment for returned instruments by providing that returning banks are obligated to settle for a returned check, either with the payor bank or a prior returning bank. This is true even if the returning bank handled the item as a collecting bank during the forward collection process. The depositary bank is obligated to pay the bank returning the check the amount of the returned check at the close of the banking day on which it receives the check.

Any provisional settlements between the banks during the forward collection process become final upon expiration of the time for payment of a returned check by the depositary bank. The settlement between the payor bank and returning bank, and between the returning banks, becomes final upon expiration of the time for payment of a returned check by the depositary bank. As a result of these provisions, the provisional settlements that occurred during the forward collection process become final. The payor bank is repaid for its provisional settlement by the returning bank, which, in turn, is repaid by the depositary bank. The depositary bank is entitled to recover its payment from its customer. This is true even though it failed to give its customer timely notice of dishonor under the U.C.C., but it is liable to its customer for any loss resulting from the delay.

The Obligations of the Depositary Bank

The depositary bank is not without obligations in the return process. Under the proposed regulations, the depositary bank is obligated to accept returned checks and to make prompt payment for them. The depositary bank becomes accountable for the amount of the returned check at the close of the banking day on which it receives the returned check. Before that time, the depositary bank must pay the returning bank the amount of the check in proceeds that are available to the returning bank or the payor bank on that date. If the depositary bank has not received full settlement for the returned check during the forward collection process, it may recover the full amount of the returned check from the bank to which it sent the check during the forward collection process.

The depositary bank is obligated to receive notices of return during its banking day. The depositary bank also is obligated to receive returned items at any branch consistent with the address in the indorsement on the check or, if there is no address, at any branch associated with the routing number in the indorsement. If there is neither an address nor a routing number, the depositary bank is obligated to receive returned items at any branch of the bank, or any other location where the bank accepts checks as a payor bank.

Uniform Indorsement Standards for Banks

The expedited return processing contemplated by the proposed regulations and the direct return and notice of return provisions depend upon proper identification of the depositary bank through its indorsement. As the commentary notes:

> One of the major difficulties in returning a check is reading the indorsements of the depositary and collecting banks, and obtaining useful information from them. Current indorsements are often faint, blurred, incomplete and overlapping. The indorsement standards in Appendix D [of the proposed regulation] address indorsement problems by specifying the information the indorsement must contain and its location and ink color. Depositary, collecting, and returning banks are required to place their indorsements on checks as specified in Appendix D. In order to avoid confusion in routing returning checks, paying banks are not required to indorse returned checks.

The proposed regulations contemplate several means by which the necessary depositary bank indorsement may be placed on deposited checks: The depositary bank may provide the indorsement, using its high-speed processing equipment or other equipment; a collecting bank may indorse on behalf of the depositary bank; or a corporate customer of the depositary bank may indorse on behalf of the depositary bank when it encodes the items prior to deposit.

This indorsement standard requires two alterations in the indorsement process. First, depositary banks will be required to place significant additional information in their indorsements if they wish to benefit from the expedited return procedures in the regulations. If a depositary bank does not provide this information, a payor bank is absolved of its obligation to give direct notice of return. Second, other banks will be required to avoid obscuring the depositary bank indorsement, by indorsing in a different location and using a different color ink than that used by the depositary bank. Failure to comply with these indorsement standards may result in liability for a collecting bank that obscures a depositary bank indorsement.

Professor Barkley Clark has considered the issues raised by the interrelation of the Regulation CC and Article 4 midnight deadline rules.

B. CLARK, THE LAW OF BANK DEPOSITS, COLLECTIONS AND CREDIT CARDS

¶¶ 5.02[1][b], 5.02[1][c], 5.02[2][l] (3d ed. 1990).

What is the relationship between a drawee bank's strict accountability under the UCC and its duties under Regulation CC? First, it must be emphasized that a drawee bank does not avoid liability under the midnight deadline just because it satisfies its duty of "expeditious return" of the check under Regulation CC. Under the "two-day/four-day" test of Regulation CC, a drawee bank makes an "expeditious return" if it sends the returned check in a manner such that it would normally be received by the depositary bank by 4:00 P.M. two business days after presentment for local checks (and four business days after presentment for nonlocal checks). For example, if the drawee bank returned a local check direct to the depositary bank on the second business day after presentment, such a return would satisfy Regulation CC. However, it would not satisfy the UCC midnight deadline. Therefore, the drawee bank would be strictly accountable for the amount of the item. The federal regulation does not preempt the UCC midnight deadline except in very limited situations. The drawee bank could find itself in a real pickle if it guided its behavior according to the rules of Regulation CC and totally forgot the midnight deadline under Article 4. The Federal Reserve Board could have done away with the UCC midnight deadline altogether, viewing the duty of expeditious return as sufficient. Instead, both bodies of law continue to apply.

But Regulation CC will have a major impact on midnight deadline litigation under the UCC. This is because § 229.34(a) of the federal regulation creates a new warranty of compliance with the UCC midnight deadline. A drawee bank that misses the midnight deadline will also violate the Regulation CC warranty. Under § 229.34(c) of Regulation CC, damages for breach of warranty include "expenses related to the returned check, if any." This language was taken straight from § 4–207(3) [R 4–207(c), R 4–208(d)], which is limited to check forgery cases. Under Comment 5 to that section, "expenses" may include attorney fees. Therefore, the courts are now invited to award attorney fees to a payee or collecting bank that pins loss on the drawee bank for missing the UCC midnight deadline. This is a sharp departure from the UCC itself, where no court has ever allowed recovery of attorney fees in standard midnight deadline litigation such as kiting cases. The "expenses" covered as damages under the new warranty could also include interest and incidental costs. This is a major change in the law.

* * *

Even though Regulation CC does not do away with the midnight deadline as codified in Regulation J and the UCC, there are three situations where it is extended slightly. Such an extension could serve as a handy defense to a midnight deadline claim. First, if the paying bank attempts to expedite return of a dishonored check by using a means of delivery that would ordinarily result in the check's receipt by the bank to which it is sent on or before the next banking day following the midnight deadline, the UCC midnight deadline will be extended one day. Second, the midnight deadline is extended further "if a paying bank uses a highly expeditious means of transportation, even if this means of transportation would ordinarily result in delivery after the receiving bank's next banking day." The Commentary to Regulation CC makes it clear that these two extension rules are intended to cover cases where the paying bank has a courier that leaves after midnight to deliver its forward collection checks. Even though the returns may get out the door slightly after the midnight deadline, the speed of the courier is such that the check would be received by the returning or depositary bank only one day beyond the paying bank's midnight deadline, so that the overall return is expeditious. In other words, it is receipt, not dispatch, that is paramount. A West Coast paying bank could use the second extension to return checks by air courier directly to an East Coast depositary bank, even though they arrive after the close of that bank's banking day. Third, Regulation CC allows a returning bank (not the paying bank) a one-day extension of the midnight deadline if it converts a "raw" return into a "qualified" return by MICR-encoding the return information.

The first two exceptions, which will have some impact on the drawee bank's strict accountability under § 4–302 [R 4–302], should not be given wider berth than they deserve. For example, suppose that two banks are caught in a kiting scheme. Both banks have retained checks beyond the midnight deadline as part of allowing the customer to draw on uncollected funds. One afternoon, one of the banks discovers the kite and hand-delivers return checks to the other bank. These checks are delivered one day beyond the UCC midnight deadline but within the "expeditious return" standard set forth in Regulation CC. Is the drawee bank accountable for the hand-delivered checks? Although it missed the midnight deadline, it might argue that the case falls within the first exception described above, that is, the bank used a means of delivery (hand) that would ordinarily result (and did result in this case) in receipt by the depositary bank on or before the next banking day following the midnight deadline. In other words, the drawee bank missed the UCC midnight deadline, but got one extra day under Regulation CC. This argument, though ingenious, is a losing one. It is clear that the drafters of Regulation CC intended the one-day extension to apply only in cases where the drawee bank consistently uses a special type of delivery, such as courier service, instead of mail. As a reward for this practice, the midnight deadline is extended one day. In the case at hand, however, the hand-delivery was employed only as an afterthought in response to discovery of the kite. The exception was not intended to allow drawee banks to win kiting cases after missing the midnight deadline.

REYNOLDS–WILSON LUMBER COMPANY v. PEOPLES NATIONAL BANK

Oklahoma Supreme Court, 1985.
699 P.2d 146.

PER CURIAM.

The plaintiff-appellant, Reynolds–Wilson Lumber Company, d/b/a T R Cattle Company [hereinafter "TRC"], is the payee of a $150,000 sight draft drawn against the account of Perdue & McCarthy Cattle Company [hereinafter "P & M"] with the defendant-appellee, The Peoples National Bank, Kingfisher, Oklahoma [hereinafter "PNB"]. TRC sought to recover the amount of the draft on a theory of absolute or strict liability arising from PNB's alleged breach of a statutory duty under 12A O.S.1981 §§ 4–301 [R 4–301] and 4–302 [R 4–302] either to honor or return the draft before PNB's midnight deadline. The trial court, sitting without a jury, made written findings of fact and conclusions of law, and rendered judgment thereon for PNB. The Court of Appeals reversed the trial court's judgment. We agree with the Court of Appeals but grant certiorari to revise its opinion.

The basic facts are not in dispute. TRC sold some cattle to P & M. In accordance with a pre-existing practice which had developed in previous dealings between TRC and P & M, an employee of TRC prepared a draft, dated February 22, 1980, payable to the order of "T R Cattle Co." in the amount of $150,000, and specified thereon that it was in "part payment 3000 hd $ $50.00/hd". The draft was signed "Perdue & McCarthy Cattle Co., By: Bernice Stephenson" (Ms. Stephenson being the TRC employee who prepared the draft). The draft bore the printed legend: "Value received and charge to account of," below which was written in longhand the following: "To Perdue & McCarthy Ctl. Co. Peoples National Bank Kingfisher, Oklahoma Acct # 0001627." The draft was on the face of an envelope. There were no papers or documents placed in the envelope, which was sealed.

After the draft was prepared, it was deposited the same day in TRC's bank account with the Union State Bank of Carrizo Springs, Texas, [hereinafter "USB"], and USB immediately gave TRC provisional credit for the item.

USB mailed the draft directly to PNB, together with an accompanying "collection letter." These were received by PNB before the end of its business day on Friday, February 29, 1980. The USB "collection letter" was addressed to PNB; it indicated that USB's depositor was TRC and that the accompanying draft was drawn by P & M on "you," i.e., on PNB.

On the same day the draft and "collection letter" were received, PNB's cashier contacted a principal of P & M by telephone, advised that the draft had been received, and told him that P & M "needed to wire funds that very day" to pay the draft. The PNB cashier was advised that funds were not then available, but should be by the following Monday, March 3.

Later, on February 29, the manager of TRC telephoned the PNB cashier. They discussed the fact that P & M did not have funds to cover the draft that day, but should have sufficient funds by Monday. TRC's manager then told the PNB cashier to hold the draft until the following Monday, and pay it then.

On the following Monday, March 3, (which was PNB's next business day), P & M did not deposit any funds to its account with PNB to cover the draft. During that day, the TRC manager again telephoned the PNB cashier. TRC's manager was advised that no funds had been deposited to P & M's account with PNB that day. They discussed that the P & M principal with whom the PNB cashier had communicated the preceding Friday was "out of town." The TRC manager did not instruct the PNB cashier to hold the draft any further, nor was there any discussion concerning further retention of the draft by PNB.

PNB did not return the draft prior to midnight, March 3. On the following Friday, March 7, the P & M principal, with whom PNB's cashier had been dealing, returned from his out-of-town trip and advised PNB in person that funds were not available to pay the draft. PNB then returned the draft unpaid to USB, which received it on March 12.

The draft was subsequently mailed by USB to PNB a second time, along with a letter from USB's attorney demanding payment. These were received by PNB on March 20, 1980. The next day, PNB's attorneys responded by letter to USB's attorney, taking the position that PNB had orally advised TRC the day the draft was received that it "could not be honored" (it is not clear whether the receipt referred to in this letter was PNB's initial receipt of February 29, or second receipt on March 20). PNB's attorneys also advised that unless they could be furnished with "persuasive authority" to the contrary, their advice to PNB would be to decline the demand for payment. The draft was not returned by PNB, and USB subsequently sent out a "tracer" to locate the draft. The "tracer" was received by PNB on April 17, and the draft returned unpaid by PNB to USB that same day.

The judgment of the trial court for PNB and against TRC was predicated on several conclusions of law. To these contested conclusions we now turn.

The trial court's principal conclusion was that PNB was not a payor bank which, under 12A O.S.1981 § 4–302(a) [R 4–302(a)(1)], became accountable for the draft when it retained it beyond midnight of March 3, 1980. Rather, the trial court held that the draft was drawn "*through or at*" PNB rather than on PNB, and that PNB was therefore only a collecting and presenting bank, obligated to make collection in accordance with the "collection letter" which accompanied the draft. The court further ruled that (a) under 12A O.S.1981 § 3–504 [R 3–501] presentment could only be made by mail or in person, not by phone; (b) that presentment did not occur until March 7, when a principal of P & M came to PNB; (c) that the draft was dishonored by P & M on March 7; and (d) that PNB's return of the draft on March 7 was within the time required after the presentment and dishonor which had occurred on that date.

The trial court's legal conclusion that PNB was not a payor bank is incorrect. A "payor bank" is one by which an item is payable as drawn or accepted. 12A O.S.1981 § 4–105(b) [R 4–105(3)]. It includes a drawee bank. Official Comment 2 to § 4–105 [comment 4 to R 4–105]. The question then is whether the draft in question was drawn on PNB as sole drawee or as co-drawee with P & M, or, as the trial court concluded, drawn on P & M as sole drawee, payable "at or through" PNB.

The trial court cited no decisional authority for its conclusion that PNB was not a payor bank. On the other hand, the cases which have been decided under the Uniform Commercial Code in other jurisdictions hold that designations such as that utilized here, to-wit: "To Perdue & McCarthy Ctl. Co. Peoples National Bank Kingfisher, Oklahoma Acct # 0001627." result in both P & M and PNB being drawees, with the further result that PNB is a payor bank. See Pecos County Bank v. El Paso Livestock Auction Co., Inc., 586 S.W.2d 183 [Tex.Civ.App.1979]; Farmers Cooperative Livestock Market, Inc. v. Second National Bank of London, 427 S.W.2d 247 [Ky.App.1968]; New Ulm State Bank v. Brown, 558 S.W.2d 20 [Tex.Civ.App.1977] and Engine Parts v. Citizens Bank of Clovis, 92 N.M. 37, 582 P.2d 809 [1978].

Thus in Pecos County, supra, the following designation, "Value Received and Charged to Account of Mesa Packing Company Pecos County State Bank Fort Stockton, Texas," was held on summary judgment to result in both Mesa Packing Company and the bank being drawees. The Texas court held that there was no genuine issue of material fact as to the construction to be given the draft, and, as a matter of law, construed it to create co-drawees. In Pecos County, supra, the court relied on New Ulm, supra, which had construed the designation "R & A Farms New Ulm State Bank New Ulm, Texas," as creating co-drawees.

PNB does not attempt to distinguish these cases, but instead simply brushes them aside because they were decided in other jurisdictions. We find them persuasive, however, in the absence of any Oklahoma decisions on the point, and in view of the policy of the Oklahoma Uniform Commercial Code " * * * to make uniform the law among the various jurisdictions * * * ". 12A O.S.1981 § 1–102(2)(c).

As previously noted, the trial court concluded without citation of decisional authority that the draft here in issue was payable "*through or at*" PNB, but was not drawn on PNB, with the result that PNB was a collecting bank but not a payor bank. But to be a "payable through" or "payable at" item, it must expressly so state on its face. See 12A

O.S.1981 §§ 3–120 and 3–121 [R 4–106]. The draft here nowhere states that it is payable "through" or "at" PNB. Applicable rules of construction dictate that the bank in such cases be held at least a co-drawee and payor, absent express designation to the contrary. As stated in Engine Parts, supra, at 813:

> "To make a draft payable 'through' or 'at' a bank, and thus designate the bank as a mere conduit for payment and not as a 'payor' bank directly ordered to pay, the drawer of the draft, must expressly write the word 'through,' 'pay through,' 'at,' 'payable at,' or similar words before the name of the bank *on the instrument itself.*"

The trial court apparently considered two other factors as indicating that PNB was a collecting and presenting bank but not a payor. First, it emphasized that the letter from USB accompanying the draft when it was received by PNB on February 29 was a "collection letter." Thus, the court stated in its Conclusion of Law No. 4 that "Collection letter attached to draft sent to PNB, instructs that it is envelope draft for collection, papers attached. PNB must act according to instructions and is not liable to T R Cattle Co. for following instructions." The short answer to this conclusion is that it does not matter what USB's letter stated. The construction to be given the draft is to be ascertained from the face of the draft itself. See Engine Parts, supra, at 812, where it is stated that:

> "* * * Engine Parts argues that the collection letter should not be considered in determining whether the Clovis Bank was a payor bank. This latter contention is correct. The status of a negotiable instrument is to be determined from its face—from the language used or authorized to be used thereon by its drawer or maker—*and not from documents attached thereto by other parties* * * *.
>
> * * *
>
> * * * Thus, information or instructions on a collection letter attached by a depository or collecting bank are irrelevant in ascertaining who the drawee of the instrument is or whether a bank is a payor or collecting bank. * * *" [emphasis ours]

See also Engine Parts, supra, at 814–815; Farmers Cooperative, supra, at 249–250; Kane v. American National Bank and Trust Company, 21 Ill.App.3d 1046, 316 N.E.2d 177 [1974].

The second factor apparently relied on by the trial court in reaching its conclusion that PNB was not a payor bank is set forth in Conclusions of Law 8 and 9, which state as follows: "8. The Plaintiff contends that the draft is drawn on PNB because it has the account number of Perdue & McCarthy Cattle Co. on the draft. All the evidence shows that the draft was drawn by Bernice Stephenson, an employee of T R Cattle Co. She had no authority to sign checks withdrawing funds from this account. This, together with the testimony presented, makes it clear that the Plaintiff never thought the draft was any obligation of the Defendant. It is also clear that Perdue & McCarthy Cattle Co. and PNB were not co-drawees. 9. PNB is not a 'payor' bank. The Uniform Commercial Code defines a payor bank as 'a bank by which an item is payable as drawn or accepted.' (12A O.S.1971 Sec. 4–105(2) [R 4–105(3)]). The item in this case could not be paid as drawn because it had no authorized signature and was not accepted. (12A O.S.1971 Sec. 3–410(1) [R 3–409(a)])."

These conclusions suggest an unspoken or implied finding by the trial court that the designation of drawee on the draft in question was ambiguous, and that it deemed itself at liberty to consider evidence extrinsic to the draft in determining the relationship of the parties. It is our view, based on such cases as Pecos County, supra, and New Ulm, supra, which involved drawee designations indistinguishable from the one involved here, and which held as a matter of law that such designations create co-drawees, that the draft here involved was not ambiguous.

However, even if it be assumed that an ambiguity existed, and resort to extrinsic evidence were appropriate, we find nothing in this record to support a conclusion that PNB was not a co-drawee and therefore not a payor bank. This is particularly so when the record is viewed in the context of the paramount rule of construction elaborated in Engine Parts, as discussed supra, as well as the requirement of 12A O.S.1981 §§ 3–120 and 3–121 [R 4–106], that there must be an express statement on the face of the draft indicating it is to be paid "at" or "through" a bank, before that bank is to be treated as a mere conduit and not a payor.

* * *

The draft here does not state a specific time for payment. It thus constitutes a demand item under 12A O.S.1981 § 3–108 [R 3–108(a)]. Therefore, PNB, as a payor bank, became "accountable" for the draft under 12A O.S.1981 § 4–302(a) [R 4–302(a)(1)] once it failed to return or send notice of dishonor by midnight, March 3, 1980. "Accountable" has been uniformly construed to mean strict liability for the full amount of the draft, with no requirement that there be proof of actual damage. See Pecos County, Engine Parts and Farmers Cooperative, all supra; Rock Island Auction Sales v. Empire Packing Co., 32 Ill.2d 269, 204 N.E.2d 721 [1965]; Bank Leumi Trust Company of New York v. Bank of Mid–Jersey, 499 F.Supp. 1022 [D.N.J.1980]; Northwest National Insurance v. Midland National Bank, 96 Wis.2d 155, 292 N.W.2d 591 [1980]. See also Goodman v. Norman Bank of Commerce, Okl., 565 P.2d 372 [1977], citing in footnote 2, both Farmers Cooperative and Rock Island Auction Sales, both supra. Thus, PNB became liable on March 4. The amount of liability was unquestionably liquidated in the face amount of the draft as of that date.

Three further arguments by PNB remain to be considered. The first is that the draft in question was a *documentary* draft, which is excluded from operation of the midnight deadline rule of 12A O.S.1981 § 4–302(a) [R 4–302(a)(1)]. " 'Documentary draft' means any negotiable or nonnegotiable draft *with accompanying documents,* securities or other papers to be delivered against honor of the draft." [emphasis ours] 12A O.S.1981 § 4–104(1)(f) [R 4–104(a)(6)].

The trial court concluded as a matter of law that the draft in issue was a documentary draft, notwithstanding that it was not accompanied by any documents. The court reasoned in Conclusion No. 11(a) that the USB "collection letter" stated there were "papers included"; (b) that although it could be easily ascertained by looking at the draft envelope that there were no documents included, PNB was not required to look; (c) that the envelope was sealed; and (d) PNB was not entitled to open it.

We disagree with the trial court. Section 4–104(1)(f) [R 4–104(a)(6)] expressly specifies that a documentary draft is one accompanied by documents. Clearly there was none here, and, as the trial court found, this was easily ascertainable by looking at the draft. The trial court's conclusion that PNB had no right or duty to open the draft envelope and inspect for documents was clearly premised on the more fundamental conclusion that PNB was only a collecting bank and not a co-drawee and payor bank. But, as we have held, PNB was not a mere collecting bank. It was instead a co-drawee and payor bank. If, despite the plain language of the draft, PNB chose to focus upon the language of the "collection letter" and treat itself as a collecting bank, it did so at its peril. As stated in Engine Parts, supra at 814,

> "The mere forwarding of an item to the bank upon which it was drawn accompanied by a letter stating the item was enclosed for 'collection' and the treatment of the item by the drawee bank as a 'collection' item does not establish that the bank upon which the item was drawn is a 'collecting' bank. Farmers Coop. Livestock Mkt., supra."

The second remaining argument by PNB is based on estoppel. In this connection, the trial court held in Conclusion No. 13 that "the action of the Plaintiff's agent, Jerry Hill [TRC's manager], in directing PNB to hold the draft until March 3rd, 1980, after being told that the draft could not be paid on February 29th, 1980, estoppes [sic] the Plaintiff from bringing action because of a failure to timely return the draft."

Again, we find this legal conclusion to be incorrect. As we have held, PNB's midnight deadline was Monday, March 3. It was legally entitled to hold the draft in question until midnight of March 3, without incurring any liability, irrespective of what TRC may have requested. In agreeing to TRC's request to hold the item until Monday to see if P & M covered it by then with a deposit of sufficient funds, PNB in no way was prejudiced, nor did it in any way change its position to its detriment. Of critical importance here is the testimony of both PNB's cashier and TRC's manager. Both testified to the effect (a) that

TRC's request was only that PNB hold the item until March 3; (b) that although they talked again on March 3, there was no further request by TRC that PNB hold the draft any longer; and (c) that there was, in short, no other discussion on the subject of further retention of the draft. There is no conflict in the evidence as to the foregoing, and PNB therefore held the draft past midnight of March 3 at its peril.

There is some suggestion in the briefs that PNB gave oral notice of dishonor on March 3 when its cashier advised TRC's manager that sufficient funds had not been deposited to cover the draft, and that this notice absolved PNB from further responsibility under 12A O.S.1981 § 4–302 [R 4–302]. This suggestion may be summarily rejected. The law is clear that if an item is being considered for dishonor, is available for return and is not being held for protest, the item itself must be returned. See Colorado National Bank v. First National Bank, 459 F.Supp. 1366 [W.D.Mich.1978]; Blake v. Woodford Bank and Trust Co., 555 S.W.2d 589 [Ky.App.1977]; and Northwest National, supra. Further even if the draft were unavailable or were being held for protest, neither of which is claimed by PNB, the law is also well established that oral notice of dishonor is inadequate under §§ 4–301 [R 4–301] and 4–302 [R 4–302], and only written notice will suffice. See Valley Bank and Trust Company v. First Security Bank of Utah, N.A., 538 P.2d 298 [Utah 1975]; Available Iron and Metal Co. v. First National Bank of Blue Island, 56 Ill.App.3d 516, 13 Ill.Dec. 940, 371 N.E.2d 1032 [1977]; accord, Security Bank and Trust Co. v. Federal National Bank and Trust Co., Okl.App., 554 P.2d 119 [1976].

The third and final remaining argument of PNB relates to the second presentment of the draft, which occurred March 20, 1980. PNB did not return the item following this second presentment until April 17, 1980, and only then in response to a "tracer" from USB. As previously outlined herein, PNB's lawyer wrote to USB's lawyer on March 21, stating it would be his advice to PNB to deny the demand for payment contained in the letter from USB's attorney, which letter had accompanied the draft when presented by USB the second time. But the draft itself was kept by PNB and not returned until April 17.

The trial court made no conclusion specifically addressing the issue of whether PNB breached a midnight deadline following the second presentment by failing timely to return the item before midnight of March 21. Of course, under our reasoning PNB was a payor bank and obligated to act on the item before its midnight deadline in the absence of some authority to the contrary. And, as we have previously noted, where the draft was available for return, only that method of dishonor may be used. The letter from PNB's attorneys would not suffice.

PNB contends that where a draft is represented there is no need to give additional notice of dishonor upon the second presentment, citing as authority the Court of Appeals' opinion, Goodman v. Norman Bank of Commerce, Okl.App., 551 P.2d 661 [1976]. Although TRC admits that the Goodman decision would decide the issue in PNB's favor, it argues that the opinion should not be followed.

In Goodman—relying on Leaderbrand v. Central State Bank of Wichita, 202 Kan. 450, 450 P.2d 1 [1969]—the Court of Appeals held that once a check has been timely dishonored because of insufficient funds in the account on which it is drawn, a later presentment for payment while the account remains insufficient does not require an additional notice of dishonor by the payor bank. The terms of 12A O.S.1981 § 3–511(4) [R 3–502(f)]—which direct that "[w]here a draft has been dishonored by nonacceptance a later presentment for payment and any notice of dishonor and protest for nonpayment are excused unless in the meantime the instrument has been accepted"—were applied in Goodman to *demand* items as well as to *time* items. The majority position is contrary to this and applies 12A O.S.1981 § 4–302 [R 4–302] strictly when demand drafts are involved, whether it is the first presentment or re-presentment.

We believe that the majority view presents a better-reasoned reading of the UCC, as well as a far more feasible view under which the bulk processing national bank system can operate. The Court of Appeals' decision in Goodman, supra, is therefore *disapproved and overruled.* Accordingly, we hold that PNB breached the requirements of § 4–302 [R 4–302] by failing to return the draft by midnight, March 21, 1980, following its second presentment the preceding day, and thereby became accountable for the item.

Certiorari is granted; the Court of Appeals' opinion is revised and the trial court's judgment is reversed, with directions to render judgment for TRC in the amount of $150,000, plus interest and costs.

* * *

All Justices concur.

Note

The instrument in this case is commonly called a trade draft. A copy of a trade draft is set out in Chapter 1 at page 34, and also in the *Newark Steel Drum* case on page 125. Such drafts are often drawn by sellers of goods for the price of goods delivered. The draft in the principal case is unusual in that it purports to be signed on behalf of the buyer. That is, it is a draft drawn by the buyer on itself. Usually, the draft is just signed by or on behalf of the seller. Both the *New Ulm* and *Newark Steel Drum* drafts were signed in the usual manner.

Trade drafts can be drawn either on the buyer itself or on the buyer's bank, or on both. Such drafts, whether drawn on the bank, on the bank customer, or on both, are usually not signed by a person who has been given authority by the bank customer to draw checks on the customer's account. Therefore, the bank has no authority to pay the drafts and will make inquiry of the bank customer as to whether the draft should be paid. That is usually true even though there are funds in the customer's account sufficient to cover the draft. Discovering whether the customer wishes to pay often takes some time and the applicability of the midnight deadline may be inappropriate. However, if the draft is drawn on the bank and is not a documentary draft, the midnight deadline rules do apply.

It is also worth noting that trade drafts, whether or not drawn on the bank, are sent through the banking system separately from ordinary checks, with a "collection letter" rather than a "cash letter." Also, the drafts are not ordinarily electronically encoded with the bank customer's account number.

Some drafts are clearly drawn on the bank customer only. Other trade drafts are completed somewhat as follows: "To First National Bank. Pay $10,000 to John Seller and charge to account of Bill Buyer." In such a case, the draft is clearly drawn on the Bank. Also, obviously, some drafts are drawn a fourth way: as was the draft in the principal case. Under such a draft, one might well conclude, as did the court, that the bank and the bank customer are co-drawees of the check. If so, the bank must handle the draft according to the usual Article 4 check rules. Banks probably believe that drafts drawn in the way the one in the principal case was drawn are in fact drawn on the customer, not the bank. If so, the bank is a collecting bank only and is liable only for failure to properly exercise its duties as collecting bank. See R 4–106(c) and comment (c) to that section which rejects the conclusion of the principal case that the bank is a drawee.

As noted in the principal case, even though the draft is drawn on the bank, the liability rules are relaxed if the draft is a documentary draft. The court held that an "envelope draft" with nothing in the envelope is not a documentary draft. But see the following case.

WILEY, TATE & IRBY v. PEOPLES BANK & TRUST CO.

United States Court of Appeals, Fifth Circuit, 1972.
462 F.2d 179.

CLARK, CIRCUIT JUDGE. * * *

The hands on the clock had turned past the midnight deadline fixed by the Mississippi Uniform Commercial Code (MUCC), not once but many times before the Payor Bank returned unpaid the demand instruments sued on here. In such a circumstance, the only avenue of escape from the Code's automatic visitation of accountability upon the bank was for it to establish that the instruments were documentary drafts, which are excepted from the deadline. A trial before the lower court, sitting without jury, resulted in a determination that the instruments were not documentary drafts and a judgment in favor of payees for the face amount of the instruments together with interest from the date of demand. We conclude that the items were documentary drafts and reverse.

Plaintiffs Marcus Wiley, James Tate and James Irby, were partners engaged in buying and selling used cars under the trade name,

Wiley, Tate & Irby. Over an extended period of time Wiley, Tate & Irby sold a number of automobiles to Billy Houston, a sole proprietor doing business as Houston Auto Sales (Houston). In connection with each purchase Houston executed and delivered to Wiley, Tate & Irby a negotiable instrument drawn on the defendant, Peoples Bank & Trust Company of Tupelo, Mississippi (Payor Bank). Upon delivery of each negotiable instrument, the respective automobiles sold were at once turned over to Houston. All transactions were consummated at Wiley, Tate & Irby's place of business in Milan, Tennessee.

In each instance Wiley, Tate & Irby deposited the instrument they received from Houston in the Milan Banking Company (Depositary Bank) and thereupon were authorized by that bank to draw against such money. The Depositary Bank transferred the instrument to Union Planters National Bank of Memphis, Tennessee (Intermediary Bank), which transferred the same to the Payor Bank.

Nine instruments are involved in this suit. The instruments contained a number of variations both in text and form but each of them complied with the MUCC definition of a check. They were drawn on a bank, signed by the maker, and contained an unconditional order to pay a sum certain on the demand of the payee. Eight of the instruments were written on envelopes. One was prepared on a regular check form.

All of the instruments except the printed check form were on envelopes which arrived at the Payor Bank sealed. One of the instruments had been presented several times and returned unpaid on each occasion. Two of the instruments were presented on two occasions and returned unpaid both times. No envelope was ever opened during the periods of time the instruments remained in the possession of the Payor Bank. When opened at the time of trial, four of the envelopes contained automobile title documents while the other four were empty. When the check form was received it had automobile title papers attached by means of a staple and the face of the instrument stated, "Title attached." All of the instruments in suit were retained by the Payor Bank from the various dates of their last (or only) presentment until September 25, 1968, when they were bundled together by the Payor Bank and returned with notice of non-payment. The interval between these dates of final presentment and the date of their last return ranged from a minimum of 12 days to a maximum of over three and a half months. All of these times were well past the midnight deadline established by the MUCC.

Each of the instruments arrived at the Payor Bank with a printed collection letter form issued by the Intermediary Bank, addressed to the Payor Bank showing that the item or items covered were drawn on Houston Auto Sales and had been endorsed by the Depositary Bank and by Wiley, Tate & Irby. The pertinent parts of this collection letter are as follows:

WE ENCLOSE FOR COLLECTION AND CREDIT WHEN PAID.

RETURNS

(Here each letter contained a description of the covered item or items showing drawee, amount and endorser.)

Deliver documents only on payment of drafts attached. Return all unpaid items immediately. Do not protest items of less than $1,000.00.

PROTEST all items of $1,000.00 or over not paid except those bearing this (N.P.) (26–8) stamps, or similar authority from a preceding endorser. Wire non-payment of all items $1,000.00 and over. (Emphasis added.)

Liability was affixed on Payor Bank under MUCC § 4–302 [R 4–302], which provides:

* * *

The trial court's reasoning was (1) that each instrument presented was a demand item drawn on the Payor Bank and (2) that none of the items constituted a documentary draft because the drawer and the drawee were one and the same person; therefore no honor of the draft by the drawee was contemplated or necessary. We agree with (1) and disagree with (2).

Three MUCC definitions form the basis for our disagreement. The term "documentary draft" means any negotiable or non-negotiable draft with accompanying documents, securities or other papers to be delivered against the honor of the draft. A "check" is a draft drawn on a bank and payable on demand. To "honor" means to pay. Thus a check with accompanying documents which are to be delivered when payment is made is a documentary draft. The center of our disagreement with the court below is found in the meaning to be ascribed to the word "Honor." Honor as used in the MUCC is a term of art. The documents accompanying these items were expressly delivered against *payment;* so, because honor means pay, they remained documentary drafts exempt from the midnight deadline.

* * *

The error of the lower court in holding these drafts were not documentary drafts prevented development of the obvious alternative issue as to whether Payor Bank complied with its duties in connection with the collection of such documentary items as prescribed by the MUCC, in light of the Intermediary Bank's collection letter. Should the plaintiffs raise this alternative issue in the court below, the trial court is the appropriate forum to make such determinations in the first instance.

* * *

The cause is reversed and remanded for further proceedings consistent with this opinion.

Reversed and remanded.

Note

1. The usual check is drawn by the depositor on her account. In such a case, the drawee bank has a signature card on file and the only questions the bank must answer in deciding whether to pay the check are (1) is the signature genuine, (2) are there sufficient funds in the account, and (3) is there a stop order or other reason not to pay. (Of course the bank may also improperly pay if there is a forged indorsement, but there is very little the bank can do to avoid that risk.) However, as the two preceding cases indicate, a "check" need not be drawn by the depositor. Anyone may draw a check on someone else's account and send it through the banking system to the drawee bank. And there are many business situations in which that, in fact, happens. In such a case, the bank might just return the check unpaid indicating that there is an unauthorized signature. In fact, however, in many cases, the "check" was drawn pursuant to a business deal between the bank's depositor and the drawer and the depositor will want the bank to pay the draft. Therefore, the usual practice in such cases is for the bank to call the depositor to learn whether the depositor wishes the draft to be paid. If the bank cannot immediately contact the depositor, it may hold the draft beyond its midnight deadline trying to contact the depositor. Also if the depositor says it wishes to pay but its account is insufficient to cover the check, banks in a number of cases have waited for a few days for the depositor to "cover" the draft and have then returned the draft when it did not do so.

If the draft is not a documentary draft and is drawn on the bank § 4–302 (R 4–302) treats it like any other check and the drawee bank is absolutely liable for the amount of the draft if it does not return it within its midnight deadline. However, documentary drafts are not subject to the midnight deadline of section 4–302 (R 4–302). Therefore, in fact situations like those in the two preceding cases, banks that have failed to return drafts within their midnight deadlines can avoid section 4–302 (R 4–302) liability if they can prove either that the draft was not drawn on them, or that it was a documentary draft.

2. Why do you suppose section 4–302 (R 4–302) distinguishes between documentary drafts and other drafts? What difference in the situation justifies a different policy? What is a drawee's responsibility for return of an unpaid documentary draft? See OR 3–419; R 3–420.

3. If the draft is not drawn on the depositor's bank, but it is merely the collecting or payable through bank, what is its duty as to return of unpaid items and its liability for breach of that duty? See OR 4–202, 4–103(5), R 4–103(e).

Problems

1. Reeves drew drafts on Himco payable through Boardwalk National Bank. Reeves deposited the drafts in Farmers Bank which allowed Reeves to draw against the uncollected drafts. Farmers forwarded the drafts to Boardwalk, which presented the drafts to Himco. Himco, which maintained an account with Boardwalk, gave Boardwalk a check for $15,000 (the amount of the drafts) payable to Boardwalk and took possession of the drafts. Later the same day, Himco discovered that Reeves had breached

the contracts under which the drafts had been drawn. Himco returned the drafts to Boardwalk and had Boardwalk return to it the $15,000 check. Boardwalk returned the drafts to Farmers showing that they had been dishonored. Assume that Farmers is a holder in due course. May it recover $15,000 from Boardwalk? See OR and R 4–201, 4–202 and 3–418. See also Farmers & Merchants Nat'l Bank of Bridgeton, New Jersey v. Boardwalk National Bank, 101 N.J.Super. 528, 245 A.2d 35 (1968).

2. Plaintiff, West Side Bank, presented to defendant, Marine National Bank, a $262,000 check for payment. Marine took all the steps in the "process of posting" that it would ordinarily take in paying a check. Marine then received a stop payment order from the drawer of the check. Marine promptly reversed the entry charging the item to the customer's account, removed the check from the paid file, canceled the paid stamp, and returned the check to West Side. All of these activities took place before the midnight deadline under OR 4–104(1)(h) and 4–302(1) and before the clearing house agreement deadline for return. West Side brought suit, claiming that it was too late to honor the stop payment order because final payment of the item had been made. See West Side Bank v. Marine National Exchange Bank, 37 Wis.2d 661, 155 N.W.2d 587 (1968).

(a) Under original Article 4, when is the payment of an item final? What is the effect of a payor bank's finally paying an item? See OR 4–213.

(b) What is the Article 4 deadline for return of an item? See OR and R 4–302. If Marine returned the check to West Side before this deadline, why was this not enough to make the return proper?

(c) Under original Article 4, had Marine completed the process of posting? See OR 4–109.

(d) Should OR 4–303 apply in this case? Compare the language of OR 4–213(1)(c) with OR 4–303(1)(d). Is deciding whether the stop-order should have been honored a question of the "priority" of the items or of whether final payment has occurred?

(e) How would the 1990 revisions to 4–303 and 4–213, now R 4–215, affect the outcome of the case?

(f) If Marine met the clearing house rules deadline for return of an item (return had to be made by the close of the second business day following the day of presentment), does this supercede any argument that Marine brings under Article 4? See OR and R 4–103.

(g) What effect would Subpart C of Regulation CC have on the outcome in West Side? See Regulation CC 229.30.

COFFEE TRADE SERVICES, INC. v. FIRST FIDELITY BANK, N.A.

United States District Court for the District of New Jersey.
Civil Action No. 89–2399.

DEBEVOISE, DISTRICT JUDGE.

This is an action brought by plaintiff Coffee Trade Services Inc. ("Coffee Trade") against the bank where it maintained two commercial accounts, defendant First Fidelity Bank, N.A., New Jersey ("First Fidelity"), alleging (1) violations of the Expedited Funds Availability Act (the "Act"), 12 U.S.C. sections 4001–10, and the regulations promulgated thereunder in 12 C.F.R. Part 229, (2) violations of Article 4 of the Uniform Commercial Code (the "UCC"), N.J.S.A. section 12A:4–101 *et seq.*, (3) negligence, and (4) estoppel. Coffee Trade moves for a preliminary injunction and for summary judgment on the First, Second and Fourth Counts of the complaint and for a dismissal of First Fidelity's counterclaim for restitution. Jurisdiction is established by virtue of 12 U.S.C. sec. 4010, 28 U.S.C. sections 1331, 1332, 1337 and by the doctrine of pendent jurisdiction.

I. Background of the Dispute

This dispute emanates from a seemingly routine banking transaction made complicated by a repeated series of errors on the part of First Fidelity. Coffee Trade is a New York corporation engaged in the business of buying and selling coffee as on the international commodity market. In August 1988, Coffee Trade opened two corporate checking accounts with First Fidelity, the first used primarily for commercial checking, the second primarily for wire transfers. In connection with the opening of these accounts, First Fidelity required Coffee Trade to authorize and execute several corporate resolutions waiving certain rights regarding deposits and borrowing. Coffee Trade executed these documents on October 28, 1988.

On December 20, 1988, Coffee Trade deposited in its second account a check payable to Coffee Trade drawn upon a third-party's account with the Laredo National Bank, Laredo, Texas in the amount of $449,000. Sidney C. Abramowitz, a principal of Coffee Trade and its director of finance claims that Debra Smith, a First Fidelity Vice President and the loan officer responsible for the Coffee Trade accounts, advised him in late December 1988 that the December 20th deposit had cleared.

Although Smith does not state what, if anything, she told Abramowitz, she does not directly deny his account:

> I have known Mr. Abramowitz for approximately ten years, and because of the nature of the account, spoke with him on virtually a daily basis. In the two week period following the date of the deposit, he asked if the [c]heck had cleared. Based on the computer records to which I had access, it appeared to me that Coffee Trade's account balance did not show that the [c]heck had failed to clear. I explained that a check drawn on a Texas bank could take some time to come back through the system.

First Fidelity does not dispute Coffee Trade's contention that the monthly statements regarding the second account sent by First Fidelity to Coffee Trade for the months of December, January and February indicated that the December 20th deposit had cleared.

On March 8, 1989, 78 days after the December 20th deposit, First Fidelity charged back Coffee Trade's second account for the full amount of the December 20th deposit. First Fidelity submits the affidavit of a Nancy Ostrander, whom it identifies as a "bank officer located within the Return Deposits and Operations Branch" of First Fidelity in North Brunswick in an attempt to explain the lengthy delay in the chargeback. According to Ostrander's account, the check deposited by Coffee Trade on December 20 was sent to the Philadelphia National Bank ("PNB") for clearance. In a communication dated December 29, 1988, PNB advised First Fidelity that a check in the amount of $449,000, referred to by a reference number, had been returned by PNB on the previous day. On December 28, further, "First Fidelity also received notification of this check being returned through E.A.R.N.S. (Electronic Advance Return–Item Notification System)." Id. at para. 5. Apparently since the part-time employee who was assigned the task of monitoring bank accounts was out ill, it was not until January 25, 1989 that First Fidelity charged back PNB for $449,000 "claiming that First Fidelity" never received the returned check. On February 10, 1989, PNB "again charged back First Fidelity for the Check, but First Fidelity at the time continued to believe that item or a copy thereof was not received."

Ostrander claims that First Fidelity first requested a photocopy of the check from PNB on February 10, 1989 and, when that request was not honored, in "numerous" subsequent phone calls. First Fidelity claims that it did not receive a photocopy until March 8, 1989. Upon receipt of the check First Fidelity immediately charged back Coffee Trade's account in the amount of the returned check. It was not "until some time in May" that First Fidelity learned that it had previously received the dishonored check from PNB, the absence of which precipitated the lengthy delay, but that it "apparently had inadvertently been misplaced somewhere within the operations branch."

In any case, Ostrander called Smith on the day she levied a chargeback to the Coffee Trade account apparently so that Smith could notify Coffee Trade of the chargeback. Smith did not return Ostrander's call until the next day. Finally, on March 9, 1989, Smith called Abramowitz at Coffee Trade to inform him of the chargeback.

* * *

II. Standards for Preliminary Injunction and Summary Judgment

In order to prevail on a motion for preliminary injunction, the movant "bears the burden of producing evidence sufficient to convince the court" that (1) the movant has a reasonable probability of success on the merits of the case; (2) the movant will be irreparably injured by a denial of the injunction; (3) granting preliminary relief will not result in even greater harm to the other party; and (4) granting a preliminary injunction is in the public interest.

In order to prevail on a motion for summary judgment, the moving party must establish that "there is no genuine issue as to any material fact and that [it] is entitled to a judgment as a matter of law." Fed.R.Civ.P. 56(c). Once the moving party has carried its burden under

Rule 56, "its opponent must do more than simply show that there is some metaphysical doubt as to the material facts." *Matsushita Electric Industrial Co. v. Zenith Radio Corp.,* 106 S.Ct. 1348, 1356 (1986). The opposing party must set forth specific facts showing a genuine issue for trial and may not rest upon the mere allegations or denials of the pleadings. *Sound Ship Bldg. Co. v. Bethlehem Steel Co.,* 533 F.2d 96, 99 (3d Cir.), *cert. denied,* 429 U.S. 860 (1976). The Supreme Court has explained that in evaluating the evidence presented, "[w]here the record taken as a whole could not lead a rational trier of fact to find for the non-moving party, there is no 'genuine issue for trial.' " *Matsushita, supra,* 106 S.Ct. at 1356. All evidence submitted must be viewed in the light most favorable to the party opposing the motion. *Wahl v. Rexnord,* 624 F.2d 1169, 1181 (3d Cir.1980).

III. Summary Judgment or Likelihood of Prevailing on the Merits

I consider first whether Coffee Trade has demonstrated a likelihood of prevailing on the merits and/or is entitled to summary judgment.

The Act establishes deadlines by which time collecting depository institutions must make funds finally available to depositors. The basic rule set out in the Act is that funds from out-of-state checks must be available for withdrawal within 6 business days. Subject to exceptions for government checks, more stringent time limits established by the Board of Governors of the Federal Reserve System (the "Board") due to technological advances, deposits made in banks in non-contiguous states and territories, and the safeguard exceptions of 12 U.S.C. sec. 4003,

> not more than 6 business days shall intervene between the business day on which funds are deposited in an account at a depository institution by a check drawn on a nonlocal originating depository institution and the business day on which such funds are available for withdrawal.

12 U.S.C. sec. 4002(c)(2).

The Board has elaborated two time schedules for funds availability pursuant to its authority under the Act in its Regulation CC. The first schedule is 12 CFR 229.11, effective September 1, 1988 through September 1, 1990. More stringent deadline requirements are imposed under 12 CFR 229.12, but these provisions take effect only after the transition period governed by Section 229.11 ends. *See* 53 Fed.Reg. 19372 (May 27, 1988). Under the regulations in force on the date Coffee Trades made the deposit here in question, a depository bank must make funds deposited in an account by check "available for withdrawal not later than the 7th business day following the banking day on which funds are deposited." 12 CFR 229.11(c).

Under the "safeguards exceptions" provisions of the Act, the Board may by regulation establish "reasonable exceptions" to the 6–day rule if, among other conditions, "the amount of deposits by one or more checks * * * exceeds the amount of $5,000 in any one day." 12 U.S.C. sec. 4003(b)(1). Under Regulation CC the Board has determined that the limits of 229.11 do not apply

> to the aggregate amount of deposits by one or more checks to the extent that the aggregate amount is in excess of $5,000 on any one banking day.

12 CFR 229.13(b). In this event "the depository bank may extend the time periods established under sec. 229.11 * * * by a reasonable time." 12 CFR 229.13(h)(1). For the purposes of this exception

> an extension of up to four business days is a reasonable period. An extension of more than four business days may be reasonable but the bank has the burden of so establishing.

12 CFR 229.13(h)(4). If a depository institution relies upon the exception for deposits exceeding $5,000, it must provide notice of "the day the funds shall be made available for withdrawal" and "the reason the exception was invoked." This notice must be given immediately, if the deposit is made in person, or, in other cases, mailed to the depositor "not later than the close of the next business day following the business day on which the deposit is received." 12 U.S.C. sec. 4003(f)(2)(A), (B).

Under the provisions of the Act and Regulation CC, First Fidelity had until the seventh business day after the deposit to make the funds available for withdrawal or to advise Coffee Trade that the check had been returned for insufficient funds. Although the bank initially made the funds available for withdrawal, months later it effectively rescinded that availability by charging back Coffee Trade's account for the amount of the check. First Fidelity could have extended the time limit for four business days or even longer, if it could show that a longer period was reasonable under the circumstances. But any extension of time required notice to the depositor which First Fidelity did not provide, apparently because it was unaware that the clearing bank, PNB, had properly returned the check. It is clear that First Fidelity did not honor the time limits established under the Act and Regulation CC.

First Fidelity asserts three defenses related to the Act itself: First, it claims it cannot be held liable because the delay in this case was a result of a bona fide error; second, it asserts that the Act protects its right to chargeback accounts and that its actions in this case were merely exercising that right; third, First Fidelity argues that, in any case, Coffee Trade waived its right under the Act to notice of exceptions to the 6–day rule. I will consider each of these purported defenses.

The bank first asserts that its actions were the result of a bona fide error. Under 12 U.S.C. sec. 4010(c), a bank cannot be held liable under the Act if it demonstrates by a preponderance of the evidence that the violation (1) was not intentional, (2) resulted from a bona fide error, and (3) that the error occurred notwithstanding "the maintenance of procedures reasonably adopted to avoid any such error." 12 U.S.C. sec. 4001(c)(1). The Act provides certain examples of bona fide errors:

> Examples of a bona fide error include clerical, calculation, computer malfunction and programming, and printing errors, except that

> an error of legal judgment with respect to a depository institution's obligation under this chapter is not a bona fide error.

12 U.S.C. sec. 4010(c)(2).

First Fidelity claims that its actions were shielded by the Act's bona fide error provision, first because the clearing bank returned the check to First Fidelity after the Act's availability deadline had passed. First Fidelity claims that the Act's drafters did not contemplate imposing liability for such unavoidable errors and that to do so would result in a gross injustice.

I note that there is nothing in the Act to support First Fidelity's interpretation. If PNB was actually to blame, it seems that First Fidelity could then seek satisfaction from it for any liability imposed upon it for delay. Second, and more to the point, First Fidelity's argument is simply wrong. Under 12 CFR 229.11(c), First Fidelity was required to make the funds available for withdrawal "not later than the 7th business day following the banking day on which the funds are deposited." The day the funds were deposited, Tuesday, December 20, 1988, was a banking day.[4] A business day is a calendar day other than a Saturday or Sunday, or, when December 25 falls on a Sunday, as it did in 1988, the following Monday. 12 CFR 229.2(g). Not counting the intervening Saturday, Sunday, and Monday, First Fidelity had until Friday, December 30, 1988 to either make the funds available or to notify Coffee Trade that the check had been returned. First Fidelity concedes that PNB advised it that the December 20th deposit had been returned through an electronic notification system on December 28 and again in an advice dated December 29. Had First Fidelity chosen to credit these notices, rather than attributing them to PNB's error, it could have timely notified Coffee Trade of the check's return.[5]

First Fidelity next argues that there is a material issue of fact as to whether First Fidelity's behavior constitutes a good faith error. The bank has the burden of proof in this defense. 12 U.S.C. sec. 4010(c); 12 CFR 229.21(c)(1). I note at the outset that First Fidelity has failed to establish one of the elements of this defense. Although the affidavits the bank has submitted do not make the assertion directly, they do reflect the fact that it maintained systems, such as E.A.R.N.S., that relayed information regarding check returns. What the bank fails to allege, however, much less demonstrate, is that it maintained systems to cope with situations like that presented in this case and that these systems were "reasonably adapted" to avoid errors of the sort that

4. "* * * [A]ny business day on which an office of a bank is open to the public for carrying on substantially all of its banking functions." 12 CFR 229.2(f).

5. It is quite clear that the Act's deadlines are calculated by counting business and not calendar days. The regulations do not say, as they could have and as First Fidelity apparently reads them, "the seventh calendar day, or, if the seventh calendar day is not a business day, the next business day thereafter." The regulations make clear distinctions between business days and calendar days throughout. Finally, if any doubt remains, the tables prepared by the Board to demonstrate how deadlines are calculated show that intervening non-business days are not counted. *See* 53 Fed.Reg. 19374–76 (May 27, 1988).

occurred here. The record demonstrates only that in this case, First Fidelity's response was ad hoc. Even if the chaos that attended First Fidelity's response to this matter could be characterized as systematic, the record demonstrates that it was not "reasonably adapted" to avoid this error.

Coffee Trade also argues that First Fidelity cannot avail itself of this defense because its decision to chargeback the Coffee Trade account 78 calendar days after the December 20th deposit was clearly intentional and not the result of a "clerical" error. At best, Coffee Trade argues, the decision to chargeback the account well after the Act's time periods had elapsed was an erroneous legal decision, a decision the Act expressly removes from the bona fide error defense.

Coffee Trade's arguments have merit. Although First Fidelity's failure to heed PNB's communications and misplacement of the returned check are arguably clerical errors, Smith's decision to chargeback the Coffee Trade account was an intentional, management decision. Although First Fidelity obviously intended it as a corrective action to remedy its earlier mistakes, this action had the effect of making at least some of the originally-deposited funds unavailable and resulted in an overdraft with its attendant implications for Coffee Trade's credit ratings. First Fidelity knew that this decision would essentially cause the funds it had credited to Coffee Service's account to become unavailable within the time required by the Act.

First Fidelity's chargeback would only be proper if it were permitted by the Act, or some other authority, at that late date. This is what First Fidelity argues. It claims that Section 4006(c) of the Act preserves the bank's right to chargeback. That Section provides as follows:

> No provision of the chapter shall be construed as—
>
> * * *
>
> (2) affecting a depository institution's right—
>
> (A) to accept or reject a check for deposit;
>
> (B) to revoke any provisional settlement made by the depository institution with respect to a check accepted by such institution for deposit;
>
> (C) to charge back the depositor's account for the amount of such check; or
>
> (D) to claim a refund of such provisional credit.

First Fidelity's reliance on this provision is misplaced. Section 4006(c)(2)(B) permits a bank to revoke a "provisional settlement" for a check. Section 4006(c)(2)(C) permits charge backs to "such check." Section 4006(c)(2)(D) again speaks of the right of a bank to claim a refund of "such provisional credit." The clear import of this section is that a bank has a right to chargeback a depositor's account against only a provisional settlement.

Under the Uniform Commercial Code ("UCC"), if a collecting bank has made a provisional settlement and the bank, in turn, fails to receive a settlement on the item, the bank may charge back the customer's account "[if] by its midnight deadline or within a longer reasonable time after it learns the facts it returns the item or sends notification of the facts." N.J.S.A. sec. 12A:4–212(1) [R 4–214(a)]. The Act preempts inconsistent provisions of the UCC. 12 U.S.C. sec. 4007(b). Since funds must be available for withdrawal within the time limits established by the Act, it is clear that the right to chargeback against a provisional settlement under the UCC exists only within the Act's deadline period, or, in this case, six business days. To read this section otherwise would permit chargebacks at anytime after the deposit and would eviscerate the essence of the Act. It is also clear that the extension permitted under the UCC for a "reasonable time after [the bank] learns the facts" must also be read in the context of the Act. As discussed above, the Act defines a reasonable time as four business days or a longer period if the bank can justify it. However, in either case the bank must provide notice to the depositor pursuant to the provisions of the Act. This First Fidelity failed to do.

First Fidelity next asserts that Coffee Trade waived notice of exceptions to the 6–day limit under the Act. First Fidelity claims that by executing certain corporate resolutions on October 28, 1988, which the bank required it to do before opening its account, Coffee Trade waived notice under the Act. First Fidelity points specifically to paragraph 3 of the "terms and conditions" governing all aspects of Coffee Trade's banking relationship with it:

> This corporation waives protest of any negotiable instruments deposited with or held by the Bank to which this corporation is a party; and this corporation consents to any and every renewal or extension of time or other modifications which may be granted or made with respect to such negotiable instruments, and any such renewal or extension of time or other modification shall be deemed to have been granted or made with the full and express reservation by the Bank of all of its rights of recourse against this corporation in respect of such negotiable instruments.

I note that this broad provision does not expressly waive the depositor's rights under the Act, it waives the technical requirements of notice and presentment under the UCC. For a waiver to be effective, however, its terms must be specific. Further, were all depository institutions to adopt such sweeping waivers the Congressional intent embodied in the Act would be flouted. This resolution, therefore, cannot be held to amount to a waiver of Coffee Trade's rights under the Act.

In another variation of this argument, First Fidelity argues that the Act does not preempt New Jersey's version of the UCC and that under the UCC a bank may enforce agreements where depositors have waived certain defenses. First Fidelity notes that Coffee Trade waived protest of any negotiable instrument under the corporate banking resolutions and that this waiver is expressly approved of under N.J.S.A. sec. 12A:3–511(2)(a) [R 3–504(a)(iv)]. First Fidelity argues, therefore, that its right to enforce this waiver is preserved and it is not obliged to provide notice to Coffee Trade.

Here again, were banks permitted to rely on previously-drafted corporate resolutions designed to waive certain defenses under the UCC to evade their responsibilities under the Act, the Congressional intent would be largely frustrated. Although the UCC expressly permits waiver of certain of its provisions, there is no correlative provision under the Act. The Act clearly expressly states that "this chapter and regulations prescribed under this chapter shall supersede any provision of the law of any State including the [UCC] as in effect in such State, which is inconsistent with this chapter or such provisions." 12 U.S.C. sec. 4007(b). In this case it is clear that the Act preempts the UCC provisions providing for the waiver of certain depositor's rights which, if given effect, would make Regulation CC unenforceable.

Finally, the Bank attempts to rely on certain purportedly suspicious circumstances surrounding the December 20th deposit and other innuendo which it claims somehow excuse it from its obligations under the Act. First Fidelity notes that the account to which Coffee Trade made the December 20th deposit was not normally used for check deposits and that Abramowitz wondered aloud whether the check would clear when the deposit was made. It also alleges that after the deposit was made, Coffee Trade "wired out an identical sum of money to a company allegedly affiliated with Miguel Sainz, the drawer of the check." First Fidelity less than subtly hints that Coffee Trade was involved in a collusive scam: "Can plaintiff seriously expect anyone to believe that Sainz could sign a check of this magnitude and not be aware of the state of his account?"

Even if First Fidelity's suggestions were to arouse suspicion, the bank has utterly failed to demonstrate how these circumstances amount to a defense under the Act. Were Coffee Trade involved in a fraudulent transaction, the bank would surely have recourse against it, but there is nothing in the Act that excuses a bank's violations because it subsequently claims that something suspicious is afoot. In any case, fraud or collusion is inherently implausible in this situation. Such a scheme would depend on the depository institution making errors (in this case, three of them) that would prevent it from making a timely chargeback to the account. While it is possible that a particularly gamesome con artist might float a bad check with the hope that a bank might make a mistake, this is most unlikely, especially when dealing with a check of half-a-million dollars. Coffee Trade has also provided an explanation of the allegedly suspicious circumstances. Finally, this argument is better addressed to the maker of the check and not to Coffee Services.

First Fidelity has not raised a material factual issue which would prevent the granting of summary judgment. Since First Fidelity is entitled to summary judgment, it has demonstrated, a fortiori, that it is likely to prevail on the merits and a preliminary injunction is in order. I turn now to the question of damages and to First Fidelity's assertion that Coffee Trade was unjustly enriched.[6]

The Act provides that any depository institution which fails to comply with any requirement imposed under the Act is liable to such person in an amount equal to the sum of actual damages sustained by the failure, statutory damages not less than $100 and not more than $1000 and reasonable attorney's fees as determined by the court. 12 U.S.C. sec. 4010(a).

Coffee Trade argues that the concept of actual damages encompasses all damages proximately caused by the bank's failure to comply with the Act. It submits the Abramowitz Reply Affidavit and supporting materials in order to demonstrate that it relied to its detriment on First Fidelity's advices that the check had cleared. Abramowitz states that the December 20th deposit was a payment made in connection with Coffee Trade's purchase of a debt owed to PBTC International Bank ("PBTC"). PBTC was owed $540,000 by Cafe Don Luis, a Mexican corporation engaged in the business of exporting coffee. Coffee Trade negotiated first with PBTC, to determine the lowest amount that it would accept on the debt, and then with Cafe Don Luis, to determine the most it would be willing to pay to settle its indebtedness. Ultimately, PBTC agreed to sell Coffee Trade the Cafe Don Luis debt for $395,000 and Cafe Don Luis agreed to pay Coffee Trade $449,000 to settle the debt and obtain a full release. The December 20th deposit was Cafe Don Luis' payment. Abramowitz claims that he believed the payment was drawn on a Cafe Don Luis account. On December 22, 1988, Coffee Trade paid PBTC the agreed upon sum for the Cafe Don Luis debt. On January 30, 1989, in reliance on First Fidelity's oral advices that the check had cleared (or had not failed to clear) and on the monthly statements which reflected that the check had been credited to its account, Coffee Services released the loan documents to Cafe Don Luis.

Save for a thousand dollars and change, the entire amount of the December 20th deposit has been spent. Coffee Trade has made an initial showing that the loan documents released to Cafe Don Luis were worth $449,000 or more. There is nothing in the record as it has presently been developed which casts doubt on this account. The case is still at an early stage, however. If First Fidelity develops evidence to show that Coffee Trade was not damaged in the full amount of $450,000, the parties can then address the question of where the loss falls or who is liable. However, it is clear that if Coffee Trade was actually

6. I assume for purposes of argument only that there is a defense of unjust enrichment under the Act.

damaged in the amount of the deposit, First Fidelity has no legitimate counterclaim and no defense under the UCC or otherwise since the Act preempts state laws which frustrate its purpose. Since that may be the case, I decline to rule at this time on Coffee Trade's motion for partial summary judgment as it relates to Counts 2 and 4.

I turn now to the issue of irreparable harm.

IV. Irreparable Injury

For a preliminary injunction to issue, "the feared injury or harm must be irreparable—not merely serious or substantial." *Glasco v. Hills,* 558 F.2d 179, 181 (3d Cir.1977). This is because an irreparable injury is a harm different in kind rather than degree. A severe injury may nonetheless be made whole; a loss of millions, for example, can be corrected by the payment of an equal sum. "Irreparable" means, as the word suggests, "not reparable; incapable of being rectified, remedied or made good." Random House Dictionary (2d Ed.1987). " 'The word means that which cannot be repaired, retrieved, put down again, atoned for * * * Grass that is cut down cannot be made to grow again; the injury cannot be adequately atoned for in money. The result of the cases fixes this to be the rule: the injury must be of a peculiar nature, so that compensation in money cannot atone for it * * *' " *Glasco, supra,* 538 F.2d at 181, quoting, *Gause v. Perkins,* 3 Jones Eq. 177, 69 Am.Dec. 728 (1857).

Coffee Trade asserts that it "cannot survive as a buyer and seller of coffee in the international market without a superior credit rating." Coffee Trade operates under a line of credit financed by Conti Trade Services, Inc. which is coming up for renewal in August, 1989. Abramowitz asserts that it is "extremely unlikely" that its credit line will be renewed if there is an outstanding chargeback claim against it.

First Fidelity does not dispute Abramowitz's assertions. The harm feared is clearly irreparable.

V. Harm Caused by Injunction to the Opposing Party

Coffee Trade seeks a preliminary injunction order directing First Fidelity to reverse the March 8, 1989 chargeback to Coffee Trade's account and to refrain from giving any adverse credit information regarding Coffee Trade to third parties. First Fidelity claims that it has refrained from giving adverse information to third parties over the course of the dispute, so this requirement cannot cause it great inconvenience. Neither will the chargeback, which involves a relatively small sum of money, impose a hardship upon the bank.

VI. Public Interest

Congress passed the Act in order to correct a pattern of abuses by banks and other financial institutions. Giving force to this mandate where it is merited is in accord with the public interest.

VII. Conclusion

For all of the reasons expressed above, Coffee Trade's motion for summary is granted with respect to Count 1 and denied with respect to

Counts 3 and 4. A preliminary injunction will enter requiring First Fidelity to restore the status quo ante by reopening the Coffee Trade wire account and reversing the March 8, 1989 chargeback and preventing First Fidelity from releasing any adverse financial information regarding Coffee Trade to third parties. Counsel for Coffee Trade should submit an appropriate form of order.

Note

Original 4–212 (R 4–214) gives a bank the right to charge-back a dishonored check against the depositor's account. The court in Coffee Trade determined that this right expires at the end of the period by which funds must be made available to the depositor under Regulation CC. This result was contrary to the intent of the drafters of Regulation CC, who never meant for the federal regulation to supercede a bank's right to exercise charge-back for a dishonored check. Apparently in response to the decision in *Coffee Trade*, the Federal Reserve Board revised the official commentary to Regulation CC 229.19(c) to read:

> For example, even if a check is returned or a notice of nonpayment is received after the time by which funds must be made available for withdrawal in accordance with this regulation, the depositary bank may charge back the customer's account for the full amount of the check.

E. OPERATION OF FRAUD AND NEGLIGENCE PRINCIPLES IN THE COLLECTION SYSTEM

Recall that in support of its conclusion, the *Pulaski* court emphasized that on the facts before it, there was no suggestion of fraud; that is, the collection practices at issue were not calculated to take undue advantage of processing systems and the U.C.C. deadlines. It is true in the bank collections law, as in perhaps the law generally, that the efficacy of the system is best tested when things go wrong. As the two cases that follow indicate, the more novel the imposition on the system the more the courts are called upon to discern the fundamental assumptions underlying the Article 4 check collection provisions. As you read through *Northpark* and *USF & G*, try to identify the "strategic strong points" on which, from the courts' perspective, the uniform commercial law of check collections is premised.

NORTHPARK NATIONAL BANK v. BANKERS TRUST CO.

United States District Court, Southern District of New York, 1983.
572 F.Supp. 524.

WHITMAN KNAPP, D.J.

On November 7, 1979 a customer of plaintiff—a Dallas bank—deposited with it a $62,500 check and thereby set in motion a clever fraud which would result in his bilking plaintiff out of some $60,000, and in the institution of this lawsuit to determine who should ultimately be left holding the proverbial "bag." The case is before us on defendant Federal Reserve Bank of New York's (FRBNY) motion to dismiss for failure to state a claim * * *

BACKGROUND

Two features of the modern check collection process are central to the understanding of this fraud. The first is that, notwithstanding the colloquial suggestion to the contrary, checks deposited for collection do not generally "clear." That is, provisional credits—on the customer's account at the depositary bank and on the accounts of intermediary banks involved in the collection process—become final by the mere passage of time, rather than by an advice of actual payment. See Uniform Commercial Code (UCC) § 4–213 [R 4–215]. See also 6 Reitman Banking Law § 135.08 (1981). It being statistically unlikely that a particular check will not be paid, see UCC § 4–212 [R 4–214] comment 1, the practicalities of the process call for giving actual notice (down the chain of collection) only in the event a check is not paid. Accordingly, the temporary hold which a depositary bank customarily places on the withdrawal of proceeds from a check deposited for collection is intended to give the collection chain an opportunity to notify the depositary bank, if it be necessary, that the check has not been paid. Thus, the hallmark of the normal completion of collection—i.e., the check having been paid—is the receipt of no notice by the depositary institution.

The second important feature is that the collection process has been, of course, automated by the use of check-sorting computers. See Bank Leumi Trust v. Bally's Park Place (S.D.N.Y.1981) 528 F.Supp. 349, 350–51. The vast amount of items processed allows no practical alternative. See 68 Annual Report, Board of Gov. of the Fed.Res.Syst. 233, table 9 (1981) (more than 16 billion checks handled in 1981); Aldom, Purdy, Schneider & Whittingham, Automation in Banking 13–15 (1963); UCC § 4–101 [R 4–101] comment. Along the bottom of a check's face there are so-called "MICR numbers" [2] which identify the drawer's bank, branch, and account number. A computer "reads" these numbers and automatically routes the check to the appropriate destination for collection. The initial destination depends, therefore, entirely on the MICR routing number printed on the check.

With the foregoing in mind it is clear how a fraud of this type is accomplished. Its object is to cause a worthless check deposited for collection to take a sufficiently long detour in its progress to the drawee bank, to insure that the notice of non-payment will not arrive at the depositary bank until after the expiration of the hold which it placed on the availability of the proceeds from transit items. Having received no such notice before the expiration of the hold, the depositary bank supposes the items to have been paid and allows its proceeds to be withdrawn. By the time notice arrives the malefactor has, of course, absconded with the spoils. The crucial detour is caused by imprinting the fraudulent check with the wrong MICR routing number—i.e., one

2. "MICR" stands for "Magnetic Ink Character Recognition."

that does not correspond to the bank designated on the face of the check as the drawee bank, but to a different bank, preferably one that is distant from the institution designated as the drawee bank on the face of the check. The fraudulent check in our case bore the MICR routing number of Bankers Trust Co. in New York and identified the "Bank of Detroit"—a fictitious institution—as the drawee bank.[4]

A brief chronology is now in order. The malefactor [5] deposited the fake check in his account with plaintiff on November 7, 1979. Plaintiff put a 14-day hold—through November 20—on the availability of the check's proceeds. On the next day, November 8, the check was presented to the Republic National Bank of Dallas—plaintiff's correspondent bank for out-of-state collections—which, in turn, presented the check on November 9 directly to the FRBNY for collection, without routing the item through the local Federal Reserve Bank of Dallas. See 12 C.F.R. § 210.4 (1983) (allowing "direct send" to Federal Reserve Banks). The complaint goes on to allege that the check bears a stamp showing that it had been presented to Bankers Trust Co. for collection on November 13. The precise timing of events during the next few days has not yet been established. It is clear, however, that at some time after November 13, Bankers Trust determined that the check was not drawn on it and returned the item to the FRBNY. The FRBNY, having now extracted the check from the computer-directed addressing system, then forwarded the check to the FRBC on the strength of the designation "Bank of Detroit" which the check bore on its face.[6] The complaint states that the check is stamped as having been in the hands of the FRBC on November 20. Meanwhile, back in Dallas, the malefactor withdrew $9,000 from his account on November 21 and an additional $40,250 on Saturday, November 24. The precise schedule of the check's vicissitudes after November 20 is yet undetermined. It must, however, have been sent to the Detroit branch of the FRBC, which branch, in turn, established that the "Bank of Detroit" did not exist. The check

4. The fact that the "Bank of Detroit" does not exist is immaterial to this motion. As we understand the mechanics of this fraud, it would work as well if the institution identified as the drawee bank on the face of the fraudulent check were a "real" bank, or if the account on which the check is ostensibly drawn were a "real" account. It is irrelevant whether the fraudulent check is returned unpaid because the drawee "bank" does not exist, because the account on which it is drawn at a (real) drawee bank does not exist, or because the (real) account on which it is drawn at a (real) drawee bank is without funds. The outcome of this motion should not depend, in our view, on the fortuitous choice of check "style" which the malefactor has made. In this connection we observe, moreover, that defendant's penchant for referring to the fraudulent check as a "non-check" on grounds that it was not drawn "on a bank," see UCC § 3–104(2)(b) [R 3–104(f)], is of no legal moment.

5. The complaint does not indicate whether the plaintiff's client was the malefactor or a victim who had dealt with one. At oral argument plaintiff's counsel advised us, however, that the (former) customer can now be found in a Pennsylvania jail, presumably on account of a less successful venture than the one which spawned this litigation.

6. Detroit lies in the geographic district served by the FRBC. The FRBNY is permitted further to route the check to Chicago by virtue of note 3 to 12 C.F.R. § 210.6 (1979), currently codified at 12 C.F.R. § 210.6(a)(2) (1983) with minor stylistic variations. It allows a Federal Reserve Bank to route a check based on any addressing symbol, whether or not it be consistent with other symbols on the item.

must then have followed the self-same route back to the FRBC and then to the FRBNY. The complaint alleges that the FRBNY again received the check on November 29, well after the malefactor had eloped with the plundered funds, leaving—we suppose—a barren account. What happened to the check thereafter is immaterial. Suffice it to say that the Federal Reserve Bank of Dallas advised plaintiff some time in December that the check would be returned unpaid, and upon the check's return debited plaintiff's account at the Dallas Fed for the amount of the phony check.

Discussion

The complaint is altogether parsimonious in describing the legal foundation of the charges against the FRBNY. As developed in its submission in opposition to the FRBNY's motion, the specific legal grounds for plaintiff's claim are that, having received the check unpaid from the FRBC on November 29, the FRBNY (a) failed timely to send notice or timely to forward the check down the collection chain, as required by UCC § 4–212(1) [R 4–214(a)] [7] and, therefore, forfeited its right to charge-back under that provision; that, having received the unpaid check from Bankers Trust on November 13, the FRBNY (b) failed to send notice down the collection chain of the check's delay in transit, as required by UCC § 4–202(1)(e) [R 4–202(a)(4)]; (c) failed timely to forward the check for presentment to the FRBC, as required by UCC § 4–202(1)(a) [R 4–202(a)(1)] [8]; and (d) failed to send notice of non-payment down the collection chain, as required by UCC § 4–202(1)(b) [R 4–202(a)(2)].

I

At the outset the parties have vigorously disputed whether the FRBNY is a "collecting bank" for purposes of UCC §§ 4–212 [R 4–214]

7. The relevant portion of the statute reads: § 4–212 [R 4–214]. Right of Charge–Back or Refund (1)[a] If a collecting bank has made provisional settlement with its customer for an item and itself fails by reason of dishonor, suspension of payments by a bank or otherwise to receive a settlement for the item which is or becomes final, the bank may revoke the settlement given by it, charge-back the amount of any credit given for the item to its customer's account or obtain refund from its customer whether or not it is able to return the items if by its midnight deadline or within a longer reasonable time after it learns the facts it returns the item or sends notification of the facts. These rights to revoke, charge-back and obtain refund terminate if and when a settlement for the item received by the bank is or becomes final (subsection (3) of Section 4–211 [R 4–213] and subsections (2) and (3) of Section 4–213[R 4–215]).

8. The provision reads, in part: § 4–202 [R 4–202]. Responsibility for Collection: When Action Seasonable (1) [(a)] A collecting bank must use ordinary care in (a) [(1)] presenting an item or sending it for presentment; and (b) [(2)] sending notice of dishonor or nonpayment or returning an item or other than a documentary draft to the bank's transferor or directly to the depositary bank under subsection (2) [omitted in revision] of Section 4–212 [R 4–214] after learning that the item has not been paid or accepted, as the case may be; and (c) [(3)] settling for an item when the bank receives final settlement; and (d) [omitted in revision] making or providing for any necessary protest; and (e) [(4)] notifying its transferor of any loss or delay in transit within a reasonable time after discovery thereof. (2) [(b)] A collecting bank taking proper action before its midnight deadline following receipt of an item, notice or payment acts seasonably; taking proper action within a reasonably longer time may be seasonable but the bank has the burden of so establishing.

and 4–202 [R 4–202] because the strictures of those sections apply only to such banks. Defendant argues that it cannot be a collecting bank because they are defined as "any bank handling the item *for collection* except the payor bank," UCC § 4–105(d) [R 4–105(5)] (emphasis added), and it had no authority to handle the check "for collection," as it was not drawn on a bank located in the geographic district served by the FRBNY. For the latter proposition the FRBNY refers us to 12 U.S.C. § 360 and 5 Fed.Res.Bull. 467 (1919). This argument is without merit. The purpose of the Federal Reserve Act of 1913, as amended—whose section 16 is the forerunner of what is now 12 U.S.C. § 360—was to organize the Federal Reserve Bank. There is not the slightest indication that the grant of authority in § 360 was intended as a shield against the application of UCC §§ 4–212 [R 4–214] and 4–202 [R 4–202] or, conversely, that the drafters of the UCC intended those sections to be read in conjunction with 12 U.S.C. § 360. Section 4–105(d) [R 4–105(5)] of the UCC sets out a very practical, commonsensical definition of "collecting" bank as every bank in the collection chain except the payor bank.

Defendant argues further that it is not a collecting bank because it was sent the check "by mistake." See Citizens State Bank v. Martin (1980) 227 Kan. 580, 609 P.2d 670, 676 (holding that a bank receiving a check because of an encoding error is not a collecting bank). The check, however, was not sent by mistake. It was properly addressed to the FRBNY in accordance with a MICR routing number which called for such destination. This was, of course, part of a fraudulent scheme but it surely was not a mistake.[12] Last, the FRBNY argues that it should not be subjected to UCC §§ 4–212 [R 4–214] and 4–202 [R 4–202] because "[p]laintiff should not be permitted to impose significant legal obligations on the New York Fed simply by sending it a worthless piece of paper." This is yet another strained argument. The check is no less valuable than a check drawn on insufficient funds at an account with an in-district bank. The value of the check is of no consequence to the role which the FRBNY played in the collection process or to the attendant obligations to which it should, accordingly, be subjected. We therefore hold that, on the facts of this case, the FRBNY is a collecting bank for the purpose of subjecting it to such duties as are specified in UCC §§ 4–212 [R 4–214] and 4–202 [R 4–202].

II

Plaintiff contends that the FRBNY lost its right to charge-back plaintiff's account under UCC § 4–212 [R 4–214] when it failed, "by its midnight deadline" after receiving the check from the FRBC on November 29, to return it or to send notification of having received it unpaid. We observe again that by November 29 any notification—by whatever

12. We have no occasion to consider whether a defendant ought to be considered a "collecting" bank with respect to an item it received truly by mistake—e.g., mislaid in a mail bag addressed to it. In this case the check was delivered to the FRBNY entirely by design. To the extent the Martin case can be read as holding that the FRBNY is not a collecting bank in this situation we disagree with its conclusion.

means—would have been futile because the malefactor had completed his fraud on November 24. Accordingly, the question we are asked to decide is whether, in requiring "notification" or the "return" of the item, UCC § 4–212(1) [R 4–214(a)] establishes conditions precedent to the right of charge-back or whether it defines a duty of ordinary care relative to the right to charge-back. If it were the former, the non-occurrence of the condition would result in there being no right to charge-back—i.e., the collecting bank who failed to fulfill the conditions would be absolutely liable for the item. If it were the latter, the right to charge-back would be absolute, at least until settlement became final, but a plaintiff could hold the collecting bank responsible for such damages as were proximately caused by the collecting bank's failure timely to discharge its duty to notify or to return the item. In this case, no damages could be traced by the FRBNY's alleged failure to notify on or after November 29, because the damage could not then have been prevented.

We hold that UCC § 4–212(1) [R 4–214(a)] establishes a duty of care, not a condition to the right to charge-back. At oral argument plaintiff's counsel conceded, that the only reported case which specifically addresses the question before us is Appliance Buyers Credit Corp. v. Prospect Nat. Bank (7th Cir.1983) 708 F.2d 290 (Timbers, C.J., of the 2d Cir. in the majority panel). It holds, as do we, that UCC § 4–212(1) [R 4–214(a)] imposes a duty, not a condition and that plaintiff, therefore, has the burden of establishing the actual damages caused by the collecting bank's failures. Id. at 294–95. We could safely rest our holding on the persuasive statutory exegesis in Appliance Buyers. In addition, however, we observe that comment 1 to UCC § 4–108 [R 4–109] specifically refers to UCC § 4–212 [R 4–214] as "prescrib[ing] * * * time limits * * * within which a bank, in fulfillment of its obligation to exercise *ordinary care,* must handle items entrusted to it for collection * * *" (Emphasis added.) Moreover, we would not impute to the drafters of the UCC the intention of imposing a duty the performance of which would make no practical difference whatever. To be sure, the language of UCC § 4–212(1) [R 4–214(a)] is far from clear in this regard. Although clarity and consistency have never been the UCC's hallmark, see, e.g., D. Mellinkoff, The Language of the Uniform Commercial Code, 77 Yale L.J. 185 (1976), practicality is certainly one of its virtues. We would therefore require a clear indication of legislative intention before reading into UCC § 4–212(1) [R 4–214(a)] a collecting bank's obligation to perform an empty gesture. Plaintiff has called to our attention no such indication, nor has our own research uncovered any.[15]

15. The charge-back section can be traced at least back to the April and July 1948 Proposed Final Drafts Nos. 1 and 2 of Article III on commercial paper, which then included the subject of check collections. Its forerunners were then entitled "reversal of credit." See § 711 (Draft No. 1, April 15, 1948); § 715 (Draft No. 2, July 30, 1948). Neither those sections nor their "Notes and Comments" provide any clue that the present UCC § 4–212(1) [R 4–214] should express a condition rather than a duty. See also Notes & Comments at 66 (Draft No. 1); Notes & Comments at 19–20

The clearest expression of the purpose to be served by the notification requirement in the charge-back statute is provided by comments 1 and 4 to UCC § 4–207 (1950 Edition). Notification is intended, the comments tell us, promptly to advise an unsuspecting customer and to protect him from having checks (drawn on his account) returned unpaid. See, e.g., First State Bank & Trust Co. v. George (Tex.Civ.App. 1974) 519 S.W.2d 198, 16 UCC Rep. 160. See also UCC § 4–212 [R 4–214] comment 5. Even on the plausible assumption that the duty of prompt notification was also intended to allow the customer and a collecting bank to protect their rights against third parties, there is no logical reason to suppose that such intention implies that the violator of the duty be held liable, irrespective of the causal connection between the breach and the plaintiff's inability to collect on the item. Cf. UCC §§ 4–202 [R 4–202] (duty) and 4–103(5) [R 4–103(e)] (measure of damages). Indeed, all decisions which we have been able to locate denying a defendant's right to charge-back under UCC § 4–212 [R 4–214] for failure to notify (or to forward the item), are cases in which causation is established because the defendant's failure led to a detrimental change in plaintiff's position, which change could have been avoided by prompt notification.

Accordingly, we hold the cause of action under UCC § 4–212 [R 4–214] to be legally insufficient because plaintiff has pleaded no facts which establish that it is entitled to any damages, even if it prevailed on the issue of liability.

III

Plaintiff also charges the FRBNY with violating UCC § 4–202(1)(e) [R 4–202(a)(4)] because it did not send a notice of delay in transit after it received the check unpaid from Bankers Trust. Defendant FRBNY contends, on the other hand, that UCC § 4–202(1)(e) [R 4–202(a)(4)] was not meant to apply to a situation such as this one, but rather to cases in which the physical items are lost or destroyed when transported from one location to another. See Citizens State Bank v. Martin, supra, 227 Kan. at 588, 609 P.2d at 676 (dictum).

In our view defendant's position is the correct one. The history of UCC § 4–202(1)(e) [R 4–202(a)(4)] can be traced at least back to the Proposed Final Drafts Nos. 1 and 2 of Article III on commercial paper. The relevant section in Draft No. 1 was appropriately entitled "*Lost* Items," see § 715 (Draft No. 1, April 15, 1948) (emphasis added), and in Draft No. 2 it was called "*Loss* of Cash Items in Transit." See § 713 (Draft No. 2, July 30, 1948) (emphasis added). Their respective notes and comments leave no doubt that the "delays in transit" which the

(Draft No. 2). In the 1948 version of the UCC the relevant section had already taken the title "right to charge back" and contained language to the effect that "[a collecting bank may charge back], but the collecting bank must make such charge back and return the item or send notice to its transferor by its midnight deadline." See UCC § 3–617(1) (1948 Edition). By 1950 it had been renumbered § 4–207 and had also taken substantially its present language. In the Final Text Edition of 1951 it was renumbered § 4–212. These antecedents do not point to a finding that a "condition" is implied by the language of UCC § 4–212(1) [R 4–214(a)].

drafters contemplated were those occasioned by mishaps in the mails. See Notes and Comments to Draft No. 1 at 71 (April 15, 1948); Notes and Comments to Draft No. 2 at 17 (August 2, 1948). See also UCC § 3–611(2) (1948 Edition). We have found nothing in the subsequent legislative history to persuade us that the several stylistic mutations which eventually led to UCC § 4–202(1)(e) [R 4–202(a)(4)] modified the above described legislative intent. See also N.Y.Law Revision Comm., Study of Unif.Com.Code—Article 4 at 97 (Leg.Doc. No. 65(E), 1955).

In this case the physical progress of the fraudulent check was never hindered by an accident, cf. Girard Trust Bank v. Brinks, Inc. (1966) 422 Pa. 48, 220 A.2d 827, or by it being mislaid in the mail. Accordingly, we hold that the FRBNY was under no obligation to give such notice as is specified in UCC § 4–202(1)(e) [R 4–202(a)(4)].

IV

Plaintiff also contends that the FRBNY violated its duties under UCC § 4–202(1)(a) [R 4–202(a)(1)] because it failed to forward the check to the FRBC within the time limits specified in UCC § 4–202(2) [R 4–202(b)] after having received it unpaid from Bankers Trust. This claim, for the time being at least, we must sustain.

In connection with a claim under UCC § 4–202 [R 4–202] there is no dispute that the appropriate rule for damages is the "but for" test of UCC § 4–103(5) [R 4–103(e)]. Moreover, this measure of damages for the violation of the duty of care in handling items for collection long antecedes the enactment of the UCC. See American Nat'l Bank v. Bank of Bandon (9th Cir.1917) 240 F. 624; Balsa Ecuador Lumber Corp. v. Security Nat. Bank (E.D.N.C.1956) 141 F.Supp. 470, 476; UCC § 4–103 [R 4–103] comment 6. With the foregoing in mind it is apparent that, even if it were able to establish that the FRBNY violated UCC § 4–202(1)(a) [R 4–202(a)(1)], plaintiff would be hard pressed to prove damages. It is equally clear, however, that in this procedural posture the claim may not be dismissed.

Defendant FRBNY has submitted an elaborate set of charts purporting to demonstrate that—given the benchmarks of November 13 and 20 when the check is known to have been in the hands of Bankers Trust and the FRBC respectively—the very task of physically transporting the check to Chicago compels the conclusions, first, that the FRBNY could not have violated UCC § 4–202(1)(a) [R 4–202(a)(1)]; and, second, that—if liability could be established—any possible delay must have been so short that it could not support damages because, even in the absence of such short delay, plaintiff could not have been notified in time to prevent the November 24 withdrawal. Defendant's presentation is cogent, but inappropriate on a motion to dismiss. On the question of liability the FRBNY's argument is flawed in that it assumed, for instance, that Bankers Trust returned the bogus check just before its midnight deadline on November 14.[18] However, the event

18. To support its assumptions about the timing of Bankers Trust's actions, defendant cleverly fastens on the fact that the complaint also includes a claim

which "starts the clock" of UCC § 4–202(2) [R 4–202(b)] for the FRBNY is not the end of the period in which Bankers Trust might have lawfully acted, but the moment when it, in fact, returned the check to the FRBNY. On this complaint and in the absence of any discovery on that issue, we must allow for the possibility—unrealistic as it may be—that Bankers Trust may have returned the check before 2:00 P.M., see UCC § 4–107 [R 4–108], on the same day it received it—November 13. Therefore, we cannot say as a matter of law that the complaint rules out a violation of UCC § 4–202 [R 4–202] by the FRBNY.

On the issue of damages, defendant's argument amounts, in substance, to the contention that the FRBC would have taken nine days to return the check to New York whether or not the FRBNY had forwarded it in time and, therefore, that—given any plausible delay—it would have been impossible to notify plaintiff in time to prevent the November 24 withdrawal. Although we are taken by the argument that the timing of events in Chicago is independent of the precise date on which the check arrived from New York, we are not prepared—on this record—to say so as a matter of law.

Accordingly, plaintiff will be allowed discovery for purposes of establishing the timing of the various stages by which the check progressed from New York to Chicago. Should the evidence prove that the FRBNY violated UCC § 4–202(1)(a) [R 4–202(a)(1)] by delaying the check's progress beyond the limits specified in UCC § 4–202(2) [R 4–202(b)], plaintiff will be allowed—indeed, required—further to establish that such delay caused it damage.

V

Finally, plaintiff charges that the FRBNY violated UCC § 4–202(1)(b) [R 4–202(a)(2)] by failing to send a notice of non-payment after it had received the check from Bankers Trust some time after November 13. On the other hand, defendant contends, in substance, that UCC § 4–202(1)(b) [R 4–202(a)(2)] does not impose on it the duty to notify about Bankers Trust's non-payment because the drafters of the UCC

against Bankers Trust on an allegation that it delayed the return of the check to the FRBNY beyond its midnight deadline. The time span between November 13 and 20 being, of course, fixed, it follows logically that the shorter the time which the check remained in the hands of Bankers Trust, the longer it necessarily must have been in the possession of the FRBNY. Accordingly, the FRBNY contends that, by assuming arguendo that Bankers Trust acted by its midnight deadline—an assumption contradicted by the very allegation against Bankers Trust—it vouchsafes plaintiff the "most favorable" construction of the complaint. This "generosity" is misleading since it amounts to no more than a disclaimer of liability on grounds that the complaint is drafted in the alternative. There having been no discovery on precisely what happened to the check between November 13 and 20, we are, of course, in no position to express a view as to whether the FRBNY, Bankers Trust, both, or neither violated UCC § 4–202 [R 4–202] in their handling of the check. What we may certainly not do is allow the FRBNY to defeat the complaint by making assumptions that are unsupported by the record and are based solely on inferences drawn from the fact that the complaint is understandably—in light of the absence of discovery—drafted in the alternative. See Fed.R.Civ.P. 8(e)(2) (allowing inconsistent or alternative pleadings).

intended the "notice of dishonor or non-payment" mentioned in UCC § 4–202(1)(b) [R 4–202(a)(2)] to originate with the payor bank; and that, accordingly, the FRBNY was not legally obligated to send the appropriate notice until it received it from Chicago.

The parties' submissions in this regard have amounted to no more than exchanges of unsupported conclusions. Such (necessarily incomplete) review of the UCC's sprawling legislative history as we were able to perform allows us to state that the drafters of the UCC certainly expected that the last bank in the collection chain would be the wellhead of the notification stream down that chain, such expectation being part of generally shared institutional assumptions. A review of the mutations of UCC § 4–202 [R 4–202]—going back to § 712(1) and § 708(1), both entitled "Responsibility for Collection," of the 1948 Proposed Final Drafts Nos. 1 and 2 of Article III, respectively—shows, however, no evidence whatever of an affirmative legislative intention in this connection. There is, in fact, no indication that any thought was given to the situation before us in this case. This is, of course, not at all surprising. The 1981 edition of a respected treatise on the law of check collections does not even mention "MICR fraud"—as this fraud has, appropriately, come to be known—in its sections dealing either with fraud or with the responsibility for losses due to improper encoding. See B. Clarke, The Law of Bank Deposits, Collections & Credit Cards chs. 6 and 10 (rev.ed. 1981). Indeed, the legal problems of loss due to improper encoding, let alone fraud, are of relatively recent vintage. See, e.g., Georgia Railroad Bank & Trust v. First Nat. Bank (1976) 139 Ga.App. 683, 229 S.E.2d 482 (calling itself a case of first impression) (underencoding); State ex rel. Gabalac v. Firestone Bank (1975) 46 Ohio App.2d 124, 346 N.E.2d 326 (overencoding). What we have, therefore, is a statute, UCC § 4–202(1)(b) [R 4–202(a)(2)], which—on the basis of the parties' submissions and our own research—cannot fairly be said to have been drafted in contemplation of the facts in this case. The question, then, is whether it should be interpreted to cover the situation at hand. We think it should.

Certain observations are in order concerning Article IV in general and UCC § 4–202 [R 4–202] in particular. The history of the UCC makes it abundantly clear that, especially in the context of those provisions which impose a duty of care, the Code's watchword is "flexibility." It is well known that banks' early opposition to what is now Article IV could be traced in considerable measure to the fear that the possibility of any conduct not complying with procedures affirmatively approved would be found to constitute a violation of the obligation of care. See, generally, W. Malcolm, Article 4—A Battle with Complexity, 1952 Wisc.L.Rev. 265, 280–83 (1952). The Final Text Edition of 1951 crystallized UCC § 4–103(3) [R 4–103(c)] and § 4–103(4) [R 4–103(d)] which clearly established that approval of certain procedures did not constitute disapproval of other procedures found reasonable in light of sound banking practice. See also UCC § 4–103 [R 4–103] comment 5. This observation leads to two conclusions. First, there being no mechanical test for what constitutes ordinary care in a novel situation, the ultimate standard is dictated by the imperatives of sound banking practice, seasoned by the obligation of good faith. See UCC § 1–201(19).[22] Second, flexibility is a two way street: just as a new task or procedure will certainly be acceptable if it reflects sound banking practice, so the lack of one—when such absence violates sound banking practice—should be actionable.

Concerning UCC § 4–202 [R 4–202] in particular, there are strong indications that the tasks described in UCC § 4–202(1) [R 4–202(a)] (a)[(1)] through (e)[(4)] are not an exhaustive list of the actions to be taken by a collecting bank in order to satisfy its obligation of ordinary care. See UCC § 4–202 [R 4–202] comment 1 (the section described "basic" responsibilities); comment 3 (the section describes "types" of "basic" actions); comment 4 ("ordinary care" is used in its "normal tort meaning" and "[n]o attempt is made * * * to define in toto what constitutes ordinary care or lack of it"). This leads to the further conclusion that the enumeration in UCC § 4–202(1) [R 4–202(a)] (a)[(1)] through (e)[(4)] should not be deemed—by negative implication—a bar to the reinterpretation (or expansion) of the duties owed by a bank in discharging its collection function with "ordinary care."

With the foregoing in mind the specific question before us is: What should be considered good banking practice in a situation where it comes to a banker's attention that the routing code on a check is inconsistent with the address on the face of the item? If day-to-day banking experience should demonstrate that such inconsistencies are usually the result of simple error, there would be no reason to assume that a conscientious banker should become alarmed at learning of an inconsistency or deem it his duty to notify anyone.[23] On the other hand, if day-to-day banking experience should establish that such

22. The same lesson can be learned when tracing the vicissitudes of what eventually became the standard of "ordinary care" in the Final Text Edition of 1951. Earlier a myriad of formulations had been attempted: § 731(1) of the 1948 Draft uses "proper handling"; the 1949 Edition of the UCC variously used terms like "diligence," § 3–614(2), "[lack of] negligence," § 3–614(3), "improper handling," § 3–616 and § 3–617(2); in the 1950 draft "improper handling" was again used, § 4–306, as was "diligence," § 4–312, and "negligence," § 4–103; the Spring 1951 draft even attempted a definition of "improper handling," § 4–103(2), and added "carelessness" to the repertoire, § 4–103(1)(a). Eventually, this process was abandoned in the 1951 Final Text Edition in favor of the pragmatic language of the A.B.A. Collection Code—"failure to exercise ordinary care"—which was thereafter consistently used. And in the A.B.A. Code it is sound banking practice which, ultimately, defines what is "ordinary care." See also N.Y.Law Revision Comm., Study of Unif.Com.Code Article 4 at 92 (Leg.Doc. No. 65(E), 1955).

23. The existence of footnote 3 to 12 C.F.R. § 210.6(a) (1979), currently codified at 12 C.F.R. § 210.6(a)(2) (1983), may well be persuasive evidence that this is, in fact, the actual state of affairs. This provision absolves the Federal Reserve from liability for routing an item according to any addressing symbol that may appear on it. Although the parties have submitted nothing to clarify the background of this regulation, its very existence may indicate that inconsistencies in routing symbols are often to be found, without thereby suggesting the possibility of fraud. We observe, moreover, that footnote 3 has—in our view—no other direct bearing on the FRBNY's obligation to notify. On its face that footnote appears to deal only with the potential claims that may be raised under UCC § 4–204 [R 4–204] which prescribes due care in routing an item.

inconsistencies are usually an indication of fraud,[24] then it might well be argued that a collecting bank, in satisfying its obligation of ordinary care, should take steps promptly to notify a prospective victim in the collection chain.[25]

If there is a policy implicit in the UCC's rules for the allocation of losses due to fraud, it surely is that the loss be placed on the party in the best position to prevent it. See B. Clarke, The Law of Bank Deposits, Collections & Credit Cards, ¶ 6.1 (1981).[26] At oral argument we suggested that plaintiff should be made to bear—on policy grounds—full responsibility for this loss. It is, after all, a bank's business to make certain that it doesn't deal with crooks.[27] On further reflection, however, we are not prepared to say that no share [28] of the

24. This form of fraud is not nearly as uncommon as defendant seems to suggest. At oral argument it developed that there is an aggregate of some $2 million of such fraud in the early stages of litigation. Tr. at 45–46. In the last few months we have had before us a criminal case involving precisely this scheme.

25. Defendant argues that if it were required to do so—in the absence of notification from a payor bank—it might be liable to an innocent drawer for misrepresentation or liable if the items later turned out to be properly payable. This argument is frivolous: all a collecting bank would be required to do is to tell the truth; namely, that there is an inconsistency in routing symbols and that the item, pursuant to 12 C.F.R. § 210.6(a)(2) (1983), is being forwarded elsewhere for further attempts at collection. It would be up to the depositary bank to draw its own inference in light of its experience with the customer involved. Moreover, the requirement of notification would place no undue burden on the collecting bank. All that would be required would be routine instructions that such disparity be automatically referred to a given individual whose automatic duty it would be to notify the depositary bank.

26. This policy can be illustrated by the well-known rule that the loss falls on a forger's immediate transferee. See UCC §§ 3–417(2)(a) [R 3–416], 4–207(2)(a) [R 4–207], 3–414(1) [R 3–415(a) and (b)], and 4–212(1) [R 4–214(a)]. Even the exceptions to the rule further illustrate that policy. For example, the so-called rule of Price v. Neal establishes that a drawee bank paying over a forged signature (not endorsement) bears the risk of loss, on the assumption, see UCC § 3–417 comment 3, that it could have verified the genuineness of its client's signature. See UCC §§ 3–418 [R 3–418], 3–417(1)(b) [R 3–417], and 4–207(1)(b) [R 4–208] (collectively denying recovery against innocent payee); §§ 3–401(1) [R 3–401(a)] and 3–404(1) [R 3–403(a)] (denying recovery against client). See also UCC § 3–406 [R 3–406] (exception to the rule of Price v. Neal when a drawer's fault contributes to loss); UCC § 3–405(1)(b) [R 3–404(b)(i)] and (c) [R 3–405] (rule of the "fictitious payee"); UCC § 3–405 comment 4.

27. Plaintiff's counsel seemed at a loss to suggest what, precisely, his client could have done to prevent this scheme. It could, of course, have placed a longer "hold" on the availability of funds; we know of no Texas or federal statute requiring that funds from transit items be available to clients in 14 days. See Wertling v. Manufacturers Hanover Trust Co., supra, 118 Misc.2d 722, 461 N.Y.S.2d at 160. But cf. Ch. 234, Section 1, 1983 N.Y.Laws 438 (McKinney) (to be codified at N.Y.Banking Law § 14–d) (allowing the banking board to prescribe "reasonable" time period for the availability of proceeds from items deposited for collection). The question, however, is not what plaintiff could have done in this case but who (in the collection chain) is, generally, in the best position to prevent the fraud. He who deals with a malefactor must certainly be charged with the responsibility of discovering the fraud—nobody else in the collection chain can do better. As a matter of policy, moreover, the depositary bank is in the best position to distribute the risk over its client base through insurance. See, generally, E.A. Farnsworth, Insurance Against Check Forgery, 60 Colum.L.Rev. 284, 302–03 (1960).

28. The recovery rules of the UCC are "all-or-nothing" schemes and they do not appear, insofar as we are aware, to sanction the notion of "comparative" fault. But neither does the UCC explicitly disavow it. See UCC § 1–103.

loss should be placed—on policy grounds—on a collecting bank which might be shown to have known (or to be on notice) that fraud was afoot and did nothing to stop it, although it had the "last clear chance" to do so. However, on the record before us no facts are pleaded—let alone proved—which would shed any light on whether inconsistency between the routing code and the address on the face of the item could reasonably be regarded as a mere mistake or should alert any knowledgeable banker to the probability of fraud.

CONCLUSION

The claims based on UCC §§ 4–202(1)(a) [R 4–202(a)(1)] and 4–202(1)(b) [R 4–202(a)(2)] are, accordingly, held to be legally viable. The plaintiff may, if it be so advised, amend its complaint to allege facts suggesting that routing code inconsistency should be regarded as indicating the probability of fraud; and may conduct appropriate discovery on that issue. The remaining claims against the FRBNY are dismissed for failure to state a cause of action.

So ordered.

UNITED STATES FIDELITY AND GUARANTY COMPANY v. THE FEDERAL RESERVE BANK OF NEW YORK

United States District Court, Southern District of New York, 1985.
620 F.Supp. 361.

HAIGHT, DISTRICT JUDGE:

Plaintiff Union Trust Company of Maryland ("Union Trust") and its insurer, United States Fidelity and Guaranty Company, brought this action to recover damages caused by a clever check fraud perpetrated upon Union Trust by a nonparty.

* * *

I.

As described more fully in USF & G I, 590 F.Supp. at 489–91, Union Trust was fraudulently induced to permit a depositor to withdraw funds against a worthless check. In April 1980, a man who called himself Marvin Goldstein established a checking account with Union Trust. Soon after, he deposited a check for over $880,000 in the account. The account upon which the check purported to be drawn did not exist, but a clever manipulation of the numerals on the face of the check caused it to be routed among a number of New York and Pennsylvania banks before being returned to Union Trust as uncollectible. In the meantime, Union Trust had permitted Goldstein to withdraw a substantial amount of cash from his account, having assumed from the lapse of time that the check had been paid.[2] The foregoing

2. As explained in USF & G I, 590 F.Supp. at 489, familiarity with which is assumed throughout this decision, this would ordinarily have been an entirely le-

information was pleaded in the original complaint, and discovery has confirmed its accuracy. The interesting details unearthed in discovery primarily concern not the behavior of the defendant banks in routing the bogus check but that of Union Trust's employees in accepting it and releasing funds against it. A summary of that new information follows.

On April 16, 1980, Goldstein walked into a Baltimore branch of Union Trust. He told the branch manager, John Gemmill, that he and his father were precious metals dealers and that he planned to establish a Baltimore office of his father's New York business, Goldstein Precious Metals and Stones. In preparation, he sought to open a checking account with Union Trust in the name of the business. In opening the account, Goldstein produced one piece of personal identification, a New Jersey driver's license, and a New York certificate of business proprietorship, and supplied a New York bank reference. Gemmill recorded this and other information on a "New Account Information Form." Goldstein opened the new account with a cash deposit of $15,000.

Gemmill then turned the new account form over to assistant branch manager John Clement with instructions to prepare two signature cards. Clement did so, but he unaccountably neglected to transcribe the bank reference from the new account form to the signature cards. The form and one card were then sent to central Union Trust files, while one card was retained at the local branch.

One week later, Goldstein returned to the branch and withdrew $14,000 from his account, reducing his balance to $1,000. Little was heard from him until May 6, when he deposited a check for $880,000 at a second Union Trust branch located a few blocks from the branch with which he had opened the account. Deposit of such a large check ordinarily triggers self-protective internal alerts at a bank, and Union Trust was no exception. Tellers who received for deposit checks over $100,000 were supposed to notify the branch manager, according to written Union Trust procedural guidelines. The manager was then to decide whether a "hold" should be placed on the check—that is, whether the depositor should be denied access to the deposited funds for an extended period of time in order to permit the bank to confirm the collectibility of the check. In the absence of such a hold, funds ordinarily become available to the depositor within one to two days of deposit of the check. The teller who accepted Goldstein's check, however, neither notified bank officers of the large deposit nor placed a hold on it.

The teller, however, was merely the bank's first line of defense against fraud. During the next few days, Gemmill, the branch manager, was reviewing a document known as a "balance fluctuation report," designed to alert bank officers to unusually large balance changes in the accounts under their supervision. The leap in the Goldstein Pre-

gitimate assumption; indeed, it is an assumption made thousands of times daily by every bank in the nation without adverse consequences.

cious Metals account balance from one thousand to nearly a million dollars naturally caught his attention, and he decided to investigate. Gemmill first requested, or had Clement request, credit reports on the Goldstein business from two national credit reporting services. Both services reported that they had no record of Goldstein Precious Metals and Stones. Upon receiving this information, Gemmill had Clement retrieve the Goldstein signature card in order to pursue the credit references which would ordinarily be listed on it. Because Clement had neglected to transfer the reference from the account form, however, the signature card was no help, and neither bank employee pursued this further.[3]

Wisely, Gemmill instructed Clement to look into the $880,000 check. The check was drawn on an account at First Penn of a company called Metropolitan Investment Corporation. On instructions from Clement, an employee of Union Trust's credit department called officials at First Penn and was told that no such account existed. First Penn had no banking relationship with Metropolitan Investment Corporation. This information was relayed to Clement, who told Gemmill. All of the foregoing occurred on or before Friday, May 9, within four days of the check's May 6 deposit.

According to his deposition testimony, Gemmill, who was leaving for vacation on May 9, told Clement to report to senior bank officers any activity in the Goldstein account, perhaps recognizing that the First Penn report made it unlikely that the Goldstein check would be honored. Clement remembers no such instructions. Either way, no other action was taken at that time to prevent Goldstein from withdrawing funds against the check.

On Monday, May 12, Gemmill was temporarily replaced by another bank officer. The next day, Goldstein telephoned Clement to ask instructions for making a "wire transfer" of funds, that is, for arranging the automatic transfer of funds from his account to an account in another bank. When Goldstein arrived at the branch to arrange for the transfer, he presented Clement with a bottle of expensive champagne. They discussed arrangements for the transfer, and Clement told him that the bank could only wire "collected" balances, that is, could only wire funds from the check after a sufficient time had passed to permit the bank to conclude that the check had been paid.[4] Apparently Goldstein was willing to wait. No further action was taken on Tuesday.

3. According to an affidavit filed by New York Fed, the New York bank reference, if contacted, would have reported no history of dealings with the Goldstein company.

4. As explained in USF & G I, 590 F.Supp. at 489, banks are never actually notified when a check which has been deposited with them is paid by, or "clears," the payor bank. Instead, they are only told if it fails to clear. Therefore, before releasing funds against a suspect check, banks commonly hold the check for the number of days which experience has taught them will be required for the check to reach the payor bank and for that bank to inform them if the check is uncollectible. If no word arrives in this time, it is assumed that the check has been paid.

Two days later, on Thursday, May 15, seven business days after deposit of the check, Goldstein returned and sought both to effect a wire transfer of $660,000 and to withdraw $95,000 in cash. The wire transfer was to be made to the account of a Maryland coin dealer. Apparently concluding that sufficient time had passed, Clement undertook to make the wire transfer. His first step was to check the Union Trust computer to find out whether sufficient funds were available in Goldstein's account to satisfy the transfer request. Because this act was crucial to the success of the fraud, it must be examined in some detail.

As explained in note 4, supra, banks are never notified when checks deposited with them are paid by the payor bank. The large volume of checks in the banking system would make any such notification system expensive and unwieldy. If payment is refused, however, the payor bank must notify the depositary bank of the refusal within roughly twenty-four hours of its receipt of the check. See N.Y.U.C.C. § 4–302 [R 4–302]. In order to protect themselves against uncollectible checks, banks commonly guess at the amount of time the check is likely to spend in the collection system before reaching the payor bank and place a hold on the deposited check for at least that amount of time. Union Trust's computer was charged with keeping track of such holds.

The Union Trust computer apparently registered two types of holds. When a check was deposited into a checking account such as Goldstein's, the Union Trust computer automatically placed a one- or two-day hold on the deposited check. These holds were keyed to the Federal Reserve clearing system. Member banks of the Federal Reserve system keep accounts with their local Federal Reserve bank. One of the functions of these accounts is to permit the Reserve bank to credit and debit member banks for checks cleared through the Reserve bank. Banks are ordinarily not given immediate credit for or access to the funds represented by checks such as that deposited with Union Trust by Goldstein.[5] In other words, regardless of whether a depositary bank gives its depositor immediate access to the funds represented by a deposited check, the Federal Reserve will not, in most instances, give the bank immediate credit for the check in the account which the bank maintains with the Reserve bank. Instead, the Reserve bank credits the check to a one- or two-day deferred account, equivalent to placing a hold on the check, with the length of the deferral depending primarily upon the distance the check must travel to reach the payor bank. Once the deferral period elapses, the Reserve bank grants the depositary bank a provisional credit for the amount of the check.

In reality, however, checks frequently do not clear in the one- or two-day time period allotted for this purpose by the Federal Reserve. The provisional status of the credit given by the Reserve bank signifies

5. There are a few exceptions to this rule of delayed availability—checks drawn on the United States Treasury, for example, are immediately credited to the depositary bank—but they are not relevant here.

that although a credit has been given to the account of the depositary bank, no corresponding debit has been made in the account of the payor bank. Once the payor bank receives the check, it must notify the Reserve bank within twenty-four hours whether it will honor the check. If the Reserve bank is notified that the check has been honored, it debits the account of the payor bank and removes the provisional status of the credit given the depositary bank.

The Union Trust computer automatically placed the equivalent of a hold on all deposited checks corresponding to the length of the deferral imposed by the Federal Reserve. The duration of Reserve system deferrals were never intended, however, to estimate or correspond precisely to the actual clearing time of a check. On the contrary, they intentionally underestimate this time. For that reason, as suggested above, banks frequently place their own extended hold on checks which are not likely to clear within one or two days. This prevents the depositor from withdrawing funds until the bank has satisfied itself that no word of dishonor has arrived or, in theory, will arrive. Such holds could also be recorded on the Union Trust computer, but they were not imposed automatically.

As noted above, no such hold was placed on the Goldstein check. The only hold in the Union Trust computer was a two-day Federal Reserve hold, which expired several days before May 15. Therefore, when Clement checked, he found no hold on the Goldstein funds. This, of course, did not indicate that the Goldstein check had been paid. It simply indicated that whatever precautions Union Trust had taken against premature withdrawal had expired, and the check had not been returned. Clement called the bookkeeping department of the bank, which confirmed that no hold was in effect—in other words, that, according to the bank's computer, the funds from the check were available for withdrawal.

Apparently misunderstanding the nature of the information supplied by the computer, Clement, according to his deposition testimony, concluded from his computerized inquiry not only that all holds had expired but that the check had actually cleared. Although he was aware of the First Penn report that no account existed against which the check could possibly have been drawn, he concluded that the report must have been incorrect. Without checking once again with First Penn, he authorized the wire transfer and the cash withdrawal.

Goldstein picked up the cash in person on May 15. The wire transfer was made to the bank of the Maryland coin dealer the same day. The dealer, however, had insufficient coins on hand to satisfy Goldstein's order. The dealer gave Goldstein the coins available on May 15; the remainder were delivered to him in mid-afternoon the following day. Goldstein thereafter disappeared with the cash and coins.

At about the same time Goldstein was receiving his coins on May 16, a Union Trust Vice President was informed that First Penn was returning the $880,000 check. Only later was it discovered that the Goldstein check was a fraud. The numbers printed in magnetic ink at the bottom of the check and the routing number, printed in ordinary ink in the top right hand corner, did not match, a circumstance which caused the check to be routed to several banks over several days before arriving at First Penn. It is now possible to describe the circumstances surrounding the routing of the check in more detail.

Union Trust's central check processing facility attempted to computer-process the check on May 6, the day of deposit. This machine rejected the check because the magnetic ink character recognition number ("MICR number") was not printed in magnetic ink and was the wrong size, necessitating hand processing.[8] At that time all of Union Trust's non-local checks which required hand processing were sent to PNB for processing and collection. The Goldstein check was accordingly dispatched to PNB in the early morning of May 7; because of its great value, it was sent by courier.

Based on the check's routing number, it was sent by PNB to a New York Fed processing center in Utica, New York, for forwarding to Albany State. Albany State received the check on the morning of May 9 and returned it to the Utica center of New York Fed, stamped "Sent in Error," on May 12.[9] The next day the Utica center sent the check to New York Fed's New York City office.

Despite irregularities in the check described as "glaring" by a New York Fed chief of operations, that office failed to detect the fraudulent nature of the check. Instead, on May 14, New York Fed sent the check to the Federal Reserve Bank of Philadelphia. A document accompanying the check indicated that New York Fed intended the check to be

8. It is interesting to note that Goldstein's technique of printing an improper MICR number has been used in other types of fraud. According to published reports, the scheme which resulted in the well-publicized May, 1985, conviction for fraud of the brokerage firm of E.F. Hutton & Co. also used improperly printed checks. Hutton had checks printed with incorrect MICR numbers to foil its banks' computer-aided check-processing machines, thereby lengthening the time needed for processing the checks and increasing Hutton's "float," or amount of funds on deposit by checks which have not yet been collected from the payor bank. Hutton deposited the flawed checks drawn on its own accounts at various banks in its accounts at other banks. Until the checks were paid by the former banks, Hutton received payment for use of the funds by both banks at once. The longer the time required to process the check, the greater the "double" payments Hutton received. This was where the incorrect MICR numbers came in handy. See Bleakley, How Hutton Scheme Worked, N.Y. Times, May 17, 1985, at D4, cols. 2–4.

9. In USF & G I one issue was whether New York Fed had a regulatory duty to "wire advice" to Union Trust of this return. 590 F.Supp. at 492–94. I concluded that New York Fed had no duty to originate such advice but only to forward wire advice given to it. 590 F.Supp. at 493–94. Albany State now claims that it did wire advice. On the basis of this allegation, which New York Fed denies, plaintiffs move to amend to assert New York Fed's failure to forward the advice. See USF & G I, 590 F.Supp. at 494. I deny the motion. Plaintiffs have adduced no evidence in support of their claim that Albany State wired advice. There is only the bank's bare allegation. Therefore, the condition set out for amendment in USF & G I, 590 F.Supp. at 494, that "discovery [has] reveal[ed] that New York Fed did indeed receive wire advice" has not been fulfilled. Discovery revealed no evidence one way or the other as to wire advice.

presented for collection to First Penn rather than returned to PNB as an unpaid item. The Philadelphia Reserve bank presented the check to First Penn at 9:00 a.m. on the same day it received it, May 14. At this time, it must be remembered, Goldstein had not yet been permitted to withdraw any funds against the check by Union Trust.

If First Penn was going to dishonor the Goldstein check, it was required by the U.C.C. to notify PNB of this fact by midnight of May 15. It did not. Instead, processing of the check was not completed until 9:45 a.m. on the morning of May 16, when First Penn finally notified PNB of the dishonor. At this point it was still not too late to recover the fraudulently gained funds, for the second shipment of gold coins had not yet been made to Goldstein. Quick action might have caught him. Quick action, however, was not forthcoming. PNB did not pass word of the dishonor to Union Trust until mid-afternoon of May 16, too late to prevent Goldstein from slipping away. He has never been located.

II.

Albany State and the three defendant banks all move for summary judgment on plaintiffs' claims. Each is in a somewhat different factual posture, and each accordingly raises somewhat different legal issues. Overhanging all of the arguments, however, is the issue of the effect of Union Trust's behavior in its dealings with Goldstein. It cannot be contended that Union Trust's behavior was anything but reckless. Gemmill opened an account with a man who presented only one form of personal identification, an out-of-state driver's license. Whether or not this alone was poor commercial practice, it placed particular importance on the bank reference which he provided, for the reference was Union Trust's only independent means of confirming Goldstein's identity. Yet Clement left the reference off the signature card, and neither man made an effort to track it down when it was needed. In addition, the teller who accepted the check for deposit did so without presenting it to a branch manager, in breach of bank regulations.[12] This failure was particularly serious, for it deprived the banking system of its one opportunity for the check to be examined by an experienced professional who was unhurried by time pressures and simultaneously had access to information about the depositor. The most astounding act of carelessness, however, was the bank's release of funds against a check which it had been told was drawn on a nonexistent account. Such an act was more than mere negligence, for it entailed acting in the face of a known and obvious risk. Viewed in its entirety, Union Trust's conduct was breathtakingly foolhardy; nay, commercially suicidal.[13]

12. In retrospect, the teller's failure to place a hold on the check, while poor practice, was of less consequence. Union Trust's standard, and apparently proper, hold for a check drawn on a Pennsylvania bank was five to six days. Since Goldstein withdrew funds on the seventh day, the hold would not have prevented execution of his scheme.

13. This is not the whole of the bank's carelessness. First, discovery revealed that after being rejected by the automatic sorting machinery the check was examined by a Union Trust supervisor, but this su-

New York Fed argues, with backing from Albany State, that such almost incomprehensible conduct should act as a bar to any recovery based on the dramatically lesser negligence of other banks in the check's chain of collection.

A.

In understanding this claim, it is helpful to review the basis of New York Fed's alleged liability. Section 4–202(1) [R 4–202(a)] of the U.C.C. imposes upon all banks which handle checks sent for collection a duty of ordinary care both in forwarding checks for collection and in returning checks deemed uncollectible. Care must be exercised both in the promptness of action and in the choice of action. Timing is handled by the "midnight deadline" rule; banks exercise care in the timing of an action by responding, generally, before midnight of the business day following the day on which the check is received. N.Y.U.C.C. §§ 4–104 [R 4–104] and 4–202(2) [R 4–202(b)]. The proper choice of action cannot be so easily codified and is governed by a general rule of reasonableness borrowed from tort law. USF & G I, 590 F.Supp. at 491–92. This is the duty New York Fed is accused of failing to satisfy.

At the time of USF & G I, the lack of discovery made it impossible to define precisely New York Fed's alleged breach of care, since its exact actions were then unknown. It now appears that plaintiffs' claim is twofold: that New York Fed should have, in the exercise of ordinary care, either 1) recognized the risk of fraud inherent in the check and sent it for return to PNB rather than collection from First Penn or 2) recognized that the routing of the check to Albany State caused a significant risk that Union Trust would release funds before the check cleared and sent wire notice to Union Trust or PNB that the check had taken the long route to First Penn. Union Trust argues that these actions would have permitted it either to prevent the fraud or to catch Goldstein before he absconded with the cash and coins.

It is by no means a foregone conclusion that New York Fed's failure to take these actions, given the realities of modern check processing, was negligent. USF & G I, 590 F.Supp. at 499. On the other hand, as discussed above, Union Trust's recklessness was gross and obvious. New York Fed argues, on several grounds, that the tenuous nature of its alleged negligence should not serve as a basis for recovery in the face of Union Trust's conduct.

The primary difficulty with defendant's theory is that it is not expressly sanctioned by the UCC. Plaintiffs' suit is for violation of a duty imposed in the first instance by the UCC, and it is to that body of law which resort must first be had to determine the rights and liabilities of the parties. Although the UCC in some specific circum-

pervisor failed to detect the "glaring" facial irregularities in the check and instead forwarded it to PNB. Second, Clement's wire transfer of $660,000 exceeded the amount of money he was authorized by bank regulations to transfer. Third, several of Goldstein's actions known to Clement labelled him as "shady," including his transparent attempt at a bribe and his request that the money be wired to a coin dealer, who presumably would convert the funds into highly liquid assets.

stances apportions liability on the basis of relative fault—most notably in the law of forged signatures and endorsements, it incorporates no general rule of comparative or contributory negligence. In the area with which we are concerned, check collection, the Code imposes upon collecting banks a duty of due care and subjects them to "but for" liability for violations of the duty. There is no express requirement that the plaintiff demonstrate its own due care as a prerequisite to recovery, nor is there any mention of comparative negligence.[14] There is simply no mention of the effect, if any, of a plaintiff's negligence on its recovery under § 4–202(1) [R 4–202(a)].

The question cannot be permitted to end there, however. Article 4 of the Code, governing check collection, was developed in the 1950s, prior to the advent of large scale fraud upon the check collection system. The rules of liability which govern the allocation of losses arising from check transit were not—could not have been—designed with such fraud in mind. In these circumstances, to adhere blindly to the limitations imposed by those rules, if to do so would violate the policies which the UCC otherwise seeks to promote, would be unwise and unjust. Nor does the Code demand such adherence. As Judge Knapp noted in his seminal Northpark decision, "the history of the UCC makes it abundantly clear that, especially in the context of those provisions which impose a duty of care, the Code's watchword is 'flexibility.' " I do not, therefore, find the lack of a rule of contributory or comparative negligence in Article 4 to be an insuperable barrier to defendants' claim that such a rule should be imposed. Rather, the decision turns upon whether to do so would, on the one hand, be consistent with the aims of § 4–202(1) [R 4–202(a)] and Article 4 as a whole and, on the other, would promote the policies which animate the rules of liability found elsewhere in the Code.

B.

In making its claim, New York Fed argues primarily by analogy to tort law. Because, the argument goes, the ordinary care standard of § 4–202(1) [R 4–202(a)] is borrowed from tort law, tort principles of comparative or contributory negligence should apply. As plaintiffs point out, however, this is not a tort case. The standard of care, though reliant on a concept borrowed from tort law, is imposed by the UCC. In allegedly violating § 4–202(1) [R 4–202(a)], defendants did not breach a duty imposed by tort law; they breached a duty imposed by statute, the UCC. It is the policies served by the UCC, therefore, rather than those served by tort law, which must determine whether plaintiffs' negligence should affect its recovery under § 4–202(1) [R 4–202(a)]. Because, as discussed below, the aims of tort law are not identical with those of the UCC, I decline to borrow the tort rule.

14. The latter is not surprising. The UCC predated the widespread acceptance of comparative negligence of the 1970s. More important, the concept of comparative negligence is anathema to a code which had as a primary aim the fostering of swift resolution of disputes through the clear delineation of commercial liabilities. See Perini Corp. v. First National Bank of Habersham County, 553 F.2d 398, 405 (5th Cir.1977).

Tort law is designed primarily to apportion loss. Because it is typically imposed upon lay parties with little or no appreciation of its finer points, only secondarily can it hope to guide behavior so as to minimize harm. Rather, it most often becomes relevant only after the fact; the courts are asked to decide who must bear or respond for a loss previously incurred, and to what degree. As such, its guiding principle is fairness. In tort law courts have equated fairness with fault. The rule of comparative negligence is a perfect expression of this principle.

The UCC, however, was designed to facilitate commerce primarily by guiding and making predictable the consequences of behavior. It is imposed primarily upon a comparatively sophisticated group, businessmen and bankers, who look to its provisions to direct their business transactions. This is not to overlook its loss allocation function. Rules designed to guide behavior are inevitably turned against those who fail to follow them, and even the most carefully planned transactions may end in dispute. This function, however, is secondary to the creation of a system of rules to bring order and predictability to commercial transactions.

Interestingly, this fact is forcefully demonstrated by a series of provisions in the Code which were designed, unlike the bulk of the Code, to distribute loss. Several provisions of Article 3 determine which party must bear loss which results from the use of a forged signature or endorsement on a negotiable instrument. Tort law would ordinarily distribute such a loss on the basis of fault: that party or parties whose carelessness resulted in the forgery would bear the consequences of it. The UCC, however, for the most part does not look at actual fault.[15] Instead, it places responsibility on the party which ordinarily would be in the best position to prevent the loss.[16] See Northpark, supra, 572 F.Supp. at 535 and n. 26; Underpinning & Foundation Constructors, Inc. v. Chase Manhattan Bank, N.A., 46 N.Y.2d 459, 468, 414 N.Y.S.2d 298, 302, 386 N.E.2d 1319 (1979). Such a result accomplishes two purposes: first, it increases the efficiency and fraud-resistance of the banking system by placing upon those best able to guard against it the responsibility for preventing fraud,[17] and, second, it speeds the resolution of disputes by establishing clear rules of liability which do not depend heavily upon the specific facts of individu-

15. The exception, discussed infra, is UCC § 3–406 [R 3–406].

16. In most cases, loss falls on the forger's immediate transferee. N.Y.U.C.C. §§ 3–417(2)(a) [R 3–416], 4–207(2)(a) [R 4–207(a)(2)], 3–414(1) [R 3–415(a) and (b)], and 4–212(1) [R 4–214(a)]. However, when a check is paid over a forged signature, loss is placed upon the drawee bank, which in theory could have checked its client's signature. N.Y.U.C.C. § 3–417, comment 3. See generally, Northpark, supra, 572 F.Supp. at 535 n. 26.

17. Because such parties are generally commercial banks, they are presumed to be aware of the UCC's rules of liability and to take precautions to guard against forgeries. The rule of absolute liability regardless of fault would, one would think, tend to increase their efforts at protecting against forgeries, since to avoid liability they would be forced to guard against not only their own carelessness but the carelessness and deviousness of others. In theory, by placing this burden upon the shoulders of those best able to guard against fraud the UCC achieves such fraud resistance in the most efficient manner.

al instances of fraud. See Perini Corp. v. First National Bank, 553 F.2d 398, 405–06 (5th Cir.1977) (describing this policy as promoting "finality"). Therefore, while the purpose of these rules is, as with tort law, to apportion loss, they are guided not by the policy which guides tort loss apportionment—fairness in the circumstances—but by the policies which shape the UCC—the promotion of efficient and predictable commerce.

Because tort law and the UCC are designed to serve different ends, I find it inappropriate to borrow a rule of comparative or contributory negligence from tort law for use in the UCC. Nevertheless, the question remains open whether such a rule should be implied from within the UCC itself.

C.

The policies which underlie the UCC were explored above. As relevant here, they were usefully summed up by Judge Knapp in Northpark: "[i]f there is a policy implicit in the UCC's rules for the allocation of losses due to fraud, it is surely that the loss be placed on the party in the best position to prevent it." 572 F.Supp. at 535. See similarly, Leigh Co. v. Bank of New York, 617 F.Supp. 147 (S.D.N.Y. 1985), at 151. These rules are most elaborately developed in connection with the law of forged endorsements and signatures. Liabilities for forgeries are assigned in the first instance without regard to fault. Instead, as noted above, the drafters placed liability upon the party which they determined would typically be best situated to prevent a particular type of forgery.

Creation of this type of rule is essentially a legislative task, outside the scope of the proper exercise of judicial power. Even assuming that courts are competent to determine which party most commonly can prevent a particular type of forgery, the decision whether to assign liability to that party in all circumstances, without regard to fault, is best left to the legislature. This is particularly true where, as here, the legislature has already undertaken to create a complex network of laws in the area. For that reason, I rejected in USF & G I New York Fed's request that I create such a rule, on grounds of public policy, assigning strict liability for MICR fraud to depositary banks. 590 F.Supp. at 500 and n. 23.

Nor is it particularly clear that depositary banks are best situated in all, or even most, cases to detect MICR fraud. If such fraud is carried out with more sophistication than demonstrated by Goldstein, the deposit and collection of funds may escape the notice of even a careful bank. In such cases, the bank best situated to detect the fraud might be the first bank to refuse payment, Albany State in this case. That bank would be the first with concrete knowledge that the check is flawed.[18] On the other hand, the fraud could not be confirmed until the

18. It appears that the first banks in the collection chain, Union Trust, PNB, and New York Fed here, would not automatically be suspicious of a check bearing a routing number inconsistent with its listed name of the payor bank. According to

check has been examined by the purported payor. Which of these banks should be assigned liability under all circumstances, if any of them should, is a choice I declined and decline to make.

If such legislative assignments of strict liability comprised the whole of the UCC's system for distributing loss due to forgeries, it might properly be concluded that the concept of contributory or comparative negligence had no role to play within the UCC. However, all rules governing liability for forged signatures are subject to the following provision, which incorporate what is, in effect, a rule of contributory negligence: Any person who by his negligence substantially contributes to a material alteration of the instrument or to the making of an unauthorized signature is precluded from asserting the alteration or lack of authority against a holder in due course or against a drawee or other payor who pays the instrument in good faith and in accordance with the reasonable commercial standards of the drawee's or payor's business. N.Y.U.C.C. § 3–406 [R 3–406].[19]

Section 3–406 [R 3–406] is consistent with the remainder of the Code. It places a burden of due care on a person well situated to prevent a forgery: the drawer of the check. Drawers are forced to draw their checks so as to prevent alterations and to safeguard their blank checks so as to prevent their falling into unauthorized hands.[20]

While § 3–406 [R 3–406] does not directly apply to the case at bar, I am persuaded that it is appropriate to apply its spirit by analogy to apportionment of loss due to MICR fraud. The depositary bank, like the drawer of the check, is well situated to protect the system against MICR fraud. The depositary bank has an opportunity to examine the check free of the time pressures which prevent collecting banks from giving checks more than a cursory glance. Perhaps more important, the depositary bank is in the unique position of being able to examine both the depositor and the check. No other bank in the collecting

the deposition testimony of a Union Trust employee, such checks may be intentionally and properly circulated. They are used, when one bank maintains an account at a second bank. Union Trust, in fact, participated in such an arrangement. On these checks, Union Trust's routing number appeared in the upper right corner of the checks, and the checks were drawn on an account held by Union Trust, but the name of a second bank, Union Trust's customer bank which maintained the account at Union Trust, appeared where one would otherwise have expected Union Trust's name. The employee called such checks "due-from" checks. The Goldstein check, of course, had other irregularities which might have attracted attention: the MICR numbers were neither in magnetic ink nor of the proper size and style, and they were nonsensical. The discrepancy between the Albany State and First Penn designations alone, however, would not automatically have suggested fraud to a collecting bank.

19. A more complex and specific provision, N.Y.U.C.C. § 4–406 [R 4–406], establishes non-exclusive circumstances which constitute per se negligence by checking account customers who are victims of forged signatures.

20. According to the Code, "[t]he most obvious case is that of the drawer who makes use of a signature stamp or other automatic signing device and is negligent in looking after it." N.Y.U.C.C. § 3–406, comment 7. Again, this shows the commercial orientation of the Code; businessmen are warned to watch those with access to signing machines.

chain can examine the depositor, a crucial disadvantage given the seeming difficulty of detecting this type of fraud.

In many cases examination of the depositor and check might well reveal nothing unusual or alarming, in which event the collecting banks will be obliged, to avoid liability, to demonstrate their compliance with § 4–202 [R 4–202]. As this case proves, however, a careful examination of either depositor or check, or both, might well reveal the fraud and protect the banking system. Because the depositary bank is uniquely situated to perform such an examination, it is entirely consistent with the policies served by the UCC to place upon it the duty to do so. Conversely, to refuse to imply such a duty would be equally inconsistent with those policies. It would permit the individual or entity in the best position, at least in those circumstances, to prevent the fraud to evade any duty to do so. Not only would such an approach be inefficient, it could well be, as this case demonstrates, entirely unjust.

Moreover, because only the depositary bank possesses this ability to examine both the depositor and the check, it is appropriate to place upon it the initial burden of care. In the banking system, the depositary bank is the first line of defense against MICR fraud, and the most efficient point at which to take precautions against it. It may properly be prevented from holding other banks liable if it has not adequately fulfilled this role.[22]

I hold that a depositary bank which is a victim of MICR fraud may be precluded from recovering damages from collecting banks under UCC § 4–202(1) [R 4–202(a)] if those banks can demonstrate that the negligence of the depositary bank played a substantial role in the success of the fraud.[23] I have no hesitation in holding that, for the

22. To this extent, this imposed rule differs from § 3–406 [R 3–406], which requires an otherwise liable bank seeking to evade liability to demonstrate not only the drawer's lack of due care but its own exercise of due care. The rules of liability of which § 3–406 [R 3–406] is a part are quite different, however, from § 4–202 [R 4–202]. "Otherwise liable" banks are not liable, as is the case with banks liable under § 4–202 [R 4–202], because of their negligence. They are strictly liable. It is arguably appropriate to require them to demonstrate their own exercise of care before evading the severe standard of strict liability. Further, drawers, who may be made liable under § 3–406 [R 3–406], stand on a much different footing than the banks which would be liable. They are generally individuals and corporations, and the forgeries are presumably carried out without their awareness. Because of this, they do not possess the tools to protect against fraud—for example, the chance to ask a customer for identification or to check a signature card—which the strictly liable banks do. Indeed, it is these tools to protect against forgery which the UCC uses to justify holding those particular banks liable. See Northpark, supra, 572 F.Supp. at n. 26. By contrast, depositary banks under § 4–202(1) [R 4–202(a)] differ from the collecting banks in their ability not only to examine the check but the depositor. They thus have advantage over the collecting banks. It is therefore appropriate to place liability on their shoulders should they fail to exercise due care, even if the collecting banks have also failed to do so.

23. It might be contended that application of comparative negligence would be more fair. The UCC, however, contains no provision for comparative negligence. See Northpark, supra, 572 F.Supp. at n. 28. Even in New York the legislature has left the UCC's all-or-nothing rules alone while statutorily adopting comparative negligence in other areas. See N.Y.Civ.P.L.R. § 1411. Contributory negligence serves

reasons stated previously, it has been demonstrated as a matter of law that the recklessness of Union Trust played a substantial—nay, indispensable—role in the success of this fraud. I grant summary judgment in favor of defendants Albany State, New York Fed, and PNB.

III.

First Penn stands on a somewhat different footing, since it is alleged to be liable not under § 4–202(1) [R 4–202(a)] but § 4–302 [R 4–302]. Section 4–302 [R 4–302] makes a payor bank which fails to return a dishonored check within its midnight deadline liable for resulting damages. It has been repeatedly recognized, however, that § 4–302 [R 4–302] does not shift the burden of loss to a payor bank which misses its deadline if the payee was already aware when presenting the check that it would not be accepted or paid except by mistake. Although Union Trust did not know that the Goldstein check would not be paid when it forwarded the check for collection, it learned long before releasing funds to Goldstein that First Penn had no account from which to pay the check. The same policy reasons which preclude recovery under § 4–302 [R 4–302] by those who forward checks which they have reason to know are uncollectible also argue in favor of precluding Union Trust from recovering. It had reason to know of the uncollectibility of Goldstein's check. Therefore, it can and should be estopped from claiming that at the time it suffered the loss it was not aware that First Penn would refuse the check.

To hold otherwise would be inequitable to First Penn. First Penn informed Union Trust that it had no account relationship with the purported drawer of the check. It should not now be held liable because Union Trust chose to ignore that information and subsequently release funds against the check.

Also relevant is National Savings and Trust Co. v. Park Corp., in which it was held that a bank may recover funds paid by mistake on a bad check unless the plaintiff has changed its position in reliance on the payment. Because Union Trust had been informed before allowing Goldstein to withdraw funds that First Penn would not pay the check, Union Trust may be estopped from claiming that it permitted withdrawal in reliance on First Penn's deemed payment at the expiration of its midnight deadline. Under both lines of authority, First Penn is entitled to summary judgment on plaintiffs' claims.

VI.

For the reasons stated above, all defendants are entitled to summary judgment on plaintiffs' claims. The third-party claims are therefore moot. The Clerk is directed to dismiss both complaints with prejudice.

It is SO ORDERED.

the UCC's aims of efficiency and finality by definitively assigning liability. * * * It would be improper to impose the more tort-oriented comparative negligence in the absence of legislative approval of such a step.

Note

1. What impact, if any, will Reg. CC have on the MICR fraud issue?

> The regulation, by its definition of payor bank, also makes MICR fraud essentially impossible for items over $2,500. Regulation CC section 229.2(z)(3) defines a payor bank as the bank whose routing number appears on the check in magnetic or fractional form, and to whom the check is sent for collection. This definition renders the printed name on the check entirely irrelevant to the determination of which bank is the payor bank in a MICR fraud scheme. The MICR encoded bank will receive the item first, and even though the name of another bank may be printed on the check, the encoded bank will be considered the paying bank. Thus, that bank will be required to expeditiously return the item, or send notice of dishonor. Further, the bank will not forward the check to another bank in an attempt to collect it. Any delay in notice of dishonor sought by the MICR criminal is thus eliminated. In addition, the provision resolves any dispute over which bank is the paying bank for purposes of fixing liability.

Note, *The Expedited Funds Availability Act of 1987: Beyond Toasters and Totally Free Checking,* 67 Wash.U.L.Q. 513, 528 (1989).

2. To appreciate the *Northpark* court's focus on the duty/condition precedent tension in OR 4–212, consider Professor Farnsworth's description of the operation of conditions precedent in the common law of contracts.

> Almost any event can be made a condition. The event may be largely within the control of the obligor, as when the owner of a house conditions the duty to pay for painting the house on the owner's 'honest satisfaction' with the job. It may be largely within the control of the obligee, as when an insurer conditions its duty to pay for loss due to fire on the insured's furnishing proof of loss within 60 days of the loss. It may be largely within the control of a third person, as when a purchaser of a house conditions the promise to go through with the deal on a bank's approval of a mortgage application. Or it may be largely beyond the control of anyone, as when an insurer conditions its duty to pay under a fire insurance policy on damage as a result of fire. Each obligor comes under a duty as soon as the contract is made, but that duty is conditional. The obligor need not render performance until the occurrence of the event on which the obligor's duty is conditioned—the homeowner's honest satisfaction with the paint job, the insured's furnishing of proof of loss, the bank's approval of the mortgage application, or damage as a result of fire.
>
> Although a condition is usually an event of significance to the obligor, this need not be the case. In exercising their freedom of contract the parties are not fettered by any test of materiality or reasonableness. If they agree, they can make even an apparently insignificant event a condition. Their freedom is subject only to the doctrine of unconscionability and a few other constraints discussed in the sections that follow.

> Conditions that are agreed to by the parties, as in the examples given above, are commonly referred to as 'express conditions.' Parties often use language such as 'if,' 'on condition that,' 'provided that,' 'in the event that,' and 'subject to' to make an event a condition, but other words may suffice. For example, a party may condition a duty to pay on the sufficiency of a particular fund or source, by providing that payment is to be made only from that fund or source. A court determines whether an agreement makes an event a condition by the process of interpretation.
>
> Even if the agreement does not make an event a condition, the court may supply a term that does so. Thus, if an obligor's duty cannot be performed without some act by the obligee, such as giving notice to the obligor, the court will supply a term making that act a condition of the obligor's duty. Such conditions are often referred to as 'implied' conditions, since a court determines whether to supply a term that makes an event a condition and what term to supply by the process of implication.

E. Allan Farnsworth, Contracts § 8.2, at pp. 564–65 (2d ed. 1990).

3. Is the *Northpark* court's approach to the "good faith" issue consistent with the definition in revised 3–103(a)(4) and 4–104(c)?

4. The *USF & G* court explains that tort law apportions loss according to actual fault and fairness, while the U.C.C.'s aim is to promote efficiency and predictability in commerce. Because the goals of tort law and the U.C.C. are deemed dissimilar, the court chooses not to apply tort principles of comparative or contributory negligence to the conduct of the plaintiff-depositary bank. Instead, it finds a basis for the contributory negligence defense implicit within the U.C.C. by drawing an analogy between the facts of the case and the situation covered by OR 3–406, which essentially provides a contributory negligence rule to apportion loss in the case of forged signatures. The court contends that the appropriate focus under the U.C.C. is to determine who is in the best position to avoid the loss. Because the plaintiff had the first and best opportunity to prevent the fraud, and failed to do so, it was precluded from recovering from the other banks in the collection chain. The rule seems to concentrate on whether plaintiff's negligence played a "substantial role" in the fraud.

Do you find the *USF & G* court's distinction between the normative bases of tort and commercial law convincing? Is the uniform commercial law really not concerned with fairness to the same extent as the tort law? Why did the *USF & G* court not apply a comparative negligence rule instead of the all or nothing approach that it took? Cf. David M. Phillips, *The Commercial Culpability Scale,* 92 Yale L.J. 228–30 (1982).

5. With regard to the question of the role of contributory/comparative negligence in the bank collections law, consider section 229.38(c) of Regulation CC:

> (c) *Comparative Negligence.* If a person, including a bank, fails to exercise ordinary care or act in good faith under this subpart [C] in indorsing a check * * * accepting a returned check or notice of nonpayment * * * or otherwise, the damages incurred by that person

under § 229.38(a) shall be diminished in proportion to the amount of negligence or bad faith attributable to that person.

Problems

1. County issued a welfare check to Smith in the amount of $100. Smith deposited it in his account. The depositary bank wrongly encoded the check for $10,100 and credited Smith's account in that amount. The check was forwarded to the drawee bank whose computer processed it as a $10,100 check and it charged that amount to County's account. Seven months later County discovered the encoding error and demanded that drawee bank recredit its account for the $10,000. (Smith has disappeared with the surplus money.) Can County recover? Can drawee bank recover from depositary bank? See *State ex rel. Gabalac v. Firestone Bank,* 346 N.E.2d 326 (Ohio App.1975).

2. X Corp. maintained a checking account with First Bank. On July 1, X Corp. deposited five checks with First Bank, all five of which were drawn by Acme Products, Co. on Second Bank. Each of the five Acme checks was in an amount less than $100. When the checks arrived at Second Bank, they were stamped "NSF" and returned to First Bank. Three days after receiving the returned checks, First Bank, on its own initiative, re-presented the checks to Second Bank. Second Bank then held the checks for ten days, awaiting an Acme deposit that never arrived, before returning them once again to First Bank.

Does X Corp. have a viable cause of action against First or Second Bank or both of them? See OR and R 4–201; *David Graubart, Inc. v. Bank Leumi Trust Co.,* 399 N.E.2d 930 (N.Y.1979); *Continental National Bank v. Sanders,* 581 S.W.2d 293 (Tex.Civ.App.1979).

3. In payment for a commodity, Buyer drew a sight draft on itself payable to the order of Seller's Bank and payable through Louisiana Bank. Seller deposited the draft in his account and received a provisional credit. It was forwarded for collection by Seller's Bank but not in a timely manner. When the draft arrived at Louisiana Bank, it was dishonored "NSF." Does Seller's Bank have the right to debit Seller's account in the amount of the draft? Compare OR 4–201, 4–202, 4–204(2)(a), 4–211, and 4–212 with R 4–201, 4–202, 4–204(b)(1), 4–213, and 4–214; *Gulf Coast State Bank v. Emenhiser,* 562 S.W.2d 449 (Tex.1978).

Chapter 7

CONSUMER FUNDS TRANSFER SYSTEMS*

A. INTRODUCTION

SAFEWAY JOINS THE CHARGE TO CHARGE IT—SUPERMARKET NOW ACCEPTS CREDIT, DEBIT PAYMENTS**

By Albert B. Crenshaw—Washington Post Staff Writer

Isabel Ernst of Georgetown thinks paying for her groceries with plastic is a neat idea. "I get frequent-flyer miles," she said Friday during a shopping trip to the Safeway store on Wisconsin Avenue NW. Lillian Owen, also of Georgetown, agreed.

"It's wonderful," she said.

Henry Franks of Cheverly, shopping with his wife in Landover last Wednesday, didn't see any real advantage, however. "It's just as easy to write a check," he said.

Safeway Inc. is betting that Ernst and Owen are the wave of the future. Giant Food Inc., so far, agrees with Franks.

Safeway, the perennial No. 2, is installing equipment in all of its area stores that will allow customers to pay for their groceries either with a regular bank credit card—Visa, MasterCard or Discover—or with any automated teller machine (ATM) card that has access to the Most network.

If things work out as Safeway hopes, new customers will be drawn to its stores by the added convenience of being able to pay with plastic, and customers old and new will spend more of their money at Safeway.

* Throughout this text, the designation "OR" refers to an Article in its original form; "R" denotes a revised Article. E.g., OR 3-303 refers to Original Article 3; R 3-303 refers to Revised Article 3.

** The Washington Post, April 13, 1992, Bus. Sec., pp. 1, 20–21.

Jerry Snider, of Snider's Supermarket in Silver Spring, has accepted Visa, MasterCard and Most for nearly a year now and says purchases "are significantly larger" for customers using credit cards than those using checks or cash.

The credit card portion of the system works much the same as in a department store or other retail outlet.

However, the ability to use an ATM card, though common in some parts of the country, remains relatively novel here. By using the ATM card, the customer authorizes immediate transfer of the amount of the purchase from his or her bank to Safeway's.

This kind of transfer, called point-of-sale debit, is another step in the nation's steadily evolving payments system. Where cash and checks once were used for virtually all the payments made in the retail marketplace, credit cards have all but supplanted them for certain kinds of transactions.

The next step, its proponents hope, is the point-of-sale debit, in which a plastic card and a computer terminal become the medium for an instantaneous transfer of funds between buyer and seller.

Few Customer Fees

In Safeway's case, the electronic transfer is carried out via the Most network, an electronic funds switching system run by Internet Inc. of Reston.

The customer at the checkout counter slides the ATM card through a magnetic reader, which identifies the card and asks for the user's personal identification number. The customer enters the number, which is verified electronically. A small screen displays the amount of the customer's purchase and the customer approves the amount.

This convenience comes at a price, although for the most part, it is Safeway that will pay. Some customers may see extra fees on their bank statements, however.

Safeway charges the customer nothing for using either a debit card or a credit card, although some banks charge a fee, treating point-of-sale transactions as if the customer were getting cash by using another bank's ATM. Crestar Bank, for example, will charge its ATM cardholders 25 cents to make a debit transaction at Safeway. NationsBank and Dominion Bank, on the other hand, do not charge for these transactions.

A survey by Continental Federal Savings & Loan, which has a contract with Safeway to handle the point-of-sale funds transfers, indicated that about 70 percent of customers will not face any charges.

Safeway pays a fee to Continental for the service, but officials said it will be offset by the savings from getting its money more quickly, fewer losses from theft and bad checks, and greater sales volume. As a result, the company said, customers will not find themselves paying for the new convenience in higher grocery prices.

Customers Curious

About 25 of Safeway's 144 stores here already are offering the credit card and debit services, and the company is adding about five stores each week. All area stores are expected to be ready by early summer.

"We think it's going to be a real addition to service," Safeway spokesman Larry Johnson said. The system has worked well where it already is operational, he said, and "we have been very happy with it."

Customer reaction has been "overwhelmingly favorable," he said.

Debit-card customers will be able to use their cards to get cash as well, subject only to the limits of their bank—"as long as the system says it's there," Johnson said.

With checks, Safeway limits the extra cash the customer can get to relatively modest amounts—$15, $25 or $50—with exact limits varying by store, he said.

Giant, for its part, accepts credit cards at pharmacies and flower shops and at the Gourmet Giant store in McLean. A spokesman said it is "exploring the possibility" of taking credit cards "in other areas."

Point-of-sale debit, however, "is on the back burner," the spokesman said. "the technology is there [but] we don't feel the public is ready to utilize it [enough] at this point to make it worth the investment."

Safeway has not begun advertising the new payment methods and will not until it is up and running in all stores. Several hours of observation in two stores last week indicated that most customers were unaware of the system.

Some cast curious glances at the keypads and electronic displays installed next to the check-writing platforms at checkout stands, but most continued to pay with cash and checks.

Store officials said they do not have figures yet on how much volume the system is capturing, but they said they believe it will rise sharply when the chain begins advertising and as customers try it. Interviews with shoppers leaving the store tended to support that assumption.

Bobbie Fry of Cheverly said she probably would use the system, once she sees it in action. Referring to ATM machines, which she said she didn't use at first but now does, she said, "It took me a while to learn to use the money mover."

System Costs Decline

Systems such as Safeway's have been in service for several years in other parts of the country, particularly in the South and West, but the large grocery chain's move represents a breakthrough for ATM technology here.

While Exxon Corp. and Mobil Corp. introduced debit cards at service stations in the mid–1980s, other retailers remained reluctant to adopt this form of payment.

Now, however, many small retailers—and some doctors and dentists, along with the Arlington County treasurer—are trying it.

The key, according to bankers and retailers here, has been the decline in the costs of using the system, coupled with studies showing the actual costs of other forms of payment.

"It's a whole different ballgame" from just three or four years ago, said Lou Ann Armstrong of Continental Federal.

She said the cost of the hardware necessary for scanning the customers' cards and obtaining on-line approvals has declined dramatically in the past few years, making the up-front cost for retailers a lot less daunting.

Further, she said, it now appears that in addition to any marketing appeal the system might have, there are enough savings to the retailer to allow the bank to collect transaction fees from the retailer while leaving the system cost-effective.

According to one survey, it costs a grocery store 53 cents to take a check but only 31 cents to take a point-of-sale payment, including all fees.

Profits for Banks

Indeed, banks now are actively pushing expansion of debit cards as a source of profit.

"Banks are in it for the fee income," Armstrong said. "It is an area where we can provide service and [receive] fee income, much like the merchant side of credit cards."

Continental Federal has been revamping its credit card services to merchants and realized that it could fold point-of-sale debit into the package, she said.

Continental is a part-owner of Internet and thus more aware of the possibilities, she said.

Continental's management "saw what was happening in the marketplace for debit card acceptance and felt this would be a good sell throughout the Washington area," Armstrong added.

For both banks and networks like Most, point-of-sale debit also is where the growth is.

Richard G. Lyons, Jr., chief operating officer of Internet, said conventional ATM transactions on the Most system, which had been increasing by about 35 percent a year in the late 1980s, now are growing by 10 percent to 12 percent a year. Debit-card transactions, in contrast, are growing almost exponentially.

Two years ago, Most was processing about 29,000 debit-card transactions a month. A year ago, the number had climbed to 94,000, and this month it will be 250,000 on the 8 million ATM cards it has in circulation.

Most expects to have a million transactions a month by year-end, Lyons said.

Reduction in Fees

Technology allows debit and credit card processing to be tied together in one system at the store. Safeway plans to integrate the new Independence card electronic benefits transfer system—a debit-card like system for dispensing food stamps now being implemented in Maryland—into its system.

This integration, coupled with a major push by Visa and MasterCard into the grocery store market, has helped persuade merchants to take the plunge.

For all the convenience many see in being able to use plastic, several shoppers cautioned, and Safeway's Johnson agreed, that consumers should be very careful about charging their groceries. Anyone who regularly carries a balance on his or her credit card could be adding a double-digit interest cost to their food bill.

And for those shoppers who want to keep only the current amount of technology in their lives, Safeway and Chevy Chase Savings Bank said last week that Chevy Chase has acquired the ATM terminals in Safeway stores that had been run by Perpetual Savings Bank before its failure.

Credit cards, of course, charge merchants a fee for allowing customers to charge purchases. Snider said the fee "sure does" take a bite out of income from credit card sales, but he said that considering how much banks are charging for their services, plus the cost of totaling and handling checks, credit remains cost-effective.

He particularly praised Visa for charging grocers a reduced fee, now matched by MasterCard.

"If we had to pay the same price as a restaurant or department store, I don't think it would be feasible," he said.

Snider and Safeway officials both said the economics of the new payment systems are such that they will not add to grocery prices.

Snider said passing on costs was "something we never intended to do" anyway, but now that he has worked with the system, "I don't think it's that much of a cost to us."

The foregoing article describes the extent to which technological developments in the payment system have been reflected in the availability of consumer payment options. This chapter treats the two payment media that have developed along lines dictated by the consumer protection movement. The review of electronic funds transfer (EFT) and credit card legal regimes invites comparison with the law of U.C.C. Articles 3 and 4. At each instance of dissonance between the two bodies of law, "new payment system," or "NPS," governing EFT and credit cards, and Articles 3 and 4 governing checks and promissory notes, it is appropriate to determine whether the different treatment is necessitated by technological differences or results from the distinct perspectives that informed the formulation of the two legal regimes. An approach to that dissonance was foreshadowed in the first chapter of this book. Though EFT and credit cards are subject to different statutory and regulatory enactments, see Chapter 1, their fundamental affinity supports their coincident treatment here.

In the course of the article just quoted, the author comments that the increased convenience provided by Safeway's acceptance of credit cards will "come at a price," but that it is Safeway that will pay that price. Is that accurate? To the extent that Safeway's payment system costs increase, won't the increased costs be borne, at least in part, by cash customers who pay the same price for food as do credit card users? Recall that when Safeway forwards the credit card slips for collection, Safeway receives less than a hundred cents of the dollar; there is a discount. Does that circumstance suggest why some gas stations charge for use of a credit card but relatively few other retail establishments choose to do so? What is the difference between buying gasoline for your car and buying that interesting glass figurine at the mall?

The Safeway article introduces many of the issues that confronted the drafters of the credit card/EFT law and that continue to determine consumer acceptance of these newer media. Why does the availability of payment with plastic, particularly credit cards, lead to more spending? To what extent should that conclusion, if indeed it is accurate, impact the apposite law? If it is the access to a line of credit that explains differences between check and credit card law, what body of law should determine the rights of consumer buyers and merchants with regard to the consumer's use of a check that accesses an "overdraft line of credit"? For that matter, what body(ies) of law govern(s) such instruments now? Do the same rules govern so-called "Visa" and "MasterCard" checks that consumers are invited, by card issuers, to use just as they would personal checks? What are the broader economic consequences of greater access to credit and to what extent should the commercial law, either state or federal, be considerate of those consequences when formulating the rights among customers and their financial institutions? These are some of the questions you should keep in mind as you consider the material in this chapter.

Toward the end of the Safeway article, the author notes that a Safeway official "praised Visa for charging a reduced fee, now matched by MasterCard." That should alert the antitrust lawyers. Insofar as Visa and MasterCard are the two biggest players, with perhaps Discover making some headway, the antitrust law may be implicated by any coordinated actions the two systems make. To the extent that Visa and MasterCard market point-of-sale products, the antitrust issues are multiplied.

> Both Visa and MasterCard were born in the 1960s. In 1973, total outstandings for the two systems were less than $7 billion; by mid–1988, total revolving bank credit (most of which represents bank credit cards) had soared to over $100 billion. This is a fifteen fold increase in fifteen years, and the sky is the limit. Visa and MasterCard totally dominate the bank credit card market, and the outstandings are split about evenly between the two giants. The plastic all-purpose bank credit card is here to stay. Now the credit card can double as a debit [POS] card, allowing the consumer to effect point-of-sale transfers from card-holder deposit account to merchant deposit account. In fact, the change in name from "MasterCharge" to "MasterCard" reflects the marketing of the card in dual function.

Barkley Clark, The Law of Bank Deposits, Collections and Credit Cards p. 11–2 (3d ed. 1990, Supp.1992). The world described by Professor Clark would seem to accommodate even greater integration of the payment media in the years to come. But what does it intimate about the development of the payments law? Will Visa and MasterCard ultimately determine the law that governs their product?

The law governing EFT and credit cards is presented in an integrated form in this chapter, with pertinent references to the distinctions between the bodies of governing law. This approach seems consistent with the state of these two "new" payment systems, as disclosed in the Washington Post article and excerpt from Barkley Clark's treatise.

Up until now, the primary emphasis of this casebook has been on the Uniform Commercial Code as it relates to more traditional forms of payment such as checks and promissory notes. As we noted when we began our analysis of the payment systems in Chapter 1, however, a comprehensive survey could not be limited to those traditional media. The creativity of merchants coupled with technological advances have ensured that new methods of payment have appeared to accomplish the more efficient transfer of value. These new payment methods may very well supplant the traditional methods in the future.

Analysis of these "new" payment systems is divided into an examination of consumer funds transfer systems (consumer electronic funds transfer systems and credit card transactions), this chapter, and wholesale funds transfer systems (wire transfers and their relation to new Article 4A of the U.C.C.), the next chapter. In both these divisions, it will be helpful to examine familiar notions of contract, warranty, and tort as sources to determine the allocation of liability among the parties to a payment transaction.

B. THE SCOPE OF CONSUMER PROTECTION

Although the greater amount of electronic funds transfers, in dollar value, are accomplished between commercial as opposed to consumer transactors, electronic funds transfers are, nevertheless, commonplace to most consumers. The now familiar ATM is being joined by point of sale systems (POS) and other advances such as on-line banking which promise to challenge the prominence of checks.

A recurring problem in defining the rights of the parties to a consumer electronic funds transfer is determining the source of applicable law. The Federal Electronic Fund Transfers Act was drafted to provide individual consumer rights in the evolving electronic payment media. Section 1693 of the E.F.T.A. describes the "liability of financial institutions" in tort-like terms:

Action or Failure to Act Proximately Causing Damages

(a) Subject to subsections (b) and (c) of this section, a financial institution shall be liable to a consumer for all damages proximately caused by—

(1) the financial institution's failure to make an electronic fund transfer, in accordance with the terms and conditions of an account, in the correct amount or in a timely manner when properly instructed to do so by the consumer, except where—

(A) the consumer's account has insufficient funds;

(B) the funds are subject to legal process or other encumbrance restricting such transfer;

(C) such transfer would exceed an established credit limit;

(D) an electronic terminal has insufficient cash to complete the transaction; or

(E) as otherwise provided in regulations of the Board;

(2) the financial institution's failure to make an electronic fund transfer due to insufficient funds when the financial institution failed to credit, in accordance with the terms and conditions of an account, a deposit of funds to the consumer's account which would have provided sufficient funds to make the transfer, * * *.

Acts of God and Technical Malfunctions

(b) A financial institution shall not be liable under subsection (a)(1) or (2) of this section if the financial institution shows by a preponderance of the evidence that its action or failure to act resulted from—

(1) an act of God or other circumstance beyond its control, that it exercised reasonable care to prevent such an occurrence, and that it exercised such diligence as the circumstances required; or

(2) a technical malfunction which was known to the consumer at the time he attempted to initiate an electronic fund transfer or,

in the case of a preauthorized transfer, at the time such transfer should have occurred.

Intent

(c) In the case of a failure described in subsection (a) of this section which was not intentional and which resulted from a bona fide error, notwithstanding the maintenance of procedures reasonably adapted to avoid any such error, the financial institution shall be liable for actual damages proved.

The drafters of the U.N.P.C., attempting to strike a balance between consumer rights and financial institution responsibilities, included as Section 101 of the last Permanent Editorial Board Draft of the U.N.P.C. a provision captioned "Contract and Liability of Payor Account Institution or Drawee":

(2) A payor account institution shall be liable to its customer for all actual damages proximately caused to the customer, but not other parties, by the wrongful dishonor of an authorized order, and such damages may include consequential damages whenever

(A) the damages are for an arrest or prosecution of the customer; or

(B) the order is drawn on a consumer account; or

(C) in the case of a draw order, the dishonor results from a failure of the payor account institution to observe the reasonable commercial standards of its business; or

(D) in the case of a pay order, the dishonor results from an intentional act of the payor account institution, including an unlawful setoff or hold placed on an account, but unless otherwise agreed the good faith failure to transmit a pay order is not itself an intentional act.

(3) Whether any damages are proximately caused by a wrongful dishonor in a particular case is a question of fact on which the customer shall have the burden of proof. If actual damages are recoverable, punitive damages may also be awarded for a wrongful dishonor done in bad faith.

The E.F.T.A. has left some gaps in its coverage through which a consumer may slip. The federal statute is concerned primarily with consumer rights rather than inter-institutional liability issues. In the absence of governing agreement among parties on an issue, where will a court look to resolve a controversy?

KASHANCHI v. TEXAS COMMERCE MEDICAL BANK

United States Court of Appeals, Fifth Circuit, 1983.
703 F.2d 936.

RANDALL, CIRCUIT JUDGE:

The plaintiff, Morvarid Paydar Kashanchi, appeals from a final judgment of the district court dismissing her complaint for lack of subject matter jurisdiction. The issue on appeal is whether the term "electronic fund transfer" as used in the Electronic Fund Transfer Act ("EFTA" or "the Act"), 15 U.S.C. § 1693 (Supp. V 1981), includes a transfer of funds from a consumer's account, initiated by a telephone conversation between someone other than the owner of the account and an employee of a financial institution, when that transfer is not made pursuant to a prearranged plan or agreement under which periodic transfers are contemplated. For the reasons set forth below, we affirm.

On or about February 9, 1981, the plaintiff and her sister, Firoyeh Paydar, were the sole owners of a savings account at Texas Commerce Medical Bank in Houston, Texas. On or about that date, $4900 was transferred from their account. The transfer was allegedly initiated by a telephone conversation between an employee of the bank and someone other than the plaintiff or her sister. Upon receipt of a March 31, 1981, bank statement showing the $4900 withdrawal, Firoyeh Paydar sent a letter to the bank, dated April 15, 1981, notifying the bank that the withdrawal was unauthorized.

After the bank refused to recredit the account with the amount of the allegedly unauthorized withdrawal, the plaintiff filed this action on December 4, 1981, alleging violations by the bank of the EFTA. The district court granted the defendant's motion to dismiss on the ground that the plaintiff's cause of action was excluded from the coverage of the Act under 15 U.S.C. § 1693a(6)(E). The plaintiff timely appealed.

This is apparently the first case in which we have been called upon to interpret any of the substantive provisions of the EFTA. We begin our inquiry with the language of the statute itself, recognizing that "absent a clearly expressed legislative intent to the contrary, the plain meaning of the language is ordinarily controlling."

The parties agree that the telephonic transfer that allegedly occurred in this case falls within the broad definition of "electronic fund transfers" in the Act: [T]he term "electronic fund transfer" means any transfer of funds, other than a transaction originated by check, draft, or similar paper instrument, which is initiated through an electronic terminal, telephonic instrument, or computer or magnetic tape so as to order, instruct, or authorize a financial institution to debit or credit an account. Such term includes, but is not limited to, point-of-sale transfers, automated teller machine transactions, direct deposits or withdrawals of funds, and transfers initiated by telephone. 15 U.S.C. § 1693a(6). Some of what Congress has given, however, it has also taken away. Excluded from the definition of an electronic fund transfer is any transfer of funds which is initiated by a telephone conversation between a consumer and an officer or employee of a financial institution which is not pursuant to a prearranged plan and under which periodic or recurring transfers are not contemplated * * *. 15 U.S.C. § 1693a(6)(E). The plaintiff concedes that the unauthorized transfer of her funds was not made "pursuant to any prearranged plan," and that it was made by an employee of the bank. The question in this case is whether the telephone conversation was between the employee and a "consumer." [1]

The Act defines a consumer as "a natural person." 15 U.S.C. § 1693a(5). If we were to apply this definition to the language in the exclusion, we would have to conclude that the withdrawal of the plaintiff's funds was excluded from the coverage of the Act since a natural person, even if the person was neither the plaintiff nor her sister, made the withdrawal. The plaintiff argues, however, that we should read the term "consumer" more narrowly in this portion of the Act; she would have us interpret the provision to exclude only transfers made by the account holder.

The plaintiff maintains that the legislative history of the Act supports her narrow reading of the exclusion. She points out that the House version of the bill used the word "holder," meaning "the individual who is recognized as the owner of the account by the financial institution where the account is held," H.R. 13007, § 903(i), 95th Cong., 2d Sess., 124 Cong.Rec. 25737 (1978), where the Senate version, eventually adopted by Congress as the EFTA, uses the word "consumer." The plaintiff would have us infer that the Senate intended the word "consumer" to be synonymous with "holder." There is no indication in the legislative history, however, that this is what the Senate intended.[2]

1. Relying on the Federal Reserve Board's use of the conjunction "and" in its regulations implementing the EFTA, rather than the relative pronoun "which" used in the Act, the plaintiff maintains that the test for whether a particular transfer falls within the exclusion is two-pronged. The federal regulations exclude: Any transfer of funds that (1) is initiated by a telephone conversation between a consumer and an officer or employee of a financial institution *and* (2) is not under a telephone bill-payment or other prearranged plan or agreement in which periodic or recurring transfers are contemplated. 12 C.F.R. § 205.3(e) (1982) (emphasis added). We do not think that the difference in grammatical construction changes the nature of the exclusion.

2. One Senate version of the bill used the words "person" and "customer" instead of "consumer." The term "person" was defined as an individual who is a citizen of the United States or an alien lawfully admitted for permanent residence, or a partnership, corporation, association, trust, or any other legal entity organized under the laws of a State of the United States. The term "customer" was defined as any natural person who is a debit instrument patron of a debit instrument issuer who utilizes electronic fund transfer services primarily for personal, family or household purposes. Consumer Protection Aspects of EFT Systems, 1978: Hearings on S. 2546 and S. 2470 Before the Subcomm. on Consumer Affairs of the Senate Comm. on Banking, Housing, and Urban Affairs, 95th Cong., 2d Sess. 131 (1978). The Senate did not explain, however, why it chose the word "consumer" and the broader defini-

The only criticism leveled at the definition of consumer concerned the exclusion of corporations, particularly nonprofit corporations, from that definition.

Secondly, Congress demonstrated in other sections of the EFTA that when it wanted to limit a particular provision of the Act to an account holder, rather than to all natural persons, it was perfectly capable of adding language to do so. For example, the Act defines an "unauthorized electronic fund transfer" as "an electronic fund transfer from a consumer's account initiated by a person other than the consumer without actual authority to initiate such transfer * * *." 15 U.S.C. § 1693a(11). It is a well-established principle of statutory construction that "where Congress includes particular language in one section of a statute but omits it in another section of the same Act, it is generally presumed that Congress acts intentionally and purposely in the disparate inclusion or exclusion." In addition, reading "consumer" as the equivalent of "holder" would create redundancies in other portions of the Act. See, e.g., 15 U.S.C. § 1693a(8).[4] "[W]ords in statutes should not be discarded as 'meaningless' and 'surplusage' when Congress specifically and expressly included them, particularly where the words are excluded in other sections of the same act." Wong Kim Bo, 472 F.2d at 722; see also Meltzer v. Board of Public Instruction, 548 F.2d 559, 578 n. 38 (5th Cir.1977), cert. denied, 439 U.S. 1089, 99 S.Ct. 872, 59 L.Ed.2d 56 (1979). In short, the language of the statute would seem to exclude the transfer in this case from the coverage of the Act.

Further, the legislative history of the EFTA is consistent with the plain meaning of the language in the statute and with the presumption arising from Congress's disparate inclusion and exclusion of words of limitation. The plaintiff emphasizes that Congress designed the Act to provide a comprehensive scheme of federal regulation for all electronic transfers of funds. H.R.Rep. No. 1315, 95th Cong., 2d Sess. 2 (1978). Congress undoubtedly intended the Act's coverage to be broad; the Act itself provides that its list of electronic fund transfers is not all-inclusive. 15 U.S.C. § 1693a(6). Aware that computer technology was still in a rapid, evolutionary stage of development, Congress was careful to permit coverage of electronic services not yet in existence: "The definition of 'electronic fund transfer' is intended to give the Federal Reserve Board flexibility in determining whether new or developing electronic services should be covered by the act and, if so, to what extent." S.Rep. No. 915, 95th Cong., 2d Sess. 9 (1978), U.S.Code Cong. & Admin.News 1978, pp. 9273, 9411.

Congressional concern about electronic systems not specifically mentioned in the Act was focused, however, on future and as yet undeveloped systems, not on systems that Congress had simply failed to

tion of that word over the word "customer."

4. Section 1693a(8) provides: the term "financial institution" means a State or National bank, a State or Federal savings and loan association, a mutual savings bank, a State or Federal credit union, or any other person who, directly or indirectly, holds an account belonging to a consumer. 15 U.S.C. § 1693a(8).

discuss. For example, the report on the House version of the Act explained the need for flexibility in dealing with future electronic systems: Many aspects of electronic fund transfer systems are undergoing evolutionary changes and, thus, projections about future events necessarily involve a degree of speculation. Consequently, the appropriate approach to those new financial service concepts is, in general, to permit further development in a free market environment and, to the extent possible, in a manner consistent with the nature and purpose of existing law and regulations governing financial services. H.R.Rep. No. 1315, supra, at 33. The absence of discussion about informal personal phone transfers would seem to indicate an intent not to cover these transfers, or at least an absence of congressional concern about them, in light of the extensive discussion throughout the hearings and reports of the other existing types of electronic transfers. It is highly unlikely that this silence was a result of congressional ignorance of the problem since these informal phone withdrawals presumably had been occurring since shortly after the time of Alexander Graham Bell.

The exclusion of these informal transactions was not in the House version of the EFTA, and presumably it was not in the original version of the Senate bill either, since the minority report criticized the bill's coverage of incidental telephone instructions: In an attempt to reach the automatic telephone payments (transfers through a touch-tone telephone and computer network routing instructions to the financial institution) the Committee has also covered incidental telephone instructions by (a) depositor to a teller to make a transfer from a savings account to cover an overdraft or pay a bill. S.Rep. No. 915, supra, at 24, U.S.Code Cong. & Admin.News 1978, p. 9425. Apparently, this criticism led to the inclusion in the final version of the EFTA of the exemption which is the subject of this suit. Focusing on the Federal Reserve Board's statement that phone transfers made as an "accommodation to the consumer" are not covered by the Act, 46 Fed.Reg. 46880 (1978), and the Senate minority report's discussion of telephone instructions made by a "depositor," the plaintiff would have us conclude that only transactions made as a favor to the actual account holder were excluded from the Act.

These transfers were more probably excluded, however, not because they are made as a favor to the account holder, but because of the personal element in these transfers. On the one hand, as the plaintiff points out, all phone transfers are particularly vulnerable to fraud because there is no written memorandum of the transactions; there is no signature to be authenticated. This lack of a written record was one of the factors that motivated Congress to pass the EFTA. See H.R.Rep. No. 1315, supra, at 2, 4. The other factor, however, was the dependency of electronic fund transfer systems on computers and the resulting absence of any human contact with the transferor. The House report explains: "Consequently, these impersonal transactions are much more vulnerable to fraud, embezzlement, and unauthorized use than the traditional payment methods." Id. at 2. Senator Proxmire opened the hearings on the Senate bill with the warning that "[c]omputer systems are far from infallible, and electronic fund transfers—so totally dependent on computers—will also be error prone." The Electronic Funds Transfer Consumer Protection Act, 1977: Hearings on S. 2065 Before the Subcomm. on Consumer Affairs of the Senate Comm. on Banking, Housing, and Urban Affairs, 95th Cong., 1st Sess. 2 (1977); see also 124 Cong.Rec. 25731 (1978) (statement of Rep. Annunzio, bill sponsor). As one commentator explains, telephonic communications were included in the definition of electronic fund transfers in order to extend coverage over computerized pay-by-phone systems; informal non-recurring consumer-initiated transfers were excluded, however, because they are not prone to computer error or institutional abuse since they are handled on a personal basis: The final exemption from the purview of the EFT Act is an exclusion for nonrecurring transfers of funds that are initiated by an ordinary telephone conversation between a consumer and an officer or employee of the financial institution. In order to extend coverage over computerized "pay-by-phone" systems, the general definition of the term "electronic fund transfer" had to be broad enough to encompass transactions initiated through a telephone. Like automatic debiting of service charges and automatic crediting of interest, however, ordinary nonrecurring transfers informally initiated by a consumer's call to an officer or employee of his neighborhood bank or savings and loan association was not considered to pose a serious threat warranting the coverage and additional costs of the EFT Act. Such requests are handled on a personal basis, so the possibility of computer error or institutional abuse, believed to exist with respect to some other EFT systems, was deemed to be absent.

Brandel & Oliff, The Electronic Fund Transfer Act: A Primer, 40 Ohio St.L.J. 531, 545 (1979). Telephonic transfers made between a natural person and an employee of the financial institution share this element of human contact, regardless of whether the transfer is made by the account holder or someone else.

Finally, we note that the EFTA was passed because "[e]xisting law and regulations in the consumer protection area are not applicable to some aspects of the new financial service concepts." H.R.Rep. No. 1315, supra, at 33. See also 15 U.S.C. § 1693a. The plaintiff suggests in her reply brief that she would have no adequate legal remedy for the wrong she has suffered if she were denied relief under the EFTA. While she conceded at oral argument that she might have an action under state law for conversion or breach of contract (her deposit agreement with the bank), she maintained that a person suffering a loss resulting from the abuse of one of the other electronic fund transfer systems[5] would also have such an action under state law.

5. Congress was specifically concerned with four principal types of electronic fund transfer services: (1) automated teller machines, (2) pay-by-phone systems, (3) direct deposits and automatic payments, and (4) point-of-sale transfers.

S.Rep. No. 915, supra, at 2, U.S.Code Cong. & Admin.News 1978, p. 9404.

The plaintiff ignores the essential difference between electronic fund transfer systems and personal transfers by phone or by check. When the bank employee allegedly agreed to withdraw funds from the plaintiff's account, he or she presumably could have asked some questions to ascertain whether the caller was one of the account holders. The failure to attempt to make a positive identification of the caller might be considered negligence or a breach of the deposit agreement under state law. When someone makes an unauthorized use of an electronic fund transfer system, however, the financial institution often has no way of knowing that the transfer is unauthorized.[6] For example, in order to make a transfer at an automatic teller machine, a person need only possess the machine card and know the correct personal identification number. The computer cannot determine whether the person who has inserted the card and typed in the magic number is authorized to use the system. What might be a withdrawal negligently permitted by the financial institution in one situation might not be a negligent action in the other.

Our analysis of both the language of the EFTA and the legislative history of the Act leads us to conclude that Congress intended to exclude from the Act's coverage any transfer of funds initiated by a phone conversation between any natural person and an officer or employee of a financial institution, which was not made pursuant to a prearranged plan and under which periodic and recurring transfers were not contemplated. Accordingly, we hold that the withdrawal of funds from the plaintiff's account is not covered by the Act even though said withdrawal allegedly was not made by either the plaintiff or her sister. The district court's dismissal of the plaintiff's action for lack of subject matter jurisdiction is AFFIRMED.

Note

1. Article 4A imposes a burden on the financial institution to assure that commercially reasonable security measures are in force with regard to the authorization of a payment order. See U.C.C. §§ 4A–201 and 4A–202. This issue is treated in the next chapter.

2. Why did the E.F.T.A. not apply to the controversy in Kashanchi? Wasn't the bank's defalcation even more egregious than those policed by the Act? What could have been the legislative reason for the exclusion of such fraud from the Act's scope? What is gained by having the customer now pursue a state law conversion or breach of contract action? Doesn't that undermine the Act's and the payments law's interest in uniformity?

To what extent do the reasons for the apposite exclusion in the principal case explain the scope of the Act generally? See 12 C.F.R. §§ 205.1 & 205.3. See also U.C.C. § 4A–108.

6. One of the purposes of the EFTA was to determine who should bear the loss for these unauthorized transfers. Limitations on the consumer's liability for unauthorized transfers are contained in 15 U.S.C. § 1693g.

Problems

1. Bank debited Ms. Judd's account for an $800 withdrawal that it claims she made from her account at an ATM. Ms. Judd insists that she was at work during the hours at which the two withdrawals (totalling $800) were made. Her employer corroborated Ms. Judd's assertion in a letter to the reviewing court. In response, Bank produced evidence that the withdrawals were effected by using the access device (card) and PIN (personal access device) issued to Ms. Judd, who maintains that she neither gave anyone her access device nor disclosed her PIN to anyone.

To what extent, if any, may Ms. Judd cause the Bank to recredit her account? See 12 C.F.R. § 205.6; see also 15 U.S.C. § 1693g(b):

(b) *Burden of Proof*

> In any action which involves a consumer's liability for an unauthorized electronic fund transfer, the burden of proof is upon the financial institution to show that the electronic fund transfer was authorized or, if the electronic fund transfer was unauthorized, then the burden is upon the financial institution to establish that the conditions of liability set forth in subsection (a) of this section [12 C.F.R. § 205.6] have been met, and, if the transfer was initiated after the effective date of section 1693c of this title, that the disclosures required to be made to the consumer under section 1693c(a)(1) and (2) of this title were in fact made in accordance with such section.

See *Judd v. Citibank, N.A.,* 107 Misc.2d 526, 435 N.Y.S.2d 210 (Small Cl.1980). There is a similar burden of proof provision in the credit card law. See 15 U.S.C. § 1643(b).

2. Mr. Porter went to his financial institution's ATM on two occasions, typed in his PIN, and told the machine that he wanted to make a $100 withdrawal. Both times the machine failed to dispense any money, but left messages on the screen to the effect that it had done so. Mr. Porter brought the malfunction to the attention of a bank official who promised to investigate. Must the bank recredit Mr. Porter's account? See *Porter v. Citibank, N.A.,* 123 Misc.2d 28, 472 N.Y.S.2d 582 (Small Cl.1984).

Credit Card Transactions

Credit Cards are a payment medium familiar to most consumers, combining the features of safety and convenience with the ability to draw on a pre-approved line of credit. A credit card system is made up of member banks that issue the cards to consumers and also act as clearing houses for the card receipts within a given geographic area. Member banks negotiate with non-member banks to act as local collection agents for the card receipts. Local merchants make arrangements with a bank accepting the receipts to provide the merchant credit (or payment by check within a set period of time) for the receipts that the merchant generates from sales to cardholders. The receipts are then forwarded throughout the network, much like checks (or in electronic form), to the appropriate member bank which then draws against the consumer's line of credit. Card association rules allow for chargebacks, against merchant accounts, much like those available for check transactions.

Given the similarities between credit card and check payment mechanisms, it is not surprising that very similar questions arise as to the rights and liabilities of the parties in check and credit card transactions. Consider how the contractual nature of the credit card system affects the individuals and businesses making and receiving credit card payments.

FIRST UNITED BANK v. PHILMONT CORPORATION

Mississippi Supreme Court, 1988.
533 So.2d 449.

I.

ROBERTSON, JUSTICE, for the Court:

This appeal arises from a dispute between a bank and a merchant/customer regarding the actions of the bank in placing a "hold" or "freeze" on the merchant's bank account. After a one-day hearing, the Chancery Court issued an injunction which ordered the bank to allow the merchant access to seventy percent (70%) of the balance of the account.

The law of this case is that, absent agreement to the contrary, a customer may not draw against deposits until the credit given has become final. Because the injunction below fails to honor this principle, we reverse.

II.

A.

Gary Montgomery is the founder, sole shareholder and principal managing officer of Philmont Corporation. The Philmont Corporation in turn owns and is the developer of Oakhill Ranch and Country Club, located near Poplarville, Mississippi. Oakhill is associated with a nationwide system of camping facilities known as Camp Coast to Coast (CCC). CCC caters to owners of recreational vehicles (RVs) by providing a nationwide system of campgrounds open exclusively to members of the organization. There are over 400 campgrounds in all fifty states affiliated with CCC. Membership in a local CCC campground entitles the RV owner entry into any other affiliated campground for the nominal charge of $1.00 per night.

Philmont began this venture when it purchased a horse farm in April of 1984 for $180,000. Philmont spent in excess of $300,000.00 remodeling the farm into an RV campground.

On July 15, 1986, Philmont entered into a VISA/Mastercard Merchant Agreement with First United Bank. First United was a local non-member bank acting as agent for VISA/Mastercard member bank, Trustmark National Bank of Jackson, Mississippi. At the same time Philmont opened two accounts at First United in the name of Oakhill. One of these accounts was a standard business checking account. The other account, the one in controversy, was opened to receive the deposit of VISA/Mastercard sales slips. Philmont could also write checks from this account.

Memberships in Oakhill Ranch sold slowly in the first year of operation. The credit card account at First United reflected an average balance of only a few thousand dollars during this time.

In May, 1987, Montgomery contacted Roy Morris who was connected with a telemarketing service known as Vacation Services, Inc. Vacation Services was engaged in telemarketing memberships in a discount travel club.

Vacation Services and Philmont worked out an agreement that ran something like this: Postcards were sent to Visa and Mastercard cardholders informing them that they had qualified for a "free" trip to Orlando and provided them with an "800" number to find out how to claim their prize. When the customer called Vacation Services' telephone boiler room, located in Jackson, his VISA or Mastercard number would be recorded and the customer was sent an information packet for review. Later, upon the customer's approval and purchase of a membership in the discount travel club, the computers at Vacation Services would generate a VISA or Mastercard sales slip in the name of the customer. The name of Oakhill Ranch appeared as the merchant on these computer-generated slips. Each of these sales were in the amount of $349.00.

Philmont/Oakhill's only tie-in to this marketing scheme was the inclusion of Montgomery's business card in the information packet sent to the customer. The $349.00 purchase also included a one-year trial membership in Oakhill Ranch, although there is no mention of that fact in any of the marketing materials. Montgomery said his intent was to follow-up the leads generated by Vacation Services with Oakhill promotional material, although he had not yet done so and at the hearing was unable to produce any of the contemplated marketing mailings.

For his part in the activities of Vacation Services Montgomery received 23% of the gross sales.

Beginning in the first week of July, 1987, Philmont/Oakhill's credit card account at First United Bank experienced a flurry of activity. Between July 1 and July 14 Philmont presented for deposit nine separate transactions totaling $131,000.00. Each of these nine deposits consisted entirely of the computer generated sales slips from Vacation Services. Upon examining the account, bank officers learned that Philmont had written checks against these deposits totaling $77,000.00, leaving a balance of $53,000.00. At this time, of course, the items had not yet been paid by the credit card holder.

When all of this happened, Raymond Saucier, the manager of First United's Poplarville branch, opened a batch envelope and attempted to verify a handful of these sales by telephoning the cardholders. Of the seven customers contacted by Saucier, only two acknowledged that they had authorized the use of their credit card for a purchase of a discount travel club membership. Immediately thereafter First United put a hold on the Oakhill credit card account and instructed Montgomery that it was terminating the Merchant Agreement with Philmont. Although Saucier discussed his plan of action with the VISA member bank (Trustmark), he did not consult legal counsel before taking action. In time Trustmark received fifty-one customer protests, amounting to some $17,500.00. As a result of the freeze on the account, thirteen checks were returned to various Philmont/Oakhill creditors marked "uncollected funds."

B.

Philmont and Montgomery commenced this civil action on September 10, 1987, by filing their complaint in the Chancery Court of Pearl River County, Mississippi. First United Bank was named the sole defendant.

Eight days later the Chancery Court entered an order granting Philmont and Montgomery a preliminary injunction. As a preliminary matter the Court found that "the merchant agreement ... does not authorize First United Bank to place a hold or freeze on any funds in the bank accounts of plaintiffs."

The Court enjoined First United Bank from "freezing, withholding, impounding, or in any way preventing Philmont Corporation or Gary Montgomery from withdrawing any funds from the two bank accounts identified in the preceding paragraph and [further] * * * enjoined [Bank] from applying charge-backs to either of these accounts on account of credits to Mastercard and Visa charge sales slips."

Finally, the Court ordered that thirty percent (30%) of the funds in the merchant's accounts "may be retained by First United Bank as security pursuant to Rule 65(c), Mississippi Rules of Civil Procedure." The effect of the order of the Chancery Court was to leave a balance of $15,652.86 as security for the repayment of any future charge-backs.

The Bank now appeals to this Court.

* * *

IV.

A.

Our bottom line question is whether First United Bank has in law the authority to place what it describes as an administrative freeze on Philmont's account. The Bank argues that the law by reference to which we answer this question is the Merchant Agreement of July 15, 1987. Philmont responds that the matter is controlled by Article 4 of the Uniform Commercial Code, as enacted in this state. Miss.Code Ann. 75–4–101, et seq. (1972). Both are right.

Credit card sales slips are not checks, drafts or other negotiable instruments as defined by UCC Articles 3 and 4.

5 Anderson, The Uniform Commercial Code, 3–104:17 (1984). The sales slips do, however, qualify as "items". An item is "any instrument for the payment of money even though it is not negotiable but does not include money." Miss.Code Ann. 75–4–104(1)(g) [R 4–104(a)(9)] (1972). The sales slips are non-negotiable instruments evidencing the payment of money and they are treated as such under the terms of the Merchant Agreement.

As these sales slips are items within the meaning of Article 4, then the defendant bank is a "depositary bank" and "collecting bank" for the purpose of further Code analysis. Miss.Code Ann. 75–4–105(a) [R 4–105(2)] (1972) ("Depositary Bank means the first bank to which an item is transferred for collection"); Miss.Code Ann. 75–4–105(d) [R 4–105(5)] (1972) ("Collecting Bank means any bank handling the item for collection").

We hold the transactions at issue in this case effectively controlled by Article 4 of the Mississippi UCC. The First United Bank was acting as a depositary bank in all of its dealings with Philmont Corporation, provisionally crediting Philmont's account upon the deposit of the credit card sales slips.

Trustmark was functioning as a clearinghouse for these items, forwarding the slips to other member banks for ultimate collection.

That a transaction falls within Article 4, however, does not necessarily lead to a mechanical application of Code law. The UCC empowers parties to commercial transactions to vary by agreement the Code provisions in many significant ways:

> (1) The effect of the provisions of this chapter may be varied by agreement except that no agreement can disclaim a bank's responsibility for its own lack of good faith or failure to exercise ordinary care or can limit the measure of damages for such lack or failure; but the parties may by agreement determine the standards by which such responsibility is to be measured if such standards are not manifestly unreasonable
>
> (2) Federal Reserve regulations and operating letters, *clearing-house rules, and the like, have the effect of agreements under subsection (1), whether or not specifically assented to by all parties interested in items handled.*

Miss.Code Ann. 75–4–103 [R 4–103] (1972) (emphasis added).

Various agreements and clearing-house rules, elements of private law which depart from the terms of Article 4, are to be found in the record in this case. As the above-quoted language states, the parties to a VISA Merchant Agreement can be bound by the VISA Operating Regulations (which have the effect of clearinghouse rules).[2] Additional-

2. This appeal is centered upon the rights and duties of banks and merchants participating in the nationwide system of bank credit card collection; specifically VISA/Mastercard. An overview of this collection system—as reflected by the record—will be helpful. At the center of the credit card collection system is the "mem-

ly, these rules may be enforced against all participants in the collection system "whether or not specifically assented to" by these parties.

So in response to the original question "what law controls?," and with reference to the positions defined by the parties, our answer may be so framed:

The law which defines the rights and obligations of these parties and controls the resolution of this case is composed of:

(1) Article 4 of the Uniform Commercial Code as enacted in this state; supplanted by

(2) the Merchant Agreement, insofar as it varies the provisions of Article 4, and is not manifestly unreasonable; and

(3) the VISA Operating Regulations (clearinghouse rules), insofar as they vary the provisions of Article 4, and are not manifestly unreasonable.

B.

The question of the Bank's rights to place an administrative freeze of Philmont's account turns upon whether Philmont could withdraw the balance represented by the VISA sales slips "as of right." We answer this question by reference to the controlling public law, supplemented by private law as above.

Of consequence is the following language of UCC Section 4–213 [R 4–215]:

> (3) If a collecting bank receives a settlement for an item *which is or becomes final* * * * the bank is accountable to its customer for the amount of the item *and any provisional credit given for the item in an account with its customer becomes final.*

ber bank." These are the banks which are authorized by VISA/Mastercard to issue credit cards. At the same time, these member banks also act as clearinghouses for the collection of credit card sales slips within a defined geographic area. The member banks in turn recruit "non-member banks" to act as local agents and as points of collection for credit card sales slips. The non-member banks enter into agreements with local merchants whereby the merchants honor the VISA and/or Mastercard credit cards at their places of business and the bank agrees to accept an "assignment" of all sales slips. Frequently, the merchant will open an account at a local participating bank for the purpose of posting and processing these credit card sales slips, although this is not required by the merchant agreement. If the merchant chooses not to maintain an account at any participating bank, the member bank agrees to pay the merchant by check no later than thirty days after presentation of the sales slips. Merchant Agreement 11. If, however, the merchant has such an account with the non-member bank, the merchant's deposit of these credit card sales slips is very similar to a deposit of personal checks. The sales slips are deposited in a sealed envelope with a cellophane window through which can be seen a "batch header" card displaying the total number and total amount of the receipts contained in the envelope (or batch). Once these sales slips are deposited, the local participating bank provisionally credits the merchant's account and forwards the batch to the local member bank. The member bank then opens the envelope and processes the batch by sending each sales slip to the bank which issued the credit card used in the sales transaction. Each member bank can then assemble a monthly statement for each of its customers. The card system's regulations provide the customer with a 120–day period in which to contest any charge appearing on a monthly statement. If contested, a "charge-back" is sent back through the collection system and is ultimately the responsibility of the merchant.

> (4) Subject to any right of the bank to apply the credit to an obligation of the customer, credit given by a bank for an item in an account with its customer becomes available for withdrawal as of right
>
> (a) in any case where the bank has received a provisional settlement for the item,—*when such settlement becomes final* and the bank has had a reasonable time to learn that the settlement is final;

Miss.Code Ann. 75–4–213 (1972) (emphasis added). Philmont could not, therefore, of right demand that the Bank honor checks drawn against the deposit of credit card sales slips until the Bank's provisional credit of the account became *final.*

The Bank's right to charge-back against Philmont's account is also affected by the point when a provisional payment becomes final. UCC Section 4–212 [R 4–214] provides:

> (1) If a collecting bank has made provisional settlement with its customer and itself fails by reason of dishonor, suspension of payments by a bank or otherwise to receive a settlement for the item which is or becomes final, the bank may revoke the settlement given by it, charge-back the amount of any credit given for the item to its customer's account or obtain refund from its customer * * * *These rights to revoke, charge-back, and obtain refund terminate if and when a settlement for the item received by the bank is or becomes final* * * *.

Miss.Code Ann. § 75–4–212(1) [R 4–214(a)] (1972) (emphasis added).

The bank, therefore, has authority to refuse to honor checks drawn against credits in a customer's account so long as those credits remain provisional and the bank retains rights of charge-back or refund. The bank must, however, act in good faith. In re Williams, 61 B.R. 567, 573 (Bankr.N.D.Tex.1986).

Miss.Code Ann. § 75–4–213 [R 4–215] (1972), in relevant part, declares that a credit to a customer's account has become final when the bank: * * * (b) settles for the item without reserving a right to revoke the settlement and without having such right under statute, *clearinghouse rule or agreement;* * * * or (d) provisionally credits the customer's account and fails to revoke the provisional credit in the time and manner permitted by statute, *clearinghouse rule or agreement.*

Here the Merchant Agreement and the VISA operating regulations are at substantial variance with Article 4 with regard to the time at which the provisional credit given by the member bank to non-member banks and customers becomes final. Significantly, they give the member bank a 120–day right of charge-back. The UCC's three day charge-back rule, Miss.Code Ann. § 75–4–213(4)(b) [R 4–215(e)(2)] (1972),[3] is wholly supplanted.

The Merchant Agreement reserves to the Bank the right to charge-back against the merchant's account any disputed charges in accordance with the operating regulations. Merchant Agreement § 11. In addition the agreement states:

> *General. Merchant will: * * * (b) observe and comply with the Master Charge—The Interbank Card System's and/or the VISA U.S.A. Inc. Card System's applicable Rules and Regulations and such procedures as Bank or System may prescribe for Charge Card Sales, Pre–Charge Card Sales, Slips and Credit Slips; * * **

Merchant Agreement § 17. The use of such language in the Merchant Agreement effectively incorporates the VISA Operating Regulations into the contract as permitted by Miss.Code Ann. § 75–4–103(2) [R 4–103(b)] (1972). Regulation 2.11.4 of the manual states:

> The following circumstances shall give rise to a charge-back right which may be exercised up to a maximum of 120 calendar days from the Endorsement Date: 2.11.4.1 Cardholder Disputes Paper—
>
> > —Issuer receives a written complaint from its Cardholder who acknowledges participation in the Transaction, but states that, for a given reason, the Cardholder requested an adjustment and Credit Voucher from the Merchant and was refused.
> >
> > —Issuer receives a written complaint from its Cardholder who acknowledges participation in the Transaction and states that the Transaction was in violation of law, or the goods, services, or other thing of value described on the Paper were not received by such Cardholder or by a person authorized by him.

—VISA U.S.A. Inc. Operating Regulation 2.11.4. The Merchant Agreement and the Operating Regulations therefore reserve the right to charge-back to the merchants account any disputed sales within 120 days after the transaction took place.

In attempting to harmonize the provisions of Article 4 and these same provisions of the Merchant Agreement and Regulations, the court in In Re Twenty-four Hour Nautilus Swim & Fitness Center, 81 B.R. 71 (D.Colo.1987), stated:

> I agree with the appellee bank that here the agreement between the debtor, the appellee [merchant] and VISA defined the time and manner in which a provisional settlement of the VISA

3. Because First United was acting as an agent of Trustmark for purposes of credit card receipt collection, it was acting as both a collecting and payor bank. Thus, Section 4–213(4)(b) [R 4–215(e)(2)] would otherwise apply.

> items would become final. The agreement created the right to revoke the settlement upon dispute by a customer and for other reasons. The official comment to [UCC § 4–213] [R 4–215] provides that "[i]f under a statute, clearinghouse rule or agreement, a right of revocation of the settlement exists, the settlement is provisional."

—In re Twenty-four Hour Nautilus, 81 B.R. at 73–74.

Philmont argues that the past practice of the Bank in sight posting deposits consisting of credit card sales slips and allowing Philmont to draw against the uncollected funds is a commitment to pay checks drawn in the same manner in the future. But this is not so. First United's "freeze" was nothing more than a suspension of a previously extended courtesy. Absent agreement to the contrary—a matter not present here, a bank has no obligation to honor checks drawn against credits that have not become final.

Addressing this same argument, the court in Bay Area Bank v. Fidelity & Deposit Co. of Maryland, 629 F.Supp. 693 (N.D.Cal.1986), stated:

> In this case, not only was the Bank capable of dishonoring checks drawn against Flynn's account, but the account at all times was also subject to the terms of the written Bank Card Merchant Agreement. Under that Agreement, the Bank expressly reserved the right to debit the account at any time for the amount of unauthorized credit card sales drafts erroneously credited to the account. The Bank further retained the right to cease sight posting and to terminate the Agreement. Far from creating an irrevocable commitment, the sight postings themselves were expressly revocable under the Agreement.

—Bay Area Bank, 629 F.Supp. at 697. The court went on to say that "[t]o accept plaintiff's argument, one would have to find that the Bank had irrevocably obligated itself to pay on any and all deposits Flynn should present. This argument is belied by standard banking practice and simple common sense." 629 F.Supp. at 697 n. 5. Other courts have reasoned that by allowing a customer to write checks against uncollected funds a bank does not waive prospectively the right to dishonor such checks. Discount Auto Mart v. Bank of North Carolina, 263 S.E.2d 41 (N.C.App.1980).

We must consider, of course, whether the enlargement of the normal three-day period to 120–days is manifestly unreasonable within Miss.Code Ann. 75–4–103(1) [R 4–103(a)] (1972). Bottomline policy considerations favor the Bank's position here. Abuse of merchant accounts by drawing against uncollected sales slips has led to substantial losses suffered by banks in recent years. The bank in Watson v.

State, 521 So.2d 1290 (Miss.1988), was left with $70,000.00 in charge-backs against a $20,000.00 balance. Losses sustained by the bank in Bay Area Bank, above, attributable to uncollectible credit card sales slips exceeded $300,000.00. 629 F.Supp. at 694. The recent case of Fogel v. White, 745 S.W.2d 444 (Tex.Civ.App.1988), involving a business venture identical to that of Vacation Services, states only that "the discrepancy between the amount in consumer charge-backs and the balance remaining in the provisional credit account became very large * * *" 745 S.W.2d at 445.

The potential for loss is further enhanced if, for instance, the merchant should engraft a kiting scheme onto the credit card "float." [4]

In any event, present commercial law is of sufficient flexibility to allow the merchant ready access to the capital generated by credit card sales. The Merchant Agreement already grants the bank the option to request an Article 9 security agreement and financing statement to protect its interests. Merchant Agreement § 17. New ventures, through the use of existing commercial devices, could therefore gain ready access to the provisional credits.

Ultimately, neither Article 4 nor any theory of waiver can grant to Philmont's deposit and account credit the finality necessary for Philmont to claim a withdrawal against these deposits "as of right." Since Philmont's deposits of the credit card sales slips were at all times provisionally credited to the account, the Bank was under no duty to make these funds available to the depositor. They, therefore, acted fully within their legal rights by informing Montgomery to cease drawing against the account and by dishonoring checks so drawn.

Of course, Philmont has (and had) the right to draw against any credits which had become final, or which subsequently became final. See Miss.Code Ann. § 75–4–213 [R 4–215] (1972). In this sense the term "freeze" is a misnomer. First United has never had any authority in law to place a permanent freeze on Philmont's account. What—and all—the Bank has ever had authority to do is to withhold honoring checks drawn against credits in Philmont's account until those credits have become final.

We reverse and remand for further proceedings consistent with this opinion.

REVERSED AND REMANDED.

4. In this case that possibility may rise to more than speculation. After First United froze Philmont's account, Montgomery offered to deposit a $30,000.00 check into the account as security. Given Montgomery's testimony regarding his poverty caused by the freeze, one can only assume that he intended to obtain the $30,000.00 from another merchant account he had opened at Trustmark (which at the time consisted of $37,000.00 in uncollected sales slips generated by Vacation Services!).

C. REVERSIBILITY OF PAYMENTS

Commercial paper law provides a customer the right to stop payment on a check; the credit card law provides the cardholder the right to reverse certain credit transactions (15 U.S.C. § 1666i (1992)); but the federal EFT law includes no such right, though individual financial institutions could certainly provide their customers a reversal right. The states of Michigan (Mich.Comp.Laws Ann. § 488.16 (West Supp. 1991–92) and Wisconsin (Wis.Admin.Code [Commissioner of Banking] § 14.09 (1992)) currently provide an EFT reversal right in their state EFT laws. Does the cash (EFT) vs. credit (credit cards) distinction support the reversal right in the credit card context but not in the EFT context? How do consumer expectations differ in the two contexts and to what extent should differences of expectation affect development of the payments law? See Peter A. Alces, *A Jurisprudential Perspective for the True Codification of Payments Law,* 53 Fordham L.Rev. 83, 113 (1984):

> Permitting a right to reverse only in the credit context is consistent with commercial expectations and practical realities. Whether or not this right exists, a consumer who has drawn against a line of credit remains in possession of the funds and the leverage that goes with possession. From the typical consumer's viewpoint, only the identity of the plaintiff changes. At the end of the provided reversal period the risk of nonpayment shifts from the merchant to the * * * financial institution, but the credit risk that remains is no more than the drawee bargained for when it issued the credit device and is therefore no longer pertinent to the reversal calculus.

The U.N.P.C. contained a reversal provision:

> Section 425. *Customer's Right to Stop Payment or Reverse an Order*
>
> (1) Any drawer, including a payor account institution which draws an order to a payee in payment of its own underlying obligation, may orally or in writing, stop payment on an order. Stop payment orders must be received at such time and in such manner as to afford the account institution a reasonable opportunity to act on them prior to any action by the account institution with respect to the order described in Section 426.
>
> (2) A consumer drawer has the right to direct a payor account institution, orally or in writing, to reverse payment on an order in the amount of $50 or more until three (3) business days after that order has been finally paid under Section 420(1), and to receive a recredit to the account on which such order was drawn unless

(a) such order is for cash withdrawal; or

(b) it is a written draw order transmitted for payment to the payor account institution; or

(c) the person or persons establishing the account have elected in writing, after the disclosure required by Section 701(4), to waive such right.

(3) An oral order is only binding upon the account institution for fourteen (14) calendar days unless confirmed in writing within that period. A written order is only binding for six (6) months unless renewed in writing. Any written order shall be signed by the person exercising the right to stop or reverse payment.

(4) An account institution acting on the direction to reverse payment of an order shall be deemed to be dishonoring the order. It shall have no further liability under Section 402(2) on the order and shall have the right to recover any credit given to its customer, a prior transmittor, or subsequent transmittee. All credits and debits as between transmittors relating to such order may be revoked seriatim along the line.

(5) The burden of establishing the fact and amount of loss resulting from the payment of an order contrary to a binding stop order or order to reverse is on the drawer, but such burden shall not affect the right of the drawer to have its account recredited by a payor account institution when a binding stop order or order to reverse has been issued by the customer.

(6) The right of a drawer to stop or reverse payment as provided herein may be exercised with respect to any order by any person authorized to initiate orders on the account against which such order was drawn, provided that any person other than the drawer who exercises such right as to any order thereby assumes the obligation of the drawer as provided in Section 100 with respect to such order.

(7) Except as provided in subsection (8), any individual shall have the same right to stop or reverse payment on a draw order drawn on the individual's behalf or accepted by an account institution as would a consumer drawer if the consumer drawer had drawn the order. Such right shall be exercised by a direction to the account institution which has drawn or accepted the order within the time limits specified by subsections (1) and (2). If such account institution has drawn the order on another account institution, it shall before midnight of the business day on which it receives the direction to stop or reverse direct such payor account institution, in accordance with the direction it has received and shall recredit the individual's account for the amount of the order or return to the person any consideration, up to the amount of the order, it received for drawing the order. No drawee or payor account institution on an order so stopped or reversed by such

person shall have any further obligation to any funds claimant. Any individual who stops or reverses an order under this subsection assumes the obligation of the drawer on the order, and the individual's underlying obligation, if discharged under Section 801 when the order was transmitted, is reinstated.

(8) Neither an account institution nor any other person may stop or reverse payment on a draw order which,

(a) an account institution has reduced to writing and on which it has assumed the obligations of the drawer or on which an account institution is an accommodation party or acceptor;

(b) is issued in tangible form by the account institution to the person from whom it receives consideration for the order, or is endorsed or accepted in tangible form by the account institution; and

(c) bears prominently on its face the legend that the order is not subject to stop or reversal and should be treated as cash,

for any reason other than loss or a claim that the order is unauthorized. Any party so requesting an account institution to stop or reverse such an order shall either provide indemnity reasonably acceptable to the account institution or enjoin payment of the order by judgment of a court of competent jurisdiction in an action in which the account institution is a party.

(9) Any direction to an account institution to stop or reverse payment of an order must at least accurately identify,

(a) the account number on which such order is drawn;

(b) the dollar amount (not cents) of the order except where a draw order is prearranged;

(c) the payee of the order;

(d) the drawer or person on whose behalf the stop or reversal is directed; and

(e) the date, within one (1) calendar week, of initiation of the order.

(10) A stop payment of an order may be revoked or canceled only by a writing signed by the person directing the original stop payment.

(11) Any direction to an account institution to stop or reverse payment must be telephoned or delivered to the telephone number or address, as the case may be, specified by the account institution in its disclosure under §§ 501(2)(e) or 701(3) or, in the absence of such disclosure, to any telephone number or address of the branch or office of the account institution where the account is maintained.

(12) An order is for cash withdrawal, within the meaning of this Section, if a drawer receives cash for an order from an account institution, as where cash is withdrawn over-the-counter or from a machine, or in exchange for draw orders payable to cash, drawer or bearer.

(13) An account institution may require any person directing it to stop or reverse an order to pay any fees or charges for such service which it reasonably believes are necessary to cover the cost of providing the service.

Chapter 4 considers how the U.C.C. warranty and conversion rules operate to distribute the loss when a forged signature appears on a negotiable instrument. It is worthwhile to contrast the statutory regime provided to allocate fraud losses in the context of credit card transactions. Liability for fraud loss in the credit card context is apparently predicated on a statutory synthesis of contract, tort, and warranty principles. In reading the following case, focus on the court's treatment of the policy issues and consider how similar arguments might apply in the commercial paper context.

AMERICAN AIRLINES, INC. v. REMIS INDUSTRIES, INC.

United States Court of Appeals, Second Circuit, 1974.
494 F.2d 196.

IRVING R. KAUFMAN, CHIEF JUDGE:

The importance of the question presented on this appeal cannot be gauged by reference to the relatively small amount in controversy. Indeed, the more than fourteen thousand dollars of disputed liability arising from the unauthorized use of an executive's Air Travel Card, issued to Remis Industries, Inc., pales in significance when viewed in the light of the sums which may well depend on our determination of the ambit of statutory credit card protection afforded by the 1970 amendment to the Truth in Lending Act. Since we find that the credit card abuses which Congress sought to eliminate plague all cardholders without meaningful distinction, we decline to interpret Congress's enactment in a way that would sap the strength of the statutory safeguards it provided. It is our belief that by arbitrarily confining the scope of the Truth in Lending Act's application to a limited class of cardholders, we would undermine Congress's purpose to afford a broader and more meaningful protection to all who enter the credit card domain.

Remis Industries is a Massachusetts corporation engaged in the sale of hides and other equine by-products. Since 1943 its personnel have been using Air Travel Cards which, although issued in this instance by American Airlines, are accepted by all airlines for the purchase of tickets on credit. Remis entered into a "Universal Air Travel Plan Subscriber's Contract" with American and in May, 1971 forwarded a "Request for Travel Cards" form to American in New York. On May 19, American approved the renewal of its contract with Remis and soon thereafter issued new Air Travel Cards, including one for use by Abraham Lerner, Remis's Vice President and General Manager.

In August, 1971 Lerner received a call from a Royal Dutch Airlines representative informing him that there had been an error in the billing of six round-trip tickets from Miami to Curacao charged to his Air Travel Card on August 6. Since Lerner had not purchased these tickets, he immediately realized that his Air Travel Card had either been lost or stolen. Because of this, he promptly notified American of the card's loss.

Much to Lerner's chagrin, he soon learned that airline tickets totaling $14,008.16 had been charged to his Air Travel Card during the period of its loss and prior to his notification of American. When American duly requested payment of this amount from Remis, the company refused to pay because the charges stemmed from an unauthorized use of the credit card.

American filed suit against Remis in February, 1972 in New York State Supreme Court. On March 6, 1972, Remis removed the action to United States District Court for the Southern District of New York on grounds of diversity, 28 U.S.C. § 1441. In its answer to the complaint, Remis contended that the amount in issue resulted from an unauthorized use of Lerner's Air Travel Card; that American was negligent in permitting the Card's unauthorized use; and that, in any event, under either Massachusetts law or New York law, liability for the unauthorized use of a credit card was limited to $50.

With the issues joined, American moved for summary judgment. It argued that the "Universal Air Travel Plan Subscriber's Contract" signed by Remis obligated the company to pay for all tickets charged to its account prior to the receipt by American of notice that an Air Travel Card had been lost. The various affirmative defenses raised by Remis, American contended, were insufficient as a matter of law.

On August 8, 1972, in an opinion reported only in 4 CCH Cons. Cred.Guide ¶ 99, 123, Judge Cannella denied the motion. Finding New York law to be applicable, he held that American had failed to comply with the conditions precedent to the recovery of charges resulting from the unauthorized use of a credit card, limited in any case to $50, as contained in N.Y.G.B.L. § 512. Moreover, in so doing, Judge Cannella rejected American's assertion that 512 was not applicable in this instance because that section, by its language, extends protection only so far as the federal Truth in Lending Act, 15 U.S.C. §§ 1601, et seq.—which in turn, argued American, does not apply to credit cards issued to corporations or to credit cards used for business or commercial purposes.

Following Judge Cannella's decision, the parties stipulated that his order would be considered as granting partial summary judgment to Remis dismissing the complaint in excess of $50, and that the balance of the claim would be voluntarily dismissed by American. On April 23, 1973, this stipulation was embodied in an order issued by Judge MacMahon and, with no claim remaining to be litigated, American appealed from the April 23rd order as a final order pursuant to 28 U.S.C. § 1291.

Although we cannot agree with the rationale of Judge Cannella's opinion, we believe his conclusion—that Remis's maximum liability for the unauthorized use of its Air Travel Card is $50—is correct. Accordingly, we affirm.

I

We begin by examining N.Y.G.B.L. § 512 upon which Judge Cannella relied as the exclusive determinant of Remis's potential liability.[1] That section states:

> A provision which imposes liability upon a holder for a cash advance or loan or for the purchase or lease of property or services obtained by the unauthorized use of a credit card shall not be enforceable to the extent that it imposes a greater liability upon the holder than is imposed under the provisions of the act of Congress entitled "Truth in Lending Act" and the regulations thereunder, as such act and regulations may from time to time be amended.

McKinney's Cons.Laws of N.Y. Cumulative Pocket Suppl. for 1973–1974. The reference to the Truth in Lending Act is quite clear. Judge Cannella construed that reference as defining the dollar amount of maximum liability under New York law—$50, pursuant to 133(a) of the Truth in Lending Act, 15 U.S.C. § 1643(a)—but not the scope of section 512's coverage. That, he concluded, was governed by the definitions contained in the New York Act, N.Y.G.B.L. § 511, which on their face include all credit card holders, natural persons as well as corporations, without exception.[2] Thus, without interpreting the range of the Truth in Lending Act as a whole, the district judge determined that 512 imposed a liability limitation on the Air Travel Card issued to Remis. It is a well-settled principle of statutory construction that the plain language of a statute offers the primary guidance to its meaning. Indeed, the New York Court of Appeals has said:

1. Since neither party disputes Judge Cannella's finding that New York law governs here, we have no occasion to examine the validity of that finding on this appeal.

2. "Holder" is defined in 511(4) as: a person to whom such a credit card is issued or who has agreed with the issuer to pay obligations arising from the use of a credit card issued to another person; And, "person," in turn, 511(2), as: an individual, corporation, partnership or association, two or more persons having a joint or common interest or any other legal or commercial entity.

> (Where) the language found in the statute is clear and unambiguous, * * * the intent of the framers "is to be sought first of all, in the words and language employed, and if the words are free from ambiguity and doubt, and express plainly, clearly and distinctly, the sense of the framers of the instrument, there is no occasion to resort to other means of interpretation." McCluskey v. Cromwell, 11 N.Y. 593, 601–602.

We believe that the clear language of 512, by referring without qualification to the "provisions of the act of Congress entitled 'Truth in Lending Act,'" simply does not support the selective incorporation approach adopted below. Accordingly, although New York's statutory definitions are sufficiently broad to cover Remis, and the statutory predecessors of 512 applied without distinction to corporate and individual credit card holders, we believe that the language of the present statute requires a determination of Remis's liability under the Truth in Lending Act. If New York intended a more restricted applicability of that Act, as Remis urges, it is for the New York legislature and not this Court to amend the statute.

II

When the Truth in Lending Act, 15 U.S.C. §§ 1601 et seq. was enacted on May 29, 1968, it contained no reference to credit card transactions. Rather, its limited though important purpose was, in the words of the Act itself, "to assure a meaningful disclosure of credit terms so that the consumer will be able to compare more readily the various credit terms available to him and avoid the uninformed use of credit." 15 U.S.C. § 1601.

The statement of purpose reveals that Congress was focusing its attention on credit transactions involving the consumer—transactions "in which the party to whom credit is offered or extended is a natural person, and the money, property, or services which are the subject of the transactions are primarily for personal, family, household, or agricultural purposes." 15 U.S.C. § 1602(h). Corporate debtors or individuals who secure credit for business or commercial purposes were thought to be amply sophisticated—that is, sufficiently able to satisfy the Act's goal of utilizing credit in an "informed" manner, 15 U.S.C. § 1601—so that mandatory disclosure requirements were not warranted for that genre of credit transaction. See Warren & Larmore, Truth in Lending: Problems of Coverage, 24 Stan.L.Rev. 793, 809–810 (1972). And, in fact, the report of the Senate Committee on Banking and Currency states in pertinent part:

> Most businesses or corporations are in a good position to judge the relative worth of alternate credit plans and by and large do not require the special disclosure protections provided by the bill.

S.Rep. No. 392, 90th Cong., 1st Sess. 7 (1967). Accordingly, to implement this view, the Truth in Lending Act includes a provision, 15 U.S.C. § 1603, which reads, in relevant part:

> This subchapter does not apply to the following:

> (1) Credit transactions involving extensions of credit for business or commercial purposes, or * * * to organizations (defined to include corporations and partnerships).

Although the original Truth in Lending Act included no provisions governing the expanding world of credit card use, the House of Representatives, at least, had begun to examine this aspect of the credit field as early as 1967. In that year, Representative Wright Patman introduced the first bill, H.R. 12646, 90th Cong., 1st Sess. (1967), designed to regulate the mailing of unsolicited credit cards, and chaired the hearings before the House Committee on Banking and Currency on this subject. See Weistart, Consumer Protection in the Credit Card Industry: Federal Legislative Controls, 70 Mich.L.Rev. 1476, 1483–1485 (1972). The following year, the Senate commenced an investigation of the credit card field, the initial hearings beginning in October, 1968 before the Subcommittee on Financial Institutions of the Senate Committee on Banking and Currency, 90th Cong., 2d Sess. (1968). Id. at 1485–1486 n. 37. By 1970, these hearings bore fruit in the form of legislation, the purposes of which were threefold: (1), to prohibit the distribution of unsolicited credit cards; (2), to limit the liability of a cardholder for the unauthorized use of his card to $50; and (3), to make the fraudulent use of a credit card a crime punishable by a fine or imprisonment or both. For its own esoteric reasons, Congress enacted this legislation as an amendment to the Truth in Lending Act, adding definitional subsections, 15 U.S.C. § 1602(j-o), and substantive sections, 15 U.S.C. §§ 1642–1644.

Section 1643(a), of principal concern in this case, states, in pertinent part:

> A cardholder shall be liable for the unauthorized use of a credit card only if the card is an accepted credit card, the liability is not in excess of $50 * * *, and the unauthorized use occurs before the cardholder has notified the card issuer that an unauthorized use of the credit card has occurred or may occur as a result of loss, theft, or otherwise.

The term "cardholder" is broadly defined as "any person to whom a credit card is issued," 15 U.S.C. § 1602(m); with the term "person" defined in the Act's original definitions as "a natural person or an organization," 15 U.S.C. § 1602(d), and "organization" defined to include a corporation, 15 U.S.C. § 1602(c). Thus, upon putting together this definitional jigsaw puzzle, one finds that 1643(a) protects all credit card holders—individual and corporate alike. Clearly, this would appear to limit Remis's liability from the unauthorized use of its Air Travel Card to $50.

American argues, however, that we must read 1643(a), which after all was an amendment to the Truth in Lending Act, in the light of § 1603, the section to which we have already referred, which exempts from the Act's purview "credit transactions involving extensions of credit for business or commercial purposes, or * * * to organizations." American's brief accordingly urges that

> Since it is beyond dispute that American extended credit to Remis Industries for business or commercial purposes, and that Remis Industries is a corporation, the exemption contained in section 104 of the Truth in Lending Act (15 U.S.C. § 1603) precludes Remis Industries from invoking the limitation of liability contained in section 133 (15 U.S.C. § 1643(a)).

American's argument founders not only on well-established principles of statutory construction but also on the uniform and contrary interpretation of the relationship between § 1603 and the 1970 credit card amendment voiced by both the Federal Reserve Board, see 37 Fed.Reg. 24339, and the Federal Trade Commission, see In re Credit Card Service Corp. d/b/a Credit Card Service Bureau, CCH Trade Reg.Rep. ¶ 20, 215 (Jan. 19, 1973), appeal docketed, No. 73–1357, D.C.Cir. (Apr. 6, 1973). The rule of statutory construction to which we turn in this instance has been enunciated as follows:

> The provisions introduced by the amendatory act should be read together with the provisions of the original section that were * * * left unchanged, as if they had been originally enacted as one section. Effect is to be given to each part, and they are to be interpreted so they do not conflict. If the new provisions and the * * * unchanged portions of the original section cannot be harmonized, the new provisions should prevail as the latest declaration of the legislative will.

1A J. Sutherland, Statutes and Statutory Construction, ¶ 22.34, p. 196 (4th ed. C. Sands 1972). We are of the view that by applying § 1603 to limit the scope of both the original disclosure provisions of the Truth in Lending Act and the credit card provisions added in 1970, as American suggests, we would produce such statutory obfuscation that it would surely thwart the intent of Congress.[3] To avoid this cacophony, § 1603 cannot be construed as circumscribing the salutary protection afforded by the credit card amendment.

We note, for example, that application of § 1603 to § 1643(a) would raise a threshold question for which the Act at least provides no ready answer: at what point in the credit card process does a transaction

3. No legislative history could be found to illuminate congressional intent with respect to the relationship, if any, between § 1603 and the 1970 credit card amendment. Appellant proffers two statements by Senator Proxmire, both uttered during hearings conducted more than one year following passage of the credit card legislation on a bill at best distantly related to the credit card provisions here in question, in which he suggests that further amendment of the Truth in Lending Act would be required to eliminate the applicability of § 1603 to the credit card provisions. See Hearings on S. 652 Before the Subcomm. on Banking, Housing and Urban Affairs, 92nd Cong., 1st Sess., at 78, 113 (1971). Suffice to say, as the Court did in United States v. Philadelphia National Bank, 374 U.S. 321, 348–349, 83 S.Ct. 1715, 1733, 10 L.Ed.2d 915 (1963) quoting United States v. Price, 361 U.S. 304, 313, 80 S.Ct. 326, 4 L.Ed.2d 334 (1960): The views of a subsequent Congress form a hazardous basis for inferring the intent of an earlier one.

involving the extension of credit occur? Since the likely response is at the time the credit card issues,[4] confusion would prevail over the classification of cards issued to natural persons. Were the cards issued for business or commercial use and thus excluded from protection, or were they for personal use and hence covered under § 1643(a)? To be sure, a predominant use test might provide a solution, cf. Brill v. Newport National Bank, 4 CCH Cons.Cred.Guide ¶ 99,057 (S.D.N.Y. 1973). But the extensive, overlapping use of some types of credit cards, e.g. to purchase gasoline or meals in a restaurant, would make this test wholly unwieldy in application.

In addition to producing needless uncertainty, engrafting the scope limitations of § 1603 upon the 1970 credit card provisions would replace the uniform safeguards demanded by the nature of the problems which Congress addressed with a crazy-quilt design of cardholder protection. The "deep pocket" theory might provide a superficial basis for distinguishing corporate from individual cardholders. But, more persuasive considerations, such as the preferential position of the card issuer to insure against the risk of card loss, see Weistart, supra at 1517, and the incapacity of corporations and individuals alike to prevent the unsolicited distribution of credit cards, suggest that Congress intended to protect all credit card holders without exception.

Nor do we find particularly cogent American's argument that, unlike consumers, corporations and individuals who use credit cards for business or commercial purposes do not need the statutory safeguard of limited liability for they are capable of apportioning the risk of loss by contract. Indeed, the facts here furnish a convincing answer to this contention. In order to obtain its Air Travel Cards, Remis was required to sign a contract entitled "Universal Air Travel Plan Subscriber's Contract." It would not be illogical to presume, based on this appellation, that, in the case of Air Travel Cards and, we suspect, in the credit card field in general, bargaining is a rather euphemistic characterization of what is essentially a take-it-or-leave-it method of contract formulation. Thus, any differential in bargaining power or sophistication among cardholders would appear to be effectively neutralized by the use of form contracts in lieu of negotiation.

Finally, a statutory construction limiting the applicability of the § 1603 exemptions to the Truth in Lending Act as originally enacted, is surely buttressed by the concurrence of both the Federal Reserve Board and the Federal Trade Commission in that interpretation. The Board, charged with prescribing regulations pursuant to the Act, 15 U.S.C. § 1604, amended its so-called "Regulation Z" to make explicit that the Act's protection extends to corporate cardholders as well as to cards

4. The alternative would be at the time the credit card is used. Appellant can hardly find solace in this choice however, for it would then appear even more clearly that § 1603 does not apply to § 1643(a) since the unauthorized use of a credit card does not result in an extension of credit to the "cardholder." Thus, the exemptions contained in § 1603 would have no relevance to § 1643(a)—unless, of course, one must look to the unauthorized user to determine whether credit has been extended for business or commercial purposes as distinguished from personal needs.

issued for business or commercial purposes. 12 C.F.R. 226.13(a)(4) (1973) (amended Nov. 2, 1972). Although this amendment was adopted subsequent to the transaction at issue, the timing does not detract one whit from the relevance of the Board's views. The language of the amendment is precise in stating that the amendment's purpose was merely to clarify the existing statutory language. See 37 Fed.Reg. 24339 (1972). Similarly the Federal Trade Commission, the agency with primary enforcement responsibilities under the Truth in Lending Act, 15 U.S.C. § 1607, has also held that the Act's credit card provisions apply to all cardholders. In re Credit Card Service Corp. d/b/a Credit Card Service Bureau, supra. Since these administrative expressions concerning the Act's proper construction should be given great weight, Trafficante v. Metropolitan Life Ins. Co., 409 U.S. 205, 210, 93 S.Ct. 364, 34 L.Ed.2d 415 (1972), and especially so, where, as here, Congress delegated broad power to the supervising agencies, Mourning v. Family Publications Service, Inc., 411 U.S. 356, 371–373, 93 S.Ct. 1652, 36 L.Ed.2d 318 (1973), we believe that any abstruseness caused by the Truth in Lending Act's ambiguities should be resolved in favor of these sound agency interpretations. Accordingly, we hold that § 133(a) of the Truth in Lending Act, 15 U.S.C. § 1643(a), limiting liability exposure to $50 where the credit card use has been unauthorized, applies to all credit card holders. We therefore affirm.

Note

1. Seven months after the principal case was decided, Congress passed 15 U.S.C. § 1645, which provides, in pertinent part,

> [A] credit card issuer and a business or other organization which provides credit cards issued by the same card issuer to ten or more of its employees may by contract agree as to liability of the business or other organization with respect to unauthorized use of such credit cards * * *, but in no case may such business or card issuer impose liability upon an employee with respect to unauthorized use of such a credit card except in accordance with and subject to the limitations of section 1643 of this title.

Do you infer from that provision that Congress was not impressed by the Second Circuit's discussion of the relative bargaining power of credit card issuers and the businesses to which cards would be issued?

2. Of the several agreements that govern the legal relationships of the transactors in the credit card context (see Chapter 1), the document that resolves the fraud issues covered by the warranty provisions of Articles 3 and 4 is the agreement between the merchant who accepts the Visa or MasterCard in payment of goods or services and the bank to which the merchant discounts the charge slips. Typically such agreements will provide that

> The merchant warrants, as to each customer transaction slip, that the slip was actually signed by the person presenting the card; that it represents a bona fide sale as itemized on the sales slips; that the slip represents an unconditional obligation of the cardholder, not subject to

> any disputes, offsets, or counterclaims; that proper authorization was obtained if the transaction exceeded the applicable floor release limit; that the merchandise was actually delivered to the person who signed the transaction slip; and that the merchant has no knowledge of any fact that would impair the validity of the transaction slip.

Barkley Clark, The Law of Bank Deposits, Collections, and Credit Cards ¶ 11.02[4][b], pp. 11–10 to 11–11 (3d ed. 1990 & Supp.1992). Compare those warranties to the commercial paper and bank collections transfer warranties. Are they coextensive or does one regime or the other give the financial institution greater rights? Can the differences, if any, be justified by reference to differences fundamental to the payment systems? What must the bank show to establish a breach of warranty under the merchant agreement?

D. TORT AS A SOURCE OF LAW

Congress has recognized the potential for harm to consumers through credit card fraud and the card issuer's response to it. Both the E.F.T.A. and the Federal Truth In Lending Act were enacted to limit consumer liability for unauthorized electronic funds transfers and credit card use respectively. In each statute, the consumer's liability is dependent on her own negligence.

Compare with the Article 3 and 4 treatment of customer contributory fault, the E.F.T.A. and credit card approach to the problem. 15 U.S.C. § 1693g, the "Consumer liability" provision of the E.F.T.A., provides,

> **(a) Unauthorized electronic fund transfers; limit**
>
> A consumer shall be liable for any unauthorized electronic fund transfer involving the account of such consumer only if the card or other means of access utilized for such transfer was an accepted card or other means of access and if the issuer of such card, code, or other means of access has provided a means whereby the user of such card, code, or other means of access can be identified as the person authorized to use it, such as by signature, photograph, or fingerprint or by electronic or mechanical confirmation. In no event, however, shall a consumer's liability for an unauthorized transfer exceed the lesser of—
>
> (1) $50; or
>
> (2) the amount of money or value of property or services obtained in such unauthorized electronic fund transfer prior to the time the financial institution is notified of, or otherwise becomes aware of, circumstances which lead to the reasonable belief that an unauthorized electronic fund transfer involving the consumer's account has been or may be effected. Notice under this paragraph is sufficient when such steps have been taken as may be reasonably required in the ordinary course of business to provide the financial institution with the pertinent

information, whether or not any particular officer, employee, or agent of the financial institution does in fact receive such information.

Notwithstanding the foregoing, reimbursement need not be made to the consumer for losses the financial institution establishes would not have occurred but for the failure of the consumer to report within sixty days of transmittal of the statement (or in extenuating circumstances such as extended travel or hospitalization, within a reasonable time under the circumstances) any unauthorized electronic fund transfer or account error which appears on the periodic statement provided to the consumer under section 1693d of this title. In addition, reimbursement need not be made to the consumer for losses which the financial institution establishes would not have occurred but for the failure of the consumer to report any loss or theft of a card or other means of access within two business days after the consumer learns of the loss or theft (or in extenuating circumstances such as extended travel or hospitalization, within a longer period which is reasonable under the circumstances), but the consumer's liability under this subsection in any such case may not exceed a total of $500, or the amount of unauthorized electronic fund transfers which occur following the close of two business days (or such longer period) after the consumer learns of the loss or theft but prior to notice to the financial institution under this subsection, whichever is less.

(c) Determination of limitation on liability

In the event of a transaction which involves both an unauthorized electronic fund transfer and an extension of credit as defined in section 1602(e) of this title pursuant to an agreement between the consumer and the financial institution to extend such credit to the consumer in the event the consumer's account is overdrawn, the limitation on the consumer's liability for such transaction shall be determined solely in accordance with this section.

(d) Restriction on liability

Nothing in this section imposes liability upon a consumer for an unauthorized electronic fund transfer in excess of his liability for such a transfer under other applicable law or under any agreement with the consumer's financial institution.

(e) Scope of liability

Except as provided in this section, a consumer incurs no liability from an unauthorized electronic fund transfer.

Now consider how consumer liability for unauthorized transactions is treated in the credit card law:

§ 1643. Liability of holder of credit card

(a) Limits on liability

(1) A cardholder shall be liable for the unauthorized use of a credit card only if—

(A) the card is an accepted credit card;

(B) the liability is not in excess of $50;

(C) the card issuer gives adequate notice to the cardholder of the potential liability;

(D) the card issuer has provided the cardholder with a description of a means by which the card issuer may be notified of loss or theft of the card, which description may be provided on the face or reverse side of the statement required by section 1637(b) of this title or on a separate notice accompanying such statement;

(E) the unauthorized use occurs before the card issuer has been notified that an unauthorized use of the credit card has occurred or may occur as the result of loss, theft, or otherwise; and

(F) the card issuer has provided a method whereby the user of such card can be identified as the person authorized to use it.

(2) For purposes of this section, a card issuer has been notified when such steps as may be reasonably required in the ordinary course of business to provide the card issuer with the pertinent information have been taken, whether or not any particular officer, employee, or agent of the card issuer does in fact receive such information.

* * *

(c) Liability imposed by other laws or by agreement with issuer

Nothing in this section imposes liability upon a cardholder for the unauthorized use of a credit card in excess of his liability for such use under other applicable law or under any agreement with the card issuer.

(d) Exclusiveness of liability

Except as provided in this section, a cardholder incurs no liability from the unauthorized use of a credit card.

15 U.S.C. § 1643. How do those two separate sections of title 15 of the United States Code differ? Why should they differ? Review the following description of the E.F.T.A. consumer liability provided by the regulators.

A: *Situation 1—$500 Limit Applies*

Date and Event

June 1—C's card is stolen
June 2—$100 unauthorized transfer
June 3—C learns of theft
June 4—$25 unauthorized transfer
June 5—Close of 2 business days
June 7-8—$600 in unauthorized transfers that could have been prevented had notice been given by June 5
June 9—C notifies bank

Computation of C's liability:

Paragraph (b)(1) will apply to determine C's liability for any unauthorized transfers that occur before notice is given.

	C's liability
Amount of transfers before close of 2 business days: $125	[1] $50
Amount of transfers, after close of 2 business days and before notice to institution, that would not have occurred but for C's failure to notify within 2 business days: $600	[2] 450
C's total liability	500

[1] Maximum liability for this period.
[2] Because maximum liability is $500.

Situation 2—Both $500 and unlimited liability provisions apply

Date and Event

June 1—C's card is stolen
June 3—C learns of theft
June 5—Close of 2 business days
June 7—$200 unauthorized transfer that could have been prevented had notice been given by June 5
June 10—Periodic statement is transmitted to C (for period from 5/10 to 6/9)
June 15—$200 unauthorized transfer that could have been prevented had notice been given by June 5
July 10—Periodic statement of C's account is transmitted to C (for period from 6/10 to 7/9)
August 4—$300 unauthorized transfer that could have been prevented had notice been given by June 5
August 9—Close of 60 days after transmittal of statement showing unauthorized transfer
August 10—Periodic statement of C's account is transmitted to C (for period 7/10 to 8/9)
August 15—$100 unauthorized transfer that could have been prevented had notice been given by August 9
August 20—C notifies bank

Computation of C's liability:

Paragraph (b)(1) will apply to determine C's liability for unauthorized transfers that appear on the periodic statement and unauthorized transfers that occur before the close of the 60-day period. (The transfers need not both appear on the periodic statement *and* occur before the close of the 60-day period.) The maximum liability under (b)(1) is $500.

	C's liability
Amount of transfers before close of 2 business days: $0	$0
Amount of transfers, after close of 2 business days and before close of 60-day period, that would not have occurred but for C's failure to notify within 2 business days: $700	[1] 500

[1] Maximum liability.

Paragraph (b)(2)(ii) will apply to determine C's liability for transfers occurring after the close of the 60-day period. There is no dollar ceiling on liability under paragraph (b)(2)(ii).

Amount of transfers, after close of 60 days and before notice, that would not have occurred but for C's failure to notify within 60 days: $100	$100
C's total liability	600

Situation 3—$50/unlimited liability provisions apply

Facts same as in Situation 2, except that C does not learn of the card theft, but questions the account balance and notifies bank on August 20 of possible unauthorized transfers.

Computation of C's liability

In this situation only paragraph (b)(2) applies.

	C's liability
Amount of transfers appearing on the periodic statement or occurring during the 60-day period: $700	[1] $50
Amount of transfers, after close of 60-day period and before notice, that would not have occurred but for C's failure to notify within 60 days: $100	100
C's total liability	150

[1] Maximum liability for this period.

12 C.F.R. Pt. 205, Supp. II (1992).

How would the liability calculations differ under the credit card regime?

TRANSAMERICA INSURANCE COMPANY v. STANDARD OIL COMPANY

North Dakota Supreme Court, 1982.
325 N.W.2d 210.

VANDE WALLE, JUSTICE.

Robert Smith, former office manager of Minot Builders Supply Association (hereinafter "MBS"), fraudulently used a credit card issued to MBS by Standard Oil Company of Indiana, doing business as Amoco Oil Company (hereinafter "Amoco"), for his personal gain. Because Transamerica Insurance Company (hereinafter "Transamerica") insured MBS for wrongful acts by MBS employees, Transamerica paid MBS for the loss caused by Smith's fraud. As a result Transamerica became subrogated to MBS's claims. Transamerica brought an action against Amoco alleging that it was not liable for Smith's fraudulent charges under Federal and State credit-card laws. The district court of Ward County agreed and awarded Transamerica $26,376.53 plus costs. We reverse and remand for a reconsideration of the amount of damages consistent with this opinion.

In March 1967 MBS first obtained an Amoco credit card for use in its business. As office manager Smith's duties included requesting credit cards for MBS employees and paying bills. The cards were renewed periodically, and the charges were paid by MBS.

On May 16, 1975, Smith made a written request to Amoco for a Torch Club credit card. A Torch Club credit card is comparable to a Diner's Club card because it may be used for purchases of consumer goods and services other than those furnished at gasoline service stations. The Torch Club application was signed by Smith as office manager. It also contained the signature of Mr. Switzer as general manager and secretary-treasurer of MBS; however, the trial court determined that Mr. Switzer's signature was forged by Smith.

After receiving the application Amoco did not contact the credit references listed in the application letter or any officer of MBS. Amoco issued the Torch Club card after reviewing MBS's record of payment on its Amoco gasoline credit cards.

During the period from May 1975 until July 1978 Smith wrongfully and fraudulently used the Torch Club card to obtain goods and services in the amount of $26,376.53. MBS paid for these purchases with checks signed by Smith and an authorized officer. There is some indication that Smith forged a portion of the necessary second signatures and that he altered the records to cover his wrongful acts.

During this time MBS employed accountant firms to perform annual audits, but they did not discover the fraud.

After Smith's dishonesty was revealed, he was fired. MBS's fidelity-bond carrier, Transamerica, paid MBS its claim in full for the loss caused by Smith's fraudulent acts. Transamerica brought an action against Amoco as a subrogee under MBS's claim, alleging that it was not liable for the charges under Federal and State credit-card law. The trial court ruled in favor of Transamerica, and Amoco appealed.

In addition to the appeal on the merits, Transamerica moved to strike designations of Amoco's appendix. The portion of the appendix Transamerica objects to is a partial transcript of Transamerica v. Scheels Hardware, a North Dakota district court case also involving embezzlement by Smith. The material objected to in Amoco's appendix by Transamerica was not considered by this court in its review of the merits. Transamerica's motion is denied.

In May of 1968 the Congress passed the Truth in Lending Act, 15 U.S.C. §§ 1601–1667e (1977), which requires that creditors disclose the true cost of consumer credit so that consumers can make informed credit decisions. 15 U.S.C. § 1601 (1977). In 1970 the Congress passed an amendment to the Truth in Lending Act to regulate the credit-card industry. 15 U.S.C. §§ 1602, 1642–1644 (1977). The amendment had three purposes—to prohibit the unsolicited distribution of credit cards [15 U.S.C. § 1642 (1977)], to make the fraudulent use of credit cards a Federal crime [15 U.S.C. § 1644 (1977)], and to limit cardholder liability to 50 dollars for the unauthorized use of a credit card [15 U.S.C. § 1643 (1977)].

The original Truth in Lending Act focused upon consumer transactions and exempted extensions of credit for business purposes. 15 U.S.C. § 1603(*l*) (1977). In 1974 the Congress added a section to the Act stating that the business exemption in § 1603(*l*) does not apply to the credit-card legislation in §§ 1642–1644. 15 U.S.C. § 1645 (1977). All credit cards, whether used for business or for consumer purposes, are covered by the 50-dollar limit in § 1643. See Credit Card Service Corp., 495 F.2d 1004, 1008 (D.C.Cir.1974); American Airlines, Inc. v. Remis Industries, Inc., 494 F.2d 196, 202 (2d Cir.1974).

The version of 15 U.S.C. § 1643(a) (1977) in effect during the time of the transaction in issue is as follows: "A cardholder shall be liable for the unauthorized use of a credit card only if the card is an accepted credit card, the liability is not in excess of $50, the card issuer gives adequate notice to the cardholder of the potential liability, the card issuer has provided the cardholder with a self-addressed, prestamped notification to be mailed by the cardholder in the event of the loss or theft of the credit card, and the unauthorized use occurs before the cardholder has notified the card issuer that an unauthorized use of the credit card has occurred or may occur as the result of loss, theft, or otherwise * * *." The North Dakota Legislature also has enacted a credit-card statute, Section 51–14.1–02, N.D.C.C., which provides, in part: "A provision imposing liability on a cardholder for the unauthorized use of a credit card shall be effective only if the card is an accepted credit card, the liability imposed is not in excess of one hundred dollars, the card issuer gives adequate notice to the cardholder of the potential liability, and the unauthorized use occurs before the cardholder has notified the card issuer of the loss or theft of the card or of any unauthorized use."

The requirements for imposing liability and the legislative purposes are similar in the Federal and State legislation. In the Federal statute, though, maximum cardholder liability is $50 while in the State statute the limit is $100. We will not apply State law in contravention of the Federal statute. See Hickman v. Cliff Peck Chevrolet, Inc., 566 F.2d 44, 47 (8th Cir.1977). Therefore, the Federal statute supersedes the State statute to the extent the provisions regarding the amount of maximum cardholder liability for an unauthorized use actually conflict. See, generally, 16 Am.Jur.2d, Constitutional Law, § 291 (1979).

In 15 U.S.C. § 1643(a) and Section 51–14.1–02, N.D.C.C., a cardholder is liable for a limited amount if certain conditions are met and if the use of the credit card was unauthorized. Accordingly, the initial determination is whether or not the use of the credit card in the case at hand was unauthorized. The Federal and State definitions of "unauthorized use" are identical: "a use of a credit card by a person other than the cardholder who does not have actual, implied, or apparent authority for such use and from which the cardholder receives no benefit." 15 U.S.C. § 1602(*o*) (1977); Sec. 15–14.1–01(7), N.D.C.C. The test for determining unauthorized use is agency, and State agency law must be used to resolve this issue.

Smith did not have actual or implied actual authority to request an Amoco Torch Club credit card. The trial court correctly determined that the doctrine of ostensible authority controls in this case. The party who alleges the existence of agency based upon ostensible authority—here, Amoco—has the burden of proving agency by clear and convincing evidence. Farmers Union Oil Co. of Dickinson v. Wood, 301 N.W.2d 129, 133 (N.D.1980).

"Ostensible authority" is also called "apparent authority" and it "is such as the principal [MBS] intentionally or by want of ordinary care causes or allows a third person [Amoco] to believe the agent [Smith] to possess." Sec. 3–02–02, N.D.C.C. MBS is bound by Smith's acts under ostensible authority only to third persons who have incurred a liability in good faith and without ordinary negligence. See Sec. 3–03–03, N.D.C.C. The trial court determined that Amoco acted negligently by issuing MBS a Torch Club credit card without independently verifying Smith's authority. Because of this negligence the trial court determined that Amoco could not rely upon Smith's ostensible authority to establish the existence of agency.

The trial court's finding of fact that Amoco was negligent in issuing Smith the Torch Club card was not clearly erroneous. Credit-card issuers should make the necessary investigation prior to issuing a credit card. First National City Bank v. Mullarkey, 87 Misc.2d 1, 385 N.Y.S.2d 473 (1976). Amoco did not use the requisite reasonable diligence to ascertain whether or not Smith was acting within the scope of his authority. Therefore, Amoco is unable to rely upon the doctrine of ostensible authority when claiming Smith was authorized to request and use the Torch Club card. In Hagel v. Buckingham Wood Products, 261 N.W.2d 869, 875 (N.D.1977), this court quoted 3 Am.Jur.2d, Agency, § 78, as follows: "[A] third person dealing with a known agent must bear the burden of determining for himself, by the exercise of reasonable diligence and prudence, the existence or nonexistence of the agent's authority to act in the premises." Smith's request for a Torch Club credit card was "unauthorized" under the Federal and State credit-card legislation.

A second requirement for imposing limited cardholder liability under Federal and State law is that the card must be an accepted credit card. An "accepted credit card" is any credit card which the cardholder has requested, signed, used, or authorized another to use for the purpose of obtaining money, property, labor, or services on credit. 15 U.S.C. § 1602(*l*) (1977); Sec. 51–14.1–01(1), N.D.C.C. In the case at hand, MBS did not sign, use, or authorize Smith to use the credit card. The trial judge's finding that the Torch Club card was not an accepted credit card belonging to MBS was not clearly erroneous.

Both the Federal and the State statutes provide that when all the statutory requirements for limited liability are not met, the cardholder incurs no liability based upon the unauthorized use of any credit card. 15 U.S.C. § 1643(d) (1977); Sec. 51–14.1–02, N.D.C.C. Because the Torch Club card issued to Smith was not an accepted card, MBS and its subrogee, Transamerica, are not liable for the initial fraudulent charges made by Smith.

However, the trial court erred in not looking beyond Amoco's negligence in issuing Smith the card. After receiving the first statement from Amoco containing the fraudulent charges, MBS was negligent in not finding and reporting the fraud. If the person to whom a credit card is issued is careless, he may be held liable. 50 Am.Jur.2d, Letters of Credit, § 39 (1970). For example, in Martin v. American Express, Inc., 361 So.2d 597 (Ala.Civ.App.1978), a cardholder voluntarily permitted another who was involved in a business venture with him to use his credit card. The court held that the limit on liability in 15 U.S.C. § 1643(a) was inapplicable to these facts for policy reasons. Otherwise, an unscrupulous cardholder could allow another to charge hundreds of dollars in goods and services and then attempt to limit his liability to 50 dollars.

The Federal Truth in Lending Act does not answer the question of whether or not cardholder negligence removes the statutory liability limit. See Weistart, Consumer Protection in the Credit Card Industry: Federal Legislative Controls, 70 Mich.L.Rev. 1476, 1526 (1972). We believe that MBS's negligence in not examining its monthly statements from Amoco removes this case from the statutory limit on cardholder liability.

A bank customer has a duty to examine his bank statement promptly, using reasonable care to discover unauthorized signatures or alterations. Sec. 41–04–33(1), N.D.C.C. If the bank uses reasonable care in making the statement and if the bank customer fails to examine his statement, the customer is precluded from asserting his unauthorized signature against the bank after a certain time. Sec. 41–04–33(2), (4), N.D.C.C.[1] This commercial-paper situation parallels the facts at hand. Amoco was not negligent in billing MBS. If someone at MBS other than Smith had examined its statements from Amoco, he would have discovered Smith's fraud. It was the responsibility of MBS to institute internal procedures for the examination of the statements from Amoco which would have disclosed Smith's defalcation. It was solely within MBS's power to do so.[2] The failure of MBS to institute such procedures is the cause of that portion of the defalcation which occurred following the billing from Amoco which contained the first evidence of Smith's fraud.

Because of MBS's negligence, we will reexamine whether or not Smith acquired ostensible authority in his use of the Torch Club card after MBS became negligent. In Farmers Union Oil Co. of Dickinson v. Wood, supra, this court set forth the test to determine whether or not an ostensible authority existed. The authority must be based upon a principal's conduct which, reasonably interpreted, causes a third person to believe the agent has authority to act for the principal.

In Hagel v. Buckingham Wood Products, Inc., supra, 261 N.W.2d at 875, this court quoted with approval McGee v. Breezy Point Estates, 283 Minn. 10, 22, 166 N.W.2d 81, 89 (1969), as follows:

> "[T]he scope of apparent [ostensible] authority is determined not only by what the principal knows and acquiesces in, but also by what the principal should, in the exercise of ordinary care and

1. In Thoreson v. Citizens State Bank, 294 N.W.2d 397 (N.D.1980), an elevator manager's wife forged his signature on checks drawn on the Leeds Elevator checking account. This court determined that the elevator owner, Thoreson, did not act with reasonable care and promptness to discover the forged checks enclosed in the weekly bank statement and notify the bank. Because he did not act with reasonable care, Thoreson had the burden of proving that the bank did not exercise ordinary care in paying the forged checks in issue.

2. In Van Gohren v. Pacific National Bank of Washington, 8 Wash.App. 245, 505 P.2d 467 (1973), a bookkeeper embezzled company money by cashing forged checks, removing the canceled checks from the monthly bank statements, and altering the company books. Even a cursory look at the bank statements would have revealed the bank was charging the company's account for unauthorized checks. Discovery of the embezzlement was solely within the company's control.

prudence, know his agent is doing. "Thus, if a principal acts or conducts his business either intentionally or through negligence, or fails to disapprove of the agent's acts or course of action so as to lead the public to believe that his agent possesses authority to act or contract in the name of the principal, the principal is bound by the acts of the agent within the scope of his apparent authority as to persons who have reasonable grounds to believe that the agent has such authority and in good faith deal with him. 3 Am.Jur.(2d) Agency, § 74."

Amoco was negligent in issuing Smith the Torch Club card and therefore Amoco initially could not rely on the doctrine of ostensible authority. However, during Smith's fraudulent use of the card, Amoco was not negligent. Rather, MBS was negligent in not requiring that someone other than Smith examine its monthly statements. Smith embezzled money from MBS for three years through his fraudulent use of the Torch Club credit card. During this lengthy period of embezzlement, MBS always paid its monthly bill to Amoco. MBS contends that it is not proper for the court to consider the fact that MBS paid all the Amoco credit card charges. That contention is without merit. As a result of MBS's acts of paying for the charges and its failure to examine its statements so that it could notify Amoco of the fraud, MBS allowed Amoco to reasonably believe that Smith was authorized to use the credit card.

MBS claims that it relied upon its accountants to find fraud during annual audits. MBS made the decision to hire and rely upon accountants. This decision does not protect MBS from the inability of these accountants to discover the fraud.

We conclude that Amoco is liable for Smith's fraudulent purchases from the time the credit card was issued until MBS received the first statement from Amoco containing Smith's fraudulent charges plus a reasonable time to examine that statement. After that time, MBS's subrogee, Transamerica, is liable for the remaining fraudulent charges. We reverse the judgment and remand this case for a determination of when MBS should have examined its statements and discovered Smith's fraud, and, consistent with this opinion, for a new calculation of the damages.

ERICKSTAD, C.J., and SAND and PAULSON, JJ., concur.

PEDERSON, JUSTICE, concurring and dissenting.

I agree that the judgment should be reversed but I do not agree that the remand should be for the purpose of recalculation of the damages. On remand, the judgment should be entered for Amoco.

The application for the Torch Club credit card was made by Smith, office manager, whose authority to do so is questioned, and by Switzer, secretary-treasurer, whose authority to do so is not questioned. It is noted that Switzer testified that he was the general manager.

The court made no findings of fact as contemplated by Rule 52(a), N.D.R.Civ.P., but if we search hard enough and use our imagination, in the court's memorandum opinion we find what appears to be a finding of fact that the application for the Torch Club credit card "carried the forged signature of Mr. Switzer." That is a controlling question in this case. As a finding of fact, it is unsupported by any substantial evidence and that makes it "clearly erroneous."

Switzer testified on direct examination as follows:

> "Q [by Mr. Rau] Does that appear to be your signature on this letter? "A [by Mr. Switzer] That is very like my signature, *yes.*" [Emphasis added.]
>
> On cross-examination Switzer testified: "Q [by Mr. Durick] I am just wondering. I think signatures are quite personal and I know—I think I could identify mine. "A [by Mr. Switzer] If this were handed to me and said, 'Is this your signature?' I would have to say it certainly looks like it, *yes.*" [Emphasis added.]

Then the judge inquired as follows:

> "THE COURT: That is essentially what he is doing. In your opinion, I know you can't be totally certain, but you feel it is your signature? "THE WITNESS: *Yes.*" [Emphasis added.]

Commenting on the holding in Verry v. Murphy, 163 N.W.2d 721 (N.D.1969), this court said in Malarchick v. Pierce, 264 N.W.2d 478, 480 (N.D.1978), that:

> "We believe, however, that testimony unfavorable to one's own contention can be a 'judicial admission' if it is 'deliberate, clear and unequivocal.' "

The fact that other witnesses may have said that this was a forged signature does not reduce Switzer's answers to something less than a judicial admission. I do not agree that either the federal statute (15 U.S.C. § 1643) or the state statute (§ 51–14.1–02, NDCC) has any bearing on this case.

Note

1. Does the result reached in the principal case seem consistent with the statutory design of the Truth in Lending Act? If the cardholder's negligence can result in avoidance of the liability limits, should that circumstance be disclosed when the credit card is issued?

2. The drafters of the U.N.P.C. tried to compose a liability rule that would govern the relative rights of financial institution and customer when the customer had been charged for unauthorized use of checks, credit cards, or other media of value transfer. Section 202(2) of the last draft of the U.N.P.C. provided that

> A person is otherwise precluded from asserting as drawer that an order is unauthorized if the person's negligence substantially contributed to the order becoming unauthorized, unless a transferee or funds transferor gave value for or on a payor account institution paid an order in bad

faith or other than in accordance with the reasonable commercial standards of its business, or fraudulently and materially altered an order.

The comment to that section explained that "[n]egligence is left undefined. While it will be given content by the courts, it should generally consist of actions which could be taken by the drawer to prevent the loss at a lower cost than the discounted expectation of loss. Negligence will obviously vary with the various payment systems and the available safeguards." U.N.P.C. § 200, comment 3. See *United States v. Carroll Towing Co.*, 159 F.2d 169 (2d Cir.1947) (Negligence is a function of three variables: possibility of accident's occurring; "gravity of resulting injury"; and "burden of adequate precautions.").

E. DISCLOSURE

Both the credit card law and the EFT law contain comprehensive disclosure provisions requiring financial institutions that make credit cards and access devices available to their customers to regularly apprise their customers of the terms of their account agreements and their consumer rights in the event of error. The following two cases describe the disclosure regimes and the policies supporting them. The first case concerns error resolution in the EFT context and the second case involves disclosure of finance rate in the credit card setting.

BISBEY v. DISTRICT OF COLUMBIA NATIONAL BANK

United States Court of Appeals, District of Columbia Circuit, 1986.
793 F.2d 315.

HARRY T. EDWARDS, CIRCUIT JUDGE:

Sandra Bisbey challenges the refusal of the District Court to hold the District of Columbia National Bank ("the Bank") liable for a violation of the Electronic Fund Transfer Act of 1984 ("the Act"). The District Court found that the Bank, in its resolution of Ms. Bisbey's inquiry about her account, erroneously failed to deliver or mail to her an explanation of its investigative findings. However, the trial court concluded that the Act did not contemplate a finding of civil liability for this type of procedural mistake.

We reverse the District Court. Although there is no evidence of bad faith in this case, it is nonetheless clear that Bank officials failed to comply with provisions of the Act. Therefore, the case must be remanded for a determination of civil liability and attorney's fees.

I. BACKGROUND

A. Facts

Ms. Bisbey opened a checking account with the defendant Bank in January 1981. Subsequently, she authorized the Bank to debit her checking account for fund transfer directives submitted monthly by the

New York Life Insurance Company ("NYLIC") for payment for her insurance premiums.

In September 1981, Ms. Bisbey's account lacked sufficient funds to cover the NYLIC directive, and no transfer was made. Thus, the September request was resubmitted by NYLIC in October, along with the latter month's directive. Appellant's funds were insufficient to satisfy either submission, both of which were covered by the Bank. As a result, two overdraft notices were sent to Ms. Bisbey, each in the amount of her monthly insurance premium. The appellant, having forgotten her nonpayment in September, believed that the Bank had erroneously made two payments in October.

At this point, Ms. Bisbey informed a customer representative of the Bank that she believed that an error had occurred with regard to these preauthorized transfers. Upon request by the Bank, she confirmed her inquiry by letter. Approximately ten days later, an official of the Bank telephoned appellant and orally explained that there had been no improper duplication of her premium payments. Ms. Bisbey, however, still considered the matter unresolved, and she filed suit under the EFTA.

B. *Procedural History*

In her complaint, plaintiff alleged that the Bank unlawfully failed to properly inform her about the result of its investigation into the alleged duplication error in her checking account. She sought compensatory, treble and liquidated damages; the Bank filed a counterclaim for costs and attorney's fees, alleging that the plaintiff had brought suit in bad faith.

In relevant part, the opinion of the District Court held that the Bank had failed to comply with its statutory obligation to provide written notice of its findings when it concluded that no electronic funds transfer error had occurred. However, the trial court determined that section 915 of the Act, which provides for civil liability and attorney's fees for certain violations, was, by its own terms, not applicable to the mistake at issue. Finally, neither party was deemed to have acted in bad faith; thus, the District Court found that an award of attorney's fees was unwarranted.

II. Analysis

Section 908(d) of the Act provides:

> If [a] financial institution determines after its investigation * * * that an error did not occur, it shall *deliver or mail to consumer an explanation of its findings within 3 business days* after the conclusion of its investigation, and upon request of the consumer promptly deliver or mail to the consumer reproductions of all documents which the financial institution relied on to conclude that such error did not occur. *The financial institution shall include notice of the right to request reproductions with the explanation of its findings.*

This section imposed a duty upon the Bank to "deliver or mail" the results of its investigation to Ms. Bisbey and to advise her of her right to request reproductions of all documents which it relied upon to conclude that no error occurred.[5] The oral notice given to appellant was insufficient with respect to the required "explanation," and it did not even purport to give "notice of the right to request reproductions" as required by the statute.

The Bank's foregoing failures to comply with the statute give rise to civil liability under section 915 of the Act. That section provides that "any person who fails to comply with any provision of [the Act] with respect to any consumer, except for an error resolved in accordance with section 908, is liable to such consumer" for actual damages or for a symbolic award. Thus, under the plain terms of the Act, civil liability attaches to *all* failures of compliance with respect to *any* provision of the Act, including section 908.

An examination of other provisions of the Act supports this analysis. We note, for example, that section 908(e) specifies certain egregious *violations of section 908* which would result in an award of treble damages, such as a failure to provisionally recredit a consumer's account while simultaneously failing to perform a good faith investigation. The singling out of these particular violations and their focus on willful unlawfulness for an award of treble damages suggests that other failures to comply with the statute in the application of section 908 give rise to standard civil liability.

The Bank contends that the only "fail[ure]s to comply" to which civil liability should adhere are those which *may* be cured by the error resolution process of section 908. And, appellee maintains, it is unlikely that such procedural mistakes as occur in the course of an attempt to utilize the error resolution process would, in turn, be resolved by that same process.

This argument is patently flawed. There are "fail[ure]s of compliance" with the Act which cannot be or are unlikely to be resolved under section 908—such as a violation of section 908 itself—and which nonetheless give rise to civil liability. For example, section 910 sets forth the liability of financial institutions for damages caused by certain acts and omissions with regard to electronic fund transfers. These acts and omissions plainly constitute "fail[ure]s to comply" with the Act, yet they do not fall within the statutory definition of "error" for purposes of utilizing the error resolution procedures set forth in

5. Although it did not cross-appeal the decision against it on this issue, the Bank suggests that the phrase "deliver or mail" encompasses oral delivery of the results of an investigation and argues that this theory provides an alternative ground for dismissal of the case. We disagree. This section also requires that, at the customer's request, reproductions of documents be delivered or mailed, obviously requiring a physical transfer of documents by mail or by hand. We find it highly improbable that these phrases would possess different meanings when used so closely in conjunction. In any event, the Bank has no explanation for its failure to give appellant "notice of the right to request reproductions," as required by the last sentence in the cited section.

section 908.[6] But surely a financial institution cannot escape civil liability for a breach of section 910 merely because the breach cannot be resolved under section 908 pursuant to the "error" correction procedures. Civil liability attaches due to the "fail[ure] to comply" with the law.

Section 915 provides for an exception to civil liability for "an error resolved in accordance with section 908." Plainly, this exception has no play in this case. The Bank's failures to comply (i.e. the failure to "deliver or mail * * * an explanation" and the failure to give "notice of the right to request reproductions") were never cured. Therefore, these failures cannot be viewed as "errors resolved in accordance with section 908" within the exception to civil liability enunciated in section 915. The District Court's ruling to the contrary is simply wrong as a matter of law.

If the Bank had made a mistake in transferring funds from appellant's account and then had redressed the error pursuant to section 908 (without otherwise failing to comply with section 908), then the exception to section 915 would have to come into play. In such a case, the Bank could not be charged with civil liability for the mistaken transfer of funds because the "error" would have been fully cured pursuant to section 908. In this case, however, there is no problem with mistaken fund transfers; rather, the problem here has arisen because the Bank failed to comply with provisions in the Act when addressing a lawful inquiry about possible mistaken fund transfers.

It may seem odd that the Bank is held liable for a transaction that benefited the plaintiff. Ms. Bisbey's account contained insufficient funds to cover either of the premium requests submitted by NYLIC. Though she had no overdraft agreement, the Bank did not charge an overdraft fee. Thus, the effect of the Bank's payments was to provide her, at no cost, with insurance coverage she would not have had otherwise. Upon Bisbey's inquiry, the Bank gave her a correct report but neglected to send it in writing, as the statute requires. Ms. Bisbey conceded below that she had suffered no damage and the District Court's surmise that she may have been benefited seems correct. Despite this, the litigation has continued for nearly three years, and the statute compels a finding that the Bank is liable. Doubtless the discretion given the District Court to award only nominal damages and a "reasonable" attorney's fee was designed to mitigate the results of strict liability in cases such as this, involving a technical and non-damaging violation.

III. CONCLUSION

The "fail[ure]s to comply" with the EFTA in the instant case are plain; moreover, they are failures to which civil liability attaches for they have not been resolved in accordance with section 908. We

6. For example, under certain circumstances, a failure to make an electronic fund transfer is a violation of section 910, but that omission does not conform to any of the definitions of "error" in section 908.

therefore remand this case to the District Court for a determination of civil liability and attorney's fees pursuant to section 915.

So ordered.

RATNER v. CHEMICAL BANK NEW YORK TRUST COMPANY

United States District Court, Southern District of New York, 1971.
329 F.Supp. 270.

FRANKEL, DISTRICT JUDGE.

The central question in this case is whether defendant Bank violated the disclosure requirements of the Truth in Lending Act when it failed to show the "nominal annual percentage rate" of interest on a statement to plaintiff obligor under an "open end consumer credit plan," where the statement showed an outstanding balance but no finance charge yet incurred so that no interest rate had yet been applied. (This involved statement of the question and its terms of art should become intelligible as we proceed.) Other questions now before the court are (1) whether, assuming a failure of adequate disclosure, the plaintiff before us is entitled to sue, and (2) whether defendant Bank is absolved because, if there was a violation, it was "not intentional." Finally, the parties have agreed, with the court's concurrence, to postpone for the time being questions as to whether the case may proceed as a class action and as to the amount of plaintiff's recoverable costs and legal fees if he is entitled to such recovery.

Now before the court are defendant's motion to dismiss and plaintiff's motion for summary judgment. Upon the study of an extensive stipulation and the long, scholarly briefs for both sides, the court concludes that the facts deemed material are undisputed; that the issues ripe for decision should be resolved in plaintiff's favor; and that further submissions on the postponed issues must precede, and determine the nature of, the summary judgment to be entered for plaintiff.

I.

The Truth in Lending Act (hereinafter "The Act") is Title I, 15 U.S.C. § 1601 et seq. of the Consumer Credit Protection Act of May 29, 1968, 82 Stat. 146. Under the Act an "open end credit plan" is one "prescribing the terms of credit transactions which may be made thereunder from time to time and under the terms of which a finance charge may be computed on the outstanding unpaid balance from time to time thereunder." As everyone knows who has not sojourned lately in a cave, plans of this kind have proliferated widely in the last few years. The parties here are known as a Master Charge Card Agreement.

Under this Agreement, as is commonly the case with such plans, the cardholder may use his card to purchase goods and services and/or to borrow money, and he may at any time repay all or any part of his outstanding indebtedness. The Bank [3] sends the cardholder at the end of each month (or "billing cycle") a statement setting forth, among other things, the indebtedness outstanding at the beginning of the month ("previous balance"), all charges and credits to the account during the month (including finance charges, if any, incurred during the month) and the indebtedness outstanding at the end of the month ("new balance").

Under plans of this type generally, the cardholder may incur a service or finance charge in connection with any extension of credit, and this may be computed as a minimum charge, a percentage of the outstanding indebtedness or in other ways. Under the Master Charge plan, where the cardholder borrows money, he incurs a finance charge from the date the indebtedness is contracted. For purchases of goods and services, however, the cardholder incurs no finance charge until the 26th day after the "billing date" shown on the statement which first reflects the indebtedness. In other words, if the indebtedness is paid in full before the expiration of the 25–day grace period (called, naturally, the "free-ride"), there is no finance charge.

The Act imposes an array of disclosure requirements to further the objective of "truth in lending"—"so that the consumer will be able to compare more readily the various credit terms available to him and avoid the uninformed use of credit." Among other things, the creditor under an open end plan, before opening an account, must disclose to the prospective obligor, "to the extent applicable," the conditions for imposing finance charges, the length of any free-ride period, the method of determining finance charges, the periodic rate for computing finance charges, and "the corresponding nominal annual percentage rate determined by multiplying the periodic rate by the number of periods in a year." It is not disputed that the Agreement in this case complied with these requirements.

Once an open end account is created, the creditor must send the obligor, "for each billing cycle at the end of which there is an outstanding balance in that account or with respect to which a finance charge is imposed, a statement setting forth" a number of prescribed items of information. The full provision governing such periodic statements central in the present dispute, is given here in a footnote.[7] For his

3. The reference here and hereafter is to defendant, but the practices described, and the statutory requirements, are similar for other open end credit plans.

7. Id. § 127(b), 15 U.S.C. § 1637(b) (Supp. V): "The creditor of any account under an open end consumer credit plan shall transmit to the obligor, for each billing cycle at the end of which there is an outstanding balance in that account or with respect to which a finance charge is imposed, a statement setting forth each of the following items to the extent applicable: (1) The outstanding balance in the account at the beginning of the statement period. (2) The amount and date of each extension of credit during the period, and, if a purchase was involved, a brief identification (unless previously furnished) of the goods or services purchased. (3) The total amount credited to the account during the period. (4) The amount of any finance charge added to the account during the period, itemized to show the amounts, if any, due to the application of percentage rates and the amount, if any, imposed as a minimum or fixed charge. (5) Where one or more periodic rates may be used to

charge of an unlawful omission, plaintiff relies on paragraph "(5)," which for convenience we remove from its vital setting and repeat here in text, italicizing the words central to his thesis:

> "Where one or more periodic rates may be used to compute the finance charge, (the statement is to set forth) each such rate, the range of balances to which it is applicable, and, unless the annual percentage rate (determined under section 1606(a)(2) of this title) is required to be disclosed pursuant to paragraph (6), *the corresponding nominal annual percentage rate determined by multiplying the periodic rate by the number of periods in a year.*"

The periodic statement sent by defendant Bank to plaintiff for the monthly period ending September 15, 1969, disclosed an outstanding indebtedness of $111.41 at the beginning of the period (approximately August 15, 1969); that this amount had been paid during the free-ride period so that it had given rise to no finance charge; that plaintiff had acquired a new indebtedness of $191.58 for purchases during the monthly period (the "new balance"); and (in a line of type under the new balance), a legend and an arrow pointing to the "new balance" and indicating "no additional finance charges if (this total of $191.58 was) paid in 25 days from bill date." On the far right, on the other hand, the statement indicated as a "minimum payment" the sum of $10.00, explained on the back of the form (and in accordance with the Agreement) as the payment required "to avoid delinquency." Although no finance charge had been incurred during the period covered by the statement, but in seeming compliance with 127(b)(5) of the Act, the statement reported three periodic (monthly) percentage rates: 1.50% For purchases up to $500, 1.00% For purchases over $500, and 1.00% For cash advances. However,—and here we reach the point of the case—no "annual percentage rate" of any kind was shown.

Plaintiff sent defendant the minimum payment of $10.00. It appears that plaintiff, on his next statement, was billed for a finance charge. In the meantime, on September 24, 1969, plaintiff filed the

compute the finance charge, each such rate, the range of balances to which it is applicable, and, unless the annual percentage rate (determined under section 1606(a)(2) of this title) is required to be disclosed pursuant to paragraph (6), the corresponding nominal annual percentage rate determined by multiplying the periodic rate by the number of periods in a year. (6) Where the total finance charge exceeds 50 cents for a monthly or longer billing cycle, or the pro rata part of 50 cents for a billing cycle shorter than monthly, the total finance charge expressed as an annual percentage rate (determined under section 1606(a)(2) of this title), except that if the finance charge is the sum of two or more products of a rate times a portion of the balance, the creditor may, in lieu of disclosing a single rate for the total charge, disclose each such rate expressed as an annual percentage rate, and the part of the balance to which it is applicable. (7) At the election of the creditor, the average effective annual percentage rate of return (or the projected rate) under the plan as prescribed in subsection (a)(5) of this section. (8) The balance of which the finance charge was computed and a statement of how the balance was determined. If the balance is determined without first deducting all credits during the period, that fact and the amount of such payments shall also be disclosed. (9) The outstanding balance in the account at the end of the period. (10) The date by which, or the period (if any) within which, payment must be made to avoid additional finance charges."

complaint instituting the present lawsuit. His ultimate contention is, in the language of the complaint, that "defendant's monthly statement to plaintiff in September 1969, violated the Act and the implementing Regulation, 12 CFR 226.7, in that it failed to disclose the annual percentage rate or the nominal annual percentage rate." We proceed to that central topic.

II.

A. To begin with the statutory language most directly in issue, § 127(b)(5) (note 7, supra) appears literally to require the kind of disclosure defendant omitted—and, specifically, disclosure of the "nominal annual percentage rate" of 18% For the category of purchases under $500.[10] Defendant attacks this literal reading by referring to the introductory words of the subsection, which say that the items listed are to be disclosed "to the extent applicable." No "nominal annual percentage rate" was "applicable," defendant says, because there was no finance charge for the period covered by the statement. Hence, no "rate" of any kind "applied." (Defendant did show the "monthly periodic rate," which was not "applied" to the statement in question. Despite defendant's attempted explanation, which the court considers elsewhere, this seeming anomaly remains to haunt and undermine a substantial portion of defendant's contentions.) Expanding on this in a Reply Memorandum, defendant argues that 127(b) of the Act, concerning periodic statements, was designed to require an historical account of things that had actually happened, as contrasted with 127(a), governing the opening Agreement and its disclosures. It is worth noting that under defendant's reading, the nominal annual percentage rate would never have to be disclosed on the monthly statement—making § 127(b)(5) meaningless—because it is, by definition, never "applied" in the sense plaintiff means. But even apart from that, the argument is weak as a matter of dictionary English and utterly limp as a matter of construction of the statute and its patent purposes.

The word "applicable" is hardly confined in meaning to what has been or is being "applied." It means, to use the dictionary only as a preliminary reference, not a legal authority:

> "Capable of being applied; fit, suitable, or right to be applied; having relevance; as, this observation is *applicable* to the case under consideration."

To illustrate the nature and signification of this usage, we need look no farther than the subsection defendant invokes, 127(a), governing the so-called "prospective" disclosure made when nothing has yet happened, everything is "unknown," nothing is being applied, and, therefore, in defendant's parlance, nothing is "applicable." Subsection (a) uses the same words: it lists the items to be disclosed "to the extent

10. That "nominal" rate, it will be recalled, is derived by multiplying the monthly periodic rate (1.50% For purchases under $500) by the number of months in a year.

applicable." And it lists, inter alia, both the periodic rates "and the corresponding nominal annual percentage rate * * *."

Clearly, "applicable" means "relevant" under the plan or statement in question. And that—when the plaintiff faced a finance charge if he chose to accept defendant's invitation to pay only the $10 minimum, and take the credit—was exactly the case for both the periodic rate defendant did show and the annual rate it omitted.

The characterization of § 127(b) as "historical" is demonstrably wrong in at least one other respect. Looking strictly to the future, the tenth item required to be shown (as defendant showed it) is the "date by which, or the period (if any) within which, payment must be made to avoid additional finance charges." [12]

But there are grounds more profound than these semantical ones for rejecting defendant's view. The thrust of the Act and its fundamental weapon of compelled disclosure is "prospective." Its purpose is to put the borrower in possession of the pertinent information before the plunge, so that he may know and intelligently compare his options. This appears at the outset in the findings and declaration of purpose, § 102, 15 U.S.C. § 1601 (Supp. V):

"The Congress finds that economic stabilization would be enhanced and the competition among the various financial institutions and other firms engaged in the extension of consumer credit would be strengthened by the informed use of credit. The informed use of credit results from an awareness of the cost thereof by consumers. It is the purpose of this subchapter to assure a meaningful disclosure of credit terms so that the consumer will be able to compare more readily the various credit terms available to him and avoid the uninformed use of credit."

Throughout the legislative process of achieving truth in lending, this was the general theme, and it is at war with defendant's position. Relevant legislative history shows that Congress expected the monthly statement to make people like the plaintiff aware of their credit options. They were to have, prospectively, not only the monthly rate (which defendant gave), but the annual rate also, so they could compare it with rates of other lenders, savings bank interest rates, etc. (commonly given as annual, not monthly, rates), before deciding whether to accept the invitation to take credit from defendant, shop other lenders, or draw money from savings accounts to pay off the indebtedness. There is nothing in the legislative history showing any purpose to

12. In an earlier phase of this litigation, where "the merits of this controversy (were) not before the court," Judge Cannella gave the pertinent language the same reading it receives in this decision. As he saw the matter, 15 U.S.C. § 1637(b) lists information (including the annual percentage rate) which must be disclosed "for each billing cycle at the end of which there is an outstanding balance in that account or with respect to which a finance charge is imposed * * *; since these phrases "are in the disjunctive and not the conjunctive * * *, upon either condition the information would be required to be set forth." Ratner v. Chemical Bank New York Trust Company, 309 F.Supp. 983, 988 n. 10 (S.D.N.Y.1969).

exempt monthly statements not imposing finance charges from the basic annual rate disclosure requirement.

Earlier versions of the bill, although more limited in disclosure requirements than the final enactment, all had as their fundamental purpose to serve this "prospective" need. Thus, the basic purpose of the Senate bill (S. 5) was stated as being to "permit consumers to compare the cost of credit among different creditors and to shop effectively for the best credit buy." S.Rep. No. 392, 90th Cong., 1st Sess. 1 (1967). House Report No. 1040, 90th Cong., 1st Sess. 7, 13 (1967), U.S.Code Cong. & Admin.News 1968, p. 1962, of the Committee considering H.R. 11601 repeated the aim to "permit the consumer to 'comparison shop' for credit" by "requiring all creditors to disclose credit information in a uniform manner * * * (giving) the American consumer * * * the information he needs to compare the cost of credit and to make the best informed decision on the use of credit." A minority of House Committeemen, whose views on specific disclosure requirements for revolving credit were eventually adopted by the entire House, reported that "the purpose (of the House Bill) is to assure to the consumer sufficient, clearly understandable and readily comparable information to enable him to measure various types of consumer credit proposals with one another and then decide, with reasonable accuracy, which offer is more suitable to his economic situation, or a better buy, or whether he should dip into his savings or make other arrangements to avoid using credit in a particular situation." Id. at 106. The general focus, then, is on making various credit options known and understandable to the consumer, before he decides among them; and this is the reason for requiring disclosure of an annual rate on the monthly statement, which, of course, is a proposal to accept credit and not pay in full the New Balance. Implementing this objective, the bill that finally emerged from Conference required an annual rate of some type to be disclosed on each monthly statement, including statements not actually applying any rate. According to the Conference Report:

> "In any statement of an account under an open end plan under which a rate may be used to compute the finance charge (even though, for the particular month, the rate may yield a charge below the minimum and thus be inapplicable) the creditor must state the periodic rate and the 'nominal' annual percentage rate determined by multiplying the periodic rate by the number of periods in a year." H.Rep. No. 1397, 90th Cong., 2d Sess. 27 (1968), U.S.Code Cong. & Admin.News 1968, p. 2024.

The compromise reached in Conference concerned only the methods to be used in computing the annual rate disclosed.[13] But, as

13. The Senate bill, as amended in Committee, exempted most revolving credit plans from the annual rate disclosure requirement. The House Banking and Currency Committee, by bare majority, had carved a similar exception in H.R. 11601. See H.R.Rep. No. 1040, 90th Cong., 1st Sess. 13–17, 107–115 (1967). On the House floor, however, the original wording of H.R. 11601 was restored, and the annual percentage rate disclosure requirement was applied to open end credit. (Defen-

Congressman Wright Patman reported back to the House from the conference, "We have maintained our basic position of annual rate disclosure on revolving charge accounts." 114 Cong.Rec. 14384 (1968).

The history, in sum, is, like the statutory language on its face, compellingly favorable to plaintiff's position.

B. Defendant moves to more promising, but eventually infirm, ground when it invokes the Federal Reserve Board's Regulation Z, 12 CFR 226.[14] In pertinent part, the Regulation says, 226.7:

> "The creditor of any open end credit account shall mail or deliver to the customer, for each billing cycle at the end of which there is an outstanding debit balance in excess of $1 in that account or with respect to which a finance charge is imposed, a statement or statements which the customer may retain, setting forth * * * each of the following items to the extent applicable:
>
> (5) Each periodic rate, using the term 'periodic rate' (or 'rates'), that may be used to compute the finance charge (whether or not applied during the billing cycle), and the range of balances to which it is applicable.
>
> (6) The annual percentage rate or rates determined under 226.5(a), using the term 'annual percentage rate' (or 'rates'), and, where there is more than one rate, the amount of the balance to which each rate is applicable. * * * "

The fragment defendant takes as a weapon from this is the parenthetical phrase in paragraph (5), "(whether or not applied during the billing cycle)." There is no such phrase in paragraph (6). So, it is

dant's attempt to interpret H.R. 11601 as requiring annual rate disclosure only on monthly statements imposing a finance charge is based on its repeated argument that "finance charge" means the finance charge "applied" during the previous billing period—a construction no more acceptable in this context than elsewhere.) The compromise reached by the Senate and House Conferees distinguished between the kinds of annual rate that had to be disclosed, but required either a nominal or actual rate on all monthly statements. And so Senator Proxmire, the sponsor of the Senate bill, reported back to his colleagues that "the effect of the conference provision is to permit creditors to disclose a nominal annual percentage rate equal to 12 times the monthly rate on all monthly statements, as long as minimum or fixed charges authorized by State law did not exceed 50 cents. If State law permitted minimum charges in excess of 50 cents and if the creditor applied such minimum charges, he would be required to annualize such charges and to disclose the resulting, rate on each monthly statement." 114 Cong.Rec. 14489 (1968). Although one of the conferees' chief areas of concern appears to have been how to "annualize" a fixed minimum finance charge, there is nothing in the history to suggest that in cases where no finance charge had been imposed for the billing period, creditors were to be exempted altogether from the basic requirement of disclosing annual rates on all monthly statements. See also Remarks of Representative Sullivan, cosponsor of the House bill, 114 Cong.Rec. 14386 (1968).

14. § 105 of the Act, 15 U.S.C. § 1604 (Supp. V), says: "The (Federal Reserve) Board shall prescribe regulations to carry out the purposes of this subchapter. These regulations may contain such classifications, differentiations, or other provisions, and may provide for such adjustments and exceptions for any class of transactions, as in the judgment of the Board are necessary or proper to effectuate the purposes of this subchapter, to prevent circumvention or evasion thereof, or to facilitate compliance therewith."

argued, the nominal annual rate is not required to be given, as it is under paragraph (5) in the corresponding statutory subsection "whether or not applied during the billing cycle." But omitting arguments about excluded middles, the point is not valid. The Regulation, like the statute, reflects that "applicable" and "applied" are not the same words. It nowhere says that the nominal annual rate should be omitted, but a periodic rate included, when there is no finance charge to which either is being "applied." The Federal Reserve draftsmen appear to have done no more than attempt a useful simplification, but perhaps at the cost of some confusion, when they undertook to shorten and streamline the thoughts spread out through paragraphs (5) and (6) of the statutory subsection.

Above all, defendant's analysis does not lead to a sensible result. There is no justification in the statutory purpose for requiring inclusion of the periodic rate and omission of the annual rate on the kind of occasion here in question—when neither has been or is being "applied." The reasons for giving either, already outlined, apply equally to both. Indeed, there is much to be said for the view that if only one were to be given, it should be the annual, more useful for comparisons, not the monthly periodic rate. But the statute requires both. The language of the Regulation embraces both. It would take much more than a possibly missing parenthesis to persuade that the Board meant to alter the statute in the (probably impermissible) fashion defendant suggests.

* * *

D. Scattered through defendant's earnest and skillful arguments is the assertion that an *actual* "annual percentage rate" cannot be computed when there has been no finance charge and that "under some open end credit plans" disclosure of a "nominal" rate "would be seriously misleading to a cardholder." The answer is (1) the statute calls for the "nominal" rate and (2) defendant, whatever may be true under "some" plans, has for a long time (though after this lawsuit began) been giving annual percentage rates of the kind plaintiff claims are required. In a letter to the Federal Reserve Board, a copy of which has been filed with the court, defendant explained that this altered practice, coinciding with what plaintiff says the statute requires, came about when (1) "the concern that provides computer services to Chemical offered to print * * * an annual percentage rate on all its periodic statements"; (2) Chemical said not to do it; (3) "the computer concern * * * inadvertently" did it anyhow; (4) Chemical "discovered (this) for the first time" several months after giving the contrary instructions; and (5) "Chemical concluded, after some deliberation, that it would be disruptive and possibly confusing to its cardholders to have its program altered again." So the annual rates plaintiff demands are being disclosed, presumably without strain and without misleading cardholders. Whatever chilling things all this tells about our prospects in the computer dynasty, it dissipates many of the fears and troubles defendant hypothesizes as answers to plaintiff's claim.

III.

The basis for plaintiff's claim and the court's jurisdiction over it is § 130 of the Act, 15 U.S.C. § 1640 (Supp. V), which provides:

> "(a) Failure to disclose.
>
> Except as otherwise provided in this section, any creditor who fails in connection with any consumer credit transaction to disclose to any person any information required under this part to be disclosed to that person is liable to that person in an amount equal to the sum of
>
> (1) twice the amount of the finance charge in connection with the transaction, except that the liability under this paragraph shall not be less than $100 nor greater than $1,000; and
>
> (2) in the case of any successful action to enforce the foregoing liability, the costs of the action together with a reasonable attorney's fee as determined by the court. * * *
>
> (c) Unintentional violations; bona fide errors.
>
> A creditor may not be held liable in any action brought under this section for a violation of this part if the creditor shows by a preponderance of evidence that the violation was not intentional and resulted from a bona fide error notwithstanding the maintenance of procedures reasonably adapted to avoid any such error.
>
> * * *
>
> (e) Jurisdiction of courts.
>
> Any action under this section may be brought in any United States district court, or in any other court of competent jurisdiction, within one year from the date of the occurrence of the violation."

Defendant argues that, assuming it violated the disclosure requirements, plaintiff's suit must be dismissed on one or more of three independently sufficient grounds:

> A. That "plaintiff did not incur any finance charge in connection with the transaction which gave rise to the alleged violation * * *."
>
> B. Defendant has a "good faith defense" because it relied upon the advice of counsel in not disclosing annual rates.
>
> C. "Recognized principles of common and constitutional law preclude the imposition of a civil penalty in this action."

The court has concluded that none of these points should be sustained.

A. It is plain from the language and sense of § 130 that the basis for the liability is the creditor's failure "to disclose to any person any information required * * * to be disclosed * * *." The "finance charge in connection with the transaction" enters the picture thereafter as a starting point for the computation of damages. There is no requirement that the plaintiff prove he himself was deceived. There is no requirement that he should have been led by the deception to pay the "finance charge in connection with the transaction * * *."

The scheme of the statute, as both sides agree, is to create a species of "private attorney general" to participate prominently in enforcement. The language should be construed liberally in light of its broadly remedial purpose. Thus construed, it plainly encompasses this suit. As plaintiff demonstrates in detail, but this court finds it sufficient to note briefly, the omission with which defendant is charged occurred "in connection with (a) consumer credit transaction * * *." The fact that there was no finance charge *at the time* of the omission is of no consequence. The fact that there might never be one (i.e., if despite defendant's invitation to pay only $10 and incur a finance charge, plaintiff paid the whole balance and incurred none) is also unimportant, as is the fact that plaintiff actually did thereafter incur and pay such a charge. It is sufficient for present purposes that (1) there was a readily knowable "finance charge in connection with the transaction," and (2) this relatively trivial detail serves, after all, not as the *ground for liability* but merely as the initial step in what defendant accurately calls the statute's "sole measure of damages."

Beyond using the finance charge as such an available and handy reference point, presumably to be replaced in the normal case by the $100 minimum or $1,000 maximum, Congress made clear its broader scheme, and broader system of reimbursement, for private enforcement. It invited people like the present plaintiff, whether they were themselves deceived or not,[16] to sue in the public interest. Following familiar precedents, it encouraged such actions by providing, in addition to the incentive of public service, costs and a reasonable attorney's fee above the minimum recovery of $100.

The essential purpose seems manifest. This action is manifestly within it. The most that may be required to cope with defendant's parsing of the statutory language is that the courts may have to scale creative heights occasionally to fix the measure of damages without having an imposed finance charge as a nominal springboard (though even that is unnecessary here). This is not only within the range of judicial competence. It is the compelled alternative to telling Congress we will ignore what was validly sought because the grammar, though entirely adequate, could be better.

B. We come to what defendant tenders as its "good faith defense," under the provision, in § 130(c) of the Act, 15 U.S.C. § 1640(c), absolving from liability a creditor who shows that his "violation was not intentional and resulted from a bona fide error notwithstanding the maintenance of procedures reasonably adapted to avoid any such er-

16. Realistically, the plaintiffs in such cases are likely to be people not easily or actually deceived.

ror." The briefs range widely and learnedly on this. Enlightened by these efforts, the court deals briefly with the subject here.

It is undisputed that defendant carefully, deliberately—intentionally—omitted the disclosure in question. That defendant, in this court's view, mistook the law does not make its action any less intentional. This is normally true in criminal cases.

This conclusion is buttressed when we note the requirement in the defensive subsection that the error be shown to have been both "not intentional and (the result of) a bona fide error notwithstanding the maintenance of procedures reasonably adapted to avoid any such error." The sparse legislative history on this reinforces what the language shows amply by itself—that the absolution was meant for clerical errors.[17] A defendant invoking this excuse is required not merely to show the clerical error was unintentional, but also that due care has been taken to set up *procedures* to avoid it. The provision is wholly inapposite to deal with errors of law like defendant's, though made in entire "good faith." [18] However, much clients and others might wish it, nobody has devised—and defendant omits to mention—"procedures" Congress could have envisaged to cover such errors of law.

C. Finally, defendant argues that its interpretation of the statute was at a minimum "reasonable," and that it may not be subjected to a "penalty" for what is now held to have been a mistake of this nature. For the moment, subject to reconsideration when the question of class-action treatment is confronted, this argument may be rejected speedily. Granting that slogans on such subjects too often do service for analysis, the "remedial" character of the provision for civil recoveries quite overwhelms its allegedly "penal" aspect. Damages are liquidated, to be sure, but there is an effective upper as well as lower limit. The aim to protect consumers is the paramount aspect of the statute; the countenancing of "reasonable" violations would be grossly subversive of that. There are explicitly penal sanctions for the "unreasonable" violator who behaves "willfully and knowingly * * *." And for now, at any rate, we are concerned with only a single plaintiff, suing within a tight

17. The original version of the Senate bill contained no exemption for unintentional or bona fide violations. After businessmen and others complained during the Senate hearings that mathematical and clerical errors would be inevitable because of the complexity of annual rate computations, Hearings on S. 5 Before the Subcomm. on Financial Institutions of the Senate Comm. on Banking and Currency, 90th Cong., 1st Sess. 64 ff., 226, 374, 426–427, 529, 584, 698 (1967), and should not subject creditors to liability, id., at 374, the bill was changed to include the language of the present exemption—with additional provision for exemption where the error is corrected and adjustments made "within fifteen days after discovering the error, and prior to the institution of an action hereunder or the receipt of written notice of the error." The House bill originally required proof of a "knowing" violation to establish civil liability. This was omitted in the final House version, apparently in response to objections by the Justice Department that to require proof of "specific knowledge" might "frustrate prospective plaintiffs, and thereby weaken the enforcement provisions of the act." Hearing on H.R. 11601 Before the Subcomm. on Consumer Affairs of the House Comm. on Banking and Currency, 90th Cong., 1st Sess., pt. 1, p. 903 (1967).

18. It merits emphasis anyhow that the words "good faith" are defendant's, not from the statute.

(one-year) statute of limitations, and likely to recover a sum paltry by any pertinent standard. While the contexts differ, this court follows the only previously reported decision in holding the provision for civil recoveries "remedial" rather than "penal."

* * *

Note

1. The plaintiff in *Bisbey,* in a portion of the opinion not reproduced here, complained that the bank had failed to provisionally recredit her account in the disputed amount pending its investigation of her claim. See 12 C.F.R. § 205.11(c), providing for provisional recrediting of consumer's account if financial institution does not complete error investigation within ten days. Contrast this rule with the missed stop payment order issue under OR and R 4–403 and 4–407. What difference between the payment media would support such diametrically opposed results? Note too that section 205.11(c)(2)(iii) requires that the consumer be given "full use of the funds recredited during the investigation." Does this provide opportunity for abuse of the system by a consumer?

2. Note that in *Bisbey* there is an overlap between the EFT law and the "wrongful dishonor" law of Article 4. To the extent that the same deposit account may be accessed both by checks and electronic means within the scope of the E.F.T.A., there will be occasions when the resolution of an issue under one of the bodies of law will impact the complementary payment systems law as well.

3. In *Ratner,* how was the plaintiff prejudiced by the bank's insufficient disclosure? Consider the court's observation in footnote 16 of the opinion; what does that intimate about the disclosure regime?

4. The *Ratner* court noted that the bank's failure to satisfy the disclosure requirements allowed affected consumers to act as "private attorneys general." If such a mechanism is appropriate in the credit card context, why is it not also available with regard to violations of the Federal Trade Commission's Holder in Due Course rule, considered in Chapter 2?

5. The credit card law also provides an exception to the HDC rule, and requires disclosure of the pertinent consumer rights. But, as the following article reveals, financial institutions may be less than enthusiastic about bringing this disclosure to the attention of cardholders.

Little–Noticed Change in Credit Card Law Gives Unhappy Consumers a Chance to Get Even *

By Jonathan Kwitny—Staff Reporter of The Wall Street Journal

New York—Exhibit A: the carburetor on Abe Fuchs' 1975 Oldsmobile.

Bob Cerullo's garage in Brooklyn repaired the carburetor. Or did it?

Mr. Fuchs says no, not satisfactorily. But he paid $85 to the garage. And that, normally, would be that, unless a dissatisfied

* The Wall Street Journal, July 28, 1980, sec. 2, p. 13, col. 4. Reprinted by permission of Wall Street Journal, © 1980 Dow Jones & Co., Inc. All Rights Reserved Worldwide.

customer was willing to go through the hassle and expense of suing a merchant.

Surprise: Abe Fuchs has his money back. He got it by writing a letter that caused $85 to be deducted from the bank account of Vins Motor Service Corp., the garage that Mr. Cerullo operates.

Unpublicized Charge

It was all quite legal. Mr. Cerullo is fuming. Various banks that sponsor such credit cards as Visa and Master Charge (now Master Card) are acknowledging that a significant change in the law governing credit cards was made five years ago. The change has gone almost unnoticed by the public.

Mr. Fuchs, an accountant, happened to read the fine print on the back of his Visa statement one day many months ago. There he saw a notice citing the Fair Credit Billing Act, which took effect in October 1975. It explained that companies can reclaim money from merchants after bank credit card slips have been signed.

Blow for the Consumer

August 1979: Mr. Fuchs takes his car to Vins Motors. Mr. Cerullo says he told Mr. Fuchs that unless the carburetor was replaced the trouble would recur, but that Mr. Fuchs insisted on having the old carburetor fixed. Mr. Fuchs says Mr. Cerullo didn't tell him of the need for a new carburetor until he—Mr. Fuchs—had gone back to Vins several times seeking repairs.

He had paid the bill with his Visa card. Before October 1975, his only recourse would have been to sue Mr. Cerullo. Disputes involving small sums traditionally have left the advantage with the party holding the money. The bank sponsoring a credit card, under the old law, paid the merchant, and then claimed full collection rights against such as Mr. Fuchs.

In legal language, the bank was the "holder in due course" of the debt, entitled to collect from the card holder. The changed law took away this privilege from banks—when the amount of a bill is more than $50, when the charge is made in the customer's home state or within 100 miles of his home, when the customer has tried to resolve the dispute with the merchant, and when the customer sends his bank written notice that negotiations with the merchant have failed.

The customer then can withhold the amount of the disputed payment from his credit card payments. Banks issuing cards thus were left under the new law in the position of having to defend against customer complaints as if they were the merchants being challenged.

This brought about swift policy changes by the banks. Anthony Urso, vice president of the retail credit group at Irving Trust Co., (issuer of Mr. Fuchs' Visa card), explains: "If a customer has a complaint about an item and it is run through the normal procedures, the money is credited to his account and is charged back to the bank that controls (services) the merchant. That bank then charges the merchant. These decisions are made pretty automatically."

So Irving Trust credited $85 to Mr. Fuchs account earlier this year, when it got his letter saying he wasn't satisfied with Mr. Cerullo's carburetor job. Then Irving charged the $85 to Manufacturers Hanover Trust Co., bankers for Vins Motor Service. And Manufacturers Hanover docked Vins.

"I was shocked," says Mr. Cerullo. The garage owner says he doesn't plan to go to court to try to collect from Mr. Fuchs. That, he says, would cost more than $85. "If it gets worse, we'll stop taking cards," Mr. Cerullo says.

The Normal Public

So far it seems not to be getting worse, for Vins or other merchants, and the reason, Irving's Mr. Urso suggests, is that "I don't think this is very widely publicized to start with; the way the normal public would find out would be to have a legitimate grievance and inquire about it."

Banks certainly aren't rushing to publicize the new policy. Both Irving and Manufacturers Hanover delayed an inquiring reporter for several days and only reluctantly discussed the changed law. Both banks said they didn't have any information that would illustrate the extent of the "chargeback" problem. Both said they hoped to keep the problem small. (The changed law also applies to American Express).

Automobile repair shops seem to be among the chief potential losers, which many motorists doubtless may consider sweet revenge. An executive at Manufacturers Hanover acknowledged that merchant-consumer disputes are resolved most easily "if there was something tangible involved, something that wasn't received. In something like automotive * * * where there's nothing tangible, there's no recourse."

6. Are disclosures worth the cost? Is the disclosure of an interest rate more rational than fixing a legal ceiling on the interest rate that a card issuer may charge? Is "competition a better regulator of rates than legislative fiat"? See Joseph W. Gelb & Peter N. Cubita, *Credit Card Application and Solicitation Disclosure Legislation: An Alternative to the Rate Ceiling Approach,* 43 Bus.Law. 1557, 1557 (1988).

7. The financial community was concerned after the decision in *Ratner* about the scope of class action liability that could confront a bank as a result of what would amount to no more than a clerical error. Their concerns were allayed when the second *Ratner* opinion was issued, which found that the class action would not be available on the facts of *Ratner* for two reasons: first, the class action device would not be necessary insofar as the statutory minimum $100 penalty plus attorney's fees would provide sufficient incentive for a cardholder to pursue his own action and, second,

> The proposed recovery of $100 each for some 130,000 class members would be a horrendous, possibly annihilating punishment, unrelated to any damage to the purported class or to any benefit of defendant for what is at most a technical and debatable violation of the Truth-in-Lending Act.

Ratner v. Chemical Bank N.Y. Trust Co., 54 F.R.D. 412, 416 (S.D.N.Y.1972).

In 1980, section 1640(a)(2)(B) of the Truth in Lending Act was amended to limit the possible liability of violators of the Act. The amended statute restricts liability of the creditor to the lesser of $500,000 or one percent of the net worth of the creditor.

8. *The Uniform Consumer Credit Code.* In 1968, the National Conference of Commissioners on Uniform State Laws, the same body that drafted the Uniform Commercial Code, produced the "Uniform Consumer Credit Code," or "U3C," its attempt to regulate the entire field of consumer credit. The drafters of the U3C proceeded under the assumption that consumer credit legislation is the province of the states, but that uniformity in such legislation, among the states, is essential in light of the large volume of consumer credit transactions conducted across state lines. The U3C's coverage extends only to consumer credit transactions. Its provisions do not apply when the debtor is an organization, such as a corporation, partnership, or trust, or when the credit transaction is conducted for business purposes.

The U3C fixes maximum finance charges for consumer credit sales and consumer loans; provides limitations and restrictions on particular sales practices such as licensing requirements for lenders; specifies the terms of and imposes restrictions on the issuance of consumer credit insurance; defines the rights of debtors and creditors and establishes remedies and penalties that are available when violations occur; describes the powers and functions of the agency designated to enforce and administer the U3C; and creates a Council of Advisors on Consumer Credit to serve as consultants aiding in the administration of the Code.

The U3C does not extensively regulate disclosure requirements imposed to help consumers make informed choices among credit options. The Federal Truth in Lending Act and Federal Reserve Regulation Z both contain comprehensive disclosure requirements with which all credit providers are required to comply.

Section 123 of the Federal Truth in Lending Act provides that the Federal Reserve Board shall exempt from the disclosure provisions of the Act any class of transactions subject to state laws that contain substantially similar requirements. States seeking this exemption, however, found that their disclosure requirements had to be essentially identical to those found in the Federal Truth in Lending Act and Regulation Z in order to satisfy the Federal Reserve Board. Often, in attempting to draft parallel provisions, state legislatures muddled the disclosure requirements to the point that all that was accomplished was added confusion.

The drafters of the U3C recognized the preemptive nature of the federal disclosure requirements and chose not to attempt to draft independent provisions. Instead, section 3.201 of the U3C provides that credit providers covered under the U3C shall make disclosure in compliance with the federal regulations. This section also gives the state's Administrator the power to enforce the disclosure provisions of the Truth in Lending Act. Other than requiring compliance with the federal legislation, there are no other substantive provisions in the U3C dealing with disclosures to consumers.

Since 1968 there have been several redrafts of the U3C. The revisions were a response to the experiences of the states that had adopted the original text of the Code. The redrafts, completed primarily in the 1970s, have put even more emphasis on the consumer protection aspects of the Code and responded to other legislative and judicial developments in the consumer credit field. Eleven states have adopted the U3C. Utah, Oklahoma, Colorado, Indiana, South Carolina, Wisconsin and Wyoming all adopted it in its 1968 form. Kansas adopted Working Redraft # 4, drafted in 1973. Finally, Iowa, Maine, and Idaho adopted Working Redraft # 5, which was drafted in 1974.

Chapter 8

WHOLESALE FUNDS TRANSFERS*

A. INTRODUCTION

Though consumer electronic funds transfers and credit card transactions are subject to pervasive federal legislation, the funds transfer system that moves the most value, "wire transfers," is governed largely by state law: Article 4A of the U.C.C. The article's denomination, Article 4A, emphasizes that the state law of wholesale funds transfers is related to the bank collections law of U.C.C. Article 4.

This chapter examines the application of Article 4A to wire transfers, largely by contrasting the results in cases decided prior to the promulgation of Article 4A with the result that the new article would yield were it applied to the facts of those cases. And to appreciate better both Article 4 and Article 4A, the provisions of the two enactments are compared. Should the only differences between the two articles be those that reflect operational or technological variations between the payment regimes?

A crucial difference between the law governing checks and the law of wire transfers is the relative sophistication of the transactors most affected by the two articles. While both businesses and consumers issue, receive, and deposit checks, wire transfers are effected by businesses a great deal more often than they are effected by consumers.

Provisions of the United Nations Commission on International Trade Law (UNCITRAL) Model Law of International Credit Transfers are incorporated into this chapter to provide alternative formulations of the legal principles informing wire payment transactions. What forces might explain differences between particular U.C.C. and analogous UNCITRAL formulations?

Problem

Professor Compassionate has a daughter attending the Acme School of Law and Chiropracty in a state 2000 miles away from her home. He would

* Throughout this text, the designation "OR" refers to an Article in its original form; "R" denotes a revised Article. E.g., OR 3–303 refers to Original Article 3; R 3–303 refers to Revised Article 3.

like to send her $5,000 to cover tuition, books, and supplies. If he goes to the local Western Union telegraph office to "wire" the money, does Article 4A apply to the transaction? What would you have to know about the transaction and the way Western Union sends the money? See U.C.C. §§ 4A–102 and 4A–104. Cf. U.C.C. § 4A–108.

Perhaps the best introduction to the Article 4A conception of a funds transfer is contained in the "Prefatory Note" to the article. You should read that Note before you begin to work through the cases and materials in this chapter.

Even in those states that jumped quickly onto the Article 4A bandwagon, enacting it only months after the article was promulgated by its sponsors, it may still be some time before appellate courts begin to interpret the law. Fortunately, those states that have enacted the article have remained true to the uniform law so there will be less to distinguish the construction of a provision in one state from that offered in another. For the time being, however, the best presentation of Article 4A is dependent on cases decided prior to its promulgation. Indeed, to the extent that the pre-Article 4A cases represent the state of the wire transfers law, a product of contract, tort, and analogy to Articles 3 and 4, they provide a provocative context in which to appraise the accommodation of technological, political, and legal considerations that informed the drafting of Article 4A.

B. "MISTAKEN" PAYMENT

DELBRUECK & CO. v. MANUFACTURERS HANOVER TRUST CO.

United States Court of Appeals, Second Circuit, 1979.
609 F.2d 1047.

MOORE, CIRCUIT JUDGE:

Delbrueck & Company ("Delbrueck") appeals from the dismissal of its complaint after a bench trial held in the United States District Court for the Southern District of New York (Honorable Vincent L. Broderick, *District Judge*). The complaint charged Manufacturers Hanover Trust Company ("Manufacturers") with negligence and breach of contract in failing to revoke two transfers to the Chase Manhattan Bank ("Chase") for the account of Bankhaus I.D. Herstatt, K.G.a.A. ("Herstatt") totaling $12.5 million. The transfers were made via an electronic funds transfer system established by the New York Clearing House Association ("Clearing House") called the Clearing House Interbank Payments System and known as CHIPS.[1] Although the facts are

1. We reproduce in full Judge Broderick's discussion of the CHIPS system, 464 F.Supp. 989 at 992 n. 5:

The mechanics of effecting an interbank payment under the CHIPS system are as follows: When the paying or sending bank (Manufacturers) receives a telex from one of its customers (Delbrueck) instructing it to make a payment to a receiving bank (Chase), another member of the CHIPS system, for the account of one of the receiving bank's customers (Herstatt), the paying bank (Manufacturers) first tests and verifies the telex.

more fully presented in Judge Broderick's opinion below (464 F.Supp. 989), a brief statement of those facts is necessary for this discussion of the appeal.

Delbrueck is a German banking house and performs functions as a commercial bank, a brokerage house and an investment bank. In connection with its banking business in 1974, Delbrueck was involved in buying and selling large quantities of foreign currency. Delbrueck maintained an account with Manufacturers, a New York banking corporation, and authorized Manufacturers to make payments out of the account. These authorizations consisted of telex messages which were customarily sent the day before the transfer was to be made.

Delbrueck had entered into three foreign exchange contracts with Herstatt which are of importance for this appeal: one for $2.5 million and one for $10 million, both due on June 26, 1974, and one for $10 million due on June 27, 1974. In accordance with the authorization procedure, Delbrueck sent a telex message to Manufacturers on June 25, 1974 ordering Manufacturers to transfer on June 26, a total of $12.5 million to Chase for the account of Herstatt. In addition, early on the morning of June 26, Delbrueck authorized the payment of the $10 million due on June 27.

Thereafter, the tested and verified telex is sent to one of the CHIPS computer terminal operators and the payment order contained in the telex is programmed into the terminal by typing into the computer the relevant information—*i.e.,* the identifying codes for the party originating the transfer (Delbrueck), the remitting bank (Manufacturers), the receiving bank (Chase), the party for whom the receiving bank is receiving the transfer (Herstatt) and the amount of the transfer ($10 million and $2.5 million). This information is then transmitted to the central computer located at the Clearing House, which, based upon the identifying codes searches out all the necessary clerical information, stores the message and causes a sending form to be automatically typed at the sending bank. In this case, this step was effected on June 25, 1974.

Once the programming of the computer has been completed, the send form is sent to the appropriate area at the sending bank for approval. When a determination is made at the sending bank (Manufacturers) to make the payment, the form is returned to one of the computer terminal operators, reinserted in the computer and the release key is depressed. At that moment, the central computer at the Clearing House causes a credit ticket to be printed automatically at the terminal of the receiving bank (Chase) and a debit ticket to be printed at the terminal of the sending bank (Manufacturers). Further, the central computer automatically makes a permanent record of the transaction and debits the Clearing House account of the sending bank and credits the Clearing House account of the receiving bank. In this case, this step was effected at 11:36 and 11:37 for the $10 million and $2.5 million payment, respectively, from Manufacturers for Delbrueck to Chase for Herstatt.

The funds received by a receiving bank (*e.g.,* Chase) for the account of one of its customers (*e.g.,* Herstatt) via the receipt of a CHIPS credit message are made available to the customer and can be drawn upon by the customer in the discharge of its obligations that same day, as soon as the receiving bank is aware of the fact that the funds have been received. This running tabulation by the receiving bank is generally referred to as a "shadow balance."

At the end of the day, the central computer correlates all of the day's transactions, nets out the debits and credits, and prints out reports showing which banks owe money and which have money due them. That information is delivered to the New York Federal Reserve Bank the next business day and adjustments are made on the appropriate books of account.

Then the problems began. Herstatt was closed by the German banking authorities around 10:30 a.m. (all times referred to are Eastern Standard Time) on June 26. Chase heard of the closing and immediately froze payments out of Herstatt's account but continued to accept incoming transfers. Delbrueck sent a telex message to Manufacturers at 11:30 a.m. requesting that the $10 million transfer to be made on June 27 be stopped. On June 26 Manufacturers transferred to Chase via the CHIPS system the payments which had been ordered to be made that day, namely, $10 million transferred at 11:36 a.m. and $2.5 million at 11:37 a.m. Delbrueck called Manufacturers at around 12:00 noon and later sent a telex message, trying to stop or recall the $12.5 million in payments which had already been made. That afternoon phone calls were made to Chase by Manufacturers and Delbrueck. These calls were directed at having the funds returned, but were unsuccessful. At around 9:00 p.m. the evening of June 26, Chase formally credited Herstatt's account with the $12.5 million.

Delbrueck maintains that the transfers were revokable until 9:00 p.m. and that by failing to revoke the transfers, Manufacturers was negligent and had breached its implied creditor-depositor contract with Delbrueck. *Stella Flour & Feed Corp. v. National City Bank,* 285 A.D. 182, 136 N.Y.S.2d 139 (1st Dept.1954), *aff'd,* 308 N.Y. 1023, 127 N.E.2d 864 (1955). Thus, the crucial issue on this appeal is whether the transfers of funds via CHIPS at 11:36 and 11:37 a.m. were final.[2] We hold those transfers were irrevocable and affirm the dismissal of the complaint.

First, the form of the transactions and the manner in which the banks viewed the transactions lead to the conclusion that the 11:36 and 11:37 a.m. transfers were final. The CHIPS system was specifically created to replace cashier's checks as a means of interbank payments of large amounts. As is stated in the CHIPS manual, "CHIPS completely eliminates checks for interbank payment transfers." (App. 377). It is not disputed that cashier's checks are irrevocable when transferred to the payee bank.

In addition, the Clearing House changed its rules after the Herstatt failure to allow revocation of transfers. Although the Clearing House previously had no specific rule concerning the finality of CHIPS transfers, all member banks must have believed that once transfers were

2. Liability for alleged failure to revoke the $12.5 million credit transfers was essentially dependent upon the answer to the question posed by Delbrueck (Delbrueck Br., p. 11) "That issue [breach of contract] inescapably requires consideration of the question, when did the credit transfers to Herstatt becomes irrevocable?"

The breach of contract issue is characterized by Delbrueck as "the central issue on this appeal." Manufacturers' alleged failure to revoke was "in breach of contract [because it] did not do so." Delbrueck concedes that: "If the credit transfers were irrevocable this appeal must fail, for the contract between Manufacturers and Delbrueck requires that any stop order issued by Delbrueck be received by Manufacturers at a time when Manufacturers still had power to revoke the transfers." (Delbrueck Br., p. 3).

We address the issues 1 and 2 presented for review by Delbrueck and refer to Judge Broderick's opinion, which we endorse, as to the other issues stated. (Delbrueck Br., pp. 1, 2).

released, they were final, except for adjustments made for clerical errors. Delbrueck's conduct supports this fact, because it initially requested stop payment only on the $10 million to be paid on June 27, apparently believing that the June 26 transfers had been made and were irrevocable.

As a direct result of the Herstatt failure, this new procedure was announced on July 1, 1974. The change was necessitated by a backlog in releasing orders created by uncertainties in the financial markets due to the Herstatt failure. Orders were not being released until the transferor was certain that funds were available to cover the transfer. The new procedure outlined in the July 1 announcement allowed members to release payments but still have a right to recall them until 10:00 a.m. of the morning after the transfer. The change would not have been required if the transfers were considered revocable by member banks. And subsequently, on November 4, 1974, the CHIPS system reverted to the tacitly accepted procedure used before July 1, which was that the transfers were irrevocable.

The fact that final settling of the accounts was not done until 9:00 p.m. is irrelevant. That was a mere bookkeeping entry. As Manufacturers asserts, a cash payment or a cashier's check would not have been formally entered on Chase's books until 9:00 p.m. and even Delbrueck agrees that cash or a cashier's check would be irrevocable when transferred.

The practices associated with banking transactions can be conclusive evidence of the legal effect of those transactions. *Indianapolis Morris Plan Corp. v. Karlen,* 28 N.Y.2d 30, 36, 319 N.Y.S.2d 831, 268 N.E.2d 632 (1971); *Hanlon v. Union Bank of Medina,* 247 N.Y. 389, 391, 160 N.E. 650 (1928). Based on the nature of the CHIPS system, and the fact that the member banks viewed the transactions as irrevocable (as evidenced by the short term change instituted after the Herstatt failure) we hold that the CHIPS transfers were irrevocable when made.

The Uniform Commercial Code ("UCC") is not applicable to this case because the UCC does not specifically address the problems of electronic funds transfer. However, analogous use of concepts such as the finality of checks once "accepted" (§§ 3–410 [R 3–409], 4–303 [R 4–303]) would support the irrevocability of these transfers.

The common law supports the view that these transfers were irrevocable. Delbrueck's deposits with Manufacturers were choses in action and as such were assignable. *Miller v. Wells Fargo Bank International Corp.,* 406 F.Supp. 452 (S.D.N.Y.1975), *affirmed,* 540 F.2d 548 (2d Cir.1976); *Paragon International, N.V. v. Standard Plastics, Inc.,* 353 F.Supp. 88, 93 (S.D.N.Y.1973). In order for there to be a valid assignment of a chose in action, there must be a specific direction to transfer by the assignor and notice to the assignee. As the Miller court stated:

> In sum, an assignment requires an agreement whereby the assignor agrees to transfer presently all right, title and control over the

> subject matter of the assignment to the assignee. Such an agreement may be manifested by conduct, writing or parol, and in particular it exists where the assignor instructs his obligor to pay the specific fund owing to him to the assignee, and the assignor either delivers that order to the assignee or notifies him of it.

Miller, *supra,* 406 F.Supp. 452 at 474.

The required notice to the assignee may also be given by the obligor.

> An order by the creditor [Delbrueck] given directly to the debtor [Manufacturers] requesting him to pay a third person [Chase or Herstatt] does not in the absence of notice to that person make him an assignee of the claim.

Williston, *Contracts* § 406 at 156 (3d ed. 1960). See also *Schreiber v. Keller Engraving Co.,* 57 Misc. 644, 108 N.Y.S. 658 (Sup.Ct.1908).

Delbrueck had given Manufacturers a clear direction to transfer these funds in its telex message of June 25. However, Delbrueck argues that the transfers were revocable until the necessary notice was given to the assignee. But notice was given in this case before Delbrueck sought to revoke the transfer.

Chase was the assignee. Delbrueck's direction in the telex message was to pay

> To CHASE BANK N Y
>
> ACCT BANKHAUS ID HERSTATT KGAA
>
> (App. 358).

When Manufacturers transferred the money to Chase, Chase received a written credit slip at its computer terminal. That was notice to Chase of the assignment.

Even if one assumes that Herstatt, not Chase, was the assignee, notice to Chase will be imputed to Herstatt. Chase was the paying and receiving agent of Herstatt, and notice to an agent is imputed to the principal. *Farr v. Newman,* 14 N.Y.2d 183, 187, 250 N.Y.S.2d 272, 199 N.E.2d 369 (1965). See also *Nolan v. Williamson Music, Inc.,* 300 F.Supp. 1311, 1316 (S.D.N.Y.1960); *Ford v. Grand Union Co.,* 268 N.Y. 243, 252, 197 N.E. 266 (1935).

Delbrueck's argument that Chase was not Herstatt's agent after the declared bankruptcy will not stand. Herstatt had directed Chase to "take whatever action [Chase] felt advisable as a result of this information [i.e. the closing of Herstatt]." (App. 68). Thus, Chase's freezing of payments out of Herstatt's account was only Chase continuing to act within the scope of its agency relationship with Herstatt.

Furthermore, the Restatement (Second) of Agency states:

> The bankruptcy * * * of the principal, of which the agent has notice, terminates his authority as to transactions which he should

infer the principal no longer consents to have conducted for him. (§ 114).

Thus, where an agent has a specific contract which is vitiated by the principal's bankruptcy, the agency is terminated. *Lewis Sagal Co. v. Smith,* 35 F.2d 182, 183 (3d Cir.1929). However, Chase (the agent) could infer in this case that Herstatt (the principal) would consent to Chase gathering payments for Herstatt's account. Indeed, no inference is required because Herstatt specifically requested Chase to "take whatever action * * * advisable." Chase's authority to act as agent for Herstatt in receiving funds was not terminated by the bankruptcy.

Sokoloff v. National City Bank, 250 N.Y. 69, 164 N.E. 745 (1928) is inapposite to this situation. That case dealt with whether or not an intermediary bank can be agent for both the transferor and the transferee. Here, Chase is agent for Herstatt and Manufacturers is agent for Delbrueck. Chase's knowledge of the transfers is imputed to Herstatt, and the assignment was effective.

The other points raised by Delbrueck on appeal were adequately addressed in the well considered opinion of the court below. We are in agreement with that decision in all respects and hold that the CHIPS payments from Manufacturers to Chase were irrevocable at 11:36 and 11:37 a.m., the times of the transfers.

The dismissal of the complaint is affirmed.

Note

1. Identify the parties to the wire transfer in *Delbrueck* in the apposite Article 4A terms.

2. Consider the result if Article 4A were applied to the facts of *Delbrueck*. See 4A–209 and 4A–211.

Compare the pertinent UNCITRAL provisions:

Article 7

Acceptance or rejection of a payment order by receiving bank other than the beneficiary's bank

(1) The provisions of this article apply to a receiving bank other than the beneficiary's bank.

(2) A receiving bank accepts the sender's payment order at the earliest of the following times:

(a) when the bank receives the payment order, provided that the sender and the bank have agreed that the bank will execute payment orders from the sender upon receipt;

(b) when the bank gives notice to the sender of acceptance;

Article 9

Acceptance or rejection of a payment order by beneficiary's bank

(1) The beneficiary's bank accepts a payment order at the earliest of the following times:

(a) when the bank receives the payment order, provided that the sender and the bank have agreed that the bank will execute payment orders from the sender upon receipt;

(b) when the bank gives notice to the sender of acceptance;

(c) when the bank debits an account of the sender with the bank as payment for the payment order;

(d) when the bank credits the beneficiary's account or otherwise places the funds at the disposal of the beneficiary;

(e) when the bank gives notice to the beneficiary that it has the right to withdraw the funds or use the credit;

(f) when the bank otherwise applies the credit as instructed in the payment order;

(g) when the bank applies the credit to a debt of the beneficiary owed to it or applies it in conformity with an order of a court or other competent authority; or

(h) when the time for giving notice of rejection under paragraph (2) has elapsed without notice having been given.

(2) A beneficiary's bank that does not accept a payment order is required to give notice of rejection no later than on the banking day following the end of the execution period, unless:

(a) where payment is to be made by debiting an account of the sender with the beneficiary's bank, there are insufficient funds available in the account to pay for the payment order;

(b) where payment is to be made by other means, payment has not been made; or

(c) there is insufficient information to identify the sender.

(3) A payment order ceases to have effect if it is neither accepted nor rejected under this article before the close of business on the fifth banking day following the end of the execution period.

Article 12
Revocation

(1) A payment order may not be revoked by the sender unless the revocation order is received by a receiving bank other than the beneficiary's bank at a time and in a manner sufficient to afford the receiving bank a reasonable opportunity to act before the later of the actual time of execution and the beginning of the day on which the payment order ought to have been executed under subparagraph (a) or (b) of article 11(1).

(2) A payment order may not be revoked by the sender unless the revocation order is received by the beneficiary's bank at a time and in a manner sufficient to afford the bank a reasonable opportunity to act before the later of the time the credit transfer is completed and the beginning of the day when the funds are to be placed at the disposal of the beneficiary.

(3) Notwithstanding the provisions of paragraphs (1) and (2), the sender and the receiving bank may agree that payment orders issued

by the sender to the receiving bank are to be irrevocable or that a revocation order is effective only if it is received earlier than the time specified in paragraph (1) or (2).

(4) A revocation order must be authenticated.

(5) A receiving bank other than the beneficiary's bank that executes, or a beneficiary's bank that accepts, a payment order in respect of which an effective revocation order has been or is subsequently received is not entitled to payment for that payment order. If the credit transfer is completed, the bank shall refund any payment received by it.

(6) If the recipient of a refund is not the originator of the credit transfer, it shall pass on the refund to its sender.

(7) A bank that is obligated to make a refund to its sender is discharged from that obligation to the extent that it makes the refund direct to a prior sender. Any bank subsequent to that prior sender is discharged to the same extent.

(8) An originator entitled to a refund under this article may recover from any bank obligated to make a refund hereunder to the extent that the bank has not previously refunded. A bank that is obligated to make a refund is discharged from that obligation to the extent that it makes the refund direct to the originator. Any other bank that is obligated is discharged to the same extent.

(9) Paragraphs (7) and (8) do not apply to a bank if they would affect the bank's rights or obligations under any agreement or any rule of a funds transfer system.

(10) If the credit transfer is completed but a receiving bank executes a payment order in respect of which an effective revocation order has been or is subsequently received, the receiving bank has such rights to recover from the beneficiary the amount of the credit transfer as may otherwise be provided by law.

(11) The death, insolvency, bankruptcy or incapacity of either the sender or the originator does not of itself operate to revoke a payment order or terminate the authority of the sender.

(12) The principles contained in this article apply to an amendment of a payment order.

(13) For the purposes of this article, branches and separate offices of a bank, even if located in the same State, are separate banks.

3. From your understanding of the nature of a payment by cashier's check, is the court correct that the cashier's check provides the accurate analogy for a CHIPS wire transfer?

4. How could you read the CHIPS system adjustment of its operating rules to support a conclusion opposite of that reached by the court?

5. Delbrueck had funds on deposit at Manufacturers. Pursuant to Delbrueck instructions Manufacturers sent transfer messages to CHIPS at 11:36 and 11:37 am and debit tickets were printed out at Manufacturers and credit tickets printed out at Chase Manhattan.

That action could be viewed in a number of ways:

(1) as notice of an intention to make an assignment,

(2) as an assignment,

(3) as notice of an intention to make a payment (as distinguished from an intention to make an assignment), or

(4) as an actual payment.

Based on the facts alone, without help from banking usage or the court's conclusion, can you comfortably decide which of the four above alternatives you think should be found to have occurred?

If the check analogy is appropriate, does the assignment analogy become inappropriate? See OR 3–409(1) and R 3–408.

6. Which provisions of Article 4 concern, in the check collection context, the issues treated in 4A–209 and 4A–211? Are the Article 4 and 4A provisions parallel? Need they be?

The following case considers the application of *Delbrueck*, as well as *Delbrueck*'s application of analogous concepts, to a bank's attempt to recover a mistaken payment.

BANQUE WORMS v. BANK AMERICA INTERNATIONAL

United States District Court, Southern District of New York, 1989.
726 F.Supp. 940.

ROBERT P. PATTERSON, JR., DISTRICT JUDGE.

This is a motion and a cross-motion for summary judgment pursuant to Federal Rule of Civil Procedure 56. At stake is $1,974,267.97, currently in the possession of plaintiff Banque Worms (BW), a bank organized and existing under the laws of the Republic of France.

BACKGROUND

In the early morning hours of April 10, 1989, third party defendant Security Pacific International Bank (SPIB), a federally chartered bank with offices in New York, received two telexes from Spedley Securities Ltd. (Spedley), an Australian company. At 12:36 A.M.,[1] the first telex instructed SPIB to wire transfer $1,974,267.97 to BW through Bank America International (BAI), a federally chartered bank with offices in New York. BW had outstanding a loan to Spedley which it had called. The amount of the wire transfer would have satisfied Spedley's indebtedness to BW. The second telex at 3:37 A.M. instructed SPIB to disregard the first telex and to wire transfer the $1,974,267.97 to National Westminster Bank Australia (NWBA).

At the time of those two telexes, Spedley's account with SPIB only contained approximately $70,000. Then at 8:36 A.M. SPIB received $1,974,267.97 from Spedley to cover a single transfer.

1. The time in New York is used throughout this opinion.

At 11:30 A.M., SPIB transferred by wire $1,974,267.97 (the Funds) to BAI for BW's account. At approximately 1:45 P.M., SPIB informed BAI that the 11:30 A.M. transfer had been a mistake.

At approximately 3:30 P.M., SPIB transferred by wire $1,974,-267.97 to NWBA. SPIB's First Vice President approved that transfer to NWBA despite the absence of sufficient cover in Spedley's account because he "expect[ed] that cover would arrive before the close of business on April 10, 1989, as had occurred on previous occasions." No additional cover ever arrived from Spedley and both payments were debited to its account.

Pursuant to an indemnification from SPIB, BAI returned the Funds to SPIB on April 11, 1989. However, BW refused to give BAI debit authorization for the return of the Funds. Accordingly, on April 12, 1989, BAI demanded return of the Funds from SPIB pursuant to the indemnity agreement.

After the Funds were not returned, BW commenced this action by filing a complaint on May 4, 1989 against BAI to recover the $1,974,-267.97 plus interest and costs. On May 18, 1989, BAI claimed over against third party defendant SPIB. On June 7, 1989, SPIB asserted a counterclaim against BAI and BW which essentially demands judgment in SPIB's favor for $1,974,267.97 against whichever party is in possession of the Funds at the time of such judgment.

On August 3, 1989, SPIB forwarded the Funds with interest and costs to BAI, who recredited the Funds to BW's account. All claims by and against BAI were then dismissed. The remaining dispute is between SPIB and BW over the $1,974,267.97, currently in the possession of BW. SPIB moves and BW cross-moves for summary judgment.

DISCUSSION

SPIB contends that permitting BW to keep the Funds would constitute unjust enrichment under New York caselaw's Mistake of Fact Doctrine. Those cases hold that money paid under a mistake of fact may be recovered back, however negligent the party paying may have been in making the mistake, unless the payment has caused such a change in the position of the other party that it would be unjust to require him to refund. National Bank of Commerce of New York v. National Mechanics Banking Ass'n of New York, 55 N.Y. 211 (1873).

In all of those cases relied upon by SPIB, those parties deemed to have been unjustly enriched did not have a right to the money when the mistaken payment was made. BW relies on that distinction and argues that the Discharge for Value Rule of the Restatement of Restitution is actually the appropriate rule to govern this case because BW, unlike the parties in the cases cited above, was a creditor with a right to the payment from Spedley.

The Discharge for Value Rule states:

§ 14. DISCHARGE FOR VALUE

> (1) A creditor of another or one having a lien on another's property who has received from a third person any benefit in discharge of the debt or lien, is under no duty to make restitution therefor, although the discharge was given by mistake of the transferor as to his interests or duties, if the transferee made no misrepresentation and did not have notice of the transferor's mistake.

Restatement of the Law of Restitution 55 (1937). See also 3 G. Palmer, The Law of Restitution 490–91 (1978) ("In situations of endless variety, courts have denied restitution because money paid by one party was received in good faith by the other, in satisfaction or as security for a valid claim against a third person." (footnote omitted)).

There are no allegations of any misrepresentations by either BAI or BW. SPIB contends, however, that BW may have had notice that SPIB was making a mistake by the close of the business day because a SPIB employee contacted BAI concerning the mistake at 1:45 P.M., approximately two hours after the incorrect transfer to BAI. SPIB Br. at 21 (August 4, 1989).

Notice to BAI at 1:45 P.M. would only assist SPIB's position if BW then received notice and if the transaction was not yet complete at 1:45 P.M. SPIB argues that the transfer was not complete at 1:45 P.M. because a wire transfer on the Clearing House Interbank Payments System (CHIPS) is not complete and final until the close of the business day.

SPIB cites no caselaw to support that contention. In Delbrueck & Co. v. Manufacturers Hanover Trust Co., 609 F.2d 1047, 1049–51 (2d Cir.1979), the Second Circuit conducted an extensive examination of the nature of the CHIPS system and held that a CHIPS transaction is irrevocable and final once the transfer takes place. The "final settling of the accounts" at the end of the day is "mere bookkeeping." Id. at 1051. Accordingly, any awareness by BW of SPIB's mistake two hours after the funds were transferred by wire is not material.

Although the Discharge for Value Rule, as set forth in the Restatement of Restitution, dictates that the Court permit BW to keep the funds, SPIB argues that the Court should rule otherwise because: (1) the Restatement of Restitution has never been adopted wholesale by the New York courts; (2) New York caselaw requires BW to have relied to its detriment to prevent restitution.

The Restatement of Restitution was adopted in 1937. Although it has never been explicitly incorporated into New York law, the framers of the Restatement in drafting Section 14's Discharge for Value Rule relied upon reasoning in a New York case.

In that case, Davis & Co. had an account at First National Bank with a balance of $473. Davis & Co. owed Seaman at least $473. In addition, Davis & Co. owed Consolidated National Bank $150. First National initially paid Consolidated National Bank $150 on behalf of

Davis & Co. After First National Bank delivered the $150 to Consolidated National Bank, Seaman received a judgment that "all of the moneys with the First National Bank to the credit of Davis & Co. should be paid to Seaman." 114 N.Y.S. at 311. First National then proceeded to pay Seaman $473 from Davis & Co.'s account. That $473 payment to Seaman was a mistake, because there was only $323 in Davis & Co.'s First National account at the time due to the earlier payment to Consolidated National Bank.[3] The New York court reasoned, "[T]he Seaman action could not rightfully reach the $150 of such payment; if the defendant [First National Bank] has paid out the full sum of $473 to Seaman, it has, of course, done so at its peril, and is unfortunately the loser." Id. Seaman was a creditor with a right to the entire $473 and First National had to suffer the consequence of mistakenly paying him $150 more than Davis & Co. had in their account. Accordingly, New York law is reflected in the the Restatement's Discharge for Value Rule and dictates that SPIB suffer the loss for its mistaken payment to Spedley's creditor BW.

Furthermore, contrary to SPIB's contention, contemporary rules of equity in New York courts are consistent with the Discharge for Value Rule. A string of cases holds that restitution is inappropriate when a bank mistakenly pays funds, over a stop payment order, in satisfaction of a debt, unless the payee has notice of the error.

SPIB attempts to distinguish these cases by pointing out that they do not involve CHIPS transactions. The Second Circuit, however, utilizes New York law's "analogous use of concepts" in cases involving checks when deciding the appropriate law for CHIPS transactions. Delbrueck, 609 F.2d at 1051. Indeed, in Delbrueck the Second Circuit drew an analogy between the "acceptance" of a check under New York law and the finalization of a CHIPS transaction. Id. The equitable principles justifying the Discharge for Value Rule, as well as the related rules concerning bona fide purchasers, are just as valid whether the payment is by wire or by check.

SPIB argues that BW must show it relied to its detriment on the mistaken payment to prevent restitution to SPIB. Its authority consists entirely of the cases cited to support its Mistake of Fact Doctrine argument. No case is cited by SPIB in which detrimental reliance was required when the payee was entitled to the funds. Under the Discharge for Value Rule, as stated in the Restatement and in the stop payment cases cited supra, a party with a right to the payment need not also manifest detrimental reliance to be allowed to keep the funds.

3. First National made the mistake of paying Seaman $150 more than Davis & Co. had in its account because First National had believed incorrectly that it somehow could prevent the $150 payment to Consolidated National from becoming finalized. The court in Consolidated National Bank held that the $150 payment was final. Under the current U.C.C. law in New York it might not be final, Regal Tour Inc. v. European American Bank, 108 Misc.2d 699, 438 N.Y.S.2d 947, 949 (Civ.Ct. Queens Co.1981); but that does not affect the validity of the court's reasoning that a bank must suffer the consequences of its mistaken payment on a debtor's behalf to a creditor, who is ignorant of the mistake.

CONCLUSION

As a matter of law, this Court cannot obligate BW to return the Funds to SPIB. Since no genuine issues of material fact exist, the Court grants plaintiff's cross-motion for summary judgment against SPIB and denies SPIB's motion for summary judgment against BW.

SO ORDERED.

Note

1. Would Article 4A or the UNCITRAL Model Law apply to Banque Worms after the promulgation of both enactments? Consider Article Y, the conflict of laws provision of the UNCITRAL law:

Article Y

Conflict of laws

> (1) The rights and obligations arising out of a payment order shall be governed by the law chosen by the parties. In the absence of agreement, the law of the State of the receiving bank shall apply.
>
> (2) The second sentence of paragraph (1) shall not affect the determination of which law governs the question whether the actual sender of the payment order had the authority to bind the purported sender.

See also 4A–507.

2. In addition to sections 4A–209 and 4A–211, how would sections 4A–205 and 4A–303 impact the facts of Banque Worms? Consider as well the effect of UNCITRAL art. 16:

Article 16

Restitution of overpayment

> If the credit transfer is completed, but the amount of the payment order executed by a receiving bank is greater than the amount of the payment order it accepted, it has such rights to recover the difference from the beneficiary as may otherwise be provided by law.

3. Is the payment revocation issue in Banque Worms akin to the stop payment issue in the check law and the reversability issue in the credit card context, or are they distinguishable in substance?

4. In footnote 3 of the Banque Worms opinion, the court cited the Regal Tour case, which involved a depositary-payor bank's charge-back against its customer's account. That case construed original 4–212, 4–213, and 4–301 to support the conclusion that the bank could charge-back against a provisional credit as long as final payment had not been made. How is that rule incorporated into the Article 4A law? Does the adjustment of those original Article 4 provisions, in revised 4–214, 4–215, and 4–301 change the Article 4 calculus in ways that are more, or less, consistent with the Article 4A formulation? Is Article 4 more, or less, relevant to the charge-back issue than it was prior to the promulgation of Federal Reserve Board Regulation CC? Recall the Coffee Trade decision from Chapter 6.

Problem

Securities Settlement Corporation ("SSC") performed clearing services in connection with securities transactions in the accounts of one of its customers, Kobrin Securities ("Kobrin"). One of Kobrin's clients was another entity, Barrett Consultants ("Barrett"), to whom SSC sent monthly statements regarding Barrett's account with Kobrin. On the morning of June 4, 1985, SSC, at Kobrin's request, instructed Mellon to wire transfer $113,080 to Barrett's account with the Franklin State Bank ("FSB"). Within several hours after Mellon had sent the wire, SSC learned that Kobrin was incapable of paying the securities' purchase price. Although SSC instructed Mellon to cancel the wire transfer, the money went through to Barrett's account. Forty-five days later, Mellon sent SSC an account statement disclosing the erroneous payment to Barrett's account. What facts would determine SSC's 4A–209 right to cancel the transfer and to what extent would 4A–204 or 4A–304 determine the recovery available to SSC if it did have the 4A–209 right to cancel? The facts supporting this problem are drawn from *Mellon Bank v. Securities Settlement Corp.*, 710 F.Supp. 991 (D.N.J.1989).

C. BANK'S LIABILITY FOR "ERRONEOUS" PAYMENT

Transfers of very large sums of money by wire are extremely common. The number of transactions is so large that, inevitably, there are operational failures. The case that follows involves a bank's liability for transferring an amount in excess of that authorized by the customer. As you read the decision, be sensitive to the distinctions the court draws between the commercial paper/bank collections law and the common law that governed wire transfers prior to promulgation of Article 4A. The questions following the case shift the focus to the Article 4A regime.

WALKER v. TEXAS COMMERCE BANK

United States District Court, Southern District of Texas, 1986.
635 F.Supp. 678.

FINDINGS OF FACT AND CONCLUSIONS OF LAW

CARL O. BUE, JR., DISTRICT JUDGE.

INTRODUCTION

The characters in this unhappy tale form a sort of eternal triangle in bankruptcy. At one point is Plaintiff, Trustee in Bankruptcy for Minro Oil, Inc. ("Minro"), who alleges that Defendant breached an implied contract of deposit, and acted negligently in a wire transfer transaction. Defendant, Texas Commerce Bank–Austin, N.A. ("T.C.B."), appears at the second point, as the "deep pocket" from which the creditors of Minro hope to recover. Independent Trading Corporation ("I.T.C."), the recipient of a windfall in the sum of Twenty–Five Thousand Dollars ($25,000.00), would be at the third point, but fails to complete the design since the corporation is insolvent, another fatality in the seemingly endless recent stream of energy-related bankruptcies.

* * *

I. Findings of Fact

1. Minro was a corporation involved in the oil trading business in the State of Texas for a period of approximately one year, until placed in involuntary bankruptcy on October 17, 1980. Shortly thereafter, William Vincent Walker was appointed as the Trustee of Minro's estate. * * *

2. T.C.B. is a national banking association doing business in Houston, Texas, which maintained Minro's principal bank account during the corporation's brief existence. * * *

3. Minro customarily settled accounts with its trading partners on the 20th of every month in the form of wire transfers initiated by T.C.B. upon oral instructions from a representative of Minro. * * *

4. On or about August 20, 1980, Linda Thompson, Minro's bookkeeper, instructed T.C.B. by telephone to wire transfer the sum of Two Million Two Hundred and Twenty–Five Thousand Dollars ($2,225,000.00) to Minro's trading partner, I.T.C. Instead, T.C.B. transferred the sum of Two Million Two Hundred and Fifty Thousand Dollars ($2,250,000.00). * * *

5. Prior to contacting T.C.B., Thompson prepared an internal check request form with the amount of Two Million Two Hundred and Twenty–Five Thousand Dollars ($2,225,000.00) pencilled in on the form. * * *

6. T.C.B. notified Minro of the actual amount transferred by sending a debit advice dated August 25, 1980. * * *

7. T.C.B. received confirmation in writing from Minro, which was also dated August 25, 1980, whereby Thompson confirmed her oral instructions to T.C.B. to wire transfer the sum of Two Million Two Hundred and Twenty–Five Thousand Dollars ($2,225,000.00). * * *

8. Pursuant to custom in Thompson's office, the original of Plaintiff's Exhibit No. 1 was signed, properly addressed, stamped, and deposited in the mail for delivery. * * * Although Defendant objects to the admissibility of Plaintiff's Exhibit No. 1, the presumption of receipt is supported by T.C.B.'s own procedures. T.C.B. required customers who placed an oral transfer request to promptly confirm the request in writing. According to the usual custom and practice established by Defendant, the failure to promptly confirm an oral transfer request in writing entailed a follow-up by T.C.B. until receipt of the written confirmation. * * *

9. Upon receiving the debit advice from T.C.B. (Plaintiff's Exhibit 2), indicating that T.C.B. had wire transferred Twenty–Five Thousand Dollars ($25,000.00) more than requested, Thompson amended her transfer request form by erasing Plaintiff's Exhibit No. 3, and inserting the amount actually transferred, in order to balance Minro's daily cash ledger. * * *

10. On the same day that the debit advice was received, Thompson notified T.C.B. by telephone of the error that had been committed in the wire transfer to I.T.C., and was informed that T.C.B. would conduct an inquiry. Appropriate weight is accorded to Thompson's testimony regarding notice of the error to T.C.B., since it is essentially uncontroverted. T.C.B.'s representatives have no personal recollection regarding the notice of overpayment. Minro did not provide notice of the error in writing, and neither party made any further attempts to correct the error prior to the filing of the instant lawsuit. * * *

11. The first bank statement following the transfer to I.T.C. was dated September 29, 1980. * * * However, Thompson, as well as Minro's other remaining employees, ceased employment during the first week of October. * * *

12. According to the procedures established by T.C.B. for initiating an oral wire transfer, an authorized representative of the transferring customer, who was recognized by telephone voice and account number, placed a call to a secretary in the Petrochemical Division at T.C.B., who then typed the request and delivered it to the bank's wire transfer department for transmittal. The amount of the request was confirmed over the telephone by both parties, and later in writing. T.C.B.'s wire transfer department transmitted the instructions, placed the transfer, and prepared a debit advice. * * * However, the customer's written confirmation was checked against the secretary's typed request, rather than against the wire transfer department's actual debit. T.C.B.'s secretaries customarily retained informal records for a brief period for the purpose of comparing the written confirmation against the oral transfer request. * * *

13. An error committed by the wire transfer department could have gone undetected if it appeared that the secretary who had accepted the original request and the customer had not committed an error. Thus, the detection of errors in an oral transfer transaction essentially depended upon the diligence of the depositor in checking bank statements, the receipt of notice from third parties who received inaccurate payments, and the informal procedures implemented by the Petrochemical Division. * * *

14. After being appointed trustee in bankruptcy, Walker employed Vi Volk to conduct an audit of Minro's books and records for the purpose of locating discrepancies, and identifying potential causes of action to be pursued on behalf of Minro's creditors. * * *

15. Subsequent to Volk's discovery of the overpayment to I.T.C., Plaintiff notified T.C.B. of the relevant discrepancy on June 18, 1982. * * * By that time, I.T.C. was insolvent. However, I.T.C. had retained sufficient funds in its account to cover the Twenty–Five Thousand Dollar ($25,000.00) overpayment for a period of more than seven months following the initial transaction. * * *

16. Although Defendant has suggested plausible theories, it is unable to premise an adequate explanation upon documentary evidence

sufficient to controvert Plaintiff's allegations of an erroneous payment to I.T.C. With the exception of routine checking account statements * * *, Defendant generally relies upon the same documentary evidence introduced by Plaintiff. * * * Furthermore, T.C.B.'s representatives have no personal recollection of the transfer in question. * * *

II. Conclusions of Law

1. The question before the Court—one of first impression in this district—is whether the rights and liabilities of the parties to a wire transfer transaction are governed by Article 4 of the Uniform Commercial Code, Tex. [Bus. & Com.] Code Ann. § 4.101 et seq. ("U.C.C."). Although Minro maintained an account with T.C.B., and must be considered a customer of T.C.B. within the meaning of the U.C.C., see § 4.104(a)(1) [R 4–104(a)(1)] and § 4.104(a)(5) [R 4–104(a)(5)], for the purposes of this case, this Court shall assume, as the Second and Seventh Circuits have previously held in analogous circumstances, see Delbrueck & Co. v. Manufacturers Hanover Co., 609 F.2d 1047 (2d Cir.1979) (electronic transfer of funds), and Evra Corp. v. Swiss Bank Corp., 673 F.2d 951 (7th Cir.1982) (wire transfer transaction), that Article 4 is inapplicable, and will instead apply common law principles. Perhaps, the language of Article 4 could be stretched to encompass wire transfers, but such application was not within the contemplation of the draftsmen. Article 4 does not govern the transaction at issue because it does not specifically address the problems involved. Nevertheless, the affirmative defense asserted by the bank pursuant to U.C.C. § 4.406 [R 4–406] will be considered, since the result would be the same in this case if the provisions of Article 4 were deemed to apply to an oral transfer request.

2. The relationship between a bank and its depositor, whether derived from common law principles or premised upon Article 4 of the U.C.C., is in the nature of an implied contract. "When a customer deposits funds with a bank, the bank impliedly agrees to disburse those funds only in accordance with the depositor's instructions." LaSara Grain Co., 673 S.W.2d at 564. Thus, T.C.B. breached its implied contract with Minro when it transferred Twenty–Five Thousand Dollars more than was requested, in contravention of the depositor's instructions.

3. To the extent that prior law conflicts with the provisions of the U.C.C., it is supplanted by the Code. Prior law is applicable, however, in so far as it has not been displaced by specific provisions of the U.C.C. See U.C.C. § 1.103. Since there is no repugnancy between the U.C.C. and the application of Texas negligence principles in the instant case, Plaintiff is not barred from asserting a cause of action in tort. Indeed, other courts have applied negligence principles in defining the rights and liabilities of parties involved in similar transactions.

In Securities Fund Services, Inc. v. American National Bank and Trust Company of Chicago, for example, the district court, relying on Evra Corp., applied state negligence principles to reach the conclusion that the defendant-bank owed the plaintiff a duty to transmit a wire transfer in an accurate and timely manner, and that the bank had breached its duty of reasonable care. Moreover, the statement of a claim in negligence is consistent with the explicit language of various provisions of the U.C.C. In sum, it is the duty of a bank to exercise good faith and use ordinary care in handling the accounts of its depositors. While the U.C.C., as adopted in Texas, does not expressly state that a bank may be held liable for negligent payment of an instrument, much less speak to the negligent processing of a wire transfer transaction, numerous provisions of the U.C.C. incorporate common law principles of negligence, and indirectly support Plaintiff's position. See, e.g., U.C.C. § 3.419 [R 3–420]; § 4.202 [R 4–202]; § 4.203 [R 4–203], and § 4.406 [R 4–406]. Thus, the general proposition that a bank owes a duty of reasonable care to its customers enjoys unwavering support which originates in decisional law both before and after the enactment of the U.C.C.

Applying these general principles to the case at bar leads to the inescapable conclusion that a depositor may justifiably expect a bank to implement commercially reasonable internal procedures designed to process an oral transfer request in accordance with depositor's instructions, to verify the accuracy of, and compliance with, instructions, to detect and minimize inaccuracy, and to act promptly and diligently to remedy errors. There can be little doubt with regard to these justified expectations, given the procedures implemented by the bank, that T.C.B. has breached its duty to Minro to exercise reasonable care under the circumstances, which duty derives from the implied contract of deposit that existed between the parties.

4. The parties vigorously dispute the assignment of the burden of proof. In reliance upon Mesquite State Bank, and the citation of authorities therein, Plaintiff contends that Defendant must be assigned the burden of proving that it transferred funds in accordance with Minro's instructions. "In suits against a bank to recover deposits, the burden of proving payment under authority from the depositor is on the bank." Id. at 75. Defendant, of course, argues that Plaintiff must be assigned the traditional burden of proof. Although fuel for esoteric debate, the parties' argumentation is immaterial because Plaintiff has established by a preponderance of the evidence that T.C.B. both breached its implied contract of deposit, and failed to exercise ordinary care. Accordingly, the question of whether the bank should properly be assigned the burden of proof need not be reached in this case.

5. Without citing a single relevant authority, Defendant contends that the Texas Civil Practice & Remedies Code § 33.001 precludes a recovery from the bank since it alleges that Plaintiff's contributory negligence was more than fifty percent (50%) responsible for the loss of funds. Defendant's position on this point conflicts with U.C.C. § 4.103 [R 4–103] which unequivocably stands for the proposition that the U.C.C. prevents a bank from contracting away its obligation to exercise ordinary care in the handling of a depositor's funds. Plaintiff's more

forceful argument, premised upon Bullitt County Bank, and Bank of Southern Maryland v. Robertson's Crab House, Inc., is that a bank may not invoke the doctrine of equitable estoppel against a depositor if its own practices are commercially unreasonable, or if it has failed to exercise ordinary care. Thus, the plaintiff-depositor's failure to examine bank statements for a period of eleven months in Bank of Southern Maryland, did not preclude recovery upon a negligence theory against the bank.

* * *

7. Finally, the bank asserts U.C.C. § 4.406 [R 4–406] as a defense to liability. This Court concludes, however, that a wire transfer is not an "item paid in good faith" within the meaning of section 4.406 [R 4–406], and that the statutory language with reference to "unauthorized signature[s]" and "alteration[s]" should not be construed to include the type of error committed by T.C.B. in this wire transfer transaction.

8. Moreover, there are three reasons why section 4.406 [R 4–406] would not benefit Defendant if Article 4 controlled the disposition of this case. First, Defendant contends that the U.C.C. imposes a one year notice period upon Minro, which is not extended by 11 U.S.C. § 108(b), and which required Minro to report the overpayment to T.C.B. by August 25, 1981. See U.C.C. § 4.406(d) [R 4–406(f)]. However, Thompson's telephone notice of the erroneous payment to I.T.C. complies with the literal requirements of subsection (d). Such notice was timely, reasonable under the circumstances, and accrues to the benefit of Minro's estate. Second, though not limited to forgeries, the statute adopts a liability-shifting approach which codifies a depositor's duty to discover and report errors that are primarily due to the acts of intervening third parties—generally, third party wrongdoers. U.S.C. § 4.406(a) [R 4–406(a)]. The statute was certainly not intended to shield a bank from liability for its own errors. Thus, it is unreasonable to bootstrap a defense upon section 4.406 [R 4–406] which foists responsibility upon the depositor to exercise diligence in the discovery of bank errors. Third, the section 4.406 [R 4–406] defense is not available to a bank which has failed to exercise ordinary care in handling a depositor's account. U.C.C. § 4.406(c) [R 4–406(e)]. If the statute were deemed applicable, the exercise of ordinary care would certainly include the implementation of reasonable commercial standards for the internal handling of a wire transaction.

8. This Court has jurisdiction over the instant proceedings pursuant to 28 U.S.C. § 1334(b).

9. In the event that the foregoing Findings of Fact also constitute Conclusions of Law, they should be regarded as such. In the event that the Conclusions of Law also constitute Findings of Fact, they are adopted as such.

CONCLUSION

This Court concludes that Defendant, T.C.B., breached its implied contract of deposit with Minro, and acted negligently in wire transferring more to the account of I.T.C. than was requested by the depositor. Accordingly, Plaintiff is entitled to recover in the sum of Twenty-Five Thousand Dollars ($25,000.00), together with interest and costs.

Counsel will prepare an appropriate judgment incorporating by reference these Findings of Fact and Conclusions of Law for entry by the Court within twenty (20) days.

Note

Sections 4A–204 and 4A–304 concern a customer's duty to notify its bank of an unauthorized or erroneous payment order, but they do not treat dispositively all of the issues treated in the analogous check setting by U.C.C. § 4–406, both original and revised. To what extent, then, does the *Walker* court's common law analysis, and analogical use of 4–406, inform resolution of the same issues after the promulgation of Article 4A? What issues are resolved in the check context by 4–406 but left unresolved by 4A–204 and 4A–304?

An earlier draft of Article 4A included a provision captioned "Duty of Customer to Report Unauthorized Transfer Order" that essentially tracked U.C.C. § 4–406. The draft provision, 4A–204, was controversial and ultimately was truncated substantially in the final draft of sections 4A–204 and 4A–304.

D. BANK'S LIABILITY FOR FAILURE TO EFFECT FUNDS TRANSFER

The cases presented to this point in the chapter concern whether a payment is authorized and the legal rules, both statutory and otherwise, that determine whether and the extent to which a bank is authorized to make a funds transfer. In this portion of the chapter the focus shifts to a provocative issue: the measure of a bank's liability for failing to make a wire transfer.

EVRA CORP. v. SWISS BANK CORP.

United States Court of Appeals, Seventh Circuit, 1982.
673 F.2d 951, cert. denied, 459 U.S. 1017, 103 S.Ct. 377, 74 L.Ed.2d 511.

POSNER, CIRCUIT JUDGE.

The question—one of first impression—in this diversity case is the extent of a bank's liability for failure to make a transfer of funds when requested by wire to do so. The essential facts are undisputed. In 1972 Hymans-Michaels Company, a large Chicago dealer in scrap metal, entered into a two year contract to supply steel scrap to a Brazilian corporation. Hyman-Michaels chartered a ship, the *Pandora*, to carry the scrap to Brazil. The charter was for one year, with an option to extend the charter for a second year; specified a fixed daily rate of pay for the hire of the ship during both the initial and the option period, payable semimonthly "in advance"; and provided that if payment was not made on time the *Pandora's* owner could cancel the charter. Payment was to be made by deposit to the owner's account in the Banque de Paris et des PaysBas (Suisse) in Geneva, Switzerland.

The usual method by which Hyman–Michaels, in Chicago, got the payments to the Banque de Paris in Geneva was to request the Continental Illinois National Bank and Trust Company of Chicago, where it had an account, to make a wire transfer of funds. Continental would debit Hyman–Michaels' account by the amount of the payment and then send a telex to its London office for retransmission to its correspondent bank in Geneva—Swiss Bank Corporation—asking Swiss Bank to deposit this amount in the Banque de Paris account of the *Pandora's* owner. The transaction was completed by the crediting of Swiss Bank's account at Continental by the same amount.

When Hyman–Michaels chartered the *Pandora* in June 1972, market charter rates were very low, and it was these rates that were fixed in the charter for its entire term—two years if Hyman–Michaels exercised its option. Shortly after the agreement was signed, however, charter rates began to climb and by October 1972 they were much higher than they had been in June. The *Pandora's* owners were eager to get out of the charter if they could. At the end of October they thought they had found a way, for the payment that was due in the Banque de Paris on October 26 had not arrived by October 30, and on that day the *Pandora's* owner notified Hyman–Michaels that it was canceling the charter because of the breach of the payment term. Hyman–Michaels had mailed a check for the October 26 installment to the Banque de Paris rather than use the wire transfer method of payment. It had done this in order to have the use of its money for the period that it would take the check to clear, about two weeks. But the check had not been mailed in Chicago until October 25 and of course did not reach Geneva on the twenty-sixth.

When Hyman–Michaels received notification that the charter was being canceled it immediately wired payment to the Banque de Paris, but the *Pandora's* owner refused to accept it and insisted that the charter was indeed canceled. The matter was referred to arbitration in accordance with the charter. On December 5, 1972, the arbitration panel ruled in favor of Hyman–Michaels. The panel noted that previous arbitration panels had "shown varying degrees of latitude to Charterers"; "In all cases, a pattern of obligation on Owners' part to protest, complain, or warn of intended withdrawal was expressed as an essential prerequisite to withdrawal, in spite of the clear wording of the operative clause. No such advance notice was given by Owners of M/V Pandora." One of the three members of the panel dissented; he thought the *Pandora's* owner was entitled to cancel.

Hyman–Michaels went back to making the charter payments by wire transfer. On the morning of April 25, 1973, it telephoned Continental Bank and requested it to transfer $27,000 to the Banque de Paris account of the *Pandora's* owner in payment for the charter hire period from April 27 to May 11, 1973. Since the charter provided for payment "in advance," this payment arguably was due by the close of business on April 26. The requested telex went out to Continental's London office on the afternoon of April 25, which was nighttime in England. Early the next morning a telex operator in Continental's London office dialed, as Continental's Chicago office had instructed him to do, Swiss Bank's general telex number, which rings in the bank's cable department. But that number was busy, and after trying unsuccessfully for an hour to engage it the Continental telex operator dialed another number, that of a machine in Swiss Bank's foreign exchange department which he had used in the past when the general number was engaged. We know this machine received the telexed message because it signaled the sending machine at both the beginning and end of the transmission that the telex was being received. Yet Swiss Bank failed to comply with the payment order, and no transfer of funds was made to the account of the *Pandora's* owner in the Banque de Paris.

No one knows exactly what went wrong. One possibility is that the receiving telex machine had simply run out of paper, in which event it would not print the message although it had received it. Another is that whoever took the message out of the machine after it was printed failed to deliver it to the banking department. Unlike the machine in the cable department that the Continental telex operator had originally tried to reach, the machines in the foreign exchange department were operated by junior foreign exchange dealers rather than by professional telex operators, although Swiss Bank knew that messages intended for other departments were sometimes diverted to the telex machines in the foreign exchange department.

At 8:30 a.m. the next day, April 27, Hyman–Michaels in Chicago received a telex from the *Pandora's* owner stating that the charter was canceled because payment for the April 27–May 11 charter period had not been made. Hyman–Michaels called over to Continental and told them to keep trying to effect payment through Swiss Bank even if the *Pandora's* owner rejected it. This instruction was confirmed in a letter to Continental dated April 28, in which Hyman–Michaels stated: "please instruct your London branch to advise their correspondents to persist in attempting to make this payment. This should be done even in the face of a rejection on the part of Banque de Paris to receive this payment. It is paramount that in order to strengthen our position in an arbitration that these funds continue to be readily available." Hyman–Michaels did not attempt to wire the money directly to the Banque de Paris as it had done on the occasion of its previous default. Days passed while the missing telex message was hunted unsuccessfully. Finally Swiss Bank suggested to Continental that it retransmit the telex message to the machine in the cable department and this was done on May 1. The next day Swiss Bank attempted to deposit the $27,000 in the account of the *Pandora's* owner at the Banque de Paris but the payment was refused.

Again the arbitrators were convened and rendered a decision. In it they ruled that Hyman–Michaels had been "blameless" up until the morning of April 27, when it first learned that the Banque de Paris had not received payment on April 26, but that "being faced with this situation," Hyman–Michaels had "failed to do everything in [its] power to remedy it. The action taken was immediate but did not prove to be adequate, in that [*Continental*] Bank and its correspondent required some 5/6 days to trace and effect the lost instruction to remit. [*Hyman–Michaels*] could have ordered an immediate duplicate payment or even sent a Banker's check by hand or special messengers, so that the funds could have reached owner's Bank, not later than April 28th." By failing to do any of these things Hyman–Michaels had "created the opening" that the *Pandora's* owner was seeking in order to be able to cancel the charter. It had "acted imprudently." The arbitration panel concluded, reluctantly but unanimously, that this time the *Pandora's* owner was entitled to cancel the agreement. The arbitration decision was confirmed by a federal district court in New York.

Hyman–Michaels then brought this diversity action against Swiss Bank, seeking to recover its expenses in the second arbitration proceeding plus the profits that it lost because of the cancellation of the charter. The contract by which Hyman–Michaels had agreed to ship scrap steel to Brazil had been terminated by the buyer in March 1973 and Hyman–Michaels had promptly subchartered the *Pandora* at market rates, which by April 1973 were double the rates fixed in the charter. Its lost profits are based on the difference between the charter and subcharter rates.

Swiss Bank impleaded Continental Bank as a third-party defendant, asking that if it should be ordered to pay Hyman–Michaels, then Continental should be ordered to indemnify it. Continental filed a crossclaim against Hyman–Michaels seeking to shift back to Hyman–Michaels the cost of any judgment that Swiss Bank might obtain against it, on the ground that any errors by Continental were caused by Hyman–Michaels' negligence. Hyman–Michaels in turn counterclaimed against Continental, alleging that Continental had both been negligent and broken its contract with Hyman–Michaels in failing to effect payment on April 26, and was therefore liable to Hyman–Michaels along with Swiss Bank.

The case was tried to a district judge without a jury. In his decision, 522 F.Supp. 820 (N.D.Ill.1981), he first ruled that the substantive law applicable to Hyman–Michaels' claim against Swiss Bank was that of Illinois, rather than Switzerland as urged by Swiss Bank, and that Swiss Bank had been negligent and under Illinois law was liable to Hyman–Michaels for $2.1 million in damages. This figure was made up of about $16,000 in arbitration expenses and the rest in lost profits on the subcharter of the *Pandora.* The judge also ruled that Swiss Bank was not entitled to indemnification from Continental Bank, which made Continental's crossclaim moot; and lastly he dismissed against Continental on the ground that Continental had not breached any duty to Hyman–Michaels. The case comes to us on Swiss Bank's appeal from the judgment in favor of Hyman–Michaels and from the dismissal of Swiss Bank's claim against Continental Bank, and on Hyman–Michaels' appeal from the dismissal of its counterclaim against Continental Bank.

Logically the first question we should address is choice of law. The parties seem agreed that if Swiss law applies, Hyman–Michaels has no claim against Swiss Bank, because under Swiss law a bank cannot be held liable to someone with whom it is not in privity of contract and there was no contract between Swiss Bank and Hyman–Michaels. Illinois does not have such a privity requirement. But this creates a conflict of laws only if Hyman–Michaels has a good claim against Swiss Bank under Illinois law; if it does not, then our result must be the same regardless of which law applies. Because we are more certain that Hyman–Michaels cannot recover against Swiss Bank under Illinois law than we are that Swiss rather than Illinois law applies to this case under Illinois choice of law principles (which we must apply in a diversity suit tried in Illinois, see *Klaxon Co. v. Stentor Elec. Mfg. Co.,* 313 U.S. 487, 496–97, 61 S.Ct. 1020, 1021–22, 85 L.Ed. 1477 (1941)), we shall avoid the choice of law question and discuss Swiss Bank's liability to Hyman–Michaels under Illinois law without deciding for, to repeat, it would make no difference to the outcome whether it really is Illinois law or Swiss law that governs.

When a bank fails to make a requested transfer of funds, this can cause two kinds of loss. First, the funds themselves or interest on them may be lost, and of course the fee paid for the transfer, having bought nothing, becomes a loss item. These are "direct" (sometimes called "general") damages. Hyman–Michaels is not seeking any direct damages in this case and apparently sustained none. It did not lose any part of the $27,000; although its account with Continental Bank was debited by this amount prematurely, it was not an interest bearing account so Hyman–Michaels lost no interest; and Hyman–Michaels paid no fee either to Continental or to Swiss Bank for the aborted transfer. A second type of loss, which either the payor or the payee may suffer, is a dislocation in one's business triggered by the failure to pay. Swiss Bank's failure to transfer funds to the Banque de Paris when requested to do so by Continental Bank set off a chain reaction which resulted in an arbitration proceeding that was costly to Hyman–Michaels and in the cancellation of a highly profitable contract. It is those costs and lost profits—"consequential" or, as they are sometimes called, "special" damages—that Hyman–Michaels seeks in this lawsuit, and recovered below. It is conceded that if Hyman–Michaels was entitled to consequential damages, the district court measured them correctly. The only issue is whether it was entitled to consequential damages.

If a bank loses a check, its liability is governed by Article 4 of the Uniform Commercial Code, which precludes consequential damages unless the bank is acting in bad faith. See Ill.Rev.Stat. ch. 26, § 4–103(5) [R 4–103(e)]. If Article 4 applies to this transaction, Hyman-Michaels cannot recover the damages that it seeks, because Swiss Bank was not acting in bad faith. Maybe the language of Article 4 could be stretched to include electronic fund transfers, see § 4–102(2) [R 4–102(b)], but they were not in the contemplation of the draftsmen. For purposes of this case we shall assume, as the Second Circuit held in *Delbrueck & Co. v. Manufacturers Hanover Trust Co.,* 609 F.2d 1047, 1051 (2d Cir.1979), that Article 4 is inapplicable, and apply common law principles instead.

Hadley v. Baxendale, 9 Ex. 341, 156 Eng.Rep. 145 (1854), is the leading common law case on liability for consequential damages caused by failure or delay in carrying out a commercial undertaking. The engine shaft in plaintiffs' corn mill had broken and they hired the defendants, a common carrier, to transport the shaft to the manufacturer, who was to make a new one using the broken shaft as a model. The carrier failed to deliver the shaft within the time promised. With the engine shaft out of service the mill was shut down. The plaintiffs sued the defendants for the lost profits of the mill during the additional period that it was shut down because of the defendants' breach of their promise. The court held that the lost profits were not a proper item of damages, because "in the great multitude of cases of millers sending off broken shafts to third persons by a carrier under ordinary circumstances, such consequences [the stoppage of the mill and resulting loss of profits] would not, in all probability, have occurred; and these special circumstances were here never communicated by the plaintiffs to the defendants." 9 Ex. at 356, 156 Eng.Rep. at 151.

The rule of *Hadley v. Baxendale*—that consequential damages will not be awarded unless the defendant was put on notice of the special circumstances giving rise to them—has been applied in many Illinois cases, and *Hadley* cited approvingly. In *Siegel v. Western Union Tel. Co.,* 312 Ill.App. 86, 92–93, 37 N.E.2d 868, 871 (1941), the plaintiff had delivered $200 to Western Union with instructions to transmit it to a friend of the plaintiff's. The money was to bet (legally) on a horse, but this was not disclosed in the instructions. Western Union misdirected the money order and it did not reach the friend until several hours after the race had taken place. The horse that the plaintiff had intended to bet on won and would have paid $1650 on the plaintiff's $200 bet if the bet had been placed. He sued Western Union for his $1450 lost profit, but the court held that under the rule of *Hadley v. Baxendale* Western Union was not liable, because it "had no notice or knowledge of the purpose for which the money was being transmitted." 312 Ill.App. at 93, 37 N.E.2d at 871.

The present case is similar, though Swiss Bank knew more than Western Union knew in *Siegel;* it knew or should have known, from Continental Bank's previous telexes, that Hyman–Michaels was paying the Pandora Shipping Company for the hire of a motor vessel named *Pandora.* But it did not know when payment was due, what the terms of the charter were, or that they had turned out to be extremely favorable to Hyman–Michaels. And it did not know that Hyman–Michaels knew the *Pandora's* owner would try to cancel the charter, and probably would succeed, if Hyman–Michaels was ever again late in making payment, or that despite this peril Hyman–Michaels would not try to pay until the last possible moment and in the event of a delay in transmission would not do everything in its power to minimize the consequences of the delay. Electronic funds transfers are not so unusual as to automatically place a bank on notice of extraordinary consequences if such a transfer goes awry. Swiss Bank did not have enough information to infer that if it lost a $27,000 payment order it would face a liability in excess of $2 million. Cf. *Snell v. Cottingham,* 72 Ill. 161, 169–70 (1874); *Flug v. Craft Mfg. Co.,* 3 Ill.App.2d 56, 67, 120 N.E.2d 666, 671 (1954).

It is true that in both *Hadley* and *Siegel* there was a contract between the parties and here there was none. We cannot be certain that the Illinois courts would apply the principles of those cases outside of the contract area. As so often in diversity cases, there is an irreducible amount of speculation involved in attempting to predict the reaction of a state's courts to a new issue. The best we can do is to assume that the Illinois courts would look to the policies underlying cases such as *Hadley* and *Siegel* and, to the extent they found them pertinent, would apply those cases here. We must therefore ask what difference it should make whether the parties are or are not bound to each other by a contract. On the one hand, it seems odd that the absence of a contract would enlarge rather than limit the extent of liability. After all, under Swiss law the absence of a contract would be devastating to Hyman–Michaels' claim. Privity is not a wholly artificial concept. It is one thing to imply a duty to one with whom one has a contract and another to imply it to the entire world.

On the other hand, contract liability is strict. A breach of contract does not connote wrongdoing; it may have been caused by circumstances beyond the promisor's control—a strike, a fire, the failure of a supplier to deliver an essential input. See *Globe Ref. Co. v. Landa Cotton Oil Co.,* 190 U.S. 540, 543–44, 23 S.Ct. 754, 755–56, 47 L.Ed. 1171 (1903). And while such contract doctrines as impossibility, impracticability, and frustration relieve promisors from liability for some failures to perform that are beyond their control, many other such failures are actionable although they could not have been prevented by the exercise of due care. The district judge found that Swiss Bank had been negligent in losing Continental Bank's telex message and it can be argued that Swiss Bank should therefore be liable for a broader set of consequences than if it had only broken a contract. But *Siegel* implicitly rejects this distinction. Western Union had not merely broken its contract to deliver the plaintiff's money order; it had "negligently misdirected" the money order. "The company's negligence is conceded." 312 Ill.App. at 88, 91, 37 N.E.2d at 869, 871. Yet it was not liable for the consequences.

Siegel, we conclude, is authority for holding that Swiss Bank is not liable for the consequences of negligently failing to transfer Hyman–Michaels' funds to Banque de Paris; reason for such a holding is found in the animating principle of *Hadley v. Baxendale,* which is that the costs of the untoward consequence of a course of dealings should be borne by that party who was able to avert the consequence at least cost and failed to do so. In *Hadley* the untoward consequence was the shutting down of the mill. The carrier could have avoided it by delivering the engine shaft on time. But the mill owners, as the court noted, could have avoided it simply by having a spare shaft. 9 Ex. at 355–56, 156 Eng.Rep. at 151. Prudence required that they have a spare shaft anyway, since a replacement could not be obtained at once even if there was no undue delay in carting the broken shaft to and the replacement shaft from the manufacturer. The court refused to imply a duty on the part of the carrier to guarantee the mill owners against the consequences of their own lack of prudence, though of course if the parties had stipulated for such a guarantee the court would have enforced it. The notice requirement of *Hadley v. Baxendale* is designed to assure that such an improbable guarantee really is intended.

This case is much the same, though it arises in a tort rather than a contract setting. Hyman–Michaels showed a lack of prudence throughout. It was imprudent for it to mail in Chicago a letter that unless received the next day in Geneva would put Hyman–Michaels in breach of a contract that was very profitable to it and that the other party to the contract had every interest in canceling. It was imprudent thereafter for Hyman–Michaels, having narrowly avoided cancellation and having (in the words of its appeal brief in this court) been "put * * * on notice that the payment provision of the Charter would be strictly enforced thereafter," to wait till arguably the last day before payment was due to instruct its bank to transfer the necessary funds overseas. And it was imprudent in the last degree for Hyman–Michaels, when it received notice of cancellation on the last possible day payment was due, to fail to pull out all the stops to get payment to the Banque de Paris on that day, and instead to dither while Continental and Swiss Bank wasted five days looking for the lost telex message. Judging from the obvious reluctance with which the arbitration panel finally decided to allow the *Pandora's* owner to cancel the charter, it might have made all the difference if Hyman–Michaels had gotten payment to the Banque de Paris by April 27 or even by Monday, April 30, rather than allowing things to slide until May 2.

This is not to condone the sloppy handling of incoming telex messages in Swiss Bank's foreign department. But Hyman–Michaels is a sophisticated business enterprise. It knew or should have known that even the Swiss are not infallible; that messages sometimes get lost or delayed in transit among three banks, two of them located 5000 miles apart, even when all the banks are using reasonable care; and that therefore it should take its own precautions against the consequences best known to itself of a mishap that might not be due to anyone's negligence.

We are not the first to remark the affinity between the rule of *Hadley v. Baxendale* and the doctrine, which is one of tort as well as contract law and is a settled part of the common law of Illinois, of avoidable consequences. See Dobbs, *Handbook on the Law of Remedies* 831 (1973); cf. *Benton v. J.A. Fay & Co.,* 64 Ill. 417 (1872). If you are hurt in an automobile accident and unreasonably fail to seek medical treatment, the injurer, even if negligent, will not be held liable for the aggravation of the injury due to your own unreasonable behavior after the accident. See, e.g., *Slater v. Chicago Transit Auth.,* 5 Ill.App.2d 181, 185, 125 N.E.2d 289, 291 (1955). If in addition you failed to fasten your seat belt, you may be barred from collecting the tort damages that would have been prevented if you had done so. See, e.g., *Mount v. McClellan,* 91 Ill.App.2d 1, 5, 234 N.E.2d 329, 331 (1968). Hyman–Michaels' behavior in steering close to the wind prior to April 27 was like not fastening one's seat belt; its failure on April 27 to wire a duplicate payment immediately after disaster struck was like refusing to seek medical attention after a serious accident. The seatbelt cases show that the doctrine of avoidable consequences applies whether the tort victim acts imprudently before or after the tort is committed. See Prosser, *Handbook of the Law of Torts* 424 (4th ed. 1971). Hyman–Michaels did both.

The rule of *Hadley v. Baxendale* links up with tort concepts in another way. The rule is sometimes stated in the form that only foreseeable damages are recoverable in a breach of contract action. E.g., Restatement (Second) of Contracts § 351 (1979). So expressed, it corresponds to the tort principle that limits liability to the foreseeable consequence of the defendant's carelessness. See, e.g., *Neering v. Illinois Cent. R.R. Co.,* 383 Ill. 366, 380, 50 N.E.2d 497, 503 (1943). The amount of care that a person ought to take is a function of the probability and magnitude of the harm that may occur if he does not take care. See, e.g., *United States v. Carroll Towing Co.,* 159 F.2d 169, 173 (2d Cir.1947); *Bezark v. Kostner Manor, Inc.,* 29 Ill.App.2d 106, 111–12, 172 N.E.2d 424, 426–27 (1961). If he does not know what that probability and magnitude are, he cannot determine how much care to take. That would be Swiss Bank's dilemma if it were liable for consequential damages from failing to carry out payment orders in timely fashion. To estimate the extent of its probable liability in order to know how many and how elaborate failsafe features to install in its telex rooms or how much insurance to buy against the inevitable failures, Swiss Bank would have to collect reams of information about firms that are not even its regular customers. It had no banking relationship with Hyman–Michaels. It did not know or have reason to know how at once precious and fragile Hyman–Michaels' contract with the *Pandora's* owner was. These were circumstances too remote from Swiss Bank's practical range of knowledge to have affected its decisions as to who should man the telex machines in the foreign department or whether it should have more intelligent machines or should install more machines in the cable department, any more than the falling of a platform scale because a conductor jostled a passenger who was carrying fireworks was a prospect that could have influenced the amount of care taken by the Long Island Railroad. See *Palsgraf v. Long Island R.R.,* 248 N.Y. 339, 162 N.E. 99 (1928); cf. *Ney v. Yellow Cab Co.,* 2 Ill.2d 74, 8084, 117 N.E.2d 74, 78–80 (1954).

In short, Swiss Bank was not required in the absence of a contractual undertaking to take precautions or insure against a harm that it could not measure but that was known with precision to Hyman–Michaels, which could by the exercise of common prudence have averted it completely. As Chief Judge Cardozo (the author of *Palsgraf*) remarked in discussing the application of *Hadley v. Baxendale* to the liability of telegraph companies for errors in transmission, "The sender can protect himself by insurance in one form or another if the risk of nondelivery or error appears to be too great * * *. The company, if it takes out insurance for itself, can do no more than guess at the loss to be avoided." *Kerr S.S. Co. v. Radio Corp. of America,* 245 N.Y. 284, 291–92, 157 N.E. 140, 142 (1927).

But *Kerr* is a case from New York, not Illinois, and Hyman–Michaels argues that two early Illinois telegraph cases compel us to rule in its favor against Swiss Bank. *Postal Tel. Cable Co. v. Lathrop,* 131 Ill. 575, 28 N.E. 583 (1890), involved the garbled transmission of two telegrams from a coffee dealer—who as the telegraph company knew was engaged in buying and selling futures contracts—to his broker. The first telegram (there is no need to discuss the second) directed the broker to buy 1000 bags of August coffee for the dealer's account. This got changed in transmission to 2000 bags, and because the price fell the dealer sustained an extra loss for which he sued the telegraph company. The court held that the company had had notice enough to make it liable for consequential damages under the rule of *Hadley v. Baxendale.* It knew it was transmitting buy and sell orders in a fluctuating market and that a garbled transmission could result in large losses. There was no suggestion that the dealer should have taken his own precautions against such mistakes. In *Providence–Washington Ins. Co. v. Western Union Tel. Co.,* 247 Ill. 84, 93 N.E. 134 (1910), a telegram from an insurance company canceling a policy was misdirected, and before it turned up there was a fire and the insurance company was liable on the policy. This was the precise risk created by delay, it was obvious on the face of the telegram, and the telegraph company was therefore liable for the insurance company's loss on the policy. Again there was no suggestion that the plaintiff had neglected any precaution. Both cases are distinguishable from the present case: the defendants had more information and the plaintiffs were not imprudent.

The legal principles that we have said are applicable to this case were not applied below. Although the district judge's opinion is not entirely clear, he apparently thought the rule of *Hadley v. Baxendale* inapplicable and the imprudence of Hyman–Michaels irrelevant. See 522 F.Supp. at 833. He did state that the damages to Hyman–Michaels were foreseeable because "a major international bank" should know that a failure to act promptly on a telexed request to transfer funds could cause substantial damage; but *Siegel*—and for that matter *Lathrop* and *Providence-Washington*—makes clear that that kind of general foreseeability, which is present in virtually every case, does not justify an award of consequential damages.

We could remand for new findings based on the proper legal standard, but it is unnecessary to do so. The undisputed facts, recited in this opinion, show as a matter of law that Hyman–Michaels is not entitled to recover consequential damages from Swiss Bank.

Since Hyman–Michaels' complaint against Swiss Bank must be dismissed, Swiss Bank's third-party complaint against Continental Bank and Continental Bank's cross-claim against Hyman–Michaels are moot. That leaves only Hyman–Michaels' counterclaim against Continental Bank still to be considered. * * *

On the merits, we agree with the district judge that Hyman–Michaels did not prove its case. Continental did not break any contract with Hyman–Michaels. All it undertook to do on April 25 was to transmit a telex message to Swiss Bank, and it did so. All it undertook to do on April 27, by the evidence of Hyman–Michaels' own confirming letter, was to advise its correspondent—that is, Swiss Bank—to "persist in attempting to make . . . payment," and it did so advise its correspondent. Nor was Continental negligent on either occasion. Its telex operator had used the machine in Swiss Bank's foreign department before, for the same purpose and without incident; he had no reason to expect a mishap. And Continental used due care in assisting Swiss Bank in the latter's vain hunt for the missing telex. The district court's findings on these issues were skimpy but the facts are clear and a remand is unnecessary.

No other issues need be decided. The judgment in favor of Hyman–Michaels against Swiss Bank is reversed with directions to enter judgment for Swiss Bank. The judgment in favor of Continental Bank on Swiss Bank's third party complaint is vacated with instructions to dismiss that complaint as moot. The judgment dismissing Continental's cross-claim against Hyman–Michaels as moot, and the judgment in favor of Continental on Hyman–Michaels' counterclaim, are affirmed. The costs of the appeals shall be borne by Hyman–Michaels (EVRA Corporation).

So Ordered.

Note

1. Consider the result if Article 4A were applied to the facts of *Evra*. See U.C.C. § 4A–305. Cf. UNCITRAL arts. 17 and 18:

Article 17
Liability for interest

(1) A receiving bank that does not comply with its obligations under article 8(2) is liable to the beneficiary if the credit transfer is completed. The liability of the receiving bank is to pay interest on the amount of the payment order for the period of delay caused by the receiving bank's non-compliance. If the delay concerns only part of the amount of the payment order, the liability shall be to pay interest on the amount that has been delayed.

(2) The liability of a receiving bank under paragraph (1) may be discharged by payment to its receiving bank or by direct payment to the beneficiary. If a receiving bank receives such payment but is not the beneficiary, the receiving bank shall pass on the benefit of the interest to the next receiving bank or, if it is the beneficiary's bank, to the beneficiary.

(3) An originator may recover the interest the beneficiary would have been entitled to, but did not, receive in accordance with paragraphs (1) and (2) to the extent the originator has paid interest to the beneficiary on account of a delay in the completion of the credit transfer. The originator's bank and each subsequent receiving bank that is not the bank liable under paragraph (1) may recover interest paid to its sender from its receiving bank or from the bank liable under paragraph (1).

(4) A receiving bank that does not give a notice required under article 8(4) or (5) shall pay interest to the sender on any payment that it has received from the sender under article 5(6) for the period during which it retains the payment.

(5) A beneficiary's bank that does not give a notice required under article 10(2), (3) or (4) shall pay interest to the sender on any payment that it has received from the sender under article 5(6), from the day of payment until the day that it provides the required notice.

(6) The beneficiary's bank is liable to the beneficiary to the extent provided by the law governing the relationship between the beneficiary and the bank for its failure to perform one of the obligations under article 10(1) or (5).

(7) The provisions of this article may be varied by agreement to the extent that the liability of one bank to another bank is increased or reduced. Such an agreement to reduce liability may be contained in a bank's standard terms of dealing. A bank may agree to increase its liability to an originator or beneficiary that is not a bank, but may not reduce its liability to such an originator or beneficiary. In particular, it may not reduce its liability by an agreement fixing the rate of interest.

Article 18
Exclusivity of remedies

The remedies in article 17 shall be exclusive, and no other remedy arising out of other doctrines of law shall be available in respect of noncompliance with articles 8 or 10, except any remedy that may exist when a bank has improperly executed, or failed to execute, a payment order (a) with the specific intent to cause loss, or (b) recklessly and with actual knowledge that loss would be likely to result.

2. Does U.C.C. § 2–715 adopt the rule of *Hadley*? Is the Article 2 consequential damages rule pertinent to the consequential damages issue in wholesale funds transfers? Is the *Hadley* rule?

3. Judge Posner distinguishes the pertinent contract law from tort law and then applies both to the facts in issue. Does the Article 4A formulation, in 4A–305, adopt a more contract or more tort perspective?

4. Which of the transactors chose Swiss Bank to act as an intermediary? Is that pertinent to the loss allocation calculus? Cf. OR and R 4–402.

E. FRAUD ON THE SYSTEM

Fraud insinuates itself into the wholesale funds transfer system no less pervasively than in any other payment medium. The stakes are often a good deal higher than they are in the paper-based or other retail systems. To a significant extent, the efficacy of a system may be determined by its reaction to fraud: the fraud provisions reveal a good deal about the Article 4A predisposition toward the rights of the parties and the division of equities. The two cases that follow confront fraud on the system and allocate the fraud loss among the relatively innocent transactors. Each of the cases was decided pre-Article 4A and use analogous Article 4 and common law loss allocation principles to determine the rights and liabilities of the parties. The notes and questions following the cases encourage comparison and contrast as well as the identification of fundamental loss allocation principles.

SECURITIES FUND SERVICES, INC. v. AMERICAN NATIONAL BANK AND TRUST COMPANY OF CHICAGO

United States District Court, Northern District of Illinois, 1982.
542 F.Supp. 323.

LEIGHTON, DISTRICT JUDGE.

I

This is a civil diversity action for damages arising out of a wire transfer transaction. New England Merchants National Bank of Boston (NEMB), at the direction of plaintiff Security Fund Services (SFS), requested, by wire, a transfer of funds disbursed by SFS to an account purportedly in the American National Bank and Trust Company of Chicago (ANB), the defendant. The dispute arises from questions now being raised concerning crediting of the funds by ANB.

The complaint is in nine counts. Count I alleges that defendant engaged in reckless, willful and wanton misconduct constituting gross negligence. Count II alleges a failure to act in accordance with reasonable commercial standards. Count III alleges that defendant acted negligently and failed to exercise ordinary care. These three counts (I–III) will be collectively referred to as the negligence claims. Count IV alleges a breach by the defendant of its duties as an agent of NEMB and SFS. Count VIII alleges a breach of defendant's obligation as agent to act in strict accordance with its instructions. Counts IV and VIII will be referred to as the agency claims. Count V alleges defendant breached its duties as a bailee. Count VI alleges that the plaintiff is a third-party beneficiary to the contract that the defendant breached in failing to properly deliver the funds as directed by NEMB. Count IX alleges that defendant is estopped to deny the existence of a deposit contract and that it breached its duties under that contract. The cause is before the court on defendant's motion to dismiss all nine counts. For the following reasons, Counts I–IV and VII–VIII are allowed to stand, while Counts V, VI and IX are dismissed.

* * *

II

SFS is the Shareholder Service Agent for Templeton Growth Fund Ltd. (Templeton). SFS processes and records the purchases and redemptions of Templeton shares. In October, 1980, one of Templeton's shareholders was Mr. John Bushman, acting as a trustee for approximately 260,000 shares valued at more than $2 million. On or about October 14, 1980, SFS received instructions, bearing Bushman's signature, requesting that his shares be redeemed and the proceeds be wired to his account at ANB. The account number was said to be 204471. SFS processed the redemption, and directed NEMB, custodian of Templeton's funds, to make the requested wire transfer. NEMB did so and directed the amount of the redemption, the sum of $2,017,867.50, credited to the account of "John Bushman, Trustee // 204471." The transferred funds and accompanying written instructions were received by ANB on or about October 15, 1980. However, the true facts were that ANB had no account in the name of John Bushman, either individually or as trustee. Account 204471 was registered to Gerald S. Haberkorn, Inc. Notwithstanding this discrepancy, ANB credited the funds to Haberkorn's account without addressing any inquiry to either NEMB, SFS, or Templeton. On or about November 4, 1980, SFS learned that the redemption instructions had been forged and that the real John Bushman had no knowledge of the redemption and had no account or relationship with ANB. And, on inquiry, SFS learned from ANB that the funds were credited to Haberkorn's account. Haberkorn had previously agreed to sell approximately $2 million worth of diamonds and jewels to two individuals who promised to pay by wiring the funds into Haberkorn's account at ANB.

After the transfer of funds, Haberkorn delivered the merchandise to the two individuals. Neither the funds transferred into Haberkorn's account nor the jewels purchased with those funds have been recovered. SFS, upon discovery of the forgery, reissued the redeemed shares to the real John Bushman, Trustee, pursuant to an agreement between it and

Templeton. The shares were paid for in cash by SFS. In having made whole Templeton and John Bushman, Trustee, SFS brings this suit, contending that it has succeeded to their interests in all claims and rights arising out of these events. In Counts IV and VIII of the complaint, it alleges that ANB, by accepting the transfer of the funds from NEMB with instructions to credit the account of John Bushman, Trustee, became an agent for NEMB, the company which was its agent. Further, SFS claims that ANB's subsequent actions constituted a breach of its duty to act in strict accordance with the instructions it had received, and to inform its principal of all material facts concerning the transaction. Thus, SFS contends that ANB acted as its agent in this transaction.

III

An agency relation may be implied from the facts of the particular case and need not be express. "The existence of an agency relationship and its nature and extent may be shown by reference to the situation of the parties, the property and the acts of the parties." This rule of Illinois law is well known. Judge Roszkowski of this court had occasion to apply and follow it in Evra Corp. v. Swiss Bank Corp., 522 F.Supp. 820 (N.D.Ill.1981), reversed on other grounds, 673 F.2d 951 (7th Cir. 1982). It is helpful for this case to analyze this recent decision.

* * *

Judge Roszkowski concluded that Swiss Bank breached the duty of care that it owed Evra Corp. By analogy, he reasoned that since there was a contract between plaintiff and Continental, Continental owed plaintiff a duty of care, and Swiss Bank, as Continental's correspondent bank, owed plaintiff that same duty. Citing Delbrueck v. Manufacturers Hanover Trust Co., 609 F.2d 1047 (2d Cir.1979), which analogized the conceptual use of the finality of checks once accepted to irrevocable wire transfers, he found a similarity between a "collecting bank" as defined in Art. IV of the U.C.C., Ill.Rev.Stat. ch. 26, § 4–105(d) [R 4–105(5)] (1979), and Swiss Bank's role as "corresponding bank." This U.C.C. provision states that a collecting bank is "any bank handling the item for collection except the payor bank," U.C.C. § 4–105(d) [R 4–105(5)].

A corresponding bank is one which "regularly performs services for another in a place or market to which the other does not have direct access." Black's Law Dictionary (1979). Under U.C.C. § 4–201(1) [R 4–201(a)], "(u)nless a contrary intent clearly appears * * * the (collecting) bank is an agent or subagent of the owner of the item." Thus, as Judge Roszkowski held in Evra, a correspondent bank in a wire transfer may be presumed to be an agent of the initiator of the transaction until such time as the transaction is completed. Swiss Bank was held to be the agent of Evra Corp. with the same duty of care owed to it by Continental.

In the present case, SFS (like Evra) is the initiator of the wire transfer. NEMB (like Continental Bank) is the custodial bank for funds disbursed by SFS. ANB, as the receiver of the wire transfer, is in the same position as Swiss Bank. In light of the holding in Evra, this court concludes that under the facts alleged, an agency relation existed between SFS and ANB. Accordingly, ANB owed SFS a duty of care which its actions in handling the transfer may have breached. Thus, the motion to dismiss Counts IV and VIII is denied.

The first three counts of SFS's complaint allege negligent conduct by ANB in failing to inform NEMB, Templeton, or SFS that the name and account number of the wire transfer did not coincide. ANB questions the existence of a duty owed by it to SFS. Both the plaintiff and the defendant consolidate these three counts into one general issue of negligence. The question, then, is the principle of law to be applied.

Under Illinois law, negligence must be proved by the existence of a duty owed to plaintiff by defendant, a breach of that duty, and an injury proximately resulting from that breach. The existence of such a duty is a question of law. For a legal duty to exist, the occurrence must not be simply foreseeable but "reasonably foreseeable." The plaintiff in Evra contended that the defendant Swiss Bank owed plaintiff a duty to transmit the wire transfer accurately and timely. The court found that Swiss Bank owed a duty of care to Evra to maintain a system of receiving and disposing of telex messages upon which plaintiff could rely, and that Swiss Bank breached that duty. The court stated that the facts indicated "an appalling lack of regard on the part of Swiss Bank for the more than reasonably foreseeable possibility that the negligent maintenance of its foreign exchange telex machines could result in substantial damage to one of its *customers.*" Id. at 829 (emphasis added). Thus, Evra, as one of Swiss Bank's "customers," could anticipate due care to be exercised by Swiss Bank in the handling of the wire transfer. In its opinion reversing the lower court, the Seventh Circuit held that this type of "general foreseeability" is insufficient to support an award of consequential damages. Evra Corp., 673 F.2d 951, at 959 (7th Cir.1982). However, the circuit court noted that a different case was presented where, as here, direct damages are sought. Id. at 955.

In this case, SFS can likewise be deemed to be a "customer" of ANB. Section 4–104(e) [R 4–104(a)(5)] of the U.C.C. defines a customer as "any person having an account with a bank or for whom a bank has agreed to collect items and includes a bank carrying an account with another bank." Through the agency relation discussed, ANB was acting essentially as a collecting bank for NEMB which in turn was the custodial agent of the funds disbursed by SFS. Furthermore, the official comment to U.C.C. 4–203 [R 4–203], dealing with the effect of instructions given to a collecting bank by the transferor, states that the collecting bank is liable for failure to exercise good faith or ordinary care. Thus, reading the complaint in the light most favorable to SFS, it was a "customer" of ANB which owed it a duty to use due care in handling the wire transfer. Further, the loss of the transferred funds is the reasonably foreseeable result of a deposit made where the name on the transfer instructions differs from the name on the account into which the funds are deposited. Thus, plaintiff has stated a claim in negligence, therefore, the motion to dismiss Counts I–III is denied.

Count V alleges that ANB was the bailee of the funds transferred for delivery to the account of John Bushman, Trustee, and that ANB breached its duty as bailee by misdelivering; that is, crediting the funds to the wrong account. The defendant contends that the wire transfer of the funds disbursed by SFS did not establish a bailment.

* * *

No distinctive feature of a "special deposit" or "bailment" was present here. Thus, ANB's motion to dismiss Count V of the complaint must be granted.

Count VI in SFS' complaint alleges that ANB's failure to transfer the funds to the account of John Bushman, Trustee, or failure to return them to NEMB, constituted actionable conversion. ANB correctly denies the applicability of the conversion claim to this fact situation. One of the legal elements of a conversion, is not present here. The traditional action of trover does not operate on chattels generally, but specifically on property capable of identification as being the actual property or thing wrongfully taken and converted. Kerwin v. Balhatchett, 147 Ill.App. 561, 566 (1909). The question remains whether the wire transfer involved specific property.

In In re Oxford Marketing, United States v. Kallen, 444 F.Supp. 399 (N.D.Ill.1978), the court stated that a bank deposit is a chose in action or debt. It is an intangible right and not specific property owned by the depositor or the successor trustee. * * * Illinois follows the common law rule which does not recognize an action for conversion of intangible rights. Thus, the wire transfer, like a bank deposit, can be considered intangible property. And since it is intangible, an action for conversion cannot be sustained. Furthermore, Burge v. Englwood, 213 Ill.App. 357, 363 (1919) stands for the principle that conversion cannot be maintained if the loss resulted from active or passive negligence or breach of contract.

Thus, the motion to dismiss Count VI is granted.

Count VII alleges that ANB entered into a contract with NEMB to deliver funds to the account of John Bushman, Trustee, in connection with redemption of Mr. Bushman's Templeton shares. SFS alleges it is a third party beneficiary and has the right to sue ANB for breach of that contract via the improper delivery for the funds. ANB counters that nothing in the complaint supports the legal conclusion that SFS was or could have been a third-party beneficiary in this situation.

The general rule regarding a third party's right to sue for breach of a contract between two other parties was announced in Carson Pirie Scott & Co. v. Parrett, 346 Ill. 252, 178 N.E. 498 (1931). There, the Illinois Supreme Court stated that if a contract is made for the direct benefit of a third person not a party to the contract, that third person may sue for a breach thereof. The test to be applied is whether the benefit to the third person is direct to him or is only an incidental benefit. If the benefit is direct, then he may sue; if incidental, then there is no right of recovery. This test is to be determined within the language of the contract. Furthermore, it is not necessary for the third party who is benefitted by the contract to be named therein if he is otherwise sufficiently described or designated. The question whether the benefit to a third party is direct or incidental depends on the intent of the parties, and must be determined case-by-case.

Under the alleged facts, SFS has adequately pleaded its status as third-party beneficiary. The direct or substantial benefit to SFS is the interest in properly transferring the funds so as to avoid any loss by its customer or SFS itself. Also, SFS did not need to be named within the contract since it is evident that SFS falls within the group designated to benefit from the contract; i.e., Templeton, SFS, and John Bushman, Trustee. Thus, the motion to dismiss Count VII is denied.

SFS' Count IX alleges that ANB acted as though a depositor account in the name of John Bushman, Trustee, actually existed. This purportedly occurred because ANB failed to inquire or give notice to NEMB or SFS of the discrepancy between the name and account number. SFS' reliance on ANB's silence or inaction fostered a belief that an account for John Bushman, Trustee, actually existed, and thus prevented SFS from acting to avoid the loss of the funds. Thus, SFS alleges that ANB is estopped to deny the existence of a deposit contract between ANB and John Bushman. Plaintiff further alleges that by virtue of having reimbursed Bushman and Templeton through its reissuance of the redeemed shares, it has succeeded to their interests and can sue on the deposit contract. The problem with these allegations is that there is no contract between ANB and Bushman. It is undisputed that Bushman did not have an account at ANB and in fact had no relationship with ANB. Rather, Bushman was the beneficiary of a contract for deposit based on the wire transfer between ANB and NEMB. Thus, the contract which SFS seeks to estop ANB from denying does not exist and Count IX should be dismissed.

Accordingly, and for these reasons, the motion to dismiss is granted as to Counts IV, V and IX and denied as to the other counts.

So ordered.

BRADFORD TRUST COMPANY OF BOSTON v. TEXAS AMERICAN BANK—HOUSTON

United States Court of Appeals, Fifth Circuit, 1986.
790 F.2d 407.

Opinion

W. Eugene Davis, Circuit Judge:

This diversity case presents the question of who should bear the loss flowing from a fraudulently induced $800,000 wire transfer. We must choose between the institution that honored the forged order of its customer to wire funds and the bank to whom the funds were wired which did not credit the account as directed. On cross-motions for summary judgment the district court applied the Texas comparative negligence statute, Tex.Rev.Civ.Stat.Ann. art. 2212a (Vernon Supp. 1985), and apportioned the loss equally between the two parties. Both parties appeal and argue that the other party should bear the entire loss. We decline to apply comparative negligence principles and reverse the judgment of the district court. We conclude that the initial bank that honored the forged order must bear the entire loss.

I.

In an ingenious scheme, two con artists, using aliases of Hank and Dave Friedman, arranged to buy rare coins and gold bullion from Colonial Coins, Inc. (Colonial) in Houston for $800,000. The imposters informed Colonial that they would wire funds from their bank in Boston to Colonial's account at Texas American Bank—Houston N.A. (Texas American) to pay for the coins. Colonial agreed and gave the Friedmans its account number at Texas American.

The imposters next sent a forged letter and stock power to Bradford Trust Company (Bradford), the agent for a mutual fund, directing the liquidation of $800,000 from the mutual fund account of Frank Rochefort. The forged order also instructed Bradford to wire the $800,000 from this account to Colonial's account in Texas American in Houston. Bradford, without following internal procedures recently instituted because of a similar scam,[3] ordered its correspondent bank, State Street Bank of Boston (State Street) to wire the funds to Texas American. The text of the transfer included the number of Colonial's account at Texas American, but stated that it was for the account of Frank S. Rochefort. When the funds were received, Texas American notified Colonial that the funds had been deposited into Colonial's account. With this assurance, Colonial released the coins to the imposters.

Bradford became aware of the scam when an astonished Rochefort received notice of the withdrawal and informed Bradford that he had not authorized it. Bradford reinstated Rochefort's account and demanded that Texas American and Colonial reimburse it. Texas American and Colonial refused and this lawsuit followed. Bradford compromised its claim against Colonial, which was dismissed from the litigation. The district court, on summary judgment, applied the Texas comparative negligence statute and divided the loss equally between Bradford and Texas American. Bradford appeals, contending that Texas American should bear the entire loss because its negligence in failing to follow Bradford's order to deposit the funds in Rochefort's

3. In April of 1980, Bradford was the victim of a similar fraudulent scheme. As a result, new security procedures were instituted. For transactions over $100,000, the new procedures required thorough review of the documents, shareholder confirmation when the shareholder instructed Bradford to wire the money to a person or to an address other than that on record, and approval by senior management.

account was the primary cause of the loss. Texas American cross-appeals, arguing that Bradford should suffer the entire loss because Bradford dealt with the imposter, honored the forged order to pay and hence was in the best position to prevent the loss.

II.

A.

The district court, having no well-defined body of law that clearly applied to resolve the dispute in this case, relied on the Texas comparative negligence statute as authority to divide the damages between the parties. The district court cited as authority Duncan v. Cessna Aircraft Co., 665 S.W.2d 414 (Tex.1984), which applied comparative negligence principles to a strict products liability case.

Although we feel the same equitable tug the district court undoubtedly felt to apply comparative negligence principles, we are persuaded that it would be a mistake to do so in this commercial case.

The comparative negligence statute expressly extends to actions "to recover damages for negligence resulting in death or injury to persons or property * * *." Art. 2212a, supra. This language clearly extends comparative negligence principles to cases of physical harm to persons and property; whether this statute was intended to apply to other types of damage is doubtful. Although it is not inconceivable that a Texas court would interpret property broadly enough to include a loss such as that at issue here, we are persuaded that a federal diversity court should not adopt such a questionable interpretation.

This is particularly true where, as here, neither party to the appeal urges us to apply comparative negligence principles.

We are also influenced by our recognition that in commercial disputes between seasoned bankers and other businessmen, certainty of result is more important than in traditional tort litigation. In commercial relationships known risks can be priced or shifted to others; if disputes arise, a bright line rule results in faster, easier settlements. The principal reason for a comparative negligence rule in physical harm cases—avoiding the harsh distributional results of precluding the recovery of the slightly negligent plaintiff who has suffered a devastating loss—has considerably less force in the commercial banking world.

B.

Having decided that the Texas comparative negligence statute does not apply to this case, we widen our search for Texas law that does apply. Unfortunately, we have found no direct authority that resolves the question. Neither the Electronic Fund Transfer Act, 15 U.S.C. § 1693a(6)(B), nor the Uniform Commercial Code apply. Other courts faced with resolving controversies relating to wire transfers have applied the UCC by analogy. Delbrueck, supra, at 1051; Securities Fund Services v. American National Bank and Trust Co., 542 F.Supp. 323 (N.D.Ill.1982). Because of the close analogy between allocation of fraud losses in negotiable instruments and wire transfers we look to both Texas court decisions before Texas adopted the UCC and the UCC for guidance. Two factors emerge from these sources that are helpful in analyzing the question of who should bear the loss in this case: 1) which party was in the best position to avoid the loss; and 2) which solution promotes the policy of finality in commercial transactions?

The first factor, which party is in the best position to avoid the loss, is a principal reason underlying a number of loss allocation calls in the UCC. For example, it provides the essential reason for requiring the drawee bank to bear the loss if it pays on the drawer's forged signature. Tex.Bus. & Com.Code Ann. § 3.404 [R 3–403] (Vernon 1968); Greenville Avenue State Bank v. Lang, 421 S.W.2d 748 (Tex.Civ.App.1967). This is because the bank, which can verify its customer's signature, is in the best position to discover the forgery and avoid the loss. Similarly, if an endorsement on an instrument is forged, the loss is ordinarily placed on the party in the collection chain who accepted the instrument from the forger. Tex.Bus. & Com.Code Ann. § 3.417(a)(1) [R 3–417] (Vernon 1968) and comment 3. Again, the UCC recognizes that the party dealing directly with the forger has an opportunity to verify the endorser's identity and is in the best position to avoid the loss. Indeed, the common thread running through the imposter cases is to "throw the loss resulting from dealing with an imposter on the person who dealt with the imposter, and presumably, had the best opportunity to take precautions that would have detected the fraud, rather than on a subsequent holder, who had no similar opportunity."

Bradford dealt directly with the imposter. It received the forged order directing the liquidation of Rochefort's account. If Bradford had followed procedures it had in place that called for verification of the customer's order, the loss would not have occurred. Instead of following those procedures and verifying Rochefort's order, Bradford set the fraudulent scheme into motion by liquidating Rochefort's account and wiring the funds to Texas American. Although Texas American should have recognized the discrepancy between the account number and the name of the owner of the account to whom the wire directed the funds be credited, we are persuaded that Texas American's fault was secondary to that of Bradford's. It is far from certain that the loss would have been prevented even if Texas American had noticed the discrepancy between the account number and the holder of the account and had called this discrepancy to Bradford's attention. To conclude that this action by Texas American would have avoided the loss requires us to assume that such a call to Bradford would have caused Bradford to contact Rochefort and verify his order. On the other hand, it is certain that if Bradford had called Rochefort to verify his purported order to transfer funds to Colonial this scheme would have been discovered and no loss would have been suffered.

Two wire transfer cases decided by Texas courts before the adoption of the UCC follow this same reasoning. In Western Union Telegraph Co. v. American State Bank, 277 S.W. 226 (Tex.Civ.App.1925), an individual who identified himself as Joe Spinks, deposited two checks in American State Bank. Before the bank learned that the checks were bogus, it received a telegram from Joe Spinks requesting the bank to wire him $650. The bank instructed Western Union to wire the money to Spinks. When the bank discovered Spinks was an imposter, it sued Western Union to recover the money. The Texas Court of Appeals in reversing a judgment entered by the district court in favor of the bank stated that: "[t]he duty devolves on the Bank to identify its customers, and when they accepted the unknown as Joe Spinks, they laid the groundwork for subsequent trouble." 277 S.W. at 227. In Western Union Telegraph Co. v. Cosby, 99 S.W.2d 662 (Tex.Civ.App.1936), an imposter representing himself as Cosby, a business partner of Langlois, called Langlois and asked Langlois to wire him $400. Langlois, thinking it really was Cosby, ordered Western Union to send him the money. Cosby then sued Western Union to recover the money once he discovered the error. The court of appeals again reversed the district court's judgment against Western Union stating that, "where two innocent parties have been deceived, the loss must be borne by the one who primarily made such loss possible."

For the reasons set forth above, we are persuaded that Bradford, by honoring the forged order to transmit Rochefort's funds after dealing directly with the imposter, was in the best position to avoid the loss.

We have also considered how our allocation of the loss in this case squares with the desired policy of finality in commercial transactions. The UCC in section 3.418 [R 3–418] adopted the principle established in the time honored decision of Price v. Neal, 3 Burr. 1355 (1762) in which the court held that a drawee who accepts or pays an instrument on the forged signature of the drawer is bound on his acceptance and cannot recover back his payment. Section 3.418 [R 3–418] provides in part: "* * * payment or acceptance of any instrument is final in favor of a holder in due course or a person who has in good faith changed his position in reliance on the payment." The reporters in the official comments to this section give two justifications for adopting this rule: "The traditional justification for the result is that the drawee is in a superior position to detect a forgery because he has the maker's signature and is expected to know and compare it; a less fictional rationalization is that it is highly desirable to end the transaction on an instrument when it is paid rather than reopen and upset a series of commercial transactions at a later date when the forgery is discovered."

In Perini Corporation v. First National Bank of Habersham County, 553 F.2d 398 (5th Cir.1977), we considered who should bear the loss as between the drawee bank that paid on forged signatures of the drawer and the depository bank which accepted the instruments without proper endorsements. In deciding this Georgia diversity case, we resolved conflicting UCC rules by relying primarily on the finality policy and concluded that the drawee bank must bear the entire loss.

Assessing the loss in this case to Bradford and ending the transaction when Bradford paid under Rochefort's forged order rather than inquiring into and upsetting later transactions after the forgery was discovered clearly serves this bedrock policy of finality.

C.

Bradford urges us to find that Texas American's failure to follow Bradford's instructions in the wire transfer was the primary, overriding cause of the loss. Bradford argues that its earlier negligence in accepting the forged order of Rochefort to pay would have been inconsequential had Texas American handled the transfer with due care and in accordance with ordinary standards and practices of the banking industry. We agree with Bradford that Texas American was negligent in failing to notice the discrepancy between the account number and the name of the owner of the account to which the funds were to be credited. Even if allocation of the loss depended entirely upon a determination of which party was more at fault, however, this would not alter our decision to lay the loss at Bradford's feet. We are persuaded that Bradford's act in honoring the forged authorization without following its own internal procedures to verify the genuineness of the request was the primary cause of the loss. The fault of Texas American failing to note the discrepancy between the account number and the name of the owner of the account to whom the money was to be credited was less grave than that of Bradford.

Bradford argues that liability is imposed on Texas American by sub-part (b) of Regulation J of the Federal Reserve System, 12 C.F.R. § 210.56(b) (1981) which governs federal reserve wire transfers of funds. We disagree. This regulation, at most, placed a duty on Texas American to follow the instructions contained in Bradford's wire. Texas American owed this duty without regard to Regulation J and as indicated above, we agree with the district court that Texas American breached this duty and was guilty for negligence in failing to follow those instructions. For the reasons stated above, despite the negligence of Texas American, we conclude that Bradford must bear the loss. Accordingly, the judgment of the district court is reversed and the action is remanded to the district court for entry of judgment in favor of Texas American and against Bradford.

REVERSED and REMANDED.

Note

1. In Article 4A terms, label the parties in the two principal cases and contrast the Article 4 and Article 4A characterizations. That will support comparison of the result under the apposite Article 4A and analogous Article 4 provisions. See sections 4A–202, 4A–203, 4A–205 and 4A–207. Which of those provisions is (are) applicable to each of the two principal cases above? See also UNCITRAL model law arts. 5 and 10:

Article 5

Obligations of sender

(1) A sender is bound by a payment order or an amendment or revocation of a payment order if it was issued by the sender or by another person who had the authority to bind the sender.

(2) When a payment order or an amendment or revocation of a payment order is subject to authentication other than by means of a mere comparison of signature, a purported sender who is not bound under paragraph (1) is nevertheless bound if

(a) the authentication is in the circumstances a commercially reasonable method of security against unauthorized payment orders, and

(b) the receiving bank complied with the authentication.

(3) The parties are not permitted to agree that a purported sender is bound under paragraph (2) if the authentication is not commercially reasonable in the circumstances.

(4) A purported sender is, however, not bound under paragraph (2) if it proves that the payment order as received by the receiving bank resulted from the actions of a person other than

(a) a present or former employee of the purported sender, or

(b) a person whose relationship with the purported sender enabled that person to gain access to the authentication procedure.

The preceding sentence does not apply if the receiving bank proves that the payment order resulted from the actions of a person who had gained access to the authentication procedure through the fault of the purported sender.

(5) A sender who is bound by a payment order is bound by the terms of the order as received by the receiving bank. However, the sender is not bound by an erroneous duplicate of, or an error or discrepancy in, a payment order if

(a) the sender and the receiving bank have agreed upon a procedure for detecting erroneous duplicates, errors or discrepancies in a payment order, and

(b) use of the procedure by the receiving bank revealed or would have revealed the erroneous duplicate, error or discrepancy.

If the error or discrepancy that the bank would have detected was that the sender instructed payment of an amount greater than the amount intended by the sender, the sender is bound only to the extent of the amount that was intended. Paragraph (5) applies to an error or discrepancy in an amendment or a revocation order as it applies to an error or discrepancy in a payment order.

(6) A sender becomes obligated to pay the receiving bank for the payment order when the receiving bank accepts it, but payment is not due until the beginning of the execution period.

Article 10

Obligations of beneficiary's bank

(1) The beneficiary's bank is, upon acceptance of a payment order, obligated to place the funds at the disposal of the beneficiary, or otherwise to apply the credit, in accordance with the payment order and the law governing the relationship between the bank and the beneficiary.

(2) When an instruction is received that appears to be intended to be a payment order but does not contain sufficient data to be a payment order, or being a payment order it cannot be executed because of insufficient data, but the sender can be identified, the beneficiary's bank shall give notice to the sender of the insufficiency, within the time required by article 11.

(3) When the beneficiary's bank detects that there is an inconsistency in the information relating to the amount of money to be transferred, it shall, within the time required by article 11, give notice to the sender of the inconsistency if the sender can be identified.

(4) When the beneficiary's bank detects that there is an inconsistency in the information intended to identify the beneficiary, it shall, within the time required by article 11, give notice to the sender of the inconsistency if the sender can be identified.

(5) Unless the payment order states otherwise, the beneficiary's bank shall, within the time required for execution under article 11, give notice to a beneficiary who does not maintain an account at the bank that it is holding funds for its benefit, if the bank has sufficient information to give such notice.

2. How many, if any, of the common law causes of action considered in *Securities Fund* survive the promulgation of Article 4A? What is the impact of U.C.C. § 1–103 on that issue? Cf. the commercial paper conversion rules of original 3–419 and revised 3–420. Why is the conversion action, both common law and statutory, viable in the paper-based system of Article 3 but inapposite in a wire transfer? Does Article 4A preempt the conversion theory? See also UNCITRAL model law art. 18, reproduced supra.

3. The *Bradford Trust* court chose not to utilize comparative negligence principles. Is the court's discussion of the issue consistent with U.C.C. § 4A–203? Is it consistent with revised 3–405? Need it be? What might support imposition of different loss allocation rules in the two analogous contexts?

After the promulgation of Article 4A, is there room for common law or statutory comparative negligence?

4. The *Bradford Trust* court cited the wire transfer rules of Federal Reserve Board Regulation J. Article 4A has now been incorporated into the federal regulation. 12 C.F.R. § 210.25. The CHIPS system as well as the National Automated Clearing House Association have also adopted Article 4A as part of their private agreements.

*

Index

[References are to pages.]

[References are to pages.]

[References are to pages.]

[References are to pages.]

[References are to pages.]

†